Essentials *of* Economics

Essentials *of* Economics

Fifth Edition

Bradley R. Schiller
American University, Washington, D.C.

Boston Burr Ridge, IL Dubuque, IA Madison, WI New York San Francisco St. Louis
Bangkok Bogotá Caracas Kuala Lumpur Lisbon London Madrid Mexico City
Milan Montreal New Delhi Santiago Seoul Singapore Sydney Taipei Toronto

Essentials of Economics

Published by McGraw-Hill/Irwin, a business unit of The McGraw-Hill Companies, Inc., 1221 Avenue of the Americas, New York, NY, 10020.

This book is printed on acid-free paper.

domestic 1 2 3 4 5 6 7 8 9 0 VNH/VNH 0 9 8 7 6 5 4
international 1 2 3 4 5 6 7 8 9 0 VNH/VNH 0 9 8 7 6 5 4

ISBN 0-07-287747-2

Vice president and editor-in-chief: *Robin J. Zwettler*
Publisher: *Gary Burke*
Executive editor: *Paul Shensa*
Developmental editor: *Katie Crouch*
Editorial assistant: *Heila Hubbard*
Marketing manager: *Martin D. Quinn*
Lead producer, Media technology: *Kai Chiang*
Senior project manager: *Kari Geltemeyer*
Manager, New book production: *Heather D. Burbridge*
Lead designer: *Pam Verros*
Photo research coordinator: *Kathy Shive*
Photo researcher: *Jennifer Blankenship*
Lead supplement producer: *Becky Szura*
Senior digital content specialist: *Brian Nacik*
Cover and interior design: *Jenny El-Shamy*
Cover image: *Counterweights, 1926 by Wassily Kandinsky (1866–1944) Stadtisches Museum, Mulheim, Germany/Bridgeman Art Library*
© 2003 Artists Rights Society (ARS), New York / ADAGP, Paris
Estate: Contrepoids, 1926, E.R.II.n°778
Typeface: *10/12 New Aster*
Compositor: *GTS Companies/York, PA Campus*
Printer: *Von Hoffmann Corporation*

Library of Congress Cataloging-in-Publication Data

Schiller, Bradley R., 1943–
Essentials of economics / Bradley R. Schiller.—5th ed.
p. cm.
Various multi-media instructional aids are available to supplement the text.
Includes index.
ISBN 0-07-287747-2 (alk. paper)—ISBN 0-07-111194-8 (international : alk. paper)
1. Economics. I. Title.
HB171.5.S2923 2005
330—dc22

2003065972

INTERNATIONAL EDITION ISBN 0-07-111194-8

www.mhhe.com

About the Author

Bradley R. Schiller has over three decades of experience teaching introductory economics at American University, the University of California (Berkeley and Santa Cruz), and the University of Maryland. He has given guest lectures at more than 100 colleges ranging from Fresno, California, to Istanbul, Turkey. Dr. Schiller's unique contribution to teaching is his ability to relate basic principles to current socioeconomic problems, institutions, and public policy decisions. This perspective is evident throughout *Essentials of Economics.*

Dr. Schiller derives this policy focus from his extensive experience as a Washington consultant. He has been a consultant to most major federal agencies, many congressional committees, and political candidates. In addition, he has evaluated scores of government programs and helped design others. His studies of discrimination, training programs, tax reform, pensions, welfare, Social Security, and lifetime wage patterns have appeared in both professional journals and popular media. Dr. Schiller is also a frequent commentator on economic policy for television, radio, and newspapers.

Dr. Schiller received his Ph.D. from Harvard in 1969. His B.A. degree, with great distinction, was completed at the University of California (Berkeley) in 1965. He is now a professor of economics in the School of Public Affairs at American University.

Contents in Brief

Contents

chapter 14

Monetary Policy 312

chapter 15

Economic Growth 332

chapter 16

Theory and Reality 352

Section IV INTERNATIONAL

Preface

Economics entails hard choices. No one knows this better than instructors assigned to teach a survey of economics in a single term. There are simply too many topics to cover in so short a time.

Focus on Core Concepts

Few textbooks confront this scarcity problem directly. Some one-semester books are nearly as long as full-blown principles texts. The shorter ones tend to condense topics and omit the additional explanations, illustrations, and applications that are especially important in survey courses. Students and teachers alike get frustrated trying to pick out the essentials from abridged principles texts.

Essentials of Economics lives up to its name by making the difficult choices. The standard table of contents has been pruned to the core. The surviving topics are the very essence of economic concepts. In Section II on microeconomics, for example, the focus is on the polar models of perfect competition and monopoly. These models are represented as the endpoints of a spectrum of market structures (see figure on p. 130). Intermediate market structures—for example, oligopoly, monopolistic competition—are noted but not analyzed. The goal here is simply to convey the sense that market structure is an important determinant of market outcomes. The contrast between the extremes of monopoly and perfect competition is sufficient to convey this essential message. The omission of other market structures from the outline also leaves more space for explaining and illustrating *how* market structure affects market behavior.

The same commitment to essentials is evident in the section on macroeconomics. Rather than attempt here to cover all the salient macro models, the focus is on a straightforward presentation of the aggregate supply-demand framework. The different interpretations of the classical, Keynesian, and monetarist models are discussed. But there is no discussion of neo-Keynesianism, rational expectations, public choice, or Marxist models. The level of abstraction required for such models is simply not necessary or appropriate in an introductory survey course. Texts that include such models tend to raise more questions than survey instructors can ever hope to answer. In *Essentials*, students are exposed only to the ideas needed for a basic understanding of how macroeconomies function.

Central Theme

The central goal of this text is to convey a sense of how economic *systems* affect economic *outcomes*. When we look back on the twentieth century, we see how some economies flourished, while others languished. Even the "winners" had recurrent episodes of slow, even negative growth. The central analytical issue is how various economic systems influenced those diverse growth records. Was the relatively superior track record of the United States a historical fluke or a by-product of its commitment to market capitalism? Were the long economic expansions of the 1980s and 1990s the result of enlightened macro policy, more efficient markets, or just good luck? What role did policy, markets, and (bad) luck play in the economic slowdown of 2001? What forces deserve credit for the economic recovery that followed?

We know how President Bush answered this question. Like his predecessors, President Bush wanted credit for all good economic outcomes and no blame for the bad outcomes (see Headline). But that's just politics. In economics, we want students to at least have an overview of how the economy works and a set of basic tools for identifying cause-and-effect relationships. Students get the bird's-eye view of the macroeconomy with a simple model (see page 252) that relates macro determinants to macro outcomes. Then they get enough tools to sort out the competing claims for credit or blame.

A recurrent theme in *Essentials* is the notion that economic institutions and policies *matter*. Economic prosperity isn't a random occurrence. The right institutions and policies can foster or impede economic progress. The challenge is to know when and how to intervene.

This central theme is the focus of Chapter 1. Our economic accomplishments and insatiable materialism set the stage for a discussion of production possibilities. The role of economic systems and choices is illustrated with the starkly different "guns versus butter" decisions in North and South Korea, Russia, and the United States. The potential for both market failure (or success) and government failure (or success) is highlighted. After reading Chapter 1, students should sense that "the economy" is important to their lives and that our collective choices on how the economy is structured are important.

A Global Portrait of the U.S. Economy

To put some meat on the abstract bones of the economy, *Essentials* offers a unique portrait of the U.S. economy. Few students easily relate to the abstraction of the economy. They hear about specific dimensions of the economy but rarely see all the pieces put together. Chapter 2 tries to fill this void by providing a bird's-eye view of the U.S. economy. This descriptive chapter is organized around the three basic questions of WHAT, HOW, and FOR WHOM to produce. The current answer to the WHAT question is summarized with data on GDP and its components. Historical and global comparisons are provided to underscore the significance of America's $11 trillion economy. Similar perspectives are offered on the structure of production and the U.S. distribution of income. An early look at the role of government in shaping economic outcomes is also provided. This colorful, global portrait is a critical tool in acquainting students with the broad dimensions of the U.S. economy and is unique to this text.

Real-World Emphasis

The decision to include a descriptive chapter on the U.S. economy reflects a basic commitment to a real-world context. Students rarely get interested in stories about the mythical widget manufacturers that inhabit so many economics textbooks. But glimmers of interest—even some enthusiasm—surface when real-world illustrations, not fables, are offered.

Every chapter starts out with real-world applications of core concepts. As the chapters unfold, empirical illustrations continue to enliven the in-text analysis. Most chapters end with a **Policy Perspectives** section that challenges the student to apply new concepts to real-world issues.

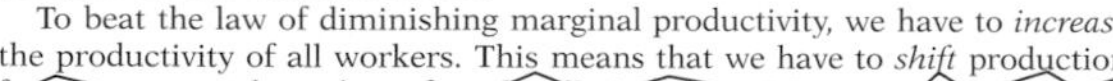

Invest in Labor or Capital?

The U.S. labor force continues to grow by more than a million workers per year. If capital investments don't keep pace, these added workers will strain production facilities. The law of diminishing marginal productivity would push wages lower and reduce living standards. Hardly a very cheerful prospect for the next millenium.

To beat the law of diminishing marginal productivity, we have to *increase* the productivity of all workers. This means that we have to *shift* production

The real-world approach of *Essentials* is reinforced by the boxed **Headlines** that appear in every chapter. Like the prior Headline on President Bush, the other 77 Headlines offer up-to-date domestic and international applications of economic concepts. Some new examples include the advent of fee-based music downloads (p. 96); OPEC's supply-management problems (p. 164); soaring salaries for college coaches (p. 188); new doubts about the value of recycling (p. 215); the unsettling effects of terrorism (p. 264); the stimulus from the 2003 tax cuts (p. 287); the threats posed by soaring budget deficits (p. 357). This is just a sampling of the stream of real-world applications that cascades throughout this text.

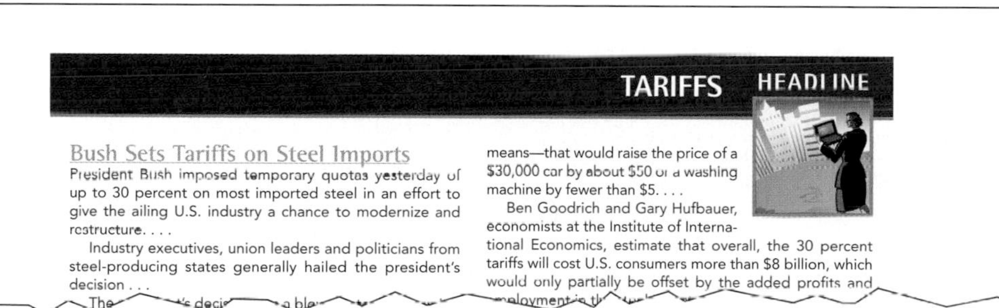
TARIFFS HEADLINE

Bush Sets Tariffs on Steel Imports

President Bush imposed temporary quotas yesterday of up to 30 percent on most imported steel in an effort to give the ailing U.S. industry a chance to modernize and restructure. . . .

Industry executives, union leaders and politicians from steel-producing states generally hailed the president's decision . . .

means—that would raise the price of a $30,000 car by about $50 or a washing machine by fewer than $5. . . .

Ben Goodrich and Gary Hufbauer, economists at the Institute of International Economics, estimate that overall, the 30 percent tariffs will cost U.S. consumers more than $8 billion, which would only partially be offset by the added profits and

Theory and Reality

In becoming acquainted with the U.S. economy, students will inevitably learn about the woes of the business cycle. As the course progresses, they will not fail to notice a huge gap between the pat solutions of economic theory and the dismal realities of recession. This experience will kindle one of the most persistent and perplexing questions students have, namely: If the theory is so good, why is the economy such a mess? Economists like to pretend that the theory is perfect but politicians aren't. That's part of the answer, to be sure. But it isn't entirely fair to either politicians or economists. In reality, the design and implementation of economic policy is impeded by incomplete information, changing circumstances, goal trade-offs, and politics. Chapter 16 examines these real-world complications. A Headline on the "black art" of economic modeling (p. 368), together with new examples of the politics of macro policy, enliven the discussion. In the end, students get a much more complete explanation of why the real world doesn't always live up to the promises of economic theory.

New Feature: Living Econ

Building on the real-world emphasis of *Essentials,* **Living Econ** is a brand-new end-of-chapter section that promotes economic literacy by relating the chapter concepts to what is most important to every student: his or her own life. Created by Linda Wilson of the University of Texas at Arlington and Mark Maier of Glendale Community College, **Living Econ** explores provocative and relevant questions such as:

- Is college a good deal?
- Where will I end up?
- How do high prices affect me?
- Should I litter to create jobs?
- How confident am I?
- How do I create money?

By bringing the concepts alive, this section gives students the opportunity to consider why economics matters to them. This glimpse into the big picture will help them see what it takes to think like an economically literate citizen. For those who want a bit more discussion of the topics in **Living Econ,** additional material can be found in the Study Guide.

Is College a Good Deal?

Even though college enrollment is a multimillion dollar decision, many students start college without thinking about the economic consequences. You may be aware of some the benefits. On average a college graduate earns over $1 million more during his or her lifetime than a high school graduate. (Of course the actual amount depends on your effort and career choice.)

On the cost side, tuition and books are a major expense for college students. However, Chapter 5 points out a cost that is often overlooked, the implicit cost of foregone earnings. You could have worked additional hours instead of going to school and you would have received promotions if you

Web Activities

To Keep *Essentials* connected to the real world, each chapter offers **Web Activities** at the end of each chapter. These require the student to access data or materials on a website, then use, summarize, or explain it in the context of the chapter's core economic concepts. The *Instructors Resource Manual* provides answers to these problems as well as additional URLs and web-based exercises.

New in This Edition

Besides the new Internet content, there is a lot of new material in this fifth edition. Although the structure of the text is unchanged, the content has been extensively refreshed throughout. All of the statistics have been updated. New problems and discussion questions have been added to every chapter. New cartoons and photos have been added. And new examples, illustrations, and Headlines appear throughout. In fact, so much material is new that a brief checklist can't do justice to this edition's freshness. The following list should therefore be regarded as a mere sampler:

- *Chapter 1: The Challenges of Economics* The "guns versus butter" debate comes to life with the contrast of North Korea's famine and military build-up, as well as a depiction of the real "Cost of War" in Iraq.

- *Chapter 2: The U.S. Economy* New global contrasts of output levels, production processes, and income distributions add substance to the core WHAT, HOW, and FOR WHOM questions.
- *Chapter 3: Supply and Demand* New evidence on how higher liquor prices quell campus drinking highlights the role of prices in changing consumer behavior.
- *Chapter 4: Consumer Demand* The emergence of fee-based music downloads showcases the importance of price elasticity. Also highlighted are the effects of New York City's new tax on cigarettes.
- *Chapter 5: Supply Decisions* The expansion of McDonald's in China illustrates the distinction between investment decisions and production decisions.
- *Chapter 6: Competition* The escalating international competition in the U.S. catfish market is a great illustration of competitive dynamics.
- *Chapter 7: Monopoly* As Linux has learned, lawsuits can be an effective entry barrier. Paying rivals to suppress innovation helps maintain market power, as well. These are some of the insights into monopoly behavior offered in Chapter 7.
- *Chapter 8: The Labor Market* The government sets a wage *minimum* but not a wage *maximum*. Is that why corporate CEO pay seems so out of whack?
- *Chapter 9: Government Intervention* Opinion polls still register high levels of doubt about the efficacy of government intervention. How do *government* failure and *market* failure compare?
- *Chapter 10: The Business Cycle* Just as the economics profession was getting complacent about the "New Economy," along came another recession. This chapter explores the basics for pursuing full employment, price stability, and economic growth.
- *Chapter 11: Aggregate Supply and Demand* The external shocks to both AS and AD from terrorist attacks underscore the potential instability of macro equilibrium. The critical role of consumer confidence in keeping the wheels of commerce turning is also highlighted.
- *Chapter 12: Fiscal Policy* The sequence of President Bush's tax cuts spotlights the potential of this macro policy lever.
- *Chapter 13: Money and Banks* The changing forms of payment help illustrate the essential characteristics of "money" and the role of banks.
- *Chapter 14: Monetary Policy* The Fed pulled out all the stops to revive the economy after the 2001 terrorist attacks and recession. This chapter explains how monetary policy works.
- *Chapter 15: Economic Growth* New evidence on the role of institutions in fostering growth enlivens the discussion. The presumed limits to growth are also explored.
- *Chapter 16: Theory and Reality* Everyone's favorite chapter keeps getting better. After reviewing the potential of economic policy, an array of real-world policy obstacles is surveyed. The "black art" of macroeconomic models and the politics of fiscal and monetary policy get their due.
- *Chapter 17: International Trade* Steel tariffs and the continuing dispute over China's currency highlight trade potential and problems. The Policy Perspective focuses on the various opponents to a strengthened World Trade Organization.

Supportive Pedagogy

The emphasis on real-world applications motivates students to read and learn basic economic concepts. This pedagogical goal is reinforced with several in-text student aids. These include

- *Chapter-opening questions* Each chapter begins with a short, empirically based introduction to key concepts. Three core questions are posed to motivate and direct student learning.
- *In-margin definitions* Key concepts are highlighted in the text and defined in the margins. Key definitions are also repeated in subsequent chapters to reinforce proper usage.
- *Precise graphs* All the analytical graphs are plotted and labeled with precision. This shouldn't be noteworthy, but other texts are surprisingly deficient in this regard.

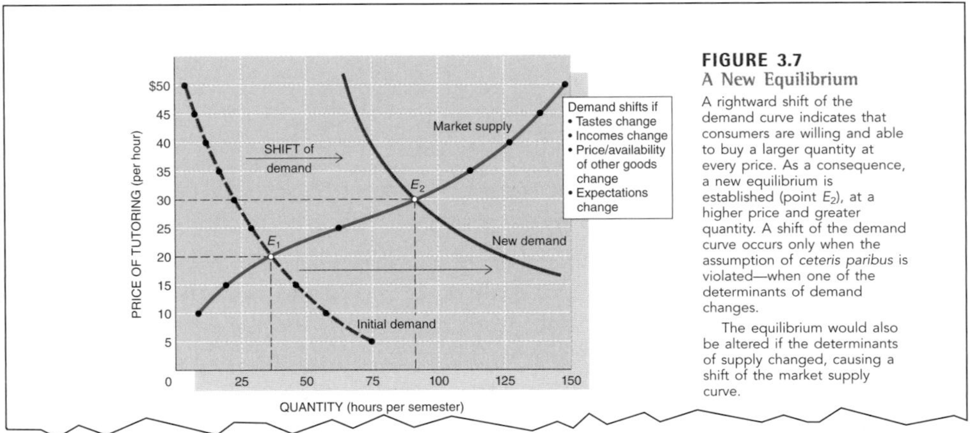

FIGURE 3.7
A New Equilibrium
A rightward shift of the demand curve indicates that consumers are willing and able to buy a larger quantity at every price. As a consequence, a new equilibrium is established (point E_2), at a higher price and greater quantity. A shift of the demand curve occurs only when the assumption of *ceteris paribus* is violated—when one of the determinants of demand changes.

The equilibrium would also be altered if the determinants of supply changed, causing a shift of the market supply curve.

- *Synchronized tables and graphs* The graphs are made more understandable with explicit links to accompanying tables. Notice in Figure 3.2 (p. 161), for example, how the lettered rows of the table match the lettered points on the graph.
- *Complete annotations* All the graphs and tables have self-contained annotations, as do the Headline boxes, the photos, and the cartoons. These captions facilitate both initial learning and later review.
- *Chapter summaries* Key points are summarized in bulleted capsules at the end of each chapter.
- *Key-term review* A list of key terms (the ones defined in the margin) is provided at the end of each chapter. This feature facilitates review and self-testing.
- *Questions for discussion* These are intended to stimulate thought and discussion about the nature of core concepts and their application to real-world settings. This edition has many more questions and exercises than earlier editions.
- *Numerical problems* Numerical problems are set out at the end of each chapter. These problems often require students to use material from earlier tables, graphs, or Headlines. Answers to all problems are provided in the *Instructor's Resource Manual* along with clarifying annotations.

- *End-of-text glossary* The chapter-specific definitions and key-term reviews are supplemented with a comprehensive glossary at the end of the text.
- *Web-based exercises* Up to four problems at the end of each chapter require students to retrieve and use material from specific websites. Answers and additional suggestions are contained in the *Instructor's Resource Manual*.
- *Living Econ* This new end-of-chapter feature gives students personal insights into how the economy relates to their everyday activities.

Contents: Microeconomics

The micro sequence of the text includes only six chapters. In this brief space students get an introduction to the essentials of consumer demand, producer supply decisions, market structure (competition versus monopoly), and labor market behavior. In each case the objective is to spotlight the essential elements of market behavior, for example, the utility-maximizing behavior of consumers, the profit-maximizing quest of producers, and the interactions of supply and demand in setting both wages and prices. The monopoly chapter (Chapter 7) offers a step-by-step comparison of competitive and monopoly behavior, in both the short and long run. Contrasts with centrally planned economies are also strewn throughout the discussion to highlight the unique character of *market* outcomes.

The final chapter in the micro core examines the purposes of government intervention. The principal sources of market failure (public goods, externalities, market power, inequity) are explained and illustrated. So, too, is the nature of government intervention and the potential for *government* failure. Students should end the micro core with a basic understanding of how markets work and when and why government intervention is somctimes necessary.

Contents: Macroeconomics

The macro sequence begins with a historical and descriptive introduction to the business cycle. The rest of the opening macro chapter explains and illustrates the nature and consequences of unemployment and inflation. This discussion is predicated on the conviction that students have to understand *why* business cycles are feared before they'll show any interest in the policy tools designed to tame the cycle. The standard measures of unemployment and inflation are explained, along with specific numerical goals set by Congress and the president.

The basic analytical framework of aggregate supply and aggregate demand (AS/AD) is introduced in Chapter 11. The focus is on how different shapes and shifts of AS and AD curves affect macro outcomes. The AS/AD framework is also used to illustrate the basic policy options that decision makers confront. The stylized model of the economy illustrated in Figure 11.1 (p. 252) is used repeatedly to show how different macro determinants affect macro outcomes (e.g., see the highlighting of fiscal policy in Figure 12.1 on p. 279).

The fiscal-policy chapter surveys the components of aggregate demand and shows how changes in government spending or taxes can alter macro equilibrium. The multiplier is illustrated in the AS/AD framework and the potential consequences for price inflation are discussed. The chapter ends with a discussion of budget deficits and surpluses.

The monetary dimensions of the macroeconomy get two chapters. The first introduces students to modern concepts of money and the process of deposit creation. Chapter 14 focuses on how the Federal Reserve regulates bank reserves and lending to influence macro outcomes.

Supply-side concerns are addressed in Chapter 15. The potential of tax cuts, deregulation, and other supply-side policy options to improve both short- and long-term macro performance is explored. The chapter also offers a discussion of why economic growth is desirable, despite mounting evidence of environmental degradation and excessive consumption.

The final chapter in the macro section is every student's favorite. It starts out with a brief review of the nature and potential uses of fiscal, monetary, and supply-side policy options. Then the economic record is examined to highlight the contrast between theory and reality. The rest of the chapter identifies the obstacles that prevent us from eliminating the business cycle in the real world. These obstacles include everything from faulty forecasts to pork-barrel politics.

Contents: International Perspective

No introduction to economics can omit discussion of the global economy. But how can international topics be included in such a brief survey? *Essentials* resolves this dilemma with a two-pronged approach. The major thrust is to integrate global perspectives throughout the text. Many of the Headline boxes feature international illustrations of core concepts. In addition, the basic contrast between market and command economies that sets the framework for Chapter 1 is referred to repeatedly in both the micro and macro sections. The U.S. economy is described in a global context (Chapter 2) and analyzed throughout as an open economy with substantial foreign trade and investment sectors. Students will not think of the U.S. economy in insular terms as they work through this text.

The second global dimension to this text is a separate chapter on international trade. Chapter 17 describes U.S. trade patterns, then it explains trade on the basis of comparative advantage. Consistent with the real-world focus of the text, a discussion of protectionist pressures and obstacles is also included. Exchange rate determinations are also explained, along with the special interests who favor currency appreciations and depreciations. The objective is to convey a sense not only of why trade is beneficial but also why trade issues are so politically sensitive.

Text Supplements

Study Guide

From the student's perspective, the most important text supplement is the *Study Guide*. The new *Study Guide* has been completely updated by Professor Linda Wilson (University of Texas at Arlington). The *Study Guide* develops quantitative skills and the use of economic terminology, and enhances critical thinking capabilities. Each chapter of the *Study Guide* contains these features:

- *Quick Review* Key points in the text chapter are restated at the beginning of each *Study Guide* chapter.
- *Learning Objectives* The salient lessons of the text chapters are noted at the outset of each *Study Guide* chapter.

- *Using Key Terms* Students are asked to complete a crossword puzzle using key terms.
- *True-False Questions* Ten true-false questions are provided in each chapter.
- *Multiple-Choice Questions* Twenty multiple-choice questions per chapter are provided.
- *Problems and Applications* These exercises stress current issues and events and problem-solving techniques. Headline boxes are the focus of questions and problems.
- *Common Student Errors* The basis for common student errors is explained, along with the correct principles. This unique feature is very effective in helping students discover their own mistakes.
- *Answers* Answers to *all* problems, exercises, and questions are provided at the end of each chapter.

Instructor's Resource Manual

Prepared by Mark Maier of Glendale Community College in collaboration with Todd Easton of the University of Portland, the *Instructor's Resource Manual* (*IRM*) is designed to assist instructors as they cope with the demands of teaching a survey of economics in a single term. Each chapter of the *Instructor's Resource Manual* contains the following features:

- *NEW! What Is This Chapter All About* A brief summary of the chapter.
- *NEW! New to This Edition* A list of changes and updates to the chapter since the last edition.
- *Lecture Launchers* Designed to offer suggestions on how to launch specific topics in each chapter.
- *Common Student Errors* To integrate the lectures with the student *Study Guide,* this provides instructors with a brief description of some of the most common problems that students have when studying the material in each chapter.
- *Headlines* A list of Headlines from the text is provided for easy reference.
- *Annotated Outline* An annotated outline for each chapter can be used as lecture notes.
- *NEW! Structured Controversies* Chapter-related topics are provided for sparking small-group debates that require no additional reading. Also accessible on the website.
- *NEW! Mini-Debates* Additional chapter-related debate topics that require individual students to do outside research in preparation. Also accessible on the website.
- *NEW! Mini-Debate Projects* Seven projects are provided, cutting across all the chapters. These include several focus questions and outside research.
- *Answers to the Chapter Questions and Problems* The IRM provides answers to the end-of-chapter questions and problems in the text, along with explanations of how the answers were derived.
- *Answers to Web Activities* Answers to Web Activities from the textbook are provided in the IRM as well as on the website.
- *Print Media Exercise* Provides a ready-to-use homework assignment using current newspapers and/or periodicals to find articles that illustrate the specific issues.

Test Bank

The *Test Bank to accompany Essentials of Economics* follows the lead of the textbook in its application of economic concepts to worldwide economic issues, current real-world examples, and the role of government in the economy. The *Test Bank* has been prepared by Linda Wilson of the University of Texas at Arlington and Diane Keenan of Cerritos College. The *Test Bank* contains roughly 2,000 objective, predominantly multiple-choice questions. Each multiple-choice question is coded as to level of difficulty and is given a text-page reference where the student will find a discussion of the concept on which the question is based. Questions based on the boxed Headline material are segregated to facilitate their use. Approximately 600 questions are new or revised from the last edition.

PowerPoints

Anthony Zambelli of Cuyamaca College has prepared a comprehensive set of PowerPoint presentations to correspond with the fifth edition. These slides offer the rare opportunity to build animated graphs on-screen, so students see the importance of each step. Consisting of over 500 slides, the PowerPoints present the text's key graphs and illustrations along with lecture notes.

News Flashes

As up-to-date as *Essentials of Economics* is, it can't foretell the future. As the future becomes the present, however, I will write News Flashes describing major economic events and relating them to specific topics in the text. Four to six News Flashes are posted on our website each year (www.mhhe.com/economics/schilleressentials5).

www.mhhe.com/economics/schilleressentials5

With brand-new interactive content developed by Mark Maier of Glendale Community College, Todd Easton of the University of Portland, and Jeffrey Phillips of Morrisville State College, the 5th edition website offers

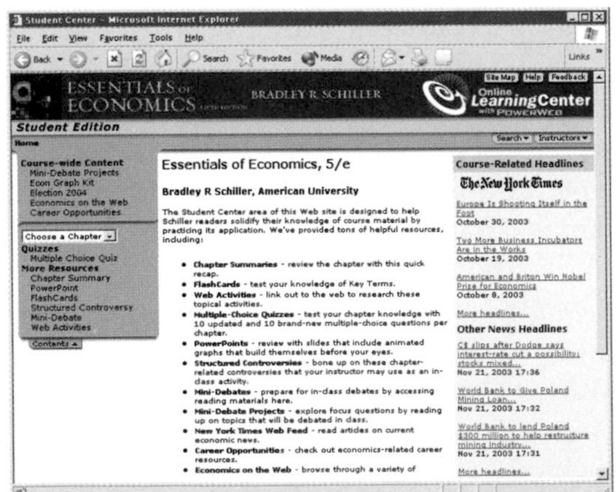

Students have easy access to Chapter Summaries, Key Terms, PowerPoints, a *New York Times* Web Feed, and the following features that include brand-new content:

- Self-quizzes—Now 20 multiple-choice questions per chapter (10 are new!), with a self-grading function that allows students to see results and e-mail them to the professor

- NEW! In-Class Debates
- NEW! Extending the Debate—For in-class debates, including additional reading
- NEW! Debate Projects—Seven projects that provide focus questions and require outside research.

Instructors also have online access to the Instructor's Manual, PowerPoint slides, and helpful grading resources for the Web Activities, Structured Controversies, Mini-Debates, and Mini-Debate Projects.

Acknowledgments

Users of the first four editions have been generous in sharing their experiences and offering suggestions for revision. In addition, the fifth edition benefited from very detailed reviews provided by:

Sue Bartlett, *University of South Florida*
John Bockino, *Suffolk Community College*
Rob Catlett, *Emporia State University*
Bruce Christopherson, *Bellevue Community College*
Mark Friedman, *Minnesota State University—Mankato*
Arlene Geiger, *CUNY—John Jay College of Criminal Justice*
Perry Haan, *Hondros College*
Robert Harmel, *Midwestern State University*
Syed Hussain, *University of Wisconsin—Oshkosh*
Judy Kamm, *Lindenwood University*
Felix B. Kwan, *Maryville University in St. Louis*
Linda M. Kwiatkowski, *Hondros College*
Judy Lee, *Leeward Community College*
Kjartan T. Magnusson, *Salt Lake Community College*
Earl L. Martin, Jr., *Hondros College*
Gayle A. Morris, *Edinboro University of Pennsylvania*
Sunday C. Nzeako, *CUNY—John Jay College of Criminal Justice*
Z. Edward O'Relley, *North Dakota State University*
Janet Ratliff, *Morehead State University*
Robert C. Rencher, Jr., *Liberty University*
Barbara Ross-Pfeiffer, *Kapi'olani Community College*
Gerald Smith, *Minnesota State University—Mankato*
Kenneth A. Small, *University of California at Irvine*
Laura Sosa, *Mercer County Community College*
Wendy Stock, *Montana State University*
Charles Wilf, *Duquesne University*

At McGraw-Hill, I was fortunate to have Katie Crouch as my development editor once again and Kari Geltemeyer as my able project manager. Together they kept all the pieces together as the book and supplements worked their way through the production process. Jon Vaupel provided critical and timely research assistance. Thanks are also due to Martin Quinn, my marketing director, for personal and corporate support of McGraw-Hill's sales efforts.

Last, but far from least, I have continued to benefit from the advice and support of Paul Shensa, my on-and-off editor of 30 years.

Final Thoughts

Hopefully, the brevity, content, style, and novel supplements of *Essentials* will induce you to try it out in your introductory survey course. The ultimate measure of the book's success will be reflected in student motivation and learning. As the author, I would appreciate hearing how well *Essentials* lives up to that standard.

Bradley R. Schiller

Essentials *of* Economics

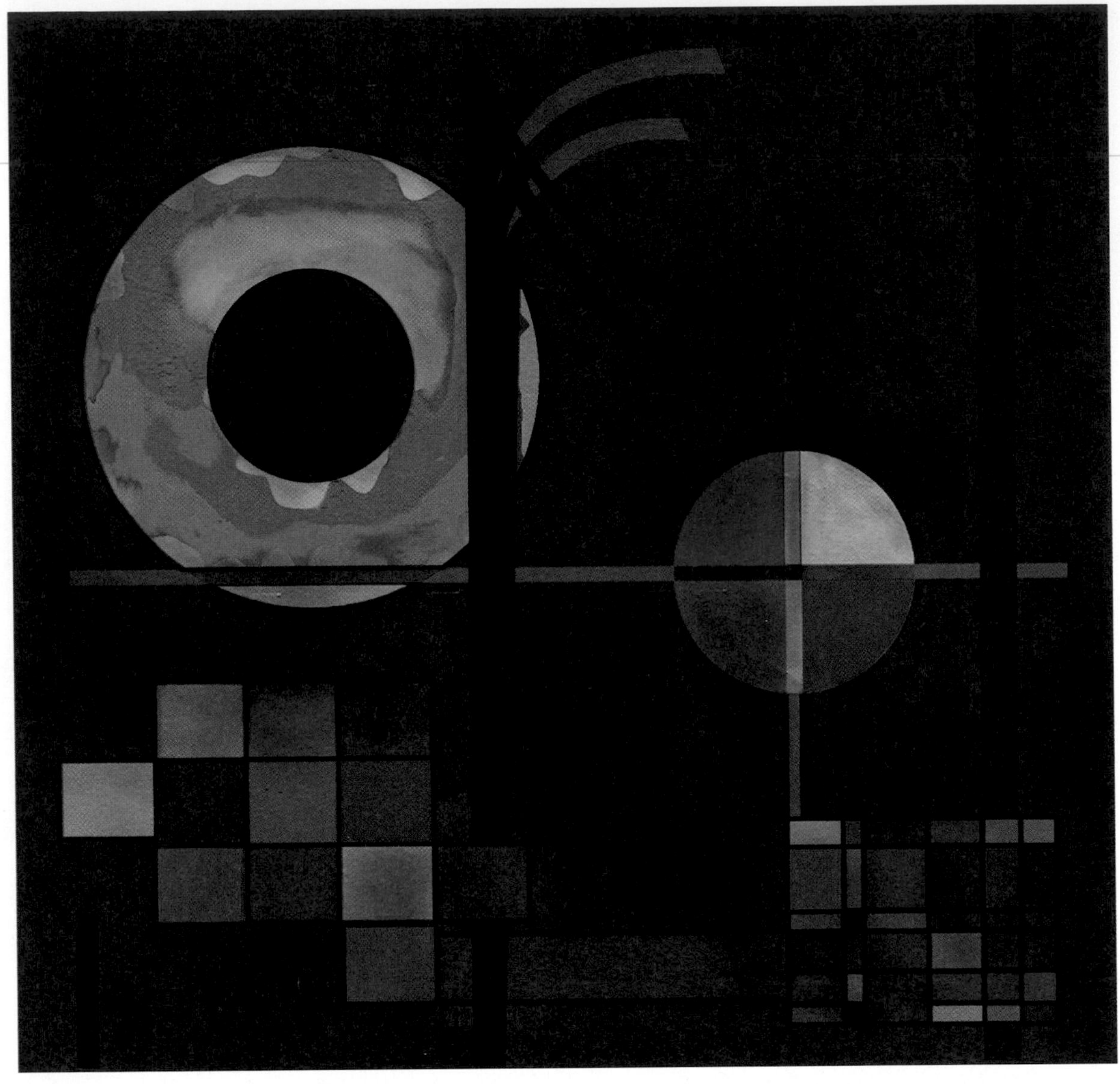

The Challenge of Economics

CHAPTER 1

The twentieth century was very good to the United States of America. At the beginning of that century, life was hard and short. Life expectancy was only 47 years for whites and a shockingly low 33 years for blacks and other minorities. Those people who survived infancy faced substantial risk of early death from tuberculosis, influenza, pneumonia, or gastritis. Measles, syphilis, whooping cough, malaria, typhoid, and smallpox were all life-threatening diseases at the turn of the last century.

Work was a lot harder back then, too. In 1900, one-third of all U.S. families lived on farms, where the workday began before sunrise and lasted all day. Those who lived in the cities typically worked 60 hours a week for wages of only 22 cents an hour. Hours were long, jobs were physically demanding, and workplaces were often dirty and unsafe.

People didn't have much to show for all that work. By today's standards nearly everyone was poor back then. The average income per person was less than $4,000 per year (in today's dollars). Very few people had telephones and even fewer had cars. There were no television sets, no home freezers, no microwaves, no dishwashers or central air-conditioning, and no computers. Even indoor plumbing was a luxury. Only a small elite went to college; an eighth-grade education was the norm.

All of this, of course, sounds like ancient history. Today, most of us take new cars, central air and heat, remote-control TVs, flush toilets, cell phones, and even long weekends for granted. We seldom imagine what life would be like without the abundance of goods and services we encounter daily. Nor do we often imagine how hard work might be had factories, offices, and homes not been transformed by technology.

We ought to ponder, however, how we got so affluent. Was it our high moral standards that made us rich? Was it our religious convictions? Did politics have anything to do with it? Did extending suffrage to women, ending prohibition, or repealing the military draft raise our living standards? Did the many wars fought in the twentieth century enhance our material well-being? Was the tremendous expansion of the public sector the catalyst for growth? Were we just lucky?

Some people say America has prospered because our nation was blessed with an abundance of natural resources. But other countries are larger. Many others have more oil, more arable land, more gold, more people, and more math majors. Yet few nations have prospered as much as the United States. Indeed, many countries today are no better off than the United States was a century ago.

Students of history can't ignore the role that economic *systems* might have played in these developments. In the mid-nineteenth century, Karl Marx predicted that the capitalist *system* of private ownership would eventually self-destruct. The capitalists who owned the land, the factories, and the machinery would continue exploiting the working class until it rose up and overthrew the social order. Long-term prosperity would be possible only if the state owned the means of production and managed the economy.

Things didn't work out as Marx predicted. People in the U.S. working class that Marx worried about now own their own home, a couple of cars, TVs, and DVDs, and they take expensive vacations they locate on the Internet. By contrast, the nations that adopted Marxian systems—Russia, China, North Korea, East Germany, Cuba—fell behind more market-oriented economies. The gap in living standards between communist and capitalist nations got so wide that communism effectively collapsed. People in those countries wanted a different economic system—one that would deliver the goods capitalist consumers were already enjoying. In the last decade of the twentieth century, formerly communist nations scrambled to transform their economies from centrally planned ones to more market-oriented systems. They sought the rules, the mechanisms, the engine that would propel their living standards upward.

Even in the United States the quest for greater prosperity continues. As rich as we are, we always want more. Fewer than four out of ten Americans feel that they have "most everything" they want. How will we get still *more* goods and services? Will the economic system that served us so well in the twentieth century continue to churn out more goods and services in the twenty-first century? A combination of terrorist attacks, wars in Afghanistan and Iraq, a brief recession, and a stock-market collapse in 2000–03 made many Americans anxious about the future. A 2003 public-opinion poll showed that as many as one out of three Americans expected their children to have *fewer* goods and services than they do (see Headline).

Is America's affluence an accident or the result of an effective economic system?

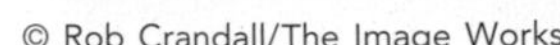
© Rob Crandall/The Image Works.

Hisham Ibrahim/Getty Images.

GROWTH PROSPECTS HEADLINE

Will Your Kids Be Better Off?

Question: Do you expect your children's generation to enjoy a higher standard of living than your generation?

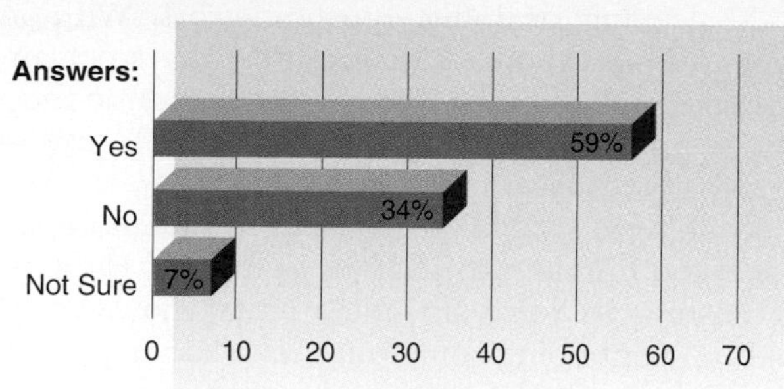

Source: NBC/*Wall Street Journal* poll, January 2003.

NOTE: For living standards to keep rising, the economy must continue to grow. Will that happen? How?

And what about people in other nations? The Russian standard of living today resembles the American standard during the Great Depression of the 1930s. Even that pitiful standard is the envy of the billion or so people in Africa, Asia, and South America who subsist on incomes of less than $1 a day. How can they ever catch up with American living standards (where families are officially designated as poor if they have less than $60 a day)?

To answer these questions we need a better sense of what an economic system is and how it works. That is the foremost goal of this course. We want to know what kind of system a "market economy" really is. How does it work? Who determines the price of a textbook in a market economy? Who decides how many textbooks will be produced? Will everyone who needs a textbook get one? And why are gasoline prices so high? How about jobs? Who decides how many jobs are available or what wages they pay in a market economy? What keeps an economy growing? Or stops it in its tracks?

To understand how an economy works and what to expect from it, we'll have to ask and answer a lot of questions. Three central questions will be paramount, however. They are:

- What are the basic goals of an economic system?
- How does a market economy address these goals?
- What role should government play in shaping economic outcomes?

We won't answer all of these questions in this first chapter. But we will get a sense of what the study of economics is all about and why the answers to these central questions are both important and controversial.

The Central Problem of Scarcity

The land area of the United States stretches over 3.5 million square miles. We have a population of over 290 million, about half of whom work. We also have over $30 trillion worth of buildings and machinery. With so many resources, the United States can produce an enormous volume of output. As we've observed, however, consumers always want more, more, more. We want not only faster cars, more clothes, and larger TVs but also more roads, better schools, and more police protection. Why can't we have everything we want?

The answer is fairly simple: ***our* wants *exceed our* resources.** As abundant as our resources might appear, they are not capable of producing everything we want. The same kind of problem makes doing homework so painful. You have only 24 hours in a day. You can spend it watching movies, shopping, hanging out with friends, sleeping, or doing your homework. With only 24 hours in a day, you've got to make choices. **Economics** offers a framework for explaining how we make such choices. The goal of economic theory is to figure out how we can best cope with scarcity. How can we use our scarce resources in the best possible way?

economics The study of how best to allocate scarce resources among competing uses.

To answer this question, economists analyze the nature of the choices we make. Consider again your decision to read this chapter right now. Hopefully, you'll get some benefit from finishing it. You'll also incur a *cost,* however. The time you spend reading could be spent doing something else. You're probably missing a good show on TV right now. Giving up that show is the *opportunity cost* of reading this chapter. You have sacrificed the opportunity to watch TV in order to finish this homework. In general, whatever you decide to do with your time will entail an **opportunity cost,** that is, the sacrifice of a next-best alternative. The rational thing to do is to weigh the benefits of doing your homework against the implied opportunity cost, then make a choice.

opportunity cost The most desired goods and services that are forgone in order to obtain something else.

The larger society faces a similar dilemma. For the larger economy, time is also limited. So, too, are the resources needed to produce desired goods and services. To get more houses, more cars, or more movies, we need not only time but also resources to produce these things. These resources—land, labor, capital, and entrepreneurship—are the basic ingredients of production. They are called **factors of production.** The more factors of production we have, the more we can produce in a given period of time.

factors of production Resource inputs used to produce goods and services; e.g., land, labor, capital, entrepreneurship.

As we noted earlier, our available resources always fall short of our output desires. The central problem here again is **scarcity,** a situation where our desires for goods and services exceed our capacity to produce them.

scarcity Lack of enough resources to satisfy all desired uses of those resources.

Three Basic Economic Questions

The central problem of scarcity forces every society to make difficult choices. Specifically, every nation must resolve three critical questions about the use of its scarce resources:

- WHAT to produce
- HOW to produce
- FOR WHOM to produce

We will first examine the nature of each question, then review the mechanisms different countries use for answering these three basic questions.

WHAT to Produce

The WHAT question is quite simple. We've already noted that there isn't enough time in the day to do everything you want to. Nor are there enough resources in the economy to produce all the goods and services society desires. ***Because wants exceed resources, we have to decide WHAT we want most, sacrificing less desired activities and goods.***

Production Possibilities Figure 1.1 illustrates this basic dilemma. Suppose there are only two kinds of goods, "consumer goods" and "military goods." In this case, the question of WHAT to produce boils down to finding the most desirable combination of these two goods.

To make that selection, we first need to know how much of each good we *could* produce. That will depend on how many resources we have available.

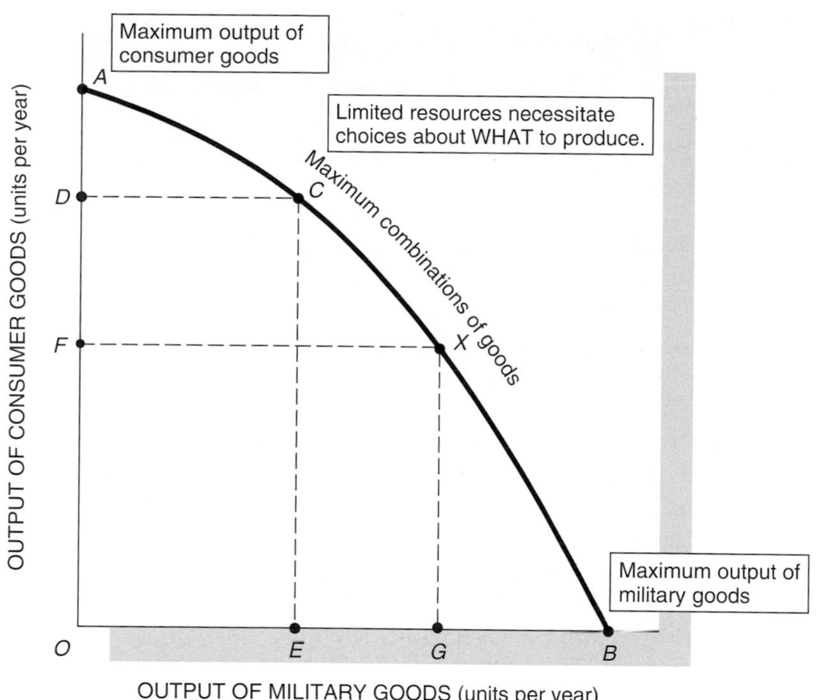

FIGURE 1.1
A Production-Possibilities Curve

A production-possibilities curve describes the various combinations of final goods or services that could be produced in a given time period with available resources and technology. It represents a menu of output choices. Point *C* indicates that we could produce a *combination* of *OD* units of consumer goods and the quantity *OE* of military output. To get more military output (e.g., at point *X*), we have to reduce consumer output (to *OF*). Our objective is to select the best possible mix of output from the choices on the production-possibilities curve.

The first thing we need to do, then, is to count up our factors of production. The factors of production include:

- **Land** (including natural resources)
- **Labor** (number and skills of workers)
- **Capital** (machinery, buildings, networks)
- **Entrepreneurship** (skill in creating products, services, and processes)

The more we have of these factors, the more output we can produce. Our technological ability is also critical. The more advanced our technology—our technological and managerial abilities—the more output we will be able to produce with available factors of production. If we inventoried all our resources and technology, we could figure out what the physical *limits* to production are.

To simplify the computation, suppose we wanted to produce only consumer goods. How much *could* we produce? Surely, not an infinite amount. After assessing our stocks of land, labor, capital, and technology, we'd discover that there was a *finite* limit on such output. The *limit* is represented by point *A* in Figure 1.1. That is to say, the vertical distance from the origin (point *O*) to point *A* represents the *maximum* quantity of consumer goods that could be produced this year. To produce the quantity *A* of consumer goods, we would have to use *all* available factors of production. At point *A* no resources would be available for producing military goods. The choice of *maximum* consumer output implies *zero* military output.

We could make other choices about WHAT to produce. Point *B*, for example, illustrates another extreme. The horizontal distance from the origin (point *O*) to point *B* represents our *maximum* capacity to produce military goods. To get that much military output, we would have to devote all available resources to that single task. At point *B*, we wouldn't be producing *any* consumer goods. We would be well protected but ill-nourished and poorly clothed (wearing last year's clothes).

Our choices about WHAT to produce are not limited to the extremes of points *A* and *B*. We could instead produce a *combination* of consumer and military goods. Point *C* represents one such combination. To get to point *C*,

TABLE 1.1
Specific Production Possibilities

The choice of WHAT to produce eventually boils down to specific goods and services. Here the choices are defined in terms of missiles or houses. More missiles can be produced only if some resources are diverted from home construction. Only one of these output combinations can be produced in a given time period. Selecting that mix is a basic economic issue.

	Possible Output Combinations					
Output	A	B	C	D	E	F
Missiles	0	50	100	150	200	250
Houses	100	90	75	55	30	0

production possibilities The alternative combinations of goods and services that could be produced in a given time period with all available resources and technology.

we have to forsake maximum consumer goods output (point *A*) and use some of our scarce resources to produce military goods. At point *C* we are producing only *OD* of consumer goods and *OE* of military goods.

Point *C* is just one of many combinations we *could* produce. We could produce *any* combination of output represented by points along the curve in Figure 1.1. For this reason we call it the **production-possibilities** curve; it represents the alternative combinations of goods and services that could be produced in a given time period with all available resources and technology. It is, in effect, an economic menu from which some combination of goods and services must be selected.

The production-possibilities curve puts the basic issue of WHAT to produce in graphic terms. The same choices can be depicted in numerical terms as well. Table 1.1, for example, illustrates specific tradeoffs between missile production and home construction. The output mix *A* allocates all resources to home construction, leaving nothing to produce missiles. If missiles are desired, the level of home construction must be cut back. To produce 50 missiles (mix *B*), home construction activity must be cut back to 90. Output mixes *C* through *F* illustrate other possible choices. Only one mix of output—one choice—can be made at any time. The question of WHAT to produce thus boils down to choosing one specific mix of output—a single point on the production-possibilities curve.

The Choices Nations Make There is no single point on the production-possibilities curve that is right for all nations at all times. In the United States, the share of total output devoted to "guns" has varied greatly. During World War II, we converted auto plants to produce military vehicles. Clothing manufacturers cut way back on consumer clothing in order to produce more uniforms for the army, navy, and air force. The government also forcibly drafted 12 million men and women to bear arms. By shifting resources from the production of consumer goods to the production of military goods, we were able to move down along the production-possibilities curve in Figure 1.1 toward point *X*. By 1944 fully 40 percent of all our output consisted of military goods. Consumer goods were so scarce that everything from butter to golf balls had to be rationed.

Figure 1.2 illustrates the rapid military buildup during World War II. The figure also illustrates how quickly we reallocated factors of production to consumer goods after the war ended. By 1948, less than 4 percent of U.S. output was military goods. We had moved close to point *A* in Figure 1.1.

Peace Dividends We changed the mix of output dramatically again to fight the Korean War. Since then, we have been slowly, if somewhat erratically, moving along the production-possibilities curve to an ever smaller military share. Less than 4 percent of total output now consists of military goods.

As we reduced the size of the military, we freed up more resources for the production of civilian goods and services. In the last 20 years, the U.S. armed forces have been reduced by nearly 600,000 personnel. As these personnel found civilian jobs, they increased consumer output. That increase in nonmilitary output is called the *peace dividend*. Notice in Figure 1.3 how the output of consumer goods increases from OC_1 to OC_2 as the mix of output

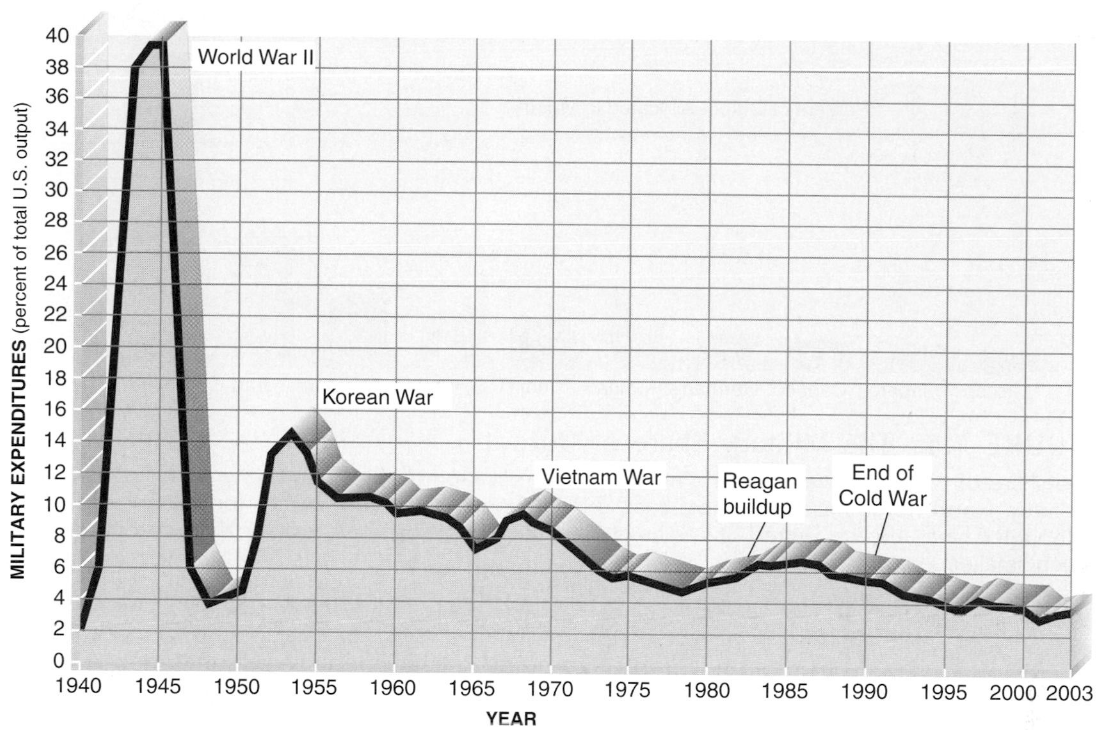

FIGURE 1.2 Military Share of Total U.S. Output

The share of total output devoted to national defense has risen sharply in wars and fallen in times of peace. The defense buildup of the 1980s increased the military share to more than 6 percent of total output. The end of the Cold War reversed that buildup, releasing resources for other uses (the peace dividend).

Source: Congressional Research Service.

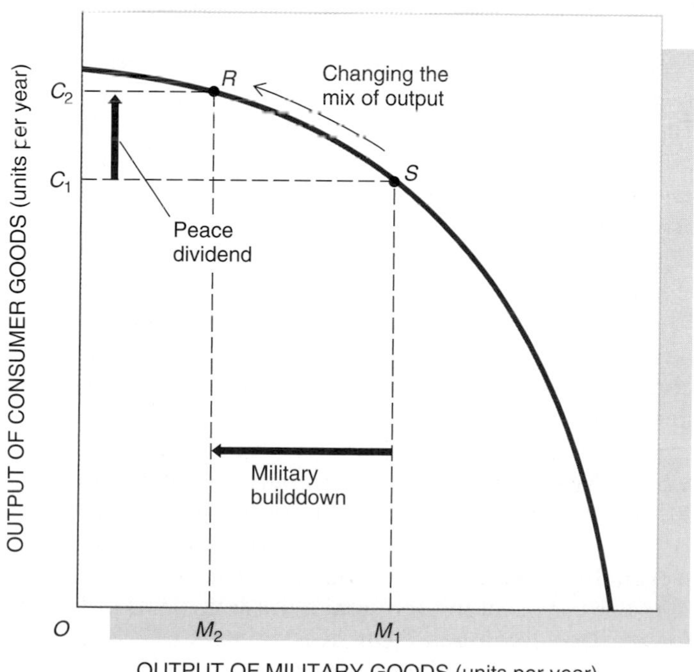

FIGURE 1.3
The Cost of War

A reduction in military output releases factors of production that can be used to produce consumer goods. The military builddown associated with the move from point *S* to point *R* enables consumption output to increase from C_1 to C_2. A military buildup reverses the process reducing output of consumer goods. The economic cost of war is measured by the implied reduction in nondefense output.

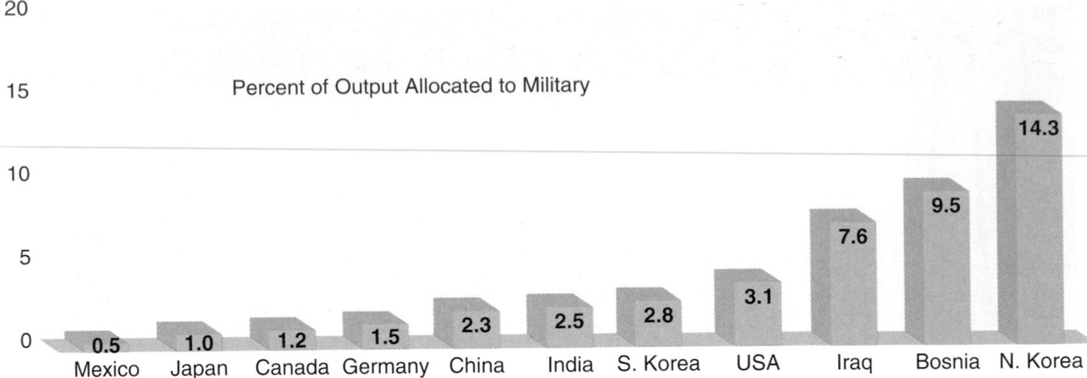

FIGURE 1.4 The Military Share of Output

The share of output allocated to the military is an indication of the opportunity cost of maintaining an army. North Korea has the highest cost, using 14 percent of its resources for military purposes. Although China and the United States have much larger armies, their military *share* of output is much smaller.

Source: World Bank (2001 data).

moves from point S to point R. That increase in consumer output is the peace dividend of a military builddown (from OM_1 to OM_2 in Figure 1.3).

The Cost of War When a nation mobilizes for war, the process is reversed. To wage war against Iraq, for example, the government spent more than $150 billion. The *economic* cost of that effort was measured in lost consumer output. The money spent by the government on war might otherwise have been spent on schools, highways, or other nondefense projects. The National Guard personnel called up for the war would otherwise have stayed home and produced consumer goods.

In some countries the opportunity cost of military output seems far too high. North Korea, for example, has the fourth-largest army in the world. Yet North Korea is a relatively small country. Consequently, it must allocate a huge share of its resources to feed, clothe, and arm its military. As Figure 1.4 illustrates, 14 percent of North Korean output consists of military goods and services. That compares with a military share of only 3 percent in the United States.

North Korea's military has a high price tag. North Korea is a very poor country, with output per capita in the neighborhood of $1,000 per year. That is substantially less than the American standard of living was in 1900 and a tiny fraction of today's output per capita (around $38,000). Although one-third of North Korea's population lives on farms, the country cannot grow enough food to feed its population. The farm sector needs more machinery, seeds, and fertilizer; better-trained labor; and improved irrigation systems. So long as the military absorbs one-seventh of total output, however, North Korea can't afford to modernize its farm sector. The implied shortfall in food and other consumer goods is the *opportunity cost* of a large military sector (see Headline).

The Best Possible Mix North Koreans apparently believed that a large military establishment was essential to their well-being and security. Recurrent famines and persistently low living standards compelled them to rethink that choice, however. In seeking to normalize relations with South Korea, the North Koreans are now seeking to change the mix of output in favor of more consumer goods. In September 2000, Russia pursued the same policy, cutting its military force by 30 percent (see Headline).

OPPORTUNITY COST HEADLINE

North Korea Says It Is Running Out of Food

TOKYO; March 3 (Tuesday)—North Korea issued its most dire assessment yet of its food shortages on Monday, saying that a hungry population already living on starvation rations could run out of food in as little as two weeks.

The official state news agency reported that daily rations for most people had already been cut to seven ounces a day, far below what is generally considered necessary for survival. It said that even if that ration is cut in half, "the stock will run out in mid-March."

Because of North Korea's secretive nature, it is virtually impossible to know whether its statements about the shortages are accurate. If true, millions of people could be at immediate risk of famine and starvation.

—Kevin Sullivan

Source: *Washington Post*, March 2, 1998, p. A11.

N. Korea Expanding Missile Programs

Despite international pressure to curtail its missile program, North Korea is building at least two new launch facilities for the medium-range Taepo Dong 1 and has stepped up production of short-range missiles, according to U.S. intelligence and diplomatic sources.

The projects, and a conclusion by U.S. intelligence agencies that North Korea intends to test-fire a second missile capable of striking Japan, are inflaming regional tensions, U.S. officials and Korea experts said.

—Dana Priest *and* Thomas W. Lippman

Source: *Washington Post*, November 20, 1998, p. 1.

NOTE: North Korea's inability to feed itself is due in part to its large army. Resources used for the military aren't available for producing food.

CHANGING THE OUTPUT MIX HEADLINE

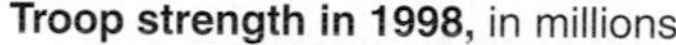

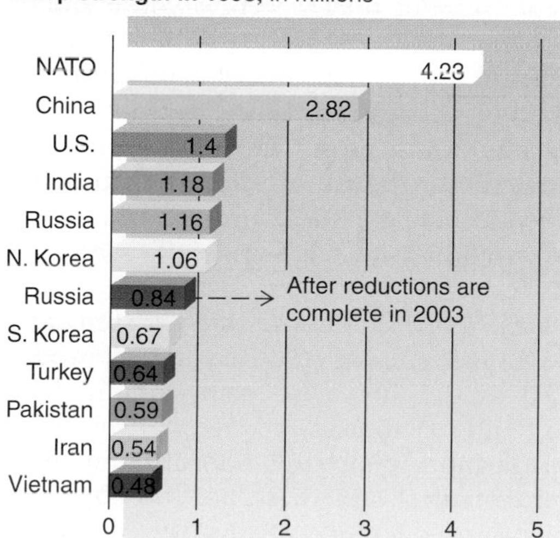

Russia Tightens Its Belt

Financially strapped Russia announced cuts in its armed forces over the next three years. Here is a comparison with troop strengths of other nations:

Source: Military Balance, from *Washington Post*, September 9, 2000, p. 1.

NOTE: To raise living standards, Russia decided it had to shift more resources out of the military and into private-sector production.

What else might these women be producing?

AP/Wide World Photos

Ultimately, the designation of any particular mix of output as "best" rests on the value judgments of a society. A militaristic society would prefer a mix of output closer to point *B* in Figure 1.1. A community of pacifists would prefer a mix of output closer to point *A*. At any moment in time, ***there is one specific mix of output that is optimal for a country,*** that is, a mix that represents the best possible allocation of resources across competing uses. Locating and producing that optimal mix of output is the essence of the WHAT challenge. Of all the points along the production-possibilities curve, every nation wants to find the single point that represents the best possible mix of output.

The optimal mix of output changes when values or circumstances change. During the Cold War that persisted from 1948 to 1989, there was a general consensus that the United States needed to maintain a huge arsenal of weapons. Not everyone agreed with that conclusion, but both the Republican and Democratic political parties supported the proposition. As a result, national defense spending absorbed as much as 6.5 percent of total output in the mid-1980s. When the Soviet Union collapsed, the need for American military preparedness diminished. People felt safer and therefore placed less priority on military output. A different mix of output—one that included more nonmilitary goods—was desired. In 2001 President George W. Bush suggested that we might have moved too far in that direction. He proposed to enhance America's military readiness by producing more "guns." After the September 11, 2001 terrorist attacks on New York City and Washington, D.C. there was a broad public consensus to devote a larger share of output to national defense and homeland security.

Although society's answer to the WHAT question may change over time, ***there is only one best possible (optimal) mix of output at any given time. The first economic goal of any society is to produce that optimal mix of output.***

The same desire for an optimal mix of output drives your decisions on the use of scarce time. There is only one *best* way to use your time on any given day. If you use your time in that way, you will maximize your well-being. Other uses won't necessarily kill you, but they won't do you as much good.

Economic Growth The selection of an optimal mix depends in part on how future-oriented one is. If you had no concern for future jobs or income, there would be little point in doing homework now. You might as well party all day if you're that present-oriented. On the other hand, if you value future jobs and income, it makes sense to allocate some present time to studying. Then you'll have more human capital (knowledge and skills) later to pursue job opportunities.

The larger society confronts the same choice between present and future consumption. We could devote all our present resources to the production of consumer goods and services. If we did, however, there wouldn't be any factors of production available to build machinery, factories, or telecommunications networks. A complete dedication to present consumption would also leave no resources for research activities. Yet these are the kinds of **investment** that enhance our capacity to produce. If we want the economy to keep growing—and our living standards to rise—we must allocate some of our scarce resources to investment rather than consumption. The resultant **economic growth** will expand our production possibilities outward, allowing us to produce more of all goods. The phenomenon of economic growth is illustrated in Figure 1.5 by the outward *shift* of the production-possibilities curve.

investment Expenditures on (production of) new plant and equipment (capital) in a given time period, plus changes in business inventories.

economic growth An increase in output (real GDP): an expansion of production possibilities.

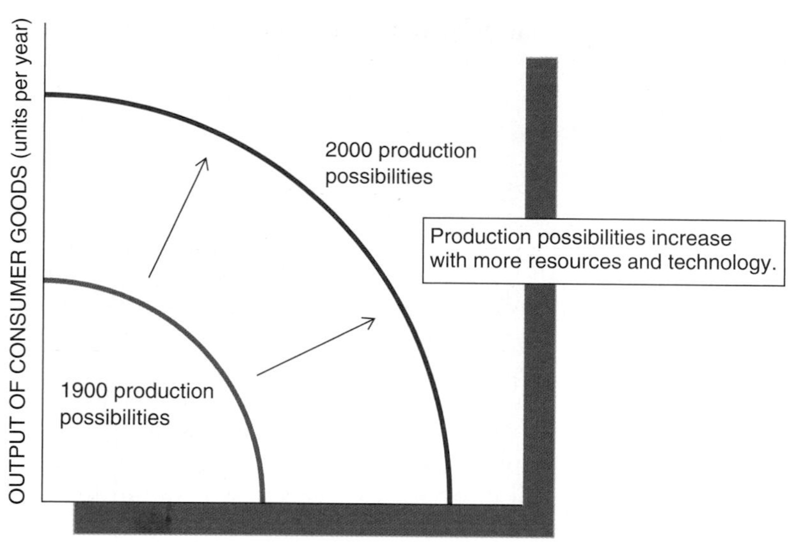

FIGURE 1.5
Economic Growth

Since 1900, the U.S. population has quadrupled. Investment in machinery and buildings has increased our capital stock even faster. These additional factors of production, together with advancing technology, have expanded (shifted outward) our production possibilities.

The tradeoff between consumption and investment required to attain such growth adds another level of complexity to the WHAT decision.

HOW to Produce

The second basic economic question concerns HOW we produce output. Should this class be taught in an auditorium or in small discussion sections? Should it meet twice a week or only once? Should the instructor make more use of computer aids? Should, heaven forbid, this textbook be replaced with online text files? There are numerous ways of teaching a course. Of these many possibilities, one way is presumably best, given the resources and technology available. That best way is HOW we want the course taught. Educational researchers and a good many instructors spend a lot of time trying to figure out the best way of teaching a course.

Chicken farmers do the same thing. They know they can fatten chickens up with a lot of different grains and other food. They can also vary breeding patterns, light exposure, and heat. They can use more labor in the feeder process, or more machinery. Faced with so many choices, the chicken farmers try to find the *best* way of raising chickens.

The HOW question isn't just an issue of getting more output from available inputs. It also encompasses our use of the environment. Should the waste from chicken farms be allowed to contaminate groundwater or local waterways? Or do we want to keep the water clean for other uses? Humanitarian concerns may also come into play. Should live chickens be processed without any concern for their welfare? Or should the processing be designed to minimize trauma? The HOW question encompasses all such issues. Although people may hold different views on these questions, everyone shares a common goal: ***to find an optimal method of producing goods and services.*** The best possible answer to the HOW question will entail both efficiency in the use of factors of

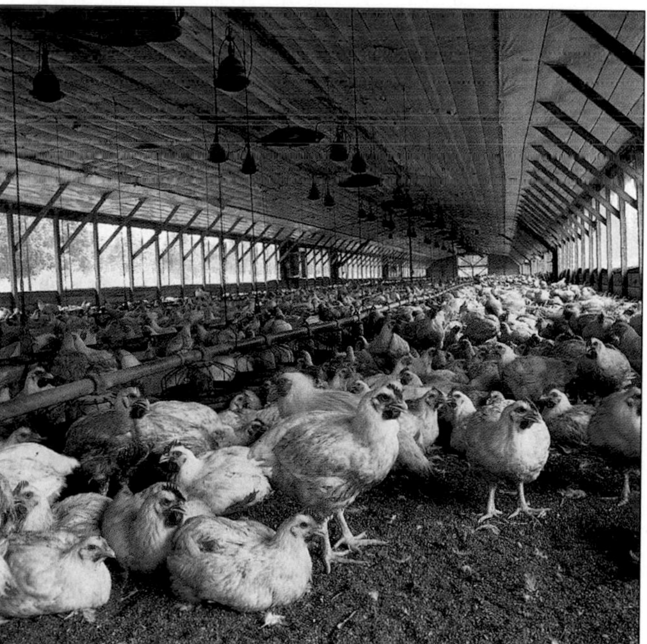

Should chicken farmers be free to process chickens and to dispose of waste in any way they desire? Or should the government regulate how chickens are produced?

Norm Thomas/Photo Researchers, Inc.

production and adequate safeguards for the environment and other social concerns.

FOR WHOM to Produce

The third basic economic question every society must confront is FOR WHOM? The answers to the WHAT and HOW questions determine how large an economic pie we'll bake and how we'll bake it. Then we have to slice it up. Should everyone get an equal slice of the pie? Or can some people have big pieces of the pie while others get only crumbs? In other words, ***the FOR WHOM question focuses on how an economy's output is distributed across members of society.***

A pie can be divided up in many ways. Personally, I like a distribution that gives me a big slice even if that leaves less for others. Maybe you feel the same way. Whatever your feelings, however, there is likely to be a lot of disagreement about what distribution is best. Maybe we should just give everyone an equal slice. But should everyone get an equal slice even if some people helped bake the pie while others contributed nothing? The Little Red Hen of children's fables felt perfectly justified eating all the pie herself after her friends and neighbors refused to help sow the seeds, harvest the grain, or bake the pie! Should such a work-based sense of equity determine how all goods are distributed?

Karl Marx's communist vision of utopia entailed a very different FOR WHOM answer. The communist ideal is "from each according to his ability, to each according to his need." In that vision, all pitch in to bake the pie according to their abilities. Slices of the pie are distributed, however, based on need (hunger, desire) rather than on productive contributions. In a communal utopia there is no direct link between work and consumption.

Incentives There is a risk entailed in distributing slices of the pie based on need rather than work effort. People who work hard to bake the pie may feel cheated if nonworkers get just as large a slice. Worse still, people may decide to exert less effort if they see no tangible reward to working. If that happens, the size of the pie may shrink and everyone will be worse off.

This is the kind of problem welfare programs create. Welfare programs are intended to provide a slice of the pie to people who don't have enough income to satisfy basic needs. As welfare benefits rise, however, the incentive to work diminishes. If people choose welfare checks over paychecks, total output will decline.

The same problem emerges in the tax system. If Paul is heavily taxed to provide welfare benefits to Peter, Paul may decide that hard work and entrepreneurship don't pay. To the extent that taxes discourage work, production, or investment, they shrink the size of the pie that feeds all of us.

The potential tradeoffs between taxes, welfare, and work don't compel us to dismantle all tax and welfare programs. They do emphasize, however, how difficult it is to select the right answer to the FOR WHOM question. The optimal distribution of income must satisfy our sense of fairness as well as our desire for more output.

The Mechanisms of Choice

By now, two things should be apparent. First, every society has to make difficult choices about WHAT, HOW, and FOR WHOM to produce. Second, those choices aren't easy. ***There are conflicts and tradeoffs with every***

choice. More of one good implies less of another. A more efficient production process may pollute the environment. Helping the poor may dull work incentives. In every case, society has to weigh the alternatives and try to find the best possible answer to each question.

How does "society" actually make such choices? What are the mechanisms we use to decide WHAT to produce, HOW, and FOR WHOM?

The Political Process

Many of these basic economic decisions are made through the political process. Consider again the decision to shrink the military share of output in the 1990s. Who made that decision? Not me. Not you. Not the mass of consumers who were streaming through real and virtual malls. No, the decisions on military buildups and builddowns were made in the political arena. The U.S. Congress made those decisions on behalf of consumers and producers. Congress also makes decisions about how many interstate highways to build, how many Head Start classes to offer, and how much space exploration to pursue.

Should *all* decisions about WHAT to produce be made in the political arena? Should Congress also decide how much ice cream will be produced, and how many DVD players? What about essentials, like food and shelter? Should decisions about the production of those goods be made in Washington, D.C., or should the mix of output be selected some other way?

The Market Mechanism

The market mechanism offers an alternative decision-making process. In a market-driven economy the process of selecting a mix of output is as familiar as grocery shopping. If you desire ice cream and have sufficient income, you simply buy ice cream. Your purchases signal to producers that ice cream is desired. By expressing the *ability and willingness to pay* for ice cream, you are telling ice cream producers that their efforts are going to be rewarded. If enough consumers feel the same way you do—and are able and willing to pay the price of ice cream—ice cream producers will churn out more ice cream.

The same kind of interaction helps determine which crops we grow. There is only so much good farmland available. Should we grow corn or beans? If consumers prefer corn, they will buy more corn and shun the beans. Farmers will quickly get the market's message and devote more of their land to corn, cutting back on bean production. In the process, the mix of output will change—moving us closer to the choice consumers have made.

The central actor in this reshuffling of resources and outputs is the **market mechanism.** ***Market sales and prices send a signal to producers about what mix of output consumers want.*** If you want something and have sufficient income, you buy it. If enough people do the same thing, the total sales of that product will rise, and perhaps its price will as well. Producers, seeing sales and prices rise, will be inclined to increase production. To do so, they will acquire a larger share of our available resources and use it to produce the goods we desire. No direct communication between us and the producer is required; market sales and prices convey the message and direct the market, much like an "invisible hand."

market mechanism The use of market prices and sales to signal desired outputs (or resource allocations).

It was this ability of "the market" to select a desirable mix of output that so impressed the eighteenth-century economist Adam Smith. He argued that nations would prosper with less government interference and more reliance on the invisible hand of the marketplace. As he saw it, markets were efficient mechanisms for deciding what goods to produce, how to produce them, and even what wages to pay. Smith's writings (*The Wealth of Nations,* 1776) urged government to pursue a policy of **laissez faire**—leaving the market alone to make basic economic decisions.

laissez faire The doctrine of "leave it alone," of nonintervention by government in the market mechanism.

Central Planning

Karl Marx saw things differently. In his view, a freewheeling marketplace would cater to the whims of the rich and neglect the needs of the poor. Workers would be exploited by industrial barons and great landowners. To "leave it to the market," as Smith had proposed, would encourage exploitation. In the mid-nineteenth century, Karl Marx proposed a radical alternative: overturn the power of the elite and create a communist state in which everyone's needs would be fulfilled. Marx's writings (*Das Kapital,* 1867) encouraged communist revolutions and the development of central planning systems. The (people's) government, not the market, assumed responsibility for deciding what goods were produced, at what prices they were sold, and even who got them.

Central planning is still the principal mechanism of choice in some countries. In North Korea and Cuba, for example, the central planners decide how many cars to produce and how much bread. They then assign workers and other resources to those industries to implement their decisions. They also decide who will get the bread and the cars that are produced. Individuals cannot own factors of production nor even employ other workers for wages. The WHAT, HOW, and FOR WHOM outcomes are all directed by the central government.

Mixed Economies

Few countries still depend so fully on central planners (government) to make basic economic decisions. China, Russia, and other formerly communist nations have turned over many decisions to the market mechanism. Likewise, no nation relies exclusively on markets to fashion economic outcomes. In the United States, for example, we let the market decide how much ice cream will be produced and how many cars. We use the political process, however, to decide how many highways to construct, how many schools to build, and how much military output to produce.

Because most nations use a combination of government directives and market mechanisms to determine economic outcomes, they are called **mixed economies.** There is huge variation in that mix, however. The government-dominated economic systems in North Korea, Cuba, Laos, and Libya are starkly different from the freewheeling economies of Singapore, Bahrain, New Zealand, or the United States.

mixed economy An economy that uses both market and nonmarket signals to allocate goods and resources.

Undesirable Choices

Although differences across nations in their relative reliance on markets or government are huge, the common use of *both* market signals and government directives raises an interesting question. Why don't we let the market make *all* our output decisions? If the market does such a good job in producing the right amount of ice cream, couldn't it also decide how many highways to build or how much weaponry to produce?

Market Failure

The market does not work equally well in all situations. In fact, in some circumstances, the market mechanism might actually fail to produce the goods and services society desires. National defense is an example. Most people want to feel that their nation's borders are secure and that law and order will prevail in their communities. But few people can afford to buy an army or maintain a legal system. Even if someone were rich enough to pay for such security, he or she might decline to do so. After all, a military force and a legal system would benefit everyone in the community, not just those individuals who paid for it. Recognizing this, few people would willingly pay for national security or a system of criminal justice. They would rather spend their income on ice cream and DVD players, hoping someone else would pay for law and order. If everyone waited for a free ride, no money would be spent on national defense or a legal system. Society would end up with neither output, even though both services were widely desired.

In other situations, the market might produce *too much* of a good or service. If there were no government regulation, then anyone who had enough money could purchase and drive a car. Little kids from wealthy families could hit the highways, and so could adults with a history of drunken driving. Moreover, no one would have to spend money on emissions-control systems, lead-free gasoline, or mufflers. We could drive as fast as we wanted.

Some people would welcome unregulated roadways as a new utopia. Others, however, would be concerned about safety and pollution. They would realize that the *market's* decisions about who could drive and what kinds of cars were produced might not be so perfect. They would want the government to intervene. To assure safer and cleaner driving, people might agree to let the government regulate speed, auto emissions, and even drivers.

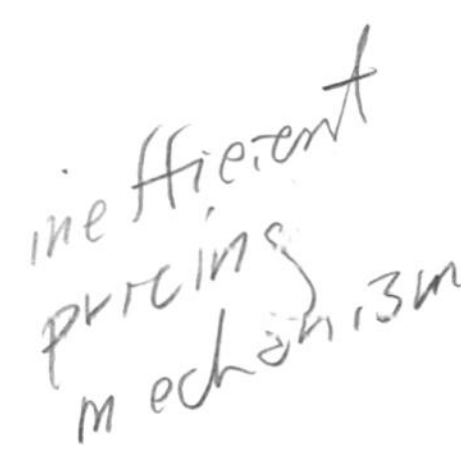

The Wrong Mix of Output These and other situations suggest that the market alone might not always pick the best possible mix of output. The problem is illustrated in Figure 1.6. In principle there is a single *best* mix of output among the array of choices along the production-possibilities curve. Suppose that we could somehow divine where that mix is. In Figure 1.6 that best-possible mix is arbitrarily placed at point *X*.

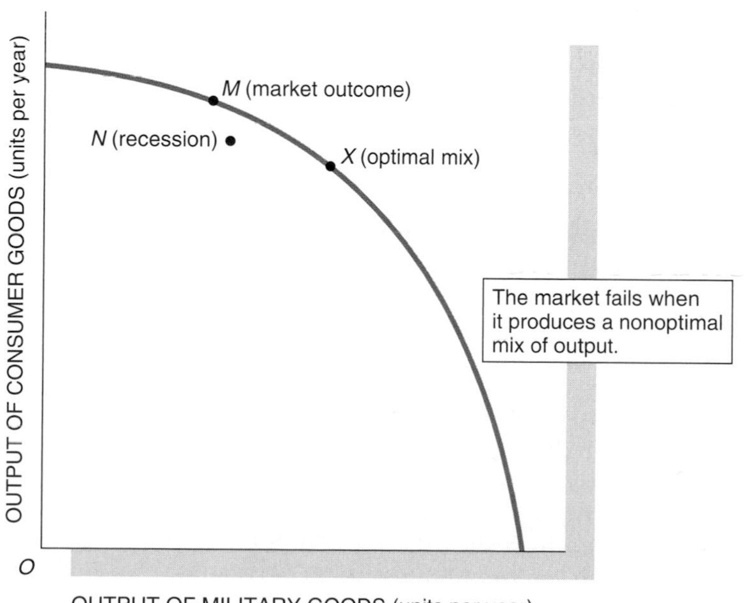

FIGURE 1.6
Market Failure

The market mechanism will allocate resources to produce a specific mix of output. In this case, however, the market-generated mix (point *M*) is not consistent with society's most desired mix (point *X*). When this happens, the market has failed.

An unregulated market might generate too much pollution. Such a market failure requires government intervention.

Gary Milburn/Tom Stack & Associates

The question now is what mix of output will the *market* produce? Suppose that the market generates the mix of output represented by point M in Figure 1.6. Clearly, the market outcome (point M) is *not* the most desirable outcome (point X). In this case, we would conclude that the market had *failed*. **Market failure** means that the market does not produce the best possible mix of output. In Figure 1.6, the market produces too much civilian output and too little military output. When the market fails to produce the right mix of output, government intervention may be required to get to point X.

market failure An imperfection in the market mechanism that prevents optimal outcomes.

The market mechanism might also fail to make full use of the economy's production possibilities. If some workers cannot find jobs, the mix of output may end up *inside* the production-possibilities curve, as at point N in Figure 1.6. This is what happened during the Great Depression of the 1930s and in a dozen or so lesser recessions since then. When the market fails in this way, the goal of economic policy is to restore full employment by moving back onto the production-possibilities curve. To get there, government intervention may be necessary.

Too Much Pollution The market mechanism might also select the wrong choice about HOW to produce. Consider the message that unregulated markets communicate to producers. In an unregulated market, no price would be charged for using air or waterways, since neither are owned by any individual. Producers, therefore, would regard the use of air and waterways as a "free" good. Under such circumstances it would be a lot cheaper for a factory to dump its waste into nearby waterways than to dispose of it more carefully. It would also be cheaper for power plants to let waste gases and soot go up in smoke than to install environmental safeguards. The resulting pollutants are an **externality**—a cost imposed on innocent third parties. Consumers would be worse off as the quality of the air and water deteriorated.

externalities Costs (or benefits) of a market activity borne by a third party; the difference between the social and private costs (or benefits) of a market activity.

Profit-driven producers would seldom worry about externalities in a completely unregulated marketplace. Were profit-and-loss considerations the only determinant of HOW goods were produced, we might end up destroying the environment. To prevent such a calamity, we look to the government to regulate HOW goods are produced, thereby rectifying market failures.

Too Much Poverty The market might also fail to distribute goods and services in the best possible way. A market system rewards people according to their value in the marketplace. Sports stars, entertainers, and corporate executives end up with huge paychecks while others toil for meager wages. Big paychecks provide access to more output; people with little paychecks get much less of what is produced.

Is this market-based system of distributing output fair? Should rich people live in mansions while poor people sleep in abandoned cars? Many observers object that the market should not be the sole arbiter of who gets shelter. If a consensus emerges that the market's way of slicing up the pie is too unfair, then taxes and income transfers (e.g., welfare benefits, Social Security) may be used to reslice the pie. Such government intervention may generate a more desirable answer to the FOR WHOM question.

Government Failure

It is relatively easy to find evidence of market failure. It is not so easy, however, to fix every failure. Karl Marx, you may recall, believed the government could always find and implement the right answers. In practice, however, central planning wasn't notably more successful than the market mechanism in answering the WHAT, HOW, and FOR WHOM questions. Indeed, the collapse of communism in the early 1990s was precipitated by recurrent failures to resolve basic economic questions. ***Just because the market fails doesn't mean that the government will necessarily offer better answers to the WHAT, HOW, and FOR WHOM questions.***

The possibility for **government failure**—intervention that fails to improve (possibly even worsens) market outcomes—is illustrated in Figure 1.7. Again, we assume the optimal mix of output is located at point X and that the market itself produces the suboptimal mix at point M. In this case, the goal of government intervention is to move the economy closer to point X. It is possible, however, that misguided intervention might move the economy to point G_1, farther away from the optimal mix. That worsening of the mix of output would represent government failure.

government failure Government intervention that fails to improve economic outcomes.

— in whose opinion

Government intervention might not just worsen the *mix* of output but even reduce the total *amount* of output. When the government regulates an industry, it typically employs a lot of inspectors, lawyers, and bureaucrats. It also burdens private industry with paperwork and other bureaucratic red tape. The resources used to write, enforce, and comply with government regulations produce neither consumer goods nor military goods. As a result, the final mix of output may end up at point G_2 in Figure 1.7. At G_2 the inefficiencies associated with government intervention prevent the economy from fully utilizing its productive capacity. If public opinion is any index of government failure, then the potential for failure appears alarmingly high. The accompanying Headline reveals that fewer than half of all Americans trust the federal government to do the right thing.

The government could also fail the HOW question. The centrally planned economies of Eastern Europe experienced some of the world's worst environmental problems. The huge steel mills outside Krakow, Poland, spewed

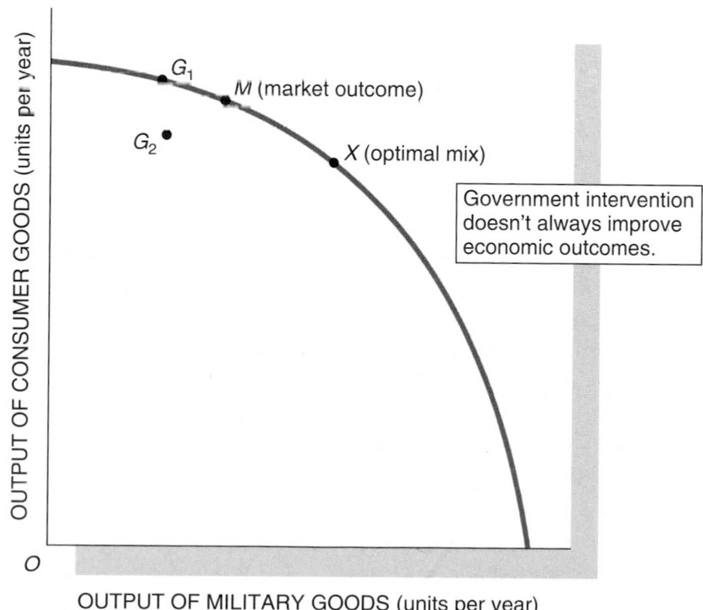

FIGURE 1.7
Government Failure

The goal of government intervention is to correct market failure. It is possible, however, that government policy might move the economy farther away from the optimal mix (to point G_1) or even inside the production-possibilities curve (point G_2).

HEADLINE GOVERNMENT FAILURE

Declining Faith in Government

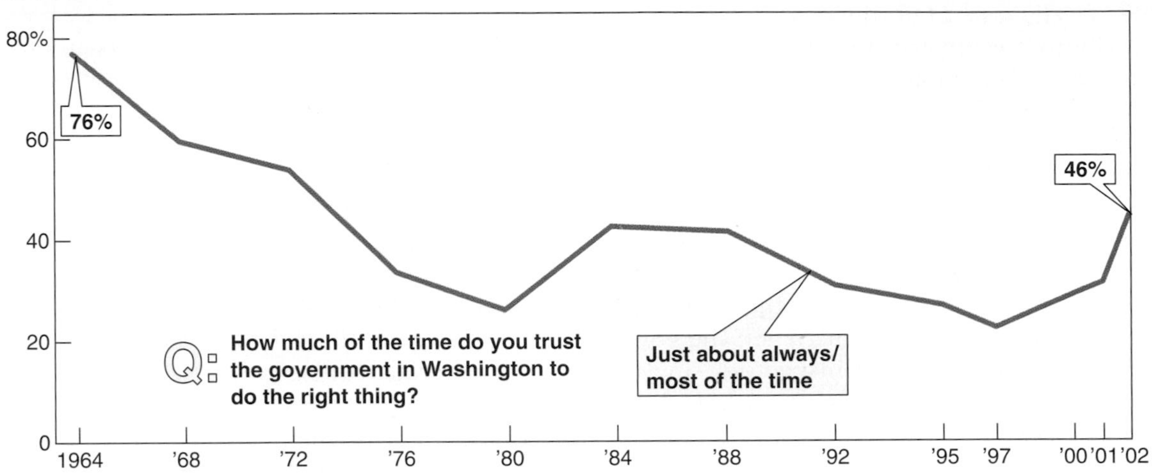

Source: *Washington Post,* February 26, 1996, p. A6. © 1996, the *Washington Post*. Reprinted with permission; ABC News poll, August 1997. CBS News Poll, January 2001. Gallup poll, September 2002.

NOTE: Government intervention is supposed to correct market failures. Most people feel, however, that the government is likely to fail as well.

more sulfur into the air than all of Western Europe's steel mills combined. The air in Budapest was so polluted that Hungarians paid for brief inhalations of compressed clean air. The factory and sewage waste from Hungary, Czechoslovakia, and Bulgaria made the Danube Europe's most polluted waterway. Worse yet, Soviet planners allowed Chernobyl to become a nuclear nightmare. Clearly, ***there is no guarantee that the visible hand of government will be any cleaner than the invisible hand of the marketplace.***

We don't have any government guarantees for the FOR WHOM question either. When the government starts reslicing the economic pie, politics may overwhelm charity. Only a small fraction of all income transfers in the United States goes to poor people. Rich people get more Social Security and Medicare benefits than poor people get in welfare benefits. And "corporate welfare" (tax breaks and subsidies) far outstrip poor people's welfare as well. As a consequence, the FOR WHOM answer generated by government intervention isn't always more equitable than that of the marketplace. Indeed, a Harvard University/*Washington Post* survey revealed that only 11 percent of all Americans believe government efforts to improve income distribution have succeeded. Forty-nine percent believe the government has made the FOR WHOM answer worse.

We have to recognize, then, that government might fail to satisfy our distributional goals.

What Economics Is All About

With so many possibilities for market and government failure, it's amazing that we ever get things right. Public policy is driven, however, by the conviction that it is better to be half right than completely wrong. That is to say, the policy challenge is to *improve* economic outcomes, even if we can't always attain perfect outcomes. To this end, ***we rely on a combination of market signals and government interventions to forge better answers to the WHAT, HOW, and FOR WHOM questions.*** That is the essence of a *mixed* economy.

The first goal of economic theory is to help society find better answers to the three basic questions. This requires us to first *understand* how the economy functions. How do people decide which goods to buy? How do producers decide what prices to charge? What forces determine how many job seekers will be employed? Who is helped and who is hurt by inflation?

The second goal of economic theory is to *predict* how changes in government policy or market institutions will affect economic outcomes. Will government-financed student loans affect how many students attend college? Will a drop in interest rates stimulate sales of new cars? Will a higher minimum wage reduce the number of available jobs? How will corporate mergers affect the quality or price of Internet features?

Macro vs. Micro

The study of economics is typically divided into two parts: macroeconomics and microeconomics. Macroeconomics focuses on the behavior of an entire economy—the big picture. In macroeconomics we study such national goals as full employment, control of inflation, and economic growth, without worrying about the well-being or behavior of specific individuals or groups. The essential concern of **macroeconomics** is to understand and improve the performance of the economy as a whole.

macroeconomics The study of aggregate economic behavior, of the economy as a whole.

Microeconomics is concerned with the details of this big picture. In microeconomics we focus on the individuals, firms, and government agencies that actually make up the larger economy. Our interest here is in the behavior of individual economic actors. What are their goals? How can they best achieve these goals with their limited resources? How will they respond to various incentives and opportunities?

microeconomics The study of individual behavior in the economy, of the components of the larger economy.

A primary concern of macroeconomics, for example, is to determine the impact of aggregate consumer spending on total output, employment, and prices. Very little attention is devoted to the actual content of consumer spending or its determinants. Microeconomics, on the other hand, focuses on the specific expenditure decisions of individual consumers and the forces (tastes, prices, incomes) that influence those decisions.

The distinction between macro- and microeconomics is also reflected in discussions of business investment. In macroeconomics we want to know what determines the aggregate rate of business investment and how those expenditures influence the nation's total output, employment, and prices. In microeconomics we focus on the decisions of individual businesses regarding the rate of production, the choice of factors of production, and the pricing of specific goods.

The distinction between macro- and microeconomics is a matter of convenience. In reality, macroeconomic outcomes depend on micro behavior, and micro behavior is affected by macro outcomes. Hence one cannot fully understand how an economy works until one understands how all the participants behave and why they behave as they do. But just as you can drive a car without knowing how its engine is constructed, you can observe how an economy runs without completely disassembling it. In macroeconomics we observe that the car goes faster when the accelerator is depressed and that it slows when the brake is applied. That is all we need to know in most situations. There are times, however, when the car breaks downs. When it does, we have to know something more about how the pedals work. This leads us into micro studies. How does each part work? Which ones can or should be fixed?

Theory vs. Reality

The distinction between macroeconomics and microeconomics is one of many simplifications we make in studying economic behavior. The economy is much too vast and complex to describe and explain in one course (or one lifetime). Accordingly, we focus on basic relationships, ignoring unnecessary detail. What this means is that we formulate theories, or *models,* of economic behavior, then use those theories to evaluate and design economic policy.

The economic models that economists use to explain market behavior are like maps. To get from New York to Los Angeles you don't need to know all the details of topography that lie between those two cities. Knowing where the interstate highways are is probably enough. An interstate route map therefore provides enough information to get to your destination.

The same kind of simplification is used in economic models of consumer behavior. Such models assert that when the price of a good increases, consumers will buy less of it. In reality, however, people *may* buy *more* of a good at increased prices, especially if those high prices create a certain snob appeal or if prices are expected to increase still further. In predicting consumer responses to price increases, we typically ignore such possibilities by *assuming* that the price of the good in question is the *only* thing that changes. This assumption of "other things remaining equal (unchanged)" (in Latin, ***ceteris paribus***) allows us to make straightforward predictions. If instead we described consumer responses to increased prices in any and all circumstances (allowing everything to change at once), every prediction would be accompanied by a book full of exceptions and qualifications. We would look more like lawyers than economists.

ceteris paribus The assumption of nothing else changing.

Although the assumption of *ceteris paribus* makes it easier to formulate economic theory and policy, it also increases the risk of error. Obviously, if other things do change in significant ways, our predictions (and policies) may fail. But, like weather forecasters, we continue to make predictions, knowing that occasional failure is inevitable. In so doing, we are motivated by the conviction that it is better to be approximately right than to be dead wrong.

Politics vs. Economics

Politicians cannot afford to be quite so complacent about predictions, however. Policy decisions must be made every day. And a politician's continued survival may depend on being more than approximately right. Economists can contribute to those policy decisions by offering measures of economic impact and predictions of economic behavior. But in the real world, those measures and predictions will always contain a substantial margin of error.

Even if the future were known, economic policy could not rely completely on economic theory. There are always political choices to be made. The choice of more consumer goods ("butter") or more military hardware ("guns"), for example, is not an economic decision. Rather it is a sociopolitical decision based in part on economic tradeoffs (opportunity costs). The "need" for more butter or more guns must be expressed politically—ends versus means again. Political forces are a necessary ingredient in economic policy decisions. That is not to say that all political decisions are right. It does suggest, however, that economic policies may not always conform to economic theory.

Both politics and economics are involved in the continuing debate about laissez faire and government intervention. The pendulum has swung from laissez faire (Adam Smith) to central government control (Karl Marx) and to an ill-defined middle ground where the government assumes major responsibilities for economic stability (John Maynard Keynes) and for answers to the WHAT, HOW, and FOR WHOM questions. In the 1980s the Reagan administration pushed the pendulum a bit closer to laissez faire by cutting taxes, reducing government regulation, and encouraging market incentives. The first Bush administration pushed the pendulum back a bit by expanding the government's role in education, regulation, and research. When the economy slumped in 1990–91, however, President Bush rejected advice to intervene, preferring to let the market right itself.

President Clinton thought the government should play a more active role in resolving basic economic issues. Just after he was elected, he published a "Vision for America" that spelled out a greater role for government in assuring health care, providing skills training, protecting the environment, and regulating working conditions. In this vision, well-intentioned government officials could correct market failures. The Democratic-controlled Congress of 1993–94 offered little support for Clinton's vision, however, and the Republican-controlled Congress of 1995–98 rejected it. President George W. Bush has made clear that he, too, favors less government intervention and more reliance on the market mechanism.

In part, this enduring controversy about markets versus government reflects diverse political, rather than strictly economic, views. Some people think a big public sector is undesirable, even if it improves economic performance. They see government intervention as a threat not only to economic performance but to individual liberties as well. They prefer the invisible hand of the market to the visible hand of government intervention almost every time. On the other hand, some advocates of government intervention feel that the market mechanism is inherently corrupting of human values and call on the government to limit greed, to guarantee economic security, and to protect the environment.

The debate over markets versus government also persists because of gaps in our economic understanding. For over 200 years economists have been arguing about what makes the economy tick. None of the competing theories has performed spectacularly well. Indeed, few economists have successfully predicted major economic events with any consistency. Even annual forecasts of inflation, unemployment, and output are regularly in error. Worse still, there are never-ending arguments about what caused a major economic event long after it occurred. In fact, economists are still arguing over the causes of the Great Depression of the 1930s!

Modest Expectations

In view of all these debates and uncertainties, you should not expect to learn everything there is to know about the economy in this text or course. Our goals are more modest. We want you to develop a reasonable perspective on economic behavior and an understanding of basic principles. With this foundation, you should acquire a better view of how the economy works. Daily news reports on economic events should make more sense. Congressional debates on tax and budget policies should take on more meaning. You may even develop some insights that you can apply toward running a business or planning a career.

SUMMARY

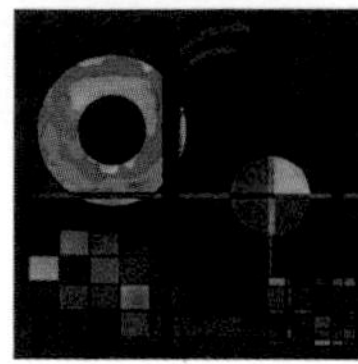

- Every nation confronts the three basic economic questions of WHAT to produce, HOW, and FOR WHOM.
- The need to select a single mix of output (WHAT) is necessitated by our limited capacity to produce. Scarcity results when our wants exceed our resources.
- The production-possibilities curve illustrates the limits to output dictated by available factors of production and technology. Points on the production-possibilities curve represent the menu of different output mixes from which we may choose.
- All production entails an opportunity cost: We can produce more of output *A* only if we produce less of output *B*. The implied reduction in output *B* is the opportunity cost of output *A*.
- The HOW question focuses on the choice of what inputs to use in production. It also encompasses choices made about environmental protection.
- The FOR WHOM question concerns the distribution of output among members of society.
- The goal of every society is to select the best possible (optimal) answers to the WHAT, HOW, and FOR WHOM questions. The optimal answers will vary with social values and production capabilities.
- The three questions can be answered by the market mechanism, by a system of central planning, or by a mixed system of market signals and government intervention.
- Price signals are the key feature of the market mechanism. Consumers signal their desires for specific goods by paying a price for these goods. Producers respond to the price signal by assembling factors of production to produce the desired output.
- Market failure occurs when the market mechanism generates the wrong mix of output, undesirable methods of production, or an inequitable distribution of income. Government intervention may fail, too, however, by not improving (or even worsening) economic outcomes.
- The study of economics focuses on the broad question of resource allocation. Macroeconomics is concerned with allocating the resources of an entire economy to achieve broad economic goals (e.g., full employment). Microeconomics focuses on the behavior and goals of individual market participants.

Terms to Remember

Define the following terms:

economics	economic growth	externalities
opportunity cost	market mechanism	government failure
factors of production	laissez faire	macroeconomics
scarcity	mixed economy	microeconomics
production possibilities	market failure	*ceteris paribus*
investment		

Questions for Discussion

1. What opportunity costs did you incur in reading this chapter?
2. In Figure 1.7 government failure causes output to fall below its full potential. How might this happen? If government intervention moved the mix of output to a point between *M* and *X*, would this be government failure?
3. In 2003, President George W. Bush proposed a significant increase in military spending. What would that added spending cost us? Is this too much or too little? How can we decide?
4. Should the government build more shelters for the homeless? Where will it get the resources to do so?
5. Why might it be necessary to reduce consumer spending in order to attain faster economic growth? Would it be worth the sacrifice?
6. If auto-emissions controls weren't required, would people willingly buy and install them? Explain.
7. McDonald's recently asked its suppliers to process chickens more humanely. How much more would you be willing to pay for chicken that was humanely processed?
8. Which government income transfers do rich people receive? Who pays for them?
9. If taxes on the rich were raised to provide more housing for the poor, how would the willingness to work be affected? What would happen to total output?
10. Why is public confidence in government so low (see Headline, p. 18)? How can government failure be avoided?

Problems

1. According to Figure 1.1, what is the opportunity cost of increasing consumer output from *OF* to *OD*?
2. Draw a production-possibilities curve based on Table 1.1, labeling combinations *A–F*. What is the opportunity cost of producing 100 missiles?
3. Assume that it takes 4 hours of labor time to paint a room and 3 hours to sand a floor. If all 24 hours were spent painting, how many rooms could be painted by one worker? If a decision were made to sand two floors, how many painted rooms would have to be given up? Illustrate with a production-possibilities curve.
4. Suppose in problem 3 that a second worker became available. Illustrate the resulting change in production possibilities. Now what would be the opportunity cost of sanding two floors?
5. According to Figure 1.3, what is the cost of a war that increases military output from M_2 to M_1? What is the opportunity cost of maintaining military output at M_1?
6. On a single graph, draw production-possibilities curves for 1945 and 2000 with consumer goods and military goods as the output choices. Label points *A* and *B* to approximate the choices made in each year (see Figure 1.2 for data).
7. Assume that the schedule below describes the production possibilities confronting an economy. Using the information from the table:
   (*a*) Draw the production-possibilities curve. Be sure to label each alternative output combination (*A* through *E*).
   (*b*) Calculate and illustrate on your graph the opportunity cost of building one convenience store per week.

(*c*) What is the cost of producing a second convenience store? What might account for the difference?
(*d*) Why can't more of both outputs be produced?
(*e*) Which point on the curve is the most desired one? How will we find out?

Potential Weekly Output Combinations	Homeless Shelters	Convenience Stores
A	10	0
B	9	1
C	7	2
D	4	3
E	0	4

8. In 1999 the dollar value of total output was roughly $25 billion in North Korea and $400 billion in South Korea. Use the data in Figure 1.4 to compute the cost of defense spending in each country.

Web Activities

1. Log on to www.federalreserve.gov/releases/g17/current.
   (*a*) Draw a production possibility curve for the U.S. measuring capital goods production on the horizontal axis and consumer goods on the vertical axis for 1982. Draw a point on this PPC map that represents the 1982 low capacity utilization. Label this point "A."
   (*b*) Draw a second PPC map that represents current production data.
      i. Draw a point on this PPC map that represents the current capacity utilization. Label this point *B*. Explain your choice of location for point *A*.
      ii. How does the location of the current PPC compare to that of 1982?
      iii. Is point *A* closer to the 1982 curve than is point *B* to the current curve?
2. Log on to www.bea.doc.gov/bea/glance.htm and find the data for nonresidential fixed investment.
   (*a*) How did the rate of nonresidential fixed investment change in the past two years of data available?
   (*b*) What are the implications for the nation's production-possibilities curve?
3. Log on to www.whitehouse.gov/fsbr/employment.html and find the data for the civilian labor force.
   (*a*) What has happened to the size of labor force over the last three years?
   (*b*) What implications does this have for the nation's production-possibilities curve? Explain.

Living Econ

How Can Hamburgers Be Scarce?

In a country as affluent as the United States it is sometimes hard to believe that scarcity exists. In particular it is hard to believe that a product such as hamburgers is scarce. In fact, you can approach a number of fast food restaurants, anytime day or night almost, and order what seems to be an endless quantity of hamburgers. But the resources used to produce hamburgers and all other goods and services are scarce in the sense that they could be put to other uses.

More than 600,000 fast food cooks use energy and other resources to prepare our burgers. Over nine billion pounds of cattle are destined for hamburger meat every year in the United States; to make one quarter pound of beef typically requires more than one pound of feed grain and 100 gallons of water. All of these resources could be used to produce other goods or services.

On an individual level, every time you buy a hamburger you choose not to buy something else. If you work in a fast food restaurant, you will have less time for other pursuits. So, whether in your personal life or at the national level, there are finite resources and choices must be made about how to use them.

APPENDIX

Using Graphs

Economists like to draw graphs. In fact, we didn't even make it through the first chapter without a few graphs. The purpose of this appendix is to look more closely at the way graphs are drawn and used.

The basic purpose of a graph is to illustrate a relationship between two *variables*. Consider, for example, the relationship between grades and studying. In general, we expect that additional hours of study time will lead to higher grades. Hence we should be able to see a distinct relationship between hours of study time and grade-point average.

Suppose that we actually surveyed all the students taking this course with regard to their study time and grade-point averages. The resulting information can be compiled in a table such as Table A.1.

According to the table, students who don't study at all can expect an F in this course. To get a C, the average student apparently spends 8 hours a week studying. All those who study 16 hours a week end up with an A in the course.

These relationships between grades and studying can also be illustrated on a graph. Indeed, the whole purpose of a graph is to summarize numerical relationships.

We begin to construct a graph by drawing horizontal and vertical boundaries, as in Figure A.1. These boundaries are called the *axes* of the graph. On the vertical axis we measure one of the variables; the other variable is measured on the horizontal axis.[1]

In this case, we shall measure the grade-point average on the vertical axis. We start at the *origin* (the intersection of the two axes) and count upward, letting the distance between horizontal lines represent half (0.5) a grade point. Each horizontal line is numbered, up to the maximum grade-point average of 4.0.

The number of hours each week spent doing homework is measured on the horizontal axis. We begin at the origin again, and count to the right. The *scale* (numbering) proceeds in increments of 1 hour, up to 20 hours per week.

When both axes have been labeled and measured, we can begin to illustrate the relationship between study time and grades. Consider the typical student who does 8 hours of homework per week and has a 2.0 (C) grade-point average. We illustrate this relationship by first locating 8 hours on the horizontal axis. We then move up from that point a distance of 2.0 grade points, to point *M*. Point *M* tells us that 8 hours of study time per week is typically associated with a 2.0 grade-point average.

The rest of the information in Table A.1 is drawn (or *plotted*) on the graph in the same way. To illustrate the average grade for people who study 12

[1]The vertical axis is often called the *Y* axis; the horizontal axis, the *X* axis.

TABLE A.1
Hypothetical Relationship of Grades to Study Time

Study Time (hours per week)	Grade-Point Average
16	4.0 (A)
14	3.5 (B +)
12	3.0 (B)
10	2.5 (C +)
8	2.0 (C)
6	1.5 (D +)
4	1.0 (D)
2	0.5 (F +)
0	0 (F)

hours per week, we move upward from the number 12 on the horizontal axis until we reach the height of 3.0 on the vertical axis. At that intersection, we draw another point (point *N*).

Once we have plotted the various points describing the relationship of study time to grades, we may connect them with a line or curve. This line (curve) is our summary. In this case, the line slopes upward to the right—that is, it has a *positive* slope. This slope indicates that more hours of study time are associated with *higher* grades. Were higher grades associated with *less* study time, the curve in Figure A.1 would have a *negative* slope (downward from left to right).

Slopes

The upward slope of Figure A.1 tells us that higher grades are associated with increased amounts of study time. That same curve also tells us *by how much* grades tend to rise with study time. According to point *M* in Figure A.1, the average student studies 8 hours per week and earns a C (2.0 grade-point average). In order to earn a B (3.0 grade-point average), a student apparently needs to study an average of 12 hours per week (point *N*). Hence an increase of 4 hours of study time per week is associated with a 1-point increase in grade-

FIGURE A.1
The Relationship of Grades to Study Time

The upward (positive) slope of the curve indicates that additional studying is associated with higher grades. The average student (2.0, or C grade) studies 8 hours per week. This is indicated by point *M* on the graph.

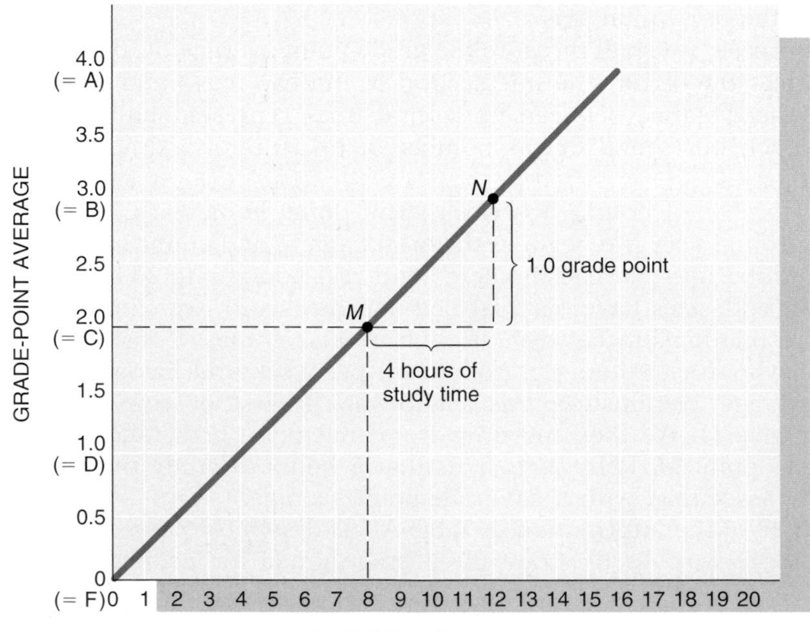

point average. This relationship between *changes* in study time and *changes* in grade-point average is expressed by the steepness, or *slope,* of the graph.

The slope of any graph is calculated as

- $\text{Slope} = \dfrac{\text{vertical distance between two points}}{\text{horizontal distance between two points}}$

Some people simplify this by saying

$$\text{Slope} = \frac{\text{the rise}}{\text{the run}}$$

In our example, the vertical distance (the "rise") between points M and N represents a change in grade-point average. The horizontal distance (the "run") between these two points represents the change in study time. Hence the slope of the graph between points M and N is equal to

$$\text{Slope} = \frac{3.0 \text{ grade} - 2.0 \text{ grade}}{12 \text{ hours} - 8 \text{ hours}} = \frac{1 \text{ grade point}}{4 \text{ hours}}$$

In other words, a 4-hour increase in study time (from 8 to 12 hours) is associated with a 1-point increase in grade-point average (see Figure A.1).

Shifts

The relationship between grades and studying illustrated in Figure A.1 is not inevitable. It is simply a graphical illustration of student experiences, as revealed in our hypothetical survey. The relationship between study time and grades could be quite different.

Suppose that the university decided to raise grading standards, making it more difficult to achieve every grade other than an F. To achieve a C, a student now would need to study 12 hours per week, not just 8 (as in Figure A.1). Whereas students could previously expect to get a B by studying 12 hours per week, now they have to study 16 hours to get that grade.

Figure A.2 illustrates the new grading standards. Notice that the new curve lies to the right of the earlier curve. We say that the curve has *shifted* to reflect a change in the relationship between study time and grades. Point R indicates that 12 hours of study time now "produces" a C, not a B (point N on the old curve). Students who now study only 4 hours per week (point S) will fail. Under the old grading policy, they could have at least gotten a D. ***When a curve shifts, the underlying relationship between the two variables has changed.***

A shift may also change the slope of the curve. In Figure A.2, the new grading curve is parallel to the old one; it therefore has the same slope. Under either the new grading policy or the old one, a 4-hour increase in study time leads to a 1-point increase in grades. Therefore, the slope of both curves in Figure A.2 is

$$\text{Slope} = \frac{\text{vertical change}}{\text{horizontal change}} = \frac{1}{4}$$

This, too, may change, however, Figure A.3 illustrates such a possibility. In this case, zero study time still results in an F. But now the payoff for additional studying is reduced. Now it takes 6 hours of study time to get a D (1.0 grade point), not 4 hours as before. Likewise, another 4 hours of study time (to a total of 10) raises the grade by only two-thirds of a point.

FIGURE A.2
A Shift

When a relationship between two variables changes, the entire curve *shifts.* In this case a tougher grading policy alters the relationship between study time and grades. To get a C one must now study 12 hours per week (point *R*), not just 8 hours (point *M*).

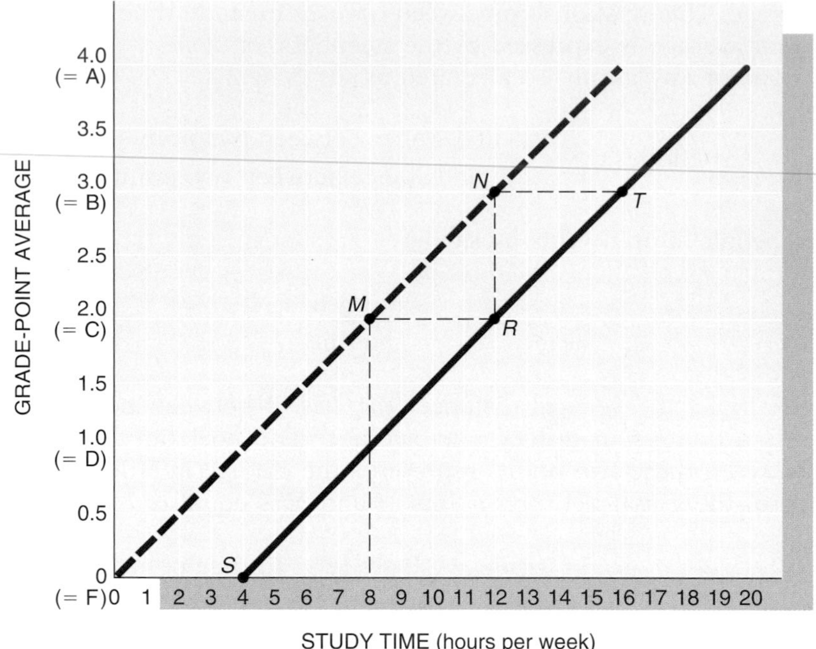

It takes 6 hours to raise the grade a full point. The slope of the new line is therefore

$$\text{Slope} = \frac{\text{vertical change}}{\text{horizontal change}} = \frac{1}{6}$$

The new curve in Figure A.3 has a smaller slope than the original curve and so lies below it. What all this means is that it now takes a greater effort to *improve* your grade.

FIGURE A.3
A Change in Slope

When a curve shifts, it may change its slope as well. In this case, a new grading policy makes each higher grade more difficult to reach. To raise a C to a B, for example, one must study 6 additional hours (compare points J and K). Earlier it took only 4 hours to move up the grade scale a full point. The slope of the line has declined from 0.25 (= 1 − 4) to 0.17 (= 1 − 6).

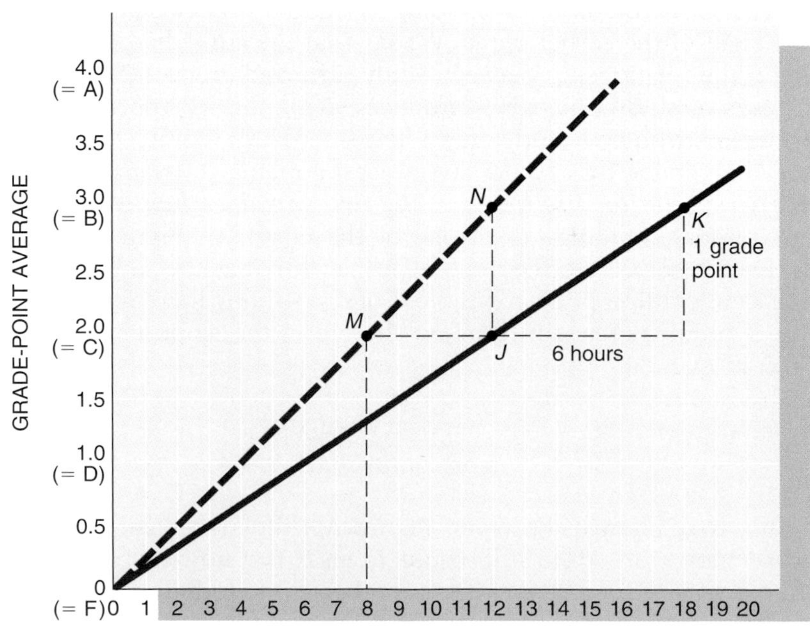

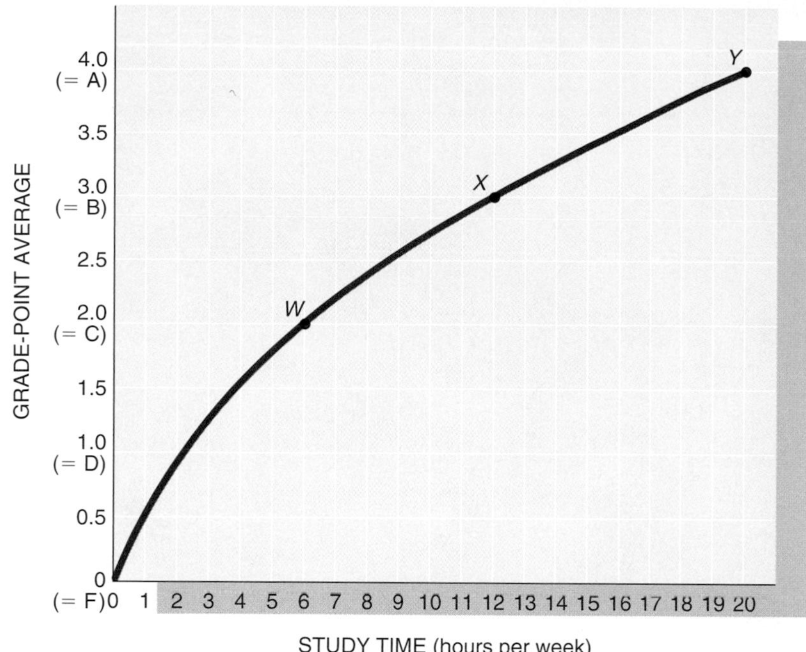

FIGURE A.4
A Nonlinear Relationship

Straight lines have a constant slope, implying a constant relationship between the two variables. But the relationship (and slope) may vary. In this case. It takes 6 extra hours of study to raise a C (point *W*) to a B (point *X*) but 8 extra hours to raise a B to an A (point *Y*). The slope is decreasing as we move up the curve.

Linear vs. Nonlinear Curves

In Figures A.1–A.3, the relationship between grades and studying is represented by a straight line—that is, a *linear* curve. A distinguishing feature of linear curves is that they have the same (constant) slope throughout. In Figure A.1, it appears that *every* 4-hour increase in study time is associated with a 1-point increase in average grades. In Figure A.3, it appears that every 6-hour increase in study time leads to a 1-point increase in grades. But the relationship between studying and grades may not be linear. Higher grades may be more difficult to attain. You may be able to raise a C to a B by studying 4 hours more per week. But it may be harder to raise a B to an A. According to Figure A.4, it takes an additional 8 hours of studying to raise a B to an A. Thus the relationship between study time and grades is *nonlinear* in Figure A.4; the slope of the curve changes as study time increases. In this case, the slope decreases as study time increases. Grades continue to improve, but not so fast, as more and more time is devoted to homework. You may know the feeling.

Causation

Figure A.4 does not itself guarantee that your grade-point average will rise if you study 4 more hours per week. In fact, the graph drawn in Figure A.4 does not prove that additional study ever results in higher grades. The graph is only a summary of empirical observations. It says nothing about cause and effect. It could be that students who study a lot are smarter to begin with. If so, then less able students might not get higher grades if they studied harder. In other words, the *cause* of higher grades is debatable. At best, the empirical relationship summarized in the graph may be used to support a particular theory (e.g., that it pays to study more). Graphs, like tables, charts, and other statistical media, rarely tell their own stories; rather, they must be *interpreted* in terms of some underlying theory or expectation.

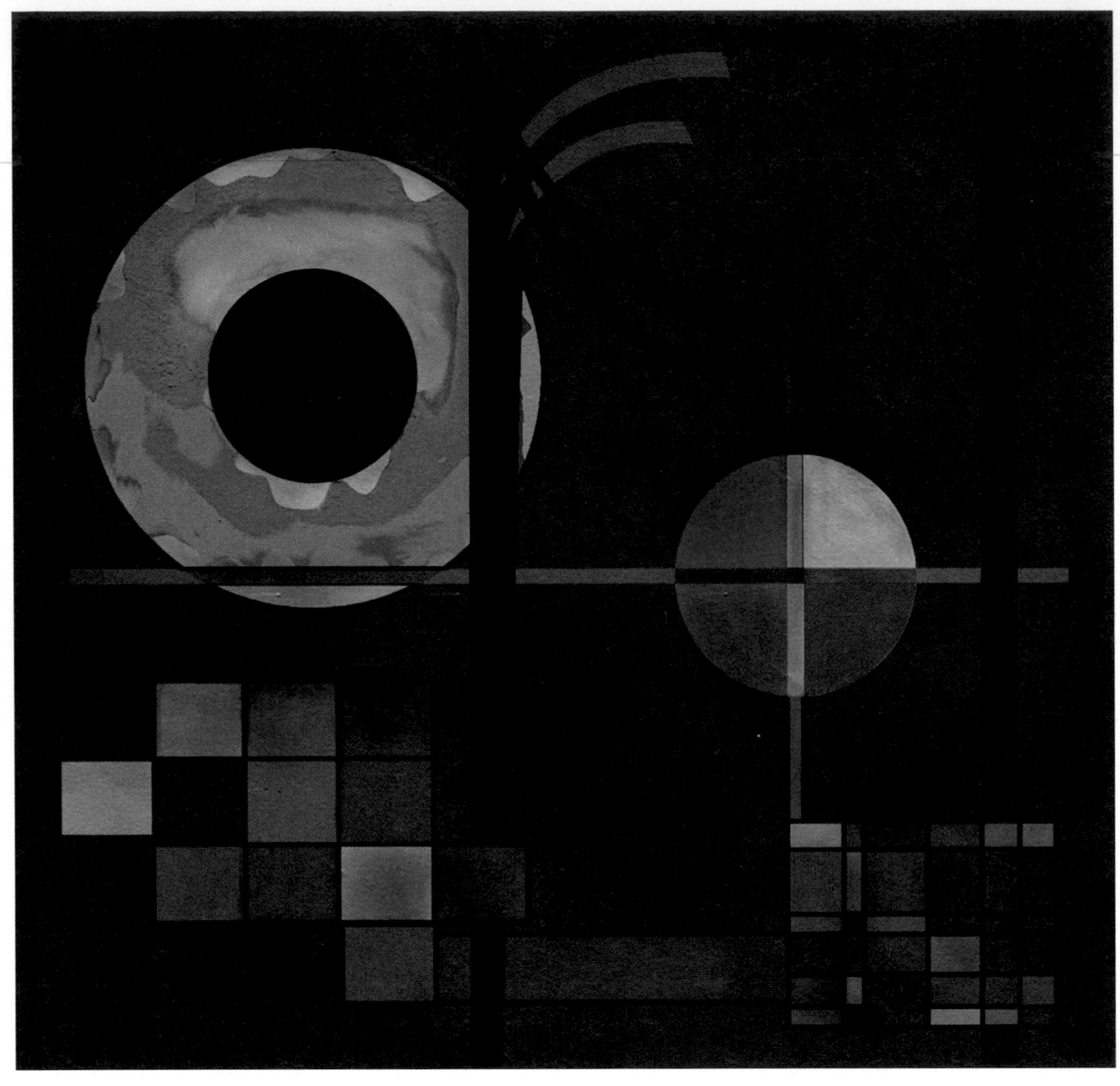

The U.S. Economy

CHAPTER 2

We are surrounded by the economy but never really see it. We see only fragments, never the entirety. We see boutiques at the mall, never total retail sales. We visit virtual stores in cyberspace but can't begin to describe the dimensions of e-commerce. We pump gas at the service station but have no notion of how many millions of barrels of oil are consumed each day. We know every detail on our paychecks but don't have a clue about how much income the entire workforce earns. Nor can many of us tell how our own income stacks up against that of the average U.S. household, much less that of earlier generations or other nations. Such details simply aren't a part of our daily agendas. For most people, the "economy" is just a vague reference to a mass of meaningless statistics.

The intent of this chapter is to provide a more user-friendly picture of the U.S. economy. This profile of the economy is organized around the three core questions of WHAT, HOW, and FOR WHOM. Our interest here is to see how these questions are answered at present in the United States—that is,

- WHAT goods and services does the United States produce?
- HOW is that output produced?
- FOR WHOM is the output produced?

We focus on the big picture, without going into too much statistical detail. Along the way, we'll see how the U.S. economy stacks up against other nations.

What America Produces

In Chapter 1 we used the two-dimensional possibilities curve to describe WHAT output combinations can be produced. In reality, the mix of output includes so many different products that we could never fit them on a graph. We can, however, sketch what the U.S. mix of output looks like and how it has changed over the years.

How Much Output

The first challenge in describing the actual output of the economy is to somehow add up the millions of different products produced into a meaningful summary. The production-possibilities curve did this in *physical* terms, for only two products. We ended up with specific quantities of two goods. In principle, we could list all of the millions of products produced each year. But such a list would be longer than this textbook and a lot less useful. We need a summary measure of how much is produced.

The top panel of Table 2.1 illustrates the problem of obtaining a summary measure of output. Even if we produced only three products—oranges, disposable razors, and insurance policies—there is no obvious way of summarizing total output in *physical* terms. Should we count *units* of output? In that case, oranges would appear to be the most important good produced. Should we count the *weight* of different products? In that case, insurance policies wouldn't count at all. Should we tally their *sizes*? As you ponder these various physical measures of output, a summary statement seems impossible.

If we use monetary *value* instead of physical units to compute total output, we would have more success. In a market economy, every good and service commands a specific price. Hence the value of each product can be observed easily. ***By multiplying the physical output of each good by its price, we can determine the total value of each good produced.*** Notice in the bottom panel of Table 2.1 how easily these separate values can be added up. The resultant sum ($4.2 billion, in this case) is a measure of the *value of* total output.

gross domestic product (GDP) The total value of final goods and services produced within a nation's borders in a given time period.

Gross Domestic Product The summary measure of output most frequently used is called **gross domestic product (GDP).** ***GDP refers to the total value of all final goods and services produced in a country during a given time period: it is a summary measure of a nation's output.*** GDP enables us to add oranges and razors and even insurance policies into a meaningful summary of economic activity (see Table 2.1).

TABLE 2.1
The Measurement of Output

It is impossible to add up all output when it is counted in *physical* terms. Accordingly, total output is measured in *monetary* terms, with each good or service valued at its market price. GDP refers to the total market value of all goods and services produced in a given time period. According to the numbers in this table, the total *value* of the oranges, razors, and insurance policies produced is $4.2 billion.

Output	Amount
Measuring output	
. . . **in physical terms**	
Oranges	6 billion
Disposable razors	3 billion
Insurance policies	7 million
Total	?
. . . **in monetary terms**	
6 billion oranges @ 20¢ each	$1.2 billion
3 billion razors @ 30¢ each	0.9 billion
7 million policies @ $300 each	2.1 billion
Total	$4.2 billion

TABLE 2.2
Inflation Adjustments

If prices rise, so do the *values* of output. In this example, the nominal value of output doubles from Year 1 to Year 2, even though physical output remains unchanged. *Real* GDP corrects for such changing price levels. In this case *real* GDP in Year 2, measured in Year 1 prices, is unchanged at $4.2 billion.

	Physical Output		Unit Prices		Value of Output (billions)		
Product	**Year 1**	**Year 2**	**Year 1**	**Year 2**	**Year 1 (@Year 1 prices)**	**Year 2 (@Year 2 prices)**	**Year 2 (@Year 1 prices)**
Oranges	6 billion	6 billion	$0.20	$0.40	$1.2	$2.4	$1.2
Razors	3 billion	3 billion	0.30	0.60	0.9	1.8	0.9
Insurance	7 million	7 million	300.00	600.00	2.1	4.2	2.1
					$4.2	$8.4	$4.2

Real GDP Although GDP is a convenient summary of total output produced in a year, it has some shortcomings. GDP is based on both physical output and prices. Accordingly, from one year to the next either rising prices or an increase in physical output could cause GDP to increase.

Notice in Table 2.2 what happens when all prices double. The measured value of total output also doubles—from $4.2 to $8.4 billion. That sounds like an impressive jump in output. In reality, however, no more goods are being produced; *physical quantities* are unchanged. So the apparent jump in GDP is an illusion caused by rising prices (inflation).

To provide a clearer picture of how much output we are producing, GDP numbers are routinely adjusted for inflation. These inflation adjustments delete the effects of rising prices by valuing output in *constant* prices. The end result of this effort is referred to as **real GDP,** an inflation-adjusted measure of total output.

real GDP The inflation-adjusted value of GDP; the value of output measured in constant prices.

In 2003, the U.S. economy produced roughly $11 *trillion* of output. That was a lot of oranges, razors, and insurance policies—not to mention the tens of thousands of other goods and services produced.

International Comparisons The $11 trillion of output that the United States produced in 2003 looks particularly impressive in a global context. The output of the entire world in 2003 was only $50 trillion. Hence the U.S. economy produces over 20 percent of the entire planet's output. With less than 5 percent of the world's population, that's a remarkable feat. It clearly establishes the United States as the world's economic giant.

Figure 2.1 provides some specific country comparisons for a recent year. The U.S. economy is two and a half times larger than Japan's, the world's third-largest. It is 12 times larger than Mexico's. In fact, the U.S. economy is so large that its output exceeds by a wide margin the *combined* production of *all* countries in Africa and South America.

Per Capita GDP Another way of putting these trillion-dollar figures into perspective is to relate them to individuals. This can be done by dividing a nation's total GDP by its population, a calculation that yields **per capita GDP.** Per capita GDP tells us how much output is potentially available to the average person. It doesn't tell us how much any specific person gets. ***Per capita GDP is simply an indicator of how much output each person would get if all output were divided evenly among the population.***

per capita GDP Total GDP divided by total population: average GDP.

In 2003, per capita GDP in the United States was approximately $34,000—more than five times the world average. Individual country comparisons are

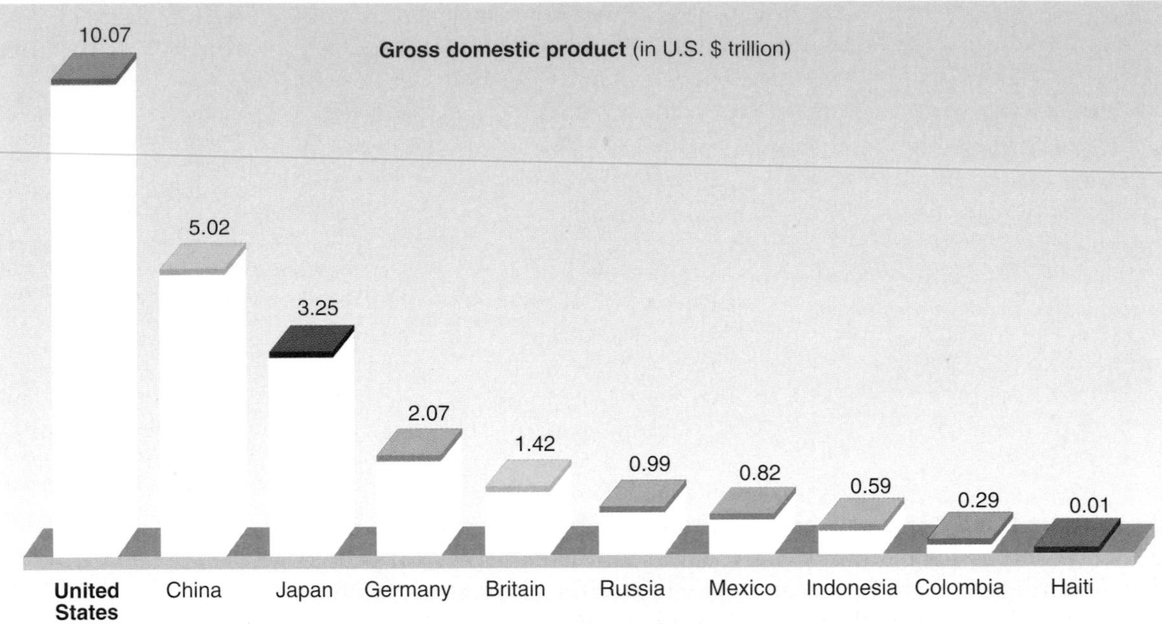

FIGURE 2.1 Real GDP (Output) of Specific Countries (2001)

The United States is by far the world's largest economy. America's annual output of goods and services is three times that of Japan's and equal to all of Western Europe. The output of Third World countries is only a tiny fraction of U.S. output.

Source: From *World Development Indicators, 2003* (Washington, DC: World Bank, 2003).

even more startling. In Ethiopia and Haiti, per capita incomes are less than \$2,000—less than six dollars per day. *Homeless* people in the United States fare better than that—typically *much* better. Americans classified as poor have more food, more shelter, and more amenities than most people in the less developed nations even hope for. That is the reality depicted in the statistics of Table 2.3.

Historical Comparisons Still another way of digesting the dimensions of the American economy is to compare today's living standards with those of

TABLE 2.3
Per Capita Incomes around the World (2001)

The American standard of living is five times higher than the world average. People in the poorest nations of the world (e.g., Haiti, Ethiopia) barely survive on per capita incomes that are a tiny fraction of U.S. standards.

United States	$34,280
Japan	25,550
France	24,080
Spain	19,860
Greece	17,520
Mexico	8,240
World average	**7,370**
China	3,950
Jordan	3,880
Indonesia	2,830
India	2,820
Haiti	1,870
Ethiopia	800

Source: From *World Development Indicators, 2003.*

earlier times. People who the U.S. government currently classifies as poor not only enjoy a much higher living standard than the human masses in Third World nations, but they are also more comfortable than the *average* American family was in the 1950s. We now spend over a billion dollars a year on closet organizers alone, an expenditure people of other nations and earlier generations would find incomprehensible. Although many of us still complain that we don't have enough, we enjoy an array of goods and services that earlier generations only dreamed about.

What's even more amazing is that our abundance keeps growing. America's real GDP has increased by about 3 percent a year. That may not sound like much, but it adds up. With the U.S. population growing by only 1 percent a year, continued **economic growth** also implies more output per person. Like interest accumulating in the bank, economic growth keeps adding to our standard of living. If real GDP keeps growing 2 percentage points faster than our population, per capita incomes will double again in approximately 35 years.

economic growth An increase in output (real GDP); an expansion of production possibilities.

There is no certainty that the economy will continue to grow at that speed. From 1929 to 1939, real GDP didn't grow at all. As a consequence, U.S. living standards *fell* during the Great Depression. In other nations, the struggle between population growth and economic growth is a persistent source of anxiety. In the 1990s, output per capita actually *declined* in Haiti, Ethiopia, Kenya, Venezuela, Nigeria, and many other nations.

Social Welfare Although the United States has claim to being the world's largest economy, we must not confuse GDP with broader measures of social welfare. First of all, GDP measures only output produced for the market. It does not include home production or volunteer activities, even though these nonmarket activities affect our personal and community well-being. Neither do GDP statistics directly measure the noise, congestion, and pollution that often accompany increased output. Maybe we'd all be better off with a little less output and its related "bads." Finally, we have to recognize that GDP statistics *do* include the services of divorce lawyers, prison guards, and trash collectors. With more love, fewer crimes, and less pollution our social welfare might increase even if GDP declined.

Although GDP is an incomplete measure of social welfare, it is still important. The people in poor nations certainly appreciate the importance of more output and even Americans still strive for higher levels of material well-being. GDP statistics gauge how well we are doing in that regard.

However imperfect, the level of output (GDP) is undoubtedly the single best measure of a nation's economic well-being. Indeed, back in 1776 Adam Smith recognized that the wealth of nations was best measured by its output rather than by the amount of gold it possessed or the resources it owned. Today that standard of wealth is reflected in real GDP statistics.

The Mix of Output

In addition to the *level* of output, we also care about its *content*. As we observed in Chapter 1, there are many possible output combinations for any given level of GDP. In Chapter 1 we examined the different mixes of military and civilian output nations choose. More broadly, the content of output is described in terms of its major end uses. ***The major uses of total output include***

- ***Household consumption***
- ***Business investment***
- ***Government services***
- ***Exports***

Consumer Goods Consumer goods account for two-thirds of America's total output. Consumer goods include everything from breakfast cereals to videos—anything and everything consumers buy.

Three types of consumer goods are often distinguished: *durable goods, nondurable goods,* and *services.* Consumer durables are expected to last at least three years. They tend to be big-ticket items like cars, appliances, and furniture. They are generally expensive and often purchased on credit. Because of this, consumers tend to postpone buying durables when they are worried about their incomes. Conversely, consumers tend to go on durables-spending sprees when times are good. This spending pattern makes durable goods output highly *cyclical,* that is, very sensitive to economic trends.

Nondurables and services are not as cyclical. Nondurables include clothes, food, gasoline, and other staples that consumers buy frequently. Services are the largest and fastest-growing component in consumption. At present, over half of all consumer output consists of medical care, entertainment, utilities, and other services.

investment Expenditures on (production of) new plant and equipment (capital) in a given time period, plus changes in business inventories.

Investment Goods Investment goods are a completely different type of output. **Investment** goods include the plant, machinery, and equipment that are produced for use in the business sector. These investment goods are used

1. To replace worn-out equipment and factories, thus *maintaining* our production possibilities.
2. To increase and improve our stock of capital, thereby *expanding* our production possibilities.

We also count as investment goods those products that businesses hold as inventory for later sale to consumers.

The economic growth that has lifted our living standards so high was fueled by past investments. To attain even higher living standards, we must continue to devote some of our scarce resources to the production of new plant and equipment. This requires us to limit our immediate consumption (i.e., save) so scarce resources can be used for investment. Only 15 percent of America's GDP today consists of investment goods (see Figure 2.2).

Note that the term *investment* here refers to real output—plant and equipment produced for the business sector. This is not the way most

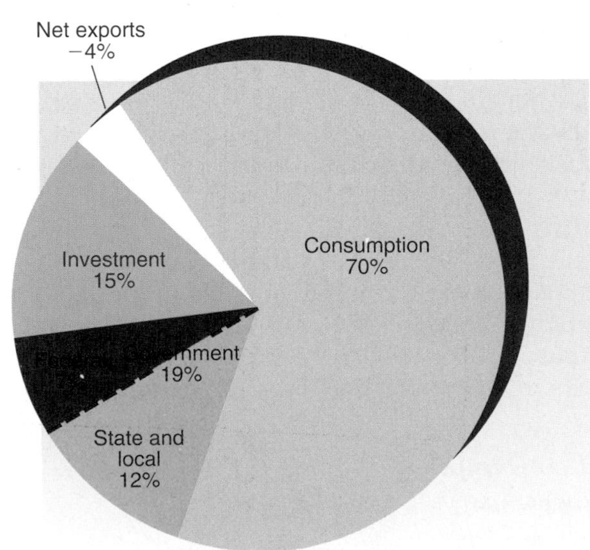

FIGURE 2.2
The Uses of GDP

Total GDP amounted to nearly $11 trillion in 2003. Over two-thirds of this output consisted of private consumer goods and services. The next-largest share (19 percent) of output consisted of public-sector goods and services. Investment absorbed 15 percent of GDP. Finally, because imports exceeded exports, we ended up consuming 4 percent more than we produced.

Source: U.S. Department of Commerce.

people use the term. People often speak, for example, of "investing" in the stock market. Purchases of corporate stock, however, do not create goods and services. Such *financial* investments merely transfer ownership of a corporation from one individual to another. Such *financial* investments may at times enable a corporation to purchase real plant and equipment. Tangible (economic) investment does not occur, however, until that plant and machinery are actually produced. Only tangible investment is counted in the mix of output.

Government Services The third type of output included in GDP is government services. Federal, state, and local governments purchase resources to police the streets, teach classes, write laws, and build highways. The resources used by the government sector for these purchases are unavailable for either consumption or investment. The production of government services currently absorbs nearly one-fifth of total output (Figure 2.2).

Notice the emphasis again on the production of real goods and services. The federal government *spends* well over $2 trillion a year. Much of that spending, however, is in the form of income transfers, not resource purchases. **Income transfers** are payments to individuals for which no direct service is provided. Social Security benefits, welfare checks, food stamps, and unemployment benefits are examples of income transfers. Such transfer payments account for half of all federal spending (see Figure 2.3). This spending is *not* part of our output of goods and services. ***Only that part of federal spending used to acquire resources and produce services is counted in GDP.*** In 2003, federal purchases (production) of goods and services accounted for only 6 percent of total output.

income transfers Payments to individuals for which no current goods or services are exchanged; e.g., Social Security, welfare, unemployment benefits.

State and local governments use far more of our scarce resources than does the federal government. These are the governments that build roads; provide schools, police, and firefighters; administer hospitals; and provide social services. The output of all these state and local governments accounts for roughly 12 percent of total GDP. In doing so, they employ four times as many people (16 million) than does the federal government (4 million).

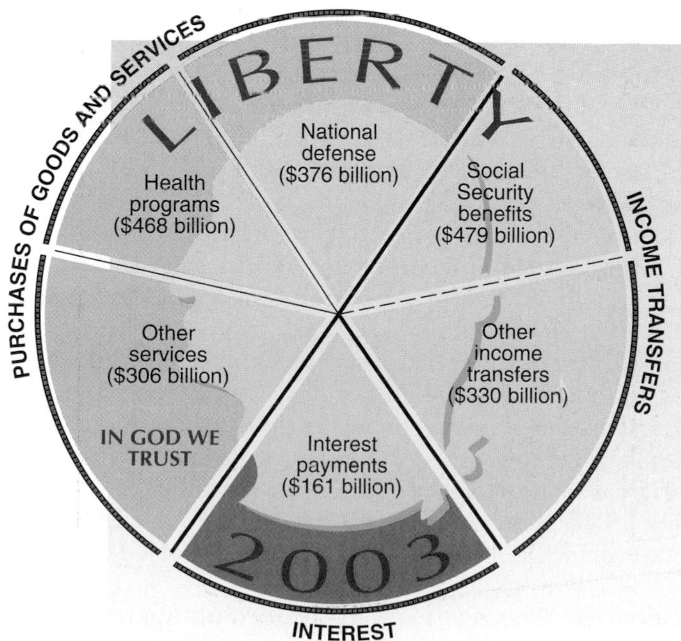

FIGURE 2.3
Federal Outlays, by Type

The federal government spent over $2.2 trillion in fiscal year 2003. Just over half of all this spending was for goods and services (including national defense, health programs, and all other services). Over $800 billion was spent on income transfers (Social Security benefits, government pensions, welfare, unemployment benefits, etc.). Interest payments on the national debt accounted for the rest of the budget.

Source: U.S. Office of Management and Budget.

Net Exports Finally, we should note that some of the goods and services we produce each year are used abroad rather than at home. That is to say, we **export** some of our output to other countries, for whatever use they care to make of it. Thus GDP—the value of output *produced* within the United States—can be larger than the sum of our own consumption, investment, and government purchases if we export some of our output.

exports Goods and services sold to foreign buyers.

International trade is not a one-way street. While we export some of our own output, we also **import** goods and services from other countries. These imports may be used for consumption (Scotch whiskey, Japanese DVD players), investment (German ball bearings), or government (French radar screens). Whatever their use, imports represent goods and services that are used by Americans but are not produced in the United States.

imports Goods and services purchased from foreign sources.

The GDP accounts subtract imports from exports. The difference represents *net* exports. In 2003, the value of exports was less than the value of imports. This implies that we *used* more goods and services than we *produced* in that year. Hence, we have to subtract net imports from consumption, investment, and government services to figure out how much we actually *produced.* That is why net exports appear as a negative item in Figure 2.2.

Changing Industry Structure

As we noted earlier, many of the products we consume today did not exist ten or even two years ago. We have also observed how much the volume of output has grown over time. Throughout this process of economic growth, the mix of output has changed dramatically.

Decline in Farming One of the most dramatic changes in the mix of output was the decline in the relative size of the farm sector. In 1900 farming was the most common occupation in the American economy. As Figure 2.4 illustrates, nearly four out of ten workers were employed in agriculture back then.

Today the mix of output is radically different. Between 1900 and 2000 over 25 *million* people left farms and sought jobs in the cities. As a result, less than 2 percent of the workforce is now employed in agriculture. And their number keeps shrinking a bit further every year as new technology makes it possible to grow *more* food with *fewer* workers.

Decline of Manufacturing Share Most of the farmers displaced by technological advances in the early 1900s found jobs in the expanding manufacturing sector. The Industrial Revolution that flourished in the late 1800s led to a massive increase in manufacturing activity (e.g., steel, transportation systems, automobiles, airplanes). Between 1860 and 1920, the manufactured share of GDP doubled, reaching a peak at 27 percent. World War II also created a huge demand for ships, airplanes, trucks, and armaments, requiring an enlarged manufacturing sector. After World War II, the manufactured share of output declined, and now accounts for less than 20 percent of total output.

The *relative* decline in manufacturing does not mean that the manufacturing sector has actually shrunk. As in farming, technological advance has made it possible to increase manufacturing output tremendously, even though employment has grown only modestly. Just in the last 50 years, manufactured *output* has increased fourfold even though manufacturing *employment* has increased only 20 percent. As a result, the volume of manufacturing output has increased, even while the manufacturing *share* of GDP has declined.

Growth of Services The *relative* decline in manufacturing is due primarily to the rapid expansion of the service sector. America has largely

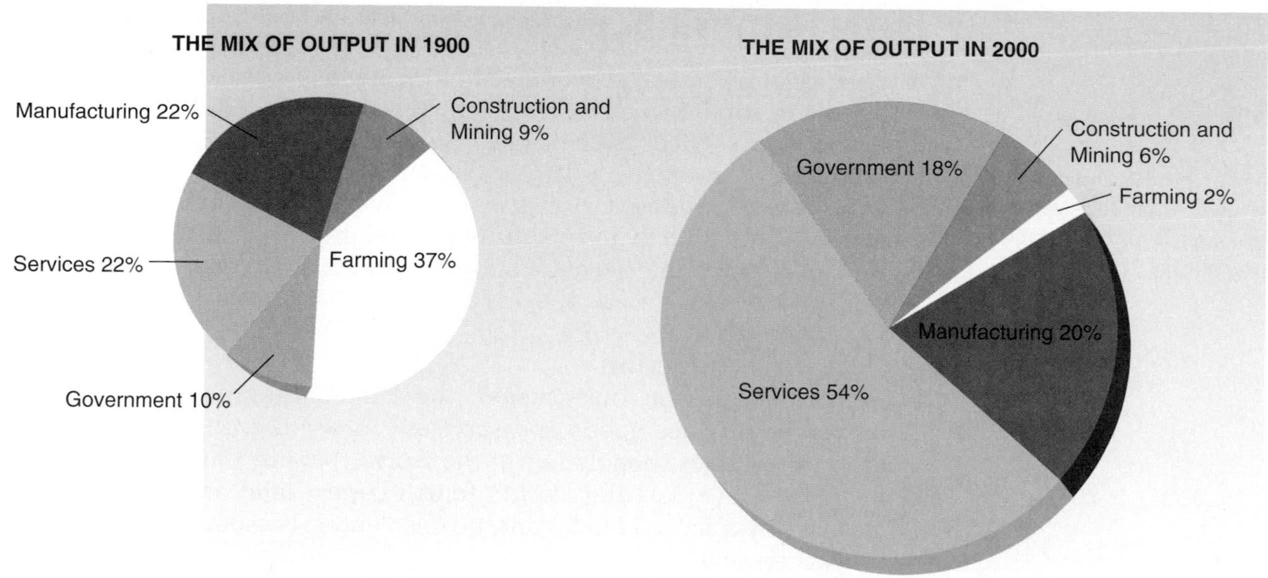

FIGURE 2.4 A Century of GDP Changes

In the 20th century the total output of the U.S. economy increased thirteenfold. As the economy has grown, the farm sector has shrunk and the manufactured *share* of total output has declined. Since 1930 the American economy has been predominantly a service economy, with output and job growth increasingly concentrated in retail trade, education, health care, entertainment, personal and business services, and government.

Source: U.S. Departments of Commerce and Labor.

become a service economy. A hundred years ago less than 25 percent of the labor force was employed in the service sector; today service industries (including government) generate over 70 percent of total output. Among the fastest growing service industries are health care, computer science and software, financial services, retail trade, business services, and law. According to the U.S. Department of Labor, this trend will continue; 98 percent of net job growth between 2005 and 2015 will be in service industries.

Growth of Trade International trade also plays an increasingly important role in how goods are produced. Roughly one-eighth of the output Americans produce is exported. As noted earlier, an even larger share of output is imported (hence the negative "net exports" in Figure 2.2).

What is remarkable about these international transactions is how they have grown. The import ratio—imports divided by GDP—has increased from 5 percent in the 1920s to over 13 percent today. This increasing globalization of the U.S. economy is likely to continue. The slow but continuing removal of trade barriers (e.g., the North American free-trade zone) facilitates this globalization. Advances in communications and transportation technologies also make international trade and investment easier. You can click onto a British clothier's website just as easily as onto the site of a U.S. merchant. And consumers in other nations can easily purchase goods from American cybermerchants. Then FedEx or another overnight delivery service can move the goods across national borders. As a result, the volume of both imports and exports keeps growing rapidly. The growth of trade is also fueled by the increased consumption of *services* (e.g., travel, finance, movies, computer software) rather than goods. With trade in services, you don't even need overnight delivery services.

How America Produces

International trade has also affected HOW goods and services are produced. Hundreds of foreign-owned firms (e.g., Toyota, BMW, Shell, Air France) produce goods or services in the United States. Any output they produce within U.S. borders is counted in America's GDP. By contrast, U.S.-owned **factors of production** employed elsewhere (e.g., a Nike shoe factory in Malaysia) don't contribute directly to U.S. output. Foreign firms typically bring not only factors of production across national borders but often new technology as well.

factors of production Resource inputs used to produce goods and services, e.g., land, labor, capital, entrepreneurship.

Factors of Production

Even without foreign investments, the United States would have ample resources to produce goods and services. To begin with, the United States has the third-largest population in the world (behind China and India). The United States also has the world's fourth-largest land area (behind Russia, China, and by a hair, Canada) and profuse natural resources (e.g., oil, fertile soil, hydropower).

Abundant labor and natural resources give the United States a decided advantage. But superior resources alone don't explain America's economic dominance. After all, China has five times as many people as the United States and equally abundant natural resources. Yet China's annual output is less than one-half of America's output.

Capital Stock In part, America's greater economic strength is explained by the abundance of capital. America has accumulated a massive stock of capital—over $30 *trillion* worth of machinery, factories, and buildings. As a result of all this prior investment, American production tends to be very **capital intensive.** The contrast with *labor-intensive* production in poorer countries is striking. A Chinese farmer mostly works with his or her hands and crude implements, whereas an American farmer works with computers, automated irrigation systems, and mechanized equipment. Russian business managers don't have the computer networks or telecommunications systems that make American business so efficient.

capital intensive Production processes that use a high ratio of capital to labor inputs.

Factor Quality The greater **productivity—**output per worker—of American workers reflects not only the capital intensity of the production process but also the *quality* of both capital and labor. America invests each year not just in *more* plant and equipment but in *better* plant and equipment. Today's new computer is faster and more powerful than yesterday's. Today's laser surgery makes yesterday's surgical procedures look primitive. Even textbooks get better each year. Such improvements in the quality of capital expand production possibilities.

productivity Output per unit of input, e.g., output per labor hour.

Labor quality also improves with education and skill training. Indeed, one can invest in human capital, much like one invests in physical capital. **Human capital** refers to the productive capabilities of labor. In the Stone Age, one's productive capacity was largely determined by physical strength and endurance. In today's economy, human capital is largely a product of education, training, and experience. Hence a country can acquire more human capital even without more bodies.

human capital The knowledge and skills possessed by the work force.

Over time, the United States has invested heavily in human capital. In 1940, only one out of twenty young Americans graduated from college; today, over 30 percent of young people are college graduates. High school graduation rates have jumped from 38 percent to over 85 percent in the same time

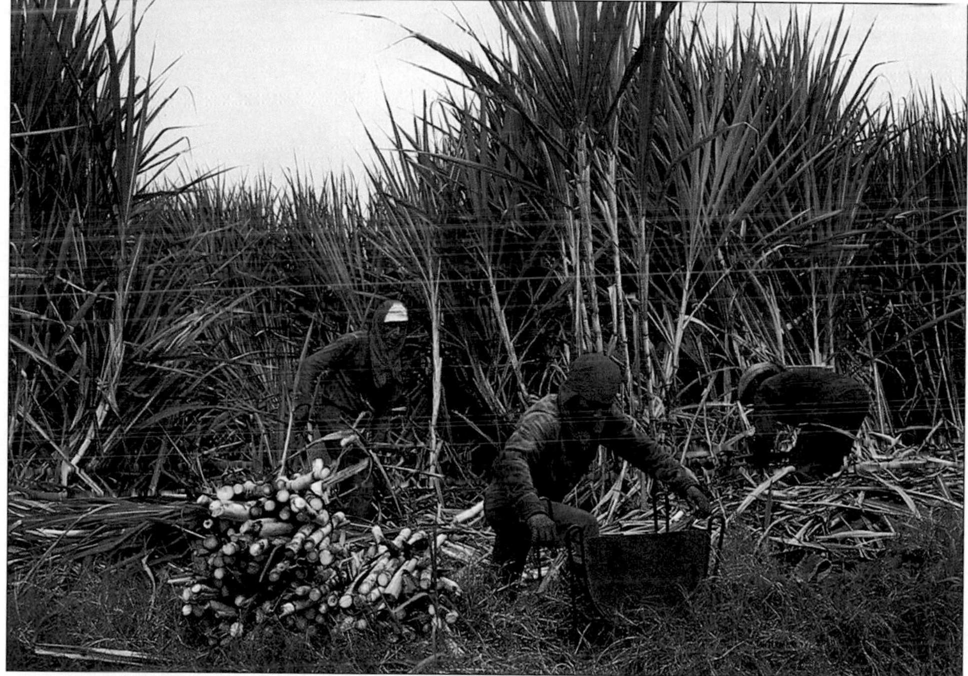

America's enormous output is made possible by huge investments in physical and human capital. In poorer countries, how output is produced is constrained by low levels of education and the scarcity of plant and equipment.

Top: © Brian F. Peterson/Corbis; *Bottom:* © Vivian Moos/Corbis

period. In the poor countries of the Third World only one out of two youths ever *attends* high school, much less graduates (see Headline on the next page). As a consequence, over one billion people—one-sixth of the world's population—is unable to read or even write their own names.

America's tremendous output is thus explained not only by a wealth of resources but by their quality as well. ***The high productivity of the U.S. economy results from using highly educated workers in capital-intensive production processes.***

HEADLINE HUMAN CAPITAL

The Education Gap between Rich and Poor Nations

Virtually all Americans attend high school and roughly 85 percent graduate. In poor countries relatively few workers attend high school and even fewer graduate. Half of the workers in the world's poorest nations are illiterate.

Source: From *World Development Indicators, 2003* (Washington, DC: World Bank, 2003).

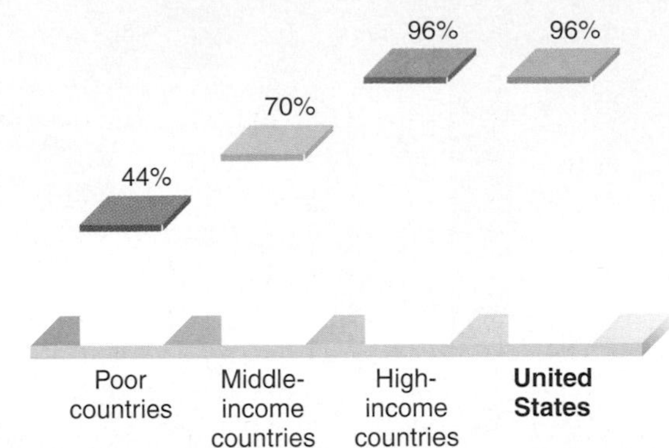

NOTE: The high productivity of the American economy is explained in part by the quality of its labor resources. Workers in poorer, less developed countries get much less education or training.

Factor Mobility Our continuing ability to produce the goods and services that consumers demand also depends on our agility in *reallocating* resources from one industry to another. Every year, some industries expand and others contract. Thousands of new firms are created each year and almost as many others disappear. In the process, land, labor, capital, and entrepreneurship move from one industry to another in response to changing demands and technology. In 1975, Federal Express, Compaq Computer, Microsoft, America Online, Amgen, and Oracle didn't even exist. Today these companies collectively employ over 200,000 people. These workers came from other firms and industries that weren't growing as fast.

Business Organization

The factors of production released from some industries and acquired by others are organized into productive entities we call businesses. A business is an organization that uses factors of production to produce specific goods or services. Actual production activity takes place in the 20 million business firms that participate in the U.S. product markets.

Business Types Business firms come in all shapes and sizes. A basic distinction is made, however, among three different legal organizations:

- Corporations
- Partnerships
- Proprietorships

The primary distinction among these three business forms lies in their ownership characteristics. A single proprietorship is a firm owned by one individual. A partnership is owned by a small number of individuals. A corporation is typically owned by many—even hundreds of thousands of—individuals, each of whom owns shares (stock) of the corporation. An important characteristic of corporations is that their owners (stockholders) are not personally responsible (liable) for the debts or actions of the company. This limited liability makes it easier for corporations to pool the resources of thousands of individuals.

Corporate America Because of their limited liability, corporations tend to be much larger than other businesses. Single proprietorships are typically quite small, because few individuals have vast sources of wealth or credit. The typical proprietorship has less than $10,000 in assets, whereas the average corporation has assets in excess of $4 million. As a result of their size, corporate America dominates market transactions, accounting for almost 90 percent of all business sales.

We can describe who's who in the business community, then, in two very different ways. In terms of numbers, the single proprietorship is the most common type of business firm in America. Proprietorships are particularly dominant in agriculture (the family farm), retail trade (the corner grocery store), and services (your dentist). In terms of size, however, the corporation is the dominant force in the U.S. economy (see Figure 2.5). The four largest nonfinancial corporations in the country (General Electric, ExxonMobil, Wal-Mart, Verizon) alone have more assets than *all* the 15 million proprietorships doing business in the United States. Even in agriculture, where corporate entities are still comparatively rare, the few agribusiness corporations are so large as to dominate many thousands of small farms.

Government Regulation

Although corporate America dominates the U.S. economy, it does not have the last word on WHAT, HOW, or FOR WHOM goods are produced. In our mixed economy, the government has a significant voice in all of these decisions. Even before America became an independent nation, royal charters bestowed the right to produce and trade specific goods. Even the European discovery of America was dependent on government financing and the establishment of exclusive rights to whatever treasures were found. Today over 50 federal agencies and thousands of state and local government entities

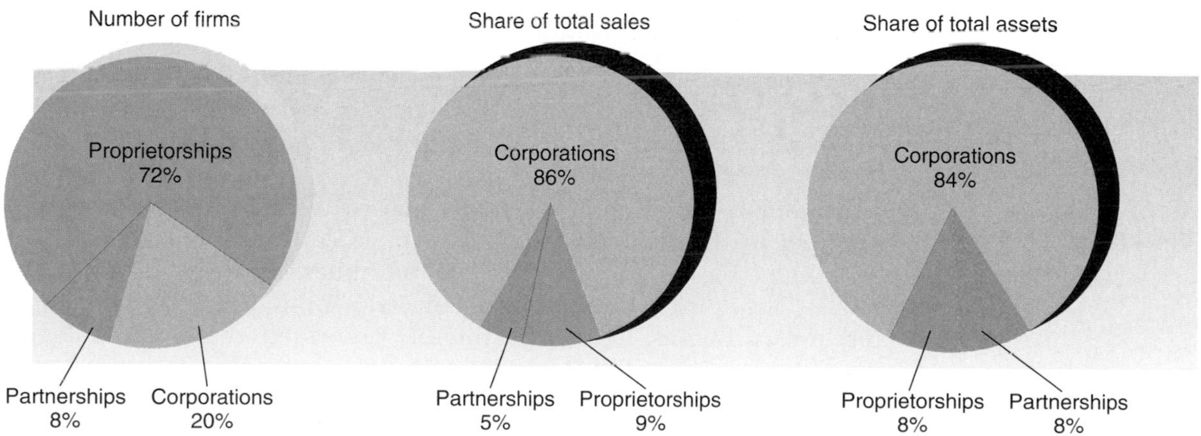

FIGURE 2.5 U.S. Business Firms: Numbers vs. Size

Proprietorships (individually owned companies) are the most common form of American business firm. Corporations are so large, however, that they account for most business sales and assets. Although only 20 percent of all firms are incorporated, corporations control 86 percent of all sales and 84 percent of all assets.

Source: U.S. Department of Commerce, *Statistical Abstract of the United States*, 2002.

regulate the production of goods. In the process, they profoundly affect HOW goods are produced.

Providing a Legal Framework One of the most basic functions of government is to establish and enforce the rules of the game. In some bygone era maybe a person's word was sufficient to guarantee delivery or payment. Businesses today, however, rely more on written contracts. The government gives legitimacy to contracts by establishing the rules for such pacts and by enforcing their provisions. In the absence of contractual rights, few companies would be willing to ship goods without prepayment (in cash). Without legally protected ownership rights, few individuals would buy or build factories. Even the incentive to write textbooks would disappear if government copyright laws didn't forbid unauthorized photocopying. By establishing ownership rights, contract rights, and other rules of the game, the government lays the foundation for market transactions.

Protecting Consumers Much government regulation is intended to protect the interests of consumers. One way to do this is to prevent individual business firms from becoming too powerful. In the extreme case, a single firm might have a **monopoly** on the production of a specific good. As the sole producer of that good, a monopolist could dictate the price, the quality, and the quantity of the product. In such a situation, consumers would likely end up with the short end of the stick—paying too much for too little.

monopoly A firm that produces the entire market supply of a particular good or service.

To protect consumers from monopoly exploitation, the government tries to prevent individual firms from dominating specific markets. Antitrust laws prohibit mergers or acquisitions that would threaten competition. The U.S. Department of Justice and the Federal Trade Commission also regulate pricing practices, advertising claims, and other behavior that might put consumers at an unfair disadvantage in product markets. The "trustbusters" also forced Microsoft to change its licensing procedures in order to assure consumers more choice in computer operating and applications software. The Justice Department even sought to break up the company so as to create more competition in both markets. By changing HOW software systems are developed, the trustbusters hoped to encourage more innovation and lower prices.

Government also regulates the safety of many products. Consumers don't have enough expertise to assess the safety of various medicines, for example. If they rely on trial and error to determine drug safety, they might not get a second chance. To avoid this calamity, the government requires rigorous testing of new drugs, food additives, and other products.

Protecting Labor The government also regulates how our labor resources are used in the production process. As recently as 1920, children between the ages of 10 and 15 were employed in mines, factories, farms, and private homes. They picked cotton and cleaned shrimp in the South, cut sugar beets and pulled onions in the Northwest, processed coal in Appalachia, and pressed tobacco leaves in the Mid-Atlantic states. They often worked six days a week in abusive conditions, for a pittance in wages. Private employers got cheap labor, but society lost valuable resources when so much human capital remained uneducated and physically abused. First the state legislatures, then the U.S. Congress intervened to protect children from such abuse by limiting or forbidding the use of child labor and making school attendance mandatory. In poor nations, governments do much less to limit use of child labor. In Africa, for example, 40 percent of children under age 14 work to survive or to help support their families.

Government regulations further change HOW goods are produced by setting standards for workplace safety and even minimum pay, fringe benefits, and overtime provisions. After decades of bloody confrontations, the government also established the right of workers to organize and set rules for union–management relations. Unemployment insurance, Social Security benefits, disability insurance, and guarantees for private pension benefits also had the effect of protecting labor from the vagaries of the marketplace. They have had a profound effect on how much people work, when they retire, and even on how long they live.

Protecting the Environment In earlier times, producers didn't have to concern themselves with the impact of their production activities on the environment. The steel mills around Pittsburgh blocked out the sun with clouds of sulfurous gases that spewed out of their furnaces. Timber companies laid waste to broad swaths of forestland, without regard to animal habitats or ecological balance. Paper mills used adjacent rivers as disposal sites, and ships at sea routinely dumped their waste overboard. Neither cars nor airplanes were equipped with controls for noise or air pollution.

In the absence of government intervention, such side effects would be common. Decisions on how to produce would be based on private costs alone, not on how the environment is affected. However, such **externalities**—spillover costs imposed on the broader community—affect our collective well-being. To reduce the external costs of production, the government limits air, water, and noise pollution and regulates environmental use.

externalities Costs (or benefits) of a market activity borne by a third party.

Striking a Balance

All of these government interventions are designed to change HOW goods and services are produced. Such interventions reflect the conviction that the market alone would not always select the best possible way of producing goods and services. The market's answer to the HOW question would be based on narrow, profit-and-loss calculations, not on broader measures of societal well-being. To redress this market failure, the government regulates production behavior.

As noted in Chapter 1, there is no guarantee that government regulation of HOW goods are produced always makes us better off. Excessive regulation may inhibit production, raise product prices, and limit consumer choices. In other words, *government* failure might replace *market* failure, leaving us no better off and possibly even worse off.

For Whom America Produces

However imperfect our answers to the WHAT and HOW questions might be, they cannot obscure how rich America is. As we have observed, the American economy produces a $11 trillion economic pie. The final question we have to address is how that pie will be sliced. Will everyone get an equal slice, or will some Americans be served gluttonous slices while others get only crumbs?

Were the slices of the pie carved by the market mechanism, the slices surely would not be equal. Markets reward individuals on the basis of their contribution to output. ***In a market economy, an individual's income depends on***

- ***The quantity and quality of resources owned.***
- ***The price that those resources command in the market.***

That's what concerned Karl Marx so much. As Marx saw it, the capitalists (owners of capital) had a decided advantage in this market-driven distribution. By owning the means of production, capitalists would continue to accumulate wealth, power, and income. Members of the proletariat would get only enough output to assure their survival. Differences in income within the capitalist class or within the working class were of no consequence in the face of these class divisions. All capitalists were rich, all workers poor.

Marx's predictions of how output would be distributed turned out to be wrong in two ways. First, labor's share of total output has risen greatly over time. Second, differences *within* the labor and capitalist classes have become more important than differences between the classes. Many workers are rich and a good many capitalists are poor. Moreover, the distinction between workers and capitalists has been blurred by profit-sharing plans, employee ownership, and widespread ownership of corporate stock. Accordingly, in today's economy it is more useful to examine how the economic pie is distributed across *individuals* rather than across labor and capitalist *classes*.

The Distribution of Income

Figure 2.6 illustrates how uneven the individual slices of the income pie are. Imagine dividing up the population into five subgroups of equal size, but sorted by income. Thus, the top fifth (or quintile) would include that 20 percent of all households with the most income. The bottom fifth would include the 20 percent of households with the least income. The rest of the population would be spread across the other three quintiles.

Figure 2.6 shows that the richest fifth of the population gets nearly *half* of the income pie. By contrast, the poorest fifth gets a tiny sliver. The dimensions of this inequality are spelled out in Table 2.4. Both the figure and the table underscore how unequally the FOR WHOM question is settled in the United States.

As shocking as U.S. income inequalities might appear, incomes are distributed even less equally in many other countries. The Headline on page 48 displays the share of total income received by the top decile (tenth) of households in various countries. In general, inequalities tend to be larger in poorer countries. As countries develop, the **personal distribution of income** tends to become more equal.

personal distribution of income The way total personal income is divided up among households or income classes.

FIGURE 2.6
Slices of the U.S. Income Pie

The richest fifth of U.S. households gets half of all the income—a huge slice of the income pie. By contrast, the poorest fifth gets only a sliver. Should the government do more to equalize the slices or let the market serve up the pie?

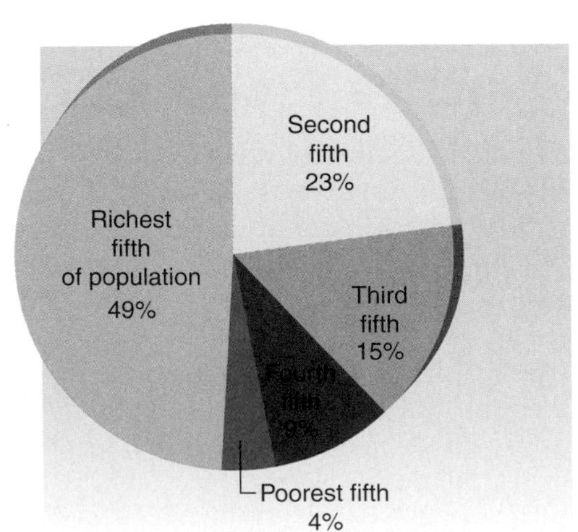

Income Group	2001 Income (dollars)	Average Income	Share of Total Income (percent)
Lowest fifth	0–$17,970	$10,136	3.5%
Second fifth	17,971–33,314	25,468	8.8
Third fifth	33,315–53,000	42,629	14.7
Fourth fifth	53,000–83,500	66,839	23.0
Highest fifth	above 83,500	145,470	50.0

Source: U.S. Department of Commerce, Bureau of the Census.

TABLE 2.4
Distribution of Personal Income, 2001

The size distribution of income indicates how total income is distributed among income classes. That fifth of our population with the lowest incomes received only 3.5 percent of total income. The highest income class (fifth) received nearly half of total income.

Income Mobility

Another important feature of any income distribution is how long people stay in any one position. Being poor isn't such a hardship if your poverty only lasts a week or even a month. Likewise, unequal slices of the economic pie aren't so unfair if the slices are redistributed frequently. In that case, everyone would have a chance to be rich or poor on occasion.

In reality, the slices of the pie are not distributed randomly every year. Some people do get large slices every year, and some other people always seem to end up with crumbs. Nevertheless, such *permanent* inequality is more the exception than the rule in the U.S. economy. One of the most distinctive features of the U.S. income distribution is how often people move up and down the income ladder. This kind of income *mobility* makes lifelong incomes much less unequal than annual incomes. In many nations, income inequalities are much more permanent.

In-Kind Income

When assessing the degree of inequality, we also have to recognize that *income* inequalities aren't a perfect gauge of how *output* is distributed. Income is the primary but not the only ticket to the GDP supermarket. Many goods and services are distributed directly as **in kind income** rather than through market purchases. Many poor people, for example, live in public housing and pay little or no rent. As a consequence, they receive a larger share of total *output* than their money incomes imply. People with low incomes also receive food stamps, which allow them to purchase more food than their money incomes would allow. In this sense, food-stamp recipients are better off than the distribution of personal income (which omits food stamps) implies.

in-kind income Goods and services received directly, without payment in a market transaction.

Students who attend public schools and colleges also consume more goods and services than they directly pay for; public education is subsidized by all taxpayers. As a consequence, the distribution of money income understates the share of output received by students in public schools. All older Americans, regardless of income, also get subsidized health care from the Medicare program.

So long as some goods and services need not be purchased in the marketplace, ***the distribution of money income is not synonymous with the distribution of goods and services.*** Accordingly, the distribution of money receipts is not a complete answer to the question of FOR WHOM we produce. This measurement problem is particularly important when comparisons are made over time. For example, the federal government officially classifies people as "poor" if their money income is below a certain threshold. By this standard, we have made little progress in reducing the number of poor people in America during the last 20 years. In that time, however, we

HEADLINE INEQUALITY

Income Share of the Rich

Incomes are distributed much less equally in poor countries than in rich ones. In most developing countries the top tenth of all households receives 30–50 percent of all income. In the United States and other developed countries inequality is much less severe.

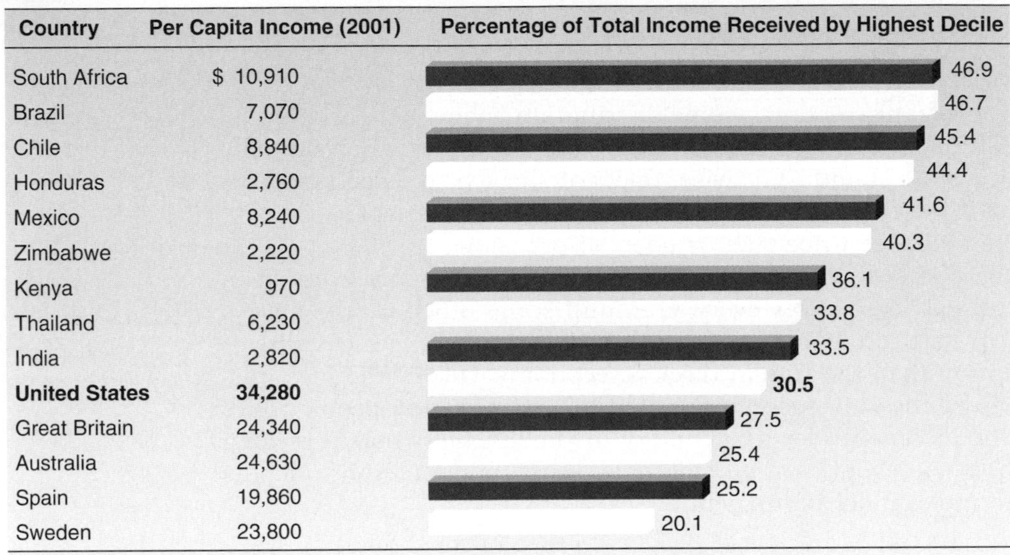

Country	Per Capita Income (2001)	Percentage of Total Income Received by Highest Decile
South Africa	$ 10,910	46.9
Brazil	7,070	46.7
Chile	8,840	45.4
Honduras	2,760	44.4
Mexico	8,240	41.6
Zimbabwe	2,220	40.3
Kenya	970	36.1
Thailand	6,230	33.8
India	2,820	33.5
United States	**34,280**	**30.5**
Great Britain	24,340	27.5
Australia	24,630	25.4
Spain	19,860	25.2
Sweden	23,800	20.1

Source: From *World Development Report Indicators,2003* (Washington, DC: World Bank)

Source: From *World Development Indicators, 2003* (Washington, DC: World Bank).

have provided a vastly increased amount of in-kind benefits to low-income people. Hence their living standards (*real* income) have risen much more than the *money* statistics indicate. In this case, money statistics exaggerate real inequalities.

The distinction between money incomes and real incomes also affects international comparisons. Many people in less developed countries rely more on home production than on market participation for essential goods and services. As a consequence, the measured distribution of money income overstates inequalities. This overstatement also affects comparisons between the United States and such countries as Sweden and Great Britain. In those countries, the governments provide more direct goods and services (e.g., housing, medical care) than the U.S. government does. Hence *real* income is more evenly distributed in those countries than money incomes imply.

Taxes and Transfers

In-kind benefits like food stamps. Medicaid, and public housing are examples of government intervention in the FOR WHOM question. Their goal is to increase the share of output received by people who receive little income from the market. Such in-kind benefits are part of the larger tax-transfer system.

progressive tax A tax system in which tax rates rise as incomes rise.

Taxes Taxes are also a critical mechanism for redistributing market incomes. A **progressive tax** does this by imposing higher tax *rates* on people

© AFP/Corbis

Income inequalities are more vivid in poor nations than in rich ones.

with larger incomes. Under such a system a rich person pays not only more taxes but also a larger *portion* of his or her income. Thus ***a progressive tax makes after-tax incomes more equal than before-tax incomes.***

The federal income tax is designed to be progressive. Individuals with less than $7,000 of income paid no income tax in 2003 and might even have received a spendable tax credit from Uncle Sam. Middle-income households confronted an average tax rate of 20 percent, and rich households faced a federal income tax rate of 35 percent.

The rest of the American tax system is less progressive. Social Security payroll taxes and state and local sales taxes have the opposite effect on the FOR WHOM question. These are **regressive taxes** that impose higher tax rates on lower-income households. This may seem strange, but this reverse redistribution results from the way such taxes are levied. The amount of sales tax you pay, for example, depends on how much you spend. As a rule, poor people spend nearly all of their income, whereas rich people save a lot. As a consequence, poor people end up spending a greater *percentage* of their incomes on sales taxes. Thus sales and other regressive taxes tend to make the after-tax distribution of income less equal.

regressive tax A tax system in which tax rates fall as incomes rise.

When all taxes are added up the tax system appears to have little impact on the FOR WHOM question. The progressive nature of the federal income tax is just about offset by the regressive nature of other sales, payroll, and property taxes. As a result, ***the tax system does not equalize incomes very much.***

Transfers Taxes are only half of the redistribution story. Equally important is who gets the income the government collects. The government completes the redistribution process by transferring income to consumers and providing services. The largest income-transfer program is Social Security, which pays over $500 billion a year to 50 million older or disabled persons. Although rich and poor alike get Social Security benefits, low-wage workers get more retirement benefits for every dollar of earnings. Hence the benefits of the Social Security program are distributed in a *progressive* fashion. Income transfers reserved exclusively for poor people—welfare benefits, food stamps, Medicaid, and the like—are even more progressive. As a result, ***the income-transfer system gives lower-income households more output than the market itself would provide.*** In the absence of transfer payments and taxes, the lowest income quintile would get only 1 percent of total income. The tax-transfer system raises their share to 4 percent. That's still not much of a slice, but it's more of the income pie than they got in the marketplace. To get a still larger slice, they need more market income or more government-led income redistribution.

SUMMARY

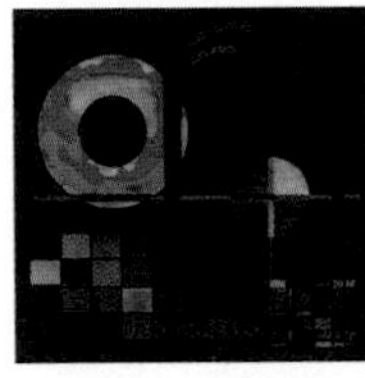

- The answers to the WHAT, HOW, and FOR WHOM questions are reflected in the dimensions of the economy. These answers are the product of market forces and government intervention.
- Gross domestic product (GDP) is the basic measure of how much an economy produces. Real GDP measures the inflation-adjusted value of output.
- The United States produces roughly $11 trillion of output, more than one-fifth of the world's total. American GDP per capita is five times the world average.
- The high level of U.S. per capita GDP reflects the high productivity of American workers. Abundant capital, education, technology, training, and management all contribute to high productivity.
- Over 70 percent of U.S. output consists of services. The service industries continue to grow faster than goods-producing industries.
- Most of America's output consists of consumer goods and services. Investment goods account for only 18 percent of total output.
- Proprietorships and partnerships outnumber corporations nearly five to one. Nevertheless, corporate America produces 90 percent of total output.
- Government intervenes in the economy to establish the rules of the (market) game and to correct the market's answers to the WHAT, HOW, and FOR WHOM questions. The risk of government failure spurs the search for the right mix of market reliance and government regulation.
- Incomes are distributed very unequally among households, with households in the highest income class (quintile) receiving 15 times more income than the average low-income (quintile) household.
- The tax system alone does little to equalize incomes. Tax-financed transfer payments like Social Security and welfare do redistribute a significant amount of income, however.

Terms to Remember

Define the following terms:

gross domestic product	exports	externality
real GDP	imports	personal distribution of income
per capita GDP	factors of production	in-kind income
economic growth	capital intensive	progressive tax
investment	productivity	regressive tax
income transfers	human capital	
	monopoly	

Questions for Discussion

1. Americans already enjoy living standards that far exceed world averages. Do we have enough? Should we even try to produce more?
2. Why do we measure output in value terms rather than in physical terms? For that matter, why do we bother to measure output at all?
3. Why do people suggest that the United States needs to devote more output to investment goods? Why not produce just consumption goods?
4. The U.S. farm population has shrunk by over 25 million people since 1900. Where did they all go? Why did they move?
5. Rich people have over 15 times as much income as poor people. Is that fair? How should output be distributed?
6. If taxes were more progressive, would total output be affected?
7. Why might income inequalities diminish as an economy develops?
8. Why is per capita GDP so much higher in the United States than in Mexico?
9. Do we need more or less government intervention to decide WHAT, HOW, and FOR WHOM? Give specific examples.

Problems

1. Draw a production-possibilities curve with consumer goods on one axis and investment goods on the other axis.
   (*a*) Identify the opportunity cost of increased investment.
   (*b*) What will happen to future production possibilities if investment increases? Illustrate.
   (*c*) What will happen to future production possibilities if only consumer goods are produced?
2. Suppose the following data describe output in two different years:

Item	Year 1	Year 2
Apples	20,000 @25¢ each	30,000 @ 30¢ each
Computers	700 @ $800 each	650 @ $900 each
Video rentals	6,000 @ $1.50 each	7,000 @ $2.00 each

   (*a*) Compute GDP in each year.
   (*b*) By what percentage did GDP increase between Year 1 and Year 2?
   (*c*) Now compute *real* GDP in Year 2 by using the prices of Year 1.
   (*d*) How has real GDP changed from Year 1 to Year 2?
3. GDP per capita in the United States was approximately $38,000 in 2004. What will it be in the year 2014 if GDP per capita grows each year by
   (*a*) 0 percent
   (*b*) 2 percent
   (*c*) 4 percent
4. According to Figure 2.4
   (*a*) Has the *quantity* of manufactured output increased or decreased since 1900?
   (*b*) By how much (in percentage terms)?
   (*c*) Why has the manufacturing *share* of GDP fallen?
5. Assume that total output is determined by the formula:

$$\text{number of workers} \times \underset{\text{(output per work)}}{\text{productivity}} = \text{Total output}$$

(a) If the number of workers increases by 1.0 percent a year and productivity doesn't improve, how fast will output grow?
(b) If productivity *and* the number of workers increase by 1 percent a year, how fast will output grow?

6. According to Table 2.4,
(a) What is the *average* income in the U.S.?
(b) What percent of the income of people in the highest fifth would have to be taxed away to achieve that average?

7. According to the Headline on p. 48, what percent of their income would the highest-decile households in Brazil have to give up to end up with an *average* income?

8. Suppose that the following table describes the spending behavior of individuals at various income levels:

Income	Total Spending	Sales Tax	Sales Tax Paid as Percentage of Income
$ 1,000	$ 1,000	______	______
2,000	1,800	______	______
3,000	2,400	______	______
5,000	3,500	______	______
10,000	6,000	______	______
100,000	40,000	______	______

Assuming that a sales tax of 10 percent is levied on all purchases, calculate
(a) The amount of taxes paid at each income level
(b) The fraction of income paid in taxes at each income level
Is the sales tax progressive or regressive in relation to income?

Web Activities

1. Log on to www.economagic.com/popular.htm and find the statistics for real gross domestic product.
(a) Compare this period's real GDP to one year ago.
(b) Has the economy experienced economic growth? Explain.

2. Log on to www.bea.doc.gov/bea/glance.htm and find the statistics on balance of payments for goods and services for the last two years of data available.
(a) The balance of payments on the current account is often referred to by the media as the *trade deficit*. Which is larger, imports or exports of goods and services?
(b) Does this imbalance in trade cause the value of GDP to increase or decrease?

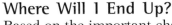

Living Econ

Where Will I End Up?

Based on the important characteristics of the U.S. economy what can we say about the future prospects of college students? Most of you will work in the service sector, a part of the economy that includes over 70 percent of all current employment and nearly 100 percent of all new jobs.

Even though many service sector jobs are in government, chances are you will produce consumption goods in the private sector. Most likely you'll work for a corporation because they produce most of U.S. output. On average households earned about $42,000 in 2001, a figure that is likely to rise over time and, as a college graduate, your earnings will average more than sixty percent above those who complete only high school.

Of course it is misleading to talk about an *average* person. Even though non-service sector jobs are on the decline, the economy still needs manufacturers, farmers, and construction and mine workers. In addition, there are more than 20 million small proprietorships providing jobs to a number of individuals, even if these jobs are not their primary income source. And, average incomes hide the great discrepancy between the lowest 20% of households with incomes in 2001 below $18,000 and the top 20% of households with incomes over $83,500.

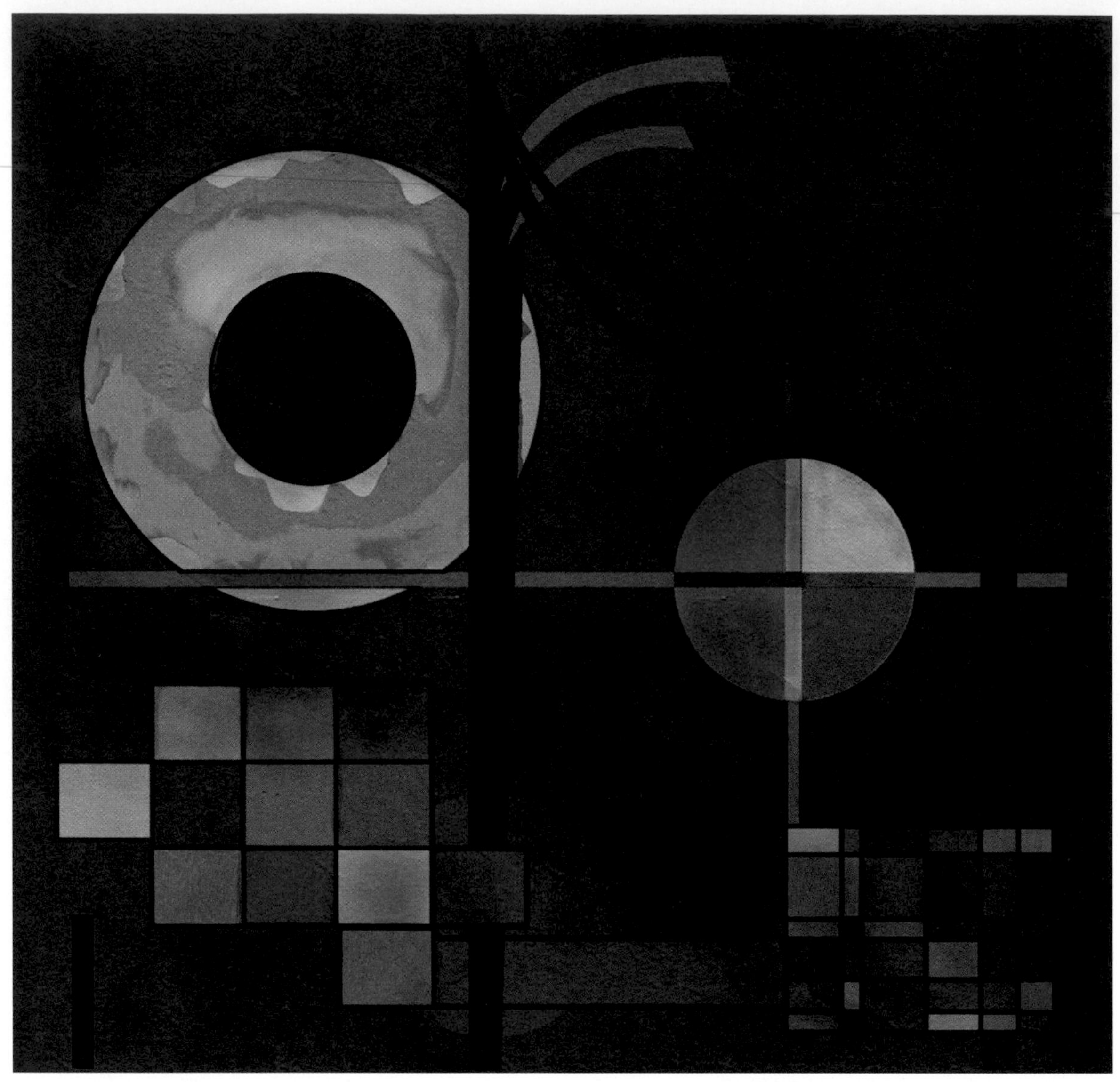

Supply and Demand

CHAPTER 3

A couple of years ago a Florida man tried to sell his kidney on eBay. As his offer explained, he could supply only one kidney because he needed the other to survive. He wanted the bidding to start out at $25,000, plus expenses for the surgical removal and shipment of his kidney. He felt confident he could get at least that much money since thousands of people have potentially fatal kidney diseases.

He was right. The bids for his kidney quickly surpassed $100,000. Clearly, there were lots of people with kidney disease who were willing and able to pay high prices to get a lifesaving transplant.

The seller never got the chance to sell his kidney to the highest bidder. Although organ transplants are perfectly legal in the United States, the purchase or sale of human organs is not. When eBay learned the pending sale was illegal, they shut down the man's auction.

Despite its illegality, there is clearly a market in human kidneys. That is to say, there are people who are willing to *sell* kidneys, and others who are willing to *buy* kidneys. Those are sufficient conditions for the existence of a market. The market in kidneys happens to be illegal in the United States, but it is still a market, although illegal. The markets for drugs, prostitution, and nuclear warheads are also illegal, but still reflect the intentions of potential buyers and sellers.

Fortunately, we don't have to venture into the underworld to see how markets work. You can watch markets work by visiting eBay or other electronic auction sites. Or you can simply go to the mall and watch people shop. In either location you will observe people deciding whether to buy or sell goods at various prices. That's the essence of market activity. The goal in this chapter is to assess how markets actually function. How does the invisible hand of the market resolve the competing interests of buyers (who want low prices) and sellers (who want high prices)? Specifically,

- What determines the price of a good or service?
- How does the price of a product affect its production or consumption?
- Why do prices and production levels often change?

Market Participants

Over 290 million individual consumers, about 20 million business firms, and tens of thousands of government agencies participate directly in the U.S. economy. Millions of foreigners also participate by buying and selling goods in American markets.

Goals

All of these economic actors participate in the market in order to achieve specific goals. Consumers strive to maximize their own happiness, businesses try to maximize profits; government agencies are supposed to maximize the general welfare. Foreigners pursue these same goals, as consumers, producers, or government agencies. In every case, they strive to achieve these goals by buying the best-possible mix of goods, services, or factors of production.

Constraints

The desire of all market participants to maximize something—profits, private satisfaction, or social welfare—is not their only common trait. Another element common to all participants is their *limited resources.* You and I cannot buy everything we desire; we simply don't have enough income. As a consequence, we must make *choices* among available products. We're always hoping to get as much satisfaction as possible for the few dollars we have to spend. Likewise, business firms and government agencies must decide how *best* to use their limited resources to maximize profits or public welfare. This is the scarcity problem we examined in Chapter 1. It is central to all economic decisions.

Specialization and Exchange

market Any place where goods are bought and sold.

To maximize the returns on our limited resources, we participate in the **market,** buying and selling various goods and services. Our decision to participate in these exchanges is prompted by two considerations. First, most of us are incapable of producing everything we desire to consume. Second, even if we *could* produce all our own goods and services, it would still make sense to specialize, producing only one product and trading it for other desired goods and services.

Suppose you were capable of growing your own food, stitching your own clothes, building your own shelter, and even writing your own economics text. Even in this little utopia, it would still make sense to decide how *best* to expend your limited time and energy and to rely on others to fill in the gaps. If you were *most* proficient at growing food, you would be best off spending your time farming. You could then exchange some of your food output for the clothes, shelter, and books you desired. In the end, you'd be able to consume more goods than if you had tried to make everything yourself.

Our economic interactions with others are thus necessitated by two constraints:

- Our inability as individuals to produce all the things we desire.
- The limited amount of time, energy, and resources we possess for producing those things we could make for ourselves.

Together, these constraints lead us to specialize and interact. Most of the interactions that result take place in the market.

Market Interactions

Figure 3.1 summarizes the kinds of interactions that occur among market participants. Note, first of all, that we have identified ***four separate groups of market participants:***

- ***Consumers***
- ***Business firms***
- ***Governments***
- ***Foreigners***

Domestically, the "Consumers" rectangle includes all 290 million consumers in the United States. In the "Business firms" box we have grouped all of the domestic business enterprises that buy and sell goods and services. The third participant, "Governments," includes the many separate agencies of the federal government, as well as state and local governments. Figure 3.1 also illustrates the role of foreigners.

The Two Markets

The easiest way to keep track of all this market activity is to distinguish two basic markets. Figure 3.1 does this by portraying separate circles for product markets and factor markets. In **factor markets,** factors of production are exchanged. Market participants buy or sell land, labor, or capital that can be used in the production process. When you go looking for work, for example, you are making a factor of production—your labor—available to producers. You are offering to *sell* your time and talent. The producers will hire you—*buy*

factor market Any place where factors of production (e.g., land, labor, capital, entrepreneurship) are bought and sold.

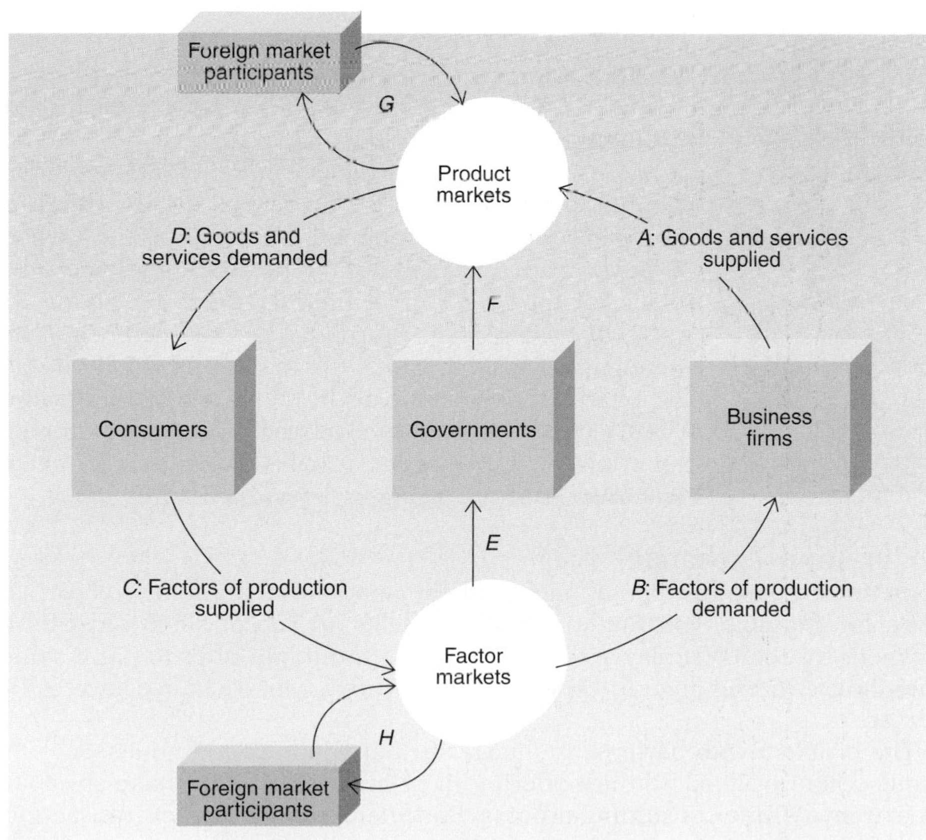

FIGURE 3.1
Market Interactions

Business firms participate in markets by supplying goods and services to product markets (point *A*) and purchasing factors of production in factor markets (*B*). Individual consumers participate in the marketplace by supplying factors of production such as their own labor (*C*) and purchasing final goods and services (*D*). Federal, state, and local governments also participate in both factor (*E*) and product markets (*F*) Foreigners participate by supplying imports, purchasing exports (*G*), and buying and selling resources (*H*).

your services in the factor market—if you are offering the skills they need at a price they are willing to pay.

Interactions within factor markets are only half the story. At the end of a hard day's work, consumers go to the grocery store (or the movies) to purchase desired goods and services—that is, to buy *products*. In this context, consumers again interact with business firms. This time, however, their roles are reversed: consumers are doing the *buying* and businesses are doing the *selling*. This exchange of goods and services occurs in **product markets.**

product market Any place where finished goods and services (products) are bought and sold.

Governments also supply goods and services to product markets. The consumer rarely buys national defense, schools, or highways directly; instead, such purchases are made indirectly through taxes and government expenditure. In Figure 3.1, the arrows running from governments through product markets to consumers serve to remind us, however, that all government output is intended "for the people." In this sense, the government acts as an intermediary, buying factors of production and providing certain goods and services consumers desire.

A market exists wherever buyers and sellers interact.

© Stephen Chernin/Getty Images

In Figure 3.1, the arrow connecting product markets to consumers (point D) emphasizes the fact that consumers, by definition, do not supply products. To the extent that individuals produce goods and services, they do so within the government or business sector. An individual who is a doctor, a dentist, or an economic consultant functions in two sectors. When selling services in the market, this person is regarded as a "business"; when away from the office, he or she is regarded as a "consumer." This distinction is helpful in emphasizing the role of the consumer as the final recipient of all goods and services produced.

Locating Markets Although we will refer repeatedly to two kinds of markets, it would be a little foolish to go off in search of the product and factor markets. Neither a factor market nor a product market is a single, identifiable structure. The term *market* simply refers to any place where an economic exchange occurs—where a buyer and seller interact. The exchange may take place on the street, in a taxicab, over the phone, by mail, in cyberspace, or through the classified ads of the newspaper. In some cases, the market used may in fact be quite distinguishable, as in the case of a retail store, the Chicago Commodity Exchange, or a state employment office. But whatever it looks like, ***a market exists wherever and whenever an exchange takes place.***

Dollars and Exchange

Sometimes people exchange one good for another in the marketplace. On eBay, for example, you might convince a seller to accept some old CDs in payment for the DVD player she is selling. Or you might offer to paint someone's house in exchange for "free" rent. Such two-way exchanges are called **barter.**

barter The direct exchange of one good for another, without the use of money.

The problem with bartered exchanges is that you have to find a seller who wants whatever good you are offering in payment. This can make shopping an extremely time-consuming process. Fortunately, most market transactions are facilitated by using money as a form of payment. If you go shopping for a DVD player, you don't have to find a seller craving old CDs; all you have to do is find a seller willing to accept the dollar price you are willing to pay. Because money facilitates exchanges, ***nearly every market transaction involves an exchange of dollars for goods (in product markets) or resources (in factor markets).*** Money thus plays a critical role in facilitating market exchanges and the specialization they permit.

Supply and Demand

The two sides of each market transaction are called **supply** and **demand.** As noted earlier, we are *supplying* resources to the market when we look for a job—that is, when we offer our labor in exchange for income. But we are *demanding* goods when we shop in a supermarket—that is, when we are prepared to offer dollars in exchange for something to eat. Business firms may *supply* goods and services in product markets at the same time that they are *demanding* factors of production in factor markets.

supply The ability and willingness to sell (produce) specific quantities of a good at alternative prices in a given time period, ceteris paribus.

demand The ability and willingness to buy specific quantities of a good at alternative prices in a given time period, ceteris paribus.

Whether one is on the supply side or the demand side of any particular market transaction depends on the nature of the exchange, not on the people or institutions involved.

Demand

Although the concepts of supply and demand are useful for explaining what's happening in the marketplace, we are not yet ready to summarize the countless transactions that occur daily in both factor and product markets. Recall that ***every market transaction involves an exchange and thus some element of both supply and demand.*** Then just consider how many exchanges you alone undertake in a single week, not to mention the transactions of the other 290 million or so consumers among us. To keep track of so much action, we need to summarize the activities of many individuals.

Individual Demand

We can begin to understand how market forces work by looking more closely at the behavior of a single market participant. Let us start with Tom, a senior at Clearview College. Tom has majored in everything from art history to government in his three years at Clearview. He didn't connect to any of those fields and is on the brink of academic dismissal. To make matters worse, his parents have threatened to cut him off financially unless he gets serious about his course work. By that they mean he should enroll in courses that will lead to a job after graduation. Tom thinks he has found the perfect solution: web design. Everything associated with the Internet pays big bucks. Plus, the girls seem to think webbies are "cool." Or at least so Tom thinks. And his parents would definitely approve. So Tom has enrolled in web-design courses.

Unfortunately for Tom, he never developed computer skills. Until he got to Clearview College he thought mastering Sony's latest alien-attack video game was the pinnacle of electronic wizardry. His parents had given him a wired iMac, but he used it only for surfing hot video sites. The concept of using his computer for course work, much less developing some web content, was completely foreign to him. To compound his problems, Tom didn't have a clue about streaming, interfacing, animation, or the other concepts the web-design instructor outlined in the first lecture.

Given his circumstances, Tom was desperate to find someone who could tutor him in web design. But desperation is not enough to secure the services of a web architect. In a market-based economy, you must also be willing to *pay* for the things you want. Specifically, ***a demand exists only if someone is willing and able to pay for the good***—that is, exchange dollars for a good or service in the marketplace. Is Tom willing and able to pay for the web-design tutoring he so obviously needs?

Let us assume that Tom has some income and is willing to spend some of it to get a tutor. Under these assumptions, we can claim that Tom is a participant in the *market* for web-design services.

opportunity cost The most desired goods or services that are forgone in order to obtain something else.

But how much is Tom willing to pay? Surely, Tom is not prepared to exchange *all* his income for help in mastering web design. After all, Tom could use his income to buy more desirable goods and services. If he spent all his income on a web tutor, that help would have an extremely high **opportunity cost.** He would be giving up the opportunity to spend that income on other goods and services. He might pass his web-design class but have little else. It doesn't sound like a good idea to Tom. Even though he says he would be willing to pay *anything* to pass the web-design course, he probably has lower prices in mind. Indeed, it would be more reasonable to assume that there are *limits* to the amount Tom is willing to pay for any given quantity of web-design tutoring. These limits will be determined by how much income Tom has to spend and how many other goods and services he must forsake in order to pay for a tutor.

Tom also knows that his grade in web design will depend in part on how much tutoring service he buys. He can pass the course with only a few hours of design help. If he wants a better grade, however, the cost is going to escalate quickly.

Naturally, Tom wants it all—an A in web design and a ticket to higher-paying jobs. But here again the distinction between *desire* and *demand* is relevant. He may *desire* to master web design, but his actual proficiency will depend on how many hours of tutoring he is willing to *pay* for.

demand schedule A table showing the quantities of a good a consumer is willing and able to buy at alternative prices in a given time period, ceteris paribus.

We assume, then, that when Tom starts looking for a web-design tutor he has in mind some sort of **demand schedule,** like that described in Figure 3.2. According to row *A* of this schedule, Tom is willing and able to buy only one hour of tutoring service per semester if he must pay $50 an hour. At such an outrageous price he will learn minimal skills and pass the course. Just the bare minimum is all Tom is willing to buy at that price.

At lower prices, Tom would behave differently. According to Figure 3.2, Tom would purchase more tutoring services if the price per hour were less. At lower prices, he would not have to give up so many other goods and services for each hour of technical help. The reduced opportunity costs implied by lower service prices increase the attractiveness of professional help. Indeed, we see from row *I* of the demand schedule that Tom is willing to purchase 20 hours per semester—the whole bag of design tricks—if the price of tutoring is as low as $10 per hour.

Notice that the demand schedule doesn't tell us anything about *why* this consumer is willing to pay specific prices for various amounts of tutoring. Tom's expressed willingness to pay for web-design tutoring may reflect a desperate need to finish a web-design course, a lot of income to spend, or a relatively small desire for other goods and services. All the demand schedule tells us is what the consumer is *willing and able* to buy, for whatever reasons.

Also observe that the demand schedule doesn't tell us how many hours of design help the consumer will *actually* buy. Figure 3.2 simply states that Tom

	Demand Schedule	
	Price of Tutoring (per hour)	Quantity of Tutoring Demanded (hours per semester)
A	$50	1
B	45	2
C	40	3
D	35	5
E	30	7
F	25	9
G	20	12
H	15	15
I	10	20

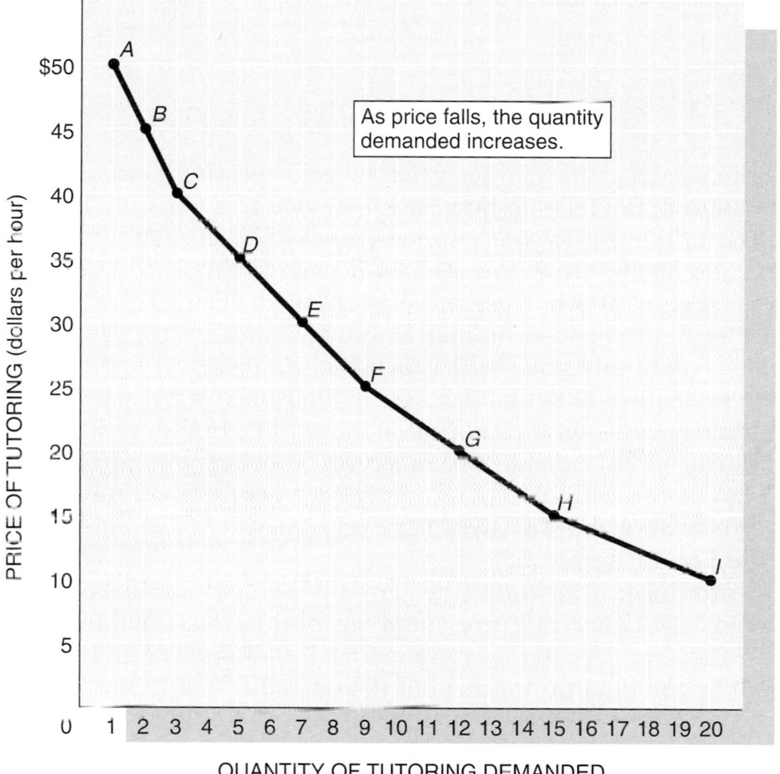

FIGURE 3.2
A Demand Schedule and Curve

A demand schedule indicates the quantities of a good a consumer is able and willing to buy at alternative prices (*ceteris paribus*). The demand schedule indicates that Tom would buy 5 hours of web-design tutoring per semester if the price were $35 per hour (row *D*). If web tutoring were less expensive (rows *E–I*). Tom would purchase a larger quantity.

A demand curve is a graphical illustration of a demand schedule. Each point on the curve refers to a specific quantity that will be demanded at a given price. If, for example, the price of web-design tutoring were $35 per hour, this curve tells us the consumer would purchase 5 hours per semester (point *D*). If web services cost $30 per hour, 7 hours per semester would be demanded (point *E*). Each point on the curve corresponds to a row in the schedule.

is *willing and able* to pay for one hour of tutoring per semester at $50 per hour, for two hours at $45 each, and so on. How much service he purchases will depend on the actual price of web services in the market. Until we know that price, we cannot tell how much service will be purchased. Hence ***demand is an expression of consumer buying intentions, of a willingness to buy, not a statement of actual purchases.***

A convenient summary of buying intentions is the **demand curve,** a graphical illustration of the demand schedule. The demand curve in Figure 3.2 tells us again that this consumer is willing to pay for only one hour of web-design tutoring per semester if the price is $50 per hour (point *A*), for two if the price is $45 (point *B*), for three at $40 a hour (point *C*), and so on.

demand curve A curve describing the quantities of a good a consumer is willing and able to buy at alternative prices in a given time period, ceteris paribus.

HEADLINE LAW OF DEMAND

Higher Alcohol Prices and Student Drinking

Raise the price of alcohol substantially and some college students will not drink or will drink less. That's the conclusion from a Harvard survey of 22,831 students at 158 colleges. Students faced with a $1 increase above the average drink price of $2.17 will be 33 percent less likely to drink at all or as much. So raising the price of alcohol in college communities could significantly lessen student drinking and its associated problems (alcohol-related deaths, property damage, unwanted sexual encounters, arrests). This could be done by raising local excise taxes, eliminating bar promotions, and forbidding all-you-can-drink events.

Source: Jenny Williams, Frank Chaloupka, and Henry Wechsler, "Are There Differential Effects of Price and Policy on College Students Drinking Intensity?" Cambridge, MA: National Bureau of Economic Research, 2002.

NOTE: The Law of Demand predicts that the quantity demanded of any good—even beer and liquor—declines as its price increases.

Once we know what the market price of web tutoring actually is, a glance at the demand curve tells us how much service this consumer will buy.

What the notion of *demand* emphasizes is that the amount we buy of a good depends on its price. We seldom if ever decide to buy only a certain quantity of a good at whatever price is charged. Instead, we enter markets with a set of desires and a limited amount of money to spend. How much we actually buy of any good will depend on its price.

A common feature of demand curves is their downward slope. As the price of a good falls, people tend to purchase more of it. In Figure 3.2 the quantity of web tutorial services demanded increases (moves rightward along the horizontal axis) as the price per hour decreases (moves down the vertical axis). This inverse relationship between price and quantity is so common we refer to it as the **law of demand.**

law of demand The quantity of a good demanded in a given time period increases as its price falls, ceteris paribus.

College administrators think the Law of Demand could be used to curb student drinking. Low retail prices and bar promotions encourage student to drink more alcohol. As the accompanying Headline explains, higher prices would reduce the quantity of alcohol demanded.

Determinants of Demand

The demand curve in Figure 3.2 has only two dimensions—quantity demanded (on the horizontal axis) and price (on the vertical axis). This seems to imply that the amount of tutorial services demanded depends only on the price of that service. This is surely not the case. A consumer's willingness and ability to buy a product at various prices depend on a variety of forces. ***The determinants of market demand include***

- ***Tastes*** (desire for this and other goods).
- ***Income*** (of the consumer).
- ***Other goods*** (their availability and price).
- ***Expectations*** (for income, prices, tastes).
- ***Number of buyers.***

If Tom didn't have to pass a web-design course, he would have no taste (desire) for web-page tutoring and thus no demand. If he had no income, he would not have the ability to pay and thus would still be out of the web-design market. The price and availability of other goods affect the opportunity cost of tutoring services, while expectations for income, grades, and graduation prospects would all influence his willingness to buy such services.

Ceteris Paribus

If demand is in fact such a multidimensional decision, how can we reduce it to only the two dimensions of price and quantity? This is the ***ceteris paribus*** trick we encountered earlier. To simplify their models of the world, economists focus on only one or two forces at a time and *assume* nothing else changes. We know a consumer's tastes, income, other goods, and expectations all affect the decision to buy web-design services. But ***we focus on the relationship between quantity demanded and price.*** That is to say, we want to know what *independent* influence price has on consumption decisions. To find out, we must isolate that one influence, price, and assume that the determinants of demand remain unchanged.

ceteris paribus The assumption of nothing else changing.

The *ceteris paribus* assumption is not as far-fetched as it may seem. People's tastes (desires) don't change very quickly. Income tends to be fairly stable from week to week. Even expectations for the future are slow to change. Accordingly, the price of a good may be the only thing that changes on any given day. In that case, a change in price may be the only thing that prompts a change in consumer behavior.

Shifts in Demand

The determinants of demand do change, of course, particularly over time. Accordingly, ***the demand schedule and curve remain unchanged only so long as the underlying determinants of demand remain constant.*** If the *ceteris paribus* assumption is violated—if tastes, income, other goods, or expectations change—the ability or willingness to buy will change. When this happens, the demand curve will **shift** to a new position.

shift in demand A change in the quantity demanded at any (every) given price.

Suppose, for example, that Tom won $1,000 in the state lottery. This increase in his income would greatly increase his ability to pay for tutoring services. Figure 3.3 shows the effect of this windfall on Tom's demand for tutoring services. The old demand curve, D_1, is no longer relevant. Tom's

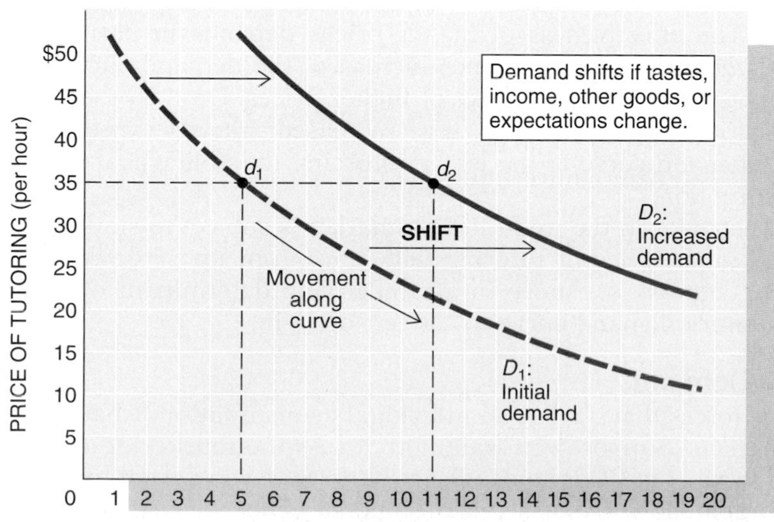

FIGURE 3.3
A Shift in Demand

A demand curve shows how the quantity demanded changes in response to a change in price, *if* all else remains constant. But the determinants of demand may themselves change, causing the demand curve to *shift*. In this case, an increase in income increases demand from D_1 to D_2. After this shift. Tom demands 11 hours (d_2), rather than 5 (d_1), at the price of $35. The quantity demanded at all other prices increases as well.

lottery winnings enable him to buy more tutoring services at any price. This is illustrated by the new demand curve, D_2. According to this new curve, lucky Tom is now willing and able to buy 11 hours per semester at the price of \$35 per hour (point d_2). This is a large increase in demand, as previously (before winning the lottery) he demanded only 5 hours at that price (point d_1).

With his higher income, Tom can buy more tutoring services at every price. Thus ***the entire demand curve shifts to the right when income goes up.*** Both the old (prelottery) and the new (postlottery) demand curves are illustrated in Figure 3.3.

Income is only one of four basic determinants of demand. Changes in any of the other determinants of demand would also cause the demand curve to shift. Tom's taste for web-design tutoring might increase dramatically, for example, if his other professors made the quality of personal web pages a critical determinant of course grades. His taste (desire) for web-design services might increase even more if his parents promised to buy him a new car for passing *all* his courses. Whatever its origins, ***an increase in taste (desire) or expectations also shifts the demand curve to the right.*** The accompanying Headline shows how such shifts can affect the equilibrium price of a product.

Movements vs. Shifts

It is important to distinguish shifts of the demand curve from movements along the demand curve. ***Movements along a demand curve are a response to price changes for that good.*** Such movements assume that determinants of demand are unchanged. By contrast, ***shifts of the demand curve occur when the determinants of demand change.*** When tastes, income, other goods, or expectations are altered, the basic relationship between price and quantity demanded is changed (shifts).

For convenience, the distinction between movements along a demand curve and shifts of the demand curve have their own labels. Specifically, take care to distinguish

- ***Changes in quantity demanded:*** movements along a given demand curve, in response to price changes of that good.
- ***Changes in demand:*** shifts of the demand curve due to changes in tastes, income, other goods, or expectations.

The Headline on p. 62 told how higher alcohol prices could reduce college drinking. The effectiveness of higher prices depends in part, however, on *ceteris paribus*. If student incomes increased, the demand curve might shift to the right, offsetting the impact of higher prices. On the other hand, if the penalties for campus drinking were increased, altered expectations might shift the demand curve to the left, reinforcing the policy goal of lower alcohol consumption.

Tom's behavior in the web-tutoring market is subject to similar influences. A change in the *price* of tutoring will move Tom up or down his demand curve. By contrast, a change in an underlying determinant of demand will shift his entire demand curve to the left or right.

market demand The total quantities of a good or service people are willing and able to buy at alternative prices in a given time period, the sum of individual demands.

Market Demand

The same forces that change an individual's consumption behavior also move entire markets. Suppose you wanted to assess the **market demand** for web-tutoring services at Clearview College. To do that, you'd want to identify every student's demand for that service. Some students, of course, have no need

SHIFTS OF DEMAND HEADLINE

Natural Gas Prices Rise as Temps Fall

WASHINGTON—Natural gas prices are climbing quickly, shocking millions of homeowners across the country as they open their winter energy bills.

Futures prices for natural gas are up more than 130% from last year and are the highest since April 2001.

What's behind the increase:

- It's colder this winter than last winter, which was the ninth warmest in the USA since recordkeeping began in 1895, according to The Weather Channel. Last winter was the warmest on record for the Northeast. Lower temperatures this year are leading to increased demand. Forecasters anticipate lower temperatures to continue in coming weeks.
- Oil prices have been rising for months because of a general strike in Venezuela and concerns about what will happen to oil supplies if the USA goes to war against Iraq. Because natural gas can often be used in place of oil, especially in industry, a rise in oil prices usually translates into higher natural gas prices.

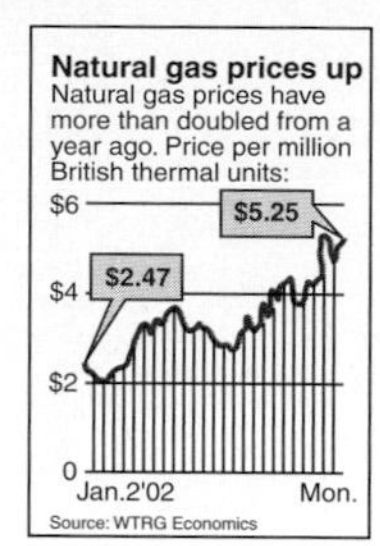

—Barbara Hagenbaugh

Source: *USA Today*, January 14, 2003, p. B1.

NOTE: Demand increases (shifts) when tastes increase (due, here, to colder weather), when the price of substitute goods (e.g., oil) increase, or when other determinants of demand (income, expectations) change.

or desire for professional web-design services and are not willing to pay anything for such tutoring; they do not participate in the web-design market. Other students have a desire for such services but not enough income to pay for them; they, too, are excluded from the web-design market. A large number of students, however, not only have a need (or desire) for tutoring but also are willing and able to purchase such services.

What we start with in product markets, then, is many individual demand curves. Fortunately, it is possible to combine all the individual demand curves into a single **market demand** for web-design services. Suppose you would be willing to buy one hour of tutoring services per semester at a price of $80 per hour. George, who is also desperate to learn web design, would buy two at that price; and I would buy none, since my publisher (McGraw-Hill) creates a web page for me (try mhhe.com/economics/Schiller). What would our combined (market) demand for hours of design services be at that price? Clearly, our individual inclinations indicate that we would be willing to buy a total of three hours of tutoring services per semester if the price were $80 per hour. Our combined willingness to buy—our collective market demand—is nothing more than the sum of our individual demands. The same kind of aggregation can be performed for all consumers, leading to a summary of the total market demand for web-design tutoring services at Clearview College. This ***market demand is determined by the number of potential buyers and their respective tastes, incomes, other goods, and expectations.***

The Market Demand Curve

Table 3.1 provides the basic market demand schedule for a situation in which only three consumers participate in the market. Figure 3.4 illustrates the same market situation with demand curves. The three individuals who

TABLE 3.1 The Market Demand Schedule

Market demand represents the combined demands of all market participants. To determine the total quantity of tutoring demanded at any given price, we add up the separate demands of the individual consumers. Row *G* of this schedule indicates that a *total* quantity of 39 hours of service per semester will be demanded at a price of $20 per hour.

		Quantity of Tutoring Demanded (hours per semester)						
	Price per Hour	Tom	+	George	+	Lisa	=	Total Demand
A	$50	1		4		0		5
B	45	2		6		0		8
C	40	3		8		0		11
D	35	5		11		0		16
E	30	7		14		1		22
F	25	9		18		3		30
G	20	12		22		5		39
H	15	15		26		6		47
I	10	20		30		7		57

participate in the market demand for web services at Clearview College obviously differ greatly, as suggested by their respective demand schedules. Tom *has* to pass his web-design classes or confront college and parental rejection. He also has a nice allowance (income), so can afford to buy a lot of tutorial help. His demand schedule is portrayed in the first column of Table 3.1 (and is identical to the one we examined in Figure 3.2). George, as we already noted, is also desperate to acquire some job skills and is willing to pay relatively high prices for web-design tutoring. His demand is summarized in the second column under "Quantity of Tutoring Demanded" in Table 3.1.

The third consumer in this market is Lisa. Lisa already knows the nuts and bolts of web design, so she doesn't have as desperate a need for tutorial services. She would like to upgrade her skills, however, especially in animation

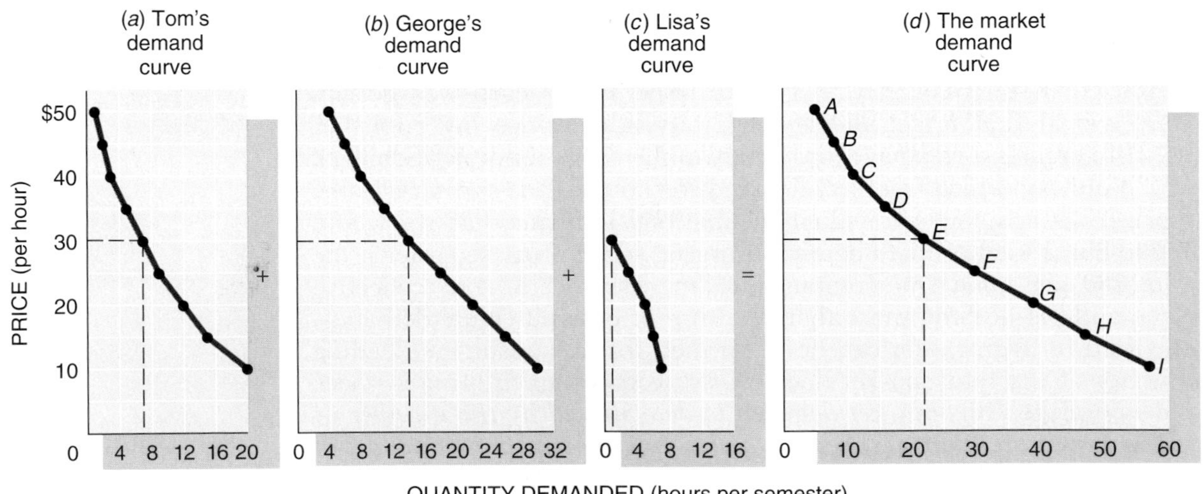

FIGURE 3.4 Construction of the Market Demand Curve

The market demand curve expresses the *combined* demands of all market participants. At a price of $30 per hour, the total quantity of web-design services demanded would be 22 hours per semester (point *E*): 7 hours demanded by Tom, 14 by George, and 1 by Lisa.

and e-commerce applications. But her limited budget precludes paying a lot for help. She will buy some technical support only if the price falls to $30 per hour. Should tutors cost less, she'd even buy quite a few hours of design services.

The differing personalities and consumption habits of Tom, George, and Lisa are expressed in their individual demand schedules and associated curves, as depicted in Table 3.1 and Figure 3.4. To determine the *market* demand for tutoring services from this information, we simply add up these three separate demands. The end result of this aggregation is, first, a *market* demand schedule (the last column in Table 3.1) and, second, the resultant *market* demand curve (the curve in Figure 3.4*d*). These market summaries describe the various quantities of tutoring services that Clearview College students are *willing and able* to purchase each semester at various prices.

The Use of Demand Curves

So why does anybody care what the demand curve for web-design tutoring looks like? What's the point of doing all this arithmetic and drawing so many graphs?

If you were a web designer at Clearview College, you'd certainly like to have the information depicted in Figure 3.4. What the market demand curve tells us is how much tutoring service could be sold at various prices to Clearview students. Suppose you hoped to sell 30 hours at a price of $30 per hour. According to Figure 3.4 (point *E*), students will buy only 22 hours at that price. Hence, you won't attain your sales goal. You could find that out by posting ads on campus and waiting for a response. It would be a lot easier, however, if you knew in advance what the demand curve looked like.

Would this many fans show up if concert prices were higher?

AP/Wide World Photos

People who promote music concerts need the same kind of information. They want to fill the stadium with screaming fans. But fans have limited income and desires for other goods. Accordingly, the number of fans who will buy concert tickets depends on the price. If the promoter sets the price too high, there will be lots of empty seats at the concert. If the price is set too low, the promoter may lose potential sales revenue. What the promoter wants to know is what price will induce a quantity demanded that conforms to the number of available seats. If the promoter could consult a demand curve, the correct price would be evident.

Supply

Even if we knew what the demand for every good looked like, we couldn't predict what quantities would be bought. The demand curve tells us only how much consumers are willing and able to buy at specific prices. We don't know the price yet, however. To find out what price will be charged, we've got to know something about the behavior of people who *sell* goods and services. That is to say, we need to examine the *supply* side of the marketplace. The **market supply** of a good reflects the collective behavior of all firms that are willing and able to sell that good at various prices.

market supply The total quantities of a good that sellers are willing and able to sell at alternative prices in a given time period, ceteris paribus.

Determinants of Supply

Let's return to the Clearview campus for a moment. What we need to know now is how much tutorial web service people are willing and able to provide. Generally speaking, web-page design can be fun, but it can also be drudge work, especially when you're doing it for someone else. Software programs like PhotoShop, Flash, and Fireworks have made web-page design easier and more creative. But teaching someone else to design web pages is still work. So few people offer to supply web services just for the fun of it. Web designers do it for money. Specifically, they do it to earn income that they, in turn, can spend on goods and services they desire.

How much income must be offered to induce web designers to do a job depends on a variety of things. The ***determinants of market supply include***

- ***Technology***
- ***Factor costs***
- ***Other goods***
- ***Taxes and subsidies***
- ***Expectations***
- ***Number of sellers***

The technology of web design, for example, is always getting easier and more creative. With a program like PageOut, for example, it's very easy to create a bread-and-butter web page. A continuous stream of new software programs (e.g., Fireworks, Dreamweaver) keeps stretching the possibilities for graphics, animation, interactivity, and content. These technological advances mean that web-design services can be supplied more quickly and cheaply. They also make *teaching* web design easier. As a result, they induce people to supply more web-design services at every price.

How much tutoring is offered at any given price also depends on the cost of factors of production. If the software programs needed to create web pages are cheap (or, better yet, free!), web designers can afford to charge lower prices. If the required software inputs are expensive, however, they will have to charge more money per hour for their services.

Other goods can also affect the willingness to supply web-design services. If you can make more income waiting tables than you can designing web pages, why would you even boot up the computer? As the prices paid for other goods and services change, they will influence people's decisions about whether to offer web services.

In the real world, the decision to supply goods and services is also influenced by the long arm of Uncle Sam. Federal, state, and local governments impose taxes on income earned in the marketplace. When tax rates are high, people get to keep less of the income they earn. Some people may conclude that tutoring is no longer worth the hassle and withdraw from the market.

Expectations are also important on the supply side of the market. If web designers expect higher prices, lower costs, or reduced taxes, they may be more willing to learn new software programs. On the other hand, if they have poor expectations about the future, they may just sell their computers and find something else to do.

Finally, we note that the number of available web designers will affect the quantity of service offered for sale at various prices. If there are lots of willing web designers on campus, a large quantity of tutoring services will be available.

The Market Supply Curve

Figure 3.5 illustrates the market supply curve of web services at Clearview College. Like market demand, the market supply curve is the sum of all the individual supplier decisions about how much output to produce at any given price. The market supply curve slopes upward to the right, indicating that

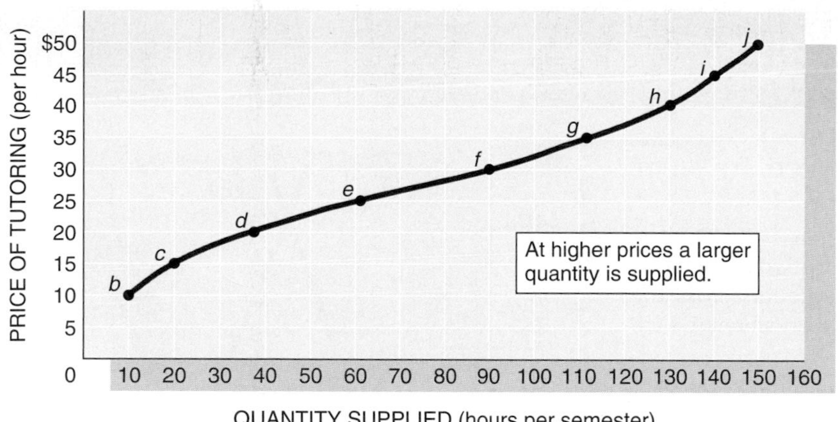

FIGURE 3.5
The Market Supply Curve

The market supply curve indicates the *combined* sales intentions of all market participants. If the price of tutoring were $25 per hour (point *e*), the *total* quantity of tutoring service supplied would be 62 hours per semester. This quantity is determined by adding together the supply decisions of all individual producers.

larger quantities will be offered at higher prices. This basic **law of supply** reflects the fact that increased output typically entails higher costs and so will be forthcoming only at higher prices. Higher prices may also increase profits and so entice producers to supply greater quantities.

law of supply The quantity of a good supplied in a given time period increases as its price increases, ceteris paribus.

Note that Figure 3.5 illustrates the *market* supply. We have not bothered to construct separate supply curves for each person who is able and willing to supply web services on the Clearview campus. We have skipped that first step and gone right to the *market* supply curve. Like the market demand curve, however, the market supply curve is based on the supply decisions of individual producers. The curve itself is computed by adding up the quantities each producer is willing and able to supply at every given price. Point *f* in Figure 3.5 tells us that those individuals are collectively willing and able to produce 90 hours of tutoring per semester at a price of $30 per hour. The rest of the points on the supply curve tell us how many hours of tutoring will be offered at other prices.

None of the points on the market supply curve (Figure 3.5) tells us how much tutoring service is actually being sold on the Clearview campus. ***Market supply is an expression of sellers' intentions, of the ability and willingness to sell, not a statement of actual sales.*** My next-door neighbor may be *willing* to sell his 1986 Honda Civic for $8,000, but it is most unlikely that he will ever find a buyer at that price. Nevertheless, his *willingness* to sell his car at that price is part of the *market supply* of used cars.

Shifts in Supply

As with demand, there is nothing sacred about any given set of supply intentions. Supply curves *shift* when the underlying determinants of supply change. Thus we again distinguish

- ***Changes in quantity supplied:*** movements along a given supply curve.
- ***Changes in supply:*** shifts of the supply curve.

Our Latin friend *ceteris paribus* is once again the decisive factor. If the price of tutoring services is the only thing changing, then we can ***track changes in quantity supplied along the supply curve*** in Figure 3.5. But if *ceteris paribus* is violated—if technology, factor costs, other goods, taxes, or expectations change—then ***changes in supply are illustrated by shifts of the supply curve.*** The accompanying Headline illustrates how a leftward shift in the supply of electricity worsened California's 2000–2001 energy crisis.

HEADLINE SUPPLY SHIFT

California Forced to Turn the Lights Off

LOS ANGELES, Jan. 17—Out of power and out of options, California ordered rolling blackouts across the state today, its most desperate move yet in an energy crisis that is spinning out of control.

The widely scattered blackouts affecting some half-million customers began at midday. With only minutes of warning, sections of San Francisco, Silicon Valley, the state capital of Sacramento and a few other smaller cities went dark . . .

The immediate cause of the blackouts was a large power plant suddenly going offline in Northern California this morning. More important is that some wholesale energy suppliers refused to sell power to California's financially struggling utility companies, which are having great difficulty paying for power.

After a week of dire warnings and coast-to-coast negotiations on the state's predicament, managers of California's electrical system—or power grid—said they resorted to blackouts because demand overwhelmed dwindling supplies and a frantic effort to beg or borrow electricity from other states failed.

"This situation is not going to get any prettier unless we find some magical megawatts from somewhere," Patrick Dorinson, a spokesman for the California Independent System Operator, the agency that distributes power through most of the state, said this afternoon.

The operators of the state's power grid said that some wholesale power providers declined to sell energy to California until the operators called the suppliers today pleading for more power hour by hour and invoking Energy Secretary Bill Richardson's emergency order requiring the providers to come to California's aid. Richardson extended that order again today.

—Rene Sanchez and William Booth

Source: *Washington Post*, January 18, 2001, p. 1.

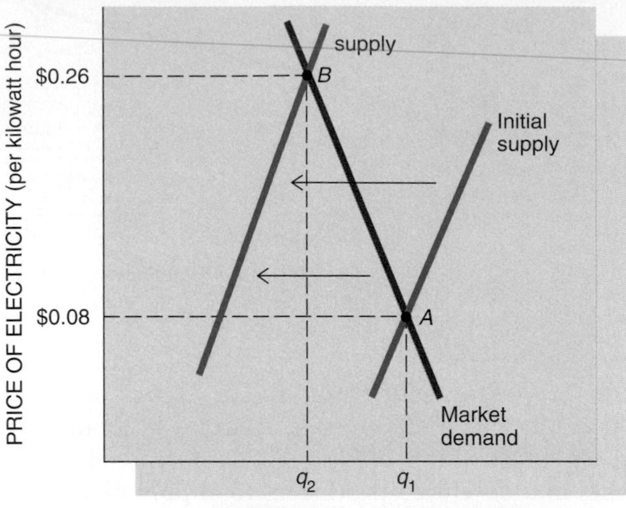

NOTE: If an underlying determinant of supply changes, the entire supply curve shifts. Mechanical breakdowns and supplier anxiety about prospects for getting paid reduced the quantity of electricity supplied at any given price in early 2001.

Equilibrium

We can now determine the price and quantity of web-tutoring services being sold at Clearview College. The market supply curve expresses the *ability and willingness* of producers to sell web services at various prices. The market demand curve illustrates the *ability and willingness* of Tom, George, and Lisa to buy web services at those same prices. When we put the two curves together, we see that ***only one price and quantity are compatible with the existing intentions of both buyers and sellers.*** This **equilibrium price** occurs at the intersection of the two curves in Figure 3.6. Once it is established, web tutoring services will cost $20 per hour. At that price, campus web designers will sell a total of 39 hours of tutoring service per semester—the same amount that students wish to buy at that price.

equilibrium price The price at which the quantity of a good demanded in a given time period equals the quantity supplied.

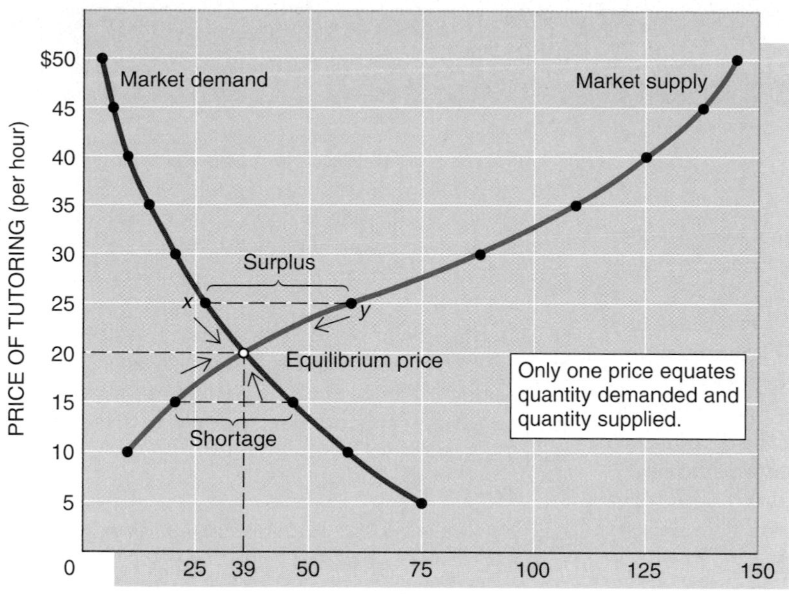

Price per Hour	Quantity Supplied (hours per semester)		Quantity Demanded (hours per semester)
$50	148		5
45	140		8
40	130	market	11
35	114	surplus	16
30	90		22
25	62		30
20	39	**equilibrium**	39
15	20	market	47
10	10	shortage	57

FIGURE 3.6
Market Surplus or Shortage

Only at equilibrium is the quantity demanded equal to the quantity supplied. In this case, the equilibrium price is $20 per hour, and 39 hours is the equilibrium quantity. At higher prices, a market surplus exists—the quantity supplied exceeds the quantity demanded. At prices below equilibrium, a market shortage exists.

The intersection of the demand and supply curves in the graph represents equilibrium price and output in this market.

Market Clearing

An equilibrium doesn't imply that everyone is happy with the prevailing price or quantity. Notice in Figure 3.6, for example, that some students who want to buy web tutoring don't get any. These would-be buyers are arrayed along the demand curve *below* the equilibrium. Because the price they are *willing* to pay is less than the equilibrium price, they don't get any tutoring.

Likewise, there are would-be sellers in the market who don't sell as many web services as they might like. These people are arrayed along the supply curve *above* the equilibrium. Because they insist on being paid a price that is higher than the equilibrium price, they don't actually sell anything.

Although not everyone gets full satisfaction from the market equilibrium, that unique outcome is efficient. The equilibrium price and quantity reflect a compromise between buyers and sellers. No other compromise yields a quantity demanded that is exactly equal to the quantity supplied.

The Invisible Hand The equilibrium price is not determined by any single individual. Rather it is determined by the collective behavior of many buyers and sellers, each acting out his or her own demand or supply schedule. It is this kind of impersonal price determination that gave rise to Adam Smith's

HEADLINE MARKET SHORTAGE

For Fans, What's 4 Nights for U2?

After an 80-hour ordeal—four nights stuffed in a car, three days breathing bus exhaust, scarfing Cokes and franks, running blocks for pit stops—the three University of Maryland seniors who camped out at RFK Stadium prevailed. They beat the scalpers to U2 concert tickets.

At 8 A.M. today they would be, if all went as planned, first in line at the RFK box office. By 9 A.M. the 52,000-seat stadium will sell out, predicted a Ticketmaster official.

"It's what you got to do to get good seats," said Crawford Conniff, 22, stretched out near the stadium among traffic island dandelions.

"We have unlimited time," said Mike Collins, 22. "If we had a job making 50 grand, we could pay $150 to scalpers."

Actually, $150 sounds cheap for the $28.50 face-value tickets. Today's ticket sale for the Aug. 15 concert, one of the summer's hottest, is likely to ignite an orgy of profiteering.

When the band played Los Angeles, scalpers scored up to $1,200 a ticket for prime seats. In Washington, as early as Tuesday, ticket brokers had stationed students, unemployed, and even homeless people at ticket outlets to snap up hundreds of choice seats.

—Laura Blumenfeld

Source: ©1992, the Washington Post. *Washington Post,* April 25, 1992, p. Al. Reprinted with permission.

NOTE: A below-equilibrium price creates a market shortage. When that happens, another method of distributing tickets—like time in line—must be used to determine who gets the available tickets.

characterization of the market mechanism as the invisible hand. In attempting to explain how the market mechanism works, the famed eighteenth-century economist noted a certain feature of market prices. The market behaves as if some unseen force (the invisible hand) were examining each individual's supply or demand schedule, then selecting a price that assured an equilibrium. In practice, the process of price determination is not so mysterious; rather, it is a simple one of trial and error.

Surplus and Shortage

Suppose for the moment that someone were to spread the word on the Clearview campus that tutors were available at only $15 per hour. Tom, George, and Lisa would be standing in line to get help with their web classes, but campus web designers would not be willing to supply the quantity desired at that price. As Figure 3.6 confirms, at $15 per page, the quantity demanded (47 hours per semester) would greatly exceed the quantity supplied (20 hours per semester). In this situation, we speak of a **market shortage,** that is, an excess of quantity demanded over quantity supplied. At a price of $15 a page, the shortage amounts to 27 hours of web service.

market shortage The amount by which the quantity demanded exceeds the quantity supplied at a given price: excess demand.

When a market shortage exists, not all consumer demands can be satisfied. Some people who are *willing* to buy tutoring services at the going price ($15) will not be able to do so. To assure themselves of good grades. Tom, George, Lisa, or some other consumer may offer to pay a *higher* price, thus initiating a move up the demand curve of Figure 3.6. The higher prices offered will in turn induce other enterprising students to offer more web tutoring, thus ensuring an upward movement along the market supply curve. Thus a higher price tends to call forth a greater quantity supplied, as reflected in the upward-sloping supply curve. Notice, again, that the *desire* to tutor web design has not changed: only the quantity supplied has responded to a change in price.

The accompanying Headline illustrates what happens at music concerts when tickets are priced below equilibrium. More fans were willing to pay

MARKET SHORTAGE HEADLINE

Buyers Line Up for Sony's PlayStation 2

Teenage boys line up outside an electronics store as the hour approaches midnight. If that scene sounds vaguely familiar, undoubtedly you remember the last videogame system that every teenager in America (and even some adults) had to have. Now, they must have another one. And at 12:01 A.M. today, the Sony PlayStation 2 went on sale.

"I want to be the first kid on the block to have one," said James Willis, 35, in line in front of the Electronic Boutique at the Fashion Centre at Pentagon City. The store planned to open at midnight and remain open until 2:30 A.M. to meet the perceived needs of hard-core game customers, some of whom signed up for the $299 videogame console as long ago as last December.

But most major electronics retailers, including CompUSA, Best Buy, and Circuit City, said they would open at the normal hour this morning, doling out the games on a first-come, first-served basis.

Sony expects to ship 1.3 million to 1.4 million PlayStation 2s to the U.S. market this year, But the demand appears to be much higher. One analyst, Greg Durkin at Alexander Associates, estimated that demand for the game system could be as high as 4 million customers.

—Nicholas Johnston and Mike Musgrove

Source: *Washington Post*, October 26, 2000, p. EI.

NOTE: If price is below equilibrium, the quantity demanded exceeds the quantity supplied. The willingness to pay $299 didn't assure purchase of a PlayStation 2 in 2000.

$28.50 for the 1992 U2 concerts than the stadiums could accommodate. At below equilibrium prices, the market mechanism was no longer the sole arbiter of FOR WHOM the concert is produced. Admission required not just the ticket price but also the willingness to stand in line—sometimes for days. Consumers with a low opportunity cost for their time (e.g., nonworking students) are more likely to stand in line. Once they get the tickets, they may even resell them at higher prices to high-paid businesspeople who have more income and a higher opportunity cost for waiting in line. Such "scalping" would not be possible if the initial price of the tickets had been set by supply and demand.

A similar situation occurred when Sony started selling the PlayStation 2 in October 2000. At the initial price of $299, the quantity demanded greatly exceeded the quantity supplied (see Headline on this page). To get a PlayStation 2, people had to spend hours in line or pay a premium price in resale markets like eBay.

A very different sequence of events occurs when a market surplus exits. Suppose for the moment that the web designers at Clearview College believed tutoring services could be sold for $25 per hour rather than the equilibrium price of $20. From the demand and supply schedules depicted in Figure 3.6, we can foresee the consequences. At $25 per hour, campus web designers would be offering more web-tutoring services (point *y*) than Tom, George, and Lisa were willing to buy (point *x*) at that price. A **market surplus** of web services would exist, in that more tutoring was being offered for sale (supplied) than students cared to purchase at the available price.

market surplus The amount by which the quantity supplied exceeds the quantity demanded at a given price: excess supply.

As Figure 3.6 indicates, at a price of $25 per hour, a market surplus of 32 hours per semester exists. Under these circumstances, campus web designers would be spending many idle hours at their computers, waiting for customers to appear. Their waiting will be in vain, because the quantity of tutoring demanded will not increase until the price of tutoring falls. That is the clear message of the demand curve. The tendency of quantity demanded to increase as price falls is illustrated in Figure 3.6 by a movement along the

HEADLINE MARKET SURPLUS

U2 Tour Turning Out 2 Be "Disaster" in Ticket Sales

Industry insiders tell me U2's "PopMart" tour, which hits Denver tonight, is the lowest-grossing stadium tour in the history of rock 'n' roll. "It's a disaster," they're saying. The lavish production, which arrived in Denver with 500 tons of equipment in 75 trailer trucks, sold out in Las Vegas when it opened last week but attracted only 30,500 fans in second-date San Diego. Sales are soft in numerous U.S. markets on the band's projected world tour. There's a lot out there competing for our fun-ticket bucks—and U2 tickets cost $37.50 to $52.50 plus service charges.

—Bill Husted

Source: *Denver Post,* May 1, 1997, p. A2. Reprinted by permission of the *Denver Post.*

NOTE: Empty seats in a stadium, on an airplane, or in a theater imply a market surplus: a larger quantity is supplied than demanded at the existing price.

demand curve from point x to lower prices and greater quantity demanded. As we move down the market demand curve, the desire for tutoring does not change, but the quantity people are able and willing to buy increases. Web designers at Clearview would have to reduce price from $25 (point y) to $20 per hour in order to attract enough buyers.

U2 learned the difference between market shortage and surplus the hard way. The group began another tour in April 1997, with scheduled concerts in 80 cities over a period of 14 months. This time around, however, U2 was charging as much as $52.50 a ticket—nearly double the 1992 price. By the time they got to the second city, they were playing in stadiums with lots of empty seats (see Headline). The apparent market surplus led critics to label the 1997 PopMart tour a disaster. For their 2001 Elevation Tour, U2 offered festival seating for only $35. By this process of trial and error, U2 ultimately located the equilibrium price for their concerts.

What we observe, then, is that ***whenever the market price is set above or below the equilibrium price, either a market surplus or a market shortage will emerge.*** To overcome a surplus or shortage, buyers and sellers will change their behavior. Only at the *equilibrium* price will no further adjustments be required.

Business firms can discover equilibrium market prices by trial and error. If they find that consumer purchases are not keeping up with production, they may conclude that price is above the equilibrium. To get rid of their accumulated inventory, they will have to lower their prices (by a Grand End-of-Year Sale, perhaps). In the happy situation where consumer purchases are outpacing production, a firm might conclude that its price was a trifle too low and give it a nudge upward. In either case, the equilibrium price can be established after a few trials in the marketplace.

Changes in Equilibrium

The collective actions of buyers and sellers will quickly establish an equilibrium price for any product. No particular equilibrium price is permanent, however. The equilibrium price established in the Clearview College web-services market, for example, was the unique outcome of specific demand and supply schedules. Those schedules are valid for only a certain time and place. They will rule the market only so long as the assumption of *ceteris paribus* holds. In reality, tastes, incomes, the price and availability of other

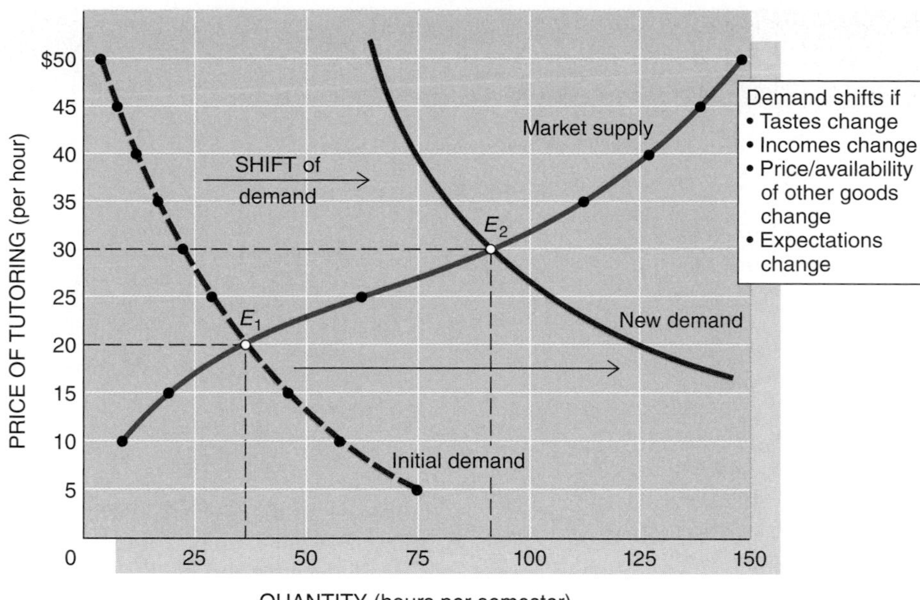

FIGURE 3.7
A New Equilibrium

A rightward shift of the demand curve indicates that consumers are willing and able to buy a larger quantity at every price. As a consequence, a new equilibrium is established (point E_2), at a higher price and greater quantity. A shift of the demand curve occurs only when the assumption of *ceteris paribus* is violated—when one of the determinants of demand changes.

The equilibrium would also be altered if the determinants of supply changed, causing a shift of the market supply curve.

goods, or expectations could change at any time. When this happens, *ceteris paribus* will be violated and the demand curve will have to be redrawn. Such a shift of the demand curve will lead to a new equilibrium price and quantity. Indeed, ***the equilibrium price will change whenever the supply or demand curve shifts.***

We can illustrate how equilibrium prices change by taking one last look at the Clearview College web-services market. Our original supply and demand curves, together with the resulting equilibrium (point E_1), are depicted in Figure 3.7. Now suppose that the professors at Clearview begin requiring more technical expertise in their web-design courses. These increased course requirements will affect market demand. Tom, George, and Lisa will suddenly be willing to buy more web services (tutors) at every price than they were before. That is to say, the *demand* for web services will increase. We can represent this increased demand by a rightward *shift* of the market demand curve, as illustrated in Figure 3.7.

Note that the new demand curve intersects the (unchanged) market supply curve at a new price (point E_2); the equilibrium price is now \$30 per hour. This new equilibrium price will persist until either the demand curve or the supply curve shifts again.

Supply and Demand Shifts The accompanying Headline illustrates what can happen to the equilibrium price when *both* demand and supply shift. Colder temperatures in the 2000–01 winter increased the demand for natural gas (heating oil). At the same time, shrinking reserves and pipeline problems reduced the supply of gas. As a result, the price of natural gas nearly tripled between January 2000 and January 2001.

The kinds of price changes described here are quite common. A few moments in a stockbroker's office or a glance through the stock pages of the daily newspaper should be testimony enough to the fluid character of market prices. If thousands of stockholders decide to sell IBM shares tomorrow, you can be sure that the market price of that stock will drop. Notice how often other prices—in the grocery store, the music store, or at the gas station—change. Then determine whether it was supply, demand, or both curves that shifted.

HEADLINE BEEF PRICES ON THE WAY UP

Canadian Import Ban, Demand Cited

Stock up the freezer if you like steak because beef prices at the supermarket are on their way up.

And they're likely to stay there for a while.

U.S. cattle prices are at a record high, say economists with the U.S. Department of Agriculture. They've increased 34% since July, and this month, the benchmark price of Nebraska choice steers went from $90 to $116 per 100 pounds. A year ago, the price per 100 pounds was $64.

"We've seen increases in the last 10 days," said Jim Robb, director of the Livestock Marketing Information Center in Denver. "Choice T-bone steak and New York strip steak, those prices are double what they were three weeks ago."

Prices are up because of a set of circumstances that Robb calls "Completely unprecedented." First, consumer demand for beef has increased nearly 10% since 1998 after declining for 20 years.

Recent increases in consumption may be due in part [to] the increasing popularity of high protein diets, such as this summer's blockbuster South Beach diet and the venerable Atkins diet.

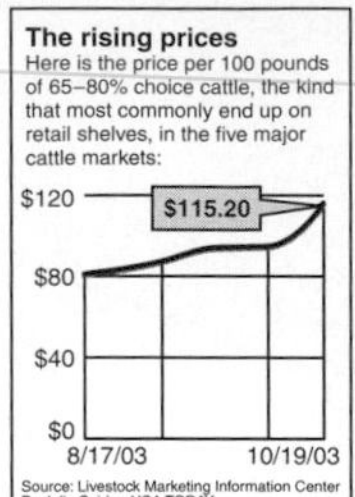

The rising prices
Here is the price per 100 pounds of 65–80% choice cattle, the kind that most commonly end up on retail shelves, in the five major cattle markets:
$120
$115.20
$80
$40
$0
8/17/03
10/19/03
Source: Livestock Marketing Information Center
By Julie Snider, USA TODAY

Second, as Wayne Purcell of the Research Institute on Livestock Pricing at Virginia Tech points out, the U.S. banned imports of Canadian cattle and beef five months ago. The ban was imposed because of the discovery of a case of mad cow disease there last spring and reduced cattle and meat imports to the USA by 9%.

Consumers already may be feeling the impact, whether they're eating out or at home.

—Elizabeth Weise

Source: *USA TODAY*, October 24, 2003, p. 1.

NOTE: If demand increases (shifts right) and supply decreases (shifts left), the equilibrium price can increase sharply.

Disequilibrium Pricing

The ability of the market to achieve equilibrium price and quantity is evident. Nevertheless, people are often upset with those outcomes. At Clearview College, the students buying tutoring services are likely to feel that the price of such services is too high. On the other hand, campus web designers may feel that they are getting paid too little for their tutorial services.

Price Ceilings

Sometimes consumers are able to convince the government to intervene on their behalf by setting a limit on prices. In many cities, for example, poor people and their advocates have convinced local governments that rents are too high. High rents, they argue, make housing prohibitively expensive for the poor, leaving them homeless or living in crowded, unsafe quarters. They ask government to impose a *limit* on rents in order to make housing affordable for everyone. Two hundred local governments—including New York City, Boston, Washington, D.C., and San Francisco—have responded with rent controls. In all cases, rent controls are a **price ceiling**—an upper limit imposed on the price of a good or service.

price ceiling Upper limit imposed on the price of a good.

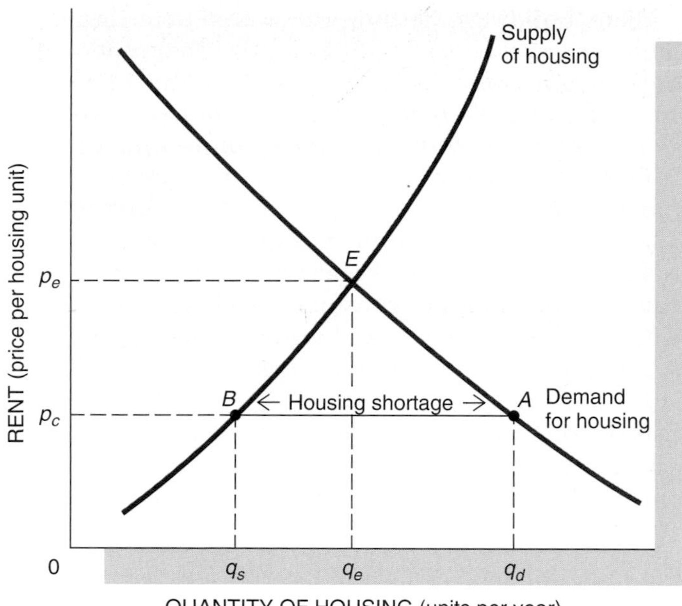

FIGURE 3.8
Price Ceilings Create Shortages

Many cities impose rent controls to keep housing affordable. Consumers respond to the below-equilibrium price ceiling (p_c) by demanding more housing (q_d vs. q_e). But the quantity of housing supplied diminishes as landlords convert buildings to other uses (e.g., condos) or simply let rental units deteriorate. New construction also slows. The result is a housing shortage ($q_d - q_s$) and an actual reduction in available housing ($q_e - q_s$).

Rent controls have a very visible effect in making housing more affordable. But such controls are *disequilibrium* prices and will change housing decisions in less visible and unintended ways. Figure 3.8 illustrates the problem. In the absence of government intervention, the quantity of housing consumed (q_e) and the prevailing rent (p_e) would be established by the intersection of market supply and demand curves (point E). Not everyone would be housed to their satisfaction in this equilibrium. Some of those people on the low end of the demand curve (below p_e) simply do not have enough income to pay the equilibrium rent p_e. They may be living with relatives or roommates they would rather not know. Or, in extreme cases, they may even be homeless.

To remedy this situation, the city government imposes a rent ceiling of p_c. This lower price seemingly makes housing more affordable for everyone, including the poor. At the controlled rent p_c, people are willing and able to consume a lot more housing: the quantity demanded increases from q_e to q_d at point A.

But what about the quantity of housing *supplied*? Rent controls do not increase the number of housing units available. On the contrary, price controls tend to have the opposite effect. Notice in Figure 3.8 how the quantity *supplied* falls from q_e to q_s when the rent ceiling is enacted. When the quantity supplied slides down the supply curve from point E to point B, there is less housing available than there was before. Thus ***price ceilings have three predictable effects; they***

- ***Increase the quantity demanded.***
- ***Decrease the quantity supplied.***
- ***Create a market shortage.***

You may well wonder where the "lost" housing went. The houses did not disappear. Some landlords simply decided that renting their units was no longer worth the effort. They chose, instead, to sell the units, convert them to condominiums, or even live in them themselves. Other landlords stopped maintaining their buildings, letting the units deteriorate. The rate of new construction slowed. too, as builders decided that rent control made new construction less profitable. Slowly but surely the quantity of housing declines from q_e to q_s. Hence ***there will be less housing for everyone when rent controls are imposed to make housing more affordable for some.***

Figure 3.8 illustrates another problem. The rent ceiling p_c has created a housing shortage—a gap between the quantity demanded (q_d) and the quantity supplied (q_s). Who will get the increasingly scarce housing? The market would have settled this FOR WHOM question by permitting rents to rise and allocating available units to those consumers willing and able to pay the rent p_e. Now, however, rents cannot rise and we have lots of people clamoring for housing that is not available. A different method of distributing goods must be found. Vacant units will go to those who learn of them first, patiently wait on waiting lists, or offer a gratuity to the landlord or renting agent. In New York City, where rent control has been the law for 60 years, people "sell" their rent-controlled apartments when they move elsewhere.

Price Floors

Artificially high (above-equilibrium) prices create similar problems in the marketplace. A **price floor** is a minimum price imposed by the government for a good or service. The objective is to raise the price of the good and create more income for the seller. Federal minimum wage laws, for example, forbid most employers from paying less than $5.15 an hour for labor.

price floor Lower limit imposed on the price of a good.

Price floors were also common in the farm sector. To stabilize farmers' incomes, the government offers price guarantees for certain crops. In 1985, for example, the government set a price guarantee of 18 cents per pound for domestically grown cane sugar. If the market price of sugar falls below 18 cents; the government promises to buy at the guaranteed price. Hence farmers know they can sell their sugar for 18 cents per pound, regardless of market demand.

Figure 3.9 illustrates the consequences of the price floor. The price guarantee (18¢) lies above the equilibrium price p_e (otherwise it would have no effect). At that higher price, farmers supply more sugar (q_s versus q_e). However, consumers are not willing to buy that much sugar: at that price; they demand only the quantity q_d. Hence, the ***price floor has three predictable effects; it***

- ***Increases the quantity supplied.***
- ***Reduces the quantity demanded.***
- ***Creates a market surplus.***

In 2001 the market surplus amounted to more than a *million tons* of sugar. The federal government ended up buying this surplus for more than $350 million. As for consumers, they ended up paying more for sugar than an unregulated market would charge. They also had to pay higher taxes to finance the government's sugar purchases. Furthermore, the mix of output now included more sugar than people would want if they had to pay the true costs of sugar directly. This is a classic case of **government failure:** society ends up with the wrong mix of output (too much sugar), an increased tax burden (to pay for the surplus), and an altered distribution of income (enriched sugar growers).

government failure Government intervention that fails to improve economic outcomes.

Laissez Faire

The apparent inefficiencies of price ceilings and floors imply that market outcomes are best left alone. This is a conclusion reached long ago by Adam

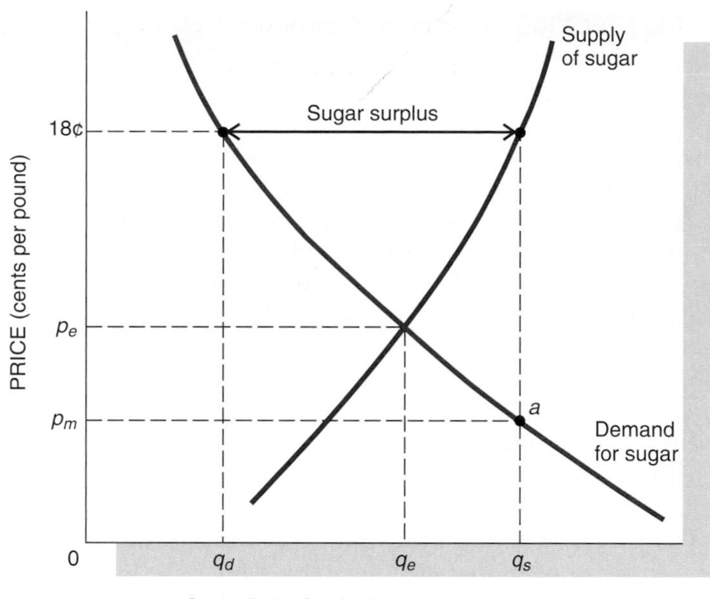

FIGURE 3.9
Price Floors Create Surplus

The U.S. Department of Agriculture sets a minimum price for sugar at 18 cents. If the market price drops below 18 cents, the government will buy the resulting surplus.

Farmers respond by producing the quantity q_s. Consumers would purchase the quantity q_s, however, only if the market price dropped to p_m (point *a* on the demand curve). The government thus has to purchase and store the surplus $q_s - q_d$.

Smith, the founder of modern economic theory. In 1776 he advocated a policy of **laissez faire—**literally, "leave it alone." As he saw it, the market mechanism was an efficient procedure for allocating resources and distributing incomes. The government should set and enforce the rules of the marketplace, but otherwise not interfere. Interference with the market—through price ceilings, floors, or other regulation—was likely to cause more problems than it could hope to solve.

laissez faire The doctrine of "leave it alone," of nonintervention by government in the market mechanism.

The policy of laissez faire is motivated not only by the potential pitfalls of government intervention but also by the recognition of how well the market mechanism can work. Recall our visit to Clearview College, where the price and quantity of tutoring services had to be established. There was no central agency that set the price of tutoring service or determined how much tutoring service would be done at Clearview College. Instead, both the price of web services and its quantity were determined by the **market mechanism**—the interactions of many independent (decentralized) buyers and sellers.

market mechanism The use of market prices and sales to signal desired outputs (or resource allocations).

WHAT, HOW, FOR WHOM Notice how the market mechanism resolved the basic economic questions of WHAT, HOW, and FOR WHOM. The WHAT question refers to how much web tutoring to include in society's mix of output. The answer at Clearview College was 39 hours per semester. This decision was not reached in a referendum but instead in the market equilibrium (see Figure 3.6). In the same way but on a larger scale, millions of consumers and a handful of auto producers decide to include 15 million cars and trucks in each year's mix of output.

The market mechanism will also determine HOW these goods are produced. Profit-seeking producers will strive to produce web services and automobiles in the most efficient way. They will use market prices to decide not only WHAT to produce but also what resources to use in the production process.

Finally, the invisible hand of the market will determine who gets the goods produced. At Clearview College, who got tutorial help in web design? Only those students who were willing and able to pay $20 per hour for that service.

FOR WHOM are all those automobiles produced each year? The answer is the same: those consumers who are willing and able to pay the market price for a new car.

Optimal, Not Perfect Not everyone is happy with these answers, of course. Tom would like to pay only $10 an hour for web tutoring. And some of the Clearview students do not have enough income to buy any assistance. They think it is unfair that they have to master web design on their own while richer students can have someone tutor them. Students who cannot afford cars are even less happy with the market's answer to the FOR WHOM question.

Although the outcomes of the marketplace are not perfect, they are often optimal. Optimal outcomes are the best possible, given the level and distribution of incomes and scarce resources. In other words, we expect the choices made in the marketplace to be the best possible choices for each participant. Why do we draw such a conclusion? Because Tom and George and everybody in our little Clearview College drama had (and continue to have) absolute freedom to make their own purchase and consumption decisions. And also because we assume that sooner or later they will make the choices they find most satisfying. The results are thus *optimal,* in the sense that everyone has done as well as can be expected, given his or her income and talents.

The optimality of market outcomes provides a powerful argument for *laissez faire.* In essence, the laissez-faire doctrine recognizes that decentralized markets not only work, but also give individuals the opportunity to maximize their satisfaction. In this context, government interference is seen as a threat to the attainment of the "right" mix of output and other economic goals. Since its development by Adam Smith in 1776, the laissez-faire doctrine has had a profound impact on the way the economy functions and what government does (or doesn't do).

POLICY PERSPECTIVES

Free Tuition in California!

In 2000 the state of California introduced a free-tuition program for residents of that state. Beginning in 2003, any high school senior in the state with at least a B average and family income below certain thresholds is guaranteed free admission to public universities in that state. Should a student prefer to go to a private college, the state will pay $9,708 per year in tuition.

What makes the Cal Grant Program so remarkable—and expensive—is how high the qualifying income threshold is. For students in four-person families, the qualifying income threshold is $66,200. Because that threshold is so high, as many as one-third of all graduating high school seniors in California will be eligible for free tuition.

The state will also provide free tuition for high school students with a C average if their families have incomes of less than half the threshold of B students. Specifically, a C student from a family with income of less than $34,800 can get free tuition as well.

Demand Effects California's free-tuition program will have a major impact on the *demand* for college. By reducing the effective price of tuition to zero, the state will induce a movement down the demand curve to a much greater quantity demanded. By making college so accessible, the program will also alter expectations, shifting demand to the right. The tuition subsidy for attending private schools represents additional income that will also shift the demand curve rightward. As a result, the state expects at least 100,000 more students to demand a college education.

Supply Responses But where will all these students enroll? California's colleges were already overflowing before this new tuition program was introduced. In fact, state subsidies had long kept tuition below its equilibrium level. The resulting shortage forced thousands of qualified students to attend schools elsewhere. An increase in demand will only exacerbate the shortage problem.

To make this program work, the state will have to increase the *supply* of college educational services. This may require the state to build more classrooms, hire more professors, construct more dorms, and pave more parking lots. Or the state may expand the use of electronic classrooms rather than brick-and-mortar classrooms. In either case, the state will now have to focus on the *supply* side of the market to assure the increased demand can be accommodated. The budget pressures that hit the state in 2002–2003 precluded such a response. This imbalance between supply and demand caused a *shortage* in the college market and a lot of frustrated applicants.

SUMMARY

- Consumers, business firms, government agencies, and foreigners participate in the marketplace by offering to buy or sell goods and services, or factors of production. Participation is motivated by the desire to maximize utility (consumers), profits (business firms), or the general welfare (government agencies).
- All interactions in the marketplace involve the exchange of either factors of production or finished products. Although the actual exchanges can take place anywhere, we say that they take place in product markets or factor markets, depending on what is being exchanged.
- People who are willing and able to buy a particular good at some price are part of the market demand for that product. All those who are willing and able to sell that good at some price are part of the market supply. Total market demand or supply is the sum of individual demands or supplies.
- Supply and demand curves illustrate how the quantity demanded or supplied changes in response to a change in the price of that good. Demand curves slope downward; supply curves slope upward.
- The determinants of market demand include the number of potential buyers and their respective tastes (desires), incomes, other goods, and expectations. If any of these determinants changes, the demand curve shifts. Movements along a demand curve are induced only by a change in the price of that good.
- The determinants of market supply include technology, factor costs, other goods, taxes, expectations, and the number of sellers. Supply shifts when these underlying determinants change.
- The quantity of goods or resources actually exchanged in each market depends on the behavior of all buyers and sellers, as summarized in

market supply and demand curves. At the point where the two curves intersect, an equilibrium price—the price at which the quantity demanded equals the quantity supplied—will be established.

- A distinctive feature of the market equilibrium is that it is the only price–quantity combination that is acceptable to buyers and sellers alike. At higher prices, sellers supply more than buyers are willing to purchase (a market surplus); at lower prices, the amount demanded exceeds the quantity supplied (a market shortage). Only the equilibrium price clears the market.
- Price ceilings and floors are disequilibrium prices imposed on the marketplace. Such price controls create an imbalance between quantities demanded and supplied.
- The market mechanism is a device for establishing prices and product and resource flows. As such, it may be used to answer the basic economic questions of WHAT to produce, HOW to produce it, and FOR WHOM. Its apparent efficiency prompts the call for laissez faire—a policy of government nonintervention in the marketplace.

Terms to Remember

Define the following terms:

market	demand curve	market shortage
factor market	law of demand	market surplus
product market	*ceteris paribus*	price ceiling
barter	shift in demand	price floor
supply	market demand	government failure
demand	market supply	laissez faire
opportunity cost	law of supply	market mechanism
demand schedule	equilibrium price	

Questions for Discussion

1. What does the supply and demand for human kidneys look like? If a market in kidneys were legal, who would get them? How does a law prohibiting kidney sales affect the quantity of kidney transplants or their distribution?
2. In the web-tutoring market, what forces might cause
   (*a*) A rightward shift of demand?
   (*b*) A leftward shift of demand?
   (*c*) A rightward shift of supply?
   (*d*) A leftward shift of supply?
   (*e*) An increase in the equilibrium price?
3. Did the price of tuition at your school change this year? What might have caused that?
4. What was the market situation for the 1992 and 1997 U2 concerts (pp. 72 and 74). Why didn't the concerts' promoters set equilibrium prices?
5. When concert tickets are priced below equilibrium, who gets them? Is this distribution of tickets fairer than a pure market distribution? Is it more efficient? Who gains or loses if all the tickets are resold (scalped) at the market-clearing price?

6. Is there a shortage of on-campus parking at your school? How might the shortage be resolved?
7. If departing tenants sell access to rent-controlled apartments, who is likely to end up with the apartments? How else might scarce rent-controlled apartments be distributed?
8. If rent controls are so counterproductive, why do cities impose them? How else might the housing problems of poor people be solved?
9. In 2003, Cruz Bustamante, the lieutenant governor of California, proposed a price ceiling on gasoline. Is this a good idea?
10. Why did Sony set the initial price of the PlayStation 2 below equilibrium (see Headline, p. 73). Should Sony have immediately raised the price?

Problems

1. Using Figure 3.7 as a guide, determine the approximate size of the market surplus or shortage that would exist at a price of (*a*) $40 (*b*) $20.
2. Illustrate the different market situations for the 1992 and 1997 U2 concerts, assuming constant supply and demand curves. What is the equilibrium price? (see Headlines on pp. 72 and 74).
3. Given the following data, (*a*) construct market supply and demand curves and identify the equilibrium price; and (*b*) identify the amount of shortage or surplus that would exist at a price of $4.

Participant	Quantity Demanded (per week)				
A. Price	$5	$4	$3	$2	$1
B. Demand side					
Al	1	2	3	4	5
Betsy	0	1	1	1	2
Casey	2	2	3	3	4
Daisy	1	3	4	4	6
Eddie	1	2	2	3	5
Market total	—	—	—	—	—

Participant	Quantity Supplied (per week)				
A. Price	$5	$4	$3	$2	$1
C. Supply side					
Alice	3	3	3	3	3
Butch	7	5	4	4	2
Connie	6	4	3	3	1
Dutch	6	5	4	3	0
Ellen	4	2	2	2	1
Market total	—	—	—	—	—

4. Suppose that the good described in problem 3 became so popular that every consumer demanded one additional unit at every price. Illustrate this increase in market demand and identify the new equilibrium. Which curve has shifted? Along which curve has there been a movement of price and quantity?
5. Illustrate each of the following events with supply or demand shifts in the domestic car market:
   (*a*) The U.S. economy falls into a recession.
   (*b*) U.S. auto workers go on strike.
   (*c*) Imported cars become more expensive.
   (*d*) The price of gasoline increases.

6. Graph the effects on price and quantity of California's free-tuition program (see Policy Perspectives beginning p. 80).
7. Assume the following data describe the gasoline market

Price per gallon	$1.00	1.25	1.50	1.75	2.00	2.25	2.50
Quantity demanded	26	25	24	23	22	21	20
Quantity supplied	16	20	24	28	32	36	40

   (*a*) What is the equilibrium price?
   (*b*) If supply at every price is reduced by 5 gallons, what will the new equilibrium price be?
   (*c*) If the government freezes the price of gasoline at its initial price, how much of a surplus or shortage will exist when supply is reduced as described above?
   (*d*) Illustrate your answers on a graph.
8. Graph the response of students to higher alcohol prices, as discussed in the Headline on p. 62.
9. Graph the changes in the beef market during 2003, as described in the Headline on p. 76.

Web Activities

1. Log on to www.whitehouse.gov/fsbr/income.html and find the data on real per capita income.
   (*a*) What has happened to the value of real per capita income?
   (*b*) Assuming that the size of the workforce has remained relatively constant, use supply and demand analysis to explain why real income has increased.
2. Log on to www.cnn.com or www.msnbc.com and do a search using the keywords "crude oil prices." Find an article that discusses recent changes in the price of crude oil.
   (*a*) Discuss the reasons stated in the article explaining why the price of crude oil has changed.
   (*b*) Use supply and demand graphs to illustrate what is being discussed in the article.
3. Log on to www.ebay.com and record the price bids for some item during a 30-minute period. Use supply and demand analysis to explain the initial shortage in the market and how the bidding process is correcting the imbalance.

Living Econ

How Can I Communicate with a Large Corporation?

Most of us spend a fair amount of time in the product market. On a typical morning you might stop at the coffee shop on your way to class, purchase your lunch at a fast food restaurant, gas up your vehicle at the corner gas station, and rent a DVD from the video store.

But for all the time we spend in the product market, few of us ever take the time to communicate directly with a business or producer. Or, at least that's what we think. Yet companies must know what we want to buy and what we're willing to pay because we keep going back into the product market and offering them additional dollars for more stuff. So how can a business know this information if we don't call or e-mail them?

You and I send a very strong signal to producers every time we go into the product market. When we make a purchase, we tell producers, "I like this product and I'm willing to pay this price for it." If we choose not to buy the product, we are also sending a signal. Maybe we are stating, "This price is too high," or perhaps we are announcing, "This product is ugly and totally useless." Either way, producers are listening to what we have to say through the purchasing choices we make. The next time you buy a pair of jeans at the mall, picture yourself yelling, "I love these pants and they are definitely worth $78."

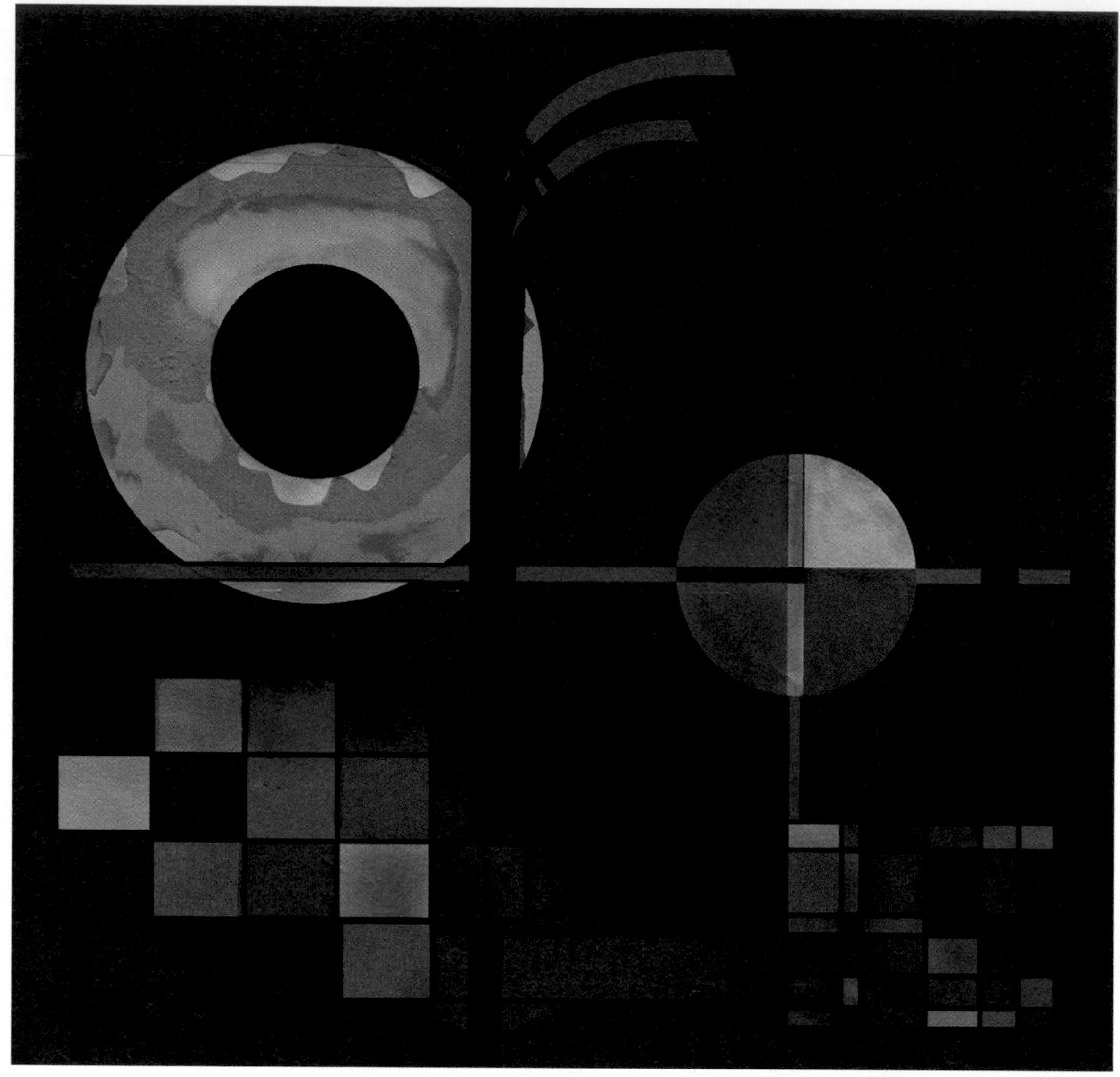

Consumer Demand

CHAPTER 4

"Shop until you drop" is apparently a way of life for many Americans. The *average* American (man, woman, or child) spends roughly $24,000 per year on consumer goods and services. This adds up at the cash register to a consumption bill of over $7 *trillion* a year.

A major concern of microeconomics is to explain this shopping frenzy. What drives us to department stores, grocery stores, and every Big Sale in town? More specifically,

- How do we decide how much of any good to buy?
- How does a change in a product's price affect the quantity we purchase or the amount of money we spend on it?
- What factors other than price affect our consumption decisions?

The law of demand, first encountered in Chapter 3, gives us some clues for answering these questions. But we need to look beyond that law to fashion more complete answers. Knowing that demand curves are downward-sloping is important, but that knowledge won't get us very far in the real world. In the real world, producers need to know the exact quantities demanded at various prices. Producers also need to know what forces will shift consumer demand.

The specifics of consumer demand are also important to public policy decisions. Suppose a city wants to relieve highway congestion and encourage more people to use public transit. Will public appeals be effective in changing commuter behavior? Probably not. But a change in relative prices might do the trick. Experience shows that raising the *price* of private auto use (e.g., higher parking fees, bridge tolls) and lowering transit fares *are* effective in changing commuters' behavior. Economists try to predict just how much prices should be altered to elicit the desired response.

Your school worries about the details of consumer demand as well. If tuition goes up again, some students will go elsewhere. Other students may take fewer courses. As enrollment begins to drop, school administrators may ask economics professors for some advice on tuition pricing. Their advice will be based on studies of consumer demand.

Patterns of Consumption

A good way to start a study of consumer demand is to observe how consumers spend their incomes. Figure 4.1 provides a quick summary. Note that half of all consumer spending is for food and shelter. Out of the typical consumer dollar, 36 cents is devoted to housing—everything from rent and repairs to utility bills and grass seed. Another 15 cents is spent on food, including groceries and trips to McDonald's. We also spend a lot on cars: transportation expenditures (car payments, maintenance, gasoline, insurance) eat up 21 cents out of the typical consumer dollar.

Taken together, housing, transportation, and food expenditures account for 70 percent of the typical household budget. Most people regard these items as the "basic essentials." However, there is no rule that says 14.9 cents of every consumer dollar must be spent on food, or that 36.4 percent of one's budget is "needed" for shelter. What Figure 4.1 depicts is how the average consumer has *chosen* to spend his or her income. We could choose to spend our incomes in other ways.

A closer examination of consumer patterns reveals that we do in fact change our habits on occasion. In the last 10 years, our annual consumption of red meat has declined from 125 pounds per person to 115 pounds. In the same time, our consumption of chicken has increased from 47 pounds to 70 pounds. We now consume less coffee, whiskey, beer, and eggs, but more wine, asparagus, and ice cream compared to 10 years ago. Cell phones and DVD players are regarded as essentials today, even though no one had these products 15 years ago. What prompted these changes in consumption patterns?

Some changes in consumption are more sudden. In the recession of 1990–91, Americans abruptly stopped buying new cars. Does that mean that cars were no longer essential? When oil prices rose sharply in 2000 people *drove* their cars less. Does that mean they *liked* driving less? Or did changes in income and prices alter consumer behavior?

Determinants of Demand

In seeking explanations for consumer behavior, we have to recognize that economics doesn't have all the answers. But it does offer a unique perspective that sets it apart from other fields of study.

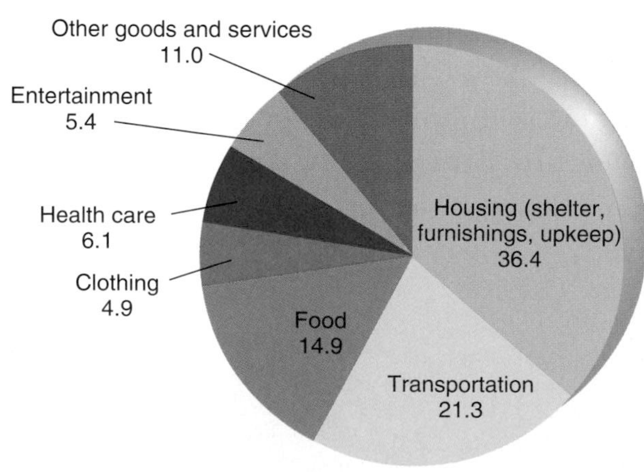

FIGURE 4.1
How the Consumer Dollar Is Spent

Consumers spend their incomes on a vast array of goods and services. This figure summarizes those consumption decisions by showing how the average consumer dollar is spent. The goal of economic theory is to explain and predict these consumption choices.

Source: U.S. Department of Labor, 2001 Consumer Expenditure Survey.

The Sociopsychiatric Explanation

Consider first the explanations of consumer behavior offered by other fields of study. Psychiatrists and psychologists have had a virtual field day formulating such explanations. The Austrian psychiatrist Sigmund Freud (1856–1939) was among the first to describe us poor mortals as bundles of subconscious (and unconscious) fears, complexes, and anxieties. From a Freudian perspective, we strive for ever higher levels of consumption to satisfy basic drives for security, sex, and ego gratification. Like the most primitive of people, we clothe and adorn ourselves in ways that assert our identity and worth. We eat and smoke too much because we need the oral gratifications and security associated with mother's breast. Self-indulgence, in general, creates in our minds the safety and satisfactions of childhood. Oversized homes and cars provide us with a source of warmth and security remembered from the womb. On the other hand, we often buy and consume some things we expressly don't desire, just to assert our rebellious feelings against our parents (or parent substitutes). In Freud's view, it is the constant interplay of id, ego, and superego drives that motivates us to buy, buy, buy.

Sociologists offer additional explanations for our consumption behavior. They emphasize our yearning to stand above the crowd, to receive recognition from the masses. For people with exceptional talents, such recognition may come easily. But for the ordinary person, recognition may depend on conspicuous consumption. A larger car, a newer fashion, a more exotic vacation become expressions of identity that provoke recognition, even social acceptance. Thus we strive for ever higher levels of consumption—so as to *surpass* the Joneses, not just to keep up with them.

Not *all* consumption is motivated by ego or status concerns, of course. Some food is consumed for the sake of self-preservation, some clothing for warmth, and some housing for shelter. The typical American consumer has more than enough income to satisfy these basic needs, however. In today's economy, consumers have a lot of *discretionary* income that can be used to satisfy psychological or sociological longings. As a result, single women are able to spend a lot of money on clothing and pets, while men spend freely on entertainment, food, and drink (see the accompanying Headline). As for teenagers, they show off their affluence in purchases of electronic goods, cars, and clothes (see Figure 4.2).

The Economic Explanation

Although psychiatrists and sociologists offer many reasons for these various consumption patterns, their explanations all fall a bit short. At best, sociopsychiatric theories tell us why teenagers, men, and women *desire* certain goods and services. They don't explain which goods will actually be *purchased*. Desire is only the first step in the consumption process. To acquire goods and services, one must be willing and able to *pay* for one's wants. Producers won't give you their goods just because you want to satisfy your Freudian desires. They want money in exchange for their goods. Hence ***prices and income are just as relevant to consumption decisions as are more basic desires and preferences.***

In explaining consumer behavior, then, economists focus on the demand for goods and services. To say that someone **demands** a particular good means that he or she is able and willing to buy it at some price(s). In the marketplace, money talks: *the willingness and ability to pay* are critical. Many people with a strong desire for a Porsche Carrera have neither the ability nor

demand The ability and willingness to buy specific quantities of a good at alternative prices in a given time period, ceteris paribus.

HEADLINE CONSUMPTION PATTERNS

Men vs. Women: How They Spend

Are men really different from women? If spending habits are any clue, males do differ from females. That's the conclusion one would draw from the latest Bureau of Labor Statistics (BLS) survey of consumer expenditures. Here's what BLS found out about the spending habits of young (under age 25) men and women who are living on their own.

Common traits

- Young men have slightly more income to spend ($12,168) than do young women ($12,029). Both sexes go deep into debt, however, by spending $3,000–$5,000 more than their incomes.
- Neither sex spends much on charity, reading, or health care.

Distinctive traits

- Young men spend 30 percent more at fast food outlets, restaurants, and carryouts.
- Men spend twice as much on alcoholic beverages and smoking.
- Men spend twice as much as women do on television, cars and stereo equipment.
- Young women spend a lot more money on clothing, personal-care items, and their pets.

Source: U.S. Bureau of Labor Statistics, 2000–01 Consumer Expenditure Survey.

NOTE: Consumer patterns vary by gender, age, and other characteristics. Economists try to isolate the common influences on consumer behavior.

FIGURE 4.2
Affluent Teenagers

Teenagers spend over $200 billion a year. Much of this spending is for cars, stereos, and other durables. The percentage of U.S. teenagers owning certain items is shown here.

Source: Teenage Research Unlimited (2003 data).

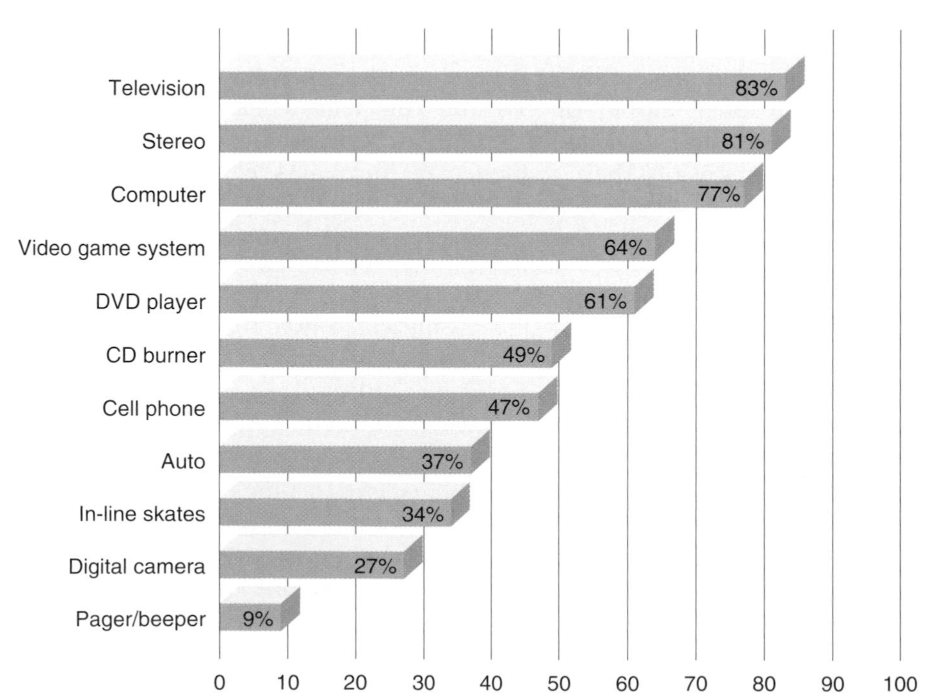

the willingness to actually buy it; they do not *demand* Porsche Carreras. Similarly, there are many rich people who are willing and able to buy goods they only remotely desire; they *demand* all kinds of goods and services.

What determines a person's willingness and ability to buy specific goods? As we saw in Chapter 3, economists have identified four different influences on consumer demand: tastes, income, expectations, and the prices of other goods. Note again that desire (tastes) is only one determinant of demand. Other determinants of demand (income, expectations, and other goods) also influence whether a person will be willing and able to buy a certain good at a specific price.

You may desire *this car, but are you* able and willing *to buy it?*
AP/Wide World Photos

As we observed in Chapter 3, the **market demand** for a good is simply the sum of all individual consumer demands. Hence ***the market demand for a specific product is determined by***

- ***Tastes*** (desire for this and other goods).
- ***Income*** (of consumers).
- ***Expectations*** (for income, prices, tastes).
- ***Other goods*** (their availability and price).
- ***The number of consumers in the market.***

market demand The total quantities of a good or service people are willing and able to buy at alternative prices in a given time period; the sum of individual demands.

In the remainder of this chapter we shall see how these determinants of demand give the demand curve its downward slope. Our objective is not only to explain consumer behavior but also to see (and predict) how consumption patterns change in response to *changes* in the price of a good or to *changes* in the underlying determinants of demand.

The Demand Curve

Utility Theory

The starting point for an economic analysis of demand is straightforward. Economists accept consumer tastes as the outcome of sociopsychiatric and cultural influences. They don't look beneath the surface to see how those tastes originated. Economists simply note the existence of certain tastes (desires), then look to see how those tastes affect consumption decisions. We assume that the more pleasure a product gives us, the higher the price we would be willing to pay for it. If gobbling buttered popcorn at the movies really pleases you, you're likely to be willing to pay dearly for it. If you have no great taste or desire for popcorn, the theater might have to give it away before you'd eat it.

Total vs. Marginal Utility Economists use the term **utility** to refer to the expected pleasure, or satisfaction, obtained from goods and services. **Total utility** refers to the amount of satisfaction obtained from your *entire* consumption of a product. By contrast, **marginal utility** refers to the amount of satisfaction you get from consuming the *last* (i.e., marginal) unit of a product.

utility The pleasure of satisfaction obtained from a good or service.

total utility The amount of satisfaction obtained from entire consumption of a product.

marginal utility The satisfaction obtained by consuming *one* additional (marginal) unit of a good or service.

Diminishing Marginal Utility The concepts of total and marginal utility explain not only why we buy popcorn at the movies but also why we stop eating it at some point. Even people who love popcorn (i.e., derive great total utility from it), and can afford it, don't eat endless quantities of popcorn. Why not? Presumably because the thrill diminishes with each mouthful. The first box of popcorn may bring sensual gratification, but the second or third box is likely to bring a stomachache. We express this change in perceptions by noting that the *marginal* utility of the first box of popcorn is higher than the additional or *marginal* utility derived from the second box.

The behavior of popcorn connoisseurs is not that unusual. Generally speaking, the amount of additional utility we obtain from a product declines as we continue to consume larger quantities of it. The third slice of pizza is not as desirable as the first, the sixth soda not so satisfying as the fifth, and so forth. Indeed, this phenomenon of diminishing marginal utility is so nearly universal that economists have fashioned a law around it. This **law of diminishing marginal utility** states that each successive unit of a good consumed yields less *additional* utility.

law of diminishing marginal utility The marginal utility of a good declines as more of it is consumed in a given time period.

The law of diminishing marginal utility does *not* say that we won't like the third box of popcorn, the second pizza, or the sixth soda; it just says we won't like them as much as the ones we've already consumed. Note also that time is important here: if the first pizza was eaten last year, the second pizza, eaten now, may taste just as good. The law of diminishing marginal utility applies to short time periods.

The expectation of diminishing marginal utility is illustrated in Figure 4.3. The graph on the left depicts the *total* utility obtained from eating popcorn. Notice that total utility continues to rise as we consume the first five boxes (ugh!) of popcorn. But total utility increases by smaller and smaller increments. Each successive step of the total utility curve in Figure 4.3 is a little shorter.

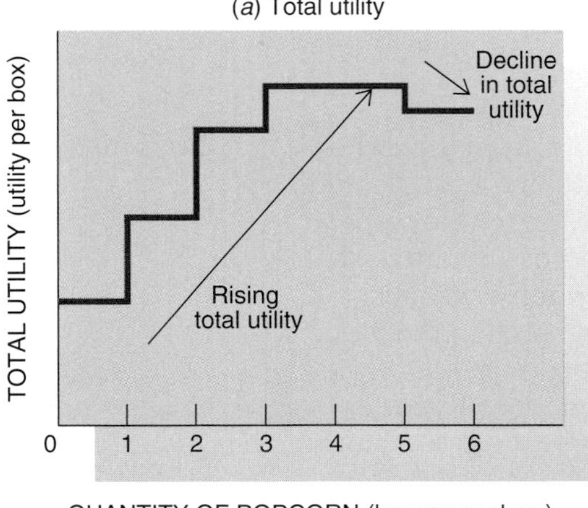

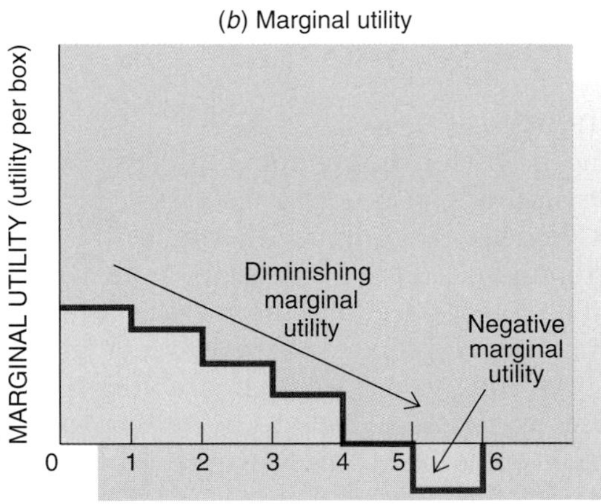

FIGURE 4.3 Total vs. Marginal Utility

The *total* utility (*a*) derived from consuming a product comes from the *marginal* utilities of each successive unit. The total utility curve shows how each of the first five boxes of popcorn contributes to total utility. Note that each successive step is smaller. This reflects the law of diminishing marginal utility.

The sixth box of popcorn causes the total-utility steps to descend; the sixth box actually *reduces* total utility. This means that the sixth box has *negative* marginal utility.

The marginal utility curve (*b*) shows the change in total utility with each additional unit. It is derived from the total utility curve. Marginal utility here is positive but diminishing for the first five boxes.

The height of each step of the total utility curve in Figure 4.3 represents *marginal* utility—the increments to total utility. The graph on the right in Figure 4.3 illustrates these marginal increments—the height of each step of the total utility curve (left graph). This graph shows more clearly how *marginal* utility diminishes.

Do not confuse *diminishing* marginal utility with dislike. Figure 4.3 doesn't imply that the second box of popcorn isn't desirable. It only says that the second box isn't as satisfying as the first. It still tastes good, however. How do we know? Because its *marginal* utility is positive (right graph), and therefore *total* utility (left graph) rises when the second box is consumed. ***So long as marginal utility is positive, total utility must be increasing.***

The situation changes abruptly with the sixth box of popcorn. According to Figure 4.3, the good sensations associated with popcorn consumption are completely forgotten by the time the sixth box arrives. Nausea and stomach cramps dominate. Indeed, the sixth box is absolutely *distasteful,* as reflected in the downturn of total utility and the *negative* value for marginal utility. We were happier—in possession of more total utility—with only five boxes of popcorn. The sixth box—yielding *negative* marginal utility—has reduced total satisfaction. This is the kind of sensation you'd also experience if you ate too many hamburgers (see cartoon).

You can have too much of a good thing. No matter how much we like a product, marginal utility is likely to diminish as we consume more of it.

Marginal utility not only explains why we stop eating before we explode but also why we pay so little for drinking water. Water has a high *total* utility: we would die without it. But its *marginal* utility is low, so we're not willing to pay much for another glass of it.

Not all goods approach zero (much less negative) marginal utility. Yet the more general principle of diminishing marginal utility is experienced daily. That is to say, ***additional quantities of a good eventually yield increasingly smaller increments of satisfaction.*** Total utility continues to rise, but at an ever slower rate as more of a good is consumed. There are exceptions to the law of diminishing marginal utility, but not many. (Can you think of any?)

Price and Quantity

Marginal utility is essentially a measure of how much we *desire* particular goods. But which ones will we *buy?* Clearly, we don't always buy the products we most desire. *Price* is often a problem. All too often we have to settle for goods that yield less marginal utility simply because they are available at a lower price. This explains why most people don't drive Porsches. Our desire ("taste") for a Porsche may be great, but its price is even greater. The challenge for most people is to somehow reconcile our tastes with our bank balances.

In deciding whether to buy something, our immediate focus is typically on a single variable, namely *price.* Assume for the moment that a person's tastes, income, and expectations are set in stone and that the prices of other goods are fixed as well. This is the ***ceteris paribus*** assumption we first encountered in Chapter 1. It doesn't mean that other influences on consumer behavior are unimportant. Rather, the *ceteris paribus* simply allows us to focus on one variable at a time. In this case, we are focusing on *price.* What

ceteris paribus The assumption of nothing else changing.

FIGURE 4.4
A Demand Schedule and Curve

Because marginal utility diminishes, consumers are willing to buy larger quantities of a good only at lower prices. This demand schedule and curve illustrate the specific quantities demanded at alternative prices. Notice that points *A* through *J* on the curve correspond to the rows of the demand schedule. If popcorn sold for 25 cents per ounce, this consumer would buy 12 ounces per show (point *F*). More popcorn would be demanded only if the price were reduced (points *G–J*).

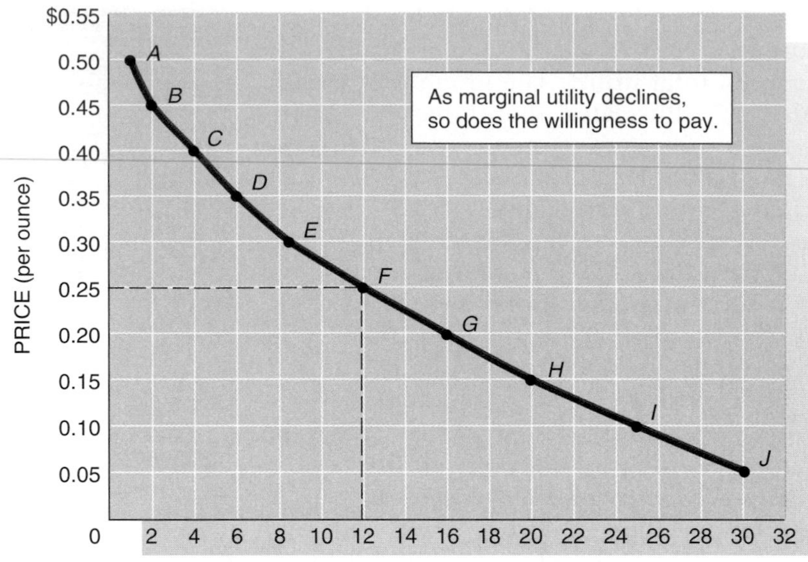

	Price (per ounce)	Quantity Demanded (ounces per show)
A	$0.50	1
B	0.45	2
C	0.40	4
D	0.35	6
E	0.30	9
F	0.25	12
G	0.20	16
H	0.15	20
I	0.10	25
J	0.05	30

we want to know is how high a price a consumer is willing to pay for another unit of a product.

The concepts of marginal utility and *ceteris paribus* enable us to answer this question. The more marginal utility a good delivers, the more you're willing to pay for it. But marginal utility *diminishes* as increasing quantities of a product are consumed. Hence you won't be willing to pay so much for additional quantities of the same good. The moviegoer who is willing to pay 50 cents for that first mouth-watering ounce of buttered popcorn may not be willing to pay so much for a second or third ounce. The same is true for the second pizza, the sixth soda, and so forth. ***With given income, taste, expectations, and prices of other goods and services, people are willing to buy additional quantities of a good only if its price falls.*** In other words, as the marginal utility of a good diminishes, so does our willingness to pay.

law of demand The quantity of a good demanded in a given time period increases as its price falls, ceteris paribus.

demand curve A curve describing the quantities of a good a consumer is willing and able to buy at alternative prices in a given time period, ceteris paribus.

This inverse relationship between the quantity demanded of a good and its price is referred to as the **law of demand.** Figure 4.4 illustrates this relationship again, for the case of popcorn. Notice that the **demand curve** slopes downwards: More popcorn is purchased at lower prices.

The law of demand and the law of diminishing marginal utility tell us nothing about why we crave popcorn or why our cravings subside. That's the job of psychiatrists, sociologists, and physiologists. The laws of economics simply describe our market behavior.

Price Elasticity

The theory of demand helps explain consumer behavior. Often, however, much more specific information is desired. Imagine you owned a theater and were actually worried about popcorn sales. Knowing that the demand curve is downward-sloping wouldn't tell you a whole lot about what price to charge. What you'd really want to know is *how much* popcorn sales would change if you raised or lowered the price.

Airlines want the same kind of hard data. Airlines know that around Christmas they can charge full fares and still fill all their planes. After the holidays, however, people have less of a desire to travel. To fill planes in February, the airlines must offer discount fares. But how far should they lower ticket prices? That depends on *how much* passenger traffic *changes* in response to reduced fares.

Apple Computer confronted a similar problem in 2003. Apple was launching its new iTunes Music Store that offered downloadable songs. The problem was the price. Earlier file-sharing services (e.g. Napster, Kazaa) had offered free downloads. But court rulings had made free file-sharing illegal. So iTunes had to charge a fee. Apple decided a price of 99 cents per song was appropriate. At that price, the quantity demanded was shockingly high (see Headline). Even Apple was surprised at how little the quantity demanded declined when the price increased from zero to 99 cents.

The central question in all these decisions is the response of quantity demanded to a change in price. ***The response of consumers to a change in price is measured by the price elasticity of demand.*** Specifically, the **price elasticity of demand** refers to the *percentage* change in quantity demanded divided by the *percentage* change in price—that is

price elasticity of demand The percentage change in quantity demanded divided by the percentage change in price.

- Price elasticity $(E) = \dfrac{\text{percentage change in quantity demanded}}{\text{percentage change in price}}$

HEADLINE PRICE ELASTICITY

iTunes Music Store Hits Five Million Downloads

Apple to Ship One Millionth iPod This Week

WWDC 2003, San Francisco—June 23, 2003—Apple® today announced that music fans have downloaded over five million songs from the iTunes® Music Store since its launch eight weeks ago today. In addition, over 46 percent of the songs have been purchased as albums, and over 80 percent of the over 200,000 songs available on the online store have been purchased at least once. Apple also announced that it will ship its one millionth iPod™ this week. Apple introduced the third generation of its ultra-portable digital music player in April, and it has become a huge hit with music lovers worldwide. . . .

The iTunes Music Store lets customers easily search a broad catalog of over 200,000 tracks to instantly locate any song by title, artist or album. With just one click, they can purchase the songs they want and download them directly into their iTunes 4 music library for just 99 cents per song, without any subscription fees.

Source: Apple Computer Corporation.

NOTE: According to the Law of Demand, quantity demanded declines when price rises. The price elasticity of demand measures how price sensitive consumers are.

Suppose we increased the price of popcorn by 20 percent. We know from the law of demand that the quantity of popcorn demanded will fall. But we need to observe market behavior to see *how far* sales drop. Suppose that unit sales (quantity demanded) fall by 10 percent. We could then compute the price elasticity of demand as

$$E = \frac{\text{percentage change in quantity demanded}}{\text{percentage change in price}} = \frac{+10\%}{-20\%} = -0.5$$

Since price and quantity demanded always move in opposite directions, E is a negative value (-0.5 in this case). For convenience, however, the absolute value of E (without the minus sign) is used. What we learn here is that popcorn sales decline at half (0.5) the rate of price increases. Moviegoers cut back grudgingly on popcorn consumption when popcorn prices rise.

Elastic vs. Inelastic Demand

We characterize the demand for various goods in one of three ways: *elastic, inelastic,* or *unitary elastic.* If E is larger than 1, we say demand is elastic: Consumer response is large relative to the change in price.

If E is less than 1, we say demand is inelastic. This is the case with popcorn, where E is only 0.5. ***If demand is inelastic, consumers aren't very responsive to price changes.***

If E is equal to 1, demand is unitary elastic. In this case, the percentage change in quantity demanded is exactly equal to the percentage change in price.

Consider the case of smoking. Many smokers claim they'd "pay anything" for a cigarette after they've run out. But would they? Would they continue to smoke just as many cigarettes if prices doubled or tripled? Research suggests not: Higher cigarette prices *do* curb smoking. There is at least *some* elasticity in the demand for cigarettes. But the elasticity of demand is low; Table 4.1 indicates that the elasticity of cigarette demand is only 0.4.

Although the average adult smoker is not very responsive to changes in cigarette prices, teen smokers apparently are. As the accompanying

TABLE 4.1
Elasticity Estimates

Price elasticities vary greatly. When the price of gasoline increases, consumers reduce their consumption only slightly. When the price of fish increases, however, consumers cut back their consumption substantially. These differences reflect the availability of immediate substitutes, the prices of the goods, and the amount of time available for changing behavior.

Type of Elasticity	Estimate
Relatively elastic ($E > 1$)	
Airline travel, long run	2.4
Fresh fish	2.2
New cars, short run	1.2–1.5
Unitary elastic ($E = 1$)	
Private education	1.1
Radios and televisions	1.2
Shoes	0.9
Relatively inelastic ($E < 1$)	
Cigarettes	0.4
Coffee	0.3
Gasoline, short run	0.2
Long-distance telephone calls	0.1

Sources: Compiled from Hendrick S. Houthakker and Lester D. Taylor, *Consumer Demand in the United States, 1929–1970* (Cambridge, MA: Harvard University Press, 1966); F. W. Bell, "The Pope and Price of Fish," *American Economic Review,* December 1968; and Michael Ward, "Product Substitutability and Competition in Long-Distance Telecommunications," *Economic Inquiry,* October 1999.

PRICE ELASTICITY OF DEMAND HEADLINE

Dramatic Rise in Teenage Smoking

Smoking among youths in the United States rose precipitously starting in 1992 after declining for the previous 15 years. By 1997, the proportion of teenage smokers had risen by one-third from its 1991 trough.

A prominent explanation for the rise in youth smoking over the 1990s was a sharp decline in cigarette prices in the early 1990s, caused by a price war between the tobacco companies. Gruber and Zinman find that young people are very sensitive to the price of cigarettes in their smoking decisions. The authors estimate that for every 10 percent decline in the price, youth smoking rises by almost 7 percent, a much stronger price sensitivity than is typically found for adult smokers. As a result, the price decline of the early 1990s can explain about a quarter of the smoking rise from 1992 through 1997. Similarly, the significant decline in youth smoking observed in 1998 is at least partially explainable by the first steep rise in cigarette prices since the early 1990s. The authors also find that black youths and those with less educated parents are much more responsive to changes in cigarette prices than are white teens and those with more educated parents.

Source: National Bureau of Economic Research, *NBER Digest* October 2000, p. 1.

NOTE: The effectiveness of higher cigarette prices in curbing teen smoking depends on the price elasticity of demand.

Headline indicates, teen smoking drops by almost 7 percent when cigarette prices increase by 10 percent. Thus, the price elasticity of *teen* demand for smoking is

$$E = \frac{\text{percent drop in quantity demanded}}{\text{percent increase in price}} = \frac{-7\%}{+10\%} = -0.7$$

Hence, higher cigarette prices can be an effective policy tool for curbing teen smoking. The decline in teen smoking after prices jumped in 1998 confirms this expectation.

According to Table 4.1, the demand for airline travel is even more price-elastic. Whenever a fare cut is announced, the airlines get swamped with telephone inquiries. If fares are discounted by 25 percent, the number of passengers may increase by as much as 60 percent. As Table 4.1 shows, the elasticity of airline demand is 2.4, meaning that the percentage change in quantity demanded (60 percent) will be 2.4 times larger than the price cut (25 percent).

Price Elasticity and Total Revenue

The concept of price elasticity refutes the popular misconception that producers charge the highest price possible. Except in the very rare case of completely inelastic demand ($E = 0$), this notion makes no sense. Indeed, higher prices may actually *lower* total sales revenue.

The **total revenue** of a seller is the amount of money received from product sales. It is determined by the quantity of the product sold and the price at which it is sold. Specifically

total revenue The price of a product multiplied by the quantity sold in a given time period: $p \times q$.

$$\bullet \quad \text{Total revenue} = \text{price} \times \text{quantity sold}$$

If the price of popcorn is 25 cents per ounce and 12 ounces are sold (point F in Figure 4.5), total revenue equals \$3.00 per show. This total revenue is illustrated by the shaded rectangle in Figure 4.5. (Recall that the area of a rectangle is equal to its height, p, times its width, q.)

FIGURE 4.5
Elasticity and Total Revenue

Total revenue is equal to the price of the product times the quantity sold. It is illustrated by the area of the rectangle formed by $p \times q$. The shaded rectangle illustrates total revenue ($3.00) at a price of 25 cents and a quantity demanded of 12 ounces. When price is reduced to 20 cents, the rectangle and total revenue expand (see dashed lines) because demand is elastic ($E > 1$) in that price range. Price cuts reduce total revenue only if demand is inelastic ($E < 1$).

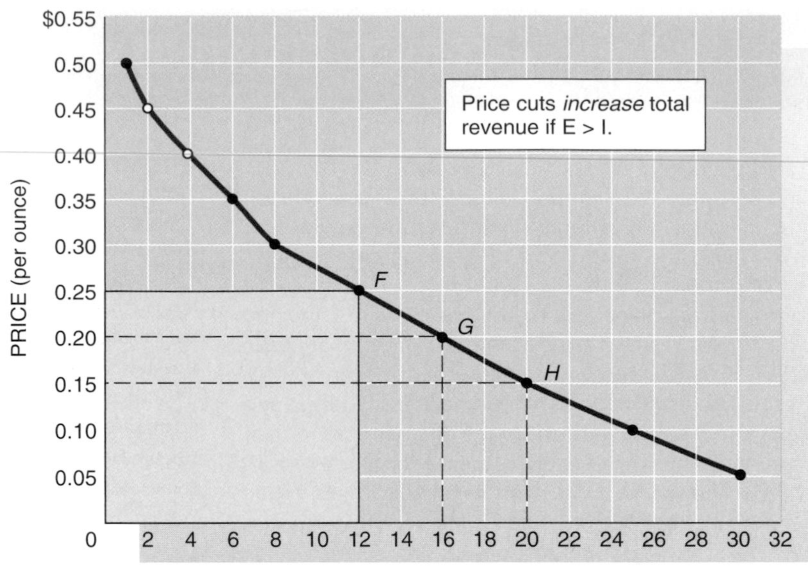

	Price	×	Quantity Demanded	=	Total Revenue
A	$0.50		1		$0.50
B	0.45		2		0.90
C	0.40		4		1.60
D	0.35		6		2.10
E	0.30		8		2.40
F	0.25		12		3.00
G	0.20		16		3.20
H	0.15		20		3.00
I	0.10		25		2.50
J	0.05		30		1.50

Effect of a Price Cut Now consider what happens to total revenue when the price of popcorn is reduced. Will total revenue decline along with the price? Maybe not. Remember the law of demand: as price falls, the quantity demanded *increases*. Hence, total revenue *might* actually *increase* when the price of popcorn is reduced. Whether it does or not depends on *how much* quantity demanded goes up when price goes down. This brings us back to the concept of elasticity.

Suppose we reduce popcorn prices from 25 cents to only 20 cents per ounce. What happens to total revenue? We know from Figure 4.5 that total revenue at point *F* was $3.00. At the lower price of 20 cents, unit sales increase significantly (to 16 ounces). In fact, they increase so much that total revenue actually increases as well. Total revenue at point *G* ($3.20) is larger than at point *F* ($3.00). Because total revenue *rose* when price *fell,* demand must be *elastic* in this price range.

Total revenue can't continue rising as price falls. At the extreme, price would fall to zero and there would be no revenue. So somewhere along the demand curve falling prices will begin to pinch total revenue. In Figure 4.5, this happens when the price of popcorn drops from 20 cents to 15 cents. Unit sales again increase (to 20 ounces) but not enough to compensate for

If Demand Is:	When Price Increases, Total Revenue Will:	When Price Decreases Total Revenue Will:
Elastic ($E > 1$)	Decrease	Increase
Inelastic ($E < 1$)	Increase	Decrease
Unitary elastic ($E = 1$)	Not change	Not change

TABLE 4.2
Price Elasticity of Demand and Total Revenue

The impact of higher prices on total revenue depends on the price elasticity of demand. Higher prices result in higher total revenue only if demand is inelastic. If demand is elastic, *lower* prices result in *higher* revenues.

the price decline. As a result, total revenue at point H ($3.00) is less than at point G ($3.20). Total revenue fell in this case because the consumer response to a price reduction was small in comparison to the relative size of the price cut. In other words, demand was price *inelastic*. Thus we can conclude that

- A price cut reduces total revenue if demand is inelastic ($E < 1$).
- A price cut increases total revenue if demand is elastic ($E > 1$).
- A price cut does not change total revenue if demand is unitary elastic ($E = 1$).

Table 4.2 summarizes these responses as well as responses to price increases.

Once we know the price elasticity of demand, we can predict how consumers will respond to changing prices. We can also predict what will happen to total revenue when a seller raises or lowers the price.

Determinants of Elasticity

Table 4.1 (p. 96) indicated the actual price elasticity for a variety of familiar goods and services. These large differences in elasticity are explained by several factors.

Necessities vs. Luxuries Some goods are so critical to our everyday life that we regard them as necessities. A hair brush, toothpaste, and perhaps textbooks might fall into this category. Our taste for such goods is so strong that we can't imagine getting along without them. As a result, we don't change our consumption of necessities much when the price increases; ***demand for necessities is relatively inelastic.***

A luxury good, by contrast, is something we'd *like* to have but aren't likely to buy unless our income jumps or the price declines sharply; vacation travel, new cars, and HDTV sets are examples. We want them, but we can get by without them. Thus ***demand for luxury goods is relatively elastic.***

Availability of Substitutes Our notion of what goods are necessities is also influenced by the availability of substitute goods. The high elasticity of demand for fish recorded in Table 4.1 reflects the fact that consumers can always eat chicken, beef, or pork if fish prices rise. On the other hand, most coffee drinkers cannot imagine any substitute for a cup of coffee. As a consequence, when coffee prices rise, consumers do not reduce their purchases very much at all. Likewise, the low elasticity of demand for gasoline reflects the fact that most cars can't run on alternative fuels. In general, ***the greater the availability of substitutes, the higher the price elasticity of demand.*** This is a principle that New York City learned when it raised the price of cigarettes from $6 to $7.50 a pack. In-city sales plummetted (see Headline), as smokers turned to adjoining states and cities, Indian reservations, and the Internet for cigarette purchases.

Price Relative to Income Another important determinant of elasticity is the price of the good itself. If the price of a product is very high in relation to

HEADLINE PRICE ELASTICITY

Cigarette Tax, Highest in Nation, Cuts Sales by Half

The number of cigarettes sold in New York City has been cut almost in half since the city began charging the highest cigarette tax in the nation last month, driving the price of many cigarettes to $7.50 a pack, according to figures released yesterday.

Only 15,630,000 packs of cigarettes were sold in the city during July, the first month of the tax, which represents a 47 percent drop from the 29,220,000 packs sold last July, according to Sam Miller, a spokesman for the city's Department of Finance.

The Bloomberg administration raised the city's cigarette tax from 8 cents a pack to $1.50 a pack, which must be paid on top of the state's $1.50-a-pack tax. Mayor Michael R. Bloomberg has long described the measure as more of a public health initiative, intended to get people to quit smoking, than a moneymaker. . . .

Just how many New Yorkers have quit, though, is hard to assess.

But many smokers are going elsewhere. Barry Wallace, an owner of the Poospatuck Smoke Shop, on the small Poospatuck Reservation on Long Island near Mastic, sells Marlboros for $3.90 a pack. Mr. Wallace said that he was seeing some new customers, but not a tremendous increase, and that it was unclear if it was because of the new tax or simply the crowds that flock to Long Island every summer.

"We're still trying to determine if it's the summer or the tax thing," he said. "There are a lot of Web sites now selling cigarettes from other states and reservations. The equation is different now.

—Michael Cooper

Source: *New York Times*, October 16, 2002, p. B1.

NOTE: Demand for cigarettes in general is inelastic. However, demand for New York City's high-tax cigarettes is elastic because smokers can purchase cigarettes elsewhere.

the consumer's income, then price *changes* will be important. Airline travel and new cars, for example, are quite expensive, so even a small percentage change in their prices can have a big impact on a consumer's budget (and consumption decisions). The demand for such big ticket items tends to be elastic. By contrast, coffee is so cheap for most people that even a large *percentage* change in price doesn't affect consumer behavior very much.

POLICY PERSPECTIVES

Caveat Emptor: The Role of Advertising

Producers who understand price elasticity have a big advantage in the marketplace. They know how to move consumers up and down an existing market demand curve. But what if producers could get around the *ceteris paribus* assumption and *change* consumer demand? That would open up a whole new set of profit opportunities. Remember that the demand curve itself will *shift* if tastes, incomes, the price/availability of other goods, or expectations *change.*

Most producers are quick to see the profit opportunity here. If they can change consumer's tastes, they can *shift* the demand curve and sell *more* output at *higher* prices. How will they do this? By advertising. As noted earlier, psychiatrists see us as complex bundles of basic drives, anxieties, and layers of consciousness. They presume that we enter the market with confused senses of guilt, insecurity, and ambition. Economists, on the other hand, regard the consumer as the rational *Homo economicus,* aware of his or her wants and knowledgeable about how to satisfy them. In reality, however, we

ADVERTISING HEADLINE

Where the Pitch Is Loudest

Countries where advertisers spend the most per person.

Country	Ad Spending per Capita
United States	$438
Japan	$263
United Kingdom	$249
Germany	$238
France	$167
Canada	$157
Spain	$122
Italy	$121
Brazil	$52

Source: *Ad Age Global* (February 2001).

NOTE: Advertising tries to change consumer tastes and shift demand.

do not always know what we want or which products will satisfy us. This uncertainty creates a vacuum into which the advertising industry has eagerly stepped.

The efforts of producers to persuade us to buy, buy, buy are as close as the nearest television, radio, magazine, or billboard. American producers now spend over $200 *billion* per year to change our tastes. This spending works out to over $400 per consumer, the highest per capita advertising rates in the world (see Headline). Much of this advertising (including product labeling) is intended to provide information about existing products or to bring new products to our attention. A great deal of advertising, however, is also designed to exploit our senses and lack of knowledge. Recognizing that we are guilt-ridden, insecure, and sex-hungry, advertisers offer us pictures and promises of exoneration, recognition, and love: all we have to do is buy the right product.

One of the favorite targets of advertisers is our sense of insecurity. Brand images are developed to give consumers a sense of identity. Smoke a Marlboro cigarette and you're a virile cowboy. Drink the right beer or vodka and you'll be a social success. Use the right perfume and you'll be irresistibly sexy. Wear Brand X jeans and you'll be way cool. Or at least that's what advertiers want you to believe.

Are Wants Created? Advertising cannot be blamed for all of our "foolish" consumption. Even members of the most primitive tribes, uncontaminated by the seductions of advertising, adorned themselves with rings, bracelets, and pendants. Furthermore, advertising has grown to massive proportions only in the last four decades, but consumption spending has been increasing throughout recorded history.

Although advertising cannot be charged with creating our needs, it does encourage specific outlets for satisfying those needs. The objective of all

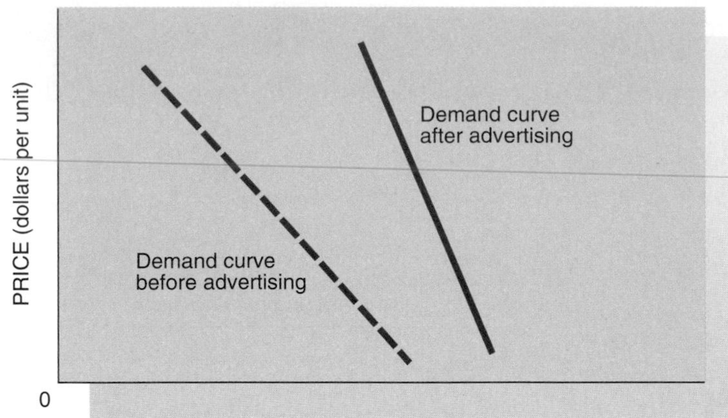

FIGURE 4.6
The Impact of Advertising on a Demand Curve

Advertising seeks to increase our taste for a particular product. If our taste (the product's perceived marginal utility) increases, so will our willingness to buy. The resulting change in demand is reflected in a rightward shift of the demand curve, often accompanied by diminished elasticity.

advertising is to alter the choices we make. Just as brand images are used to attract us to particular products, so are pictures of hungry, ill-clothed children used to persuade us to give money to charity. In the same way, public-relations gimmicks are employed to sway our votes for public servants. In the case of consumer products, advertising seeks to increase tastes for particular goods and services and therewith our willingness to pay. ***A successful advertising campaign is one that shifts the demand curve for a product to the right,*** inducing consumers to increase their purchases of a product at every price (see Figure 4.6). Advertising may also increase brand loyalty, making the demand curve less elastic, thereby reducing consumer responses to price increases. By influencing our choices in this way, advertising alters the distribution of our consumption expenditures, if not their level.

SUMMARY

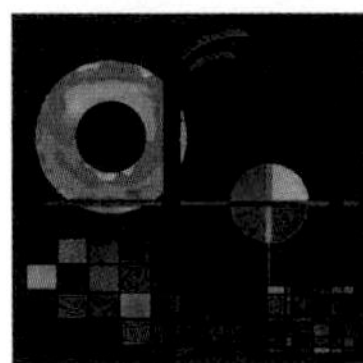

- Our desires for goods and services originate in the structure of personality and social dynamics and are not explained by economic theory. Economic theory focuses on *demand*—that is, our ability and willingness to buy specific quantities of a good at various prices.
- *Utility* refers to the satisfaction we get from consumer goods and services. *Total utility* refers to the amount of satisfaction associated with all consumption of a product. *Marginal utility* refers to the satisfaction obtained from the last unit of a product.
- The law of diminishing marginal utility says that the more of a product we consume, the smaller the increments of pleasure we get from each additional unit. This is the foundation for the law of demand.
- The price elasticity of demand (E) is a numerical measure of consumer response to a change in price (*ceteris paribus*). It equals the percentage change in quantity demanded divided by the percentage change in price.
- If demand is elastic ($E > 1$), a small change in price induces a large change in quantity demanded. "Elastic" demand indicates that consumer behavior is very responsive to price changes.
- If demand is *elastic,* a price increase will reduce total revenue. Price and total revenue move in the *same* direction only if demand is *inelastic.*

- The shape and position of any particular demand curve depend on a consumer's income, tastes, expectations, and the price and availability of other goods. Should any of these things change, the assumption of *ceteris paribus* will no longer hold, and the demand curve will *shift.*
- Advertising seeks to change consumer tastes and thus the willingness to buy. If tastes do change, the demand curve will shift.

Terms to Remember

Define the following terms:

demand	law of diminishing marginal utility	price elasticity of demand
market demand	*ceteris paribus*	total revenue
utility	law of demand	
total utility	demand curve	
marginal utility		

Questions for Discussion

1. Why do people routinely stuff themselves at all-you-can-eat buffets? Explain in terms of both utility and demand theories.
2. What does the demand for education at your college look like? What is on each axis? Is the demand elastic or inelastic? How could you find out?
3. What would happen to unit sales and total revenue for this textbook if the publisher reduced its price?
4. If *all* soda advertisements were banned, how would Pepsi sales be affected? How about total soda consumption?
5. How has the Internet affected the elasticity of demand for air travel?
6. Identify three goods each for which your demand is (*a*) elastic or (*b*) inelastic. What accounts for the differences in elasticity?
7. Utility companies routinely ask state commissions for permission to raise utility rates. What does this suggest about the price elasticity of demand? Why is demand so (in)elastic?
8. Why is the demand for New York City cigarettes so much more price elastic than the overall market demand for cigarettes (see Headline, p. 100)?
9. BuyMusic, a Windows-based music download site, was introduced in July 2003. How will that affect the demand for iTunes (see Headline, p. 95)? The price elasticity of demand?

Problems

1. The following is a demand schedule for shoes:

Price (per pair)	$100	$80	$60	$40	$20
Quantity demanded (in pairs per year)	10	14	18	22	26

(*a*) Illustrate the demand curve on the following graph.
(*b*) How much will consumers spend on shoes at the price of (i) $80 and (ii) $60? As the price drops from $80 to $60 a pair, is demand elastic or inelastic?

(*c*) If advertisers convinced people that to be stylish they needed more shoes, how would the demand curve be altered? Illustrate this change on the following graph.

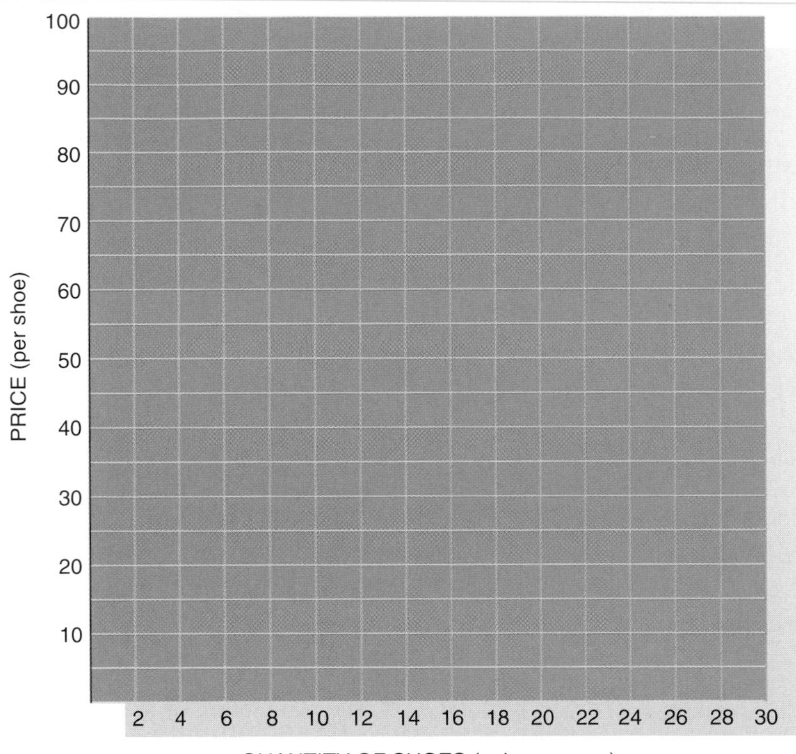

2. According to the elasticity computation on p. 96, by how much would popcorn sales fall if the price increased by 20 percent?_____ By 50 percent_____?
3. According to Table 4.1, by how much will unit sales of (a) coffee, (b) shoes, and (c) airline travel decline when price goes up by 10 percent? What will happen to total revenue in each case?
4. According to the Headline on p. 62, what is the price elasticity of demand for alcohol among college students?
5. According to Table 4.1, by how much would coffee sales decline if the price of coffee doubled? If Starbucks doubled *its* coffee prices, what would happen to Starbucks' sales? How do you explain these responses?
6. In 1998 President Clinton proposed an additional $1.10 per pack tax that would have increased cigarette prices roughly 60 percent. According to the Headline on p. 97 by how much would teen smoking have dropped in response to such a tax?
7. Suppose the following table reflects the total satisfaction (utility) derived from eating pizza:

Quantity consumed	1	2	3	4	5	6	7
Total utility	47	92	122	135	137	120	70

(*a*) What is the marginal utility of each pizza?
(*b*) What causes the marginal utility to diminish?

8. Economists estimate price elasticities by using *average* price and quantity to compute percentage changes. Thus,

$$E = \frac{Q_1 - Q_2}{\frac{Q_1 + Q_2}{2}} \div \frac{P_1 - P_2}{\frac{P_1 + P_2}{2}}$$

Using this formula. (a) compute E for a popcorn price increase from 20 cents to 40 cents per ounce (Figure 4.5), and (b) compute E for New York City cigarettes (see Headline p. 100 and text).

Web Activities

1. Log on to www.whitehouse.gov/fsbr/income.html. Click on the chart for disposable personal income. Link into income and find the trend in real disposable personal income. Given the trend in these data, what has probably happened to consumer demand? Explain.
2. Log on to www.msnbc.com. Complete a keyword search using the search words "consumer demand." Find an article that suggests a change in demand.
   (*a*) Analyze the article and identify the determinants of demand that are changing.
   (*b*) What is the likely implication of this change on the market price?
3. Log on to www.census.gov/population/www/projections/popproj.html and click on "total resident population." What are the high and low projections for the U.S. population in the year 2025? What is the likely impact on the demand for housing in the United States? Explain.
4. Log on to www.bls.gov/cex. Click the overview button then click on "News Release" and then the link for consumer expenditures survey.
   (*a*) What has happened to consumer income before taxes in the last two years reported?
   (*b*) What has happened to the average expenditures for food purchased away from home as a percentage of income before taxes? What are some possible explanations for this trend?
   (*c*) What two categories of expenditures have had the largest percentage increase in the last two reported years?

Living Econ

Am I a Spendthrift?

Sometimes you may have felt irresponsible because you bought items without much regard for their prices. This chapter explains why people often are relatively unaffected by price changes. When you picked up your morning coffee, the cost was small compared to other purchases. When you filled up the car with gas, it was a necessity for you to drive to school. And, when you paid the parking fee, probably you had few substitutes. In the short run, all of these items have low price elasticity of demand. So you shouldn't be surprised—or guilty—that higher prices don't affect your behavior very much.

However, you may also carefully shop for clothing, comparing prices because there are many substitutes. If you are in the market for a new computer, you'll shop around because it is a relatively high ticket item. And, you'll think about whether or not to go out to dinner because it isn't a necessity. In each case the item has high price elasticity.

Sellers are well aware of the ways in which your behavior depends on price elasticity. The next time you are shopping check out which items come with lower prices—or at least have the appearance of a discount. Chances are they have higher price elasticity of demand than items not on sale.

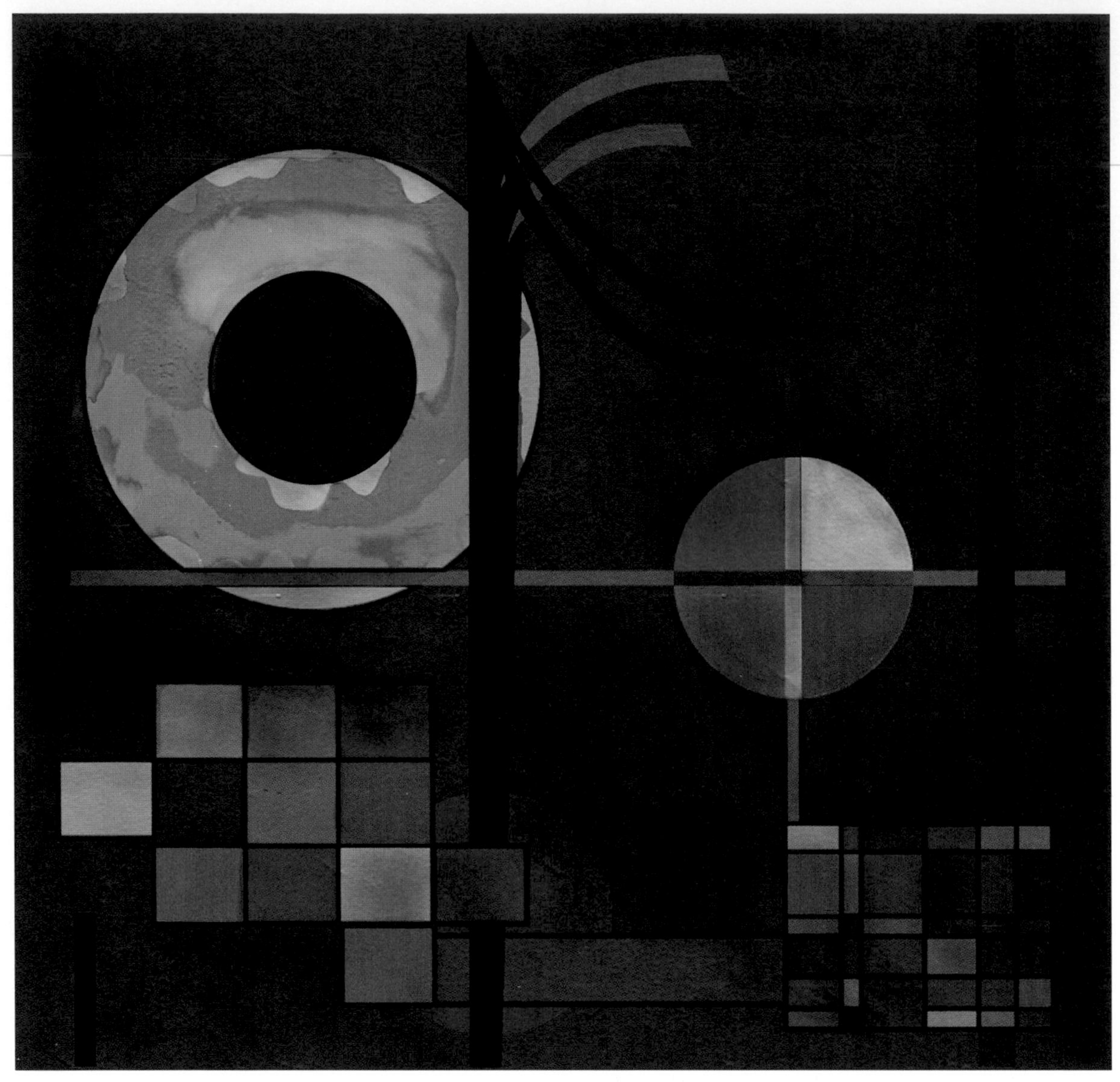

Supply Decisions

CHAPTER 5

Most consumers think producers reap huge profits from every market sale. Most producers wish that were true. The average producer earns a profit of only four to six cents on every sales dollar. And those profits don't come easily. Producers earn a profit only if they make the correct supply decisions. They have to keep a close eye on prices and costs and produce the right quantity at the right time. If they do all the right things, they *might* make a profit. Even when a producer does everything right, however, profits are not assured. Over 50,000 U.S. businesses failed last year, despite their owners' best efforts to make a profit.

In this chapter we look at markets from the supply side, examining two distinct concerns. First, how much output *can* a firm produce? Second, how much output will it *want* to produce? As we'll see, the answers to these two questions are rarely the same.

The question of how much *can* be produced is largely an engineering and managerial problem. The question of how much *should* be produced is an *economic* issue. If costs escalate as capacity is approached, it might make sense to produce less than capacity output. In some situations, the costs of production might even be so high that it doesn't make sense to produce *any* output from available facilities. The end result will be a supply decision, that is, an expressed *ability* and *willingness* to produce a good at various prices.

This chapter focuses on those supply decisions. We first look at the capacity to produce, then at how choices are made about how much to supply. The discussion revolves around three questions:

- What limits a firm's ability to produce?
- What costs are incurred in producing a good?
- How do costs affect supply decisions?

Once we have answered these questions, we should be able to understand how supply-side forces affect the price and availability of the goods and services we demand.

Capacity Constraints: The Production Function

supply The ability and willingness to sell (produce) specific quantities of a good at alternative prices in a given time period, ceteris paribus.

factors of production Resource inputs used to produce goods and services, e.g., land, labor, capital, entrepreneurship.

production function A technological relationship expressing the maximum quantity of a good attainable from different combinations of factor inputs.

No matter how large a business is or who owns it, all businesses confront one central fact: you need resources to produce goods. To produce corn, a farmer needs land, water, seed, equipment, and labor. To produce fillings, a dentist needs a chair, a drill, some space, and labor. Even the "production" of educational services (e.g., this economics class) requires the use of labor (your teacher), land (on which the school is built), and some capital (bricks and mortar or electronic classrooms). In short, unless you are producing unrefined, unpackaged air, you need **factors of production**—that is, resources that can be used to produce a good or service.

The factors of production used to produce a good or service provide the basic measure of economic cost. If someone asked you what the cost of your econ class was, you'd probably quote the tuition you paid for it. But tuition is the *price* of *consuming* the course, not the *cost* of *producing* it. The cost of producing your economic class is measured by the amounts of land, labor, and capital it requires. These are *resource* costs of production.

An essential question for production is, How many resources are actually needed to produce a given product? You could use a lot of resources to produce a product or use just a few. What we really want to know is how *best* to produce. What is the *smallest* amount of resources needed to produce a specific product? Or we could ask the same question from a different perspective: What is the *maximum* amount of output attainable from a given quantity of input resources?

These aren't easy questions to answer. But if we knew the technology of the production process and the efficiency of managerial organizations, we could come up with an answer. The answer would tell us the *maximum* amount of output attainable from a given quantity of resources. These limits to the production of any good are reflected in the **production function.** The production function tells us the maximum amount of good *X* producible from various combinations of factor inputs. With one chair and one drill, a dentist can fill a maximum of 32 cavities per day. With two chairs, a drill, and an assistant, a dentist can fill up to 55 cavities per day.

A production function is a technological summary of our ability to produce a particular good. Table 5.1 provides a partial glimpse of one such function. In this case, the desired output is designer jeans, as produced by Tight Jeans Corporation. The essential inputs in the production of jeans are land, labor (garment workers), and capital (a factory and sewing machines). With these inputs, Tight Jeans can produce and sell fancy jeans to status-conscious consumers.

As in all production endeavors, we want to know how many pairs of jeans we can produce with available resources. To make things easy, we shall assume that the factory is already built. We will also assume that only one leased sewing machine is available. Thus, both land and capital inputs are fixed. Under these circumstances, only the quantity of labor can be varied. In this case, the quantity of jeans we can produce depends directly on the amount of labor we employ. ***The purpose of a production function is to tell us just how much output we can produce with varying amounts of factor inputs.*** Table 5.1 provides such information for jeans production.

Column A of Table 5.1 confirms the obvious: you can't manufacture jeans without any workers. Even though land, capital (an empty factory and idle machine), and even denim are available, essential labor inputs are missing, and jeans production is impossible. Maybe advances in robotics will change

	A	B	C	D	E	F	G	H	I
Labor input (workers per day)	0	1	2	3	4	5	6	7	8
Output (pairs of jeans per day)	0	15	34	44	48	50	51	51	47

TABLE 5.1
A Production Function

A production function tells us the *maximum* amount of output attainable from alternative combinations of factor inputs. This particular function tells us how many pairs of jeans we can produce in a factory that has only 1 sewing machine and varying quantities of labor. With only one operator, we can produce a maximum of 15 pairs of jeans per day, as indicated in column *B*. To produce more jeans, we need more labor.

that reality. For now, however, the factory depicted in Table 5.1 isn't nearly that advanced. It still needs live bodies in the production process.

Column B in Table 5.1 shows what happens to jeans output when only one worker is employed. With only one machine and one worker, the jeans start rolling out the front door. Maximum output under these circumstances (row 2, column B) is 15 pairs of jeans per day. Now we're in business!

The remaining columns of Table 5.1 tell us how many additional jeans we can produce if we hire still more workers, still leasing only one sewing machine. With one machine and two workers, maximum output rises to 34 pairs per day (column C). If a third worker is hired, output could increase to 44 pairs.

This information on our production capabilities is illustrated in Figure 5.1. Point *A* illustrates the cold, hard fact that we can't produce any jeans without some labor. Points *B* through *I* show how production increases as additional labor is employed.

Efficiency

Every point on the production function in Figure 5.1 represents the *most* output we could produce with a given number of workers. Point *D*, for example, tells us we could produce as many as 44 pairs of jeans with three workers. We must recognize, however, that we might also produce less. If the workers goof off or the sewing machine isn't maintained well, total output might be less than 44 pairs per day. In that case, we wouldn't be making the best possible use of scarce resources: we would be producing *inefficiently*. In Figure 5.1 this would imply a rate of output *below* point *D*. Only if we produce with maximum *efficiency* will we end up at point *D* or some other point on the production function.

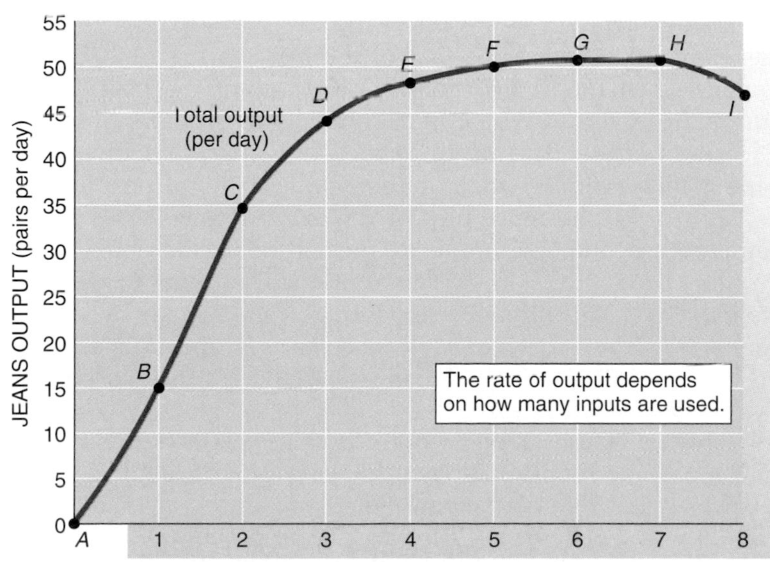

FIGURE 5.1
Short-Run Production Function

In the short run some inputs (e.g., land, capital) are fixed in quantity. Output then depends on how much of a variable input (e.g., labor) is used. The short-run production function shows how output changes when more labor is used. This figure is based on Table 5.1.

Capacity

Although the production function emphasizes how output increases with more workers, the progression can't go on forever. Labor isn't the only factor of production needed to produce jeans. We also need capital. In this case, we have only a small factory and one sewing machine. If we keep hiring workers, we will quickly run out of space and available equipment. ***Land and capital constraints place a ceiling on potential output.***

Notice in Figure 5.1 how total output peaks at point *G*. We can produce a total of 51 pairs of jeans at that point by employing six workers. What happens if we hire still more workers? According to Figure 5.1, if we employed a seventh worker, total output would not increase further. At point *H*, total output is 51 pairs, just as it was at point *G*, when we hired only six workers.

Were we to hire an *eighth* worker, total jeans output would actually *decline*, as illustrated by point *I*. An eighth worker would actually *reduce* total output by increasing congestion on the factory floor, delaying access to the sewing machine, and just plain getting in the way. Given the size of the factory and the availability of only one sewing machine, no more than six workers can be productively employed. Hence, the *capacity* production of this factory is 51 pairs of jeans per day. We could hire more workers, but output would not go up.

Marginal Physical Product

The land and capital constraints that limit output have some interesting effects on the productivity of individual workers. Consider that seventh worker at the jeans factory. If she were hired, total output would not increase: total output is 51 pairs of jeans when either six or seven workers are employed. Accordingly, that seventh worker contributes nothing to total output.

The contribution of each worker to production is measured by the change in *total* output that occurs when the worker is employed. The name for this concept is **marginal physical product (MPP)** and is measured as

marginal physical product (MPP) The change in total output associated with one additional unit of input.

- $\text{Marginal physical product (MPP)} = \dfrac{\text{change in total output}}{\text{change in input quantity}}$

In this case, total output doesn't change when the seventh worker is hired, so her MPP equals zero.

Contrast that experience with that of the *first* worker hired. Notice again what happens when the first worker is employed at the jeans factory: total output jumps from zero (point *A* in Figure 5.1) to 15 pairs of jeans per day (point *B*). This *increase* in output reflects the marginal physical product (MPP) of that first worker—that is, the *change* in total output that results from employment of one more unit of (labor) input.

If we employ a second operator, jeans output more than doubles, to 34 pairs per day (point *C*). Whereas the marginal physical product of the first worker was only 15 pairs, a second worker increases total output by 19 pairs.

The higher MPP of the second worker raises a question about the first. Why was the first's MPP lower? Laziness? Is the second worker faster, less distracted, or harder working?

The higher MPP of the second worker is not explained by superior talents or effort. We assume in this exercise that all units of labor are equal—that is, one worker is just as good as another. Their different marginal products are explained by the structure of the production process, not by their respective abilities. The first garment worker had not only to sew jeans but also to unfold bolts of denim, measure the jeans, sketch out the patterns, and cut them to approximate size. A lot of time was spent going from one task to another. Despite the worker's best efforts (and assuming perfect efficiency), this person simply could not do everything at once.

A second worker alleviates this situation. With two workers, less time is spent running from one task to another. Now there is an opportunity for each worker to specialize a bit. While one is measuring and cutting, the other can continue sewing. This improved ratio of labor to other factors of production results in the large jump in total output. The superior MPP of the second worker is not unique to this person: it would have occurred even if we had hired the workers in the reverse order. What matters is the amount of capital or land each unit of labor can work with. In other words, ***a worker's productivity (MPP) depends in part on the amount of other resources in the production process.***

Law of Diminishing Returns

Unfortunately, output cannot keep increasing at this rate. Look what happens when a third worker is hired. Total jeans production continues to increase. But the increase from point *C* to point *D* in Figure 5.1 is only 10 pairs per day. Hence the MPP of the third worker (10 pairs) is *less* than that of the second (19 pairs). Marginal physical product is *diminishing*.

Resource Constraints What accounts for this decline in MPP? The answer again lies in the ratio of labor to other factors of production. A third worker begins to crowd our facilities. We still have only one sewing machine. Two people cannot sew at the same time. As a result, some time is wasted as the operators wait for their turns at the machine. Even if they split up the various jobs, there will still be some downtime, since measuring and cutting are not as time-consuming as sewing. In this sense, we cannot make full use of a third worker. ***The relative scarcity of other inputs (capital and land) constrains the marginal physical product of labor.***

Resource constraints are even more evident when a fourth worker is hired. Total output increases again, but the increase this time is very small. With three workers, we got 44 pairs of jeans per day (point *D*); with four workers, we get a maximum of 48 pairs (point *E*). Thus the marginal physical product of the fourth worker is only 4 pairs of jeans. A fourth worker really begins to strain our productive capacity. There simply aren't enough machines to make productive use of so much labor.

Negative MPP If a seventh worker is hired, the operators get in each other's way, argue, and waste denim. As we observed earlier, total output does not increase at all when a seventh worker is hired. The MPP of the seventh worker is zero. The seventh worker is being wasted, in the sense that she contributes nothing to total output. This waste of scarce resources (labor) was commonplace in communist countries, where everyone was guaranteed a job (see Headline). At Tight Jeans, however, they do not want to hire someone who doesn't contribute to output. And they certainly wouldn't want to hire an *eighth* worker, since total output actually *declines* from 51 pairs of jeans (point *H* in Figure 5.1) to 47 pairs (point *I*) when an eighth worker is hired. In other words, the eighth worker has a *negative* MPP.

The problem of crowded facilities applies to most production processes. In the short run, a production process is characterized by a fixed amount of available land and capital. Typically, the only factor that can be varied in the short run is labor. Yet, ***as more labor is hired, each unit of labor has less capital and land to work with.*** This is simple division: the available facilities are being shared by more and more workers. At some point, this constraint begins to pinch. When it does, marginal physical product starts to

HEADLINE MARGINAL PHYSICAL PRODUCT

"We Pretend to Work, They Pretend to Pay Us"

One of the attractions of communist nations was their promise of employment. Passing through the factory gate was not proof of productive employment, however. Ordered to hire all comers, state-run enterprises became bloated with surplus workers. Although payrolls climbed, output stagnated.

As it turned out, the paychecks handed out to the workers weren't very good anyway. Runaway inflation and a scarcity of consumer goods rendered the paychecks almost worthless. The futility of the situation was summed up by one worker who explained that "we pretend to work and they pretend to pay us."

When communism collapsed, the factory gates were no longer open to all. New profit-oriented owners were unwilling to pay workers whose marginal physical product was zero. In East Germany alone, over 400,000 workers lost their jobs when 126 state-owned enterprises were sold to private investors—without any decline in output.

NOTE: As more workers are hired in a given plant, marginal physical product declines. It may even fall to zero or less.

decline. This situation is so common that it is the basis for an economic principle: the **law of diminishing returns.** This law says that the marginal physical product of any factor of production (e.g., labor) will begin to diminish at some point, as more of it is used in a given production setting.

law of diminishing returns The marginal physical product of a variable input declines as more of it is employed with a given quantity of other (fixed) inputs.

Short Run vs. Long Run

The limited availability of space or equipment is the cause of diminishing returns. Once we have purchased or leased a specific factory, it sets a limit to current jeans production. When such commitments to fixed inputs (e.g., the factory and machinery) exist, we are dealing with a **short-run** production problem. If no land or capital were in place—if we could build or lease any size factory—we would be dealing with a *long-run* decision. In the **long run** we might also learn new and better ways of making jeans and so increase our production capabilities. For the time being, however, we must accept the fact that the production function in Figure 5.1 defines the *short-run* limits to jeans production. Our short-run objective is to make the best possible use of the factory we have acquired. This is the challenge producers face every day.

short run The period in which the quantity (and quality) of some inputs cannot be changed.

long run A period of time long enough for all inputs to be varied (no fixed costs).

Costs of Production

A production function tells us how much output a firm *could* produce with its existing plant and equipment. It doesn't tell us how much the firm will *want* to produce. The level of desired output depends on prices and costs. A firm *might* want to produce at capacity if the profit picture were bright enough. On the other hand, a firm might not produce *any* output if costs always exceeded sales revenue. The most desirable rate of output is the one that maximizes total **profit—**the difference between total revenue and total costs.

profit The difference between total revenue and total cost.

The production function, then, is just a starting point for supply decisions. To decide how much output to produce with that function, a firm must next examine the dollar costs of production.

Total Cost

The economic cost of producing a good is ultimately gauged by the amount of scarce resources used to produce it. In a market economy, however, we want a more convenient measure of cost. Instead of listing all the input quantities used, we want a single dollar figure. To get that dollar amount, we must identify all

Cost of Producing Jeans (15 pairs per day)				
Resource Used	×	Unit Price	=	Total Cost
1 factory		$100 per day		$100
1 sewing machine		20 per day		20
1 operator		80 per day		80
1.5 bolts of denim		30 per bolt		45
Total cost				$245

TABLE 5.2
The Total Costs of Production

The total cost of producing a good equals the market value of all the resources used in its production. In this case, we have assumed that the production of 15 pairs of jeans per day requires resources worth $245.

the resources used in production, compute their value, then add everything up. The end result will be a dollar figure for the **total cost** of production.

total cost The market value of all resources used to produce a good or service.

In the production of jeans, the resources used include land, labor, and capital. Table 5.2 identifies these resources, their unit values, and the total costs associated with their use. This table is based on an assumed output of 15 pairs of jeans per day, with the use of one machine operator and one sewing machine (point *B* in Figure 5.1). The rent on the factory is $100 per day, a sewing machine costs $20 per day, the wages of a garment worker are $80 per day. We shall assume Tight Jeans Corporation can purchase bolts of denim for $30 apiece, each of which provides enough denim for 10 pairs of jeans. In other words, one-tenth of a bolt ($3 worth of material) is required for one pair of jeans. We shall ignore any other potential expenses. With these assumptions, the total cost of producing 15 pairs of jeans per day amounts to $245, as shown in Table 5.2.

Fixed Costs Total costs will change, of course, as we alter the rate of production. But not all costs increase. In the short run, some costs don't increase at all when output is increased. These are **fixed costs,** in the sense that they do not vary with the rate of output. The factory lease is an example. Once you lease a factory, you are obligated to pay for it, whether you use it or not. The person who owns the factory wants $100 per day. Even if you produce no jeans, you still have to pay that rent. That is the essence of fixed costs.

fixed costs Costs of production that do not change when the rate of output is altered, e.g., the cost of basic plant and equipment.

The leased sewing machine is another fixed cost. When you rent a sewing machine, you must pay the rental charge. It doesn't matter whether you use it for a few minutes or all day long—the rental charge is fixed at $20 per day.

Variable Costs Labor costs are another story altogether. The amount of labor employed in jeans production can be varied easily. If we decide not to open the factory tomorrow, we can just tell our only worker to take the day off. We will still have to pay rent, but we can cut back on wages. On the other hand, if we want to increase daily output, we can also get additional workers easily and quickly. Labor is regarded as a **variable cost** in this line of work—that is, a cost that *varies* with the rate of output.

variable costs Costs of production that change when the rate of output is altered, e.g., labor and material costs.

The denim itself is another variable cost. Denim not used today can be saved for tomorrow. Hence how much we "spend" on denim today is directly related to how many jeans we produce. In this sense, the cost of denim input varies with the rate of jeans output.

Figure 5.2 illustrates how these various costs are affected by the rate of production. On the vertical axis are the costs of production, in dollars per day. Notice that the total cost of producing 15 pairs per day is still $245, as indicated by point *B*. This figure consists of $120 of fixed costs (factory and sewing machine rents) and $125 of variable costs ($80 in wages and $45 for denim). If we increase the rate of output, total costs will rise. ***How fast total costs rise depends on variable costs only,*** however, since fixed costs remain at $120 per day. (Notice the horizontal fixed cost curve in Figure 5.2.)

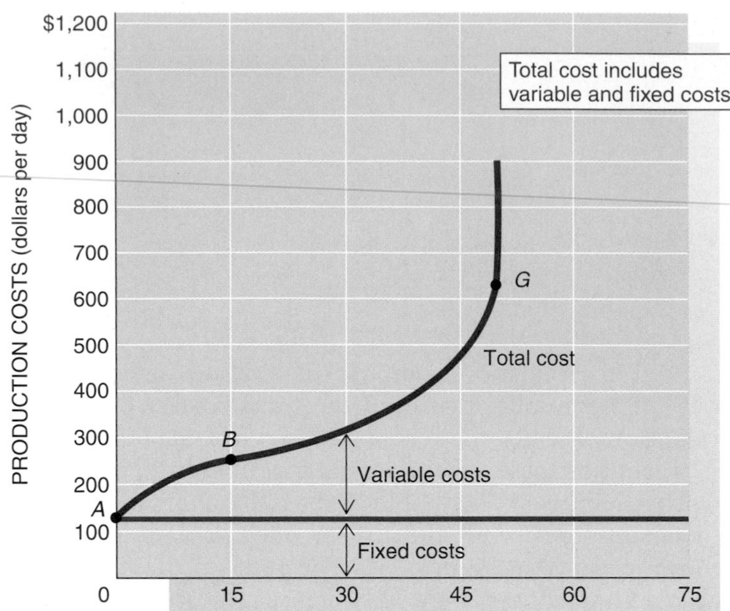

FIGURE 5.2
The Costs of Jeans Production

Total cost includes both fixed and variable costs. Fixed costs must be paid even if no output is produced (point *A*). Variable costs start at zero and increase with the rate of output. The total cost of producing 15 pairs of jeans (point *B*) includes $120 in fixed costs (rent on the factory and sewing machines) and $125 in variable costs (denim and wages). Total cost rises as output increases, because additional variable costs must be incurred.

In this example, the short-run capacity is equal to 51 pairs (point *G*). If still more inputs are employed, costs will rise but not total output.

With one sewing machine and one factory, there is an absolute limit to daily jeans production. As we observed in the production function (Figure 5.1), the capacity of a factory with one machine is 51 pairs of jeans per day. If we try to produce more jeans than this by hiring additional workers, total *costs* will rise, but total *output* will not. In fact, we could fill the factory with garment workers and drive total costs sky-high. But the limits of space and one sewing machine do not permit output in excess of 51 pairs per day. This limit to productive capacity is represented by point *G* on the total cost curve. Further expenditure on inputs will increase production costs but not output.

Although there is no upper limit to costs, there is a lower limit. If output is reduced to zero, total costs fall only to $120 per day, the level of fixed costs. This is illustrated by point *A* in Figure 5.2. As before, ***there is no way to avoid fixed costs in the short run.*** If you have leased a factory or machinery, you must pay the rent whether you produce any jeans or not.

Which Costs Matter?

The different nature of fixed and variable costs raises some intriguing questions about how to measure the cost of producing a pair of jeans. In figuring how much it costs to produce one pair, should we look only at the denim and labor time used to produce that pair? Or should we also take into account the factory rent and lease payments on the sewing machines?

A similar problem arises when you try to figure out whether a restaurant overcharges you for a steak dinner. What did it cost the restaurant to supply the dinner? Should only the meat and the chef's time be counted? Or should the cost include some portion of the rent, the electricity, and the insurance?

The restaurant owner, too, needs to figure out which measure of cost to use. She has to decide what price to charge for the steak. She wants to earn a profit. Can she do so by charging a price just above the cost of meat and wages? Or must she charge a price high enough to cover some portion of all her fixed costs as well?

To answer these questions, we need to introduce two distinct measures of cost, namely, *average* cost and *marginal* cost.

Average Cost

Average total cost (ATC) is simply total cost divided by the rate of output; that is

average total cost (ATC) Total cost divided by the quantity produced in a given time period.

$$\bullet \text{ Average total cost (ATC)} = \frac{\text{total cost}}{\text{total output}}$$

If the total cost (including both fixed and variable costs) of supplying 10 steaks is $62 then the *average* cost of the steaks is $6.20.

As we observed in Figure 5.2, total costs change as the rate of output increases. Hence, both the numerator and the denominator in the ATC formula change with the rate of output. This complicates the arithmetic a bit, as Figure 5.3 illustrates.

Figure 5.3 shows how average costs change as the rate of output varies. Row *J* of the cost schedule, for example, again indicates the fixed, variable, and total costs of producing 15 pairs of jeans per day. Fixed costs are still $120 (for factory and machine rentals); variable costs (denim and labor) are $125. Thus the total cost of producing 15 pairs per day is $245. The *average* cost for this rate of output is simply total cost ($245) divided by quantity (15), or $16.33 per day. This ATC is indicated in column 5 of the table and by point *J* on the graph.

U-Shaped ATC Curve An important feature of the ATC curve is its shape. ***Average costs start high, fall, then rise once again, giving the ATC curve a distinctive U shape.***

The initial decline in ATC is largely due to fixed costs. At low rates of output, fixed costs are a high proportion of total costs. Quite simply, it's very expensive to lease (or buy) an entire factory to produce only a few pairs of jeans. The entire cost of the factory must be averaged out over a small quantity of output. This results in a high average cost of production. To reduce *average* costs, we must make fuller use of our leased plant and equipment.

The same problem of cost spreading would affect a restaurant that served only two dinners a day. The *total* cost of operating a restaurant might easily exceed $500 a day. If only two dinners were served, the *average* total cost of each meal would exceed $250. That's why restaurants need a high volume of business to keep meal prices low.

As output increases, the fixed costs of production are distributed over an increasing quantity of output. Fixed costs no longer dominate total costs as production increases (compare columns 2 and 3 in Figure 5.3). As a result, average total costs tend to decline.

Average total costs don't fall forever, however. They bottom out at point *M* in Figure 5.3, then start rising. What accounts for this turnaround?

Marginal Cost

The upturn of the ATC curve is caused by rising *marginal* costs. **Marginal cost (MC)** ***refers to the change in total costs when one more unit of output is produced.*** In practice, marginal cost is easy to measure; just observe how much total costs increase when one more unit of output is produced. For larger increases in output, marginal cost can also be approximated by the formula

marginal cost (MC) The increase in total cost associated with a one-unit increase in production.

$$\bullet \text{ Marginal cost} = \frac{\text{change in total cost}}{\text{change in total output}}$$

Using this formula and Figure 5.3 we could confirm how marginal costs rise in jeans production. As jeans production increases from 20 pairs (row *K*) to 30 pairs (row *L*) per day, total costs rise from $270 to $360. Hence, the *change*

FIGURE 5.3
Average Total Cost

Average total cost (ATC) in column 5 of the accompanying table equals total cost (column 4) divided by the rate of output (column 1). ATC tends to fall initially, then later rise. This gives the ATC curve a U shape, as illustrated in the graph.

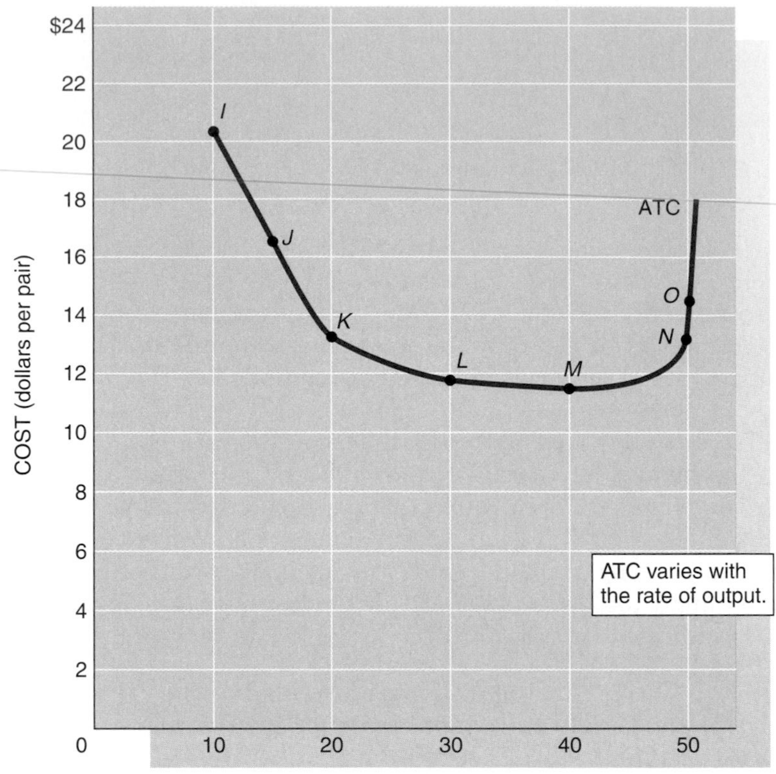

	(1) Rate of Output	(2) Fixed Costs	+	(3) Variable Costs	=	(4) Total Cost	(5) Average Total Cost
H	0	$120		$ 0		$120	—
I	10	120		85		205	$20.50
J	15	120		125		245	16.33
K	20	120		150		270	13.50
L	30	120		240		360	12.00
M	40	120		350		470	11.75
N	50	120		550		670	13.40
O	51	120		633		753	14.76

in total cost ($90) divided by the *change* in total output (10) equals $9. This is the *marginal* cost of jeans in that range of output (20 to 30 pairs).

Figure 5.4 shows how marginal costs change as jeans output increases. As output continues to increase further from 30 to 40 pairs per day, marginal costs rise. *Total* cost rises from $360 (row *L*) to $470 (row *M*), a *change* of $110. Dividing this by the *change* in output (10) reveals that *marginal* cost is now $11. Marginal costs are rising as output increases.

Rising marginal cost implies that each additional unit of output becomes more expensive to produce. Why is this? Why would a third pair of jeans cost more to produce than a second pair did? Why would it cost a restaurant more to serve the twelfth dinner than the eleventh dinner?

The explanation for this puzzle of rising marginal cost lies in the production function. As we observed earlier, output increases at an ever slower pace

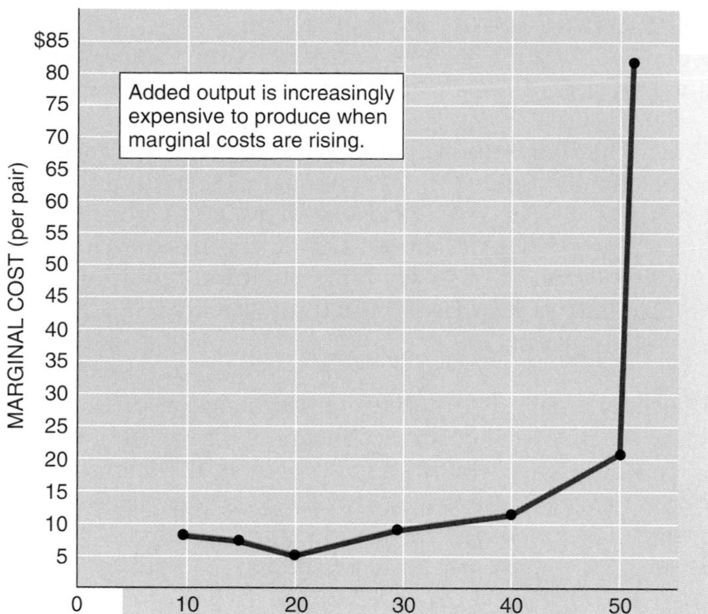

FIGURE 5.4
Marginal Cost

Marginal cost is the change in total cost that occurs when more output is produced. *MC* equals $\Delta TC/\Delta q$. When diminishing returns set in, *MC* begins rising.

	Rate of Output	Total Cost	$\frac{\Delta TC}{\Delta q} = MC$
H	0	$120	
I	10	205	$ 85/10 = $ 8.5
J	15	245	$ 40/5 = $ 8.0
K	20	270	$ 25/5 = $ 5.0
L	30	360	$ 90/10 = $ 9.0
M	40	470	$110/10 = $11.0
N	50	670	$200/10 = $20.0
O	51	753	$ 83/1 = $83.0

as capacity is approached. The law of diminishing marginal product tells us that we need an increasing amount of labor to eke out each additional pair of jeans. The same law applies to restaurants. As more dinners are served, the waiters and cooks get pressed for space and equipment. It takes a little longer (and, hence, more wages) to prepare and serve each meal. Hence, the *marginal* costs of each meal increase as the number of patrons rises.

Supply Horizons

All these cost calculations can give you a real headache. They can also give you second thoughts about jumping into Tight Jeans, restaurant management, or any other business. There are tough choices to be made. Any firm can produce many different rates of output, each of which entails a distinct level of costs. Someone has to choose which level of output to produce and thus how many goods to supply to the market. That decision has to be based not only on the *capacity* to produce (the production function) but also on the *costs* of production (the cost functions). Only those who make the right decisions will succeed in business.

The Short-Run Production Decision

The nature of supply decisions also varies with the relevant time frame. In this regard, we must distinguish *short*-run decisions from *long*-run decisions.

production decision The selection of the short-run rate of output (with existing plant and equipment).

The Short Run The *short run* is characterized by the existence of fixed costs. A commitment has been made: a factory has been built, an office leased, or machinery purchased. The only decision to make is how much output to produce with these existing facilities. This is the **production decision,** the choice of how intensively to use available plant and equipment. This choice is typically made daily (e.g., jeans production), weekly (e.g., auto production), or seasonally (e.g., farming).

Focus on Marginal Cost The most important factor in the short-run production decision is marginal costs. Producers will be willing to supply output only if they can at least cover marginal costs. If the marginal cost of producing a product exceeds the price at which it is sold, it doesn't make sense to produce that last unit. Price must exceed marginal cost for the producer to reap any profit from the last unit produced. Accordingly, ***marginal cost is a basic determinant of short-run supply (production) decisions.***

Look back at Figure 5.4. Suppose Tight Jeans is producing 40 pairs per day and selling them for \$18 each. In that case, total revenue is \$720 (\$18 × 40 pairs) and total cost is \$470, yielding a profit of \$250 per day.

Now suppose the plant manager is so excited by these profits that she increases total output to 50 pairs per day. Will profits increase proportionately? Not according to Figure 5.4. When output increases to 50 pairs, marginal cost rises to \$20. Hence it is more expensive to produce those extra 10 pairs (@ \$20 each) than they can be sold for (\$18). Marginal costs would dictate *not* supplying the additional jeans. If they are produced, total profits will decline (check this!). Hence marginal costs provide an important clue about the profitability of supplying more output.

Marginal costs may also dictate short-run pricing decisions. Suppose the average total cost of serving a steak dinner is \$12, but the marginal cost is only \$7. How low a price can the restaurant charge for the dinner? Ideally, it would like to charge at least \$12 and cover all of its costs. It could at least cover *marginal* costs, however, if it charged only \$7. At that price the restaurant would be no worse or better off for having served an extra dinner. The additional cost of serving that one meal would be covered.

It must be emphasized that covering marginal cost is a *minimal* condition for supplying additional output. A restaurant that covers only marginal costs but not average total cost will lose money. It may even go out of business. This is a lesson lots of now-defunct Internet companies learned. They spent millions of dollars building telecommunications networks to produce Internet services. The *marginal* costs of producing Internet service was low, so they sold their services at low prices. Those low prices didn't bring in enough revenue to cover *fixed* costs, however, so legions of "dot.com" companies went bankrupt. As they quickly learned, you can get by just covering marginal costs. To stay in the game, however, you've got to cover average *total* costs as well. In Chapter 6 we'll examine more closely just how marginal costs considerations affect short-run supply behavior.

The Long-Run Investment Decision

The long run opens up a whole new range of options. In the *long run,* we have no lease or purchase commitments. We are free to start all over again, with whatever scale of plant and equipment we desire. ***There are no fixed costs in the long run.*** Accordingly, long-run supply decisions are more complicated. If no commitments to production facilities have been made, a

PRODUCTION AND INVESTMENT HEADLINE

Mercedes-Benz

Mercedes-Benz says it will increase production of its Alabama-built M-Class sport utility vehicle in 1999 to about 80,000, from 65,000 in 1998.

Source: Copyright 1997, USA Today. *USA Today*, December 16, 1997 p. B1. Reprinted with permission.

McDonald's Plans Expansion in China

SHANGHAI, China—McDonald's Corp. plans to step up its pace of expansion in China. . . .

McDonald's Chief Executive Jim Cantalupo said in an interview that the world's largest restaurant chain plans to open about 100 stores next year in China, and a similar number in each of the next several years. . . .

The Oak Brook, Ill., concern has invested about $700 million to set up supplier networks and transportation systems in China, and an additional $1 billion in the dining places themselves.

—Ben Dolven

Source: *Wall Street Journal*, September 8, 2003, p. A13A.

NOTE: Production decisions focus on the (short-run) use of existing facilities. Investment decisions relate to the acquisition of productive facilities.

producer must decide how large a facility to build, buy, or lease. Hence the size (scale) of plant and equipment becomes an additional option for long-term supply decisions. In a long-run (no fixed costs) situation, a firm can make the **investment decision.**

investment decision The decision to build, buy, or lease plant and equipment; to enter or exit an industry.

No Fixed Costs Note that the distinction between short- and long-run supply decisions is not based on time. The distinction instead depends on whether commitments have been made. If no leases have been signed, no construction contracts awarded, no acquisitions made, a producer still has a free hand. With no fixed costs, the producer can walk away from the potential business at a moment's notice.

Once fixed costs are incurred, the options narrow. Then the issue becomes one of making the best possible use of the assets (e.g., factory, office space, equipment) that have been acquired. Once fixed costs have been incurred, it's hard to walk away from the business at a moment's notice. The goal then becomes to make as much profit as possible from the investments already made. The accompanying Headline illustrates the distinction between these production and investment decisions. The weekly decisions of automakers about how many cars to produce is a short-run production decision. They are deciding how fully to utilize their production capacity. By contrast, McDonald's decided to *increase* its production capacity by building more outlets in China; that was an investment decision.

Economic vs. Accounting Costs

The cost concepts we have discussed here are based on *real* production relationships. The dollar costs we compute reflect underlying resource costs—the land, labor, and capital used in the production process. Not everyone counts this way. On the contrary, accountants and businesspeople often count dollar costs only and ignore any resource use that doesn't result in an explicit dollar cost.

Return to Tight Jeans for a moment to see the difference. When we computed the dollar cost of producing 15 pairs of jeans per day, we noted the following resource inputs:

Inputs	**Cost**
1 factory rent	@ $100
1 machine rent	@ 20
1 machine operator	@ 80
1.5 bolts of denim	@ 45
Total cost	$245

The total value of the resources used in the production of 15 pairs of jeans was thus $245 per day. But this economic cost need not conform to *actual* dollar costs. Suppose the owners of Tight Jeans decided to sew jeans. Then they would not have to hire a worker or pay $80 per day in wages. *Dollar* costs would drop to $165 per day. The producers and their accountant would consider this to be a remarkable achievement. They would assert that the costs of producing jeans had fallen.

Economic Cost

An economist would draw no such conclusions. ***The essential economic question is how many resources are used in production.*** This has not changed. One unit of labor is still being employed at the factory; now it's simply the owner, not a hired worker. In either case, one unit of labor is not available for the production of other goods and services. Hence society is still incurring an opportunity cost of $245 for jeans, whether the owners of Tight Jeans write checks in that amount or not. We really don't care who sews jeans—the essential point is that someone (i.e., a unit of labor) does.

The same would be true if Tight Jeans owned its own factory rather than rented it. If the factory was owned rather than rented, the owners probably would not write any rent checks. Hence accounting costs would drop by $100 per day. But society would not be saving any resources. The factory would still be in use for jeans production and therefore unavailable for the production of other goods and services. Hence the *opportunity cost* of the factory would still be $100 per day. As a result, the economic (resource) cost of producing 15 pairs of jeans would still be $245.

The distinction between an economic cost and an accounting cost is essentially one between resource and dollar costs. *Dollar cost* refers to the explicit dollar outlays made by a producer; it is the lifeblood of accountants. **Economic cost,** in contrast, refers to the dollar *value* of all resources used in the production process: it is the lifeblood of economists. The accountant's dollar costs are usually *explicit,* in the sense that someone writes a check. The economist takes into consideration *implicit* costs as well, that is, even those costs for which no direct payment is made. In other words, economists count costs as

economic cost The value of all resources used to produce a good or service: opportunity cost.

- Economic cost = explicit costs + implicit costs

As this formula suggests, ***economic and accounting costs will diverge whenever any factor of production is not paid an explicit wage (or rent, etc.).***

The Cost of Homework These distinctions between economic and accounting costs apply also to the "production" of homework. You can pay people to write term papers for you or even buy them off the Internet. At large schools you can often buy lecture notes as well. But most students end up doing their own homework, so that they will learn something and not just turn in required assignments.

Doing homework is expensive, however, even if you don't pay someone to do it. The time you spend reading this chapter is valuable. You could be doing something else if you weren't reading right now. What would you be doing? The forgone activity—the best alternative use of your time—represents the opportunity cost of doing homework. Even if you don't pay yourself for reading this chapter, you'll still incur that *economic* cost.

Economic Profit

The distinction between economic cost and accounting cost directly affects profit computations. People who supply goods and services want to make a profit from their efforts. But what exactly *is* "profit"? In economic terms, **profit** is the difference between total revenues and *total* economic costs, that is,

profit The difference between total revenue and total cost

$$\text{Profit} = \text{total revenue} - \text{total cost}$$

Economists don't rely on accountants to compute profits. Instead, they factor in not just the explicit costs that accountants keep track of, but also the implicit costs that arise when resources are used but not explicitly paid (e.g., an owner's time and capital investment). Suppose total revenue at Tight Jeans was $300 per day. With total costs of $245 per day (see foregoing cost computation), profit would be $55 per day. If the owner did her own stitching, *accounting* costs would drop by $80 and *accounting* profits would increase by the same amount. *Economic* profits would *not* change, however. By keeping track of *all* costs (implicit and explicit) economists can keep a consistent eye on profits. In the next chapter we'll see how business firms use supply decisions to maximize those profits.

POLICY PERSPECTIVES

Invest in Labor or Capital?

The U.S. labor force continues to grow by more than a million workers per year. If capital investments don't keep pace, these added workers will strain production facilities. The law of diminishing marginal productivity would push wages lower and reduce living standards. Hardly a very cheerful prospect for the next millenium.

To beat the law of diminishing marginal productivity, we have to *increase* the productivity of all workers. This means that we have to *shift* production functions upward, as shown graphically in Figure 5.5*a*.

How can we achieve such across-the-board productivity gains? There are several possibilities. One possibility is to invest in labor by increasing education and training. Better-educated workers are apt to squeeze more output from any production facility. In the world's poorest nations, one out of every two workers is illiterate (see Headline, p. 42). In those nations, even basic literacy training can boost labor productivity substantially. In the United States, most workers have at least some college education. That isn't the end of skill training, however. Skill training in classrooms and on-the-job continue to boost U.S. labor productivity. The government encourages such training with student loans, school subsidies, and training programs. In 2003, the federal government spent over $60 billion on education and state and local governments spent ten times that much.

FIGURE 5.5
Improvements in Productivity Reduce Costs

Advances in technological or managerial knowledge increase our productive capability. This is reflected in upward shifts of the production function (*a*) and downward shifts of production cost curves (*b*).

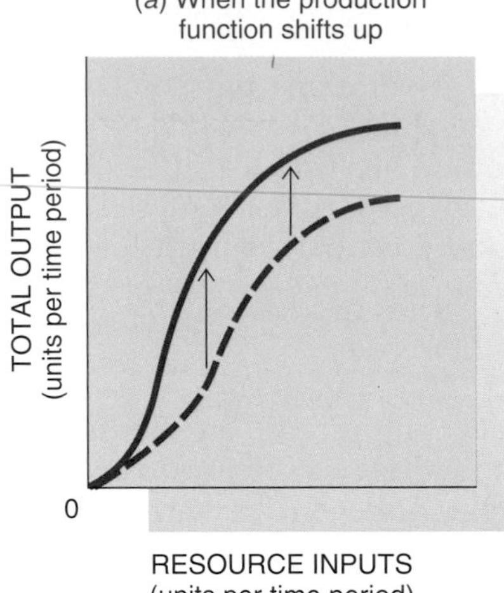

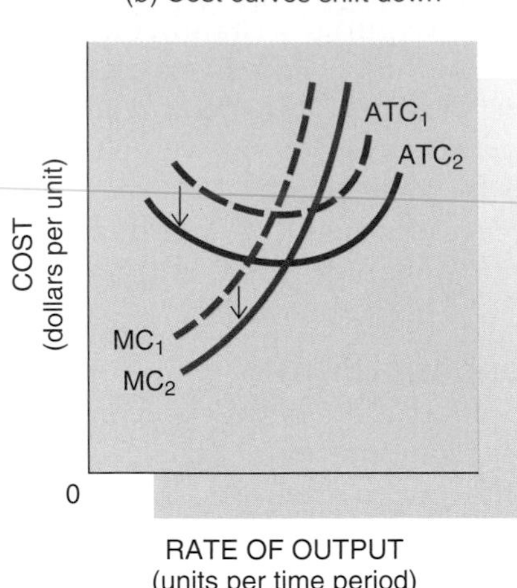

Spending on *capital* investment also boosts productivity. As we observed in Chapter 2, American workers have the productivity advantage of not just more education, but also far more capital resources in the workplace. Additional investment in capital not only adds to the stock (quantity) of resources but increases its *quality* as well. New machines, factories, and networks almost always embody the latest technology. Hence more capital investment typically results in improved technology as well, giving a double boost to production possibilities. The government can encourage such investments with targeted tax incentives.

Both human capital and nonhuman capital investments shift the production function upward, as in Figure 5.5*a*. In either case, the marginal physical product of labor rises and marginal costs fall (Figure 5.5*b*). This not only increases worker productivity, but also expands (shifts) society's production possibilities, potentially making everyone better off.

SUMMARY

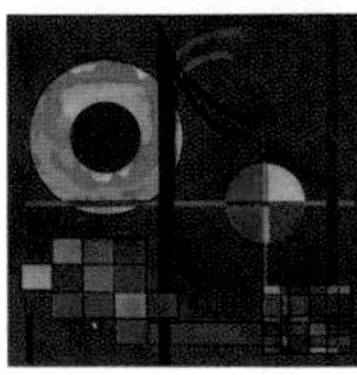

- Supply decisions are constrained by the *capacity* to produce and the *costs* of using that capacity.
- In the short run, some inputs (e.g., land and capital) are fixed in quantity. Increases in (short-run) output result from more use of variable inputs (e.g., labor).
- A production function indicates how much output can be produced from available facilities, using different amounts of variable inputs. Every point on the production function represents efficient production. Capacity output refers to the maximum quantity that can be produced from a given facility.
- Output tends to increase at a diminishing rate when more labor is employed in a given facility. Additional workers crowd existing facilities, leaving each worker with less space and machinery to work with.
- The costs of production include both fixed and variable costs. Fixed costs (e.g., space and equipment leases) are incurred even if no output is produced. Variable costs (e.g., labor and material) are incurred when plant and equipment are put to use.

- Average cost is total cost divided by the quantity produced. The ATC curve is typically U-shaped.
- Marginal cost is the increase in total cost that results when one more unit of output is produced. Marginal costs increase because of diminishing returns in production.
- The production decision is the short-run choice of how much output to produce with existing facilities. At a minimum, a producer will be willing to supply output only if price at least covers marginal cost.
- The long run is characterized by an absence of fixed costs. The investment decision entails the choice of whether to acquire fixed costs, that is, whether to build, buy, or lease plant and equipment.
- The economic costs of production include the value of *all* resources used. Accounting costs typically include only those dollar costs actually paid (explicit costs).
- Historically, advances in technology and the quality of our inputs have been the major source of productivity growth. These advances have shifted production functions up and pushed cost curves down.

Terms to Remember

Define the following terms:

supply	short run	average total cost (ATC)
factors of production	long run	marginal cost (MC)
production function	profit	production decision
marginal physical product (MPP)	total cost	investment decision
law of diminishing returns	fixed costs	economic cost
	variable costs	profit

Questions for Discussion

1. Is your school currently producing at capacity (i.e., teaching as many students as possible)? What considerations might inhibit full capacity utilization?
2. What are the production costs of your economics class? What are the fixed costs? The variable costs? What is the marginal cost of enrolling more students?
3. Suppose you set up a lawn-mowing service and recruit friends to help you. Would the law of diminishing returns apply? Explain.
4. What are the fixed costs of (*a*) a pizza shop, (*b*) an Internet service provider, (*c*) a corn farm? Which needs the highest sales volume to earn a profit?
5. Owner-operators of small gas stations rarely pay themselves an hourly wage. Does this practice reduce the economic cost of dispensing gasoline?
6. In the Headline on p. 114, why did MPP fall to zero? What was the opportunity cost of those surplus workers?
7. Why might a producer not accept a price below marginal cost?
8. What are the fixed input constraints that limit worker productivity in the typical fast-food outlet?
9. How does capital investment affect the marginal physical product of labor? Does more college education have the same kind of effect? Which is a better investment?

Problems

1. What is the marginal physical product of each successive worker in Table 5.1?
2. Compute *average* fixed costs and *average* variable costs in Figure 5.3 for all rates of output. At what rate of output
   (*a*) are average fixed costs the lowest?
   (*b*) are average variable costs the lowest?
   (*c*) is average total cost the lowest?
3. Complete the following table, then plot the marginal cost and average total cost curves on the same graph. Identify the lowest per-unit cost on the graph.

Rate of Output	Total Cost	Marginal Cost	Average Total Cost
0	$100	____	____
1	110	____	____
2	130	____	____
3	165	____	____
4	220	____	____
5	300	____	____

4. What is the value of fixed costs in the foregoing table?
5. Suppose the mythical Tight Jeans Corporation leased a *second* sewing machine, giving it the following production function:

Number of workers:	0	1	2	3	4	5	6	7	8
Quantity of output:	0	20	46	64	72	78	81	82	80

   (*a*) Graph the production function.
   (*b*) On a separate graph, illustrate marginal physical product.
   (*c*) At what level of employment does the law of diminishing returns become apparent?
   (*d*) At what level of employment does MPP become negative?
   (*e*) Why does MPP become negative?
6. Using the data in problem 3 and a wage of $10 per worker, compute the marginal cost of increasing output from 72 to 78 pairs of jeans.
7. Suppose the following data represent the total costs of production:

Units of output:	0	1	2	3	4	5	6	7	8	9
Total cost:	$20	24	29	35	42	50	59	69	80	92

   (*a*) If the firm sold 3 units at their marginal cost, what price would it receive?
   (*b*) At that price would the firm cover average total cost?
   (*c*) At what rate of output would a price equal to MC cover ATC?
8. Suppose a company incurs the following costs:

Labor	$400
Equipment	$300
Materials	$100

   It owns the building, so it doesn't have to pay the usual $800 in rent.
   (*a*) What is the total accounting cost?
   (*b*) What is the total economic cost?
   (*c*) How would accounting and economic costs change if the company sold the building and then leased it back?

Web Activities

1. Log on to www.whitehouse.gov/fsbr/employment.html and click on the link for productivity.
   (*a*) What has been the general trend for productivity in the United States since 1990?
   (*b*) What does this trend suggest has happened to production functions in the United States?
   (*c*) Assuming this change in productivity has happened to all firms, how will this change in productivity affect cost curves?
2. Log on to www.whitehouse.gov/fsbr/employment.html and click on the link for the employment cost index.
   (*a*) Are hourly employment costs a fixed or variable cost?
   (*b*) How is the average total cost curve affected by these changes in costs? In the chart you found, what has been the trend in employment costs since 2000?
   (*c*) What is the likely implication of the trend in employment cost on profits?
3. Log on to www.federalreserve.gov/releases/g17/current.
   (*a*) What is current capacity utilization rate for manufacturing in the United States?
   (*b*) If the 1972–2002 average capacity utilization rate represents the average full capacity utilization rate, what does the current utilization rate suggest about how close the manufacturing sector is to full capacity?
   (*c*) What does the current rate suggest about the ability to increase output in the short run?
4. Log on to www.msnbc.com and do a word search using "production costs." Select an article that discusses a changing cost situation faced by a firm. Discuss what the cost change means for this firm. Focus your discussion on what will happen to the firm's output level and profits.

Living Econ

Is College a Good Deal?

Even though college enrollment is a multimillion-dollar decision, many students start college without thinking about the economic consequences. You may be aware of some of the benefits. On average a college graduate earns over $1 million more during his or her lifetime than a high school graduate. (Of course the actual amount depends on your effort and career choice.)

On the cost side, tuition and books are a major expense for college students. However, Chapter 5 points out a cost that is often overlooked, the implicit cost of forgone earnings. You could have worked additional hours instead of going to school and you would have received promotions if you could dedicate more time to your job. Nonetheless, overall career earnings by most college graduates more than compensate for these forgone earnings.

You'll need to make similar computations later in life if you own a business. Remember to count the implicit cost of your own time, frequently an uncounted expense by harried businesspeople. And, when you invest in the stock market, remember to count the implicit cost of your money, meaning the interest it could have earned if you didn't use it for stock investing.

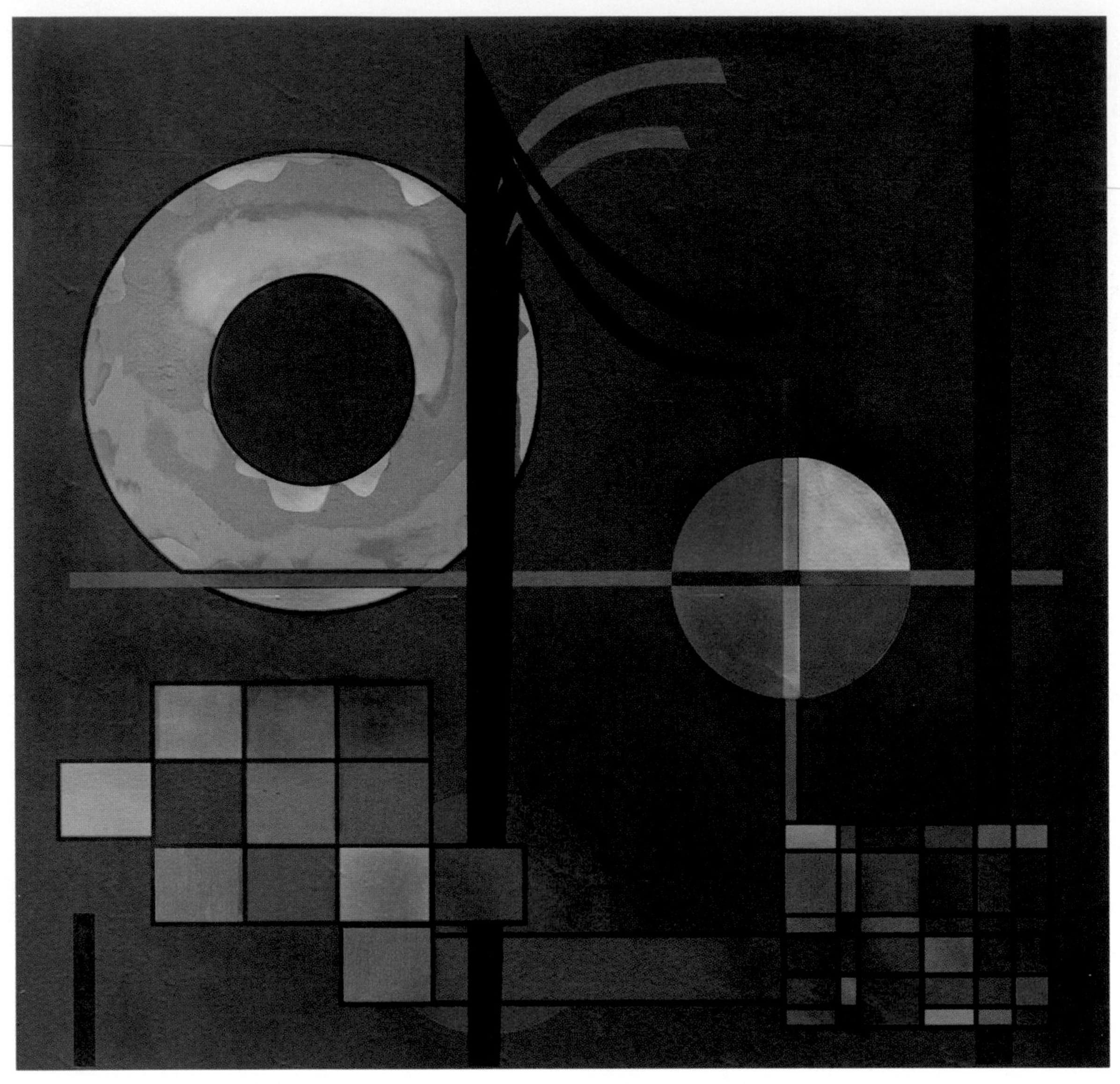

Competition

CHAPTER 6

Catfish farmers in the South are upset. During the last two decades they have invested millions of dollars in converting cotton farms into breeding ponds for catfish. They now have 150,000 acres of ponds and supply over 90 percent of the nation's catfish. Unfortunately, catfish prices have been dropping. From January 1989 to January 1992, catfish prices fell 25 percent. Prices then rose for a few years but fell again in the late 1990s and still further in 2002–03. These recurrent price declines killed any hopes the farmers had of making huge profits. Indeed, catfish prices are so low that many farmers are draining their ponds and planting crops again.

The dilemma the catfish farmers find themselves in is a familiar occurrence in competitive markets. When the profit prospects look good, everybody wants to get in on the act. As more and more firms start producing the good, however, prices and profits tumble. This helps explain why over 200,000 new firms are formed each year as well as why 50,000 others fail.

In this chapter we examine how supply decisions are made in competitive markets—markets in which all producers are relatively small. Our focus on competition centers on the following questions:

- What are the unique characteristics of competitive markets?
- How do competitive firms make supply decisions?
- How are the quantity and price of a good determined in competitive markets?

By answering these questions, we will develop more insight into supply decisions and thus the core issues of WHAT, HOW, and FOR WHOM goods and services are produced.

Market Structure

The quest for profits is the common denominator of business enterprises. But not all businesses have the same opportunity to pursue profits. Millions of firms, like the southern catfish farms, are very small and entirely at the mercy of the marketplace. A small decline in the market price of their product often spells financial ruin. Even when such firms make a profit, they must always be on the lookout for new competition, new products, or changes in technology.

Larger firms don't have to work quite so hard to maintain their standing. Huge corporations often have the power to raise prices, to change consumer tastes (through advertising), or even to prevent competitors from taking a slice of the profit pie. Such powerful firms can protect and perpetuate their profits. They are more likely to dominate markets than to be at their mercy.

market structure The number and relative size of firms in an industry.

competitive firm A firm without market power, with no ability to alter the market price of the goods it produces.

competitive market A market in which no buyer or seller has market power.

monopoly A firm that produces the entire market supply of a particular good or service.

Business firms aren't always either giants or dwarfs. Those are extremes of **market structure** that illustrate the range of power a firm might possess. Most real-world firms fall along a spectrum that stretches from the powerless to the powerful. At one end of the spectrum (Figure 6.1) we place perfectly **competitive firms**—firms that have no power over the price of goods they produce. Like the catfish farmers in the South, a perfectly competitive firm must take whatever price for its wares the market offers; it is a *price taker.* A market composed entirely of competitive firms—and without anyone dominating the demand side either—is referred to as a (perfectly) **competitive market.** ***In a perfectly competitive market, no single producer or consumer has any control over the price or quantity of the product.***

At the other end of the spectrum of market structures are monopolies. A **monopoly** is a single firm that produces the entire supply of a particular good. Despite repeated legal and technological attacks, Microsoft still has a near monopoly on computer operating systems. That position gives Microsoft the power to *set* market prices rather than simply respond to them. With nearly 75 percent of the soft drink market between them, Coke and Pepsi are a virtual duopoly (two-firm market). Together, they have the power to set prices for their beverages. All firms with such power are price *setters,* not price *takers.*

Monopolies are the extreme case of market power. In Figure 6.1 they are at the far right end of the spectrum, easily distinguished from the small, competitive firms that reside at the low (left) end of the power spectrum.

Among the 20 million or so business enterprises in the United States, there are relatively few monopolies. Local phone companies, cable TV companies, and utility firms often have a monopoly in specific geographic areas. The National Football League also has a monopoly on professional football. The

FIGURE 6.1
Market Structures

The number and relative size of firms producing a good vary across industries. Market structures range from perfect competition (a great many firms producing the same goods) to monopoly (only one firm). Most real-world firms are along the continuum of *imperfect* competition.

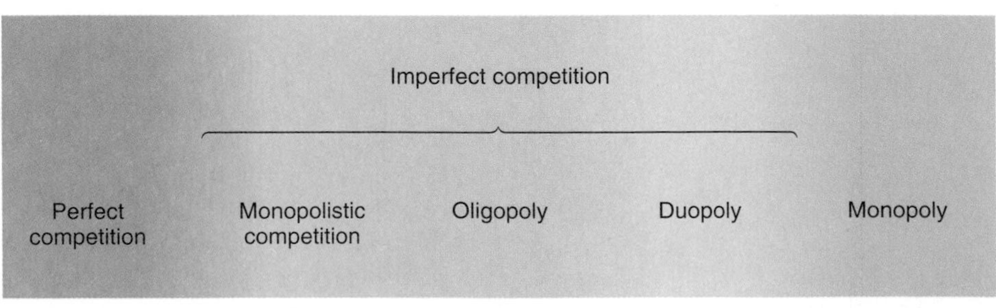

NFL owners know that if they raise ticket prices, fans won't go elsewhere to watch a football game. These situations are the exception to the rule, however. Typically, more than one firm supplies a particular product.

Consider the case of IBM. IBM is a megacorporation with over $60 billion in annual sales revenue and more than 300,000 employees. It is not a monopoly, however. Other firms produce computers that are virtually identical to IBM products. These IBM clones limit IBM's ability to set prices for its own output. In other words, other firms in the same market limit IBM's **market power.** IBM is not completely *powerless,* however, it is still large enough to have some direct influence on computer prices and output. Because it has some market power over computer prices, IBM is not a *perfectly* competitive firm.

market power The ability to alter the market price of a good or service.

Economists have created categories to distinguish the degrees of competition in product markets. These various market structures are illustrated in Figure 6.1. At one end of the spectrum is perfect competition, where lots of small firms vie for consumer purchases. At the other extreme is monopoly, where only one firm supplies a particular product.

In between the extremes of monopoly (no competition) and perfect competition lie various forms of imperfect competition, including:

- ***Duopoly:*** Only two firms supply a particular product.
- ***Oligopoly:*** A few large firms supply all or most of a particular product.
- ***Monopolistic competition:*** Many firms supply essentially the same product, but each enjoys significant brand loyalty.

How a firm is classified across this spectrum depends not only on its size, but also on how many other firms produce identical or similar products. IBM, for example, would be classified in the oligopoly category for large business computers. IBM supplies nearly 70 percent of all business computers and confronts only a few rival producers. In the personal computer market, however, IBM has a small market share (under 10 percent) and faces dozens of rivals. In that market IBM would fit into the category of monopolistic competition. Gasoline stations, fast food outlets, and even colleges are other examples of monopolistic competition: many firms are trying to rise above the crowd, to get the consumer's attention (and purchases).

Market structure has important effects on the supply of goods. How much you pay for a product depends partly on how many firms offer it for sale. This textbook would be even more expensive if other publishers weren't offering substitute goods. And long-distance telephone service didn't become inexpensive until competing firms broke AT&T's monopoly control of that market. AOL wouldn't have reduced its Internet-access prices if a throng of other service providers hadn't offered cut-rate deals. In every one of these cases, the number of firms in the market has had a significant effect on price.

The quality of the product also depends on the degree of competition in the marketplace. Why do e-mail and e-commerce features keep improving so fast? Largely because hundreds of firms are trying to gain a foothold in that marketplace. By contrast, the U.S. Department of Justice contended that the lack of effective competition allowed Microsoft to sell operating systems that were too complex and unwieldy for the typical computer user. With more firms in the market, consumers would have gotten a *better* product at a *lower* price.

In this chapter we focus on only one market structure, namely perfect competition. Our goal is to see how perfectly competitive firms make supply decisions. In the next chapter we will contrast *monopoly* behavior with this model of perfect competition.

Perfect Competition

It's not easy to visualize a perfectly competitive firm. None of the corporations you could name are likely to fit the model of perfect competition. Perfectly competitive firms are pretty much faceless. They have no brand image, no real market recognition.

No Market Power

The critical factor in perfect competition is the total absence of market power for individual firms. ***A perfectly competitive firm is one whose output is so small in relation to market volume that its output decisions have no perceptible impact on price.*** A competitive firm can sell all its output at the prevailing market price. If it tries to charge a higher price, it will not sell anything, because consumers will shop elsewhere. In this sense, a perfectly competitive firm has no *market power*—no ability to control the market price for the good it sells.

At first glance, it might appear that all firms have market power. After all, who is to stop a producer from raising prices? The critical concept here, however, is *market* price; that is, the price at which goods are actually sold. You might want to resell this textbook for $50. But you will discover that the bookstore will not buy it at that price. Anyone can change the *asking* price of a good, but actual sales will occur only at the market price. With so many other students offering to sell their books, the bookstore knows it does not have to pay the $50 you are asking. Because you do not have any market power, you have to accept the "going price" for used texts if you want to sell this book.

The same kind of powerlessness is characteristic of the small catfish farmer. Like any producer, the lone catfish farmer can increase or reduce his rate of output. But this production decision will not affect the market price of catfish.

Even a larger farmer who can alter a harvest by as much as 100,000 pounds of fish per year will not influence the market price of catfish. Why not? Because over 600 million pounds of catfish are brought to market every year, and another 100,000 pounds simply isn't going to be noticed. In other words, ***the output of the lone farmer is so small relative to the market supply that it has no significant effect on the total quantity or price in the market.***

One can visualize the difference between competitive firms and firms with market power by considering what would happen to U.S. catfish supplies and prices if one of Farmer Hollingsworth's ponds ran out of oxygen and his 100,000 catfish died (see Headline). Then contrast this with the likely consequences for U.S. auto supplies and prices if the Ford Motor Company were to close down suddenly. The one event would go unnoticed by the public; the impact of the other would be dramatic.

The same kind of contrast is evident when a firm's output is increased. Were Farmer Hollingsworth to double his production capacity (build another 10 ponds), the added catfish output would not show up in commerce statistics. U.S. catfish production is calibrated in the hundreds of millions of pounds, and no one is going to notice another 100,000 fish. Were Ford, on the other hand, to double its production, the added output would not only be noted but would tend to depress automobile prices as Ford tried to unload its heavy inventories.

Price Takers

The critical distinction between Ford and Farmer Hollingsworth is not in their motivation but in their ability to alter market outcomes. Both are out to make a buck. What makes Farmer Hollingsworth's situation different is the fact that his output decisions do not influence catfish prices. All catfish look alike, so Farmer Hollingsworth's catfish will fetch the same price as everyone else's

COMPETITIVE MARKETS HEADLINE

Southern Farmers Hooked on New Cash Crop

Catfish are replacing crops and dairy farming as a cash industry in much of the South, particularly in Mississippi's Delta region, where 80 percent of farm-bred catfish are grown.

Production has skyrocketed in the USA from 16 million pounds in 1975 to an expected 340 million pounds this year.

The business is growing among farmers in Alabama, Arkansas, and Louisiana.

Catfish farming is similar to other agriculture, experts say. One thing is the same: It takes money to get started.

"If you have a good row-crop farmer, you have a good catfish farmer," says James Hoffman of Farm Fresh Catfish Co. in Hollandale, Miss. "But you can't take a poor row-crop farmer and make him a good catfish farmer."

Greensboro, Ala., catfish farmer Steve Hollingsworth says he spends $18,000 a week on feed for the 1 million catfish in his ponds.

"Each of the ponds has about 100,000 fish," he says. "You get about 60 cents per fish, so that's about $60,000."

The investment can be lost very quickly "if something's wrong in that pond," like an inadequate oxygen level, Hollingsworth says.

"You can be 15 minutes too late getting here, and all your fish are gone," he says.

—Mark Mayfield

Source: Copyright 1989, USA Today. *USA Today*, December 5, 1989, p. 3A. Reprinted with permission.

NOTE: In competitive markets, new firms enter quickly when profitable opportunities exist. As a result of such entry, profits often don't last long.

catfish. Were he to attempt to enlarge his profits by raising his catfish prices above market levels, he would find himself without customers, because consumers would go elsewhere to buy their catfish. To maximize his profits. Farmer Hollingsworth can only strive to run an efficient operation and to make the right supply decisions. He is a *price taker,* taking the market price of catfish as a fact of life and doing the best he can within that constraint.

Ford Motor Company, on the other hand, can behave like a *price setter.* Instead of waiting to find out what the market price is and making appropriate output adjustments, Ford has the discretion to announce prices at the beginning of every model year. Fords are not exactly like Chevrolets or Toyotas in the minds of consumers. Because Fords are *differentiated,* Ford knows that sales will not fall to zero if its car prices are set a little higher than those of other car manufacturers. Ford confronts a downward-sloping rather than a perfectly horizontal demand curve for its output.

Market Demand vs. Firm Demand

To appreciate the unique nature of perfect competition, ***you must distinguish between the market demand curve and the demand curve confronting a particular firm.*** Farmer Hollingsworth's small operation does not contradict the law of demand. The quantity of catfish purchased in the supermarket still depends on catfish prices. That is to say, the *market* demand curve for catfish is downward-sloping, just as the market demand for cars is downward-sloping.

But the demand curve facing Farmer Hollingsworth has a unique shape: it is *horizontal.* Remember, if he charges a price above the prevailing market, he will lose *all* his customers. So a higher price results in quantity demanded falling to zero. On the other hand, he can double or triple his output and still sell every fish he produces at the prevailing market price. As a result, ***the demand curve facing a perfectly competitive firm is horizontal.*** Farmer Hollingsworth himself faces a horizontal demand curve because his share of

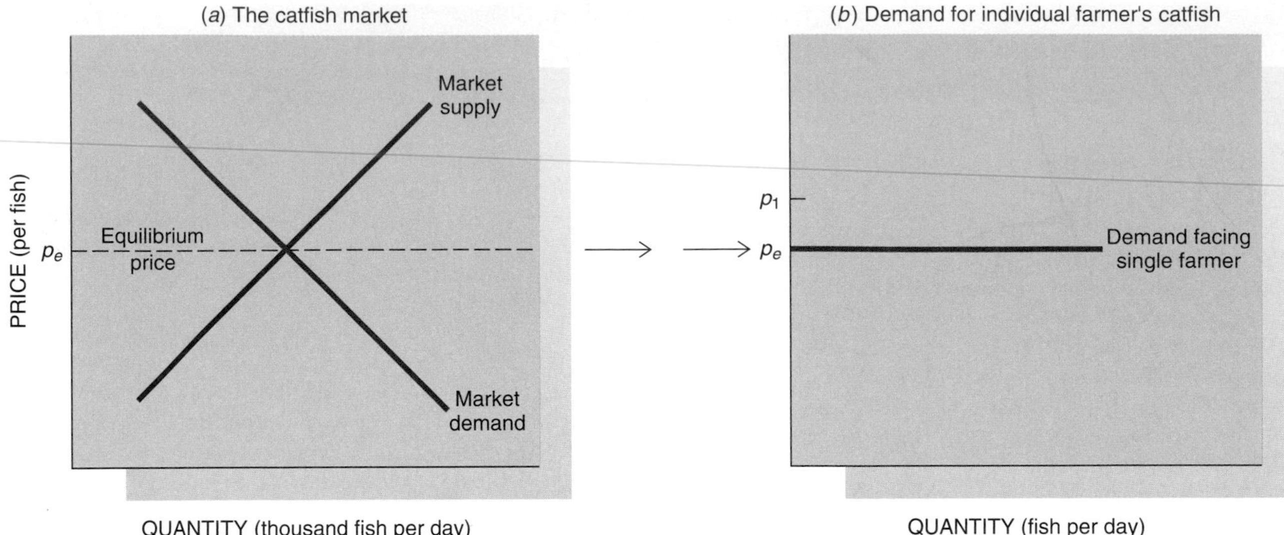

FIGURE 6.2 Market vs. Firm Demand

The *market* demand for any product is downward-sloping. The equilibrium price (p_e) of catfish is established by the intersection of *market demand* and *market supply* in the graph on the left.

This market-established price is the only one at which an individual farmer can sell catfish. If the farmer asks a higher price (e.g., p_1), no one will buy the catfish, since they can buy identical catfish from other farmers at p_e. But a farmer can sell all of his catfish at the equilibrium price. The lone farmer thus confronts a horizontal demand curve for his own output. (Notice the difference in quantities on the horizontal axes of the two graphs.)

the market is so infinitesimal that changes in his output do not disturb the market equilibrium.

Collectively, though, individual farmers do count. If 10,000 small, competitive farmers expand their catfish production at the same time, the market equilibrium will be disturbed. That is to say, a competitive market composed of 10,000 individually powerless producers still sees a lot of action. The power here resides in the collective action of all the producers, however, and not in the individual action of any one. Were catfish production to increase so abruptly, the catfish could be sold only at lower prices, in accordance with the downward-sloping nature of the *market* demand curve.

The distinction between the actions of a single producer and those of the market are illustrated in Figure 6.2. Notice that

- ***The market demand curve for a product is always downward-sloping.***
- ***The demand curve facing a perfectly competitive firm is horizontal.***

That horizontal demand curve is the distinguishing feature of *perfectly* competitive firms. If a firm can raise its price without losing *all* its customers, it is not a perfectly competitive firm. (Does McDonald's meet this condition? United Airlines? AOL? Your college?)

The Firm's Production Decision

Because a competitive firm is a price taker, it doesn't have to worry about what price to charge: Everything it produces will be sold at the prevailing *market* price. It still has an important decision to make, however. The competitive firm must decide *how much* output to sell at the going price.

Choosing a rate of output is a firm's **production decision.** Should it produce all the output it can? Or should it produce at less than its capacity output?

production decision The selection of the short-run rate of output (with existing plant and equipment).

Output and Revenues

If a competitive firm produces more output, its sales revenue will definitely increase. **Total revenue** is the price of the good multiplied by the quantity sold:

total revenue The price of a product multiplied by the quantity sold in a given time period, p × q.

- Total revenue = price × quantity

Since a competitive firm can sell all of its output at the market price, total revenue is a simple multiple of that price.

Revenues vs. Profits

If a competitive firm wanted to maximize total revenue, its strategy would be obvious: it would simply produce as much output as possible. But maximizing total revenue isn't the goal. Business firms try to maximize total *profits,* not total *revenue.*

As we saw in Chapter 5, total **profit** is the *difference* between total revenues and total costs. Hence a profit-maximizing firm must look not only at revenues but at costs as well. As output increases, total revenues go up, but profits may not. If costs rise too fast, profits may actually decline as output increases. This is a situation to be avoided.

profit The difference between total revenue and total cost.

We may embark on the search for maximizing profits with two clues:

- ***Maximizing output or revenue is not the way to maximize profits.***
- ***Total profits depend on how both revenues and costs increase as output expands.***

With these clues, we may narrow the scope of our search for the profit maximizing rate of output.

Profit Maximization

We can advance still further toward the goal of maximum profits by employing a rather primitive but quite practical maxim. This third clue tells us to produce an additional unit of output only if that unit brings in more revenue than it costs. A producer who follows this clue will move steadily closer to maximum profits. We shall explain this clue by looking first at the revenue side of production (what it brings in), then at the cost side (what it costs).

Price

For a perfectly competitive firm, it is easy to determine how much revenue a unit of output will bring in. All we have to look at is price. ***Since competitive firms are price takers, they must take whatever price the market has put on their products.*** Thus a catfish farmer can readily determine the value of the fish by looking at the market price of catfish.

Marginal Cost

Once we know what one more unit brings in (its price); all we need to know for profit maximization is the cost of producing an additional unit.

The production process for catfish farming is fairly straightforward. The "factory" in this case is a pond; the rate of production is the number of fish harvested from the pond per hour. A farmer can alter the rate of production at will, up to the breeding capacity of the pond.

Assume that the *fixed* cost of the pond is $10 per hour. The fixed costs include the rental value of the pond and the cost of electricity for keeping the pond oxygenated so the fish can breathe. These fixed costs must be paid no matter how many fish the farmer harvests.

To harvest catfish from the pond, the farmer must incur additional costs. Labor is needed to net and sort the fish. The cost of labor is *variable,* depending on how much output the farmer decides to produce. If no fish are harvested, no variable costs are incurred.

marginal cost (MC) The increase in total costs associated with a one-unit increase in production.

The **marginal costs** of harvesting refer to the additional costs incurred to harvest *one* more basket of fish. Generally, marginal costs rise as the rate of production increases. The law of diminishing returns we encountered in Chapter 5 applies to catfish farming as well. As more labor, is hired, each worker has less space (pond area) and capital (access to nets, sorting trays) to work with. Accordingly, it takes a little more labor time (marginal cost) to harvest each additional fish.

Figure 6.3 illustrates these marginal costs. The unit of production used here is baskets of fish per hour. Notice how the MC rises as the rate of output increases. At the output rate of 4 baskets per hour (point *E*), marginal cost is $13. Hence the fourth basket increases total costs by $13. The fifth basket is even more expensive, with a marginal cost of $17.

FIGURE 6.3
The Costs of Catfish Production

Marginal cost is the cost of producing one more unit. When production expands from 2 to 3 units per day, total costs increase by $9 (from $22 to $31 per day). The marginal cost of the third basket is therefore $9, as seen in row *D* of the table and point *D* in the graph.

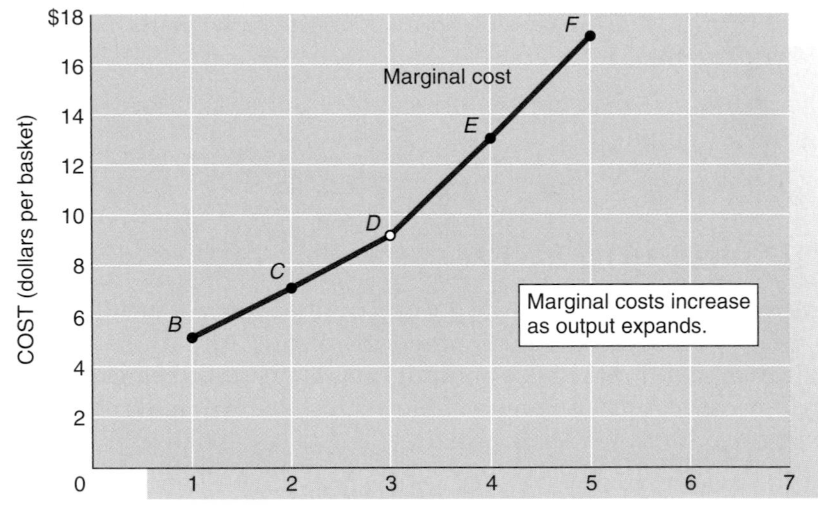

	Rate of Output (baskets per hour)	Total Cost (per hour)	Marginal Cost (per unit)	Average Total Cost (per unit)
A	0	$10	—	—
B	1	15	$ 5	$15.00
C	2	22	7	11.00
D	3	31	9	10.33
E	4	44	13	11.00
F	5	61	17	12.20

Profit-Maximizing Rate of Output

We are now in a position to make a production decision. The rule about never producing anything that costs more than it brings in boils down to a comparison of *price* and *marginal cost*. We do not want to produce an additional unit of output if its MC exceeds its price. If MC exceeds price, we are spending more to produce that extra unit than we are getting back: total profits will decline if we produce it.

The opposite is true when price exceeds MC. If an extra unit brings in more revenue than it costs to produce, it is adding to total profit. Total profits must increase in this case. Hence ***a competitive firm wants to expand the rate of production whenever price exceeds MC.***

Since we want to expand output when price exceeds MC and contract output if price is less than MC, the profit-maximizing rate of output is easily found. ***Short-run profits are maximized at the rate of output where price equals marginal cost.*** The **competitive profit-maximization rule** is summarized in Table 6.1.

Figure 6.4 illustrates the application of our profit-maximization rule in the production of catfish. The prevailing price of catfish is $13 a basket. At this price we can sell all the fish we produce, up to our short-run capacity. The fish cannot be sold at a higher price, because lots of farmers grow fish and sell them for $13. If we try to charge a higher price, consumers will buy their fish from these other producers. Hence the demand curve facing this one firm is horizontal at the price of $13 a basket.

Fish production is most profitable when MC = p.

Photo by Lou Manna/Courtesy of the Catfish Institute

The costs of harvesting catfish were already examined in Figure 6.3. The key concept illustrated here is marginal cost. The MC curve slopes upward.

competitive profit-maximization rule Produce at that rate of output where price equals marginal cost.

Decision when p > MC Also depicted in Figure 6.4 are the total revenues, costs, and profits of alternative production rates. Study the table first. Notice that the firm loses $10 per hour if it produces no fish (row *A*). At zero output, total revenue is zero ($p \times q = 0$). However, the firm must still contend with fixed costs of $10 per hour. Total profit—total revenue minus total cost—is therefore *minus* $10; the firm incurs a loss.

Row *B* of the table shows how this loss is reduced when 1 basket of fish is produced per hour. The production and sale of 1 basket per hour brings in $13 of total revenue (column 3). The total cost of producing 1 basket per hour is $15 (column 4). Hence the total loss associated with an output rate of 1 basket per hour is $2 (column 5). This may not be what

TABLE 6.1
Short-Run Decision Rules for a Competitive Firm

The relationship between price and marginal cost dictates short-run production decisions. For competitive firms, profits are maximized at that rate of output where price = MC.

Price Level	Production Decision
Price > MC	Increase output rate
Price = MC	Maintain output rate (profits maximized)
Price < MC	Decrease output rate

FIGURE 6.4
Maximization of Profits for a Competitive Firm

A competitive firm maximizes total profits at the output rate where MC = *p*. If MC is less than price, the firm can increase profits by producing more. If MC exceeds price, the firm should reduce output. In this case, profit maximization occurs at an output of 4 baskets of fish per hour.

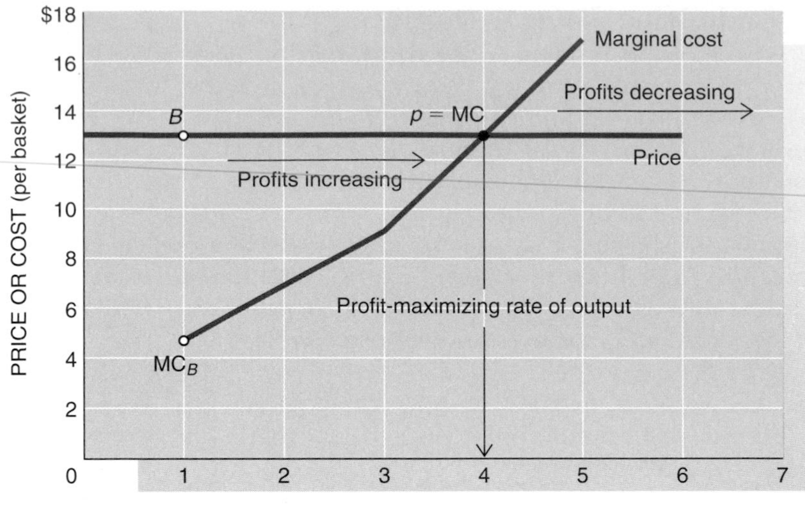

	(1) Number of Baskets (per hour)	(2) Price	(3) Total Revenue	(4) Total Cost	(5) Total Profit	(6) Price	(7) Marginal Cost
A	0	—	0	$10.00	−$10.00	—	—
B	1	$13.00	$13.00	15.00	− 2.00	$13.00	$5.00
C	2	13.00	26.00	22.00	+ 4.00	13.00	7.00
D	3	13.00	39.00	31.00	+ 8.00	13.00	9.00
E	4	13.00	52.00	44.00	+ 8.00	13.00	13.00
F	5	13.00	65.00	61.00	+ 4.00	13.00	17.00

we hoped for, but it is certainly better than the $10 loss incurred at zero output.

The superiority of producing 1 basket per hour rather than none is also evident in columns 6 and 7 of row *B*. The first basket produced fetches a price of $13. Its *marginal cost* is only $5. Hence it brings in more added revenue than it costs to produce. Under these circumstances—whenever price exceeds MC—output should definitely be expanded. That is one of the decision rules summarized in Table 6.1.

The excess of price over MC for the first unit of output is also illustrated by the graph in Figure 6.4. Point *B* ($13) lies above MC$_B$ ($5); the *difference* between these two points measures the contribution that the first basket of fish makes to the total profits of the firm. In this case, that contribution equals $13 − $5 = $8, and production losses are reduced by that amount when the rate of output is increased from zero 1 basket per hour.

So long as price exceeds MC, further increases in the rate of output are desirable. Notice what happens to profits when the rate of output is increased from 1 to 2 baskets per hour (row *C*). The price of the second basket is $13; its MC is $7. Therefore it *adds* $6 to total profits. Instead of losing $2 per hour, the firm is now making a profit of $4 per hour.

The firm can make even more profits by expanding the rate of output further. Look what happens when the rate of output reaches 3 baskets per hour (row *D* of the table). The price of the third basket is $13; its marginal cost is $9. Therefore the third basket makes a $4 contribution to profits. By increasing its rate of output to 3 baskets per hour, the firm doubles its total profits.

This firm will never make huge profits. The fourth unit of output has a price of \$13 and a MC of \$13 as well. It does not contribute to total profits, nor does it subtract from them. The fourth unit of output represents the highest rate of output the firm desires. ***At the rate of output where price = MC, total profits of the firm are maximized.***

Decision when p < MC Notice what happens if we expand output beyond 4 baskets per hour. The price of the fifth basket is still \$13; its MC is \$17. The fifth basket costs more than it brings in. If we produce that fifth basket, total profit will decline by \$4. The fifth unit of output makes us worse off. This eventuality is evident in the graph of Figure 6.4: at the output rate of 5 baskets per hours, the MC curve lies above the price curve. The lesson here is clear: ***output should not be increased if MC exceeds price.***

Maximum Profit at p = MC The outcome of the production decision is illustrated in Figure 6.4 by the intersection of the price and MC curves. At this intersection, price equals MC and profits are maximized. If we produced less, we would be giving up potential profits. If we produced more, total profits would also fall. Hence, the point where MC = p is the limit to profit-maximization.

Total Profit

To reach the right production decision, we need only compare price and marginal costs. Having found the desired rate of output, however, we may want to take a closer look at the profits we are accumulating. We could, of course, content ourselves with the statistics in the table of Figure 6.4. But a picture would be nice, too, especially if it reflected our success in production. Figure 6.5 provides such a picture.

Figure 6.5 takes advantage of the fact that total profit can be computed in one of two ways:

- Total profit = total revenue − total cost

or as,

- Total profit = average profit × quantity sold
(profit per unit)

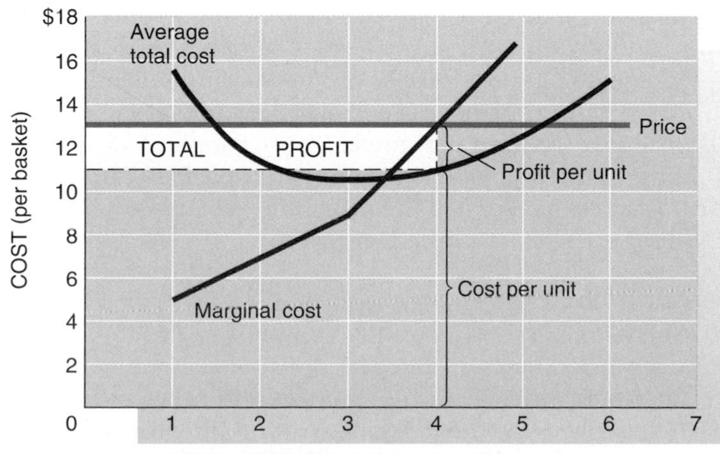

FIGURE 6.5
Illustrating Total Profit

Total profits can be computed as profit *per unit* (p − ATC) multiplied by the quantity sold. This is illustrated by the shaded rectangle. To find the profit-maximizing rate of output, we could use this graph or just the MC and price curves of Figure 6.4.

In Figure 6.5 the focus is on the second formula. To use it, we compute profit per unit as price *minus* average total cost—that is

- Profit per unit = p − ATC

The price of catfish is illustrated in Figure 6.5 by the horizontal price line at \$13. The average cost of producing catfish is illustrated by the ATC curve. Like the ATC curve we encountered in Chapter 5, this one has a U shape. Therefore, the *difference* between price and average cost—profit per unit—is illustrated by the vertical distance between the price and ATC curves. At 4 baskets of fish per hour, for example, profit per unit equals \$13 − \$11 = \$2.

To compute *total* profits, we note that

- Total profit = profit per unit × quantity
  = (p − ATC) × q
  = (\$13 − \$11) × 4

In this case, the *total* profit would be \$8 per hour. *Total* profits are illustrated in Figure 6.5 by the shaded rectangle. (Recall that the area of a rectangle is equal to its height [profit per unit] multiplied by its width [quantity sold].)

Profit per unit is not only used to compute total profits but is often of interest in its own right. Businesspeople like to cite statistics on markups, which are a crude index to per-unit profits. However, ***the profit-maximizing producer never seeks to maximize per-unit profits.*** What counts is *total* profits, not the amount of profit per unit. This is the age-old problem of trying to sell ice cream for \$5 a cone. You might be able to maximize profit per unit if you could sell 1 cone for \$5, but you would make a lot more money if you sold 100 cones at a per-unit profit of only 50 cents each.

Similarly, ***the profit-maximizing producer has no particular desire to produce at that rate of output where ATC is at a minimum.*** Minimum ATC does represent least-cost production. But additional units of output, even though they raise average costs, will increase total profits. This is evident in Figure 6.5: price exceeds MC for some output to the right of minimum ATC (the bottom of the U). Therefore, total profits are increasing as we increase the rate of output beyond the point of minimum average costs. ***Total profits are maximized only where p = MC.***

Supply Behavior

Right about now you may be wondering why we're memorizing formulas for profit maximization. Our interest in these formulas stems from our concern about supply behavior. If we don't know how firms make production decisions, we'll never figure out how the market establishes prices and quantities for the products we desire. Knowledge of supply decisions can also be valuable if you are purchasing a car, a vacation package, or even something in an electronic auction. What we're learning here is how much of a good sellers are willing to offer at any given price.

A Firm's Supply

supply The ability and willingness to sell (produce) specific quantities of a good at alternative prices in a given time period, ceteris paribus.

The most distinctive feature of perfectly competitive firms is the lack of pricing decisions. As price takers, the only decision competitive firms make is how much output to produce at the prevailing market price. Their **supply** behavior is determined by the rules for profit maximization. Specifically, ***competitive firms adjust the quantity supplied until MC = price.***

Suppose the price of catfish was only $9 per basket instead of $13. Would it still make sense to harvest 4 baskets per hour? No. Four baskets is the profit-maximizing rate of output only when the price of catfish is $13. At a price of $9 a basket, it would not make sense to produce 4 baskets, since the MC of the fourth basket ($13) would exceed its price. The decision rule (Table 6.1) in this case requires a cutback in output. At a market price of $9, the most profitable rate of output would be only 3 baskets of fish per hour (see Figure 6.4).

The marginal cost curve thus tells us how much output a firm will supply at different prices. Once we know the price of catfish, we can look at the MC curve to determine exactly how many fish Farmer Hollingsworth will harvest. In other words, ***the marginal cost curve is the short-run supply curve for a competitive firm.***

Supply Shifts Since marginal costs determine the supply decisions of a firm, anything that alters marginal cost will change supply behavior. The most important influences on marginal cost (and supply behavior) are

- ***The price of factor inputs***
- ***Technology***
- ***Expectations***

A catfish farmer will supply more fish at any given price if the price of feed declines. If fish can be bred faster because of advances in genetic engineering, productivity will increase and the farmer's MC curve will shift downward. With lower marginal costs, the firm will supply more output at any given price.

Conversely, if wages increased, the marginal cost of producing fish would rise as well. This upward shift of the MC curve would cause the firm to supply fewer fish at any prevailing price. Finally, if producers expect factor prices to rise or demand to diminish, they may be more willing to supply output now.

You can put the concept of marginal cost pricing to use the next time you buy a car. The car dealer wants to get a price that covers all costs, including a share of the rent, electricity, and insurance (fixed costs). The dealer might, however, be willing to sell the car for only its *marginal* cost—that is, the wholesale price paid for the car plus a little labor time (variable costs). So long as the price exceeds marginal cost, the dealer is better off selling the car than not selling it.

Market Supply

Up until now we have focused on the supply behavior of a single competitive firm. But what about the **market supply** of catfish? We need a *market* supply curve to determine the *market* price the individual farmer will confront. In the previous discussion, we simply picked a price arbitrarily, at $13 per basket. Now our objective is to find out where that market price comes from.

market supply The total quantities of a good that sellers are willing and able to sell at alternative prices in a given time period, ceteris paribus.

Like the market supply curves we first encountered in Chapter 3, the market supply of catfish is obtained by simple addition. All we have to do is add up the quantities each farmer stands ready to supply at each and every price. Then we will know the total number of fish to be supplied to the market at that price. Figure 6.6 illustrates this summation. Notice that ***the market supply curve is the sum of the marginal cost curves of all the firms.*** Hence whatever determines the marginal cost of a typical firm will also determine industry supply. Specifically, the ***market supply of a competitive industry is determined by***

- ***The price of factor inputs***
- ***Technology***
- ***Expectations***
- ***The number of firms in the industry***

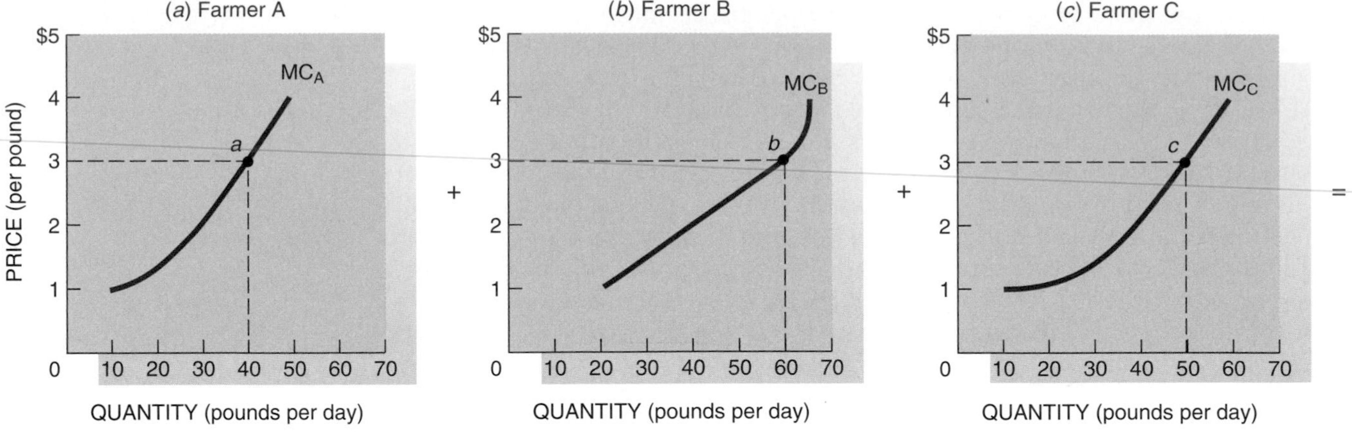

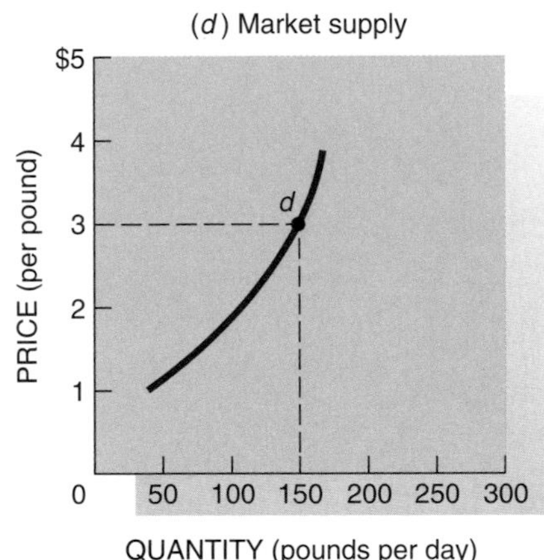

FIGURE 6.6 Competitive Market Supply

The MC curve is a competitive firm's short-run supply curve. The curve MC_A tells us that Farmer A will produce 40 pounds of catfish per day if the market price is $3 per pound.

To determine the *market supply,* we add up the quantities supplied by each farmer. The total quantity supplied to the market here is 150 pounds per day (= $a + b + c$). Market supply depends on the number of firms in an industry and their respective marginal costs.

Industry Entry and Exit

equilibrium price The price at which the quantity of a good demanded in a given time period equals the quantity supplied.

With a market supply curve and a market demand curve, we can readily identify the **equilibrium price**—that is, the price that matches the quantity demanded to the quantity supplied. This equilibrium is shown as E_1 in Figure 6.7.

If truth be told, locating a market's equilibrium is neither difficult nor terribly interesting. Certainly not in competitive markets. In competitive markets, the real action is in *changes* to market equilibrium. In competitive markets, new firms are always beating down the door, trying to get a share of industry profits. Entrepreneurs are always looking for ways to improve products or the production process. Nothing stays in equilibrium very long. Hence, to understand how competitive markets really work we have to focus on *changes* in equilibrium rather than on the identification of a static equilibrium. One of the forces driving those changes is the entry of new firms into an industry.

Entry

Suppose that the equilibrium price in the catfish industry is $13. This short-run equilibrium is illustrated in Figure 6.7 by the point E_1 at the intersection of market demand and the market supply curve S_1. At that price, the typical catfish farmer would harvest 4 baskets of fish per hour and earn a profit of $8 per hour (as seen earlier in Figure 6.5). All the farmers together would be producing the quantity q_1 in Figure 6.7.

The profitable equilibrium at E_1 is not likely to last, however. Farmers still growing cotton or other crops will see the profits being made by catfish

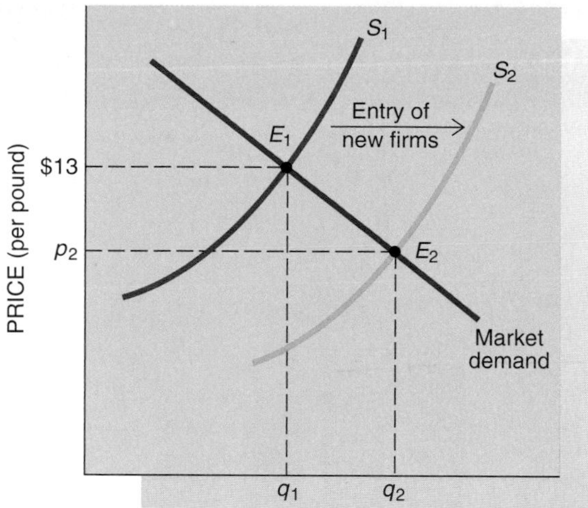

FIGURE 6.7
Market Entry
If more firms enter an industry, the market supply curve (S_1) shifts to the right (S_2). This creates a new equilibrium (E_2), where output is higher (q_2) and price is lower (p_2).

farmers and lust after them. They, too, will want to dig up their crops and replace them with catfish ponds. This is a serious problem for the catfish farmers in the South. It is fairly inexpensive to get into the catfish business. You can start with a pond, some breeding stock, and relatively little capital equipment. Accordingly, when catfish prices are high, lots of cotton farmers are ready and willing to bulldoze a couple of ponds and get into the catfish business. The entry of more farmers into the catfish industry increases the market supply and drives down catfish prices.

The impact of market entry on market outcomes is illustrated in Figure 6.7. The initial equilibrium at E_1 was determined by the supply behavior of existing producers. If those producers are earning a profit, however, other firms will want to enter the industry. When they do, the industry supply curve shifts to the right (S_2). This entry-induced shift of the market supply curve changes market equilibrium. A new equilibrium is established at E_2. At E_2, the quantity supplied is larger and the price is lower than at the initial equilibrium E_1. Hence ***industry output increases and price falls when firms enter an industry.*** This is the kind of competitive behavior that has made cell phone calls so cheap (see the following Headline).

Tendency toward Zero Economic Profits

Whether or not more cotton farmers enter the catfish industry depends on their expectations for profit. If catfish farming looks more profitable than cotton, more farmers will flood their cotton fields. As they do, the market supply curve will continue shifting to the right, driving catfish prices down.

How far can catfish prices fall? *The force that drives catfish prices down is market entry.* ***New firms continue to enter a competitive industry so long as profits exist.*** Hence the price of catfish will continue to fall until all economic profits disappear.

Notice in Figure 6.8 where this occurs. When price drops from p_1 to p_2, the typical firm reduces its output from q_1 to q_2. At the price p_2, however, the firm is still making a profit, since price exceeds average cost at the output q_2. This profit is illustrated by the colored rectangle that appears in Figure 6.8*b*.

The persistence of profits lures still more firms into the industry. As they enter the industry, the market price of fish will be pushed ever lower (Figure 6.8*a*). When the price falls to p_3, the most profitable rate of output will be q_3 (where MC = p). But at that level, price no longer exceeds average

HEADLINE ENTRY AND PRICE

Cheaper Wireless Talk

Cheaper digital networks and more competition are expected to cut the cost of wireless phone use. Per-minute average cost in the next few years:

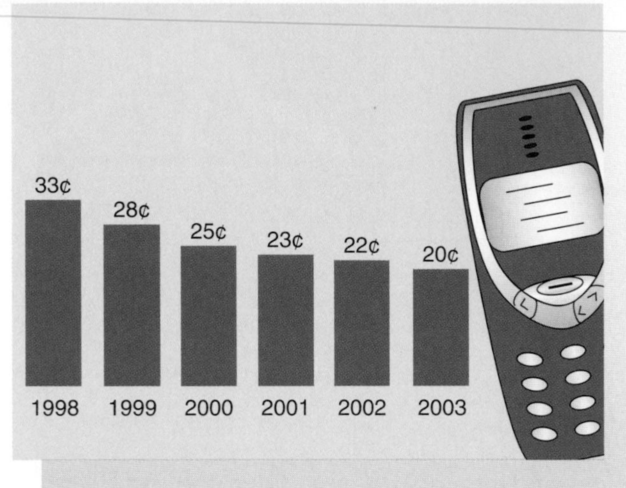

Source: *USA Today*, January 28, 1999, p. B1.

NOTE: When more firms enter an industry, the market supply increases (shifts right) and price declines.

cost. ***Once price falls to the level of minimum average cost, all economic profits disappear.*** This zero-profit outcome occurs at the bottom of the U-shaped ATC curve.

When economic profits vanish, market entry ceases. No more cotton farmers will switch to catfish farming once the price of catfish falls to the level of minimum average total cost.

Exit

In the short run, catfish prices might actually fall *below* average total cost. This is what happened in 2002–03 when Vietnamese catfish exports to the United States soared from 575,000 pounds in 1998 to over 20 *million* pounds in 2002 (see Headline). The resultant shift of market supply pushed prices so low that many U.S. catfish farmers incurred an economic *loss* (p < ATC).

Suddenly, fields of cotton looked a lot more enticing than ponds full of fish. Before long, some catfish farmers started filling in their ponds and planting cotton again. As they exited the catfish industry, the market supply curve shifted to the left and catfish prices rose a bit. Eventually, price will rise to the level of average total costs, at which point further exits will cease. Once entry and exit cease, the market price will stabilize.

Equilibrium

The lesson to be learned from catfish farming is straightforward:

- ***The existence of profits in a competitive industry induces entry.***
- ***The existence of losses in a competitive industry induces exits.***

Accordingly, we can anticipate that prices in a competitive market will continue to adjust until all entry and exit cease. At that point, the market will be in equilibrium. ***In long-run competitive market equilibrium***

- ***Price equals minimum average total cost.***
- ***Economic profit is eliminated.***

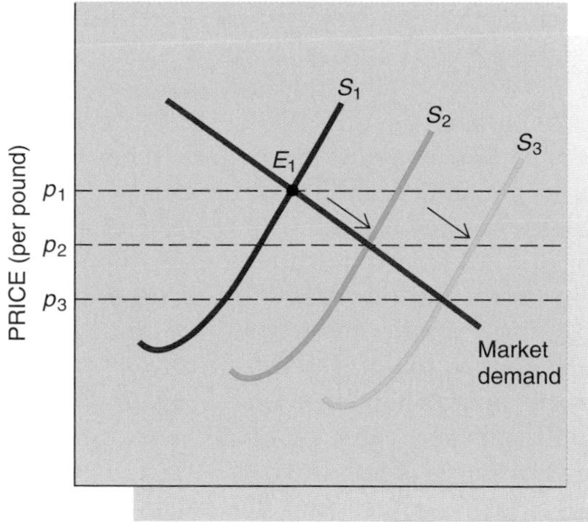

(b) Reduces profits of competitive firm

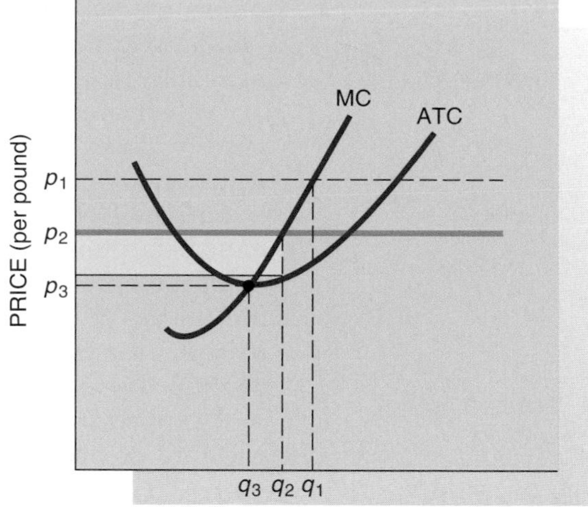

FIGURE 6.8 The Lure of Profits

If economic profits exist in an industry, more firms will want to enter it. As they do, the market supply curve will shift to the right and cause a drop in the market price (*left graph*). The lower market price, in turn, will reduce the output and profits of the typical firm (*right graph*). Once the market price is driven down to p_3, all profits disappear and entry ceases.

Catfish farmers would be happier, of course, if the price of catfish did not decline to the point where economic profits disappeared. But how are they going to prevent it? Farmer Hollingsworth knows all about the law of demand and would like to get his fellow farmers to slow production a little before all the profits disappear. But Farmer Hollingsworth is powerless to stop the forces of a competitive market. He cannot afford to reduce his own catfish production. Nobody would notice the resulting drop in market supplies, and catfish prices would continue to slide. The only one affected would be Farmer Hollingsworth, who would be denying himself the opportunity to

ENTRY AND EXIT HEADLINE

Whiskered Catfish Stir a New Trade Controversy

A Southern fishery, battered by imports, fights for help. Its crusade could affect larger US trade policy.

LAKE VILLAGE, ARK.—Alleamer Tyler works in quality control at Farm Fresh Catfish, a processing plant in this small Delta town on the edge of the Mississippi River. Her days are sometimes slower than in the past, because she doesn't test as many fish as she once did.

"The imports have made a huge impact," says Ms. Tyler, one of Farm Fresh's 100 employees . . .

Catfish producers say imports from Vietnam have soared from 575,000 pounds in 1998 to as much as 20 million pounds this year . . .

Because of Vietnamese fish imports, the US catfish production has plunged in the past year. At Farm Fresh, 95,000 pounds a day were processed last year. This year, it's down to 65,000.

—Suzi Parker

Source: Christian Science Monitor, October 3, 2001.

NOTE: Firms will enter a competitive industry when it is profitable and exit when losses are incurred. A competitive industry stabilizes when economic profits equal zero.

share in the good fortunes of the catfish market while they last. As long as others are willing and able to enter the industry and increase output, Farmer Hollingsworth must do the same or deny himself even a small share of the available profits. Others will be willing to expand catfish production so long as catfish breed economic profits—that is, so long as the rate of return in catfish production is superior to that available elsewhere. They will be able to do so as long as it is easy to get into catfish production.

Farmer Hollingsworth's dilemma goes a long way toward explaining why catfish farming is not highly profitable. Every time the profit picture looks good, everybody tries to get in on the action. This kind of pressure on prices and profits is a fundamental characteristic of competitive markets. ***As long as it is easy for existing producers to expand production or for new firms to enter an industry, economic profits will not last long.*** Industry output will expand, market prices will fall, and rates of profit will diminish. Thus the rate of profits in catfish farming is kept down by the fact that anyone with a pond and a couple of catfish can get into the business fairly easily.

Low Barriers to Entry

barriers to entry Obstacles that make it difficult or impossible for would-be producers to enter a particular market, e.g., patents.

New producers will be able to enter a profitable industry and help drive down prices and profits as long as there are no significant **barriers to entry.** Such barriers may include patents, control of essential factors of production, brand loyalty, and various forms of price control. All such barriers make it expensive, risky, or impossible for new firms to enter into production. In the absence of such barriers, new firms can enter an industry more readily and at less risk.

Not suprisingly, firms already entrenched in a profitable industry do their best to keep newcomers out, by erecting barriers to entry. As we saw, there are few barriers to entering the catfish business. When catfish imports from Vietnam soared in 2002–03, domestic farmers sought to stem the inflow with new entry barriers, including country-of-origin labeling, tougher health inspections, and outright import quotas. Such entry barriers would have impeded rightward shifts of the market supply curve and kept catfish prices higher. Without such protection, domestic farmers who couldn't keep up with falling prices and increased productivity exited the industry. Owners of T-shirt shops also fret over the low entry barriers that keep their prices and profits low (see Headline).

Market Characteristics

This brief review of catfish economics illustrates a few general observations about the structure, behavior, and outcomes of a competitive market:

- ***Many firms.*** A competitive market will include a great many firms, none of which has a significant share of total output.
- ***Identical products.*** Products are homogeneous. One firm's product is virtually indistinguishable from any other firm's product.
- ***MC = p.*** All competitive firms will seek to expand output until marginal cost equals price.
- ***Low barriers.*** Barriers to enter the industry are low. If economic profits are available, more firms will enter the industry.
- ***Zero economic profit.*** The tendency of production and market supplies to expand when profit is high puts heavy pressure on prices and profits in competitive industries. Economic profit will approach zero in the long run as prices are driven down to the level of average production costs.
- ***Perfect information.*** All buyers and sellers are fully informed of market opportunities.

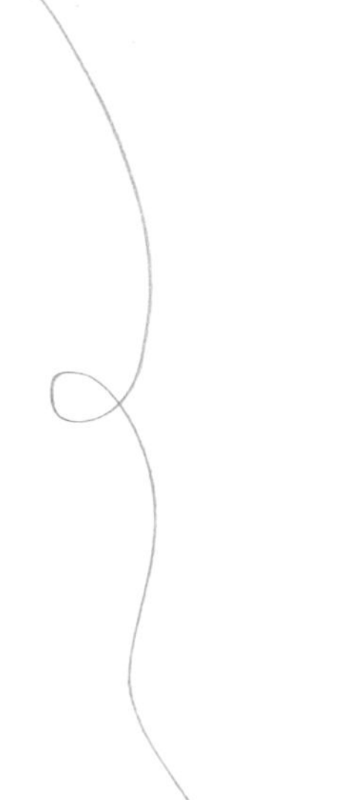

COMPETITIVE PRESSURE HEADLINE

T-Shirt Shop Owner's Lament: Too Many T-Shirt Shops

The small Texas beach resort of South Padre Island boasts white sand, blue skies (much of the time), the buoyant waters of the Gulf of Mexico and, at last count, more than 40 T-shirt shops.

And that's a problem for Shy Oogav, who owns one of those shops. "Every day you have to compete with other shops," he says. "And if you invent something new, they will copy you."

Padre Island illustrates a common condition in the T-shirt industry—unbridled, ill-advised growth. Many people believe T-shirts are the ticket to a permanent vacation—far too many people. "In the past years, everything that closed opened up again as a T-shirt shop," says Maria C. Hall, executive director of the South Padre Island Chamber of Commerce.

Mr. Oogav, a 29-year-old immigrant from Israel, came to South Padre Island on vacation six years ago, thought he had found paradise and stayed on. He subsequently got a job with one of the town's T-shirt shops, which then numbered fewer than a dozen. Now that he owns his own shop, and the competition has quadrupled, his paradise is lost. "I don't sleep at night," he says, morosely.

—Mark Pawlosky

Source: *The Wall Street Journal,* July 31, 1995, p. B1. Reprinted by permission of The Wall Street Journal,

NOTE: The ability of a single firm to increase the price of its product depends on how many other firms offer identical products. A perfectly competitive firm has no market power.

POLICY PERSPECTIVES

The Virtues of Competition

In Chapter 3 we noted that there is a strong case to be made for the market mechanism. In particular, we observed that the market mechanism permits individual consumers and producers to express their views about WHAT to produce, HOW to produce, and FOR WHOM to produce by "voting" for particular goods and services by way of market purchases and sales. How well this market mechanism works depends in part on how competitive markets are.

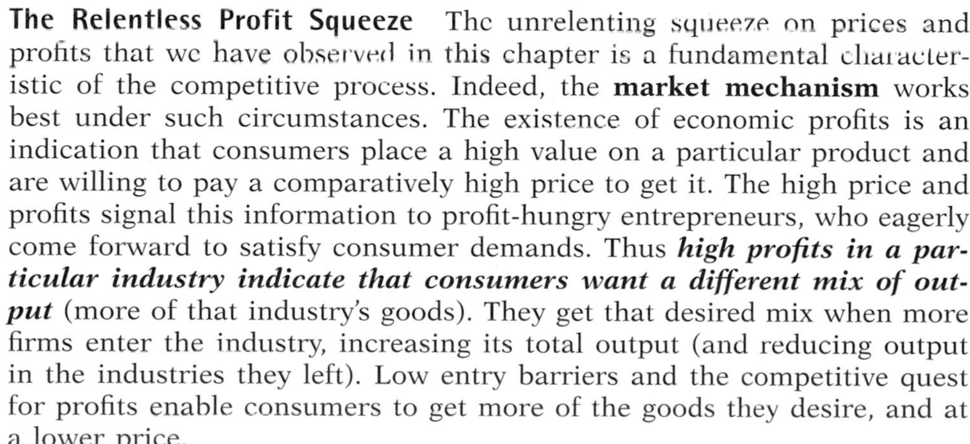

The Relentless Profit Squeeze The unrelenting squeeze on prices and profits that we have observed in this chapter is a fundamental characteristic of the competitive process. Indeed, the **market mechanism** works best under such circumstances. The existence of economic profits is an indication that consumers place a high value on a particular product and are willing to pay a comparatively high price to get it. The high price and profits signal this information to profit-hungry entrepreneurs, who eagerly come forward to satisfy consumer demands. Thus ***high profits in a particular industry indicate that consumers want a different mix of output*** (more of that industry's goods). They get that desired mix when more firms enter the industry, increasing its total output (and reducing output in the industries they left). Low entry barriers and the competitive quest for profits enable consumers to get more of the goods they desire, and at a lower price.

market mechanism The use of market prices and sales to signal desired outputs (or resource allocations).

Maximum Efficiency When the competitive pressure on prices is carried to the limit, the products in question are also produced at the least possible cost, another dimension of economic efficiency. This was illustrated by the tendency of catfish prices to be driven down to the level of minimum average costs. Once the market equilibrium has been established, society is getting the most it can from its available (scarce) resources.

Zero Economic Profits At the limit of the process, all economic profit is eliminated. This doesn't mean that producers are left empty-handed, however. To begin with, the zero profit limit is rarely, if ever, reached, because new products are continually being introduced, consumer demands change, and more efficient production processes are discovered. In fact, the competitive process creates strong pressures to pursue product and technological innovation. In a competitive market, the adage about the early bird getting the worm is particularly apt. As we observed in the catfish market, the first ones to take up catfish farming were the ones who made the greatest profits.

The sequence of events common to a competitive market situation includes the following:

- High prices and profits signal consumers' demand for more output.
- Economic profit attracts new suppliers.
- The market supply curve shifts to the right.
- Prices slide down the market demand curve.
- A new equilibrium is reached at which increased quantities of the desired product are produced and its price is lowered. Average costs of production are at or near a minimum, more of the product is supplied and consumed, and economic profit approaches zero.
- Throughout the process producers experience great pressure to keep ahead of the profit squeeze by reducing costs, a pressure that frequently results in product and technological innovation.

What is essential to note about the competitive process is that the potential threat of other firms to expand production or new firms to enter the industry keeps existing firms on their toes. Even the most successful firm cannot rest on its laurels for long. To stay in the game, competitive firms must continually improve technology, improve their products, and reduce costs.

The Social Value of Losses Not all firms can maintain a competitive pace. Throughout the competitive process, many firms incur economic losses, shut down production, and exit the industry. These losses are a critical part of the market mechanism. ***Economic losses are a signal to producers that they are not using society's scarce resources in the best way.*** Consumers want those resources reallocated to other firms or industries that can better satisfy consumer demands. In a competitive market, money-losing firms are sent packing, making scarce resources available to more efficient firms.

The dog-eat-dog character of competitive markets troubles many observers. Critics say competitive markets are "all about money," with no redeeming social attributes. But such criticism is ill-founded. The economic goals of society are to produce the best-possible mix of output, in the most efficient way, then to distribute the output fairly. In other words, society seeks optimal answers to the basic WHAT, HOW, and FOR WHOM questions. What makes competitive markets so desirable is that they are most likely to deliver those outcomes.

Because competitive markets do such a good job of allocating resources, they present a strong argument for *laissez faire*. In this context, the government should promote competition by vigilantly dismantling entry barriers that might keep new entrants out of an industry. By pursuing such *antitrust* policies, the government can maximize competition and the associated pressure to deliver the goods consumers want.

SUMMARY

- Market structure affects the behavior of firms and thus market outcomes. Market structures range from perfect competition to monopoly.
- A perfectly competitive firm has no power to alter the market price of the goods it sells. The perfectly competitive firm confronts a horizontal demand curve for its own output even though the relevant *market* demand curve is negatively sloped.
- Profit maximization induces the competitive firm to produce at that rate of output where marginal cost equals price. This represents the short-term equilibrium of the firm.
- A competitive firm's supply curve is identical to its marginal cost curve. In the short run, the quantity supplied will rise or fall with price.
- The determinants of supply include the price of inputs, technology, and expectations. If any of these determinants change, the *firm's* supply curve will shift. *Market* supply will shift if costs or the number of firms in the industry change.
- If short-term profits exist in a competitive industry, new firms will enter the market. The resulting shift of supply will drive market prices down the market demand curve. As prices fall, the profit of the industry and its constituent firms will be squeezed.
- The limit to the competitive price and profit squeeze is reached when price is driven down to the level of minimum average total cost. Additional output and profit will be attained only if technology is improved (lowering costs) or if demand increases.
- If the market price falls below ATC, firms will exit an industry. Price will stabilize only when entry and exit cease (and zero profit prevails).
- The most distinctive thing about competitive markets is the persistent pressure they exert on prices and profits. The threat of competition is a tremendous incentive for producers to respond quickly to consumer demands and to seek more efficient means of production. In this sense, competitive markets do best what markets are supposed to do—efficiently allocate resources.

Terms to Remember

Define the following terms:

market structure	total revenue	supply
competitive firm	profit	market supply
competitive market	marginal cost (MC)	equilibrium price
monopoly	competitive profit-maximization rule	barriers to entry
market power		market mechanism
production decision		

Questions for Discussion

1. What industries do you regard as being highly competitive? Can you identify any barriers to entry in those industries?
2. According to the Headline on p. 133, by how much did catfish production increase between 1975 and 1989? Where did all these catfish come from? Can you illustrate this explanation with a graph?
3. If there were more bookstores around your campus, would textbook prices rise or fall? Why aren't there more bookstores?
4. Why doesn't Coke lose all its customers when it raises its price? Why would a catfish farmer lose all his customers at a higher price?

5. How many fish should a commercial fisherman try to catch in a day? Should he catch as many as possible or return to dock before filling the boat with fish? Under what economic circumstances should he not even take the boat out?
6. In Figure 6.8 the output of the typical firm is decreasing even while industry output is increasing. How is this possible?
7. Why would anyone want to enter a profitable industry knowing that profits would eventually be eliminated by competition?
8. What rate of output is appropriate for a nonprofit corporation (e.g., a university or hospital)?
9. What would be the short- and long-run effects on the catfish industry if the Surgeon General established that catfish consumption reduces the risk of heart failure?
10. Adam Smith in *The Wealth of Nations* asserted that the pursuit of self-interest by competitive firms promoted the interests of society. What did he mean by this?

Problems

1. Use Figure 6.5 to determine
   (*a*) How many fish should be harvested at market prices of
      i. $17
      ii. $13
      iii. $9
   (*b*) How much total revenue is collected at each price?
   (*c*) How much profit does the farmer make at each of these prices?
2. Suppose the typical catfish farmer was incurring an economic loss at the prevailing price p_1. What forces would raise the price? What price would prevail in long-term equilibrium? Illustrate your answers with separate graphs for the catfish market and the typical farmer.
3. Suppose a firm has the following costs:

Output (units):	10	11	12	13	14	15	16	17	18	19
Total cost:	$50	$52	$56	$62	$70	$80	$92	$106	$122	$140

   (*a*) If the prevailing market price is $12 per unit, how much should the firm produce?
   (*b*) How much profit will it earn at that output rate?
   (*c*) If the market price dropped to $8, what should the firm do?
4. Graph the market behavior described in the Headline on p. 144.
5. Suppose that the monthly market demand schedule for Frisbees is

Price	$8	$7	$6	$5	$4	$3	$2	$1
Quantity demanded	1,000	2,000	4,000	8,000	16,000	32,000	64,000	150,000

   Suppose further that the marginal and average costs of Frisbee production for every competitive firm are

Rate of output	100	200	300	400	500	600
Marginal cost	$2.00	$3.00	$4.00	$5.00	$6.00	$7.00
Average total cost	2.00	2.50	3.00	3.50	4.00	4.50

   Finally, assume that the equilibrium market price is $6 per Frisbee.
   (*a*) Draw the cost curves of the typical firm and identify its profit-maximizing rate of output and its total profits.

(*b*) Draw the market demand curve and identify market equilibrium.
(*c*) How many Frisbees are being sold in equilibrium?
(*d*) How many (identical) firms are initially producing Frisbees?
(*e*) How much profit is the typical firm making?
(*f*) In view of the profits being made, more firms will want to get into Frisbee production. In the long run, these new firms will shift the market supply curve to the right and push the price down to average total cost, thereby eliminating profits. At what equilibrium price are all profits eliminated? How many firms will be producing Frisbees at this price?

Web Activities

1. Log on to www.fortune.com/fortune. Click on the technology section, and find an article which tells of a firm adopting a new technology.
   (*a*) What will this new technology do to the company's profits?
   (*b*) Will other firms also adopt this technology?
   (*c*) Explain why or why not.
   (*d*) Will this technology make it easier or harder for new firms to enter the industry? Explain
2. Log on to www.cnn.com or www.msnbc.com. Complete a search using the key words "beef market."
   (*a*) Explain why the market for beef in the United States is a competitive market.
   (*b*) In the article you found, what determinant of supply or demand in the market for beef is changing?
   (*c*) How will this change affect the short-run equilibrium price? The long-run equilibrium price?
3. Log on to www.census.gov, and follow this series of links: click on economic census, construction reports; click on the arrow for tables in your state.
   (*a*) How many construction establishments exist in your state?
   (*b*) Does this number constitute a competitive market? Explain.

Living Econ

Do I Make Marginal Decisions?

In this chapter you learned that a rational firm in a competitive market will seek to produce the rate of output at which marginal cost equals price. At this point the producer reaps the greatest total profit possible, given other constraints. Additional production beyond this point will actually make the firm worse off.

Well, if you are rational, you should seek to make the same types of decisions in your life (you probably already do so without thinking of your decisions in economic terms). As a consumer, your goal is to maximize satisfaction, not total profit. You are not seeking to equate marginal cost with price but instead to equate the additional opportunity cost of an activity or purchase with the additional benefit the activity or purchase provides for you.

The next time you are trying to decide if you should spend one more hour watching TV, think about the additional satisfaction of watching TV versus the value of what you give up. As long as the marginal benefit of watching TV is greater than the marginal cost of the foregone activity, you should watch another hour of TV. The end result of this economic exercise will be maximum satisfaction (even if lower grades!).

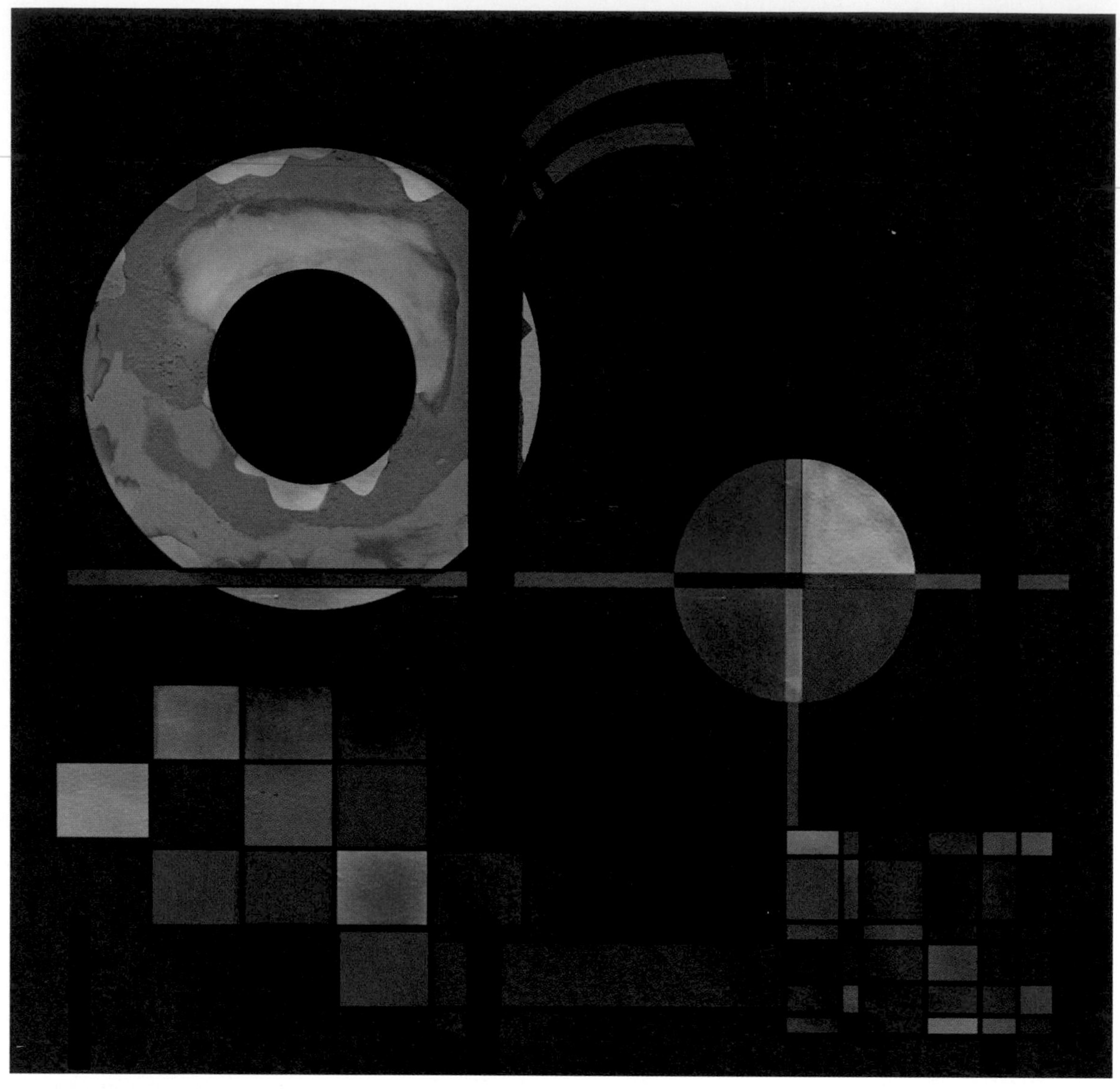

Monopoly

CHAPTER 7

In 1908 Ford produced the Model T, the car "designed for the common man." It was cheap, reliable, and as easy to drive as the horse and buggy it was replacing. Ford sold 10,000 Model T's in its first full year of production (1909). After that, sales more than doubled every year. In 1913, nearly 200,000 Model T's were sold and Ford was fast changing American patterns of consumption, travel, and living standards.

During this early development of the U.S. auto industry, Henry Ford dominated the field. There were other producers, but the Ford Motor Company was the only producer of an inexpensive "motorcar for the multitudes." In this situation, Henry Ford could dictate the price and the features of his cars. When he opened his new assembly line factory at Highland Park, he abruptly raised the Model T's price by $100—an increase of 12 percent—to help pay for the new plant. Then he decided to paint all Model T's black. When told of consumer complaints about the lack of colors, Ford advised one of his executives in 1913: "Give them any color they want so long as it's black."[1]

Henry Ford had market power. He could dictate what color car Americans would buy. And he could raise the price of Model T's without fear of losing all his customers. Such power is alien to competitive firms. Competitive firms are always under pressure to reduce costs, improve quality, and cater to consumer preferences.

In this chapter we will continue to examine how market structure influences market outcomes. Specifically, we examine how a market controlled by a single producer—a monopoly—behaves. We are particularly interested in the following questions:

- What price will a monopolist charge for its output?
- How does a monopolist keep potential competitors at bay?
- Are consumers better or worse off when only one firm controls an entire market?

[1]Charles E. Sorensen. *My Forty Years with Ford* (New York: W. W. Norton & Co., 1956), p. 127.

Monopoly Structure

market power The ability to alter the market price of a good or service.

The essence of **market power** is the ability to alter the price of a product. The catfish farmers of Chapter 6 had no such power. Because many other farms were producing and selling the same good, each catfish producer had to act as a *price taker.* Each farm could sell all the fish it harvested at the prevailing market price. If the farmer tried to charge a higher price for his catfish, the individual farmer would lose all his customers. This inability to set the price of their output is the most distinguishing characteristic of perfectly competitive firms.

Catfish don't, of course, violate the law of demand. As tasty as catfish are, people are not willing to buy unlimited quantities of them at $13 per basket. The marginal utility of extra fish, in fact, diminishes very rapidly. To induce consumers to buy more fish, the price of fish must be reduced.

market demand The total quantities of a good or service people are willing and able to buy at alternative prices in a given time period; the sum of individual demands.

This seeming contradiction between the law of demand and the situation of the competitive firm was explained by the existence of two distinct demand curves. The demand for catfish refers to the **market demand** for that good: like all other consumer demand curves, this market demand curve is downward-sloping. A second demand curve was constructed to represent the situation confronting a *single firm* in the competitive catfish market; that demand curve was horizontal.

Monopoly = Industry

We now confront an entirely different market structure. Suppose that the entire output of catfish could be produced by a single large producer. Assume that Universal Fish actually has a patent on the oxygenating equipment needed to maintain commercial-sized fish ponds. A **patent** gives a firm the exclusive right to produce or license a product. With its patent, Universal Fish can deny other farmers access to oxygenating equipment and thus establish itself as the sole supplier of catfish. Such a firm is a **monopoly—**that is, a single firm that produces the entire market supply of a good.

patent Government grant of exclusive ownership of an innovation.

monopoly A firm that produces the entire market supply of a particular good or service.

In view of the fact that a monopoly has no direct competition, you'd hardly expect it to behave like a competitive firm. Competitive firms are always under pressure from other firms in the industry to hold down costs and improve product quality. Competitive firms also have to worry about new entrants into their industry and the resultant downward pressure on prices. A monopolist, however, owns the ballpark and can set the rules of the game. Is a monopoly going to charge the same price for fish as a competitive industry would? Not likely. As we'll see, a monopolist can use its market power to charge higher prices and retain larger profits.

The emergence of a monopoly obliterates the distinction between industry demand and the demand curve facing the firm. A monopolistic firm *is* the industry. Hence there is only *one* demand curve to worry about, and that is the market (industry) demand curve. ***In monopoly situations the demand curve facing the firm is identical to the market demand curve for the product.***

Price vs. Marginal Revenue

Although monopolies simplify the geometry of the firm, they complicate the arithmetic of supply decisions. Competitive firms maximize profits by producing at that rate of output where *price* equals marginal cost. Monopolies do not maximize profits in the same way. They still heed the advice about never producing anything that costs more than it brings in. But as strange as it may seem, what is brought in from an additional sale is not the price in this case.

The contribution to total revenue of an additional unit of output is called **marginal revenue (MR).** To calculate marginal revenue, we compare the total revenues received before and after a one-unit increase in the rate of production; the difference between the two totals equals *marginal* revenue.

marginal revenue (MR) The change in total revenue that results from a one-unit increase in quantity sold.

If every unit of output could be sold at the same price, marginal revenue would equal price. But what would the demand curve look like in such a case? It would have to be *horizontal,* indicating that consumers were prepared to buy everything produced at the existing price. As we have observed, however, a horizontal demand curve only applies for small competitive firms, firms that produce only a tiny fraction of total market output. ***Only for perfectly competitive firms does price equal marginal revenue.***

The situation in monopoly is different. The firm is so big that its output decisions affect market prices. Keep in mind that a monopolist confronts the *market* demand curve, which is always downward-sloping. As a consequence, a monopolist can sell additional output only if it *reduces* prices.

Suppose Universal Fish could sell 1 ton of fish for $6,000. If it wants to sell 2 tons, however, it has to heed the Law of Demand and reduce the price per ton. Suppose it has to reduce the price to $5,000 in order to get the additional sales. In that case, we would observe

- Total revenue before price reduction = 1 ton × $6,000 per ton = $6,000
- Total revenue after price reduction = 2 tons × $5,000 per ton = $10,000
- Marginal revenue = total revenue @ 2 tons − total revenue @ 1 ton
  = $10,000 − $6,000 = $4,000

Notice how the quantity demanded in the marketplace increases as the unit price is reduced. Notice, also, however, what happens to total revenue when unit sales increase: Total revenue here *increases* by $4,000. This *change* in total revenue represents the *marginal* revenue of the second ton.

Notice in the calculation that marginal revenue ($4,000) is less than price ($5,000). This will always be the case when the demand curve facing the firm is downward-sloping. To get added sales, price must be reduced. The additional quantity sold is a plus for total revenue, but the reduced price per unit is a negative. The net result of these offsetting effects represents *marginal* revenue. Since the demand curve facing a monopolist is always downward-sloping, ***marginal revenue is always less than price for a monopolist,*** as shown in Figure 7.1.

Figure 7.1 provides another illustration of the relationship between price and marginal revenue. The demand curve and schedule represent the market demand for catfish and thus the sales opportunities for the Universal Fish monopoly. According to this information, Universal Fish can sell 1 pound of fish per hour at a price of $13. If the company wants to sell a larger quantity of fish, however, it has to reduce its price. According to the market

FIGURE 7.1
Price Exceeds Marginal Revenue in Monopoly
If a firm must lower its price to sell additional output, marginal revenue is less than price. If this firm wants to increase its sales from 1 to 2 pounds per hour, for example, price must be reduced from $13 to $12. The marginal revenue of the second pound is therefore only $11. This is indicated in row *B* of the table and by point *b* on the graph.

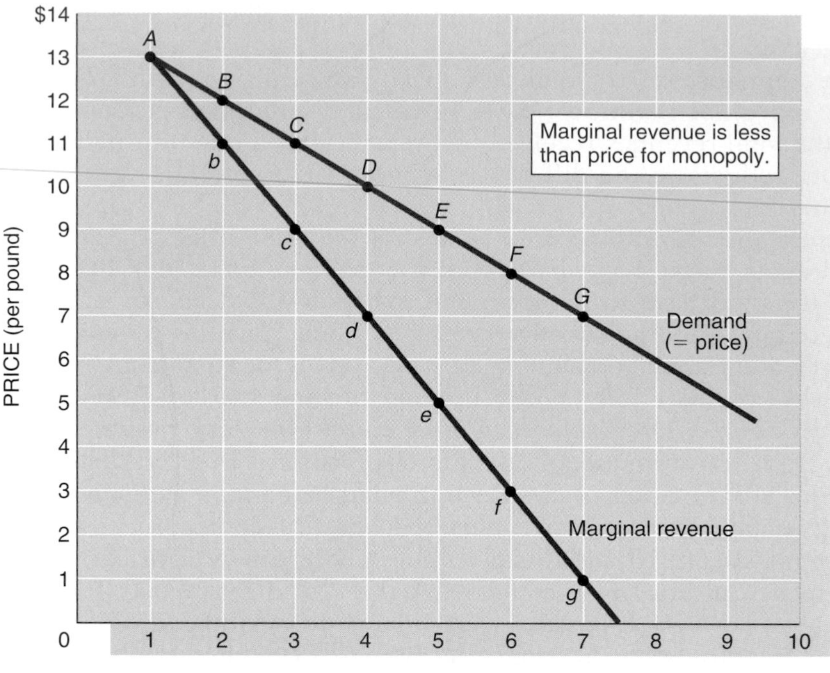

	(1) Quantity	×	(2) Price	=	(3) Total Revenue	(4) Marginal Revenue
A	1		$13		$13	
						$11
B	2		12		24	
						9
C	3		11		33	
						7
D	4		10		40	
						5
E	5		9		45	
						3
F	6		8		48	
						1
G	7		7		49	

demand curve shown here, the price must be lowered to $12 to sell 2 pounds per hour. This reduction in price is shown by a movement along the demand curve from point *A* to point *B*.

Our primary focus here is on marginal revenue. We want to show what happens to total revenue when unit sales increase by 1 pound per hour. To do this, we must compute the total revenue associated with each rate of output, then observe the changes that occur.

The calculations necessary for computing MR are summarized in Figure 7.1. Row *A* of the table indicates that the total revenue resulting from one sale per hour is $13. To increase unit sales, price must be reduced. Row *B* indicates that total revenues rise to only $24 per hour when catfish sales double. The *increase* in total revenues resulting from the added sale is thus $11. The marginal revenue of the second pound is therefore $11. This is illustrated in the last column of the table and by point *b* on the marginal revenue curve.

Notice that the MR of the second pound of fish ($11) is *less* than its price ($12). This is because both pounds are being sold for $12 apiece. In effect, the firm is giving up the opportunity to sell only 1 pound per hour at $13 in order to sell a larger quantity at a lower price. In this sense, the firm is sacrificing $1 of potential revenue on the first pound of fish in order to increase *total* revenue. Marginal revenue measures the change in total revenue that results.

So long as the demand curve is downward-sloping, MR will always be less than price. Compare columns 2 and 4 of the table in Figure 7.1. At each rate of output in excess of one pound, marginal revenue is less than price. This is also evident in the graph: ***the MR curve lies below the demand (price) curve at every point but the first.***

Monopoly Behavior

Like all other producers, a monopolist is in business to maximize total profits. A monopolist does this a bit differently from a competitive firm, however. Recall that a perfectly competitive firm is a *price taker.* It maximizes profits by adjusting its rate of output to a *given* market price. A monopolist, by contrast, *sets* the market price. Hence ***a monopolist must make a pricing decision that perfectly competitive firms never make.***

Profit Maximization

In setting its price, the monopolist, like the perfectly competitive firm, seeks to maximize total profit. To do so, the monopolist first identifies the profit-maximizing rate of output (the production decision), then determines what price is compatible with that much output.

To find the best rate of output, a monopolist will follow the general **profit-maximization rule** about equating marginal cost (what an additional unit costs to produce) and marginal revenue (how much more revenue an additional unit brings in). Hence ***a monopolist maximizes profits at the rate of output where MR = MC.***

profit-maximization rule Produce at that rate of output where marginal revenue equals marginal cost.

Note that competitive firms actually do the same thing. In their case, MR and price are identical. Hence a competitive firm maximizes profits where MC = MR = p. Thus the general profit-maximization rule (MR = MC) applies to *all* firms; only those firms that are perfectly competitive use the special case of MC = p = MR.

The Production Decision

Figure 7.2 shows how a monopolist applies the profit-maximization rule to the **production decision.** The demand curve represents the market demand for catfish; the marginal revenue curve is derived from it, as shown in Figure 7.1. The marginal cost curve in Figure 7.2 represents the costs incurred by Universal Fish in supplying the market. Universal's objective is to find that one rate of output that maximizes profit.

production decision The selection of the short-run rate of output (with existing plant and equipment).

Competitive firms make the production decision by locating the intersection of marginal cost and price. A monopolist, however, looks for the rate of output at which marginal cost equals marginal revenue. This is illustrated in Figure 7.2 by the intersection of the MR and MC curves (point *d*). Looking down from that intersection, we see that the associated rate of output is 4 pounds per hour. Thus 4 pounds is the profit-maximizing rate of output for this monopoly.

The Monopoly Price

How much should Universal Fish charge for these 4 pounds of fish? Naturally, the monopolist would like to charge a very high price. But its

FIGURE 7.2
Profit Maximization

The most profitable rate of output is indicated by the intersection of marginal revenue and marginal cost (point *d*). In this case, marginal revenue and marginal cost intersect at an output of 4 pounds per hour. Point *D* indicates that consumers will pay $10 per pound for this much output. Total profits equal price ($10) minus average total cost ($8), multiplied by the quantity sold (4).

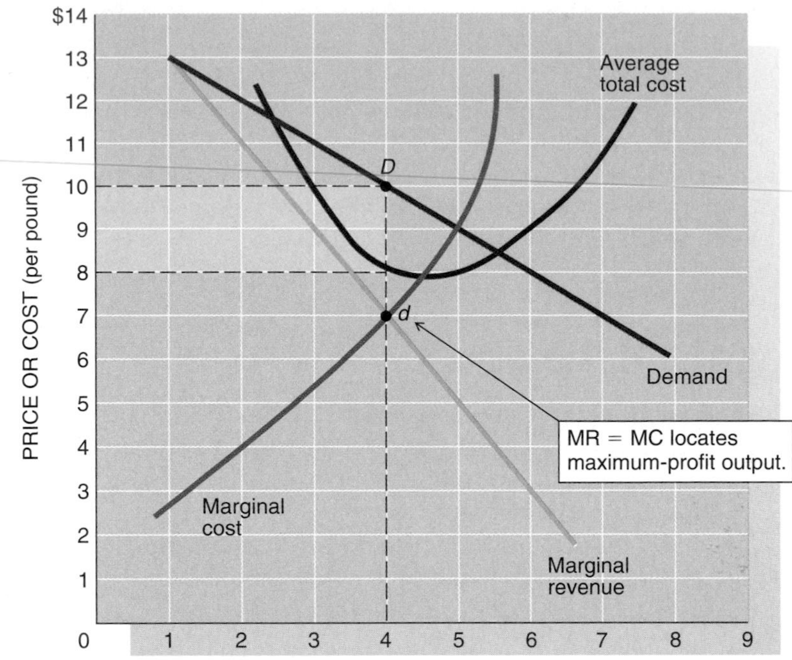

ability to charge a high price is limited by the demand curve. The demand curve always tells how much consumers are willing to pay for any given quantity. Once we have determined the quantity that is going to be supplied (4 pounds per hour), we can look at the demand curve to determine the price ($10 at point *D*) that consumers will pay for these catfish. That is to say,

- ***The intersection of the marginal revenue and marginal cost curves (point d) establishes the profit-maximizing rate of output.***
- ***The demand curve tells us the highest price consumers are willing to pay for that specific quantity of output (point D).***

If Universal Fish ignored these principles and tried to charge $13 per pound, consumers would buy only 1 pound, leaving it with 3 unsold pounds of fish. As the monopolist will soon learn, ***only one price is compatible with the profit-maximizing rate of output.*** In this case the price is $10. This price is found in Figure 7.2 by moving up from the intersection of MR = MC until reaching the demand curve at point *D*. Point *D* tells us that consumers are able and willing to buy exactly 4 pounds of fish per hour at the price of $10 each. A monopolist that tries to charge more than $10 will not be able to sell all 4 pounds of fish. That could turn out to be a smelly and unprofitable situation.

Monopoly Profits

Also illustrated in Figure 7.2 are the total profits of the Universal Fish monopoly. To compute total profits we can first calculate profit per unit, that is, price minus *average* total cost. In this case, profit per unit is $2 (price of $10 minus ATC of $8). Multiplying profit per unit by the quantity sold (4) gives us total profits of $8 per hour, as illustrated by the shaded rectangle.

Barriers to Entry

The profits attained by Universal Fish as a result of its monopoly position are not the end of the story. As we observed earlier, the existence of economic profit tends to bring profit-hungry entrepreneurs swarming like locusts. Indeed, in the competitive catfish industry of Chapter 6, the lure of high profits brought about an enormous expansion in domestic catfish farming, a flood of imported fish, and a steep decline in catfish prices. What, then, can we expect to happen in the catfish industry now that Universal has a monopoly position and is enjoying economic profits?

The consequences of monopoly for prices and output can be seen in Figure 7.3. In this case, we must compare monopoly behavior to that of a competitive *industry*. Remember that a monopoly is a single firm that comprises the entire industry. What we want to depict, then, is how a different market structure (perfect competition) would alter prices and the quantity supplied.

If a *competitive* industry were producing at point *D*, it, too, would be generating an economic profit with the costs shown in Figure 7.3. A competitive industry would not stay at that rate of output, however. All the firms in a competitive industry try to maximize profits by equating price and marginal cost. At point *D*, however, price exceeds marginal cost. Hence a competitive industry would quickly move from point *D* (the monopolist's equilibrium) to point *E*, where marginal cost and price are equal. At point *E* (the short-run competitive equilibrium), more fish are supplied, their price is lower, and industry profits are smaller.

Threat of Entry

At point *E*, catfish farming is still profitable, since price ($9) exceeds average cost ($8) at that rate of production. Although total profits at point *E* ($5 per hour) are less than at point *D* ($8 per hour), they are still attractive.

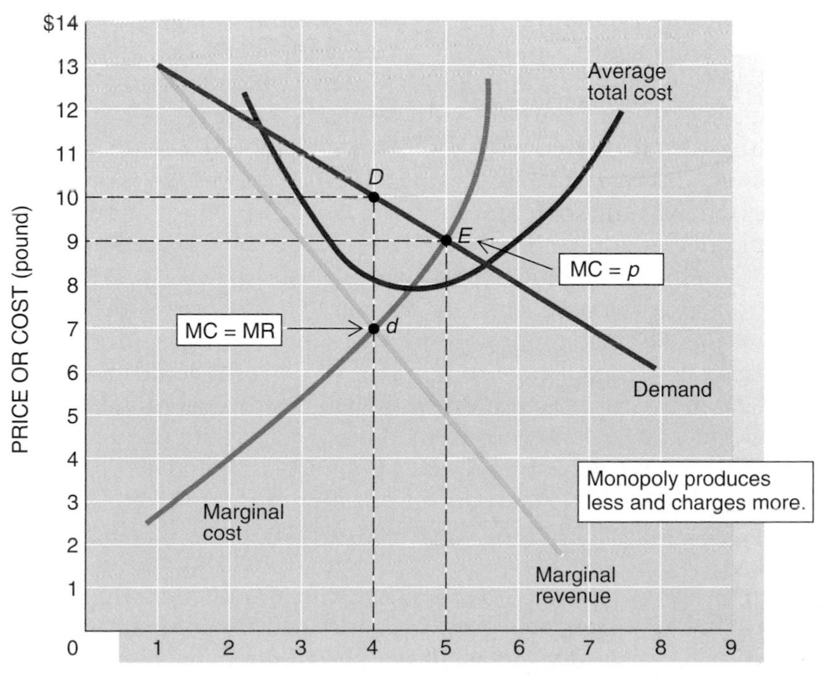

FIGURE 7.3
Monopoly vs. Competitive Outcomes

A monopoly will produce at the rate of output where MR = MC. A competitive industry will produce where MC = *p*. Hence, a monopolist produces less (q = 4) than a competitive industry (q = 5). It also charges a higher price ($10 vs. $9).

These remaining profits will lure more entrepreneurs into a competitive industry. As more firms enter, the market supply curve will shift to the right, driving prices down further. As we observed in Chapter 6, output will increase and prices will decline until all economic profit is eliminated and entry ceases (long-run competitive equilibrium).

Will this sequence of events occur in a monopoly? Absolutely not. Remember that Universal Fish is now assumed to have an exclusive patent on oxygenating equipment and can use this patent as an impassable barrier to entry. Consequently, would-be competitors can swarm around Universal's profits until their wings drop off; Universal is not about to let them in on the spoils. Universal Fish has the power to maintain production and price at point *D* in Figure 7.3. In the absence of competition, monopoly outcomes won't budge. We conclude, therefore, that ***a monopoly attains higher prices and profits by restricting output.***

barriers to entry Obstacles that make it difficult or impossible for would-be producers to enter a particular market, e.g., patents.

The secret to a monopoly's success lies in its **barriers to entry.** So long as entry barriers exist, a monopoly can control (restrict) the quantity of goods supplied. The barrier to entry in this catfish saga is the patent on oxygenating equipment. Without access to that technology, would-be catfish farmers must continue to farm cotton.

Patent Protection: Polaroid vs. Kodak

A patent was also the source of monopoly power in the battle between Polaroid and Eastman Kodak. Edwin Land invented the instant-development camera in 1947 and got a patent on his invention. Over the subsequent 29 years, the company he founded was the sole supplier of instant-photography cameras and racked up billions of dollars in profits. Along the way, the Polaroid Corporation acquired still more patents to protect Dr. Land's original invention and subsequent improvements.

Polaroid's huge profits were too great a prize to ignore. In 1976, the Eastman Kodak Company decided to enter the market with an instant camera of its own. The availability of a second camera quickly depressed camera prices and squeezed Polaroid's profits.

Polaroid cried foul and went to court to challenge Kodak's entry into the instant-photography market. Polaroid claimed that Kodak had infringed on Polaroid's patent rights and was producing cameras illegally. Kodak responded that it had developed its cameras independently and used no processes protected by Polaroid's patents.

The ensuing legal battle lasted 14 years. In the end, a federal judge concluded that Kodak had violated Polaroid's patent rights. Kodak not only stopped producing instant cameras but also offered to repurchase all of the 16 million cameras it had sold (for which film would no longer be available).

In addition to restoring Polaroid's monopoly, the court ordered Kodak to pay Polaroid for its lost monopoly profits. The court essentially looked at Figure 7.3 and figured out how much profit Polaroid would have made had it enjoyed an undisturbed monopoly in the instant-photography market. Prices would have been higher, output lower, and profits greater. Using such reasoning, the judge determined that Polaroid's profits would have been \$909.5 million higher if Kodak had never entered the market—*twice* as high as the profits actually earned. Kodak had to repay Polaroid these lost profits in 1990.

Although Polaroid won the legal battle, consumers ended up losing. What the Kodak entry demonstrated was how just a little competition (a second firm) can push consumer prices down, broaden consumer options, and

BARRIERS TO ENTRY HEADLINE

Suit Threat Slows Linux Sales

SAN FRANCISCO—Businesses continue to buy Linux software, though a bit more slowly than before, despite threats of lawsuits against users of the popular operating system.

Only 16% of 50 large-company tech managers recently surveyed by Forrester Research said that the legal challenges from tech firm SCO will deter them from buying Linux. SCO says it owns part of the computer code used to create the operating system, and wants all users to pay royalties or possibly face legal action.

Companies are taking a few extra weeks or months to evaluate the legal impact before buying. "There's a stretching of the sales cycle," says Joe Eckert of Linux software maker Suse Linux. "But it's not a panic."

SCO says its intent was not to slow sales. "Our intent was to protect our intellectual property," says SCO spokesman Marc Modersitzki.

—Michelle Kessler

Source: *USA Today*, October 3, 2003, p. 5B.

NOTE: Legal action—or even the *threat* of legal action—may dissuade a firm from entering an industry or its customers from buying its product.

improve product quality. Once its monopoly was restored, Polaroid didn't have to try as hard to satisfy consumer desires.

Other Entry Barriers

Patents are a highly visible and effective barrier. There are numerous other ways of keeping potential competitors at bay, however.

Legal Harassment An increasingly effective way of suppressing competition is to sue new entrants. Even if a new competitor hasn't infringed on a monopolist's patents or trademarks, it is still fair game for legal challenges. Recall that Kodak spent 14 *years* battling Polaroid in court. Small firms can't afford all that legal skirmishing. When Napster, one of the first companies to offer free music downloads, got sued for copyright infringement in 2000, its fate was sealed. It simply didn't have the revenues needed to wage an extended legal battle. Even before the court ruled against it, Napster chose to compromise rather than fight. Because lengthy legal battles are so expensive, even the *threat* of legal action may dissuade entrepreneurs from entering a monopolized market. Kazaa customers were scared away from using its music file-sharing network when the record companies filed suit against 261 download users in 2003. Linux sales were also slowed by legal threats, as the accompanying Headline explains.

Exclusive Licensing Nintendo allegedly used another tactic to control the video game market in the early 1990s. Nintendo forbade game creators from writing software for competing firms. Such exclusive licensing made it difficult for potential competitors to acquire the factors of production (game developers) they needed to compete against Nintendo. It was only after the giant electronics company Sony entered the market in 1995 with new technology (PlayStation) that Nintendo had to share its monopoly profits.

HEADLINE BARRIERS TO ENTRY

Judge Says Microsoft Broke Antitrust Law

A federal judge yesterday found Microsoft Corp. guilty of violating antitrust law by waging a campaign to crush threats to its Windows monopoly, a severe verdict that opens the door for the government to seek a breakup of one of the most successful companies in history.

Saying that Microsoft put an "oppressive thumb on the scale of competitive fortune," U.S. District Judge Thomas Penfield Jackson gave the Justice Department and 19 states near-total victory in their lawsuit. His ruling puts a black mark on the reputation of a software giant that has been the starter engine of the "new economy."

"Microsoft mounted a deliberate assault upon entrepreneurial efforts that, left to rise or fall on their own merits, could well have enabled the introduction of competition into the market for Intel-compatible PC operating systems," Jackson said.

In blunt language, Jackson depicted a powerful and predatory company that employed a wide array of tactics to destroy any innovation that posed a danger to the dominance of Windows. Among the victims were corporate stars of the multibillion-dollar computer industry: Intel Corp., Apple Computer Inc., International Business Machines Corp., and RealNetworks Inc.

To crush the competitive threat posed by the Internet browser, Jackson ruled, Microsoft integrated its own Internet browser into its Windows operating system "to quell incipient competition," bullied computer makers into carrying Microsoft's browser by threatening to withhold price discounts, and demanded that computer makers not feature rival Netscape's browser in the PC desktop as a condition of licensing the Windows operating system.

"Only when the separate categories of conduct are viewed, as they should be, as a single, well-coordinated course of action does the full extent of the violence that Microsoft has done to the competitive process reveal itself," Jackson wrote in the 43-page ruling.

—James V. Grimaldi

Source: *Washington Post*, April 4, 2000, p. 1.

NOTE: Microsoft tried to keep competitors out of its operating- and applications-software markets by erecting various barriers to entry. This behavior slowed innovation, restricted consumer choices, and kept prices too high.

Nintendo also kept game prices artificially high by restricting *sales* competition. In October 2002 the European Commission's antitrust department concluded that Nintendo was prohibiting retailers in low-cost nations from selling Nintendo games in high-cost nations. This practice eliminates potential price competition, keeping Nintendo profits high.

Bundled Products Another way to thwart competition is to force consumers to purchase complementary products. The U.S. Justice Department repeatedly accused Microsoft Corporation of "bundling" its applications software (e.g., Windows Explorer) with its Windows operating software. With a near monopoly on operating systems, Microsoft can charge a high price for Windows, then give "free" applications software with each system. Such bundling makes it almost impossible for potential competitors in the *applications* market to sell their products at a profitable price. The accompanying Headline cites this practice as one of the many "oppressive" tactics that Microsoft used to protect and exploit its monopoly position. Bundling helped Microsoft gain 96 percent of the Internet browser market (displacing Netscape), 94 percent of the office suites markets (displacing Word Perfect), and an increased share of money-management applications (gaining on Intuit). The federal courts concluded that consumers would have enjoyed better products and lower prices had the market for computer operating systems been more competitive. In a November 2002 ruling, however, a federal judge said Microsoft could continue bundling applications so long as it made it easier for consumers to unbundle those products.

Government Franchises In many cases, a monopoly persists just because the government gave a single firm the exclusive right to produce a particular good in a specific market. The entry barrier here is not a patent on a product but instead an exclusive franchise to sell that product. Local cable and telephone companies are often franchised monopolies. So is the U.S. Postal Service in the provision of first-class mail. Your campus bookstore might also have exclusive rights to sell textbooks on campus.

Comparative Outcomes

These and other entry barriers are the ultimate sources of monopoly power. With that power, monopolies can change the way the market responds to consumer demands.

Competition vs. Monopoly

By way of summary, we may recount the different ways in which perfectly competitive and monopolized markets behave. The likely sequence of events that occurs in each type of market structure is as follows:

Competitive Industry	**Monopoly Industry**
• High prices and profits signal consumers' demand for more output.	• High prices and profits signal consumers' demand for more output.
• The high profits attract new suppliers.	• Barriers to entry are erected to exclude potential competition.
• Production and supplies expand.	• Production and supplies are constrained.
• Prices slide down the market demand curve.	• Prices don't move down the market demand curve.
• A new equilibrium is established wherein more of the desired product is produced, its price falls, average costs of production approach their minimum, and economic profits approach zero.	• No new equilibrium is established; average costs are not necessarily at or near a minimum, and economic profits are at a maximum.
• Price equals marginal cost throughout the process.	• Price exceeds marginal cost at all times.
• Throughout the process, there is great pressure to keep ahead of the profit squeeze by reducing costs or improving product quality.	• There is no squeeze on profits and thus no pressure to reduce costs or improve product quality.

Near Monopolies

These comparative sequences aren't always followed exactly. Nor is the monopoly sequence available only to a single firm. In reality, two or more firms may rig the market to replicate monopoly outcomes and profits.

HEADLINE MIMICKING MONOPOLY

OPEC Votes to Cut Production

The Organization of Petroleum Exporting Countries, faced with declining crude oil prices and rising inventories, voted unexpectedly yesterday to cut its production by 3.5 percent in hopes of propping up prices.

OPEC succeeded for a day at least, as the price of crude on the New York Mercantile Exchange jumped 4.1 percent, to $28.24 a barrel, up $1.11, halting a six-week slide from more than $32 a barrel.

Oil traders had expected that the OPEC oil ministers, meeting in Vienna, Austria, would leave production at 25.4 million barrels a day, about a third of the world's daily output, but the oil chiefs instead decided to cut production by 900,000 barrels a day, to 24.5 million, effective Nov. 1.

—Kenneth Bredemeier

Source: *Washington Post*, September 25, 2003, p. E1.

NOTE: The 11 member-nations of OPEC collectively set their combined rate of output. In doing so, they are trying to duplicate monopoly outcomes.

Duopoly In a duopoly there are two firms rather than only one. They may literally be the only two firms in the market, or two firms may so dominate the market that they can still control price and output, even if other firms are present.

How would you expect duopolists to behave? Will they slug it out, driving prices and profits down to competitive levels? Or will they recognize that less intense competition will preserve industry profits? If they behave like true competitors, they risk losing economic profits. If they lay back, they assure themselves a continuing share of monopoly-like profits.

The two giant auction houses, Sotheby's and Christie's, figured out which strategy made more cents. Together the two companies control 90 percent of the $4 billion auction market. Rather than compete for sales by offering lower prices to potential sellers, Sotheby's and Christie's agreed to fix commission prices at a high level. When they got caught in 2000, the two firms agreed to pay a $512 million fine to auction customers.

Oligopoly In an oligopoly, *several* firms (rather than one or two) control the market. Here, too, the strategic choice is whether to compete feverishly or live somewhat more comfortably. To the extent that the dominant firms recognize their mutual interest in higher prices and profits, they may avoid the kind of price competition common in perfectly competitive industries. Coca-Cola and Pepsi, for example, much prefer to use clever advertising rather than lower prices to lure customers away from each other. With 75 percent of industry sales between them, Coke and Pepsi realize that price competition is a no-win strategy.

In some instances, an oligopoly may have explicit limits on production and price. The 11 nations that comprise the Organization of Petroleum Exporting Countries (OPEC), for example, meet every six months or so to limit output (quantity supplied) and maintain a high price for oil (see Headline). OPEC operates outside of U.S. borders and is therefore immune from U.S. laws against price fixing. The record industry doesn't enjoy such immunity,

PRICE FIXING HEADLINE

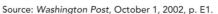

Music Firms Settle Lawsuit

Refund Pact Ends CD Price-Fixing Case

Five of the nation's largest music companies and three of the biggest music retailers agreed to refund $67.4 million to consumers some time next year to settle a multi-state price-fixing lawsuit involving the sale of music on compact discs.

The lawsuit, filed in August 2000, alleges that for five years the music companies and the retailers had an illegal marketing agreement that stifled competition and inflated prices for CDs sold at Tower Records, Musicland Stores and Trans World Entertainment.

Under the arrangement, the record companies would subsidize the cost of advertisements, instore displays and other promotions if retailers advertised CDs at the minimum prices set by the companies, which they did, the lawsuit alleged.

Source: *Washington Post*, October 1, 2002, p. E1.

NOTE: When a handful of companies dominate an industry, they may conspire to fix prices at monopoly levels.

however. In October 2002, eight music companies agreed to refund $67.4 million to consumers for inflating CD prices at Tower Records, Musicland Stores, and Trans World Entertainment (see Headline).

Monopolistic Competition Starbucks, too, has the power to set prices for its products even though many other firms sell coffee. But it has much less power than Coca-Cola or OPEC, because many firms sell coffee. A market made up of many firms each of which has some distinct brand image is called *monopolistic competition.* Each company has a monopoly on its brand image but still must contend with competing brands. This is still very different from *perfect* competition, in which no firm has a distinct brand image or price setting power. As a result, any industry dominated by relatively few firms is likely to behave more like a monopoly than like perfect competition.

WHAT Gets Produced

To the extent that dominating firms behave as we have discussed, they alter the output of goods and services in two specific ways. You remember that competitive industries tend, in the long run, to produce at minimum average total costs. Competitive industries also pursue cost reductions and product improvements relentlessly. These pressures tend to expand our production possibilities. No such forces are at work in the monopoly we have discussed here. Hence there is a basic tendency for monopolies to inhibit economic growth.

Another important feature of competitive markets is their tendency toward **marginal cost pricing.** Marginal cost pricing is important to consumers because it permits rational choices among alternative goods and services. In particular, it informs consumers of the true opportunity costs of various goods, thereby allowing them to choose the mix of output that delivers the most utility with available resources. In our monopoly example, however, consumers end up getting fewer catfish than they would like, while the economy continues to produce cotton and other goods that are less desired. Thus the mix of output shifted away from catfish when Universal took over the

marginal cost pricing The offer (supply) of goods at prices equal to their marginal cost.

industry. The presence of a monopoly therefore alters society's answer to the question of WHAT to produce.

FOR WHOM

Monopoly also changes the answer to the FOR WHOM question. The reduced supply and higher price of catfish imply that some people will have to eat canned tuna instead of breaded catfish. The monopolist's restricted output will also reduce job opportunities in the South, leaving some families with less income. The monopolist will end up with fat profits and thus greater access to all goods and services.

HOW

Finally, monopoly may also alter the HOW response. Competitive firms are likely to seek out new ways of breeding, harvesting, and distributing catfish. A monopoly, however, can continue to make profits from existing equipment and technology. Accordingly, monopolies tend to inhibit technology—how things are produced—by keeping potential competition out of the market.

Any Redeeming Qualities?

Despite the strong and general case to be made against monopoly, it is conceivable that monopolies could also benefit society. One of the arguments made for concentrations of market power is that monopolies have greater ability to pursue research and development. Another is that the lure of monopoly power creates a tremendous incentive for invention and innovation. A third argument in defense of monopoly is that large companies can produce goods more efficiently than smaller firms. Finally, it is argued that even monopolies have to worry about *potential* competition and will behave accordingly. We must pause to reflect, then, on whether and how market power might be of some benefit to society.

Research and Development

In principle, monopolies are well positioned to undertake valuable research and development. First, such firms are sheltered from the constant pressure of competition. Second, they have the resources (monopoly profits) with which to carry out expensive R&D functions. The manager of a perfectly competitive firm, by contrast, has to worry about day-to-day production decisions and profit margins. As a result, she is unable to take the longer view necessary for significant research and development and could not afford to pursue such a view even if she could see it.

The basic problem with the R&D argument is that it says nothing about *incentives*. Although monopolists have a clear financial advantage in pursuing research and development activities, they have no clear incentive to do so. They can continue to make substantial profits just by maintaining market power. Research and development are not necessarily required for profitable survival. In fact, research and development that tend to make existing products or plant and equipment obsolete run counter to a monopolist's vested interest and so may actually be suppressed.

In 2003 two drug companies admitted to paying a third company $100 million a year to suppress its new competing product. As the accompanying Headline notes, consumers were paying $73 a month for medication that the third company could produce and sell for only $32. In a truly competitive

R&D INCENTIVES HEADLINE

2 Drug Firms Agree to Settle Pricing Suit

ALBANY, N.Y., Jan. 27—Two drug companies have agreed to pay $80 million to settle allegations that they conspired to keep a cheaper, generic version of a blood pressure medication off the market.

Under the settlement announced today, Aventis Pharmaceuticals Inc. and Andrx Corp. will pay that amount to states, insurance companies and consumers nationwide.

Consumers paid too much for the drugs Cardizem CD and its generic equivalents because the companies conspired to delay the marketing of cheaper competitors, said New York state Attorney General Eliot L. Spitzer.

Spitzer said that in 1998, the German pharmaceutical giant Hoechst—which merged with Rhone-Poulenc in 1999 to form Aventis—paid Andrx just under $100 million to not market a generic form of Cardizem CD for 11 months. The agreement was to be renewed annually, he said.

This "most craven form of anti-competitive behavior" kept the drug financially out of the reach of countless people, Spitzer said.

Consumer groups have said that Cardizem sales total about $700 million a year domestically. Users of Cardizem were paying about $73 a month for the drug when a generic cost about $32 a month.

—Michael Gormley
Associated Press

Source: *Washington Post*, January 28, 2003, p. E3.

NOTE: A firm that dominates a market may not have sufficient incentive to improve its product or reduce costs. It may even try to suppress product improvements.

market, there would be too many firms to control in this way. Everyone would be scrambling to bring improved products to market.

Entrepreneurial Incentives

The second defense of market power uses the incentive argument—with an interesting twist. As we observed in Chapter 6, every business is out to make a buck, and it is the quest for profits that keeps industries running. Thus, it is argued, even greater profit prizes will stimulate more entrepreneurial activity. Little Horatio Algers will work harder and longer if they can dream of one day possessing a whole monopoly.

The incentive argument for market power is enticing but not entirely convincing. After all, an innovator can make substantial profits in a competitive market, as it typically takes a considerable amount of time for the competition to catch up. Recall that the early birds did get the worm in the catfish industry in Chapter 6 even though profit margins were later squeezed. The same thing happened in the energy-bar market: Brian Maxwell made a bundle (see Headline) even though other firms later developed competing products. Hence it is not evident that the profit incentives available in a competitive industry are at all inadequate.

Economies of Scale

A third defense of market power is the most convincing. A large firm, it is argued, can produce goods at a lower unit (average) cost than a small firm. That is, there are **economies of scale** in production. Thus if we desire to produce goods in the most efficient way—with the least amount of resources per unit of output—we should encourage and maintain large firms.

economies of scale Reductions in minimum average costs that come about through increases in the size (scale) of plant and equipment.

Consider once again the comparison we made earlier between Universal Fish and the competitive catfish industry. We explicitly assumed that Universal confronted the same production costs as the competitive industry.

Thus Universal was not able to produce catfish any more cheaply than the competitive counterpart, and we concerned ourselves only with the different production decisions made by competitive and monopolistic firms.

It is conceivable, however, that Universal Fish might use its size to achieve greater efficiency. Perhaps the firm could build one enormous pond and centralize all breeding, harvesting, and distributing activities. If successful, this centralization might reduce production costs, making Universal more efficient than a competitive industry composed of thousands of small farms (ponds).

Even though large firms may be able to achieve greater efficiencies than smaller firms, there is no assurance that they actually will. Increasing the size (scale) of a plant may actually reduce operating efficiency. Workers may feel alienated in a massive firm and perform below their potential. Centralization might also increase managerial red tape and increase costs. In evaluating the economies-of-scale argument for market power, then, we must recognize that efficiency and size do not necessarily go hand in hand. In fact, monopolies may generate *dis*economies of scale, producing at higher cost than a competitive industry. Only when there is clear evidence of economies of scale is the cost argument for industry concentration persuasive.

Even where economies of scale do exist there is no guarantee that consumers will benefit. Consider the case of multiplex theaters that offer multiple movie screens. Multiplex theaters have significant economies of scale (e.g., consolidated box office, advertising, snack bar, restrooms, projection) compared to single-screen theaters. Once they drive smaller theaters out of business, however, they rarely lower ticket prices.

Natural Monopolies

natural monopoly An industry in which one firm can achieve economies of scale over the entire range of market supply.

There is a special case where the economies-of-scale argument is potentially more persuasive. In this case—called **natural monopoly—**a single firm can produce the entire market supply more efficiently than any larger number of (smaller) firms. As the size (scale) of the one firm increases, its average total costs continue to fall. These economies of scale give the one large producer a decided advantage over would-be rivals. Hence economies of scale act as a "natural" barrier to entry.

Local telephone, cable, and utility services are classic examples of natural monopoly. They have extraordinarily high fixed costs (e.g., transmission lines and switches) and exceptionally small marginal costs. Hence, average total costs keep declining as output expands. As a result, it is much cheaper to install one system of cable or phone lines than a maze of competing ones. Accordingly, a single telephone or power company can supply the market more efficiently than a large number of competing firms.

Although natural monopolies are economically desirable, they may be abused. We must ask whether and to what extent consumers are reaping some benefit from the efficiency a natural monopoly makes possible. Do consumers end up with lower prices, expanded output, and better service? Or does the monopoly tend to keep the benefits for itself, in the form of higher profits, wages, and more comfortable offices? Typically, federal, state, and local governments are responsible for regulating natural monopolies to ensure that the benefits of increased efficiency are shared with consumers.

Contestable Markets

Governmental regulators are not necessarily the only force keeping monopolists in line. Even though a firm may produce the entire supply of a particular product at present, it may face *potential* competition from other firms. Potential rivals may be sitting on the sidelines, watching how well the monopoly fares. If it does too well, these rivals may enter the industry, undermining the monopoly structure and profits. In such **contestable markets,** monopoly behavior may be restrained by potential competition.

contestable market An imperfectly competitive industry subject to potential entry if prices or profits increase.

How contestable a market is depends not so much on its structure as on entry barriers. If entry barriers are insurmountable, would-be competitors are locked out of the market. But if entry barriers are modest, they will be surmounted when the lure of monopoly profits is irresistible. Foreign rivals already producing the same goods are particularly likely to enter domestic markets when monopoly prices and profits are high.

Structure vs. Behavior

From the perspective of contestable markets, the whole case against monopoly is misconceived. Market *structure* per se is not a problem; what counts is market *behavior.* If potential rivals force a monopolist to behave like a competitive firm, then monopoly imposes no cost on consumers or on society at large.

The experience with the Model T Ford illustrates the basic notion of contestable markets. At the time Henry Ford decided to increase the price of the Model T and paint them all black, the Ford Motor Company enjoyed a virtual monopoly on mass-produced cars. But potential rivals saw the profitability of offering additional colors and features (e.g., self-starter, left-hand drive). When they began producing cars in volume, Ford's market power was greatly reduced. In 1926, the Ford Motor Company tried to regain its dominant position by again supplying cars in colors other than black. By that time, however, consumers had more choices. Ford ceased production of the Model T in May 1927.

The experience with the Model T suggests that potential competition can force a monopoly to change its ways. Critics point out, however, that even contestable markets don't force a monopolist to act exactly like a competitive firm. There will always be a gap between competitive outcomes and those monopoly outcomes likely to entice new entry. That gap can cost consumers a lot. The absence of *existing* rivals is also likely to inhibit product and productivity improvements. From 1913 to 1926, all Model T's were black, and consumers had few alternatives. Ford changed its behavior only after *potential* competition became *actual* competition. Even after 1927, when the Ford Motor Company could no longer act like a monopolist, it still didn't price its cars at marginal cost.

POLICY PERSPECTIVES

Flying Monopoly Air

Ever wonder why it's so cheap to fly to one place, yet so expensive to fly somewhere else of equal distance? The answer is likely to be market structure. As we've observed in this and the previous chapter, the greater the number of firms in a market, the lower prices are likely to be. More competition also increases the quantity supplied.

Industry Structure From a national perspective, the airline industry looks pretty competitive. There are over 80 domestic airline companies offering scheduled passenger service and at least 150 foreign carriers serving U.S.

cities. So there are a lot of firms competing for the $100 billion that Americans spend annually on airline travel.

All those airlines don't fly to the places you want to go, however. If you're looking for a flight from Dallas (TX) to Cedar Rapids (IA), don't bother calling United Airlines. Continental, or Delta, much less Air France. None of those firms fly that route. In fact, only one airline (American) was flying that route in early 2003. Hence travelers in the Dallas–Cedar Rapids market confront a *monopoly.*

Travelers between Pittsburgh and Harrisburg confront an equally limited choice. Only one airline (US Airways) produces service on that route. Hence consumers in that market also confront a monopoly in air service.

When assessing market structure, it is essential to specify the relevant market. In this case the relevant market is best defined by specific intercity routes. The number of airlines serving a particular route is a far better measure of market power than the number of airlines flying anywhere. By this yardstick, the airline industry is beset with market power. In two-thirds of U.S. air routes, a single carrier accounts for at least half of all service. US Airways provided 70 percent of the flights departing Pittsburgh in 2003 and 85 percent of the air traffic in Charlotte. Northwest had 60 percent of the Minneapolis market and 54 percent of Detroit's. American Airlines had 58 percent of the market supply in St. Louis. United supplied 50 percent of Denver's flights. As a result of such high local concentrations, 1 out of 10 domestic routes is monopolized. Continuing mergers in the airline industry may extend monopoly power to even more routes.

"We make money the old-fashioned way . . . first we undercut the competition into bankruptcy, and then we jack up the prices!"

NOTE: Predatory pricing—or even the threat of it—can be used to eliminate competition.

Source: © Pepper and Salt, *The Wall Street Journal*, January 5, 1999, p. A3, by Roy Delgado.

Industry Behavior If market structure really matters, airline fares should vary with the number of firms serving a particular route. And so they do. A study by the U.S. General Accounting Office (GAO) found that fares from airports dominated by one or two carriers were 45–85 percent higher than at more competitive airports.

Entry Effects Another way to assess the impact of market structure on prices is to observe how airline fares *change* when airlines enter or exit a specific market. According to a 1999 antitrust suit filed by the U.S. Justice Department, American Airlines slashed fares whenever a new carrier entered a market it dominated. As soon as the new carrier was forced out of the market, American raised fares to monopoly levels again. The accompanying Headline offers some examples of this **predatory pricing.**

predatory pricing Temporary price reductions designed to drive out competition.

Barriers to Entry For the Big Six carriers (United, Delta, American, Continental, US Airways, and Northwest) to maintain high profits on specific routes, they must be able to keep new firms from entering those markets. One of the most formidable entry barriers is their ownership of slots (landing rights) and gates. At Washington, D.C.'s National Airport, for example, the Big Six owned 97 percent of available takeoff/landing slots in 2000. To offer service from that airport, a new entrant would have to buy or lease a slot from the Big Six. It would also have to secure a gate so passengers could access the plane. Would-be competitors complain that the dominant carriers unfairly withhold access to slots and gates, thereby thwarting competition.

PREDATORY PRICING HEADLINE

Following the Fares

The Justice Department says American Airlines cut its fares when low-cost carriers arrived—then raised them when they left. Fares* shown are for 1995–96 from the Dallas–Fort Worth airport to:

Before low-cost

Low-cost in the market

After low-cost exit

Colorado Springs

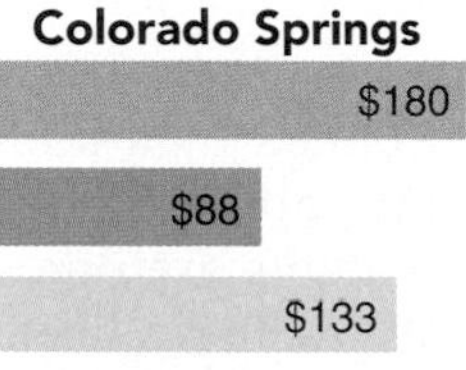

Wichita

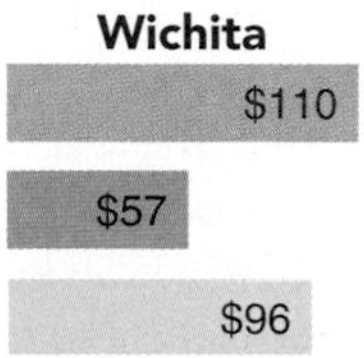

Kansas City

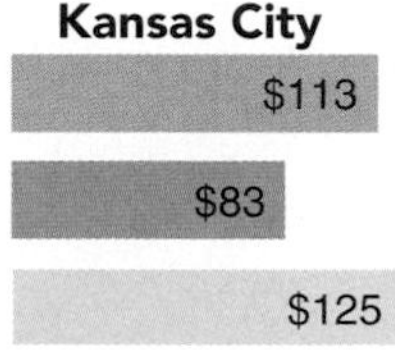

*Average for all local carriers, nonstop.
Source: *Washington Post,* May 14, 1999, p. 1.

NOTE: A monopoly carrier may use a sharp but temporary cut in fares to drive a new entrant out of the market—or to discourage others from entering.

In 1999 the U.S. Department of Transportation started examining options for giving would-be entrants more access to airline markets. One proposal focused on a lottery system for redistributing some slots. In a prior lottery, however, almost all the new entrants that were awarded slots simply resold them to the Big Six. That still left travelers with the all-too-familiar choice of either staying home or flying Monopoly Air.

SUMMARY

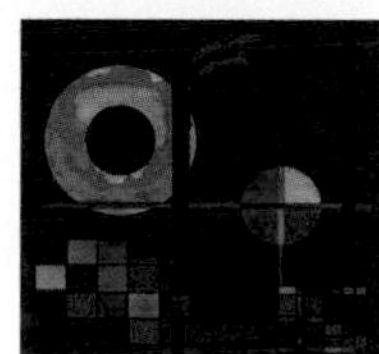

- Market power is the ability to influence the market price of goods and services. The extreme case of market power is monopoly, a situation in which only one firm produces the entire supply of a particular product. A monopolist selects the quantity to be supplied to the market and sets the market price.
- The distinguishing feature of any firm with market power is the fact that the demand curve it faces is downward-sloping. In a monopoly, the demand curve facing the firm and the market demand curve are identical.

- The downward-sloping demand curve facing a monopolist creates a divergence between marginal revenue and price. To sell larger quantities of output, the monopolist must lower product prices. Marginal revenue is the *change* in total revenue divided by the *change* in output.
- A monopolist will produce at the rate of output at which marginal revenue equals marginal cost. Because marginal revenue is always less than price for a monopoly, the monopolist will produce less output than will a competitive industry confronting the same market demand and cost opportunities. That reduced rate of output will be sold at higher prices, in accordance with the (downward-sloping) market demand curve.
- A monopoly will attain a higher level of profit than a competitive industry because of its ability to equate industry (i.e., its own) marginal revenues and costs. By contrast, a competitive industry ends up equating marginal costs and *price,* because its individual firms have no control over the market supply curve.
- Because the higher profits attained by a monopoly will attract envious entrepreneurs, barriers to entry are needed to prohibit other firms from expanding market supplies. Patents are one such barrier to entry. Other barriers are legal harassment, exclusive licensing, product bundling, and government franchises.
- The defense of market power rests on (1) the ability of large firms to pursue long-term research and development, (2) the incentives implicit in the chance to attain market power, (3) the efficiency that larger firms may attain, and (4) the contestability of even monopolized markets. The first two arguments are weakened by the fact that competitive firms are under much greater pressure to innovate and can stay ahead of the profit game if they do so. The contestability defense at best concedes some amount of monopoly exploitation.
- A natural monopoly exists when one firm can produce the output of the entire industry more efficiently than can a number of smaller firms. This advantage is attained from economies of scale. Large firms are not necessarily more efficient, however.

Terms to Remember

Define the following terms:

market power
market demand
patent
monopoly
marginal revenue (MR)
profit-maximization rule
production decision
barriers to entry
marginal cost pricing
economies of scale
natural monopoly
contestable market
predatory pricing

Questions for Discussion

1. If you owned the only bookstore on or near campus, what would you charge for this textbook? How much would you pay students for their used books?
2. Why don't competitive industries produce at the rate of output that maximizes industry profits, as a monopolist does?

3. Is single ownership of a whole industry necessary to exercise monopoly power? How might an industry with several firms achieve the same result? Can you think of any examples?
4. In addition to higher profits, what other benefits accrue to a firm with monopoly power?
5. Why don't monopolists try to establish the highest price possible, as many people allege? What would happen to sales? To profits?
6. What circumstances might cause a monopolist to charge less than the profit-maximizing price?
7. What are the entry barriers that protected Microsoft according to the Headline on p. 162? Were these barriers insurmountable?
8. What entry barriers exist in (*a*) the fast-food industry; (*b*) cable TV; (*c*) the auto industry; (*d*) illegal drug trade?
9. Why would any firm pay another firm so much money to *not* produce? (See Headline on p. 167.)
10. How could airline routes be made more competitive?

Problems

1. In Figure 7.1,
   (*a*) What is the highest price the monopolist could charge and still sell fish?
   (*b*) What is total revenue at that highest price?
   (*c*) What happens to total revenue as price is reduced from its maximum?
   (*d*) Is marginal revenue positive or negative as price declines?
   (*e*) At what price is total revenue maximized?
2. Use Figure 7.2 to answer the following questions:
   (*a*) What rate of output maximizes total profit?
   (*b*) What is MR at that rate of output? What is price?
   (*c*) If output is increased beyond that point, what is the relationship of MC to MR? How will this affect total profits?
3. Suppose the following data represent the market demand for catfish.

Price (per unit)	$20	19	18	17	16	15	14	13	12	11
Quantity demanded (units per day)	10	11	12	13	14	15	16	17	18	19
Total revenue	—	—	—	—	—	—	—	—	—	—
Marginal revenue	—	—	—	—	—	—	—	—	—	—

   (*a*) Compute total and marginal revenue to complete the table above.
   (*b*) At what rate of output is total revenue maximized?
   (*c*) At what rate of output is MR less than price?
   (*d*) At what rate of output does MR first become negative?
   (*e*) Graph the demand and MR curves.
4. Assume that the following marginal costs exist in catfish production.

Quantity produced (units per day)	10	11	12	13	14	15	16	17	18	19
Marginal cost (per unit)	$ 3	5	7	9	12	15	18	21	25	29

(a) Graph the MC curve.
(b) Use the data on market demand from problem 3 to graph the demand and MR curves on the same graph.
(c) At what rate of output is MR = MC?
(d) What price will a monopolist charge for that much output?
(e) If the market were perfectly competitive, what price would prevail? How much output would be produced?

5. Compute marginal revenues from the following data on market demand:

Price per unit	$40	36	32	25	20	12	4
Units demanded	10	12	14	17	25	50	150
Marginal revenue	—	—	—	—	—	—	—

6. If the price elasticity of demand for oil were 0.1, by how much would the price of oil have risen in response to the September 2003 OPEC production cutback? (See Headline, p. 164.)
7. If the on-campus demand for soda is as follows:

Price (per can)	$0.25	0.50	0.75	1.00	1.25	1.50	1.75	2.00
Quantity demanded (per day)	100	90	80	70	60	50	40	30

and the marginal cost of supplying a soda is 50 cents, what price will students end up paying in
(a) a perfectly competitive market?
(b) a monopolized market?

8. According to the Headline on p. 167, how much profit per year might the producers of Cardizem have been making if their average total costs were equal to that of the generic substitute.

Web Activities

1. Log on to www.usdoj.gov and do a keyword search using "monopoly." List two current activities the Department of Justice is involved in against monopolies. Explain briefly why each action is being taken.
2. Log on to www.ftc.gov/be/econrpt.htm and choose a recent economic report prepared by the FTC that discusses a monopoly market. Summarize this report and explain how the FTC is regulating the market.
3. Log on to thomas.loc.gov and complete a keyword search using "monopoly." Click on a piece of legislation, of your choosing, and print it out. How is this legislation intended to help or harm monopolies in the United States?
4. Log on to http://moneycentral.msn.com/investor/home.asp and complete a search on the CNBC website using the keyword "monopoly." Choose a recent article and explain what characteristics exist that make the market being discussed a monopoly.

Living Econ

How Much Should I Charge?

Perhaps you don't think of yourself as a monopolist, but you may have faced the same pricing issues encountered by a monopoly if you ever set the price for a fund-raising event such as a school concert, a bake sale, or even a garage sale. You had to decide whether to set a high price, a low price, or a price somewhere in between. In making this decision about price, you were exerting a degree of monopoly power, even though the market was probably contestable and you were not subject to government regulation.

As the organizer of a relatively small event, you will not likely have enough information to apply the MR = MC profit maximization rule. Instead, you probably relied on prior experience and your best judgment as a pricing guideline. But some economic principles, whether conscious or not, also were embedded in this decision.

According to the law of demand, if you set the price too high you will lose many of your potential customers. On the other hand, if you set the price too low, total costs might be greater than total revenue. The goal is obviously to find a price somewhere in the middle of these two extremes. So the next time you are faced with establishing a price, pay careful attention to revenues and costs in an effort to maximize profits.

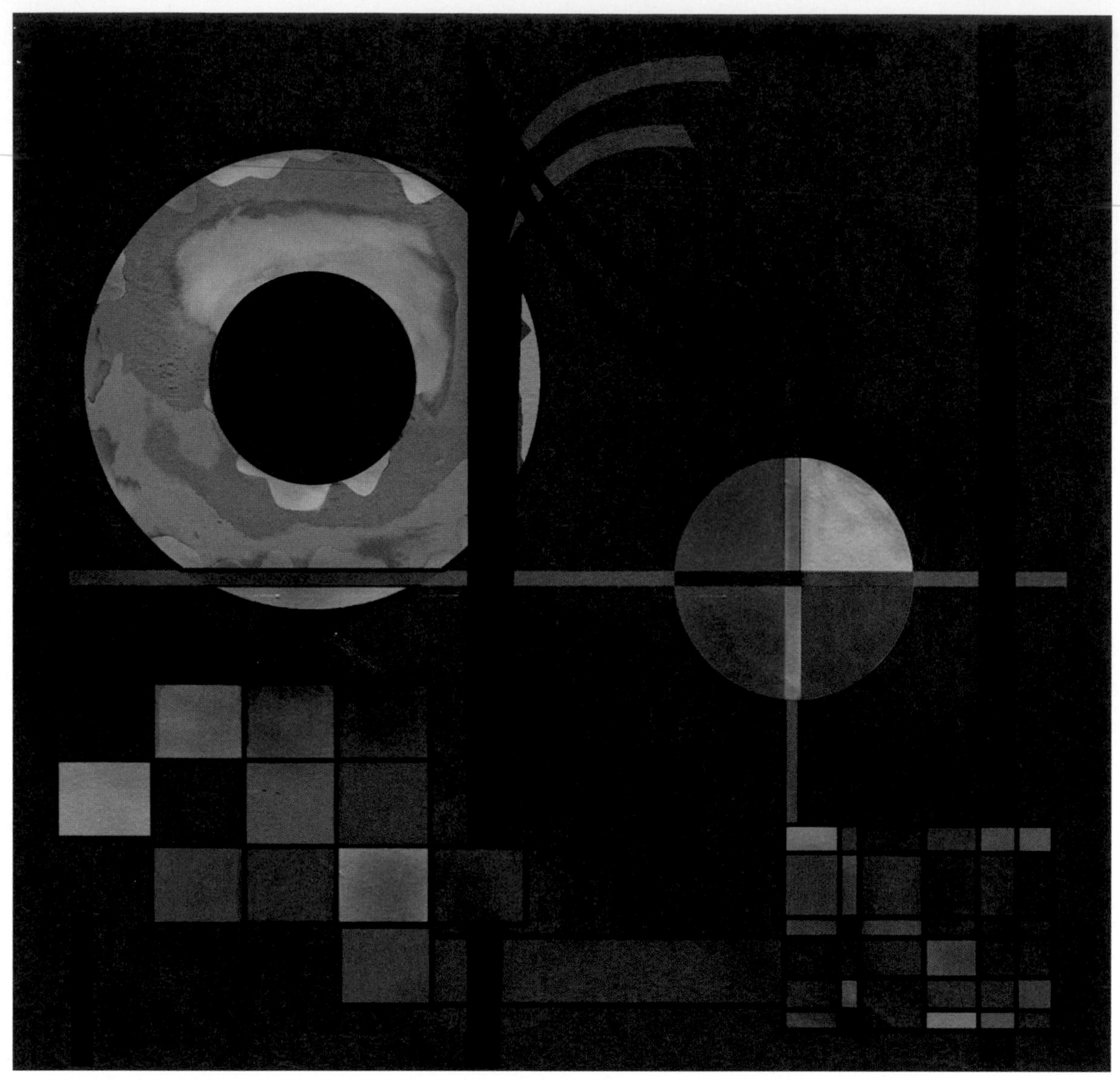

The Labor Market

CHAPTER 8

In 2004, the chairman of Walt Disney Company was two-thirds through a 10-year contract paying him $771 million for his services. Tiger Woods was in the fifth year of a Nike endorsement contract worth at least $100 million and Lebron James was in the second year of a $90 million Nike contract. Yet, the president of the United States was paid only $400,000. And the secretary who typed the manuscript of this book was paid just $19,000. What accounts for these tremendous disparities in earnings?

And why is it that the average college graduate earns over $55,000 a year while the average high school graduate earns just $32,000? Are such disparities simply a reward for enduring four years of college, or do they reflect real differences in talent? Are you really learning anything that makes you that much more valuable than a high school graduate? For that matter, what are you worth? Not in metaphysical terms but in terms of the wages that you would get paid in the marketplace.

If we are to explain why some people earn a great deal of income while others earn very little, we will have to consider both the *supply* and the *demand* for labor. In this regard, the following questions arise:

- How do people decide how much time to spend working?
- What determines the wage rate an employer is willing to pay?
- Why are some workers paid so much and others so little?

To answer these questions, we need to examine the behavior of labor *markets.*

Labor Supply

The following two ads appeared in the campus newspaper of a well-known university:

> Will do ANYTHING for money: able-bodied liberal-minded male needs money, will work to get it. Have car. Call Tom 555–0244.

> Web Architect: Computer sciences graduate, strong programming skills and software knowledge (e.g., Flash, DreamWeaver). Please call Margaret 555–3247, 9–5.

Although placed by individuals of very different talents, the ads clearly expressed Tom's and Margaret's willingness to work. We don't know how much money they were asking for their respective talents, or whether they ever found jobs, but we can be sure that they were prepared to take a job at some wage rate. Otherwise, they would not have paid for the ads in the "Jobs Wanted" column of their campus newspaper.

labor supply The willingness and ability to work specific amounts of time at alternative wage rates in a given time period, ceteris paribus.

The advertised willingness to work expressed by Tom and Margaret represents a **supply of labor.** They are offering to sell their time and talents to anyone who is willing to pay the right price. Their explicit offers are similar to those of anyone who looks for a job. Job seekers who check the current job openings at the student employment office or send résumés to potential employers are demonstrating a willingness to accept employment—that is, to *supply* labor. The 25,000 Muscovites who applied for jobs at Russia's first McDonald's were also offering to supply labor (see Headline).

Our first concern in this chapter is to explain these labor-supply decisions. As Figure 8.1 illustrates, we expect the quantity of labor supplied—the number of hours people are willing to work—to increase as wage rates rise. At the Moscow McDonald's, 25,000 job applicants were willing to work for $2.50 an hour. Were McDonald's paying a higher wage, even more job seekers might have shown up.

HEADLINE LABOR SUPPLY

In Moscow, 25,000 Apply for 630 Jobs at McDonald's

More than 25,000 Muscovites have dreams of flipping burgers beneath the golden arches as a member of the worldwide Big Mac and French fry brigade, eager to share in the West's most greasy rite of passage.

The flood of job seekers started almost immediately after a Moscow newspaper advertisement was published last month. More than 1,000 applications for the 630 available crew spots came the first day, said George Cohon, deputy chairman of Moscow McDonald's. More than 3,100 interviews have been conducted, seven days a week, with such criteria as whether applicants are legal Moscow residents.

Many job seekers are housewives and students from the prestigious Moscow University, and more than 20 percent speak two languages. Hiring is almost complete now, said Cohon, with only a few spots left to be filled. . . .

The Pushkin Square outlet, the biggest McDonald's in the world, will serve 15,000 diners a day, with 700 seats inside and 200 outside. . . .

Part-time Soviet workers make about 1½ rubles per hour, said Cohon, which is $2.50 at the commercial rate. But workers will also be rewarded every few months for productivity.

—Kara Swisher

NOTE: People supply labor by demonstrating a willingness to work. The quantity of labor supplied increases as the wage rate rises.

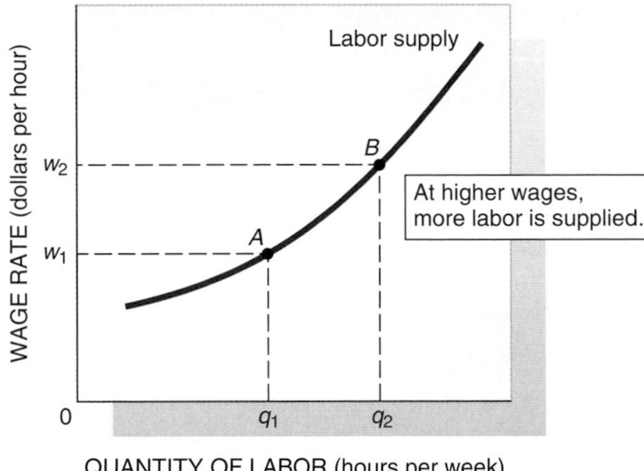

FIGURE 8.1
The Supply of Labor
The quantity of any good or service offered for sale typically increases as its price rises. Labor supply responds in the same way. At the wage rate w_1, the quantity of labor supplied is q_1 (point *A*). At the higher wage w_2, workers are willing to work more hours per week, that is, to supply a larger quantity of labor (q_2).

But how do people decide how many hours to supply at any given wage rate? Do people try to maximize their income? If they did, we would all be holding three jobs and sleeping on the commuter bus. Few of us actually live this way. Hence we must have other goals than simply maximizing our incomes.

Income vs. Leisure

The most visible benefit obtained from working is a paycheck. In general, the fatter the paycheck—the greater the wage rate offered—the more willing a person is to go to work.

As important as paychecks are, however, people recognize that working entails real sacrifices. Every hour we spend working implies one less hour available for other pursuits. If we go to work, we have less time to watch TV, go to a soccer game, or simply enjoy a nice day. In other words, there is a real **opportunity cost** associated with working. Generally, we say that ***the opportunity cost of working is the amount of leisure time that must be given up in the process.***

opportunity cost The most desired goods and services that are forgone in order to obtain something else.

Because both leisure and income are valued, we confront a tradeoff when deciding whether to go to work. Going to work implies more income but less leisure. Staying home has the opposite consequences.

The inevitable tradeoff between labor and leisure explains the shape of individual labor-supply curves. As we work more hours, our leisure time becomes more scarce—and thus more valuable. We become increasingly reluctant to give up any remaining leisure time as it gets ever scarcer. People who work all week long are reluctant to go to work on Saturday. It's not that they are physically exhausted. It's just that they want some time to enjoy the fruits of their labor. In other words, ***as the opportunity cost of job time increases, we require correspondingly higher rates of pay.*** We will supply additional labor—work more hours—only if higher wage rates are offered: this is the message conveyed by the upward-sloping labor-supply curve.

The upward slope of the labor-supply curve is reinforced with the changing value of income. Our primary motive for working is the income a job provides. Those first few dollars are really precious, especially if you have bills to pay and no other source of support. As you work and earn more, however, you discover that your most urgent needs have been satisfied. You may still want more things, but your consumption desires aren't so urgent. In other words, ***the marginal utility of income declines as you earn more.*** Accordingly, the wages offered for more work lose some of their

HEADLINE INCOME VS. LEISURE

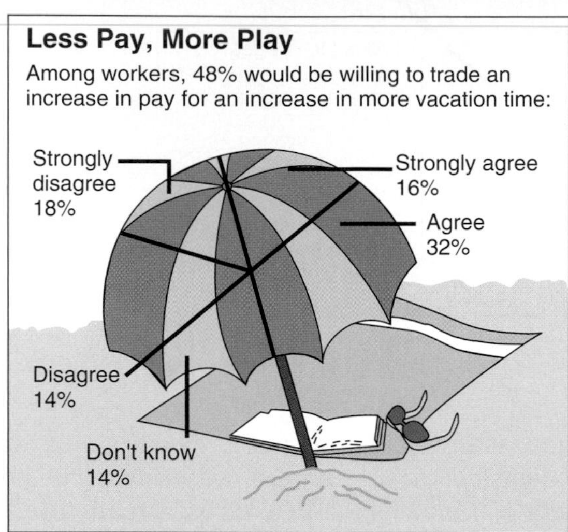

Source: *USA Today*, November 6, 2000, p. l.

NOTE: The labor supply decision entails a tradeoff between more leisure and more income. A lot of people feel they don't have enough leisure time and would give up some income to get it.

allure. You may not be willing to work more hours unless offered a higher wage rate.

The upward slope of an individual's labor-supply curve is thus a reflection of two phenomena:

- The increasing opportunity cost of labor.
- The decreasing marginal utility of income as a person works more hours.

As the accompanying Headline reveals, nearly 1 out of 2 U.S. workers would be willing to give up some pay for more leisure. As wages and living standards have risen, the urge for more money has abated. What people want is more leisure time to *spend* their incomes. As a result, ever higher wages are needed to lure people into working longer hours.

Money isn't necessarily the only thing that motivates people to work, of course. People *do* turn down higher-paying jobs in favor of lower-wage jobs that they like. Many mothers forgo high-wage "career" jobs in order to have more flexible hours and time at home. Volunteers offer their services just for the sense of contributing to their communities; no paycheck is required. Even MBA graduates say they are motivated more by the challenge of high-paying jobs rather than the money. When push comes to shove, however, money almost always makes a difference: people *do* supply more labor when offered higher wages.

market supply of labor The total quantity of labor that workers are willing and able to supply at alternative wage rates in a given time period, ceteris paribus.

Market Supply

The **market supply of labor** refers to all of the hours people are willing to work at various wages. It, too, is upward-sloping. As wage rates rise, not only do existing workers offer to work longer hours but other workers are drawn into the labor market as well. If jobs are plentiful and wages high, many students leave school and start working. Likewise, many homemakers decide that work outside the home is too hard to resist. The flow of immigrants into the labor market also increases when wages are high. As these various flows of labor-market entrants increase, the total quantity of labor supplied to the market goes up.

Labor Demand

Regardless of how many people are *willing* to work, it is up to employers to decide how many people will *actually* work. Employers must be willing and able to hire workers if people are going to find the jobs they seek. That is to say, there must be a **demand for labor.**

demand for labor The quantities of labor employers are willing and able to hire at alternative wage rates in a given time period, ceteris paribus.

The demand for labor is readily visible in the help-wanted section of the newspaper. Employers who pay for these ads are willing and able to hire a certain number of workers at specific wage rates. How do they decide what to pay or how many people to hire?

Derived Demand

In earlier chapters we emphasized that employers are profit maximizers. In their quest for maximum profits, firms seek the rate of output at which marginal revenue equals marginal cost. Once they have identified the profit-maximizing rate of output, firms enter factor markets to purchase the required amounts of labor, equipment, and other resources. Thus ***the quantity of resources purchased by a business depends on the firm's expected sales and output.*** In this sense, we say that the demand for factors of production, including labor, is a **derived demand;** it is derived from the demand for goods and services. As Boeing employees learned in 2003, when the demand for airplanes declines, so does the demand for the workers who make airplanes (see the following Headline).

derived demand The demand for labor and other factors of production results from (depends on) the demand for final goods and services produced by these factors.

Consider also the plight of strawberry pickers. Strawberry farming is a $650 million industry. Yet the thousands of pickers who toil in the fields earn only $7 an hour. The United Farm Workers union blames greedy growers for the low wages. They say if the farmers would only raise the price of strawberries by a nickel a pint, they could raise wages by 50 percent.

Unfortunately, employer greed is not the only force at work here. Strawberry growers, like most producers, would love to sell more strawberries at higher prices. If they did, there is a strong possibility that the growers would hire more pickers and even pay them a higher wage rate. But the growers must contend with the market demand for strawberries. If they increase the

DERIVED DEMAND HEADLINE

Boeing to Issue Layoff Notices

Boeing Co. plans to issue layoff notices today to 1,440 employees, as part of continuing employment reductions amid the commercial aviation industry's prolonged downturn. About 1,250 of those receiving the 60-day notices are in the Puget Sound area, where Chicago-based Boeing builds all but one of its commercial jets.

Source: *Bloomberg News,* August 22, 2003, p. 56.

NOTE: The demand for labor depends on the demand for the products labor produces.

HEADLINE UNEQUAL WAGES

Majoring in Money

Unfortunately, wisdom apparently is its only reward, as the job market for professional philosophers—or at least philosophy majors—continues to be weak, according to the latest *Monthly Labor Review.*

Daniel Hecker, an economist for the federal Bureau of Labor Statistics, computed the annual earnings of everyone who had graduated from college before 1991 and had a full-time job in 1993.

The least lucrative majors for both men and women: philosophy, religion and theology, probably because many of the paying gigs for these students are in the church, where the rewards presumably come in the next lifetime and not in the pay envelope.

Among mid-career men between the ages of 35 and 44, Hecker found that those who had majored in engineering and math as undergraduates earned the most. For similarly aged women, an economics degree was golden.

—Richard Morin

Annual Earnings by College Undergraduate Major *Men and Women Aged 35–44*

Men Top Five Majors		Women Top Five Majors	
1. Engineering	$53,286	1. Economics	$49,170
2. Mathematics	$51,584	2. Engineering	$49,070
3. Computer science	$50,509	3. Pharmacy	$48,427
4. Pharmacy	$50,480	4. Architecture	$46,353
5. Physics	$50,128	5. Computer science	$43,757
Bottom Five Majors		**Bottom Five Majors**	
1. Philosophy/Religion	$31,848	1. Philosophy/Religion	$25,788
2. Social work	$32,171	2. Education	$27,988
3. Visual and performing arts	$32,972	3. Home economics	$28,275
4. Foreign language/linguistics	$33,780	4. Social work	$28,594
5. Education	$34,470	5. Agriculture	$28,751

Source: Bureau of Labor Statistics.

NOTE: The pay of college graduates depends in part on what major they studied. Graduates who can produce goods and services in great demand get the highest pay.

price of strawberries—even by only 5 cents a pint—the quantity of berries demanded will decline. They'd end up hiring fewer workers. If profits declined, wage rates might suffer as well.

The link between the product market and the labor market also explains why graduates with engineering or computer science degrees are paid so much (see accompanying Headline). Demand for related products is growing so fast that employers are desperate to hire individuals with the necessary skills. By contrast, the wages of philosophy majors suffer from the fact that the search for meaning is no longer a growth industry.

The principle of derived demand suggests that if consumers really want to improve the lot of strawberry pickers, they should eat more strawberries. An increase in consumer demand for strawberries will motivate growers to

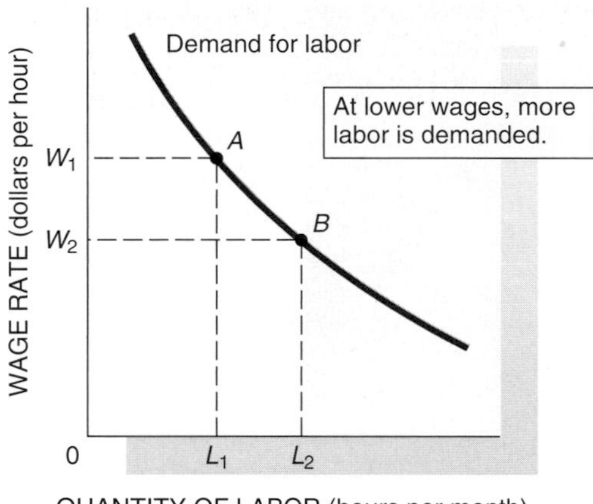

FIGURE 8.2
The Demand for Labor
The higher the wage rate, the smaller the quantity of labor demanded (*ceteris paribus*). At the wage rate W_1, only L_1 of labor is demanded. If the wage rate falls to W_2, a larger quantity of labor (L_2) will be demanded. The labor demand curve obeys the law of demand.

plant more berries and hire more labor to pick them. Until then, the plight of the pickers is not likely to improve.

The Wage Rate The number of strawberry pickers hired by the growers is not completely determined by consumer demand for strawberries. A farmer with tons of strawberries to harvest might still be reluctant to hire many workers at $30 an hour. At $7 per hour, however, the same farmer would hire a lot of help. That is to say, ***the quantity of labor demanded will depend on its price (the wage rate).*** In general, we expect that strawberry growers will be *willing to hire* more pickers at low wages than at high wages. Hence the demand for labor is not a fixed quantity; instead, there is a varying relationship between quantity demanded and price (wage rate). Like virtually all other demand curves, the labor-demand curve is downward-sloping (see Figure 8.2).

Marginal Physical Product

The downward slope of the labor-demand curve reflects the changing productivity of workers as more are hired. Each worker isn't as valuable as the next. On the contrary, each additional worker tends to be *less* valuable as more workers are hired. In the strawberry fields, a worker's value is measured by the number of boxes he or she can pick in an hour. More generally, we measure a worker's value to the firm by his or her **marginal physical product (MPP),** that is, the *change* in total output that occurs when an additional worker is hired. In most situations, ***marginal physical product declines as more workers are hired.***

marginal physical product (MPP) The change in total output associated with one additional unit of input.

Suppose for the moment that Marvin, a college dropout with three summers of experience as a canoe instructor, can pick 5 boxes of strawberries per hour. These 5 boxes represent Marvin's marginal physical product (MPP)—in other words, the *addition* to total output that occurs when the grower hires Marvin. That is

$$\text{Marginal physical product} = \frac{\text{change in total output}}{\text{change in quantity of labor}}$$

Marginal physical product establishes an *upper limit* to the grower's willingness to pay. Clearly the grower can't afford to pay Marvin more than 5 boxes of strawberries for an hour's work; the grower will not pay Marvin more than he produces.

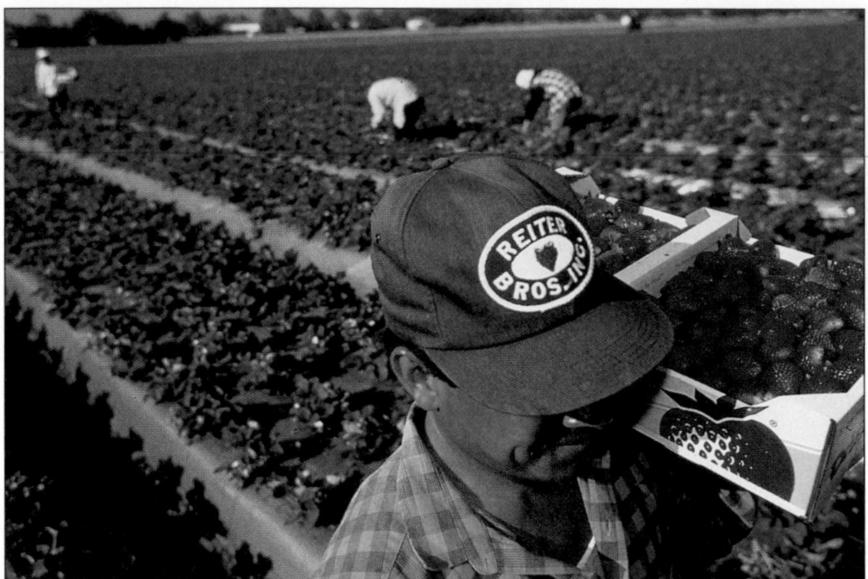

The 25,000 pickers who harvest America's $650 million strawberry crop are paid only $7 an hour. Why is their pay so low?

© David Butow/Corbis SABA.

Marginal Revenue Product

Most strawberry pickers don't want to be paid in strawberries, of course. At the end of a day in the fields, the last thing a picker wants to see is another strawberry. Marvin, like the rest of the pickers, wants to be paid in cash. To find out how much cash he might be paid, all we need to know is what a box of strawberries is worth. This is easy to determine. The market value of a box of strawberries is simply the price at which the grower can sell it. Thus Marvin's contribution to output can be measured in either marginal *physical* product (5 boxes per hour) or the dollar *value* of that product.

The dollar value of a worker's contribution to output is called **marginal revenue product (MRP).** Marginal revenue product is the *change* in total revenue that occurs when more labor is hired—that is,

$$\bullet \quad \text{Marginal revenue product} = \frac{\text{change in total revenue}}{\text{change in quantity of labor}}$$

marginal revenue product (MRP) The change in total revenue associated with one additional unit of input.

If the grower can sell strawberries for $2 a box, Marvin's marginal revenue product is 5 boxes per hour × $2 per box, or $10 per hour. This is Marvin's value to the grower. Accordingly, the grower can afford to pay Marvin up to $10 per hour. Thus ***marginal revenue product sets an upper limit to the wage rate an employer will pay.***

But what about a lower limit? Suppose that the pickers aren't organized and that Marvin is desperate for money. Under such circumstances, he might be willing to work—to supply labor—for only $6 an hour.

Should the grower hire Marvin for such a low wage? The profit-maximizing answer is obvious. If Marvin's marginal revenue product is $10 an hour and his wages are only $6 an hour, the grower will be eager to hire him. The difference between Marvin's marginal revenue product ($10) and his wage ($6) implies additional profits of $4 an hour. In fact, the grower will be so elated by the economics of this situation that he will want to hire everybody he can find who is willing to work for $6 an hour. After all, if the grower can make $4 an hour by hiring Marvin, why not hire 1,000 pickers and accumulate profits at an even faster rate?

The Law of Diminishing Returns

The exploitive possibilities suggested by Marvin's picking are too good to be true. For starters, how could the grower squeeze 1,000 workers onto one acre of land and still have any room left over for strawberry plants? You don't need two years of business school to recognize a potential problem here. Sooner or later the farmer will run out of space. Even before that limit is reached, the rate of strawberry picking may slow. Indeed, the grower's eagerness to hire additional pickers will begin to fade long before 1,000 workers are hired. The critical concept here is *marginal productivity.*

Diminishing MPP The decision to hire Marvin originated in his marginal physical product—that is, the 5 boxes of strawberries he can pick in an hour's

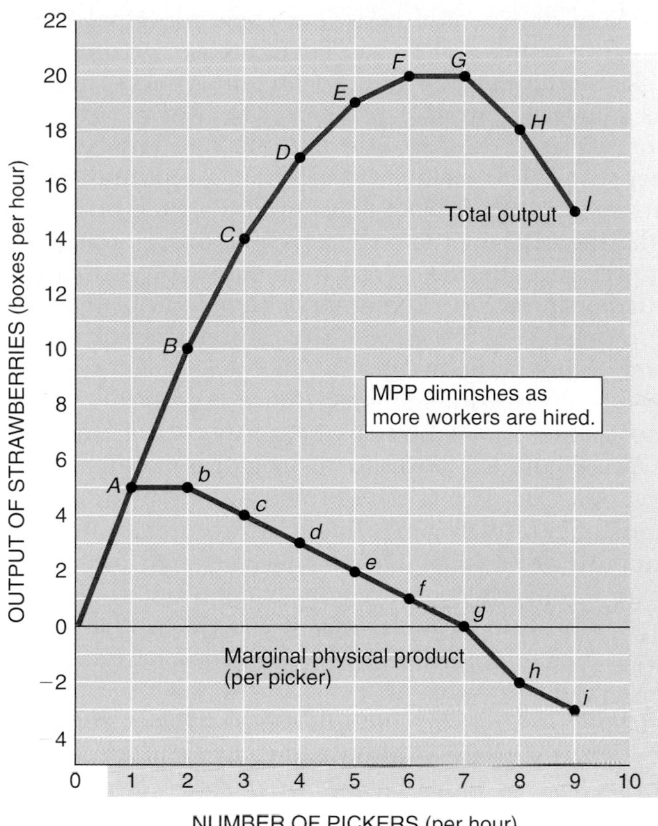

FIGURE 8.3
Diminishing Marginal Physical Product

The marginal physical product of labor is the increase in total production that results when one additional worker is hired. Marginal physical product tends to fall as additional workers are hired. This decline occurs because each worker has increasingly less of other factors (e.g., land) with which to work.

When the second worker (George) is hired, total output increases from 5 to 10 boxes per hour. Hence the second worker's MPP equals 5 boxes per hour. Thereafter, capital and land constraints diminish marginal physical product.

	Number of Pickers (per hour)	Total Strawberry Output (boxes per hour)	Marginal Physical Product (boxes per hour)
A	1 (Marvin)	5	5
B	2 (George)	10	5
C	3	14	4
D	4	17	3
E	5	19	2
F	6	20	1
G	7	20	0
H	8	18	−2
I	9	15	−3

time. To assess the wisdom of hiring additional pickers, we again have to consider what happens to total output as more workers are employed. To do so we need to keep track of marginal physical product.

Figure 8.3 shows how strawberry output changes as additional pickers are hired. We start with Marvin, who picks 5 boxes of strawberries per hour. Total output and his marginal physical product are identical, because he is initially the only picker employed. When the grower hires George, Marvin's old college roommate, we observe the total output increases to 10 boxes per hour (point *B* in Figure 8.3). This figure represents another increase of 5 boxes per hour. Accordingly, we may conclude that George's *marginal physical product* is 5 boxes per hour, the same as Marvin's. Naturally, the grower will want to hire George and continue looking for more pickers.

As more workers are hired, total strawberry output continues to increase, but not nearly as fast. Although the later hires work just as hard, the limited availability of land and capital constrain their marginal physical product. One problem is the number of boxes. There are only a dozen boxes, and the additional pickers often have to wait for an empty box. The time spent waiting depresses marginal physical product. The worst problem is space: as additional workers are crowded onto the one-acre patch, they begin to get in one another's way. The picking process is slowed, and marginal physical product is further depressed. Note that the MPP of the fifth picker is 2 boxes per hour, while the MPP of the sixth picker is only 1 box per hour. By the time we get to the seventh picker, marginal physical product actually falls to zero, as no further increases in total strawberry output take place.

Things get even worse if the grower hires still more pickers. If 8 pickers are employed, total output actually *declines*. The pickers can no longer work efficiently under such crowded conditions. Hence the MPP of the eighth worker is *negative*, no matter how ambitious or hardworking this person may be. Points *H* and *h* in Figure 8.3 illustrate this negative marginal physical product.

Our observations on strawberry production apply to most industries. Indeed, diminishing returns are evident in even the simplest production processes. Suppose you ask a friend to help you with your homework. A little help may go a long way toward improving your grade. Does that mean that your grade improvement will *double* if you get *two* friends to help? What if you get five friends to help? Suddenly, everyone's partying and your homework performance deteriorates. In general, ***the marginal physical product of labor eventually declines as the quantity of labor employed increases.***

law of diminishing returns The marginal physical product of a variable input declines as more of it is employed with a given quantity of other (fixed) inputs.

You may recognize the **law of diminishing returns** at work here. ***Marginal productivity declines as more people must share limited facilities.*** Typically, diminishing returns result from the fact that an increasing number of workers leaves each worker with less land and capital to work with.

Diminishing MRP As marginal *physical* product diminishes, so does marginal *revenue* product (MRP). As noted earlier, marginal revenue product is the increase in the *value* of total output associated with an added unit of labor (or other input). In our example, it refers to the increase in strawberry revenues associated with one additional picker.

The decline in marginal revenue product mirrors the drop in marginal physical product. Recall that a box of strawberries sells for $2. With this price and the output statistics of Figure 8.3, we can readily calculate marginal revenue product, as summarized in Table 8.1. As the growth of output

TABLE 8.1
Diminishing Marginal Revenue Product

Marginal revenue product measures the change in total revenue that occurs when one additional worker is hired. At constant product prices, MRP equals MPP × price. Hence MRP declines along with MPP.

Number of Pickers (per hour)	Total Strawberry Output (boxes per hour)	×	Price of Strawberries (per box)	=	Total Strawberry Revenue (per hour)	Marginal Revenue Product
0	0		$2		0	
						$ 10
1 (Marvin)	5		$2		$10	
						$ 10
2 (George)	10		$2		$20	
						$ 8
3	14		$2		$28	
						$ 6
4	17		$2		$34	
						$ 4
5	19		$2		$38	
						$ 2
6	20		$2		$40	
						$ 0
7	20		$2		$40	
						$−4
8	18		$2		$36	
						$−6
9	15		$2		$30	

diminishes, so does marginal revenue product. Marvin's marginal revenue product of $10 an hour has fallen to $6 by the time 4 pickers are employed and reaches zero when 7 pickers are employed.

The Hiring Decision

The tendency of marginal revenue product to diminish will clearly cool the strawberry grower's eagerness to hire 1,000 pickers. We still don't know, however, how many pickers will be hired.

The Firm's Demand for Labor

Figure 8.4 provides the answer. We already know that the grower is eager to hire pickers whose marginal revenue product exceeds their wage. Suppose the going wage for strawberry pickers is $6 an hour. At that wage, the grower will certainly want to hire at least 1 picker, because the MRP of the first picker is $10 an hour (point *A* in Figure 8.4). A second worker will be hired as well, because that picker's MRP (point *B* in Figure 8.4) also exceeds the going wage rate. In fact, ***the grower will continue hiring pickers until the MRP has declined to the level of the market wage rate.*** Figure 8.4 indicates that this intersection of MRP and the market wage rate (point *C*) occurs after 4 pickers are employed. Hence we can conclude that the grower will be willing to hire—will *demand*—4 pickers if wages are $6 an hour.

The folly of hiring more than 4 pickers is also apparent in Figure 8.4. The marginal revenue product of the fifth worker is only $4 an hour (point *D*). Hiring a fifth picker will cost more in wages than the picker brings in as revenue. The *maximum* number of pickers the grower will employ at prevailing wages is 4 (point *C*).

The law of diminishing returns also implies that all of the 4 pickers will be paid the same wage. Once 4 pickers are employed, we cannot say that any single picker is responsible for the observed decline in marginal revenue product. Marginal revenue product diminishes because each worker has less capital and land to work with, not because the last worker hired is less able than the others. Accordingly, the fourth picker cannot be identified as any

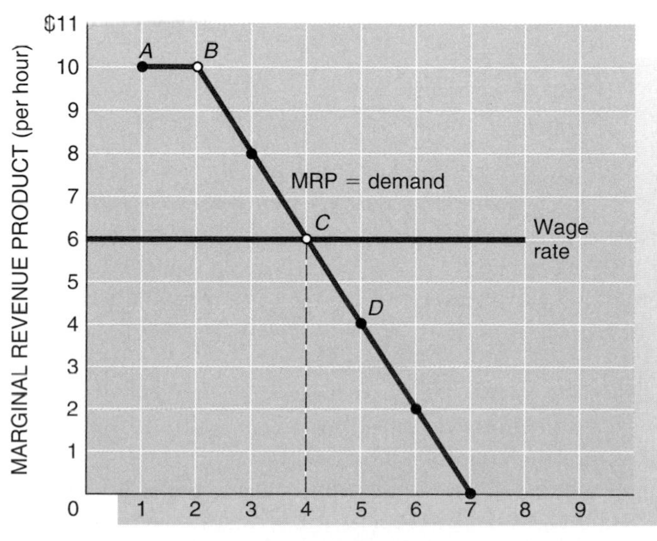

FIGURE 8.4
The Marginal Revenue Product Curve Is the Labor-Demand Curve
An employer is willing to pay a worker no more than his or her marginal revenue product. In this case, a grower would gladly hire a second worker, because that worker's MRP (point *B*) exceeds the wage rate ($6). The fifth worker will not be hired at that wage rate, however, since that worker's MRP (at point *D*) is less than $6. The MRP curve is the labor-demand curve.

HEADLINE MARGINAL REVENUE PRODUCT

Count it out. Two million dollars. Guaranteed.

What Bob Stoops will make as the University of Oklahoma football coach this season is more than the average American wage earner will see in a lifetime. It's roughly 25 times what the average college professor will pull down in the coming school year.

The figure is so sizable it disgusts some in higher education—an example, they say, of how far many colleges and universities have strayed from their basic mission, from teaching and research to the pursuit of athletic reputation and the purveyance of entertainment.

One of the anticipated returns on Oklahoma's dollar is now evident. Stoops and the defending national champion Sooners are projected among the front-runners for this year's title.

Texas will pay football coach Mack Brown $1.45 million and basketball coach Rick Barnes as much as $1 million if Barnes cashes in on enough incentives.

But the football program has sold out all of Memorial Stadium's 67 luxury suites at $65,000 a pop—and the waiting list is 50 deep. Season-ticket sales are up some 10,000 since Brown took over in 1998, and athletic donations have gone up by half to $15 million a year.

Coming off a 4–7 record and the firing of John Mackovic in 1997, "we could have hired a $250,000 coach. Money was tight." Texas athletic director DeLoss Dodds says. "But we hired somebody who could turn our business around, and he (Brown) has. If you ask me or you ask anybody 'Is he worth what we're paying?' absolutely he is. Now would we like to pay him less? Yes. But we're in a market that won't let that happen."

Millionaires Row *22 college football and 17 basketball head coaches who have annual deals worth at least $1 million:*

Football		
$2.1 million	Steve Spurrier	Florida
$2 million	Bob Stoops	Oklahoma
$1.5 million	Bobby Bowden	Florida State
$1.45 million	Mack Brown	Texas
$1.3 million	Barry Alvarez	Wisconsin
$1.3 million	Phillip Fulmer	Tennessee
Basketball		
$2.2 million	Rick Pitino	Louisville
$1.6 million	Mike Krzyzewski	Duke
$1.5 million	Tubby Smith	Kentucky
$1.2 million	Billy Donovan	Florida
$1.2 million	Matt Doherty	North Carolina

Source: *USA Today*, August 3, 2001, p. l.

NOTE: Colleges are willing to pay more for football coaches than professors. Successful coaches bring in much more revenue.

particular individual. Once 4 pickers are hired, Marvin's MRP is no higher than any other picker's. ***Each (identical) worker is worth no more than the marginal revenue product of the last worker hired, and all workers are paid the same wage rate.***

The principles of marginal revenue product apply to football coaches as well as strawberry pickers. The University of Texas's football coach earned more than $1.45 million in 2001 (see Headline). Why did he get paid nine times more than the university's president? Because his winning football team brought in 70,000 paying fans per game, plus lots of media exposure. The university thought his MRP justified the high salary.

If we accept the notion that marginal revenue product sets the wages of both football coaches and strawberry pickers, must we give up all hope for low-paid workers? Can anything be done to create more jobs or higher wages for pickers? To answer this, we need to see how market demand and supply interact to establish employment and wage levels.

Market Equilibrium

The principles that guide the hiring decisions of a single strawberry grower can be extended to the entire labor market. This suggests that the *market* demand for labor depends on

- The number of employers.
- The marginal revenue product of labor in each firm and industry.

On the supply side of the labor market we have already observed that the market supply of labor depends on

- The number of available workers.
- Each worker's willingness to work at alternative wage rates.

The supply decisions of each worker are in turn a reflection of tastes, income, wealth, expectations, other prices, and taxes.

Equilibrium Wage

Figure 8.5 brings these market forces together. ***The intersection of the market supply and demand curves establishes the equilibrium wage.*** In our previous example we assumed that the prevailing wage was $6 an hour. In reality, the market wage will be w_e, as illustrated in Figure 8.5. ***The equilibrium wage is the only wage at which the quantity of labor supplied equals the quantity of labor demanded.*** Everyone who is willing and able to work for this wage will find a job.

equilibrium wage The wage at which the quantity of labor supplied in a given time period equals the quantity of labor demanded.

Many people will be unhappy with the equilibrium wage. Employers may grumble that wages are too high. Workers may complain that wages are too low. Nevertheless, the equilibrium wage is the only one that clears the market.

Equilibrium Employment

The intersection of labor supply and demand determines not just the prevailing wage rate but the level of employment as well. In Figure 8.5, this equilibrium level of employment occurs at q_e. That is the only sustainable level of employment in that market, given prevailing supply and demand conditions.

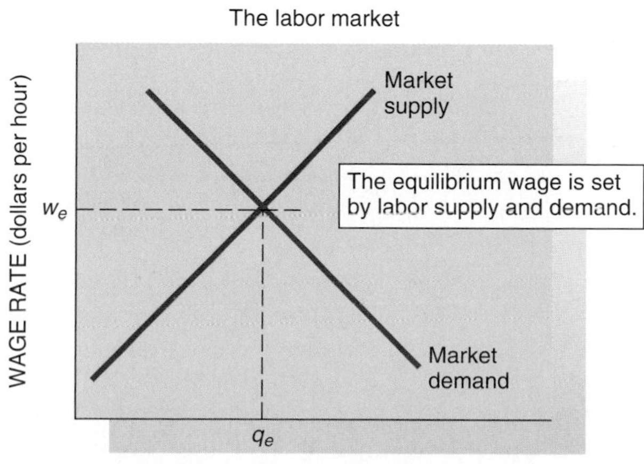

FIGURE 8.5
Equilibrium Wage

The intersection of *market supply* and *demand* determines the equilibrium wage in a competitive labor market. All of the firms in the industry can then hire as much labor as they want at that equilibrium wage. Likewise, anyone who is willing and able to work for the wage w_e will be able to find a job.

Changing Market Outcomes

The equilibrium established in any market is subject to change. If the University of Texas football teams started losing too many games, ticket and ad revenues would fall. Then the coach's salary might shrink. Likewise, if someone discovered that strawberries cure cancer, those strawberry pickers might be in great demand. In this section, we examine how changing market conditions alter wages and employment levels.

Changes in Productivity

The law of diminishing returns is responsible for the tradeoff between wage and employment levels. The downward slope of the labor-demand curve does not mean wage *and* employment can never rise together, however. ***If labor productivity (MPP) rises, wages can increase without sacrificing jobs.***

Suppose that Marvin and his friends enroll in a local agricultural extension course and learn new methods of strawberry picking. With these new methods, the marginal physical product of each picker increases by 1 box per hour. With the price of strawberries still at \$2 a box, this productivity improvement implies an increase in marginal *revenue* product of \$2 per worker. Now farmers will be more eager to hire pickers. This increased demand for pickers is illustrated by the *shift* of the labor-demand curve in Figure 8.6.

Notice how the improvement in productivity has altered the value of strawberry pickers. The MRP of the fourth picker is now \$7 an hour (point *S*) rather than \$6 (point *C*). Hence the grower can now afford to pay higher wages. Or the grower could employ more pickers than before, moving from point *C* to point *E*. ***Increased productivity implies that workers can get higher wages without sacrificing jobs or more employment without lowering wages.*** Historically, increased productivity has been the most important source of rising wages and living standards.

Changes in Price

An increase in the price of strawberries would also help the pickers. Marginal revenue product reflects the interaction of productivity and product prices. If strawberry prices were to double, strawberry pickers would become twice as valuable, even without an increase in *physical* productivity. Such a

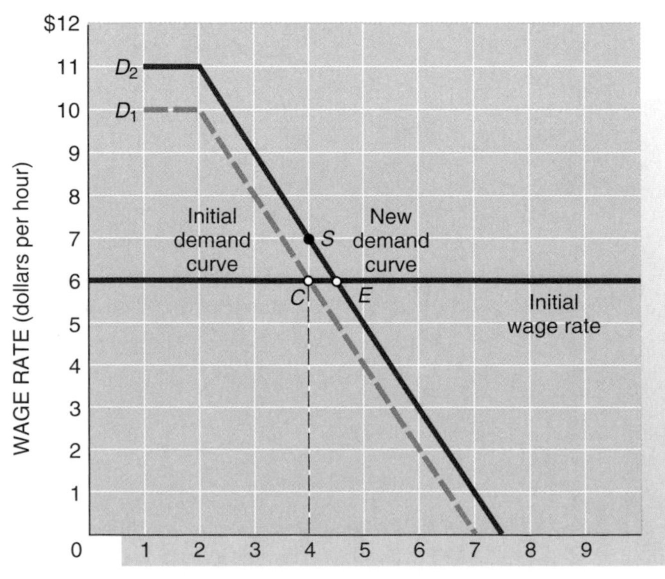

FIGURE 8.6
Increased Productivity

Wage and employment decisions depend on marginal revenue product. If productivity improves, the labor-demand curve shifts upward (e.g., from D_1 to D_2), raising the MRP of all workers. The grower can now afford to pay higher wages (point *S*) or hire more workers (point *E*).

DISEQUILIBRIUM WAGES HEADLINE

Senate GOP Blocks Minimum Wage Hike

Senate Democrats yesterday launched a new drive to raise the minimum wage but ran into a roadblock from Republicans, who sidetracked a major foreign operations bill so it could not be used as a vehicle for votes on the wage proposal and other Democratic initiatives.

Democrats argued that a minimum wage increase, last approved by Congress seven years ago, is long overdue and complained that Republicans were refusing to allow the Senate even to consider the issue.

The Democrats' proposal would raise the hourly wage floor from \$5.15 to \$6.65 in two annual steps: by 75 cents immediately after the bill is signed into law and by another 75 cents a year later.

Republicans did not respond publicly to Kennedy but have argued in the past that hardpressed employers will eliminate jobs to offset the cost of minimum wage increases.

—Helen Dewar

Source: *Washington Post*, July 12, 2003, p. 4.

Minimum-Wage History

Oct. '38	\$0.25	Jan '75	\$2.10
Oct. '39	0.30	Jan. '76	2.30
Oct. '45	0.40	Jan. '78	2.65
Jan. '50	0.75	Jan. '79	2.90
Mar. '56	1.00	Jan. '80	3.10
Sept. '61	1.15	Jan. '81	3.35
Sept. '63	1.25	Apr. '90	3.80
Feb. '67	1.40	Apr. '91	4.25
Feb. '68	1.60	Oct. '96	4.75
May. '74	2.00	Sept. '97	5.15

Source: *Houston Chronicle*, September 22, 2000, p. A9.

NOTE: The size of the job loss caused by a higher minimum wage depends on labor-market conditions.

change in product prices depends, however, on changes in the market supply and demand for strawberries.

Legal Minimum Wages

Rather than waiting for *market* forces to raise their wages, the strawberry pickers might seek *government* intervention. The U.S. government decreed in 1938 that no worker could be paid less than 25 cents per hour. Since then the U.S. Congress has repeatedly raised the legal minimum wage, bringing it to \$5.15 in 1997. As the accompanying Headline suggests, further increases are likely.

Figure 8.7 illustrates the consequences of such minimum-wage legislation. In the absence of government intervention, the labor-supply and -demand curves would establish the wage w_e. At that equilibrium q_e workers would be employed.

Demand-Side Effects When a legislated minimum wage of w_m is set, things change. Suddenly, the quantity of labor *demanded* declines. In the prior equilibrium employers kept hiring workers until their marginal revenue product fell to w_e. If a minimum wage of w_m must be paid, it no longer makes sense to hire that many workers. So employers back up on the labor demand curve from point *E* to point *D*. At *D*, marginal revenue product is high enough to justify paying the legal minimum wage. As a result of these retrenchments, however, some workers ($q_e - q_d$) lose their jobs.

Supply-Side Effects Note in Figure 8.7 what happens on the *supply* side as well. The higher minimum wage attracts more people into the labor market. The number of workers willing to work jumps from q_e (point *E*) to q_s (point *S*). Everybody wants one of those better-paying jobs.

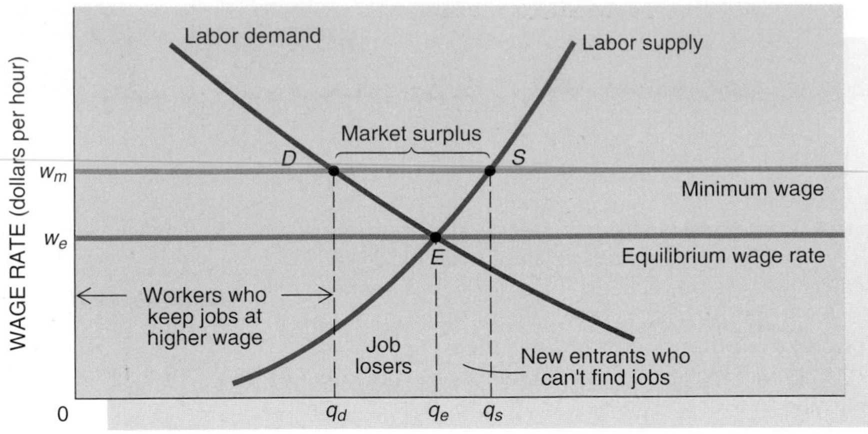

FIGURE 8.7
Minimum-Wage Effects
A minimum wage increases the quantity of labor supplied but reduces the quantity demanded. Some workers (q_d) end up with higher wages, but others ($q_s - q_d$) remain or become jobless.

There aren't enough jobs to go around, however. The number of jobs available at the minimum wage is only q_d; the number of job seekers at that wage is q_s. With more job seekers than jobs, unemployment results. We now have a market surplus (equal to q_s minus q_d). Those workers are unemployed.

Government-imposed wage floors thus have two distinct effects. ***A minimum wage***

- ***Reduces the quantity of labor demanded.***
- ***Increases the quantity of labor supplied.***

and thus,

- ***Creates a market surplus.***

The market surplus creates inefficiency and frustration, especially for those workers who are ready and willing to work but can't find a job. Not everyone suffers, however. Those workers who keep their jobs (at q_d in Figure 8.7) end up with higher wages than they had before. Accordingly, ***a legal minimum wage entails a tradeoff: some workers end up better off, while others end up worse off.*** Those most likely to end up worse off are teenagers and other inexperienced workers whose marginal revenue product is below the legal minimum wage. They will have the hardest time finding jobs when the legal wage floor is raised.

How many potential jobs are lost to minimum-wage hikes depends on how far the legal minimum is raised. The elasticity of labor demand is also important. Democrats argue that labor demand is inelastic, so few jobs will be lost. Republicans argue that labor demand is elastic, so more jobs are lost. The state of the economy is also critical. If the economy is growing rapidly, increases (shifts) in labor demand will help offset job losses resulting from a minimum-wage hike.

Labor Unions

Labor unions are another force that attempts to set aside equilibrium wages. The workers in a particular industry may not be satisfied with the equilibrium wage. They may decide to take *collective* action to get a higher wage. To do so, they form a labor union and bargain collectively with employers. This is what the United Farm Workers are trying to do in California's strawberry fields.

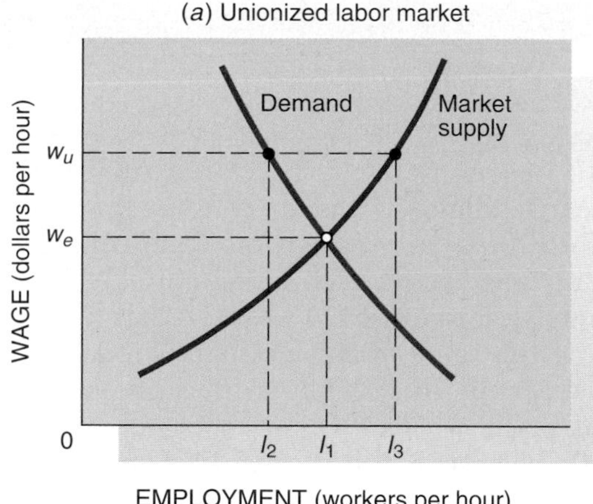

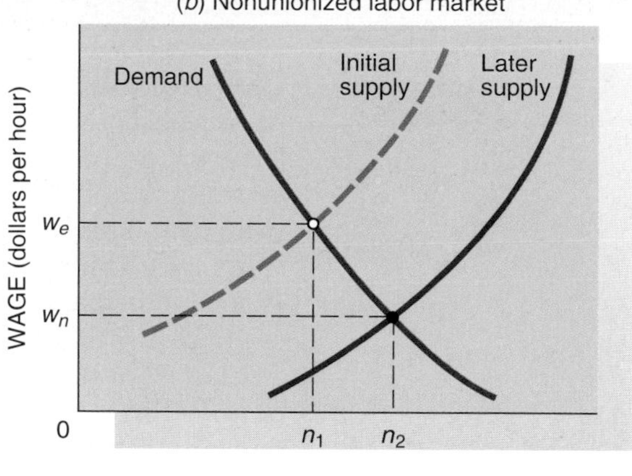

FIGURE 8.8 The Effect of Unions on Relative Wages

In the absence of unions, the average wage rate would be equal to w_e. As unions take control of the market, however, they seek to raise wage rates to w_u. The higher wage reduces the amount of employment in the unionized market from l_1 to l_2. The workers displaced from the unionizied market will seek work in the nonunionzed market, thereby shifting the nonunion supply curve to the right. The result will be a reduction of wage rates (to w_n) in the nonunionized market. Thus union wages end up higher than nonunion wages.

The formation of a labor union does not set aside the principles of supply and demand. The equilibrium wage remains at w_e, the intersection of labor supply and demand curves (see Figure 8.8*a*). If the union were successful in negotiating a higher wage (w_u in the figure), a labor-market surplus would appear ($l_3 - l_2$ in Figure 8.8*a*). These jobless workers would compete for the union jobs, putting downward pressure on the union-negotiated wage. Hence ***to get and maintain an above-equilibrium wage, a union must exclude some workers from the market.*** Effective forms of exclusion include union membership, required apprenticeship programs, and employment agreements negotiated with employers.

What happens to the excluded workers? In the case of a national minimum wage (Figure 8.7), the surplus workers remain unemployed. A union, however, sets above-equilibrium wages in only one industry or craft. Accordingly, there are lots of other potential jobs for the excluded nonunion workers. Their wages will suffer, however. As workers excluded from the unionized market (Figure 8.8*a*) stream into the nonunionized market (Figure 8.8*b*), they shift the nonunionized labor supply to the right. This influx of workers depresses nonunion wages, dropping them from w_e to w_n.

Although the theoretical impact of union exclusionism on relative wages is clear, empirical estimates of that impact are fairly rare. We do know that union wages in general are significantly higher than nonunion wages ($20.65 versus $16.42 per hour in 2003). But part of this differential is due to the fact that unions are more common in industries that have always been more capital-intensive and have paid relatively high wages. When comparisons are made within particular industries or sectors, the differential narrows considerably. Nevertheless, there is a general consensus that unions have managed to increase their relative wages from 15 to 20 percent.

POLICY PERSPECTIVES

Capping CEO Pay

As we observed at the beginning of this chapter, the chairman of the Walt Disney Company signed a 10-year contract in 1997 that may pay him an astronomical $771 million (see Headline). If Disney can pay that much to its chairman, surely it could afford to pay more than the legal minimum wage to its least skilled workers. But Disney says such a comparison is irrelevant. When challenged to defend his pay, Disney's CEO asserted that he had earned every penny of it by enhancing the value of the company's stock.

Critics of CEO pay don't accept this explanation. They make three points. First, the rise in the price of Disney's *stock* is not a measure of marginal revenue product. Only part of the increase in share prices was due to the company's performance: the rest was due to a general upswing in the stock market. Second, the revenues of the Walt Disney Company probably wouldn't be $771 million less in the absence of Eisner. Hence his marginal revenue product is less than $771 million. Finally, Eisner probably would have worked just as hard for, say, just $400 million or so. Therefore, his actual pay was more than required to elicit the desired supply response.

Critics conclude that many CEO paychecks are out of line with the realities of supply and demand. They want corporations to reduce CEO pay and revise the process used for setting CEO pay levels.

"O.K. guys, now lets go and *earn* that four hundred times our workers' salaries."

The wages of top corporate officers may not be fully justified by their marginal revenue product.

William Hamilton, New York Magazine, April 24, 2000.

Unmeasured MRP One of the difficulties in determining the appropriate level of CEO pay is the elusiveness of marginal revenue product. It is easy to measure the MRP of a strawberry picker or even a sales clerk who sells Disney toys. But a corporate CEO's contributions are less well defined. A CEO is supposed to provide strategic leadership and a sense of mission. These are critical to a corporation's success but hard to quantify.

Congress confronts the same problem in setting the president's pay. We noted earlier that the president of the United States is paid $400,000 a year. Can we argue that this salary represents his marginal revenue product? The Headline on page 196 suggests that the president's pay would be in the range of $38–58 million if he was paid on performance (MRP). The wage we actually pay the president of the United States is less a reflection of his contribution to total output than a matter of custom. His salary also reflects the price voters believe is required to induce competent individuals to forsake private-sector jobs and assume the responsibilities of the presidency. In this sense, the wage paid to the president and other public officials is set by their **opportunity wage—**that is, the wage they could earn in private industry.

The same kinds of considerations influence the wages of college professors. The marginal revenue product of a college professor is not easy to measure. Is it the number of students he or she teaches, the amount of knowledge conveyed, or something else? Confronted with such problems, most universities tend to pay college professors according to their **opportunity wage—**that is, the amount the professors could earn elsewhere.

opportunity wage The highest wage an individual would earn in his or her best alternative job.

Opportunity wages also help explain the difference between the wage of the chairman of Disney and the workers who peddle its products. The lower wage of sales clerks reflects not only their marginal revenue product at

MEASURING MRP HEADLINE

Disney Chief May Reap $771 Million

By any measure, Michael Eisner, the chief executive of the Walt Disney Co., has been one of America's most successful corporate executives. And by any measure, he has been handsomely compensated for it.

Eisner, in fact, could be poised to become one of the most richly rewarded employees in the history of American business. Thanks to a new 10-year pay package that includes generous stock options, the top executive of the entertainment conglomerate could reap nearly $771 million over the next decade, according to estimates by the compensation expert who designed Eisner's new contract. The figure doesn't include Eisner's $750,000-per-year salary or bonuses that could add another $15 million annually. . . .

But Watson said Eisner's compensation will be worth it if he can help Disney keep up its historical growth. He noted that options only have value if the company's stock keeps appreciating. Indeed, companies award executives options in order to motivate them to keep share value rising.

Under Eisner, Disney has been one of Wall Street's stellar performers. Its revenue has grown from $1.5 billion in 1984 to $18.7 billion in 1996. And its stock has soared during that period—from $3 per share to $75.37½ as of Friday, after adjusting for splits.

Even Graef Crystal, a frequently quoted critic of huge executive pay packages, grudgingly says Disney's board had to offer Eisner his huge new deal. "The package he got is awesome," he said. "But if Sony had tried to lure him away, they would have offered him Tokyo and thrown in Kyoto as a bonus."

—Paul Farhi

Source: 1997, the Washington Post. *Washington Post*, February 22, 1997, p. 81. Reprinted with permission.

NOTE: If CEOs are credited with a company's profit growth, their MRP would seem astronomical. A CEO's unique contribution to company profits isn't necessarily so evident, however.

Disney stores but also the fact that they are not trained for many other jobs. That is to say, their opportunity wages are low. By contrast, Disney's CEO has impressive managerial skills that are in demand by many corporations; his opportunity wages are high. According to the Headline above, Sony Corporation might have offered Eisner all of Tokyo as his base pay!

Opportunity wages help explain CEO pay but don't fully justify such high pay levels. If Disney's CEO pay is justified by opportunity wages, that means that another company would be willing to pay him that much. But what would justify such high pay at another company? Would his MRP be any easier to measure? Maybe *all* CEO paychecks have been inflated.

Critics of CEO pay conclude that the process of setting CEO pay levels should be changed. All too often, executive pay scales are set by self-serving committees comprised of executives of the same or similar corporations. Critics want a more independent assessment of pay scales, with nonaffiliated experts and stockholder representatives. Some critics want to go a step further and set mandatory caps on CEO pay. President Clinton rejected legislated caps but convinced Congress to limit the tax deductibility of CEO pay. Any unjustified CEO pay in excess of $1 million a year cannot be treated as a business expense but must instead be paid out of after-tax profits. This change puts more pressure on corporations to examine the rationale for multimillion-dollar paychecks.

If markets work efficiently, such government intervention should not be necessary. Corporations that pay their CEOs excessively will end up with smaller profits than companies who pay market-based wages. Over time, lean companies will be more competitive than fat companies, and excessive pay scales will be eliminated. Legislated CEO pay caps imply that CEO labor markets aren't efficient or that the adjustment process is too slow.

HEADLINE UNDERPAID PRESIDENTS

What's a President Worth?

So what if the president were paid like a CEO? On the basis of performance, a president would be worth up to $58 million a year—if he meets certain goals, compensation experts say. What those goals might be:

	Possible payout
Inflation A key to everything from credit card rates\ to grocery prices. Say the annualized rate is 2.5% or less.	**$10 million to $14 million**
Economic growth A growing economy means prosperity from Wall Street to Main Street. Gross National Product growth of 3% or more.	**$15 million to $23 million**
Crime Reduction in murders, robberies, and other serious crimes.	**$5 million to $8 million**
Employment Cut unemployment to 4%.	**$3 million to $5 million**
Intangibles Foreign policy successes, lowering the trade deficit, environmental issues, cutting the costs of government.	**$5 million to $8 million**

Total annual potential pay: $38 million to $58 million

If the nation's president and chief executive were running a major corporation, he probably would find a proposed pay raise to $400,000 laughable.

Compared with what Jack Welch makes at General Electric and Lou Gerstner makes at IBM, that's pocket change.

In the private sector, a CEO running a huge corporation would earn $34 million to $58 million a year, much of it from incentive bonuses and stock options, says compensation expert Graef Crystal of the online newsletter *crystalreport.com.*

At $400,000 a year, the president makes more than 99 percent of all workers. But he oversees a budget of $1.8 trillion, 11 times the annual revenue of the nation's largest company, General Motors. He's boss of 4.2 million employees, both civilian and military, six times as many as the largest private employer, Wal-Mart.

Yet he would have to work 2,878 years to bring home the $576 million that Walt Disney CEO Michael Eisner made last year, largely from exercising stock options he was granted as incentives.

In 1980, *Fortune* 500 CEOs averaged $625,000 a year, a little more than three times what President Carter was making. By 1990, the average CEO was making 10 times more than President Bush. And last year, in the wake of generous stock options awarded in a booming market, the CEO-to-president ratio swelled to 53-to-1.

—Del *Jones* and Gary Strauss

Source: *USA Today,* May 27, 1999, p. Al.

NOTE: If the nation's president were paid on the basis of his marginal revenue product, his salary would be a lot higher than $400,000.

SUMMARY

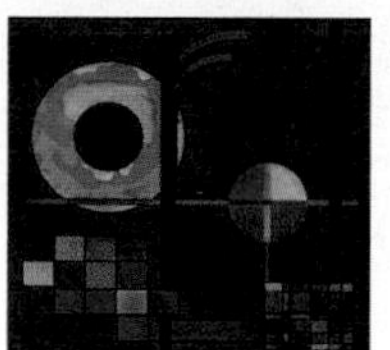

- The economic motivation to work arises from the fact that people need income to buy the goods and services they desire. As a consequence, people are willing to work—to supply labor.
- There is an opportunity cost involved in working—namely, the amount of leisure time one sacrifices. People willingly give up additional leisure only if offered higher wages. Hence the labor supply curve is upward sloping.
- A firm's demand for labor reflects labor's marginal revenue product. A profit-maximizing employer will not pay a worker more than the value of what the worker produces.
- The marginal revenue product of labor tends to diminish as additional workers are employed on a particular job (the law of diminishing returns). This decline occurs because additional workers have to share existing land and capital, leaving each worker with less land and capital to work with. The decline in MRP gives labor-demand curves their downward slope.
- The equilibrium wage is determined by the intersection of labor supply and demand curves. Attempts to set above-equilibrium wages cause labor surpluses by reducing the jobs available and increasing the number of job seekers.
- Labor unions attain above-equilibrium wages by excluding some workers from a particular industry or craft. The excluded workers increase the labor supply in the nonunion market, depressing wages there.
- Differences in marginal revenue product are an important explanation of wage inequalities. But the difficulty of measuring MRP in many instances leaves many wage rates to be determined by custom, power, discrimination, or opportunity wages.

Terms to Remember

Define the following terms:

labor supply
opportunity cost
market supply of labor
demand for labor
derived demand
marginal physical product (MPP)
marginal revenue product (MRP)
law of diminishing returns
equilibrium wage
opportunity wage

Questions for Discussion

1. Why are you doing this homework? What are you giving up? What do you expect to gain? If homework performance determined course grades, would you spend more time doing it?
2. Why does the opportunity cost of doing homework increase as you spend more time doing it?
3. The Headline on p. 182 implies that students sacrifice a lot of potential income when they major in philosophy, education, or other social work. Is such behavior rational?
4. Suppose George is making $18 an hour installing electronic chips in handheld computers. Would your offer to work for $8 an hour get

you the job? Why might a profit-maximizing employer turn down your offer?

5. Under what conditions might an increase in the minimum wage *not* reduce the number of low-wage jobs? How much of a job loss is acceptable?
6. The United Farm Workers wants strawberry pickers to join their union. They hope then to convince consumers to buy only union strawberries. Will such activities raise picker wages? What else might help?
7. Explain why marginal physical product would diminish as
   (*a*) More secretaries are hired in an office.
   (*b*) More professors are hired in the economics department.
   (*c*) More construction workers are hired to build a school.
8. Why are professors of computer science paid more than professors of English literature?
9. How might you measure the marginal revenue product of (*a*) a quarterback, (*b*) the team's coach?
10. Should President Bush's salary be performance-based (see Headline, p. 196)? Why is the president's salary so low?

Problems

1. According to Figure 8.4, how many workers would be hired if the prevailing wage were
   (*a*) $8 an hour?
   (*b*) $7 an hour?
2. The following table depicts the number of grapes that can be picked in an hour with varying amounts of labor:

Number of pickers (per hour)	1	2	3	4	5	6	7	8
Output of grapes (in flats)	20	38	53	64	71	74	74	70

   Use this information to graph the total and marginal physical product of grape pickers.
3. Assuming that the price of grapes is $1.50 per flat, use the data in problem 2 to graph the marginal revenue product of grape pickers. How many pickers will be hired if the going wage rate is $10.50 per hour?
4. In Figure 8.7.
   (*a*) How many workers lose their jobs when the minimum wage is enacted?
   (*b*) How many workers are unemployed at the minimum wage?
   (*c*) What accounts for the difference between the answers to (*a*) and (*b*)?
5. What is the approximate marginal revenue product of the University of Texas football coach (see Headline, p. 188)? Is the university overpaying him?
6. In December 2000, the Texas Rangers baseball team agreed to pay shortstop Alex Rodriguez at least $25 million per year for 10 years. If this salary were to be covered by ticket sales only, how many more tickets per game would the Rangers have to sell to cover Rodriguez's salary in the 81 home games if the average ticket price is $20? Are there any additional sources of revenue the Rangers might be able to use to cover the cost of Rodriguez's salary?

Web Activities

1. Log on to www.whitehouse.gov/fsbr/employment.html and click on the link for the civilian labor force.
   (*a*) In general, what has happened to the labor force (supply) since 1993?
   (*b*) Using the same source, click on the link for unemployment. During that same period, what was happening to the number of people unemployed?
   (*c*) Are these two numbers inconsistent?
2. Log on to www.census.gov/ftp/pub/hhes/www/img/edugraph.html and list the three top-paying degrees. Why do these degrees pay so much? In your answer, include a discussion of the opportunity wage.
3. Log on to stats.bls.gov, click on "Average Hourly Earnings" (under "Latest Numbers") and then Table B-3. Record the current average hourly wage rate for the private sector. Explain, in terms of marginal revenue product, why an employer would hire a worker at this wage rate.

Living Econ

How Much Will I Earn?

In this chapter, you learned that pay levels depend on a number of factors. You can use the list below to help you evaluate your earnings prospects after college. For most people, pay level is one of several incentives for choosing a specific career path.

- Market supply: if few other graduates compete for the same job, then pay will be higher.
- Market demand: if workers are productive in your chosen career, then pay will be higher.
- Labor unions: if the industry is unionized, then pay will be higher.
- Opportunity wages: if you have opportunities to work in other fields, then pay will be higher.

Of course, individual pay levels will vary within a specific labor market depending on your location, your skills, and even your bargaining ability. And, future labor markets will differ; in particular, today's high-paying jobs likely will attract more people into the field, causing lower future pay levels.

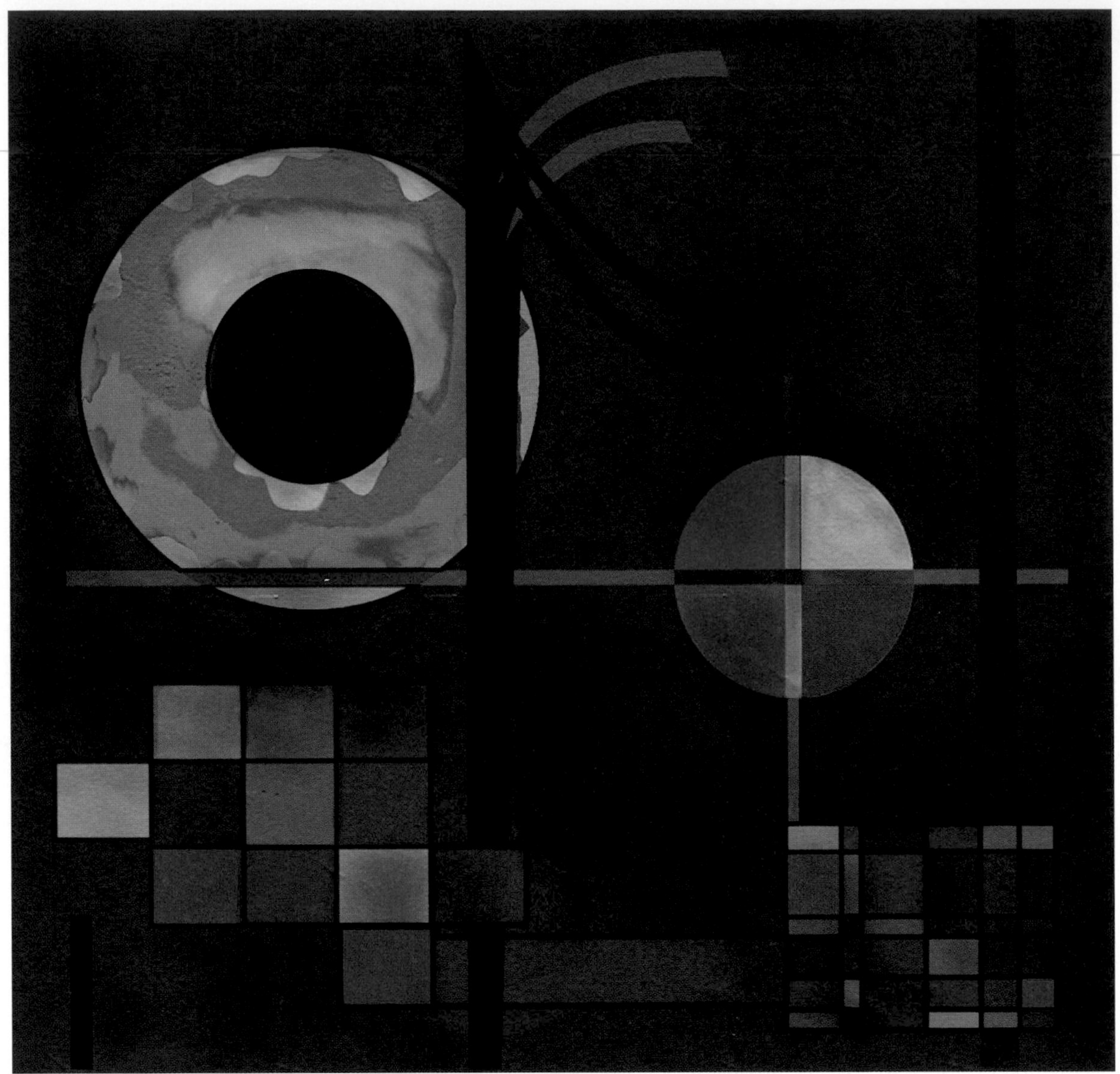

Government Intervention

CHAPTER 9

The market has a keen ear for private wants, but a deaf ear for public needs.

—Robert Heilbroner

Adam Smith was the eighteenth-century economist who coined the phrase *laissez faire*. He wanted the government to "leave it [the market] alone" so as not to impede the efficiency of the marketplace. But even Adam Smith felt the government had to intervene on occasion. He warned in *The Wealth of Nations*, for example, that firms with market power might meet together and conspire to fix prices or restrain competition. He also recognized that the government might have to give aid and comfort to the poor. So he didn't really believe that the government should leave the market *entirely* alone. He just wanted to establish a *presumption* of market efficiency.

Economists, government officials, and political scientists have been debating the role of government ever since. So has the general public. Although people are quick to assert that government is too big, they are just as quick to demand more schools, more police, and more income transfers.

The purpose of this chapter is to help define the appropriate scope of government intervention in the marketplace. To this end, we try to answer the following questions:

- Under what circumstances do markets fail?
- How can government intervention help?
- How much government intervention is desirable?

As we'll see, there is substantial agreement about how and when markets fail to give us the best WHAT, HOW, and FOR WHOM answers. There is much less agreement about whether government intervention improves the situation. Indeed, an overwhelming majority of Americans are ambivalent about government intervention. They want the government to fix the mix of output, to protect the environment, and to ensure an adequate level of income for everyone. But voters are equally quick to blame government meddling for many of our economic woes.

Market Failure

We can visualize the potential for government intervention by focusing on the WHAT question. Our goal here is to produce the best possible mix of output with existing resources. We illustrated this goal earlier with production-possibilities curves. Figure 9.1 assumes that of all the possible combinations of output we could produce, the unique combination at point *X* represents the most desirable, that is, the **optimal mix of output.**

optimal mix of output The most desirable combination of output attainable with existing resources, technology, and social values.

The Nature of Market Failure

We have observed how the market mechanism can help us find this desired mix of output. The **market mechanism** moves resources from one industry to another in response to consumer demands. If we demand more computers—offer to buy more at a given price—more resources (labor) will be allocated to computer manufacturing. Similarly, a fall in demand will encourage producers to stop making computers and offer their services in another industry. Changes in market prices direct resources from one industry to another, moving us along the perimeter of the production-possibilities curve.

market mechanism The use of market prices and sales to signal desired outputs (or resource allocations).

The big question is whether the mix of output selected by the market mechanism is the one most desired by society. If so, we don't need government intervention to change the mix of output. If not, we may need government intervention to guide the invisible hand of the market.

We use the term **market failure** to refer to less than perfect (suboptimal) outcomes. If the invisible hand of the marketplace produces a mix of output that is different from the one society most desires, then it has failed. ***Market failure implies that the forces of supply and demand have not led us to the best point on the production-possibilities curve.*** Such a failure is illustrated by point *M* in Figure 9.1. Point *M* is assumed to be the mix of output generated by market forces. Notice that the market mix (*M*) does not represent the optimal mix, which is assumed to be at point *X*. The market in this case *fails*; we get the wrong answer to the WHAT question. Specifically, too many computers are produced at point *M* and too few of other goods. We would be better off with a slightly different mix of output.

market failure An imperfection in the market mechanism that prevents optimal outcomes.

Market failure opens the door for government intervention. If the market can't do the job, we need some form of *nonmarket* force to get the right

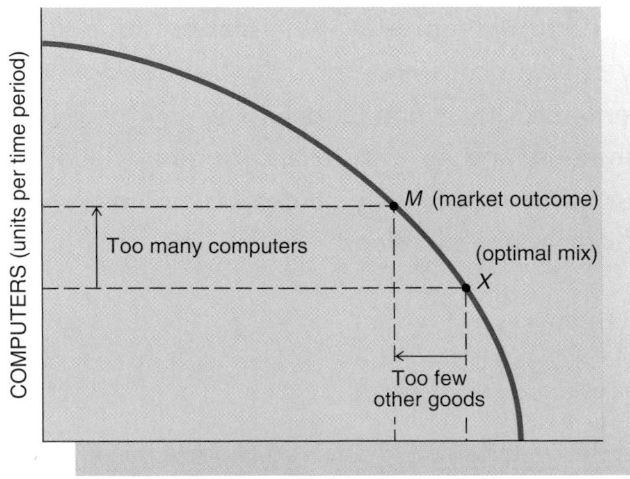

FIGURE 9.1
Market Failure

We can produce any mix of output on the production-possibilities curve. Our goal is to produce the optimal (best possible) mix of output, as represented by point X. Market forces, however, may produce another combination, like point M. In that case, the market fails—it produces a suboptimal mix of output.

answers. In terms of Figure 9.1, we need something to change the mix of output—to move us from point *M* (the market mix of output) to point *X* (the optimal mix of output). Accordingly, ***market failure establishes a basis for government intervention.***

Sources of Market Failure

Because market failure is the justification of government intervention, we need to know how and when market failure occurs. ***There are four specific sources of microeconomic market failure:***

- ***Public goods***
- ***Externalities***
- ***Market power***
- ***Equity***

We will examine the nature of these micro problems in this chapter. We will also take note of failures due to *macro* instability. Along the way we'll see why government intervention is called for in each case.

Public Goods

The market mechanism has the unique capability to signal consumer demands for various goods and services. By offering to pay higher or lower prices for some goods, we express our collective answer to the question of WHAT to produce. However, the market mechanism works efficiently only if the benefits of consuming a particular good or service are available only to the individuals who purchase that product.

Consider doughnuts, for example. When you eat a doughnut, you alone enjoy its greasy, sweet taste—that is, you derive a *private* benefit. No one else reaps any significant benefit from your consumption of a doughnut: the doughnut you purchase in the market is yours alone to consume. Accordingly, your decision to purchase the doughnut will be determined by your anticipated satisfaction as well as your income and opportunity costs.

Joint Consumption

Many of the goods and services produced in the public sector are different from doughnuts—and not just because doughnuts look, taste, and smell different from nuclear submarines. When you buy a doughnut, you exclude others from consumption of that product. If Dunkin' Donuts sells a particular pastry to you, it cannot supply the same pastry to someone else. If you devour it, no one else can. In this sense, the transaction and product are completely private.

The same exclusiveness is not characteristic of public goods such as national defense. If you buy a nuclear submarine to patrol the Pacific Ocean, there is no way you can exclude your neighbors from the protection your submarine provides. Either the submarine deters would-be attackers or it doesn't. In the former case, both you and your neighbors survive happily ever after; in the latter case, we are all blown away together. In that sense, you and your neighbors either consume or don't consume the benefits of nuclear submarine defenses *jointly*. There is no such thing as exclusive consumption here. The consumption of nuclear defenses is a communal feat, no matter who pays for them. For this reason, national defense is regarded as a **public good** or product, in the sense that ***consumption of a public good by one***

public good A good or service whose consumption by one person does not exclude consumption by others.

person does not preclude consumption of the same good by another person. By contrast, a doughnut is a **private good** because if I eat it, nobody else can consume it.

private good A good or service whose consumption by one person excludes consumption by others.

The Free-Rider Dilemma

The communal nature of public goods leads to a real dilemma. If you and I will *both* benefit from nuclear defenses, which one of us should buy the nuclear submarine? I would prefer, of course, that *you* buy it, thereby providing me with protection at no direct cost. Hence I may profess no desire for nuclear subs, secretly hoping to take a **free ride** on your market purchase. Unfortunately, you, too, have an incentive to conceal your desire for national defenses. As a consequence, neither one of us may step forward to demand nuclear subs in the marketplace. We will both end up defenseless.

free rider An individual who reaps direct benefits from someone else's purchase (consumption) of a public good.

Flood control is also a public good. No one in the valley wants to be flooded out. But each landowner knows that a flood-control dam will protect *all* the landowners, regardless of who pays. Either the entire valley is protected or no one is. Accordingly, individual farmers and landowners may say they don't *want* a dam and aren't willing to *pay* for it. Everyone is waiting and hoping that someone else will pay for flood control. In other words, everyone wants a *free ride*. Thus, if we leave it to market forces, no one will *demand* flood control and everyone in the valley will be washed away.

Exclusion The difference between public goods and private goods rests on *technical* considerations, not political philosophy. The central question is whether we have the technical capability to exclude nonpayers. In the case of national defense or flood control, we simply don't have that capability. Even city streets have the characteristics of public goods. Although we could theoretically restrict the use of streets to those who pay to use them, a toll gate on every corner would be exceedingly expensive and impractical. Here, again, joint or public consumption appears to be the only feasible alternative. As the accompanying Headline on Napster emphasizes, the technical capability to exclude nonpayers is the key factor in identifying public goods.

To the list of public goods we could add the administration of justice, the regulation of commerce, and the conduct of foreign relations. These services—which cost tens of *billions* of dollars and employ thousands of workers—provide benefits to everyone, no matter who pays for them. More importantly, there is no evident way to exclude *nonpayers* from the benefits of these services.

The free rides associated with public goods upset the customary practice of paying for what you get. If I can get all the streets, defenses, and laws I desire without paying for them, I am not about to complain. I am perfectly happy to let you pay for the services while all of us consume them. Of course, you may feel the same way. Why should you pay for these services if you can consume just as much of them when your neighbors foot the whole bill? It might seem selfish not to pay your share of the cost of providing public goods. But you would be better off in a material sense if you spent your income on doughnuts, letting others pick up the tab for public services.

Underproduction Because the familiar link between paying and consuming is broken, public goods cannot be peddled in the supermarket. People are reluctant to buy what they can get free. This is a perfectly rational response for a consumer who has only a limited amount of income to

PUBLIC GOODS HEADLINE

Napster Gets Napped

Shawn Fanning had a brilliant idea for getting more music—download it from friends' computers to the Internet. So he wrote software that enables online sharing of audio files. This peer-to-peer (P2P) online distribution system became an overnight sensation: within a year's time, 38 million consumers were using Napster's software to acquire recorded music.

At first blush, Napster's service looked like a classic public good. The service was free, and one person's consumption did not impede another person from consuming the same service. Moreover, the distribution system was configured in such a way that nonpayers could not be excluded from the service.

The definition of *public good* relies, however, on whether nonpayers *could* be excluded, not whether they are excluded. In other words, technology is critical in classifying goods as public or private. In Napster's case, encryption technology that could exclude nonpayers was available, but the company had *chosen* not to use it. After being sued by major recording companies for copyright infringement, Napster sold out. In 2001 the company joined up with Bertelsmann (BMG Records) and reconfigured its software to exclude nonpayers. Now consumers have to pay for that private good.

NOTE: A product is a public good only if nonpayers *cannot* be excluded from its consumption.

spend. Hence ***if public goods were marketed like private goods, everyone would wait for someone else to pay.*** The end result might be a total lack of public services. This is the kind of dilemma Robert Heilbroner had in mind when he spoke of the market's "deaf ear" (see quote at the beginning of this chapter).

The production-possibilities curve in Figure 9.2 illustrates the dilemma created by public goods. Suppose that point *A* represents the optimal mix of private and public goods. It is the mix of goods and services we would select if everyone's preferences were known and reflected in production decisions. The market mechanism will not lead us to point *A*, however, because the demand for public goods will be hidden. If we rely on the

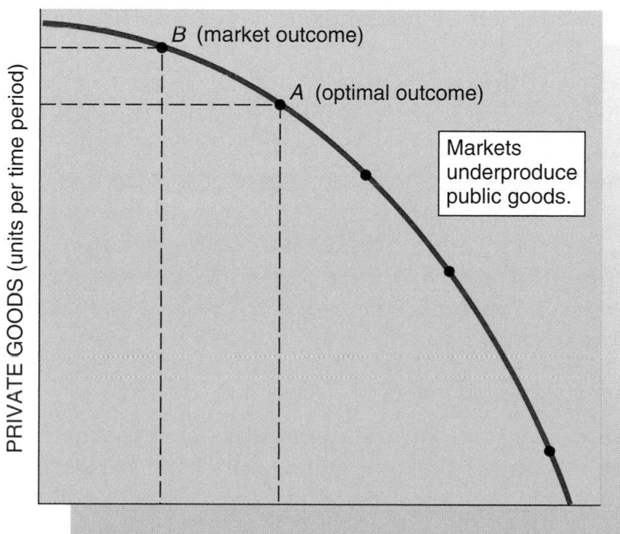

FIGURE 9.2
Underproduction of Public Goods

Suppose point *A* represents the optimal mix of output, i.e., the mix of private and public goods that maximizes society's welfare. Because consumers will not demand purely public goods in the marketplace, the price mechanism will not allocate so many resources to the production of public goods. Instead, the market will tend to produce a mix of output like point *B*, which includes fewer public goods and more private goods than is optimal.

market, nearly everyone will withhold demand for public goods, waiting for a *free ride* to point *A*. As a result, ***the market tends to underproduce public goods and overproduce private goods.*** The market mechanism will leave us at a mix of output like that at point *B*, with few, if any, public goods. Since point *A* is assumed to be optimal, point *B* must be *suboptimal* (inferior to point *A*).

Figure 9.2 illustrates how the market fails: we cannot rely on the market mechanism to allocate resources to the production of public goods, no matter how much they might be desired. If we want more public goods, we need a *nonmarket* force—government intervention—to get them. The government will have to force people to pay taxes, then use the tax revenues to pay for the production of defense, flood control, and other public goods.

Note that we are using *public good* in a different way than most people use it. To most people, the term *public good* refers to any good or service the government produces. In economics, however, the meaning is much more restrictive. ***The distinction between public goods and private goods is based on the nature of the goods, not who produces them.*** The term "public good" refers only to those goods and services that are consumed jointly, both by those who pay for them and by those who don't. Public goods can be produced by either the government or the private sector. Private goods can be produced in either sector as well.

Externalities

The free-rider problem associated with public goods provides one justification for government intervention into the market's decision about WHAT to produce. It is not the only justification, however. Further grounds for intervention arise from the tendency of costs or benefits of some market activities to spill over onto third parties.

Your demand for a good reflects the amount of satisfaction you expect from its consumption. Often, however, your consumption may affect others. The purchase of cigarettes, for example, expresses a smoker's demand for that good. But others may suffer from that consumption. In this case, smoke literally spills over onto other consumers, causing them discomfort and possibly even ill health (see Headline). Yet their loss is not reflected in the market—the harm caused to nonsmokers is *external* to the market price of cigarettes.

externalities Costs (or benefits) of a market activity borne by a third party; the difference between the social and private costs (benefits) of a market activity.

The term **externalities** refers to all costs or benefits of a market activity borne by a third party, that is, by someone other than the immediate producer or consumer. Whenever externalities are present, the preferences expressed in the marketplace will not be a complete measure of a good's value to society. As a consequence, the market will fail to produce the right mix of output. Specifically, ***the market will underproduce goods that yield external benefits and overproduce those that generate external costs.*** Government intervention may be needed to move the mix of output closer to society's optimal point.

Consumption Decisions

Externalities often originate on the demand side of markets. Consumers are always trying to maximize their personal well-being by buying products that deliver the most satisfaction (marginal utility) per dollar spent. In the process, they aren't likely to consider how the well-being of others is affected by their consumption behavior.

EXTERNALITIES HEADLINE

Passive Smoke Doesn't Kill—Or Does It?

A newly released study claiming that the danger of secondhand smoke is greatly overstated has provoked protests from antismoking advocates.

According to the study, which will appear in the prestigious *British Journal of Medicine*, exposure to secondhand smoke had no significant effect on death rates from lung cancer or heart disease. The rates were similar for those with spouses who smoked and those with nonsmoking spouses, the study found.

As word of the study's findings began to circulate, antismoking activists released a barrage of data showing the health dangers of secondhand smoke.

According to experts in the fields of cancer and heart disease, existing research shows that secondhand smoke boosts cancer and heart disease mortality by 10 percent to 30 percent. A 2002 summary of 58 studies by the International Agency for Research on Cancer blames exposure to secondhand smoke for a 22 percent increased risk of lung-cancer death in women and a 36 percent higher risk in men.

—Marilyn Chase and Vanessa O'Connell

Source: *Wall Street Journal*, May 16, 2003, p. B1.

NOTE: People who smoke feel the pleasures of smoking justify the cost (price). But nonsmokers end up bearing an external cost—secondhand smoke—that they don't voluntarily assume.

External Costs Automobile driving illustrates the problem. The amount of driving one does is influenced by the price of a car and the marginal costs of driving it. But automobile use involves not only *private costs* but *external costs* as well. When you cruise down the highway, you are adding to the congestion that slows other drivers down. You're also fouling the air with the emissions (carbon monoxide, hydrocarbons, etc.) your car spits out. The quality of the air other people breathe gets worse. Hence some people are made *worse* off when your auto consumption is making you *better* off.

Do you take account of such *external* costs when you buy a car? Not likely. Your willingness to buy a car is more likely to reflect only *your* expected satisfaction. Hence the *market* demand for cars doesn't fully represent the interests of society. Instead, market demand reflects only *private* benefits.

To account more fully for our *collective* well-being, we must distinguish the *social* demand for a product from the *market* demand whenever externalities exist. This isn't that difficult. We simply recognize that

- Social demand = market demand + externalities

In the case of autos, the externality is *negative,* that is, an external *cost*. Hence the social demand for cars is less than the (private) market demand. Put simply, this means we'd own and drive fewer cars if we took into account the external costs (pollution, congestion) that our cars caused. We don't, of course, since we're always trying to maximize our personal well-being. Market failure results.

Figure 9.3 illustrates the divergence between the social demand for automobiles and the market demand. The market demand expresses the anticipated *private* benefits of driving. Because of the *external* costs (congestion, pollution) associated with driving, the market demand *overstates* the social benefits of auto consumption. To represent the *social* demand for cars, we must subtract external costs from the private benefits. This leaves us with the *social demand* curve in Figure 9.3. Notice that the market alone would

FIGURE 9.3
Social vs. Market Demand

Whenever external costs exist, market demand overstates (lies above) social demand. At p_1 the market would demand q_M cars. Because of external costs, however, society wants only q_S cars at that price.

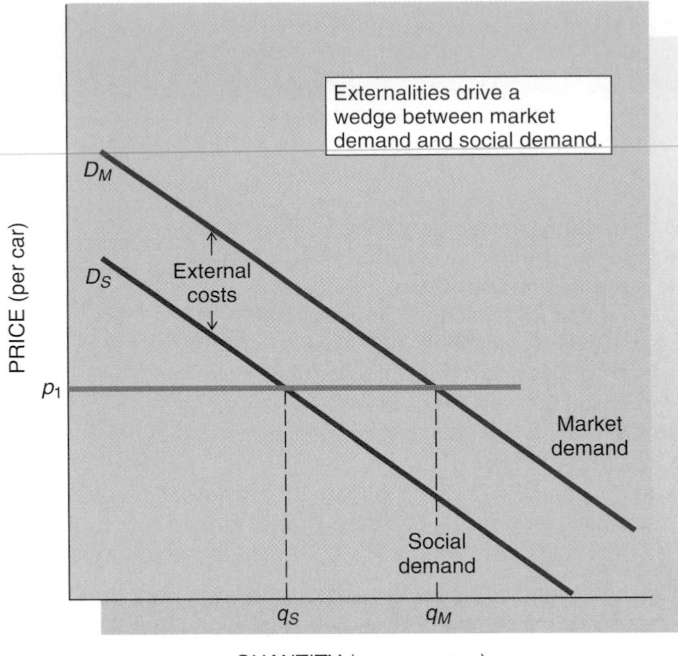

produce *more* cars at any price than is socially optimal. At the price p_1, for example, the market demands q_M cars, but society really wants only the quantity q_S.

A divergence between social and private costs can be observed even in the simplest of consumer activities, such as throwing an empty soda can out the window of your car. To hang onto the soda can and later dispose of it in a trash barrel involves personal effort and thus private marginal costs. Throwing it out the window effectively transfers the burden of disposal costs to someone else. Thus private costs can be distinguished from social costs. The resulting externality ends up as roadside litter.

The same kind of divergence between private and social costs helps to explain why people abandon old cars in the street rather than haul them to scrap yards. It also explains why people use vacant lots as open dumps. In all of these cases, ***the polluter benefits by substituting external costs for private costs.*** In other words, market incentives encourage environmental damage.

External Benefits Not all consumption externalities are negative. Completing this course will benefit you personally, but it may benefit society as well. If more knowledge of economics makes you a better-informed voter, your community will reap some benefit from your education. If you share the lessons of supply and demand with friends, they will benefit without ever attending class. If you complete a research project that helps markets function more efficiently, others will sing your praises. In all these cases, an *external* benefit augments the private benefit of education. ***Whenever external benefits exist, the social demand exceeds the market demand.*** In Figure 9.3, the social demand would lie *above* the market demand if external *benefits* were present. Society wants more of those goods and services generating external benefits than the market itself will demand. This is why governments subsidize education.

Production Decisions

Externalities also exist in production. A power plant that burns high-sulfur coal damages the surrounding environment. Yet the damage inflicted on neighboring people, vegetation, and buildings is external to the cost calculations of the firm. Because the cost of such pollution is not reflected in the price of electricity, the firm will tend to produce more electricity (and pollution) than is socially desirable. To reduce this imbalance, the government has to step in and change market outcomes.

Suppose you're operating an electric power plant. Power plants are major sources of air pollution and responsible for nearly all thermal water pollution. Hence your position immediately puts you on the most-wanted list of pollution offenders. But suppose you bear society no grudges and would truly like to help eliminate pollution. Let's consider the alternatives.

Profit Maximization Figure 9.4*a* depicts the marginal and average total costs (MC and ATC) associated with the production of electricity. By equating

(*a*) **Using cheap but polluting process**

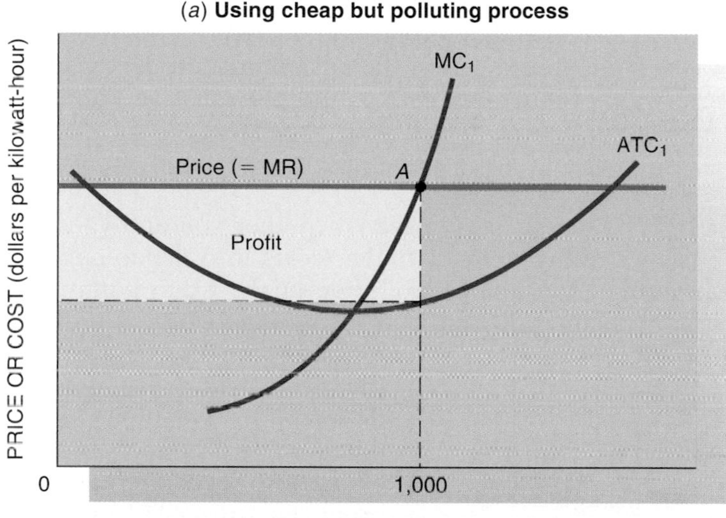

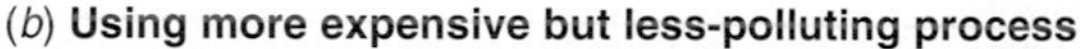

(*b*) **Using more expensive but less-polluting process**

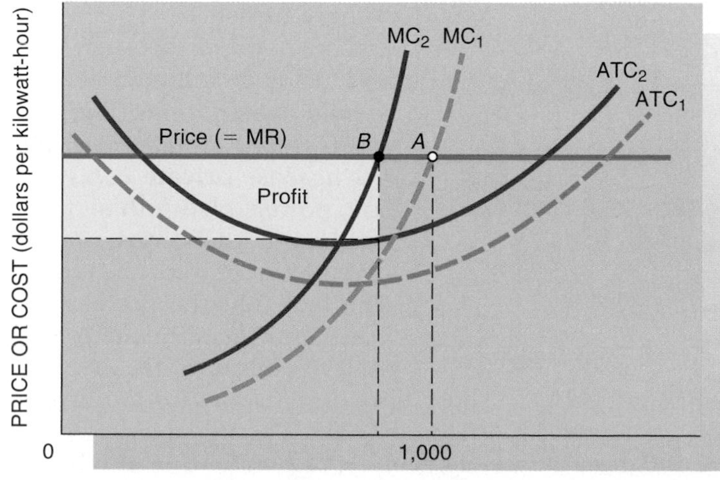

FIGURE 9.4
Profit Maximization vs. Pollution Control

Production processes that control pollution may be more expensive than those that do not. If they are, the MC and ATC curves will shift upward (to MC_2 and ATC_2). These higher costs will reduce output and profits. In this case, the profit-maximizing point moves to point *B* from point *A* and total profit shrinks. Hence a producer has an incentive to continue polluting, using cheaper technology.

marginal cost (MC) to price (= marginal revenue, MR), we observe (point *A*) that profit maximization occurs at an output of 1,000 kilowatt-hours per day. Total profits are illustrated by the shaded rectangle between the price line and the average total cost (ATC) curve.

The profits illustrated in Figure 9.4*a* are achieved in part by use of the cheapest available fuel under the boilers (which create the steam that rotates the generators). Unfortunately, the cheapest fuel is high-sulfur coal, a major source of air pollution. Other fuels (e.g., low-sulfur coal, fuel oil) pollute less but cost more. Were you to switch to one of them, the ATC and MC curves would both shift upward, as in Figure 9.4*b*. Under these conditions, the most profitable rate of output (point *B*) would be less than before (point *A*), and total profits would decline (note the smaller profit rectangle in Figure 9.3*b*). Thus pollution abatement can be achieved, but only by sacrificing some profit. If you owned this power plant, would you sacrifice profits for the sake of cleaner air?

The same kinds of cost considerations lead the plant to engage in thermal pollution. Cool water must be run through an electric utility plant to keep the turbines from overheating. And once the water runs through the plant, it is too hot to recirculate. Hence it must be either dumped back into the adjacent river or cooled off by being circulated through cooling towers. As you might expect, it is cheaper simply to dump the hot water in the river. The fish don't like it, but they don't have to pay the construction costs of cooling towers. Were you to get on the environmental bandwagon and build those towers, your production costs would rise, just as they did in Figure 9.4*b*. The fish would benefit, but at your expense.

External Cost The big question here is whether you and your fellow stockholders would be willing to incur higher costs in order to cut down on pollution. Eliminating either the air pollution or the water pollution emanating from the electric plant will cost a lot of money; eliminating both will cost much more. And to whose benefit? To the people who live downstream and downwind? We don't expect profit-maximizing producers to take such concerns into account. The behavior of profit maximizers is guided by comparisons of revenues and costs, not by philanthropy, aesthetic concerns, or the welfare of fish.

"Where there's smoke, there's money."

The moral of this story—and the critical factor in pollution behavior—is that ***people tend to maximize their personal welfare, balancing* private *benefits against* private *costs.*** For the electric power plant, this means making production decisions on the basis of revenues received and costs incurred. The fact that the power plant imposes costs on others, in the form of air and water pollution, is irrelevant to its profit-maximizing decision. Those costs are *external* to the firm and do not appear on its profit-and-loss statement. Those external costs are no less real, but they are incurred by society at large rather than by the firm.

Whenever external costs exist, a private firm will not allocate its resources and operate its plant in such a way as to maximize social welfare. In effect, society is permitting the power plant the free use of valued resources—clean air and clean water. Thus the power plant has a tremendous incentive to substitute those resources for others (such as high-priced fuel or cooling towers) in the production process. The inefficiency of such an arrangement is obvious when we recall that the function of markets is to allocate scarce resources in accordance with consumers' expressed demands. Yet here we are, proclaiming a high value for clean air and clean water while encouraging the power plant to use up both resources by offering them at zero cost to the firm.

Social vs. Private Costs

The inefficiency of this market arrangement can be expressed in terms of a distinction between social costs and private costs. **Social costs** are the total costs of all the resources that are used in a particular production activity. On the other hand, **private costs** are the resource costs that are incurred by the specific producer.

social costs The full resource costs of an economic activity, including externalities.

private costs The costs of an economic activity directly borne by the immediate producer or consumer (excluding externalities).

Ideally, a producer's private costs will encompass all the attendant social costs, and production decisions will be consistent with our social welfare. Unfortunately, this happy identity does not always exist, as our experience with the power plant illustrates. ***When social costs differ from private costs, external costs exist. In fact, external costs are equal to the difference between the social and private costs***—that is

- External costs = social costs − private costs

When external costs are present, the market mechanism will not allocate resources efficiently. The price signal confronting producers is flawed. By not conveying the full (social) cost of scarce resources, the market encourages excessive pollution. We end up with a suboptimal mix of output, the wrong production processes, and a polluted environment. This is another case of market failure.

The nature and consequences of this market failure are illustrated in Figure 9.5, which again depicts the cost situation confronting the electric power plant. Notice that we use two different marginal cost curves this time. The lower one, the *private* MC curve, reflects the private costs incurred by the power plant when it uses the cheapest production process, including high-sulfur coal and no cooling towers. It is identical to the MC curve of Figure 9.4*a*. We now know, however, that such operations impose *external* costs

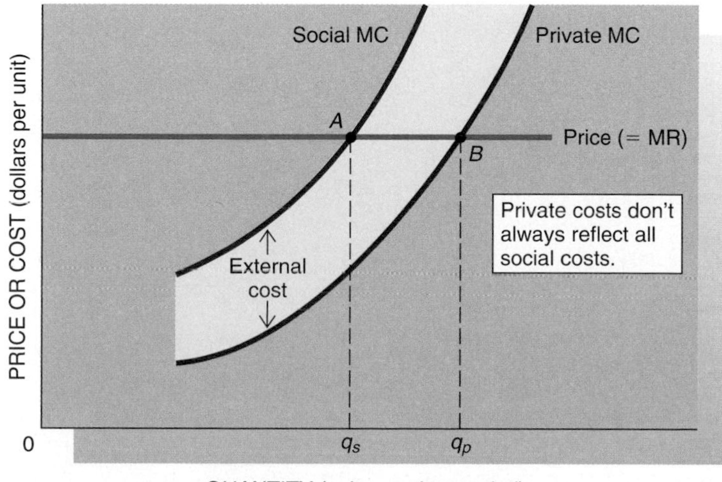

FIGURE 9.5
Market Failure

Social costs exceed private costs by the amount of external costs. Production decisions based on private costs alone will lead us to point *B*, where private MC = MR. At point *B*, the rate of output is q_p.

To maximize social welfare, we equate *social* MC and MR, as at point *A*. Only q_s of output is socially desirable. The failure of the market to convey the full costs of production keeps us from attaining this outcome.

on others in the form of air and water pollution. Hence social costs are higher than private costs, as reflected in the *social* MC curve. To maximize *social* welfare, we would equate *social* marginal costs with marginal revenue (point *A* in Figure 9.5) and thus produce at the output level q_s. The private profit maximizer, however, equates *private* marginal costs and marginal revenue (point *B*) and thus ends up producing at q_p, making more profit but also causing more pollution. As a general rule, ***if pollution costs are external, firms will produce too much of a polluting good.***

Policy Options

What should the government do to remedy these market failures?

Consider again the failure of the market to include environmental costs in production and consumption decisions. Our goal in this case is to discourage production and consumption activities that impose external costs on society. We can do this in one of two ways:

- ***Alter market incentives.***
- ***Bypass market incentives.***

Emission Fees The key to market-based environmental protection is to eliminate the divergence between private costs and social costs. The opportunity to shift some costs onto others lies at the heart of the pollution problem. If we could somehow compel producers to *internalize* all costs—pay for both private and previously external costs—the divergence would disappear, along with the incentive to pollute.

emission charge A fee imposed on polluters, based on the quantity of pollution.

One possibility is to establish a system of **emission charges,** direct costs attached to the act of polluting. Suppose that we let you keep your power plant and permit you to operate it according to profit-maximizing principles. The only difference is that we no longer agree to supply you with clean air and cool water at zero cost. Instead, we will charge you for these scarce resources. We might, say, charge you 2 cents for every gram of noxious emission you discharge into the air. In addition we might charge you 3 cents for every gallon of water you use, heat, and discharge back into the river.

Confronted with such emission charges, a producer would have to rethink the production decision. ***An emission charge increases private marginal cost and thus encourages lower output.*** Figure 9.6 illustrates this effect.

Once an emission fee is in place, a producer may also reevaluate the production process. Consider again the choice of fuels to be used in our fictional

FIGURE 9.6
Emission Fees

Emission charges can be used to close the gap between social costs and private costs. Faced with an emission charge of *t*, a private producer will reduce output from q_0 to q_1. Emission charges may also induce different investment decisions.

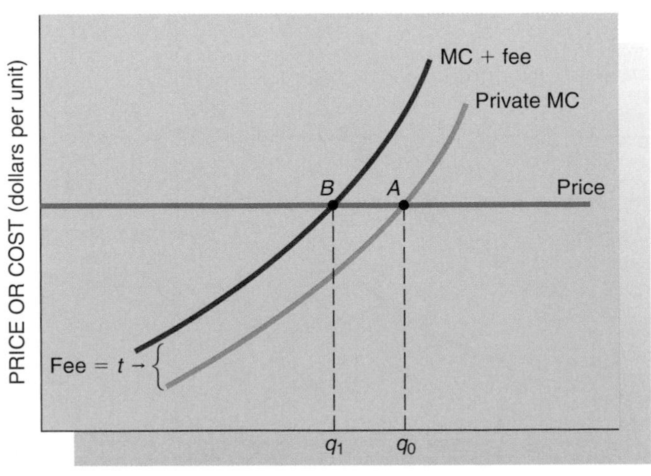

power plant. We earlier chose high-sulfur coal, for the very good reason that it was the cheapest fuel available. Now, however, there is an additional cost attached to burning such fuel, in the form of an emission charge on noxious pollutants. This higher marginal cost might prompt a switch to less-polluting fuels. The actual response of producers will depend on the relative costs involved. If emission charges are too low, it may be more profitable to continue burning and polluting with high-sulfur coal and pay a nominal fee. This is a simple pricing problem. The government could set the emission price higher, prompting the desired behavioral responses.

What works on producers will also sway consumers. Surely you've heard of deposits on returnable bottles. At one time the deposits were imposed by the beverage producer to encourage you to bring the bottle back for reuse. Thirty years ago, virtually all soft drinks and most beer came in returnable bottles. But producers discovered that such deposits discouraged sales and yielded very little cost savings. The economics of returnable bottles were further undermined by the advent of metal cans and, later, plastic bottles. Today, returnable bottles are rarely used. One result is the inclusion of over 30 billion bottles and 60 billion cans in our solid-waste-disposal problem.

We could reduce this solid-waste problem by imposing a deposit on all beverage containers. This would internalize pollution costs for the consumer and render the throwing of a soda can out the window equivalent to throwing away money. Some people would still find the thrill worthwhile, but they would be followed around by others who attached more value to money. The state of Oregon imposed a 5-cent deposit on beverage containers in 1972 and soon thereafter discovered that beverage-container litter in Oregon declined by 81 percent! Since that time, other states and communities have also imposed mandatory deposits as a mechanism for eliminating the distinction between social and private costs.

Regulation Although emission fees can be used to alter market outcomes, the incentive approach is not the only policy option. Direct regulation is another option. The federal government began regulating auto emissions in 1968 and got tough under the provisions of the Clean Air Act of 1970. The act required auto manufacturers to reduce hydrocarbon, carbon monoxide, and nitrogen oxide emissions by 90 percent within six years of the act's passage. Although the timetable for reducing pollutants was later extended, the act did stimulate auto manufacturers to reduce auto emissions dramatically: by 1990, new cars were emitting only 4 percent as much pollution as 1970 models. This dramatic reduction in per-vehicle emissions enabled auto production to increase even while pollution declined (see Headline on the following page).

Regulatory standards may specify not only the required reduction in emissions, but also the *process* by which those reductions are to be achieved. Clean air legislation mandated not only fewer auto emissions but also specific processes (e.g., catalytic converters, lead-free gasoline) for attaining them. Specific processes and technologies are also required for toxic waste disposal and water treatment. Laws requiring the sorting and recycling of trash are also examples of process regulation.

Although such hands-on regulation can be effective, this policy option also entails risks. By requiring market participants to follow specific rules, the regulations may impose excessive costs on some activities and too low a constraint on others. Some communities may not need the level of sewage treatment the federal government prescribes. Individual households may not generate enough trash to make sorting and separate pickups economically sound. Some producers may have better or cheaper ways of attaining environmental standards.

HEADLINE BYPASSING THE MARKET

Breathe Easy

America's air has become a great deal cleaner over the last generation. Since measurement began in 1970, U.S. emissions have fallen dramatically, even while GDP and travel have more than doubled. America, in other words, is producing much more while polluting less.

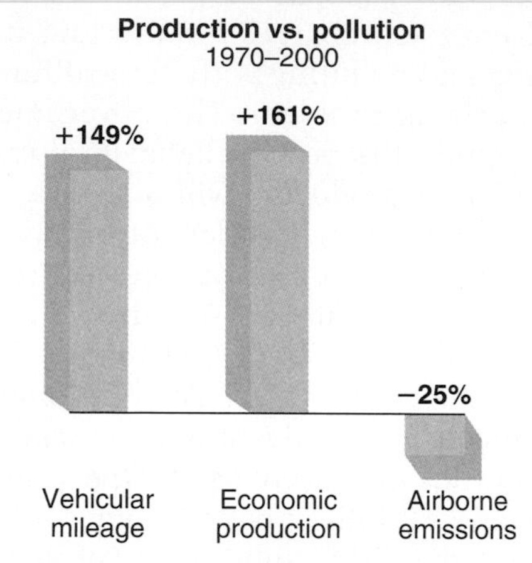

Source: *The American Enterprise*, July/August 2003, p. 17.

Ambient Air Pollution Levels (1976–2001)

Ozone	−33%
Sulfur Dioxides	−67
Nitrogen Dioxide	−42
Carbon Monoxide	−73
Particulates*	−27
Lead	−97

Note: *1996–2001

Source: *Index of Environmental Indicators, 2003*

NOTE: A combination of market incentives and government mandates has enabled output to increase even while the volume of pollution has diminished. The market alone would not have done as well.

Excessive process regulation may raise the costs of environmental protection and discourage cost-saving innovation. There is also the risk of regulated processes becoming entrenched long after they are obsolete.

Regulation also entails compliance and enforcement costs. Government agencies must monitor market behavior to assure that regulations are enforced. Market participants must learn about the regulations, implement them, and usually complete some compliance paperwork. All of these activities require scarce resources (labor) that could be used to produce other goods and services. Accordingly, regulations must not only be well designed, but also be beneficial enough to justify their opportunity costs. New York City Mayor Michael Bloomberg concluded forced recycling didn't pass this test (see the following Headline).

Market Power

When either public goods or externalities exist, the market's price signal is flawed. The price consumers are willing and able to pay for a specific good does not reflect all the benefits or costs of producing that good. As a result, the market fails to produce the socially desired mix of output.

Even when the price signals emitted in the market are accurate, however, we may still get a suboptimal mix of output. The *response* to price signals, rather than the signals themselves, may be flawed.

Restricted Supply

Market power is often the cause of a flawed response. Suppose there were only one airline company in the world. As a monopolist, the airline could

OPPORTUNITY COSTS

HEADLINE

Forced Recycling Is a Waste

As New York City faces the possibility of painful cuts to its police and fire department budgets, environmentalists are bellyaching over garbage. Mayor Michael Bloomberg's proposed budget for 2003 would temporarily suspend the city's recycling of metal, glass and plastic, saving New Yorkers $57 million.

The city's recycling program—like many others around the country—has long hemorrhaged tax dollars. Every mayor has tried to stop the waste since the program began in 1989, when local law 19 mandated the city to recycle 25 percent of its waste by 1994.

The city spends about $240 per ton to "recycle" plastic, glass, and metal, while the cost of simply sending waste to landfills is about $130 per ton.

You don't need a degree in economics to see that something is wrong here. Isn't recycling supposed to save money and resources? Some recycling does—when driven by market forces. Private parties don't voluntarily recycle unless they know it will save money, and, hence, resources. But forced recycling can be a waste of both because recycling itself entails using energy, water and labor to collect, sort, clean and process the materials.

There are also air emissions, traffic and wear on streets from the second set of trucks prowling for recyclables. The bottom line is that most mandated recycling hurts, not helps, the environment.

"You could do a lot better things in the world with $57 million," says Mayor Bloomberg. Like rebuilding from the greatest catastrophe ever to befall New York. But first Mayor Bloomberg is going to have to battle the green lobby to eliminate his city's wasteful recyling program.

—Angela Logomasini

Source: *Wall Street Journal*, March 19, 2002, p. A22.

NOTE: Recycling programs reduce pollution but also use resources that could be employed for other purposes. The benefits of recycling should exceed its opportunity costs.

charge extremely high prices without worrying that travelers would flock to a competing airline. Ideally, such high prices would act as a signal to producers to build and fly more planes—to change the mix of output. But a monopolist does not have to cater to every consumer whim. It can limit airline travel and thus obstruct our efforts to achieve an optimal mix of output.

Monopoly is the most severe form of **market power.** More generally, market power refers to any situation where a single producer or consumer has the ability to alter the market price of a specific product. If the publisher (McGraw-Hill) charges a high price for this book, you will have to pay the tab. McGraw-Hill has market power because there are relatively few economics textbooks and your professor has required you to use this one. You don't have power in the textbook market because your decision to buy or not will not alter the market price of this text. You are only one of the million students who are taking an introductory economics course this year.

market power The ability to alter the market price of a good or service.

The market power McGraw-Hill possesses is derived from the copyright on this text. No matter how profitable textbook sales might be, no one else is permitted to produce or sell this particular text. Patents are another common source of market power, because they also preclude others from making or selling a specific product. Market power may also result from control of resources, restrictive production agreements, or efficiencies of large-scale production.

Whatever the source of market power, ***the direct consequence of market power is that one or more producers attain discretionary power over the market's response to price signals.*** They may use that discretion to enrich themselves rather than to move the economy toward the optimal mix of output. In this case, the market will again fail to deliver the most desired goods and services. As we observed in Chapter 7, the government concluded that Microsoft used its virtual monopoly in computer operating systems to limit consumer choice and enrich itself.

Antitrust Policy

antitrust Government intervention to alter market structure or prevent abuse of market power.

A primary goal of government intervention in such cases is to prevent or dismantle concentrations of market power. That is the essential purpose of **antitrust** policy. The legal foundations of federal antitrust activity are contained in three laws:

- **The Sherman Act (1890).** The Sherman Act prohibits "conspiracies in restraint of trade," including mergers, contracts, or acquisitions that threaten to monopolize an industry. Firms that violate the Sherman Act are subject to fines of up to $1 million, and their executives may be subject to imprisonment. In addition, consumers who are damaged—for example, via high prices—by a conspiracy in restraint of trade may recover treble damages. The U.S. Department of Justice has used this trust-busting authority to block attempted mergers and acquisitions, force changes in price or output behavior, require companies to sell some of their assets, and even send corporate executives to jail for conspiracies in restraint of trade.
- **The Clayton Act (1914).** The Clayton Act of 1914 was passed to outlaw specific antitrust behavior not covered by the Sherman Act. The principal aim of the act was to prevent the development of monopolies. To this end the Clayton Act prohibits price discrimination, exclusive dealing agreements, certain types of mergers, and interlocking boards of directors among competing firms.
- **The Federal Trade Commission Act (1914).** The increased antitrust responsibilities of the federal government created the need for an agency that could study industry structures and behavior so as to identify anticompetitive practices. The Federal Trade Commission was created for this purpose in 1914.

In the early 1900s this antitrust legislation was used to break up the monopolies that dominated the steel and tobacco industries. In the 1980s the same legislation was used to dismantle AT&T's near monopoly of telephone service. The court forced AT&T to sell off its local telephone service companies (the Baby Bells) and allow competitors more access to long-distance service. The resulting competition pushed prices down and spawned a new wave of telephone technology and services.

Although antitrust policy has produced some impressive results, its potential is limited. There are over 20 million businesses in the United States and the trustbusters can watch only so many. Even when they decide to take action, antitrust policy entails difficult decisions. What, for example, constitutes a monopoly in the real world? Must a company produce 100 percent of a particular good to be a threat to consumer welfare? How about 99 percent? Or even 75 percent?

And what specific monopolistic practices should be prohibited? Should we be looking for specific evidence of price gouging? Or should we focus on barriers to entry and unfair market practices? In the antitrust case against Microsoft (see Headline on p. 162, Chapter 7) the Justice Department asserted that bundling its Internet Explorer with Windows was an anticompetitive practice. Microsoft chairman Bill Gates responded that the attorney general didn't understand how the fiercely competitive software market worked. Who was right?

These kinds of questions determine how and when antitrust laws will be enforced. Just the threat of enforcement, however, may help push market outcomes in the desired direction. In the Microsoft case, for example, the company changed some of it exclusionary licensing practices soon after the government filed its antitrust case. Presumably, other powerful companies also became more cautious about abusing market power when they saw the guilty verdict against Microsoft.

Equity

Public goods, externalities, and market power all cause resource misallocations. Where these phenomena exist, the market mechanism will fail to produce the optimal mix of output.

Beyond the question of WHAT to produce, we are also concerned about FOR WHOM output is to be produced. Is the distribution of goods and services generated by the marketplace fair? If not, government intervention may be needed to redistribute income.

In general, the market mechanism tends to answer the basic question of FOR WHOM to produce by distributing a larger share of total output to those with the most income. Although this result may be efficient, it is not necessarily equitable. Individuals who are aged or disabled, for example, may be unable to earn much income yet still be regarded as worthy recipients of goods and services. In such cases, we may want to change the market's answer to the basic question of FOR WHOM goods are produced.

Instead of relying exclusively on the market mechanism to determine people's income, we provide income transfers. **Transfer payments** are income payments for which no goods or services are exchanged. They are used to bolster the incomes of those for whom the market itself provides too little. Table 9.1 indicates some of the largest income transfers. Social Security benefits are far and away the largest transfer, followed by Medicare and Medicaid. Welfare checks for the poor are relatively low on this list.

transfer payments Payments to individuals for which no current goods or services are exchanged, e.g., Social Security, welfare, unemployment benefits.

To some extent, government intervention in the distribution of income can also be explained by the theory of public goods. If the public sector did not

TABLE 9.1
Income Transfers

The market mechanism might leave some people with too little income and others with too much. The government uses taxes and transfers to redistribute income more fairly.

Program	Recipient Group	Number of Recipients	Value of Transfers
Social Security	Retired and disabled workers	50 million	$432 billion
Medicare	Individuals over age 65	40 million	$241 billion
Medicaid	Medically needy individuals	37 million	$270 billion
Earned Income Tax Credit	Low-wage workers	19 million	$ 32 billion
Food Stamps	Low-income households	21 million	$ 20 billion
Temporary Aid to Needy Families	Poor families	6 million	$ 16 billion

Source: *The Economics of Poverty and Discrimination*, 9th ed. by Bradley R. Schiller, © 2004. Adapted by permission of Prentice Hall, Inc., Upper Saddle River, NJ.

provide help to the aged, the disabled, the unemployed, and the needy, what would they do? Some might find a little extra work, but many would starve, even die. Others would resort to private solicitations or criminal activities to fend off hunger or death. This would mean more homeless people and muggers on the streets. In nearly all cases, the general public would suffer, either directly or through pangs of conscience. Hence, the elimination of poverty may make a great many people better off.

But who would actually *pay* to eliminate poverty in a market economy? If I contributed heavily to the needy, then you and I would both be relieved of the burden of the poor. We could both walk the streets with less fear and better consciences. Hence you could benefit from my expenditure, just as was possible in the case of national defense. In this sense, the relief of misery is a *public* good. Were I the only taxpayer to benefit substantially from the reduction of poverty, then charity would be a private affair. As long as income support substantially benefits the public at large, then income redistribution is a *public* good, for which public funding is appropriate. This is the *economic* rationale for public income-redistribution activities. To this rationale one can add such moral arguments as seem appropriate.

Macro Instability

The micro failures of the marketplace imply that we are at the wrong point on the production-possibilities curve or inequitably distributing the output produced. There is another basic question we have swept under the rug, however. How do we get to the production-possibilities curve in the first place? To reach the curve, we must utilize all available resources and technology. Can we be confident that the invisible hand of the marketplace will use all of our resources? Or will some people remain unemployed—that is, willing to work, but unable to find a job?

And what about prices? Price signals are a critical feature of the market mechanism. But the validity of those signals depends on some stable measure of value. What good is a doubling of salary when the price of everything you buy doubles as well? Generally, rising prices enrich people who own property and impoverish people who rent. That is why we strive to avoid inflation—a situation where the *average* price level is increasing.

Historically, the marketplace has been wracked with bouts of both unemployment and inflation. These experiences have prompted calls for government intervention at the macro level. ***The goal of macro intervention is to foster economic growth—to get us on the production-possibilities curve (full employment), to maintain a stable price level (price stability), and to increase our capacity to produce (growth).*** The means for achieving this goal are examined in the macro section of this course.

POLICY PERSPECTIVES

Trust in Government?

The potential micro and macro failures of the marketplace provide specific justifications for government intervention. The question then turns to how well the activities of the public sector correspond to these implied mandates. Can we trust the government to fix the shortcomings of the market?

Information If the government is going to fix things, it must not only confirm market failure but identify the social optimum. This is no easy task. Back in Figure 9.1 we arbitrarily designated point *X* as the social optimum. In the real world, however, only the *market* outcome is visible. The social optimum isn't visible; it must be inferred. To locate it, we need to know the preferences of the community as well as the dimensions of any externalities. Likewise, if we want the government to change the market distribution of income, we need to know what society regards as fair. No one really has all the required information. Consequently, government intervention typically entails a lot of groping in the dark for *better,* if not *optimal,* outcomes.

Vested Interests Vested interests often try to steer the search away from the social optimum. Cigarette manufacturers don't want people to stop smoking. Car companies don't want consumers to reject the fuel technology they have developed. So they try to keep the government from altering market outcomes. To do so, they may generate studies that minimize the size of external costs. They may try to sway public opinion with public-interest advertising. And they may use their wealth to finance the campaigns of sympathetic politicians. In the process, it becomes more difficult to figure out where the social optimum is, much less get there.

Government Failure These are just a couple of reasons why government intervention won't always improve market outcomes. Yes, an unregulated market might produce the wrong mix of output, generate too much pollution, or leave too many people in poverty. However, government intervention might *worsen,* rather than improve, market outcomes. In that case, we would have to conclude that government intervention *failed.*

Government failure refers to any intervention that fails to improve market outcomes. Perhaps the mix of output or the income distribution got *worse* when the government intervened. Or the regulatory/administrative cost of intervention outweighed its benefits.

government failure Government intervention that fails to improve economic outcomes.

The average citizen clearly understands that government intervention doesn't always succeed as hoped. A 2002 opinion poll revealed little trust in the government to improve market outcomes. As Figure 9.7 illustrates, one out of four Americans have "not very much" trust and confidence in the federal government's ability to fix things and 1 out of 14 citizens has "none at all." Confidence levels are higher for state and local governments, but still far short of comfort levels.

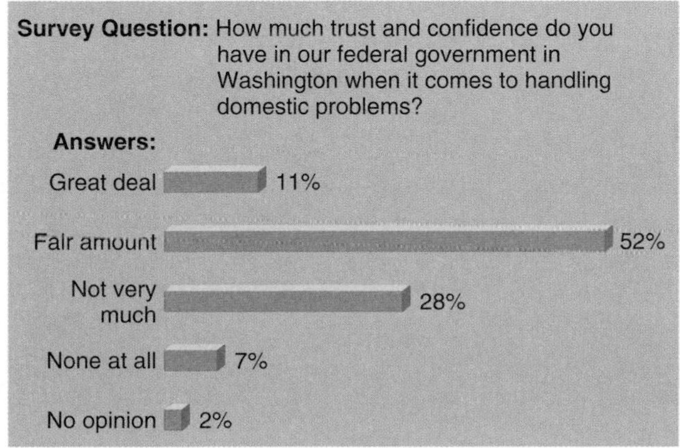

FIGURE 9.7
Low Expectations
The public has little faith in the ability of government to fix market failures.
Source: Gallup poll, September 2002.

Neither market failure nor government failure is inevitable. The challenge for public policy is to decide when *any* government intervention is justified, then intervene in a way that improves outcomes in the least costly way.

SUMMARY

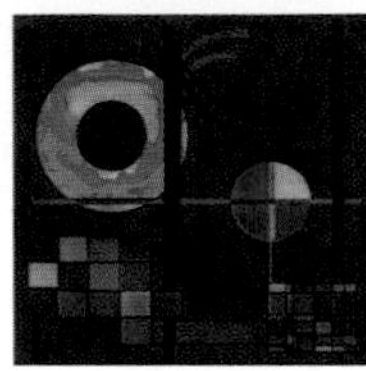

- Government intervention in the marketplace is justified by market failure, that is, suboptimal market outcomes.
- The micro failures of the market originate in public goods, externalities, market power, and an inequitable distribution of income. These flaws deter the market from achieving the optimal mix of output or distribution of income.
- Public goods are those that cannot be consumed exclusively; they are jointly consumed regardless of who pays. Because everyone seeks a free ride, no one demands public goods in the marketplace. Hence the market underproduces public goods.
- Externalities are costs (or benefits) of a market transaction borne by a third party. Externalities create a divergence between social and private costs (or benefits), causing suboptimal market outcomes. The market overproduces goods with external costs and underproduces goods with external benefits.
- Market power enables a producer to thwart market signals and maintain a suboptimal mix of output. Antitrust policy seeks to prevent or restrict market power.
- The market-generated distribution of income may be regarded as unfair. This equity concern may prompt the government to intervene with taxes and transfer payments that redistribute incomes.
- The macro failures of the marketplace are reflected in unemployment and inflation. Government intervention is intended to achieve full employment and price stability.
- Government failure occurs when intervention moves us away from rather than toward the optimal mix of output (or income).

Terms to Remember

Define the following terms:

optimal mix of output
market mechanism
market failure
public good
private good
free rider
externalities
social costs
private costs
emission charge
market power
antitrust
transfer payments
government failure

Questions for Discussion

1. Why should taxpayers subsidize public colleges and universities? What external benefits are generated by higher education?
2. If everyone seeks a free ride, what mix of output will be produced in Figure 9.2? Why would anyone voluntarily contribute to the purchase of public goods like flood control?
3. Could local fire departments be privately operated, with services sold directly to customers? What problems would be involved in such a system?

4. Identify specific government activities that are justified by different micro failures.
5. Why would auto manufacturers resist exhaust-control devices? How would their costs, sales, and profits be affected?
6. Does anyone have an incentive to maintain auto-exhaust-control devices in good working order? How can we ensure that they will be maintained?
7. Suppose we established a $10,000 fine for water pollution. Would some companies still find that polluting was economical? Under what conditions?
8. What are the costs of New York City's recycling program (see Headline, p. 215). Are these costs justified?
9. Four companies produce virtually all breakfast cereals. How might this concentration of market power affect market outcomes? What should the government do, if anything?
10. The government now spends close to $500 billion a year on Social Security benefits. Why don't we leave it to individuals to save for their own retirement?

Problems

1. (*a*) Draw a production-possibilities curve with cars on the horizontal axis and other goods on the vertical axis.
   (*b*) Illustrate on your curve the market failure that occurs in Figure 9.3.
2. Draw market-demand and social-demand curves for flu shots.
3. Suppose the following data represent the market demand for college education:

Tuition (per year)	$1,000	2,000	3,000	4,000	5,000	6,000	7,000	8,000
Enrollment demanded (in millions)	8	7	6	5	4	3	2	1

   (*a*) If tuition is set at $5,000, how many students will enroll?
   Now suppose that society gets an external benefit of $1,000 for every enrolled student (for, say, more informed voting).
   (*b*) Draw the social and market demand curves for this situation.
   (*c*) What is the optimal level of enrollments at the tuition price of $5,000?
   (*d*) How can this optimal enrollment level be achieved?
4. Assume the market demand for cigarettes is as follows:

Price per pack	$0.25	0.50	0.75	1.00	1.25	1.50	1.75	2.00	2.25	2.50
Quantity (packs per day)	100	90	80	70	60	50	40	30	20	10

   Suppose further that smoking creates external costs valued at 25 cents per pack.
   (*a*) Draw the social and market demand curves.
   (*b*) At $2 per pack what quantity is demanded in the market?
   (*c*) What is the socially optimal quantity at that price?
   (*d*) How can the optimal quantity be attained?

5. Suppose the following data represent the prices that each of three consumers is willing to pay for a good.

Quantity	Consumer A	Consumer B	Consumer C
1	$50	$40	$30
2	30	20	20
3	20	15	10

(*a*) Construct the market demand curve for this good.
(*b*) If this good were priced in the market at $40, how many units would be demanded?
(*c*) Now suppose that this is a public good, in the sense that all consumers receive satisfaction from the good even if only one person buys it. Construct the social demand curve for this good.
(*d*) Based on the social demand curve, how many units of this good are demanded by society at a price of $40?
(*e*) What is the evidence of market failure in this case?

6. Redraw Figure 9.4*b* and indicate the amount of profit that would be sacrificed if the firm adopted less-polluting technology.
7. Suppose a product can be produced with the following marginal costs:

Quantity (units)	1	2	3	4	5	6	7	8	9	10
Marginal cost	$2	$3	$4	$5	$6	$7	$8	$9	$10	$11

If the market price of the product is $6:
(*a*) How much output will a competitive firm produce?
(*b*) If each unit produced causes $1 of pollution, what is the socially desired rate of production?
(*c*) Graph your answers.

Web Activities

1. Log on to www.epa.gov and read one of the headline stories.
(*a*) What is an externality?
(*b*) What externality is the EPA attempting to correct in the headline story?
2. Log on to www.usdoj.gov/atr/index.html and read the first two articles listed under highlights. Which antitrust acts are being enforced in these legal actions by the U.S. Department of Justice?

Living Econ

Should I Litter to Create Jobs?

In this chapter you learned that government intervention may be necessary to correct market failures at the micro level. Littering is an example of a type of micro failure known as an externality. Throwing trash out the car window imposes a social cost on society because government expenditures are required to clean up our roadsides, parks, and other public spaces.

But does littering solve a potential macro failure of too few jobs? The answer lies in the concept of opportunity cost. When the government employs people to pick up cans thrown out of car windows, the level of unemployment is reduced. However, that means fewer resources are currently available for the production of other goods and services. As a result, the economy moves to a less optimal point on the production-possibilities curve. Even though there are now more jobs, the economy would be better off if the resources had been put to other uses.

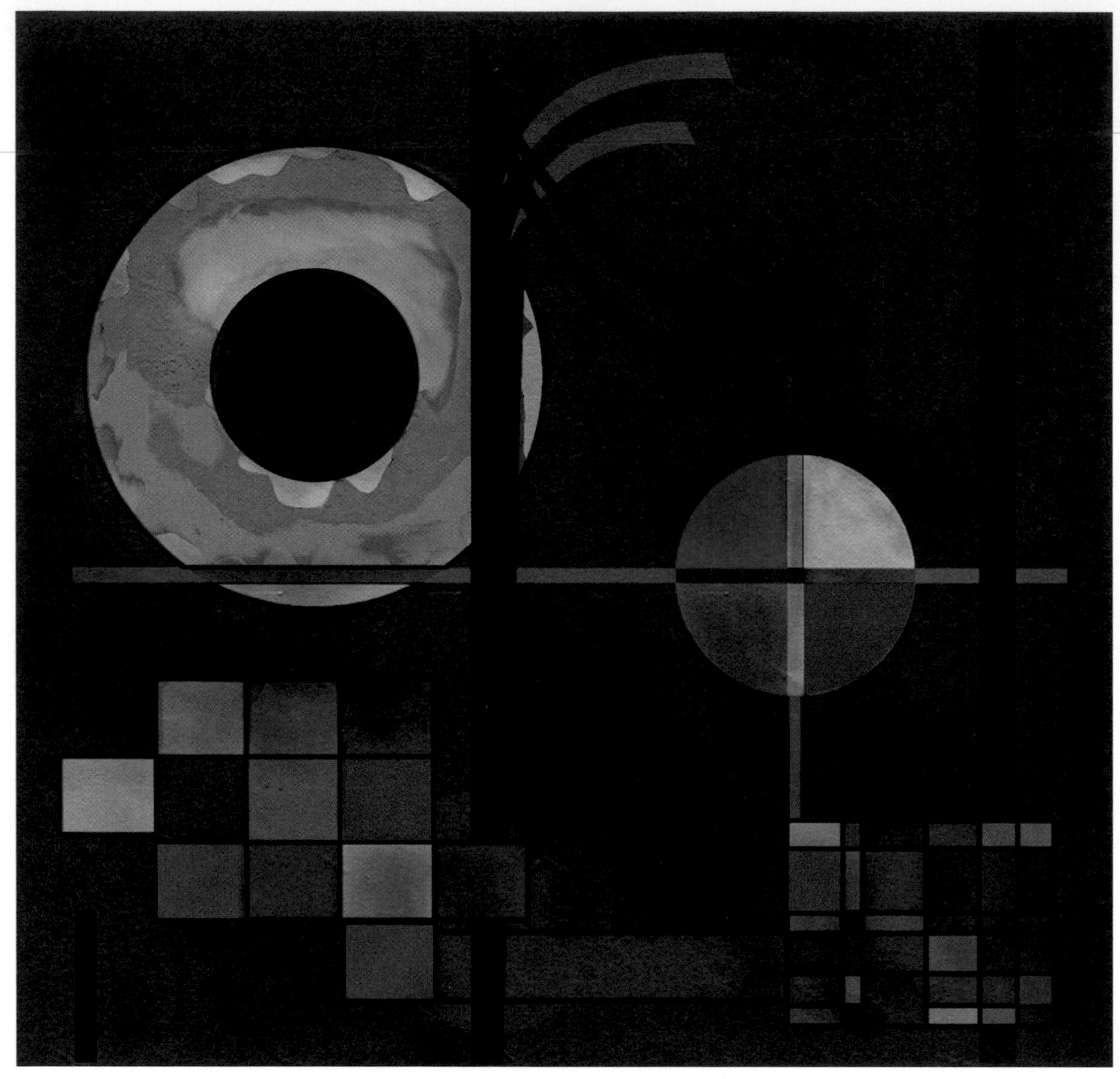

The Business Cycle

CHAPTER 10

In 1929 it looked as though the sun would never set on the American economy. For eight years in a row, the U.S. economy had been expanding rapidly. During the Roaring Twenties the typical American family drove its first car, bought its first radio, and went to the movies for the first time. With factories running at capacity, virtually anyone who wanted to work readily found a job.

Under these circumstances everyone was optimistic. In his acceptance address of November 1928, President-elect Herbert Hoover echoed this optimism by declaring: "We in America today are nearer to the final triumph over poverty than ever before in the history of any land. . . . We shall soon with the help of God be in sight of the day when poverty will be banished from this nation."

The booming stock market seemed to confirm this optimistic outlook. Between 1921 and 1927, the stock market's value more than doubled, adding billions of dollars to the wealth of American households and businesses. The stock-market boom accelerated in 1927, causing stock prices to double again in less than two years. The roaring stock market made it look easy to get rich in America.

The party ended abruptly on October 24, 1929. On what came to be known as Black Thursday, the stock market crashed. In a few hours, the market value of U.S. corporations fell abruptly, in the most frenzied selling ever seen (see Headline). The next day President Hoover tried to assure America's stockholders that the economy was "on a sound and prosperous basis." But despite his assurances and the efforts of leading bankers to stem the decline, the stock market continued to plummet. The following Tuesday (October 29) the pace of selling quickened. By the end of the year, over $40 billion of wealth had vanished in the Great Crash. Rich men became paupers overnight; ordinary families lost their savings, their homes, and even their lives.

The devastation was not confined to Wall Street. The financial flames engulfed the farms, the banks, and industry. Between 1930 and 1935, millions of rural families lost their farms. Automobile production fell from 4.5 million cars in 1929 to only 1.1 million in 1932. So many banks were forced to close that newly elected President Roosevelt had to declare a "bank holiday" in March 1933 to stem the outflow of cash to anxious depositors.

HEADLINE THE CRASH OF 1929

Market in Panic as Stocks Are Dumped in 12,894,600 Share Day; Bankers Halt It

Effect is felt on the curb and throughout nation—financial district goes wild

The stock markets of the country tottered on the brink of panic yesterday as a prosperous people, gone suddenly hysterical with fear, attempted simultaneously to sell a record-breaking volume of securities for whatever they would bring.

The result was a financial nightmare, comparable to nothing ever before experienced in Wall Street. It rocked the financial district to its foundations, hopelessly overwhelmed its mechanical facilities, chilled its blood with terror.

In a society built largely on confidence, with real wealth expressed more or less inaccurately by pieces of paper, the entire fabric of economic stability threatened to come toppling down.

Into the frantic hands of a thousand brokers on the floor of the New York Stock Exchange poured the selling orders of the world. It was sell, sell, sell—hour after desperate hour until 1:30 P.M.

—Laurence Stern

Source: *The World,* October 25, 1929.

NOTE: The stock market is often a barometer of business cycles. The 1929 crash both anticipated and worsened the Great Depression.

The Great Depression left millions of workers jobless, homeless, and hungry. Macroeconomic policy seeks to eliminate or minimize such cyclical setbacks.

© Topham/The Image Works

Throughout these years, the ranks of the unemployed continued to swell. In October 1929, only 3 percent of the workforce was unemployed. A year later over 9 percent of the workforce was unemployed. Still, things got worse. By 1933 over one-fourth of the labor force was unable to find work. People slept in the streets, scavenged for food, and sold apples on Wall Street.

The Great Depression seemed to last forever. In 1933 President Roosevelt lamented that one-third of the nation was ill-clothed, ill-housed, and ill-fed. Thousands of unemployed workers marched to the Capitol to demand jobs and aid. In 1938, nine years after the great crash, nearly 20 percent of the workforce was still unemployed.

The Great Depression shook not only the foundations of the world economy but also the self-confidence of the economics profession. No one had predicted the depression and few could explain it. How could the economy perform so poorly for so long? What could the government do to prevent such a catastrophe? Suddenly, there were more questions than answers.

The scramble for answers became the springboard for modern **macroeconomics,** the study of aggregate economic behavior. A basic purpose of macroeconomic theory is to *explain* the **business cycle—**to identify the forces that cause the overall economy to expand or contract. Macro *policy* tries to *control* the business cycle, using the insights of macro theory.

macroeconomics The study of aggregate economic behavior, of the economy as a whole.

In this chapter we focus on the nature of the business cycle and the related problems of unemployment and inflation. Our goal is to acquire a sense of why the business cycle is so feared. To address these concerns we need to know

business cycle Alternating periods of economic growth and contraction.

- What are business cycles?
- What damage does unemployment cause?
- Who is hurt by inflation?

As we answer these questions, we will get a sense of why people worry so much about the macro economy and why they demand that Washington do something about it.

Assessing Macro Performance

Doctors gauge a person's health with a few simple measurements like body temperature, blood pressure, and blood content. These tests don't tell doctors everything they need to know about a patient, but they convey some important clues about a patient's general health. In macroeconomics, the economic doctors need comparable measures of the patient's health. The macro economy is a complex construction, encompassing all economic activity. To get a quick reading of how well it is doing, economists rely on three gauges. ***The three basic measures of macro performance are:***

- ***Output (GDP) growth***
- ***Unemployment***
- ***Inflation***

The macro economy is in trouble when output growth slows down—or worse, turns negative, as during the Great Depression. Economic doctors also worry about the macro economy when they see either unemployment or inflation rising. Any one of these symptoms is painful and may be the precursor of a more serious ailment. Someone has to decide whether to intervene or instead wait to see if the economy can overcome such symptoms by itself.

GDP Growth

The first test of the economy's macro health is the rate of output growth. As we first saw in Chapter 1, an economy's *potential* output is reflected in its **production-possibilities** curve. That curve tells us how much output the economy *could* produce with available resources and technology. The relevant performance test is whether we are living up to that potential. Are we fully using available resources—or producing at less than capacity? If we are producing *inside* the production-possibilities curve, some resources (e.g., workers) are unnecessarily idle. If we are inside the production-possibilities curve, the macro economy isn't doing very well.

production possibilities The alternative combinations of goods and services that could be produced in a given time period with all available resources and technology.

In reality, output has to *keep* increasing if an economy is to stay healthy. The population increases and technology advances every year. So the production-possibilities curve keeps shifting outward. This means *output* has to keep expanding at a healthy clip just to keep from falling further behind that expanding capacity.

Business Cycles

The central concern in macroeconomics is that the rate of output won't always keep up with ever-expanding production possibilities. Indeed, when macro doctors study the patient's charts, they often discern a pattern

HEADLINE DECLINING OUTPUT

Economy Contracts in 3rd Quarter

"A recession has begun," some economists believe

In the first official sign that the nation may have tipped into recession, government figures showed that the U.S. economy shrank in late summer for the first time since 1993 and at the sharpest rate since the 1990–91 recession.

Gross domestic product (GDP), the key gauge of the output of goods and services, fell at a 0.4 percent annual rate in the July–September quarter, according to the Bureau of Economic Analysis. That was the first quarterly drop since a 0.1 percent decline in early 1993 and three back-to-back quarters in 1990–91, when GDP fell at a rate as great as 3.2 percent. In 1999 and 2000, by contrast, the economy boomed at a 4.1 percent rate.

The numbers confirm that "a recession has begun," says Bruce Steinberg, chief economist for Merrill Lynch, who forecasts the downturn will last until spring before a strong rebound takes hold.

The rough definition of a recession is at least two consecutive quarters of economic contraction.

—George Hager

Source: *USA Today*, November 1, 2001, p. B1.

NOTE: A contraction in output indicates that an economy has moved to a point inside its production-possibilities curve. Such contractions lower living standards and create more joblessness.

of fits, starts, and stops in the growth of output. Sometimes the volume of output grows at a healthy clip. At other times, the growth rate slips. And in some cases total output actually contracts, as it did in 2001 (see Headline).

Figure 10.1 illustrates this typical business-cycle chart. During an economic expansion total output grows rapidly. Then a peak is reached and output starts dropping. Once a trough is reached, the economy prospers again. This roller-coaster pattern begins to look like a recurring cycle.

Real GDP

When we talk about output expanding or contracting, we envision changes in the physical quantity of goods and services produced. But the physical volume of output is virtually impossible to measure. Millions of different goods and services are produced every year, and no one has figured out how to add up their physical quantities (e.g., 30 million grapefruits + 128 electronic

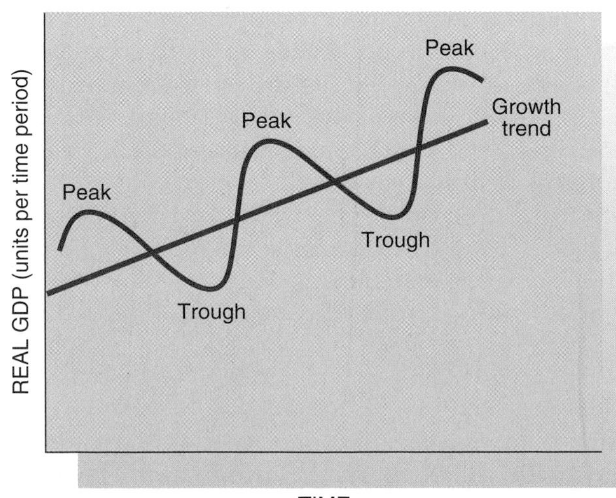

FIGURE 10.1
The Business Cycle

The model business cycle resembles a roller coaster. Output first climbs to a peak, then decreases. After hitting a trough, the economy recovers, with real GDP again increasing.

A central concern of macroeconomic theory is to determine whether a recurring business cycle exists and, if so, what forces cause it.

software downloads = ?). So ***we measure the volume of output by its market value,*** not by its physical volume (e.g., the dollar *value* of grapefruits + the dollar *value* of electronic commerce = a dollar value total). We refer to the dollar value of all the output produced in a year as *gross domestic product (GDP).*

Because prices vary from one year to the next, GDP yardsticks must be adjusted for inflation. Suppose that from one year to the next all prices doubled. Such a general price increase would double the *value* of output even if the *quantity* of output were totally unchanged. So an unadjusted measure of **nominal GDP** would give us a false reading: we might think output was racing ahead when in fact it was standing still.

nominal GDP The total value of goods and services produced within a nation's borders, measured in current prices.

To avoid such false readings, we adjust our measure of output for changing price levels. The yardstick of **real GDP** does this by valuing output at constant prices. Thus, changes in real GDP are a proxy for changes in the number of grapefruits, houses, cars, clothes, movies, and so forth we produce in a year.

real GDP The inflation adjusted value of GDP; the value of output measured in constant prices.

Economic activity in 2001 illustrates the distinction between real and nominal GDP. Nominal GDP increased from $9.825 trillion to $10.082 trillion in that year, a rise of 2.6 percent. But a big chunk of that nominal GDP growth was due to rising prices. *Real* GDP increased by a tiny 0.3 percent.

Erratic Growth

In the 1990s U.S. real GDP grew better than that almost every year. As Figure 10.2 illustrates, the annual rate of real GDP growth between 1992

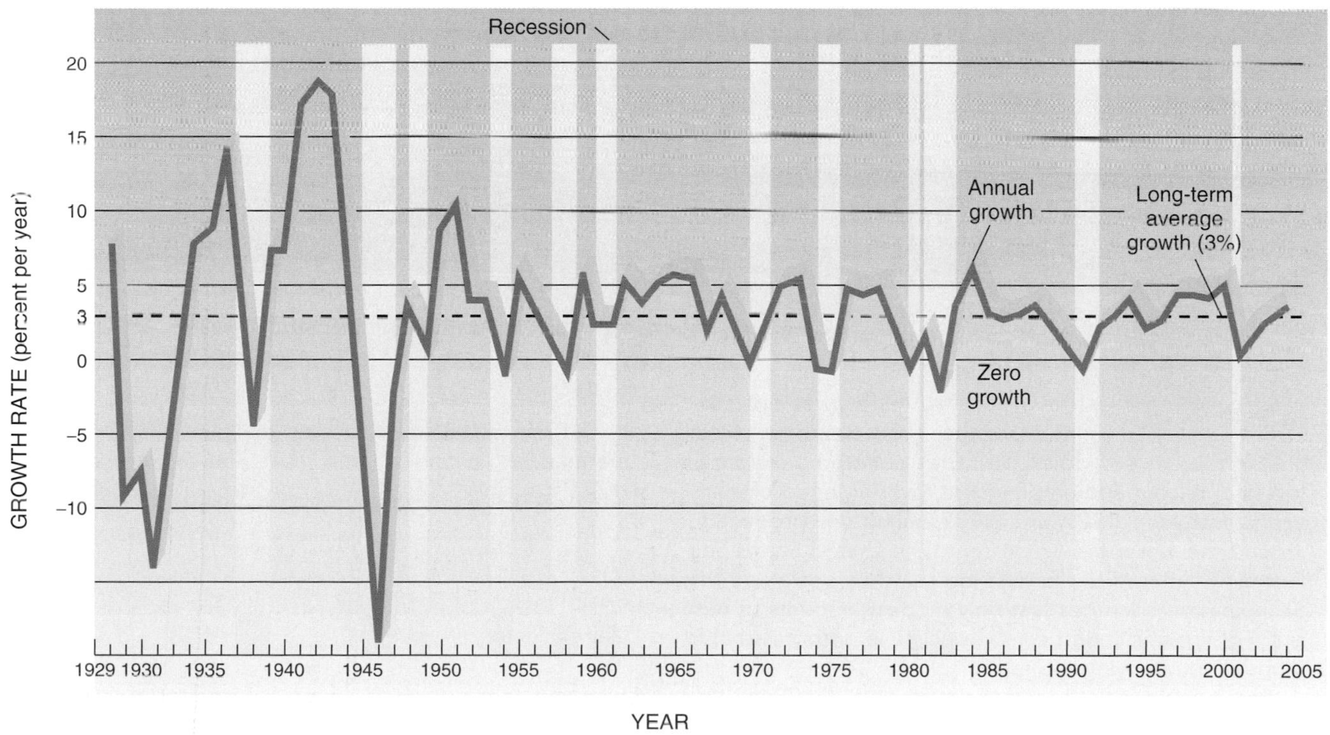

FIGURE 10.2 The Business Cycle in U.S. History

From 1929 to 2003, real GDP increased at an average rate of 3 percent a year. But annual growth rates have departed widely from that average. Years of above-average growth seem to alternate with years of sluggish growth and years in which total output actually *declines*. Such *recessions* occurred in 1980, 1981–82, 1990–91, and again in 2001.

Source: *Economic Report of the President,* 2003.

and 2000 was never less than 2.4 percent and got as high as 5.0 percent. Those may not sound like big numbers. In a $10 *trillion* economy, however, even small growth rates imply a *lot* of added output. Moreover, the GDP growth of those years exceeded the rate of expansion in production possibilities. Hence the economy kept moving closer to the limits of its (expanding) production possibilities. In the process, living standards rose and nearly every job seeker could find work.

The economy doesn't always perform so well. Look closer at Figure 10.2. The dashed horizontal line across the middle of the chart illustrates the long-term *average* real GDP growth rate, at 3.0 percent a year. Then notice how often the economy grew slower than that. Notice also the periodic economic busts when the growth rate fell below zero and total output actually *decreased* from one year to the next. This experience confirms that ***real GDP doesn't increase in consistent, smooth increments but in a pattern of steps, stumbles, and setbacks.***

The Great Depression The most prolonged setback occurred during the Great Depression. Between 1929 and 1933, total U.S. output steadily declined. Real GDP fell nearly 30 percent in those four years. Industrial output declined even further, as investments in new plant and equipment virtually ceased. Economies around the world came to a grinding halt (see Headline).

The U.S. economy started to grow again in 1934, but the rate of expansion was modest. Millions of people remained out of work. In 1936–37, the situation worsened again, and total output once more declined. As a consequence, the rate of total output in 1939 was virtually identical to that in 1929. Because of continuing population growth, GDP per capita was actually *lower* in 1939 than it had been in 1929. American families had a *lower* standard of living in 1939 than they had enjoyed 10 years earlier.

HEADLINE WORLDWIDE LOSSES

Depression Slams World Economies

The Great Depression was not confined to the U.S. economy. Most other countries suffered substantial losses of output and employment, over a period of many years. Between 1929 and 1932, industrial production around the world fell 37 percent. The United States and Germany suffered the largest losses, while Spain and the Scandinavian countries lost only modest amounts of output. For specific countries, the decline in output is shown in the accompanying table.

Some countries escaped the ravages of the Great Depression altogether. The Soviet Union, largely insulated from Western economic structures, was in the midst of Stalin's forced industrialization drive during the 1930s.

Country	Percentage Decline in Output
Chile	−22%
France	−31
Germany	−47
Great Britain	−17
Japan	−2
Norway	−7
Spain	−12
United States	−46

China and Japan were also relatively isolated from world trade and finance, and so suffered less damage from the depression.

NOTE: Trade and financial links make countries interdependent. When one economy falls into a recession, other economies may suffer as well.

Dates	Duration (months)	Percentage Decline in Output	Peak Unemployment Rank
Aug. '29–Mar. '33	43	53.4%	24.9%
May '37–June '38	13	32.4	20.0
Feb. '45–Oct. '45	8	38.3	4.3
Nov. '48–Oct. '49	11	9.9	7.9
July '53–May '54	10	10.0	6.1
Aug. '57–Apr. '58	8	14.3	7.5
Apr. '60–Feb. '61	10	7.2	7.1
Dec. '69–Nov. '70	11	8.1	6.1
Nov. '73–Mar. '75	16	14.7	9.0
Jan. '80–July '80	6	8.7	7.6
July '81–Nov. '82	16	12.3	10.8
July '90–Feb. '91	8	2.2	6.5
Mar. '01–Nov. '01	8	0.6	5.6
The next one	?	?	?

TABLE 10.1
Business Slumps, 1929–2002

The U.S. economy has experienced 13 business slumps since 1929. None of the post–World War II recessions came close to the severity of the Great Depression of the 1930s. Recent slumps have averaged 10 months in length (versus 10 *years* for the 1930s depression).

World War II World War II greatly increased the demand for goods and services and ended the Great Depression. During the war years, output grew at unprecedented rates—almost 19 percent in a single year (1942). Virtually everyone was employed, either in the armed forces or in the factories. Throughout the war, our productive capacity was strained to the limit.

Recent Recessions In the postwar years the U.S. economy resumed a pattern of alternating growth and contraction. The contracting periods are called recessions. Specifically, the term **recession** refers to a decline in real GDP that continues for at least two successive calendar quarters. As Table 10.1 indicates, there have been 11 recessions since 1944. The most severe recession occurred immediately after World War II ended, when sudden cutbacks in defense production caused sharp declines in output (−38 percent). That first postwar recession lasted only eight months, however, and raised the rate of unemployment to just 4.3 percent. By contrast, the recession of 1981–82 was much longer (16 months) and pushed the national unemployment rate to 10.8 percent. That was the highest unemployment rate since the Great Depression of the 1930s.

recession A decline in total output (real GDP) for two or more consecutive quarters.

From November 1982 until November 1989, the U.S. economy enjoyed an unusually long and robust expansion. In the process, nearly 20 million jobs were created and total output increased by over 30 percent. Once again, however, the economy ran out of steam. The expansion slowed in the winter of 1990 and then slid into another recession in July of that year.

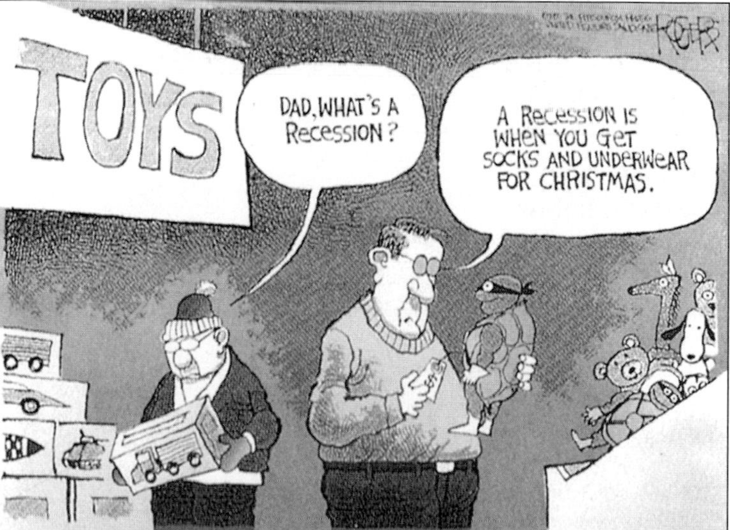

Recessions vary in length and magnitude. A deep and prolonged recession is called a depression.

Rob Rogers, reprinted by permission of United Feature Syndicate, Inc.

Yet another upswing began eight months later. Although the recovery started slowly, it picked up steam in 1993 and 1994. By 2000, the '90s expansion had become the longest in history. Economists were worried, however, that the economy might not have enough momentum to sustain the expansion. By the time President George W. Bush took office in January 2001, GDP growth had slowed to a crawl. Another recession—brief and mild—occurred shortly thereafter.

Unemployment

Although the primary measure of the economy's health is the real GDP growth rate, that measure is a bit impersonal. *People,* not just output, suffer in recessions. When output declines, *jobs* are eliminated. In the 1990–91 recession over 2 million American workers lost their jobs. The same thing happened again in the economic slowdown of 2001–2003. Other would-be workers—including graduating students—had great difficulty finding jobs. These are the human dimensions of a recession.

The Labor Force

Our concern about the human side of recession doesn't mean that we believe *everyone* should have a job. We do, however, strive to ensure that jobs are available for all individuals who *want* to work. This requires us to distinguish the general population from the smaller number of individuals who are ready and willing to work, that is, those who are in the **labor force.** The ***labor force consists of everyone over the age of 16 who is actually working plus all those who are not working but are actively seeking employment.*** As Figure 10.3 shows, only about half of the population participates in the labor market. The rest of the population (nonparticipants) are too young, in school, retired, sick or disabled, institutionalized, or taking care of household needs.

labor force All persons over age 16 who are either working for pay or actively seeking paid employment.

Note that our definition of labor-force participation excludes most household and volunteer activities. A woman who chooses to devote her energies to household responsibilities or to unpaid charity work is not counted as part of the labor force, no matter how hard she works. Because she is neither in paid employment nor seeking such employment in the marketplace, she is regarded as outside the labor market (a nonparticipant). But if she decides

FIGURE 10.3
The U.S. Labor Force, 2000

Only half of the total U.S. population participates in the civilian labor force. The rest of the population is too young, in school, at home, retired, or otherwise unavailable.

Unemployment statistics count only those participants who are not currently working and actively seeking paid employment. Nonparticipants are neither employed nor actively seeking employment.

Source: U.S. Department of Labor, and U.S. Bureau of Census

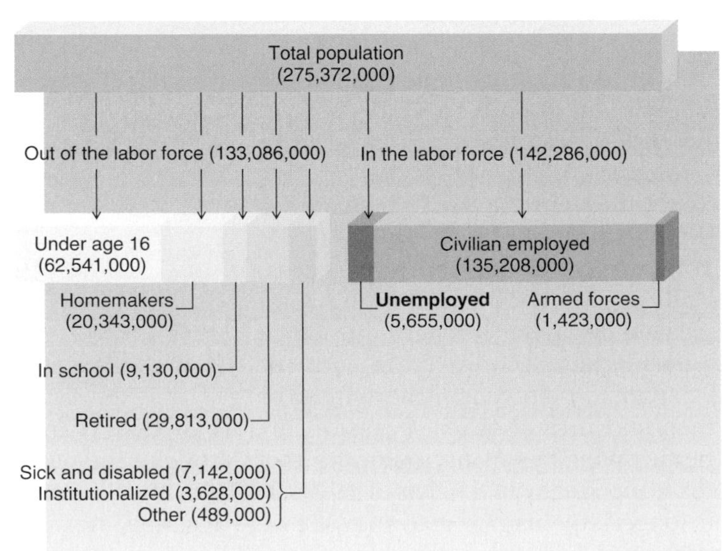

to seek a paid job outside the home and engages in an active job search, we would say that she is "entering the labor force." Students, too, are typically out of the labor force until they leave school and actively look for work, either during summer vacations or after graduation.

The Unemployment Rate

To assess how well labor-force participants are faring in the macro economy, we compute the **unemployment rate** as:

unemployment rate The proportion of the labor force that is unemployed.

- $\text{Unemployment rate} = \dfrac{\text{number of unemployed people}}{\text{size of the labor force}}$

To be counted as *unemployed,* a person must not only be jobless but also actively looking for work. A full-time student, for example, may be jobless but would not be counted as unemployed. Likewise, a full-time homemaker who is not looking for paid employment outside the home would not be included in our measure of **unemployment.**

unemployment The inability of labor-force participants to find jobs.

Figure 10.3 indicates that nearly 6 million Americans were counted as unemployed in 2000. The civilian labor force (excluding the armed forces) at that time included 141 million individuals. Accordingly, the civilian unemployment *rate* was

$$\text{Civilian unemployment rate, in 2000} = \frac{\text{5.7 million unemployed}}{\text{141 million in labor force}} = 4.0\%$$

As Figure 10.4 illustrates, the unemployment rate in 2000 was far below the recession experience of 1982. In fact, it was the lowest unemployment rate in over 30 years. Over the next three years, the unemployment rose to over 6 percent as economic growth slowed.

As noted earlier, the unemployment rate is our second measure of the economy's health. It is often regarded as an index of human misery. The people who lose their jobs in a recession experience not only a sudden loss of income but also losses of security and self-confidence. Extended periods of unemployment

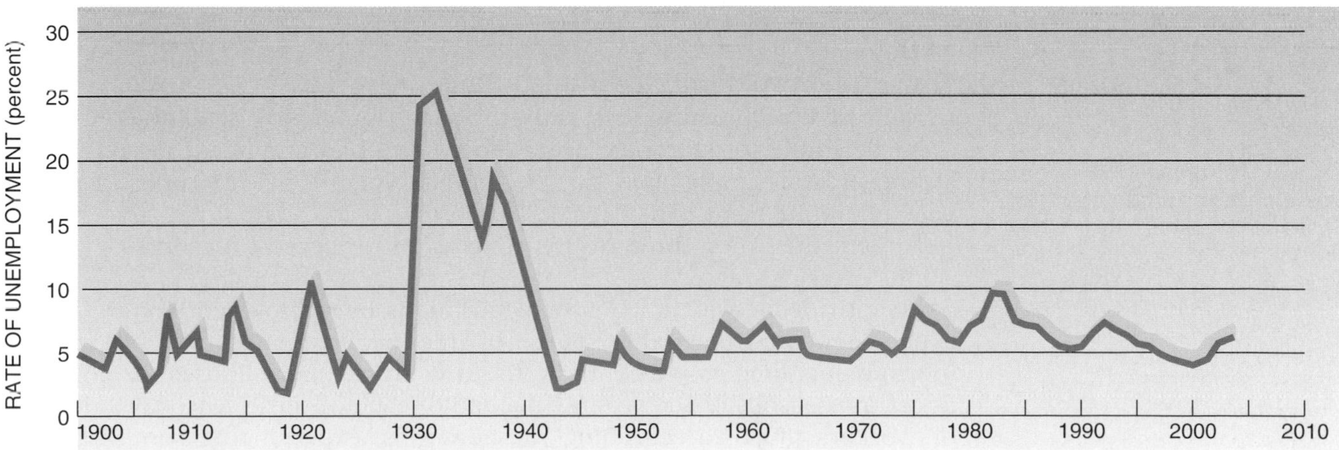

FIGURE 10.4 The Unemployment Record

Unemployment rates reached record heights during the Great Depression. The postwar record is much better than the prewar record, even though full employment has been infrequent.

Source: U.S. Department of Labor.

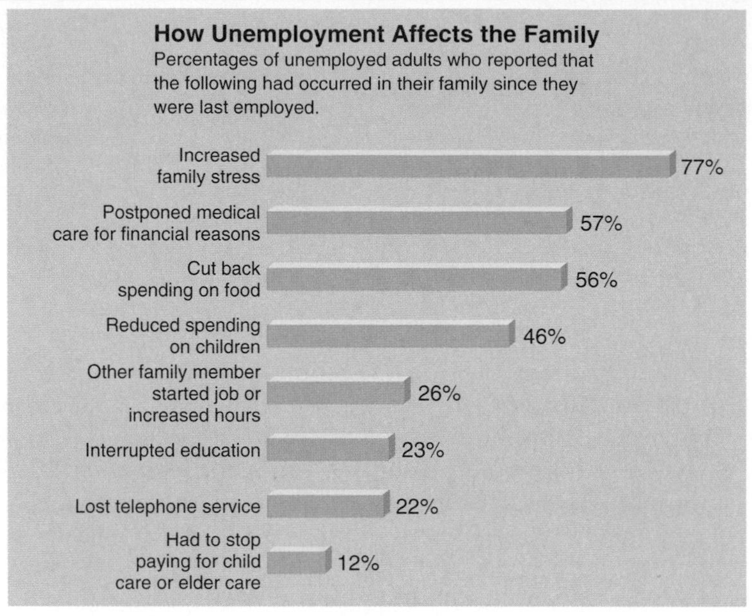

Source: Bob Laird, *USA Today*, June 27, 2003, p. 1B.

NOTE: The cost of unemployment goes beyond the implied loss of output. Unemployment may breed despair, crime, ill health, and other social problems.

may undermine families as well as finances. One study showed that every percentage increase in the unemployment rate causes an additional 10,000 divorces. An unemployed person's health may suffer too. Thomas Cottle, a lecturer at Harvard Medical School, stated the case more bluntly: "I'm now convinced that unemployment is *the* killer disease in this country—responsible for wife beating, infertility, and even tooth decay." The accompanying Headline documents some of the symptoms on which such diagnoses are based.

The Full-Employment Goal

In view of the human misery caused by high unemployment rates, it might seem desirable to guarantee every labor-force participant a job. But things are never that simple. The macroeconomic doctors never propose to *eliminate* unemployment. They instead prescribe a *low,* but not a *zero,* unemployment rate. They come to this conclusion for several reasons.

Seasonal Unemployment Seasonal variations in employment conditions are a persistent and inevitable source of unemployment. Some joblessness is inevitable as long as we continue to grow crops, build houses, or go skiing at certain seasons of the year. At the end of each of these seasons, thousands of workers must go searching for new jobs, experiencing some seasonal unemployment in the process.

Seasonal fluctuations also arise on the supply side of the labor market. Teenage unemployment rates, for example, rise sharply in the summer as students look for temporary jobs. To avoid such unemployment completely, we would either have to keep everyone in school or ensure that all students go immediately from the classroom to the workroom. Neither alternative is likely, much less desirable.

Frictional Unemployment There are other reasons for prescribing some amount of unemployment. Many workers have sound financial or personal reasons for leaving one job to look for another. In the process of moving from one job to another, a person may well miss a few days or even weeks of work without any serious personal or social consequences. On the contrary, people who spend more time looking for work may find *better* jobs.

The same is true of students first entering the labor market. It is not likely that you will find a job the moment you leave school. Nor should you necessarily take the first job offered. If you spend some time looking for work, you are more likely to find a job you like. The job-search period gives you an opportunity to find out what kinds of jobs are available, what skills they require, and what they pay. Accordingly, a brief period of job search for persons entering the labor market may benefit both the individual involved and the larger economy. The unemployment associated with this kind of job search is referred to as *frictional* unemployment.

Structural Unemployment For many job seekers, the period between jobs may drag on for months or even years because they do not have the skills that employers require. In the early 1980s, the steel and auto industries downsized, eliminating over half a million jobs. The displaced workers had years of work experience. But their specific skills were no longer in demand. They were *structurally* unemployed. The same kind of structural displacement hit the defense industry in the 1990s. Cutbacks in national defense spending forced weapons manufacturers, aerospace firms, and electronics companies to reduce output and lay off thousands of workers. The displaced workers soon discovered that their highly developed skills were not immediately applicable in nondefense industries. The same fate befell programmers and software engineers when the "dot com" boom burst in 2000–01.

High school dropouts suffer similar structural problems. They simply don't have the skills that today's jobs require. When such structural unemployment exists, more job creation alone won't necessarily reduce unemployment. On the contrary, more job demand might simply push wages higher for skilled workers, leaving unskilled workers unemployed.

Cyclical Unemployment There is a fourth kind of unemployment that is more worrisome to the macroeconomic doctors. *Cyclical* unemployment refers to the joblessness that occurs when there are simply not enough jobs to go around. Cyclical unemployment exists when the number of workers demanded falls short of the number of persons in the labor force. This is not a case of mobility between jobs (frictional unemployment) or even of job seekers' skills (structural unemployment). Rather, it is simply an inadequate level of demand for goods and services and thus for labor.

The Great Depression is the most striking example of cyclical unemployment. The dramatic increase in unemployment rates that began in 1930 (see Figure 10.4) was not due to any increase in friction or sudden decline in workers' skills. Instead, the high rates of unemployment that persisted for a *decade* were due to a sudden decline in the market demand for goods and services. How do we know? Just notice what happened to our unemployment rate when the demand for military goods and services increased in 1941!

The Policy Goal In later chapters we will examine the causes of cyclical unemployment and explore some potential policy responses. At this point, all we want to do is to set some goals for macro policy. We have seen that *zero* unemployment is not an appropriate goal. But what, then, is a desirable level of *low* unemployment? If we want to assess macro policy, we need to know what specific rate of unemployment to shoot for.

full employment The lowest rate of unemployment compatible with price stability; variously estimated at between 4 and 6 percent unemployment.

There is no total agreement about the level of unemployment that constitutes **full employment.** Most macro economists agree, however, that the optimal unemployment rate lies somewhere between 4 and 6 percent.

Inflation

When the unemployment rate falls to its full-employment level, you might expect everyone to cheer. This rarely happens, though. Indeed, when the jobless rate declines, a lot of macro economists start to fret. Too much of a good thing, they worry, might cause some harm. The harm they fear is *inflation.*

The fear of inflation is based on the price pressures that accompany capacity production. When the economy presses against its production possibilities, idle resources are hard to find. An imbalance between the demand and supply of goods may cause prices to start rising. The resulting inflation may cause a whole new type of pain. Even a low level of inflation pinches family pocketbooks, upsets financial markets, and ignites a storm of political protest. Runaway inflations do even more harm; they crush whole economies and topple governments. In Germany, prices rose more than twenty-five-fold in only one month during the *hyperinflation* of 1922–23. As the accompanying Headline describes, those runaway prices forced people to change their market behavior radically. After the Soviet Union collapsed in 1989, Russia also experienced price increases that exceeded 2,000 percent a year. Such uncontrolled inflation sent consumers scrambling for goods that became increasingly hard to find at "reasonable" prices. To avoid that kind of economic disruption, every American president since Franklin Roosevelt has expressed a determination to keep prices from rising.

Relative vs. Average Prices

inflation An increase in the average level of prices of goods and services.

Although most people worry about inflation, few understand it. Most people associate **inflation** with price increases on specific goods and services. The economy is not necessarily experiencing an inflation, however, every time the price of a cup of coffee goes up. We must be careful to distinguish the phenomenon of inflation from price increases for specific goods. ***Inflation is an increase in the average level of prices, not a change in any specific price.***

Suppose you wanted to know the average price of fruit in the supermarket. Surely you would not have much success in seeking out an average fruit—nobody would be quite sure what you had in mind. You might have some success, however, if you sought out the prices of apples, oranges, cherries, and peaches. Knowing the price of each kind of fruit, you could then compute the average price of fruit. The resultant figure would not refer to any particular product but would convey a sense of how much a typical basket of fruit might cost. By repeating these calculations every day, you could then determine whether fruit prices, *on average,* were changing. On occasion, you might even notice that apple prices rose while orange prices fell, leaving the *average* price of fruit unchanged.

The same kinds of calculations are made to measure inflation in the entire economy. We first determine the average price of all output—the average price level—then look for changes in that average. A rise in the average price level is referred to as inflation.

HYPERINFLATION HEADLINE

Inflation and the Weimar Republic

At the beginning of 1921 in Germany, the cost-of-living index was 18 times higher than its 1913 prewar base, while wholesale prices had mushroomed by 4,400 percent. Neither of these increases are negligible, but inflation and war have always been bedfellows. Normally, however, war ends and inflation recedes. By the end of 1921, it seemed that way; prices rose more modestly. Then, in 1922, inflation erupted.

Zenith of German hyperinflation

Wholesale prices rose fortyfold, an increase nearly as large as during the prior eight years, while retail prices rose even more rapidly. The hyperinflation reached its zenith during 1923. Between May and June 1923, consumer prices more than quadrupled; between July and August, they rose more than 15 times; in the next month, over 25 times; and between September and October, by ten times the previous month's increase.

The German economy was thoroughly disrupted. Businessmen soon discovered the impossibility of rational economic planning. Profits fell as employees demanded frequent wage adjustments. Workers were often paid daily and sometimes two or three times a day, so that they could buy goods in the morning before the inevitable afternoon price increase. The work ethic suffered; wage earners were both more reluctant to work and less devoted to their jobs. Bankers were on the phone hour after hour, quoting the value of the mark in dollars, as calls continuously came in from merchants who needed the exchange rate to adjust their mark prices.

In an age that preceded the credit card, businessmen traveling around the country found themselves borrowing funds from their customers each stage of the way. The cash they'd allocated for the entire trip barely sufficed to pay the way to the next stop. Speculation began to dominate production.

As a result of the decline in profitability, in the ability to plan ahead, and the concern with speculation rather than production, unemployment rose, increasing by 600 percent between September 1 and December 15, 1923. And, as the hyperinflation intensified, people found goods unobtainable.

Hyperinflation crushed the middle class. Those thrifty Germans who had placed their savings in corporate or government bonds saw their lifetime efforts come to naught. Debtors sought out creditors to pay them in valueless currency. The debts of German government and industry disappeared. Farmers, too, profited, for, like farmers elsewhere, they were debtors. Nevertheless, the hyperinflation left a traumatic imprint on the German people, a legacy which colors their governmental policy to this day.

—Jonas Prager

NOTE: When prices are rising quickly, people are forced to change their market behavior. A runaway inflation can derail an economy.

The average price level may fall as well as rise. A decline in average prices—a **deflation**—occurs when price decreases on some goods and services outweigh price increases on all others. Although we have not experienced any general deflation since 1940, general price declines were frequent in earlier periods.

deflation A decrease in the average level of prices of goods and services.

Because inflation and deflation are measured in terms of average price levels, it is possible for individual prices to rise or fall continuously without changing the average price level. We already noted, for example, that the price of apples can rise without increasing the average price of fruit, so long as the price of some other fruit (e.g., oranges) falls. In such circumstances, **relative prices** are changing, but not average prices. An increase in the relative price of apples, for example, simply means that apples have become more expensive in comparison with other fruits (or any other goods or services).

relative price The price of one good in comparison with the price of other goods.

Changes in relative prices may occur in a period of stable average prices, or in periods of inflation or deflation. In fact, in an economy as vast as ours—where literally millions of goods and services are exchanged in the factor and product markets—relative prices are always changing. Indeed, relative price changes are an essential ingredient of the market mechanism. If the relative

HEADLINE **PRICE EFFECTS**

Tuition Is Up 11.5% at Community Colleges

Tuition for the current academic year jumped by 11.5 percent at community colleges, largely because of state budget cuts, according to a survey released last week by the American Association of Community Colleges.

In more than half of the states, community-college tuition rose by more than 10 percent.

California and Virginia colleges had the highest percentage increases, at 60 percent and 42 percent, respectively. Maine and West Virginia did not raise tuition at all, although some two-year colleges in those states increased fees slightly . . .

Still, the survey found, average tuition at public two-year colleges—$1,560 annually for full-time students—remains the lowest in higher education. The 11.5-percent increase amounts to a rise of roughly $80 per semester.

—Jamilah Evelyn

Source: *Chronicle of Higher Education*, September 26, 2003.

NOTE: An increase in tuition reduces the real income of college students, forcing them to reduce spending on other goods and services.

price of apples increases, that is a signal to farmers that they should grow more apples and less of other fruits.

A general inflation—an increase in the *average* price level—does not perform this same market function. If all prices rise at the same rate, price increases for specific goods are of little value as market signals. In less extreme cases, when most but not all prices are rising, changes in relative prices do occur but are not so immediately apparent.

Redistributions

The distinction between relative and average prices helps us determine who is hurt by inflation—and who is helped. Popular opinion notwithstanding, it is simply not true that everyone is worse off when prices rise. ***Although inflation makes some people worse off, it makes other people better off.*** Some people even get rich when prices rise! These redistributions of income and wealth occur because people buy different combinations of goods and services, own different assets, and sell distinct goods, or services (including labor). The impact of inflation on individuals, therefore, depends on how the prices of the goods and services each person buys or sells actually change. In this sense, ***inflation acts just like a tax, taking income or wealth from some people and giving it to others.*** This "tax" is levied through changes in prices, changes in incomes, and changes in wealth.

Price Effects Price changes are the most familiar of inflation's pains. If you have been paying tuition, you know how the pain feels. In 1975 the average tuition at public colleges and universities was $400 per year. In 2003, in-state tuition was $4,694 and still rising (see Headline). At private universities, tuition has increased eightfold in the last 10 years, to nearly $20,000. You don't need a whole course in economics to figure out the implications of these tuition hikes. To stay in college, you (or your parents) must forgo increasing amounts of other goods and services. You end up being worse off, since you cannot buy as many goods and services as you were able to buy before tuition went up.

nominal income The amount of money income received in a given time period, measured in current dollars.

The effect of tuition increases on your economic welfare is reflected in the distinction between nominal income and real income. **Nominal income** is the amount of money you receive in a particular time period; it is measured in current dollars. **Real income,** by contrast, is the purchasing power of that money, as measured by the quantity of goods and services your dollars will buy. If the number of dollars you receive every year is always the same, your *nominal income* doesn't change, but your *real income* will fall if prices increase.

real income Income in constant dollars: nominal income adjusted for inflation.

Suppose you have an income of $6,000 a year while you're in school. Out of that $6,000 you must pay for your tuition, room and board, books, and everything else. The budget for your first year at school might look like this:

First Year's Budget

Nominal income	$6,000
Consumption	
Tuition	$3,000
Room and board	2,000
Books	300
Everything else	700
Total	$6,000

After paying for all your essential expenses, you have $700 to spend on clothes, entertainment, or anything else you want.

Now suppose tuition increases to $3,500 in your second year, while all other prices remain the same. What will happen to your nominal income? Nothing. You're still getting $6,000 a year. Your *real* income, however, will suffer. This is evident in the second year's budget:

Second Year's Budget

Nominal income	$6,000
Consumption	
Tuition	$3,500
Room and board	2,000
Books	300
Everything else	200
Total	$6,000

You now have to use more of your income to pay tuition. This means you have less income to spend on other things. After paying for room, board, books, and the increased tuition, only $200 is left for everything else. This is $500 less than in the prior year's budget. That means fewer pizzas, movies, dates, or anything you'd like to buy. The pain of higher tuition will soon be evident; your *nominal income* hasn't changed, but your *real income* has.

There are two basic lessons about inflation to be learned from this sad story:

- ***Not all prices rise at the same rate during an inflation.*** In our example, tuition increased substantially while other prices remained steady. Hence the "average" rate of price increase was not representative of any particular good or service. Typically, some prices rise very rapidly, others only modestly, and some may actually fall. Table 10.2 illustrates some recent variations in price changes. The average rate of inflation (2.1 percent in 2002) disguised very steep price hikes for bacon, lettuce, gasoline, and college tuition.

TABLE 10.2
Not All Prices Rise at the Same Rate

The average rate of inflation conceals substantial differences in the price changes of specific goods and services. The impact of inflation on individuals depends in part on which goods and services are consumed. People who buy goods whose prices are rising fastest lose more real income. In 2002 college students were particularly hard hit by inflation.

Item	Price Change in 2002 (percent)	Item	Price Change in 2002 (percent)
Food		Other	
Lettuce	+24.8	College tuition	+7.4
Eggs	+9.3	Textbooks	+6.7
Bacon	+7.1	Cable TV	+5.1
Pork chops	−1.9	Dental care	+4.1
Coffee	−4.1	Women's dresses	−0.8
Transportation		Video rentals	−8.7
Gasoline	+8.4	Computers	−22.6
Airfares	0.0		
New cars	−1.8	**Average inflation rate**	**+2.1**

Source: U.S. Bureau of Labor Statistics.

- ***Not everyone suffers equally from inflation.*** This follows from our first observation. Those people who consume the goods and services that are rising faster in price bear a greater burden of inflation; their real incomes fall more. In 2002 people who consumed BLTs suffered the most from changing food prices. Other consumers bore a lesser burden, or even none at all, depending on how fast the prices rose for the goods they enjoyed.

We conclude, then, that the price increases associated with inflation redistribute real income. In the example we have discussed, college students end up with fewer goods and services than they had before. Other consumers can continue to purchase at least as many goods as before, perhaps even more. Thus output is effectively *redistributed* from college students to others. Naturally, most college students aren't very happy with this outcome. Fortunately for you, inflation doesn't always work out this way.

Income Effects The redistributive effects of inflation are not limited to changes in prices. Changes in prices automatically influence nominal incomes also.

If the price of tuition does in fact rise faster than all other prices, we can safely make three predictions:

- The *real income* of college students will fall relative to that of nonstudents (assuming constant nominal incomes).
- The *real income* of nonstudents will rise relative to that of students (assuming constant nominal incomes).
- The *nominal income* of colleges and universities will rise.

This last prediction simply reminds us that someone always pockets higher prices. ***What looks like a price to a buyer looks like income to a seller.*** If students all pay higher tuition, the university will take in more income. It will end up being able to buy *more* goods and services (including faculty, buildings, and library books) after the price increase than it could before. Both its nominal income and its real income have risen.

Not everyone gets more nominal income when prices rise. But you may be surprised to learn that *on average* people's incomes *do* keep pace with inflation. Again, this is a direct consequence of the circular flow: what one

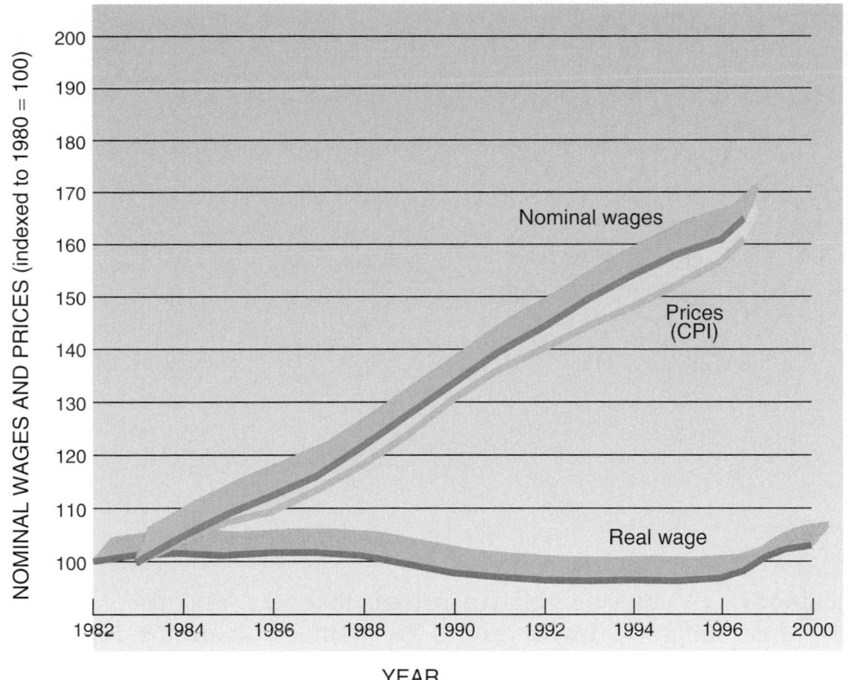

FIGURE 10.5
Nominal Wages and Prices

Inflation implies not only higher prices but higher wages as well. What is a price to one person is income to someone else. Hence inflation cannot make *everyone* worse off. This graph confirms that average hourly wages have risen along with average prices. When nominal wages rise faster than prices, *real* wages are increasing. Higher real wages reflect higher productivity (more output per worker).

Source: *Economic Report of the President,* 2003.

person pays out someone else takes in. ***If prices are rising, incomes must be rising, too.*** Notice in Figure 10.5 that nominal wages have pretty much risen in step with prices. As a result, *real* wages have been fairly stable. From this perspective, it makes no sense to say that "inflation hurts everybody." On *average,* at least, we are no worse off when prices rise, since our (average) incomes increase at the same time.

No one is exactly "average," of course. In reality, some people's incomes rise faster than inflation while others' increase more slowly. Hence the redistributive effects of inflation also originate in varying rates of growth in nominal income.

Wealth Effects The same kind of redistribution occurs between those who hold some form of wealth and those who do not. Suppose that on January 1 you deposit $100 in a savings account, where it earns 5 percent interest until you withdraw it on December 31. At the end of the year you will have more nominal wealth ($105) than you started with ($100). But what if all prices have doubled in the meantime? At the end of the year, your accumulated savings ($105) buys less than it would have at the start of the year. In other words, inflation in this case reduces the *real* value of your savings. You end up with fewer goods and services than those individuals who spent all their income earlier in the year! Table 10.3 shows how different rates of inflation alter the real value of money hidden under the mattress for 10 years.

Table 10.4 shows how the value of various assets actually changed in the 1990s. Between 1991 and 2001, the average price level rose by 32 percent. The price of stocks increased much faster, however, while the price of gold fell. Hence people who held their wealth in the form of stocks rather than gold came out far ahead. The nominal values of bonds and silver rose, but their real value fell.

TABLE 10.3
Inflation's Impact, 2004–2014

In the 1990s, the U.S. rate of inflation ranged from a low of 1.6 percent to a high of 6.1 percent. Does a range of 4–5 percentage points really make much difference? One way to find out is to see how a specific sum of money will shrink in real value.

Here's what would happen to the *real* value of $1,000 from January 1, 2004, to January 1, 2014, at different inflation rates. At 2 percent inflation, $1,000 held for 10 years would be worth $820. At 10 percent inflation that same $1,000 would buy only $386 worth of goods in the year 2014.

	Annual Inflation Rate				
Year	2 Percent	4 Percent	6 Percent	8 Percent	10 Percent
2004	$1,000	$1,000	$1,000	$1,000	$1,000
2005	980	962	943	926	909
2006	961	925	890	857	826
2007	942	889	840	794	751
2008	924	855	792	735	683
2009	906	822	747	681	621
2010	888	790	705	630	564
2011	871	760	665	584	513
2012	853	731	627	540	467
2013	837	703	592	500	424
2014	820	676	558	463	386

Robin Hood? By altering relative prices, incomes, and the real value of wealth, then, inflation turns out to be a mechanism for redistributing incomes. ***The redistributive mechanics of inflation include***

- ***Price effects.*** People who prefer goods and services that are increasing in price least quickly end up with a larger share of real income.
- ***Income effects.*** People whose nominal incomes rise faster than the rate of inflation end up with a larger share of total income.
- ***Wealth effects.*** People who own assets that are increasing in real value end up better off than others.

On the other hand, people whose nominal incomes do not keep pace with inflation end up with smaller shares of total output. The same thing is true of those who enjoy goods that are rising fastest in price or who hold assets that are declining in real value. In this sense, ***inflation acts just like a tax, taking income or wealth from one group and giving it to another.*** But we have no assurance that this particular tax will behave like Robin Hood, taking from the rich and giving to the poor. It may do just the opposite. Not knowing who will win or lose the inflation sweepstakes may make everyone fear rising price levels.

TABLE 10.4
The Real Story of Wealth

As the value of various assets changes, so does a person's wealth. Between 1991 and 2001, prices rose an average of 32 percent. But the prices of stocks, diamonds, and oil rose even faster. People who held these assets gained in *real* (inflation-adjusted) wealth. Home prices also rose more than average prices. Hence, the *real* value of homes also increased in the 1990s. Investors in silver, bonds, and gold did not fare as well.

Asset	Change in Value, 1991–2001
Stocks	+250%
Diamonds	+71
Oil	+66
Housing	+56
U.S. farmland	+49
Average price of goods	**+32**
Silver	+22
Bonds	+20
Stamps	−9
Gold	−29

Uncertainty

The uncertainties of inflation may also cause people to change their consumption, saving, or investment behavior. When average prices are changing rapidly, economic decisions become increasingly difficult. Should you commit yourself to four years of college, for example, if you are not certain that you or your parents will be able to afford the full costs? In a period of stable prices you can at least be fairly certain of what a college education will cost over a period of years. But if prices are rising, you can no longer be sure how large the bill will be. Under such circumstances, many individuals may decide not to enter college rather than risk the possibility of being driven out later by rising costs. In extreme cases, fear of rapidly increasing prices may even deter diners from ordering a meal (see cartoon).

"DO I HAVE YOUR ASSURANCE THAT PRICES WILL NOT BE INCREASED BEFORE WE ARE SERVED?"

Fear of rising prices may alter production, consumption, and investment behavior.

From *The Wall Street Journal*, by permission Cartoon Features Syndicate.

The uncertainties created by changing price levels affect production decisions as well. Imagine a firm that is considering building a new factory. Typically, the construction of a factory takes two years or more, including planning, site selection, and actual construction. If construction costs change rapidly, the firm may find that it is unable to complete the factory or to operate it profitably. Confronted with this added uncertainty, the firm may decide to do without a new plant or at least to postpone its construction until a period of stable prices returns.

Inflation need not always lead to a cutback in consumption and production. The uncertainties generated by inflation may just as easily induce people to buy *more* goods and services now, before prices rise further. In their haste to beat inflation, however, consumers and producers may make foolish decisions, buying goods or services that they will later decide they don't really need or want.

Measuring Inflation

Given all the pain associated with inflation, it's no wonder that inflation rates are a basic barometer of macroeconomic health. To gauge that dimension of well-being, the government computes several price indexes. Of these indexes, the **Consumer Price Index (CPI)** is the most familiar. As its name suggests, the CPI is a mechanism for measuring changes in the average price of consumer goods and services. It is analogous to the fruit price index we discussed earlier. The CPI does not refer to the price of any particular good but, rather, to the average price of all consumer goods.

Consumer Price Index (CPI) A measure (index) of changes in the average price of consumer goods and services.

By itself, the "average price" of consumer goods is not a very useful number. Once we know the average price of consumer goods, however, we can observe whether that average rises—that is, whether inflation is occurring. By observing how prices change, we can calculate the **inflation rate,** that is, the annual percentage increase in the average price level.

inflation rate The annual rate of increase in the average price level.

To compute the CPI, the Bureau of Labor Statistics periodically surveys families to determine what goods and services consumers actually buy. The Bureau of Labor Statistics then goes shopping in various cities across the country, recording the prices of 184 items that make up the typical market basket. This shopping survey is undertaken every month, in 85 areas and at a variety of stores in each area.

As a result of its surveys, the Bureau of Labor Statistics can tell us what's happening to consumer prices. Suppose, for example, that the market basket cost $100 in 2000, and that one year later the same basket of goods and services cost $110. On the basis of those two shopping trips, we could conclude that consumer prices had risen by 10 percent in one year—that is, that the rate of inflation was 10 percent per annum.

In practice, the CPI is usually expressed in terms of what the market basket cost in 1982–84. For example, the CPI stood at 184 in July 2003. In other words, it cost $184 in 2003 to buy the same market basket that cost only $100 in the base period (1982–84). Thus prices had increased by an average of 84 percent over that period. Each month the Bureau of Labor Statistics updates the CPI, telling us how the current cost of that same basket compares to its cost in 1982–84.

The Price-Stability Goal

In view of the inequities, anxieties, and real losses caused by inflation, it is not surprising that price stability is a major goal of economic policy. As we observed at the beginning of this chapter, every American president since Franklin Roosevelt has decreed price stability to be a foremost policy goal. Unfortunately, few presidents (or their advisers) have stated exactly what they mean by *price stability.* Do they mean *no* change in the average price level? Or is some upward creep in the CPI consistent with the notion of price stability?

price stability The absence of significant changes in the average price level; officially defined as a rate of inflation of less than 3 percent.

The Policy Goal An explicit numerical goal for **price stability** was established for the first time in the Full Employment and Balanced Growth Act of 1978. According to that act, the goal of economic policy is to hold the rate of inflation under 3 percent.

Why did Congress choose 3 percent inflation rather than zero inflation as the benchmark for price stability? Two considerations were important. First, Congress recognized that efforts to maintain absolutely stable prices (zero inflation) might threaten full employment. Recall that our goal of full employment is defined as the lowest rate of unemployment *consistent with stable prices.* The same kind of thinking is apparent here. The amount of inflation regarded as tolerable depends in part on how anti-inflation strategies affect unemployment. If policies that promise zero inflation raise unemployment rates too high, people may prefer to accept a little inflation. After reviewing our experiences with both unemployment and inflation, Congress concluded that 3 percent inflation was a safe target.

Quality Improvements The second argument for setting our price-stability goal above zero inflation relates to our measurement capabilities. Although the Consumer Price Index is very thorough, it is not a perfect measure of inflation. In essence, the CPI simply monitors the price of specific goods over time. Over time, however, the goods themselves change, too. Old products become better as a result of *quality improvements.* A television set costs more today than it did in 1955, but today's TV also delivers a bigger, clearer picture—in digital images and stereo sound. Hence increases in the price of television sets tend to exaggerate the true rate of inflation: part of the higher price represents more product.

The same kind of quality changes distort our view of how car prices have changed. Since 1958, the average price of a new car has risen from $2,867 to roughly $20,000. But today's cars aren't really comparable to those of 1958. Since that time, the quality of cars has been improved with electronic ignitions, emergency flashers, rear-window defrosters, crash-resistant bodies, air bags, antilock brakes, remote-control mirrors, seatbelts, variable-speed windshield wipers, radial tires, a doubling of fuel mileage, and a hundredfold decrease in exhaust pollutants. Accordingly, the sixfold increase in average car prices since 1958 greatly overstates the true rate of inflation.

New Products The problem of measuring quality improvements is even more apparent in the case of new products. The computers and word processors found in many offices and homes today did not exist when the Census Bureau conducted its 1972–73 survey of consumer expenditures. The 1982–84 survey included these new products, but the CPI itself was not revised until 1987. In the intervening years, the real incomes of consumers were affected by these and other goods the CPI did not include. The same thing is happening now: new products and continuing quality improvements are enriching our consumption, even though they are not reflected in the CPI. Hence there is a significant (though unmeasured) element of error in the CPI insofar as it is intended to gauge changes in the average prices paid by consumers. The goal of 3 percent inflation allows for such errors.

SUMMARY

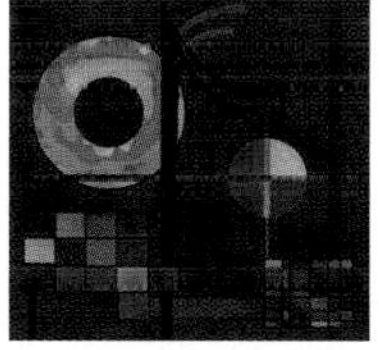

- The health of the macroeconomy is gauged by three measures: real GDP growth, the unemployment rate, and the inflation rate.
- The long-term growth rate of the U.S. economy is approximately 3 percent a year. But output doesn't increase 3 percent every year. In some years real GDP grows faster; in other years growth is slower. Sometimes total output actually declines.
- These short-run variations in GDP growth are the focus of macroeconomics. Macro theory tries to explain the alternating periods of growth and contraction that characterize the business cycle; macro policy attempts to control the cycle.
- To understand unemployment, we need to distinguish the labor force from the larger population. Only people who are working (employed) or spend some time looking for a job (unemployed) are participants in the labor force. People who are neither working nor looking for work are outside the labor force.
- The most visible loss imposed by unemployment is reduced output of goods and services. Those individuals actually out of work suffer lost income, heightened insecurity, and even reduced longevity.
- There are four types of unemployment: seasonal, frictional, structural, and cyclical. Because some seasonal and frictional unemployment is inevitable, and even desirable, full employment is not defined as zero unemployment. These considerations, plus fear of inflation, result in full employment being defined as an unemployment rate of 4–6 percent.
- Inflation is an increase in the average price level. Typically it is measured by changes in a price index such as the Consumer Price Index (CPI).
- Inflation redistributes income by altering relative prices, incomes, and wealth. Because not all prices rise at the same rate and because not all people buy (and sell) the same goods or hold the same assets, inflation does not affect everyone equally. Some individuals actually gain from inflation, whereas others suffer a drop in real income.

- Inflation threatens to reduce total output because it increases uncertainties about the future and thereby inhibits consumption and production decisions. Fear of rising prices can also stimulate spending, forcing the government to take restraining action that threatens full employment.
- The U.S. goal of price stability is defined as an inflation rate of less than 3 percent per year. This goal recognizes potential conflicts between zero inflation and full employment, as well as the difficulties of measuring quality improvements and new products.

Terms to Remember

Define the following terms:

macroeconomics
business cycle
production possibilities
nominal GDP
real GDP
recession
labor force
unemployment rate
unemployment
full employment
inflation
deflation
relative price
nominal income
real income
Consumer Price Index (CPI)
inflation rate
price stability

Questions for Discussion

1. Microsoft sells operating systems, applications software, and technical services. How would you compute changes in Microsoft's volume of output from one year to the next? How would price changes affect your computations?
2. According to the Headline on p. 228, when did the U.S. economy go into recession?
3. Could we ever achieve an unemployment rate *below* full employment? What problems might we encounter if it did?
4. Have you ever had difficulty finding a job? Why didn't you get one right away? What kind of unemployment did you experience?
5. Why might inflation accelerate as the unemployment rate declines?
6. During the period shown in Table 10.4, what happened to
   (a) The nominal price of gold?
   (*b*) The real price of gold?
7. According to Table 10.2, who was most adversely affected by price changes in 2002: consumers who (a) eat a bacon and egg breakfast, or (b) just have coffee?
8. Which of the following people would we expect to be hurt by an increase in the rate of inflation from 3 percent to 6 percent?
   (*a*) A homeowner with a $50,000 fixed-rate mortgage on his home.
   (*b*) A retired person who receives a monthly pension of $500 from her former employer.
   (*c*) An automobile worker with a cost-of-living provision in his employment contract.
   (*d*) A wealthy individual who owns coporate bonds that pay her an interest rate of 8 percent per year.

9. Would it be advantageous to borrow money if you expected prices to rise? Why, or why not? Provide a numerical example.
10. Why did the Great Depression last so long? What happened to all the jobs?

Problems

1. How much *more* output will the average American have next year if the $11 trillion U.S. economy grows by
   (*a*) 2 percent?
   (*b*) 5 percent?
   (*c*) −1.0 percent?
   Assume a population of 290 million.
2. Suppose the following data describe a nation's population:

	Year 1	Year 2
Population	200 million	203 million
Labor force	120 million	125 million
Unemployed	7.2 million	7.5 million

   (*a*) What is the unemployment rate in each year?
   (*b*) How has the *number* of unemployed changed from Year 1 to Year 2?
   (*c*) How is the apparent discrepancy between (*a*) and (*b*) explained?
3. If the average worker produces $70,000 of GDP, by how much will GDP increase if there are 140 million labor-force participants and the unemployment rate drops from 5.2 to 4.5 percent?
4. What would the *real* value be in 10 years of $500 you hid under your mattress if the inflation rate is
   (*a*) 4% (*b*) 8%
   (*Hint:* Table 10.3 provides clues.)
5. According to the data below,
   (*a*) How did nominal wages change between 1990 and 1992?
   (*b*) How did real wages change between 1990 and 1992?
   (*c*) How did nominal wages change between 1990 and 1999?
   (*d*) How did real wages change between 1990 and 1999? (Compute *percentage* changes.)

	1990	1992	1999
Average weekly wage	$345	$364	$457
CPI	131	140	167

6. Suppose you will have an annual nominal income of $40,000 for the next five years, without any increases. However, the inflation rate is 5 percent.
   (*a*) Find the real value of your $40,000 salary for each of the next five years.

(*b*) Suppose your boss agrees to raise your $40,000 salary by 5 percent for each of the next five years. Given the 5 percent inflation rate for each of those five years, what is the real value of your salary for each year?

7. The following table lists the prices of a small market basket purchased in both 2000 and 2004. Assuming that this basket of goods is representative of all goods and services
   (*a*) Compute the cost of the market basket in 2000.
   (*b*) Compute the cost of the market basket in 2004.
   (*c*) By how much has the average price level risen between 2000 and 2004?
   (*d*) The average household's nominal income increased from $45,000 to $50,000 between 2000 and 2004. What happened to its real income?

		Price (per unit)	
Item	**Quantity**	**2000**	**2004**
Coffee	20 pounds	$ 3	$ 4
Tuition	1 year	4,000	7,000
Pizza	100 pizzas	8	10
VCR rental	75 days	15	10
Vacation	2 weeks	300	500

Web Activities

1. Log on to www.whitehouse.gov/fsbr/esbr.html. List three of the leading economic indicators and explain what they suggest about the current U.S. business cycle; that is, are we currently in a period of economic expansion or recession? Your answer should include a discussion of the general trend in the indicators you have chosen and what this trend suggests about the current business cycle.
2. Log on to www.census.gov and click on the latest economic indicators (under subjects index "E"). Choose three economic indicators to examine (different indicators than described in question 1). Explain what the trends in these indicators suggest about the current U.S. business cycle.
3. Log on to www.whitehouse.gov/fsbr/esbr.html. Link into output, then click on the chart for Gross Domestic Product. What has been the trend in real GDP? What do these data suggest about the current business cycle? That is, are we in a period of economic growth or decline?

Living Econ

How Do High Prices Affect Me?

When most people read about inflation, they worry about the negative impact of high prices. After all, as Chapter 3 confirms, high prices cause the quantity demanded to fall for *individual* goods and services. But in Chapter 10 you learned that inflation means an increase in the *average* price level, not necessarily a rise in all prices. With inflation some prices fall while others rise.

Moreover, not all individuals are affected equally by inflation. As a college student you may be not be hurt by inflation, at least in the short run, if you have loans at fixed interest rates, if you work at a job with wages that rise with inflation, or if you consume lots of goods and services for which prices are rising less than the overall inflation rate, such as clothing, food, and electronics.

In the long run, your economic situation may change, putting you on the losing side of inflation. Also, high or rising inflation may disrupt the economy or cause government policymakers to put on the economic brakes, causing a drop in your income and job opportunities. So there are additional aspects of inflation to consider.

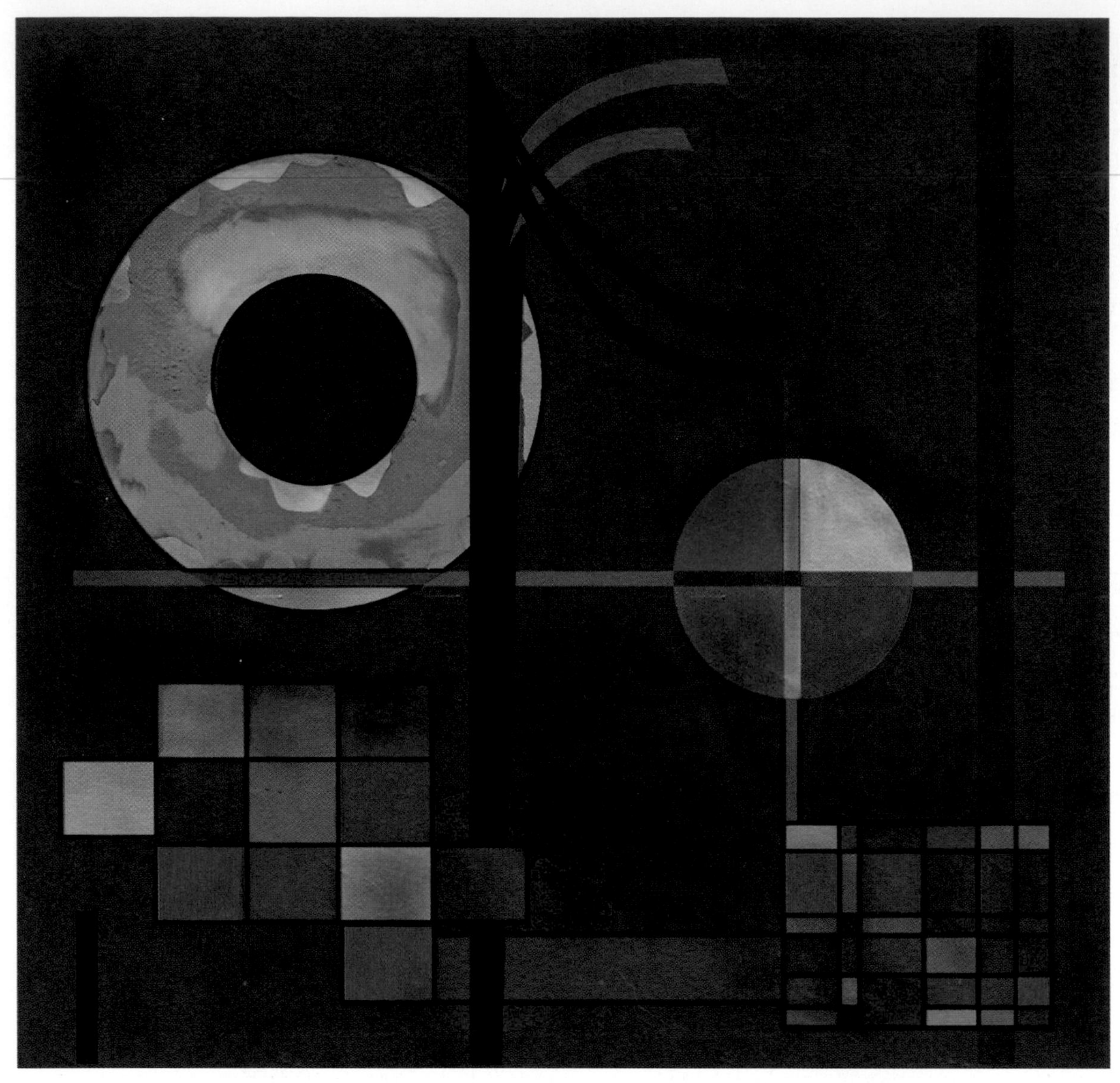

Aggregate Supply and Demand

CHAPTER 11

Recurrent recessions, unemployment, and inflation indicate that the economy isn't always in perfect health. Now it's time to start thinking about causes and cures. Why does the economy ever slip into recession? What causes unemployment or inflation rates to flare up? And what, if anything, can the government do to cure these ailments?

The central focus of **macroeconomics** is on these very questions, that is, What causes business cycles and what, if anything, the government can do about them. Can government intervention prevent or correct market excesses? Or is government intervention likely to make things worse?

To answer these questions, we need a model of how the economy works. The model must provide a clear view of how the various pieces of the economy interact. Such a model will allow us not only to see how the macro economy works but also to pinpoint potential causes of macro failure.

In developing a macro model, the following questions must be answered:

- What are the major determinants of macro outcomes?
- How do the forces of supply and demand fit into the macro picture?
- Why are there disagreements about causes and cures of macro ailments?

Answers to these questions will go a long way in explaining the continuing debates about the causes of business cycles. A macro model can also be used to identify policy options for government intervention.

A Macro View

Macro Outcomes

macroeconomics The study of aggregate economic behavior, of the economy as a whole.

Figure 11.1 provides a bird's-eye view of the macro economy. The primary outcomes of the macro economy are arrayed on the right side of the figure. These basic ***macro outcomes include***

- ***Output:*** total volume of goods and services produced (real GDP).
- ***Jobs:*** levels of employment and unemployment.
- ***Prices:*** average prices of goods and services.
- ***Growth:*** year-to-year expansion in production capacity.
- ***International balances:*** international value of the dollar; trade and payments balances with other countries.

These macro outcomes define our nation's economic welfare. As observed in Chapter 10, we gauge the health of the macro economy by its real GDP (output) growth, unemployment (jobs), and inflation (prices). To this list, we now add an international measure—the balances in our trade and financial relations with the rest of the world.

Macro Determinants

Figure 11.1 also provides an overview of the separate forces that affect macro outcomes. Three very broad forces are depicted. These ***determinants of macro performance include***

- ***Internal market forces:*** population growth, spending behavior, invention and innovation, and the like.
- ***External shocks:*** wars, natural disasters, trade disruptions, and so on.
- ***Policy levers:*** tax policy, government spending, changes in the availability of money, and regulation, for example.

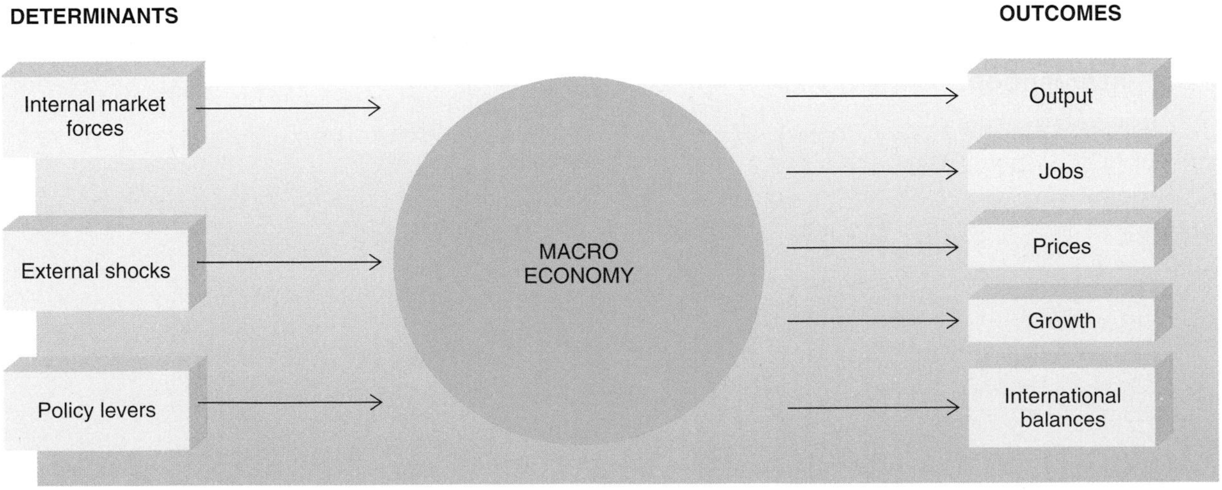

FIGURE 11.1 The Macro Economy

The primary outcomes of the macro economy are output of goods and services, jobs, prices, economic growth, and international balances (trade, currency). These outcomes result from the interplay of internal market forces (e.g., population growth, innovation, spending patterns), external shocks (e.g., wars, weather, trade disruptions), and policy levers (e.g., tax and budget decisions).

In the absence of external shocks or government policy, an economy would still function—it would still produce output, create jobs, develop prices, and maybe even grow. The U.S. economy operated this way for much of its history. Even today, many less developed countries and areas operate in relative isolation from government and international events. In these situations, macro outcomes depend exclusively on internal market forces.

Stable or Unstable?

The central concern of macroeconomic theory is whether the internal forces of the marketplace will generate desired outcomes. Will the market mechanism assure us full employment? Will the market itself maintain price stability? Or will the market *fail,* subjecting us to recurring bouts of unemployment, inflation, and declining output?

Classical Theory

Prior to the 1930s, macro economists thought there could never be a Great Depression. The economic thinkers of the time asserted that the economy was inherently stable. During the nineteenth century and the first 30 years of the twentieth century, the U.S. economy had experienced some bad years—years in which the nation's output declined and unemployment increased. But most of these episodes were relatively short-lived. The dominant feature of the industrial era was growth—an expanding economy, with more output, more jobs, and higher incomes nearly every year.

Self-Adjustment In this environment, classical economists, as they later became known, propounded an optimistic view of the macro economy. ***According to the classical view, the economy self-adjusts to deviations from its long term growth trend.*** Producers might occasionally reduce their output and throw people out of work. But these dislocations would cause little damage. If output declined and people lost their jobs, the internal forces of the marketplace would quickly restore prosperity. Economic downturns were viewed as temporary setbacks, not permanent problems.

Flexible Prices The cornerstones of classical optimism were flexible prices and flexible wages. If producers were unable to sell all their output at current prices, they had two choices. They could reduce the rate of output and throw some people out of work. Or they could reduce the price of their output, thereby stimulating an increase in the quantity demanded. According to the law of demand, price reductions cause an increase in unit sales. If prices fall far enough, all the output produced can be sold. Thus flexible prices—prices that would drop when consumer demand slowed—virtually guaranteed that all output could be sold. No one would have to lose a job because of weak consumer demand.

Flexible Wages Flexible prices had their counterpart in factor markets. If some workers were temporarily out of work, they would compete for jobs by offering their services at lower wages. As wage rates declined, producers would find it profitable to hire more workers. Ultimately, flexible wages would ensure that everyone who wanted a job would have a job.

Say's Law These optimistic views of the macro economy were summarized in Say's Law. **Say's Law—**named after the nineteenth-century economist Jean-Baptiste Say—decreed that "supply creates its own demand." In Say's

Say's Law Supply creates its own demand.

view, if you produce something, *somebody* will buy it. All you have to do is find the right price. In this classical view of the world, unsold goods could appear in the market. But they would ultimately be sold when buyers and sellers found an acceptable price.

The same self-adjustment was expected in the labor market. Sure, some people could lose jobs, especially when output growth slowed. But they could find new jobs if they were willing to accept lower wages. With enough wage flexibility, no one would remain unemployed.

There could be no Great Depression—no protracted macro failure—in this classical view of the world. Indeed, internal market forces (e.g., flexible prices and wages) could even provide an automatic adjustment to external shocks (e.g., wars, droughts, trade disruptions) that threatened to destabilize the economy. ***The classical economists saw no need for the box labeled "policy levers" in Figure 11.1; government intervention in the (self-adjusting) macro economy was unnecessary.***

The Great Depression was a stunning blow to classical economists. At the onset of the depression, classical economists assured everyone that the set-backs in production and employment were temporary and would soon vanish. Andrew Mellon, secretary of the U.S. Treasury, expressed this optimistic view in January 1930, just a few months after the stock-market crash. Assessing the prospects for the year ahead, he said: "I see nothing . . . in the present situation that is either menacing or warrants pessimism . . . I have every confidence that there will be a revival of activity in the spring and that during the coming year the country will make steady progress."[1] Merrill Lynch, one of the nation's largest brokerage houses, was urging people to buy stocks. But the depression deepened. Indeed, unemployment grew and persisted, *despite* falling prices and wages (see Figure 11.2). The classical self-adjustment mechanism simply did not work.

The Keynesian Revolution

The Great Depression destroyed the credibility of classical economic theory. As John Maynard Keynes wrote in 1935, classical economists

> were apparently unmoved by the lack of correspondence between the results of their theory and the facts of observation:—a discrepancy which the ordinary man has not failed to observe. . . .
>
> The celebrated optimism of [classical] economic theory . . . is . . . to be traced, I think, to their having neglected to take account of the drag on prosperity which can be exercised by an insufficiency of effective demand. For there would obviously be a natural tendency towards the optimum employment of resources in a Society which was functioning after the manner of the classical postulates. It may well be that the classical theory represents the way in which we should like our Economy to behave. But to assume that it actually does so is to assume our difficulties away.[2]

No Self-Adjustment Keynes went on to develop an alternative view of the macro economy. Whereas the classical economists viewed the economy as inherently stable, ***Keynes asserted that the private economy was inherently unstable.*** Small disturbances in output, prices, or unemployment were likely to be magnified, not muted, by the invisible hand of the marketplace. The

[1]David A. Shannon, *The Great Depression* (Englewood Cliffs, NJ: Prentice Hall, 1960), p. 4.

[2]John Maynard Keynes, *The General Theory of Employment, Interest and Money* (London: Macmillan, 1936), pp. 33–34.

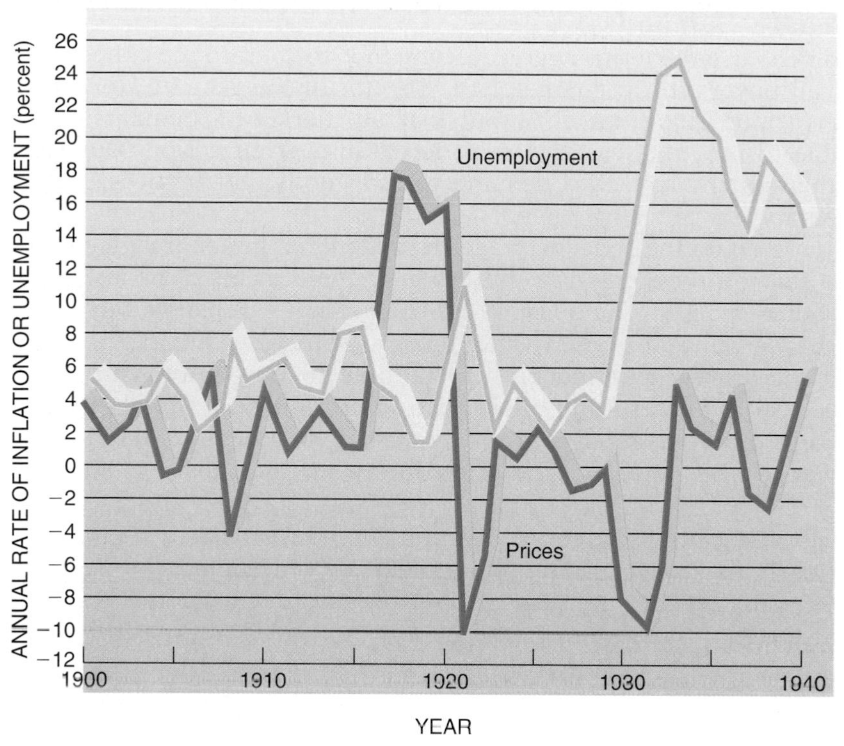

FIGURE 11.2
Inflation and Unemployment, 1900–1940

In the early twentieth century, prices responded to both upward and downward changes in aggregate demand. Periods of high unemployment also tended to be brief. In the 1930s, however, unemployment rates rose to unprecedented heights and stayed high for a decade. Falling wages and prices did not restore full employment. This macro failure prompted calls for new theories and policies to control the business cycle.

Source. U.S. Bureau of the Census. *Historical Statistics of the United States*, 1957.

Great Depression was not a unique event, Keynes argued, but a calamity that would recur if we relied on the market mechanism to self-adjust. Macro failure was the rule, not the exception, for a purely private economy.

In Keynes's view, the inherent instability of the marketplace required government intervention. When the economy falters, we cannot afford to wait for some assumed self-adjustment mechanism. We must instead intervene to protect jobs and income. Keynes concluded that policy levers (see Figure 11.1) were both effective and necessary. Without such intervention, he believed, the economy was doomed to bouts of repeated macro failure.

Modern economists hesitate to give policy intervention that great a role. Nearly all economists recognize that policy intervention affects macro outcomes. But there are great arguments about just how effective any policy lever is. A vocal minority of economists even echoes the classical notion that policy intervention may be either ineffective or, worse still, inherently destabilizing.

The Aggregate Supply–Demand Model

These persistent debates can best be understood in the familiar framework of supply and demand—the most commonly used tools in an economist's toolbox. All of the macro outcomes depicted in Figure 11.1 are the result of market transactions—an interaction between supply and demand. Hence ***any influence on macro outcomes must be transmitted through supply or demand.*** In other words, if the forces depicted on the left side of Figure 11.1 affect neither supply nor demand, they will have no impact on macro outcomes. This makes our job easier. We can resolve the question about macro stability by focusing on the forces that shape supply and demand in the macro economy.

Aggregate Demand

aggregate demand The total quantity of output demanded at alternative price levels in a given time period, ceteris paribus.

Economists use the term "aggregate demand" to refer to the collective behavior of all buyers in the marketplace. Specifically, **aggregate demand** refers to the various quantities of output that all market participants are willing and able to buy at alternative price levels in a given period. Our view here encompasses the collective demand for *all* goods and services, rather than the demand for any single good.

To understand the concept of aggregate demand better, imagine that everyone is paid on the same day. With their income in hand, people then enter the product market. The question is: How much will people buy?

To answer this question, we have to know something about prices. If goods and services are cheap, people will be able to buy more with their given income. On the other hand, high prices will limit both the ability and willingness to purchase goods and services. Note that we are talking here about the average price level, not the price of any single good.

real GDP The inflation-adjusted value of GDP; the value of output measured in constant prices.

Real GDP (Output) This simple relationship between average prices and real spending is illustrated in Figure 11.3. On the horizontal axis we depict the various quantities of output that might be purchased. We are referring here to **real GDP,** an inflation-adjusted measure of physical output.

Price Level On the vertical axis we measure prices. Specifically, Figure 11.3 depicts alternative levels of *average* prices. As we move up the vertical axis, the average price level rises; as we move down, the average price level falls.

The aggregate demand curve in Figure 11.3 has a familiar shape. The message of this downward-sloping macro curve is a bit different, however. ***The aggregate demand curve illustrates how the volume of purchases varies with average prices.*** The downward slope of the aggregate demand curve suggests that with a given (constant) level of income, people will buy more goods and services at lower prices. The curve doesn't tell us *which* goods and services people will buy; it simply indicates the total volume (quantity) of their intended purchases.

At first blush, a downward-sloping demand curve hardly seems remarkable. But because *aggregate* demand refers to the total volume of spending, Figure 11.3 requires a distinctly macro explanation. That explanation includes three separate phenomena:

- ***Real balances effect:*** The primary explanation for the downward slope of the aggregate demand curve is that cheaper prices make dollars

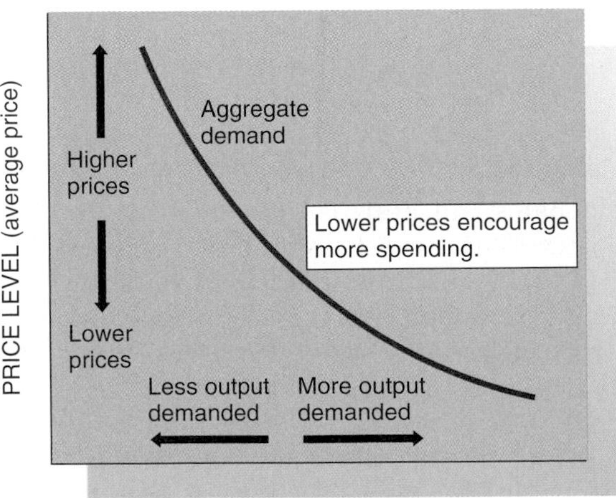

FIGURE 11.3
Aggregate Demand
Aggregate demand refers to the total output demanded at alternative price levels (*ceteris paribus*). The vertical axis here measures the average level of all prices, rather than the price of a single good. Likewise, the horizontal axis refers to the real value of all goods, not the quantity of only one product.

more valuable. That is to say, ***the real value of money is measured by how many goods and services each dollar will buy.*** In this respect, lower prices make you richer: the cash balances you hold in your pocket, in your bank account, or under your pillow are worth more when the price level falls. Lower prices also increase the value of other dollar-denominated assets (e.g., bonds), thus increasing the wealth of consumers.

When their real incomes and wealth increase because of a decline in the price level, consumers respond by buying more goods and services. They end up saving less of their incomes and spending more. This causes the aggregate demand curve to slope downward to the right.

- ***Foreign trade effect:*** The downward slope of the aggregate demand curve is reinforced by changes in imports and exports. When American-made products become cheaper, U.S. consumers will buy fewer imports and more domestic output. Foreigners will also step up their purchases of American-made goods when American prices are falling.

  The opposite is true as well. When the domestic price level rises, U.S. consumers are likely to buy more imports. At the same time, foreign consumers may cut back on their purchases of American-made products.
- ***Interest-rate effect:*** Changes in the price level also affect the amount of money people need to borrow, and so tend to affect interest rates. At lower price levels, consumer borrowing needs are smaller. As the demand for loans diminishes, interest rates tend to decline as well. This cheaper money stimulates more borrowing and loan-financed purchases.

The combined forces of these real-balances, foreign-trade, and interest-rate effects give the aggregate demand curve its downward slope. People buy a larger volume of output when the price level falls (*ceteris paribus*).

Aggregate Supply

While lower price levels tend to increase the volume of output *demanded,* they have the opposite effect on the aggregate quantity *supplied*.

Profit Margins If the price level falls, producers as a group are being squeezed. In the short run, producers are saddled with some relatively constant costs like rent, interest payments, negotiated wages, and inputs already contracted for. If output prices fall, producers will be hard-pressed to pay these costs, much less earn a profit. Their response will be to reduce the rate of output.

Rising output prices have the opposite effect. Because many costs are relatively constant in the short run, higher prices for goods and services tend to widen profit margins. As profit margins widen, producers will want to produce and sell more goods. Thus ***we expect the rate of output to increase when the price level rises.*** This expectation is reflected in the upward slope of the aggregate supply curve in Figure 11.4. **Aggregate supply** reflects the various quantities of real output that firms are willing and able to produce at alternative price levels, in a given time period.

aggregate supply The total quantity of output producers are willing and able to supply at alternative price levels in a given time period, ceteris paribus.

Costs The upward slope of the aggregate supply curve is also explained by rising costs. To increase the rate of output, producers must acquire more resources (e.g., labor) and use existing plant and equipment more intensively.

FIGURE 11.4
Aggregate Supply

Aggregate supply refers to the total volume of output producers are willing and able to bring to the market at alternative price levels (*ceteris paribus*). The upward slope of the aggregate supply curve reflects the fact that profit margins widen when output prices rise (especially when short-run costs are constant). Producers respond to wider profit margins by supplying more output.

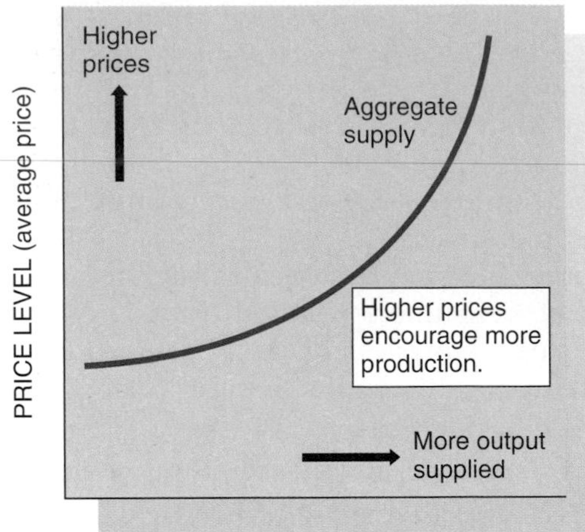

These greater strains on our productive capacity tend to raise production costs. Producers must therefore charge higher prices to recover the higher costs that accompany increased capacity utilization.

Cost pressures tend to intensify as capacity is approached. If there is a lot of excess capacity, output can be increased with little cost pressure. Hence, the lower end of the aggregate supply (AS) curve is fairly flat. As capacity is approached, however, business isn't so easy. Producers may have to pay overtime wages, raise base wages, and pay premium prices to get needed inputs. This is reflected in the steepening slope of the AS curve at higher output levels, as shown in Figure 11.4.

Macro Equilibrium

What we end up with here are two rather conventional-looking supply and demand curves. But these particular curves have special significance. Instead of describing the behavior of buyers and sellers in a single market, ***aggregate supply and demand curves summarize the market activity of the whole (macro) economy.*** These curves tell us what *total* amount of goods and services will be supplied or demanded at various price levels.

These graphic summaries of buyer and seller behavior provide some initial clues as to how macro outcomes are determined. The most important clue is point E in Figure 11.5, where the aggregate demand and supply curves intersect. This is the only point at which the behavior of buyers and sellers is compatible. We know from the aggregate demand curve that people are willing and able to buy the quantity Q_E when the price level is at P_E. From the aggregate supply curve we know that businesses are prepared to sell the quantity Q_E at the price level P_E. Hence buyers and sellers are willing to trade exactly the same quantity (Q_E) at that price level. We call this situation **macro equilibrium**—the unique combination of price level and output that is compatible with both buyers' and sellers' intentions.

equilibrium (macro) The combination of price level and real output that is compatible with both aggregate demand and aggregate supply.

Disequilibrium To appreciate the significance of macro equilibrium, suppose that another price or output level existed. Imagine, for example, that prices were higher, at the level P_1 in Figure 11.5. How much output would people want to buy at that price level? How much would business want to produce and sell?

The aggregate demand curve tells us that people would want to buy only the quantity D_1 at the higher price level P_1. In contrast, business firms would

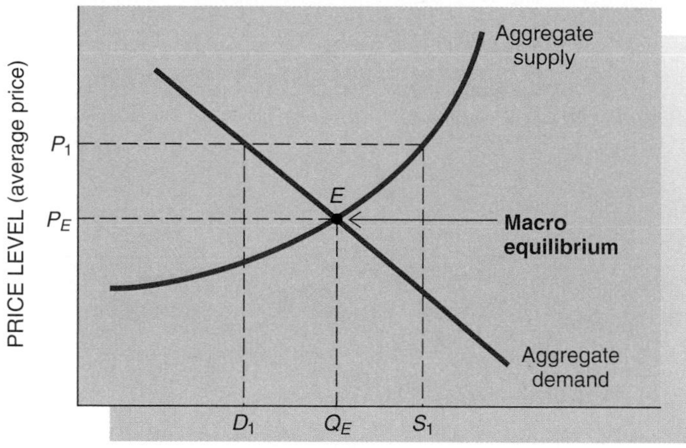

FIGURE 11.5
Macro Equilibrium
The aggregate demand and supply curves intersect at only one point (E). At that point, the price level (P_E) and output (Q_E) combination is compatible with both buyers' and sellers' intentions. The economy will gravitate to those equilibrium price (P_E) and output (Q_E) levels. At any other price level (e.g., P_1), the behavior of buyers and sellers is incompatible.

want to sell a larger quantity, S_1. This is a *disequilibrium* situation, in which the intentions of buyers and sellers are incompatible. The aggregate quantity supplied (S_1) exceeds the aggregate quantity demanded (D_1). Accordingly, a lot of goods will remain unsold at price level P_1.

Market Adjustments To sell these goods, producers will have to reduce their prices. As prices drop, producers will decrease the volume of goods sent to market. At the same time, the quantities that consumers seek will increase. This adjustment process will continue until point E is reached and the quantities demanded and supplied are equal. At that point, the lower price level P_E will prevail.

The same kind of adjustment process would occur if a lower price level first existed. At lower prices, the aggregate quantity demanded would exceed the aggregate quantity supplied. The resulting shortages would permit sellers to raise their prices. As they do so, the aggregate quantity demanded would decrease, and the aggregate quantity supplied would increase. Eventually, we would return to point E, where the aggregate quantities demanded and supplied are equal.

Equilibrium is unique; it is the only price–output combination that is mutually compatible with aggregate supply and demand. In terms of graphs, it is the only place the aggregate supply and demand curves intersect. At point E there is no reason for the level of output or prices to change. The behavior of buyers and sellers is compatible. By contrast, any other level of output or prices creates a disequilibrium that requires market adjustments. All other price and output combinations, therefore, are unstable. They will not last. Eventually, the economy will return to point E.

Macro Failure

There are ***two potential problems with the macro equilibrium*** depicted in Figure 11.5:

- ***Undesirability:*** The price–output relationship at equilibrium may not satisfy our macroeconomic goals.
- ***Instability:*** Even if the designated macro equilibrium is optimal, it may be displaced by macro disturbances.

FIGURE 11.6
An Undesired Equilibrium

Equilibrium establishes only the levels of prices and output that are compatible with both buyers' and sellers' intentions. These outcomes may not satisfy our policy goals. In this case, the equilibrium price level is too high (above P^*) and the equilibrium output rate falls short of full-employment GDP (Q_F).

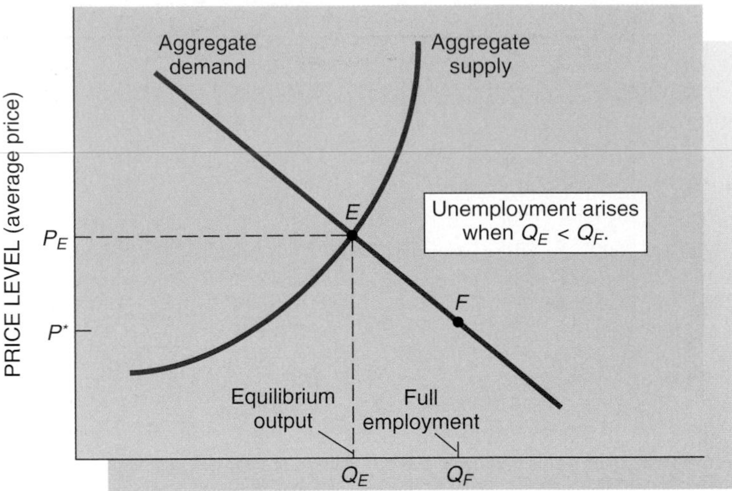

Undesirable Outcomes

The macro equilibrium depicted in Figure 11.5 is simply the intersection of two curves. All we know for sure is that people want to buy the same quantity of goods and services that businesses want to sell at the price level P_E. This quantity (Q_E) may be more or less than our full-employment capacity. This contingency is illustrated in Figure 11.6. What's new in Figure 11.6 is the designation of full-employment output, that is, capacity output. The output level Q_F in the figure represents society's full-employment goal. It refers to the quantity of output that could be produced if the labor force were fully employed. At macro equilibrium depicted here, however, only the quantity Q_E is being produced. The economy is not fully utilizing its production possibilities. This is the dilemma that the U.S. economy confronted in 2002 (see Headline).

unemployment The inability of labor-force participants to find jobs.

Unemployment The shortfall in equilibrium output illustrated in Figure 11.6 implies that the economy will be burdened with cyclical **unemployment.** Full employment is attained only if we produce at Q_F. Market forces, however, lead us to the lower rate of output at Q_E. Some workers can't find jobs.

inflation An increase in the average level of prices of goods and services.

Inflation Similar problems may arise with the equilibrium price level. Suppose that P^* represents the most desired price level. In Figure 11.6 we see that the equilibrium price level P_E exceeds P^*. If market behavior determines prices, the price level will rise above the desired level. The resulting increase in average prices is what we call **inflation.**

It could be argued, of course, that our apparent macro failures are simply an artifact. We could have drawn our aggregate supply and demand curves to intersect at point F in Figure 11.6. At that intersection we would be assured both price stability and full employment. Why didn't we draw them there, rather than intersecting at point E?

On the graph we can draw curves anywhere we want. In the real world, however, only one set of curves will correctly express buyers' and sellers' behavior. We must emphasize here that those real-world curves may *not* intersect at point F, thus denying us price stability, full employment, or both. That is the kind of economic outcome illustrated in Figure 11.6.

UNDESIRABLE OUTCOMES HEADLINE

Too Much Supply, Too Little Demand

Businesses Have Few Incentives to Expand or Hire, Economists Say

To understand why the U.S. economy can't seem to muster a stronger recovery, it helps to look for clues in Victorville, Calif., where 500 unused and unwanted passenger jets—some of them brand new—sit wingtip to wingtip in the desert.

Or in Detroit, where the Big Three continue to churn out large numbers of passenger cars that they sell at little or no profit, just to keep their factories busy.

Or in nearly every major metropolitan area, where office vacancy rates are still rising after 18 months, and have reached 25 percent in Dallas, 24 percent in Raleigh-Durham, N.C., and 18 percent in San Francisco.

But perhaps the best explanation can be found in those falling prices shoppers find for clothing, televisions, hotel rooms and cellular phone service. While the bargains are great for American consumers, they are being paid in the form of continued corporate layoffs, lackluster stock prices and a sky-high trade deficit—in short, an economy that's having trouble building up a head of steam.

Economists refer to this phenomenon as overcapacity, which is really nothing more than too much supply chasing too little demand. And it can be found these days across a wide swath: agriculture, autos, advertising, chemicals, computer hardware and software, consulting, financial services, forest products, furniture, mining, retail, steel, textiles, telecommunications, trucking, and electric generation, just to mention a few. In most every case, it is accompanied by prices that are flat or falling.

To be sure, overcapacity is a feature of every recession. A slowdown in consumer spending and a decline in business investment suddenly leave too many companies with too many workers, underutilized plants and underperforming stores. In most cases, it is only after most of that excess is cut back, and supply and demand get back into some rough balance, that businesses begin hiring and investing again, laying the foundation for another period of economic expansion.

—Steven Pearlstein

Source: *Washington Post*, August 25, 2002, p. 1.

NOTE: Market forces may generate an undesirable outcome. In this case, macro equilibrium has left the economy *inside* its production possibilities, with too much unemployment.

Unstable Outcomes

Figure 11.6 is only the beginning of our macro worries. Suppose, just suppose, that the aggregate supply and demand curves actually intersected in the perfect spot. That is to say, imagine that macro equilibrium yielded the optimal levels of both employment and prices. If this happened, could we settle back and stop fretting about the state of the economy?

Unhappily, even a perfect macro equilibrium doesn't ensure a happy ending. The aggregate supply and demand curves that momentarily bring us macro bliss are not necessarily permanent. They can *shift*—and they will, whenever the behavior of buyers and sellers changes.

Shift of AS When the United States invaded Iraq in March 2003, the price of oil shot up. This oil price hike directly increased the cost of production in a wide range of U.S. industries, making producers less willing and able to supply goods at prevailing prices. Thus the aggregate supply curve *shifted to the left*, as in Figure 11.7*a*.

The impact of a leftward supply shift on the economy is evident. Whereas macro equilibrium was originally located at the optimal point *F*, the new equilibrium was located at point *G*. At point *G*, less output was produced and prices were higher. Full employment and price stability vanished before our eyes. This is the kind of "external shock" that can destabilize any economy.

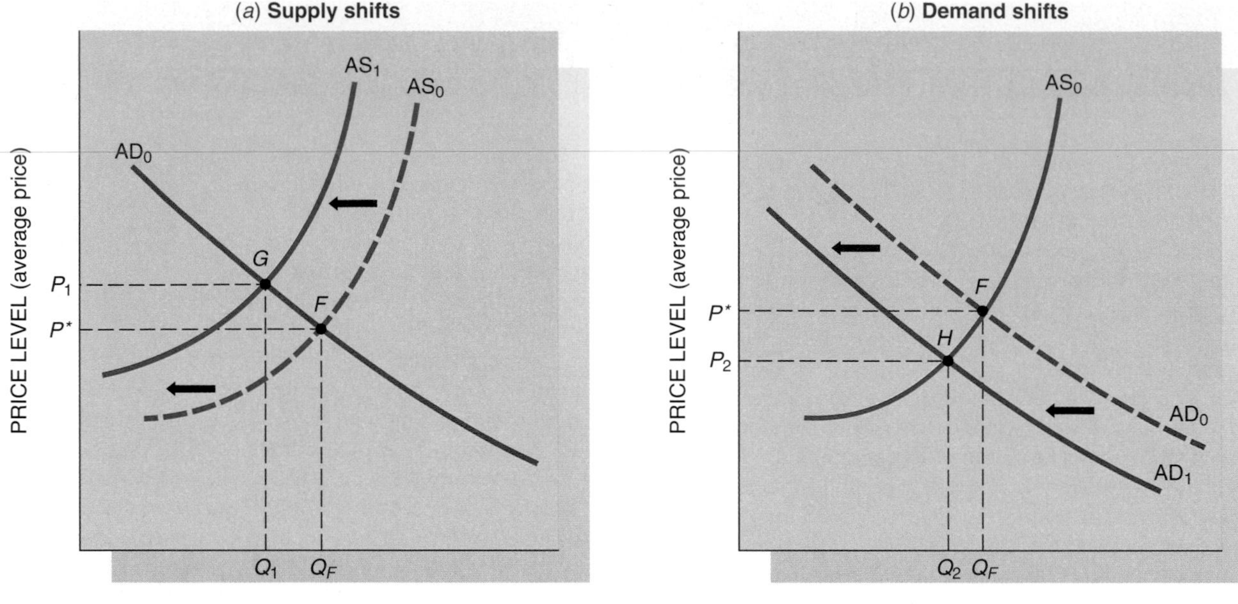

FIGURE 11.7 Macro Disturbances

(a) Supply shifts: A decrease (leftward shift) of the aggregate supply (AS) curve tends to reduce real GDP and raise average prices. When supply shifts from AS_0 to AS_1, the equilibrium moves from *F* to *G*. Such a supply shift may result from higher import prices, changes in tax policy, or other events.
(b) Demand shifts: A decrease (leftward shift) in aggregate demand (AD) tends to reduce output and price levels. A fall in demand may be due to a plunge in the stock market, an increased taste for imports, changes in expectations, higher taxes, or other events.

Shift of AD A shift of the AD curve could do similar damage. Suppose the stock market plunged tomorrow. How would consumers respond? Seeing their accumulated wealth vanish, they might decide to save more and spend less. At any price level fewer goods and services would be demanded. This change in consumer behavior would be reflected in a leftward shift of the aggregate demand curve, as in Figure 11.7*b*. The resulting disturbance would knock the economy out of its equilibrium at point *F*, leaving us at point *H*, with less output at home. This is the kind of shift that hurt the U.S. economy in 2000–01 (see Headline).

Recurrent Shifts The situation gets even crazier when the aggregate supply and demand curves shift repeatedly in different directions. A leftward shift of the aggregate demand curve can cause a recession, as the rate of output falls. A later rightward shift of the aggregate demand curve can cause a recovery, with real GDP (and employment) again increasing. Shifts of the aggregate supply curve can cause similar upswings and downswings. Thus **business cycles *result from recurrent shifts of the aggregate supply and demand curves.***

business cycle Alternating periods of economic growth and contraction.

Shift Factors

There is no reason to believe that the aggregate supply and demand curves will always shift in such undesired ways. However, there are lots of reasons to expect them to shift on occasion.

Demand Shifts The aggregate demand curve might shift, for example, if consumer sentiment changed. As noted above, a stock market plunge might

SHIFTING AD HEADLINE

Falling Stocks Smash Nest Eggs

"Wealth effect" has gone poof, and so have many investors' spending plans

For a long time, the stock market was very good to Chuck Yanus—so good that he and his wife went out and bought themselves two Suzuki motorcycles for about $10,000. In cash.

The Yanus family felt so flush that when Honda introduced its new top-of-the-line Gold Wing touring bike (price tag: $17,000-plus) this year, the couple began making plans to give one to themselves for Christmas.

But then the markets plunged, vaporizing more than $2 trillion in stock value in the nine months since stocks peaked in March. The tech-heavy Nasdaq is down a stunning 36 percent this year and about 48 percent from its exhilarating high last spring. The Dow Jones industrial average, sober avatar of the Old Economy, is better, but not enough to avoid pain: It's down about 7 percent this year, after being up 25 percent last year.

Stock portfolios that gave investors thoughts of early retirement or made almost anything seem affordable were devastated.

"When you lop 25 percent off your bottom line, it makes you stop and think," says Yanus, 46, a district manager for Sun Microsystems in Syracuse, NY. Big-ticket items like the Gold Wing are out. "I said the hell with it, let's wait," Yanus says.

For many Americans like the Yanuses, the thrill is gone. The "wealth effect"—that giddy feeling of richness that consumers got as they watched the value of their portfolios and their homes soar—has been killed, or at least badly wounded, by the prolonged market decline.

—George Hager and Dina Temple-Raston

Source: *USA Today*, December 19, 2000, p. 1B.

NOTE: A decline in the value of stocks may cause consumers to spend less on goods and services. Such a negative *wealth effect* shifts the AD curve leftward.

shatter consumer confidence, causing consumers to pare their spending plans. A tax hike might have a similar effect. Higher taxes reduce disposable (after-tax) incomes, forcing consumers to cut back spending. Higher interest rates make credit-financed spending more expensive and so might also reduce aggregate demand (especially on big-ticket items like cars and houses). This was a prominent worry in 2003–04 as interest rates rose from historic lows.

The September 2001 terrorist attacks on New York and Washington, DC, caused dramatic and abrupt shifts of aggregate demand. As the first Headline on the next page explains, the attacks caused companies and consumers to postpone spending plans. These shifts made it difficult to reach or maintain full employment.

Supply Shifts External forces may also shift aggregate supply. As noted earlier, rising oil prices are another brake on GDP growth. Higher oil prices raise the cost of producing goods and services (e.g., airline travel, heating, delivery services), making producers less willing to supply output at a given price level. A similar shift occurred in the wake of the September 2001 terrorist attacks. Higher costs for stepped-up security made it more expensive to produce and ship goods (see second Headline on next page). As a result, a smaller quantity of goods was available at any given price level.

Higher business taxes could also discourage production, thereby shifting the aggregate supply curve to the left. Tougher environmental or workplace regulations could also raise the cost of doing business, inducing less supply at a given price level. On the other hand, more liberal immigration rules might increase the supply of labor and increase the supply of goods and services (a rightward shift).

HEADLINE EXTERNAL SHOCKS

Attack Puts Chill on European Businesses

To see the depth of economic paralysis gripping Europe in the wake of the U.S. terrorist attacks, look no farther than German auto-parts maker Hella KG Hueck & Co.

Two days after the Sept. 11 tragedy, Hella directors shelved plans to build a 10 million euro ($9.2 million) factory in eastern Europe. The Lippstadt, Germany, firm wants to wait a few months before deciding whether to proceed. "We are in a hold position at the moment," said Hans Sudkamp, chief financial officer of Hella, which plans to tell its shareholders that the fallout from the attacks could drag revenue down by as much as 20 percent this year.

Companies across the continent are halting investments, holding off on new hires and canceling takeover and merger plans. Airlines and other travel-related businesses are cutting back the most. But in the two weeks since the attacks on the U.S., European firms spanning the industry spectrum—from autos and construction to luxury goods and bathroom fixtures—are freezing activity as well, showing the extent of the chill.

Compared with the Japanese economy, in or near recession for much of the past decade, and the sharply slowing U.S., Europe had appeared to be muddling through the global slowdown. Now, the negative effects of the terrorist strikes appear to be accelerating the continent's downturn.

—Christopher Rhoads

Source: *Wall Street Journal,* September 27, 2001, p. A17.

NOTE: An external shock may foster fear and uncertainty, causing market participants to postpone spending plans. This shifts the aggregate demand curve leftward.

HEADLINE SHIFTING AS

Difficult Passage

After terror attacks, shipping goods takes longer and costs more

Newark, NJ—Two days after terrorists slammed jets into the World Trade Center and the Pentagon, Quality Carriers Inc. rehired the $5,000-a-month night-shift security guard it had recently let go at its tanker-truck terminal here. The company also paid two drivers a total of $1,200 to repark any vehicles loaded with chemicals in plain view and under security lights. To get in at night, the terminal's 52 drivers now must wait for supervisors to open the gate with new electronic gadgets.

For Quality Carriers, the country's biggest liquid-bulk trucker, there is no such thing anymore as a routine delivery. New York City police guarding against chemical or biological attacks now demand a copy of its driver's license and registration before allowing him to make his twice-daily delivery of fluorosilicic acid, a fluoridation agent, to a suburban water-treatment facility that serves the city.

"Our expenses are piling up," says Thomas Schofield, a regional vice president at the unit of Quality Distribution Inc. One example: $2,500 a week in lost driving time because of stepped-up scrutiny of the company's tankers at two oil refineries in New Jersey. From now on, Mr. Schofield says, the carrier is going to try to pass along most of the added costs to its customers.

The Sept. 11 terror attacks are wrenching the nation's freight-transportation system, which moved $9 trillion of cargo last year. The network of trucks, trains, planes and ships suddenly faces a slew of new costs, delays and demands that threaten to hobble an essential part of the already-slumping U.S. economy.

—Daniel Machalaba and Rick Brooks

Source: *Wall Street Journal,* September 27, 2001, p. 1.

NOTE: If an external shock raises production costs, it reduces the willingness of producers to supply output at any given price level. This causes a leftward AS shift.

Competing Theories of Short-Run Instability

Although it is evident that either aggregate supply or demand *might* shift, economists are not in complete agreement about how often such shifts might occur or what consequences they might have. What we have seen in Figures 11.6 and 11.7 is how things might go poorly in the macro economy.

Figure 11.6 suggests that the odds of the market generating an equilibrium at full employment and price stability are about the same as finding a needle in a haystack. Figure 11.7 suggests that if we are lucky enough to find the needle, we will probably drop it again when AS or AD shifts. From this perspective, it appears that our worries about the business cycle are well founded.

The classical economists had no such worries. As we saw earlier, they believed that the economy would gravitate toward full employment. Keynes, on the other hand, worried that the macro equilibrium might start out badly and get worse in the absence of government intervention.

Aggregate supply and demand curves provide a convenient framework for comparing these and other theories on how the economy works. Essentially, ***macro controversies focus on the shape of aggregate supply and demand curves and the potential to shift them.*** With the right shape—or the correct shift—any desired equilibrium could be attained. As we will see, there are differing views as to whether and how this happy outcome might come about. These differing views can be classified as demand-side explanations, supply-side explanations, or some combination of the two.

Demand-Side Theories

Keynesian Theory Keynesian theory is the most prominent of the demand-side theories. Whereas the classical economists asserted that supply creates its own demand, Keynes argued the reverse: demand it, and it will be supplied.

The downside of this demand-driven view is that a lack of spending will cause the economy to contract. If aggregate spending isn't sufficient, some goods will remain unsold and some production capacity will be idled. This contingency is illustrated by point E_1 in Figure 11.8*a*.

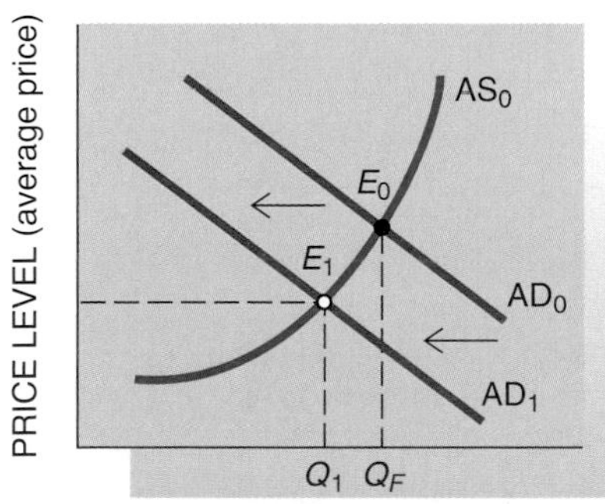

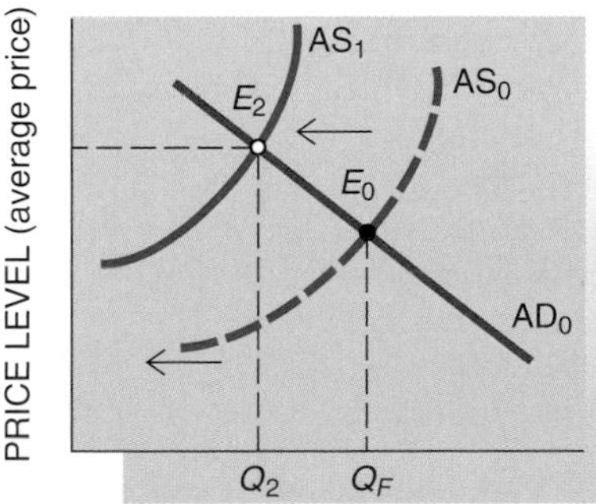

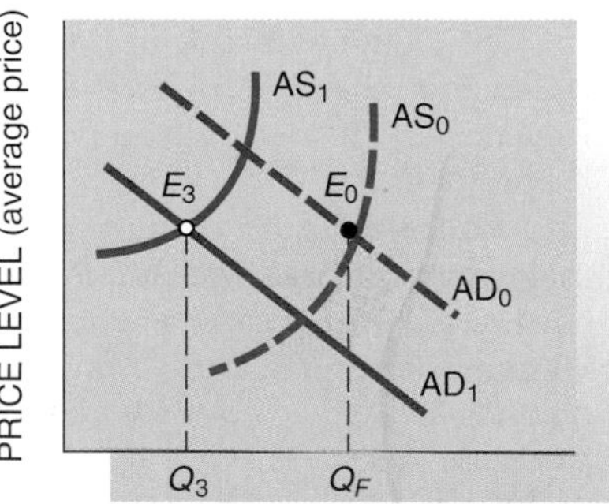

FIGURE 11.8 Origins of a Recession

Unemployment can result from several kinds of market phenomena, including

(a) Demand shifts: Total output will fall if aggregate demand (AD) declines. The shift from AD_0 to AD_1 changes equilibrium from point E_0 to E_1.

(b) Supply shifts: Unemployment can also emerge if aggregate supply (AS) declines, as the shift from AS_0 to AS_1 shows.

(c) AS/AD shifts: If aggregate demand and aggregate supply both decline, output and employment also fall (E_0 to E_3).

Keynes developed his theory during the Great Depression, when the economy seemed to be stuck at a very low level of equilibrium output, far below full employment GDP. The only way to end the depression, he argued, was for someone to start demanding more goods. He advocated a big increase in government spending to start the economy moving toward full employment. At the time, his advice was largely ignored. When the United States mobilized for World War II, however, the sudden surge in government spending shifted the AD curve to the right, restoring full employment.

In the late 1990s, the U.S. economy didn't need that kind of surge in government spending. A spectacular rise in the stock market provided the impetus for a surge in *consumer* spending. The increase in consumption shifted the AD curve to the right, increasing GDP growth.

When consumer spending is not so buoyant, Keynesian economists might advocate tax cuts to energize consumers. With more after-tax dollars in their pockets, consumers are likely to spend more. Hence ***Keynesian theory urges increased government spending or tax cuts as mechanisms for increasing (shifting) aggregate demand.*** President Bush used this Keynesian argument to convince Congress to cut taxes in 2001 and again in 2003. As the accompanying Headline suggests, this strategy was effective in shifting AD to the right. By contrast, if too much aggregate demand were pushing the price level up, Keynes advocated moving these policy levers in the opposite direction.

Monetary Theories Another demand-side theory emphasizes the role of money in financing aggregate demand. Money and credit affect the ability and willingness of people to buy goods and services. If credit isn't available or is too expensive, consumers won't be able to buy as many cars, homes,

HEADLINE DEMAND-DRIVEN GROWTH

Consumers Are Spending Big Time

Americans appear to be plowing a large chunk of their tax cuts back into the economy.

The Commerce Department reported that consumer spending rose by a robust 0.8% in August from July, following a 0.9% increase the month before. The latest figures pointed to a remarkably strong 7.4% annualized gain in inflation-adjusted consumer spending through the first two months of the third quarter, according to Bear Stearns estimates. If that spending pace was sustained through September—final data won't be available until next month—it would be the largest quarterly spending increase since 1985.

"Massive tax relief has boosted disposable income and real consumer spending," Steven Wood, an economist with Insight Economics, said in a note to clients. "This fiscal stimulus will provide a strong boost to third-quarter" growth.

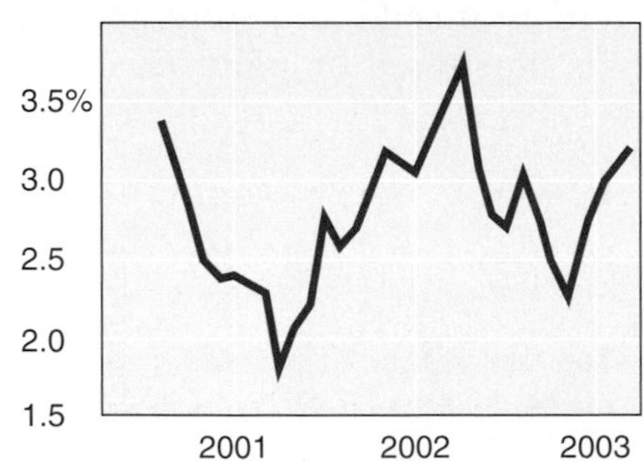

Spending Rebound

Three-month moving average of the year-over-year percentage change in consumer spending.

Source: Bureau to Economic Analysis via Economy.com

—Jon E. Hilsenrath and Patrick Barta

Source: *Wall Street Journal*, September 30, 2003, p. A2.

NOTE: A jump in consumer spending shifts the AD curve to the right. The increased demand may accelerate GDP growth.

or other expensive products. Tight money might also curtail business investment. In these circumstances, aggregate demand might prove to be inadequate. In this case, an increase in the money supply may be required to shift the aggregate demand curve into the desired position. Monetary theories thus focus on the control of money and interest rates as mechanisms for shifting the aggregate demand curve. To boost aggregate demand, the Federal Reserve cut interest rates 13 times between January 2001 and July 2003.

Supply-Side Theories

Figure 11.8*b* illustrates an entirely different explanation of the business cycle. Notice that the aggregate *supply* curve is on the move in Figure 11.8*b*. The initial equilibrium is again at point E_0. This time, however, aggregate demand remains stationary, while aggregate supply shifts. The resulting decline of aggregate supply causes output and employment to decline (to Q_2 from Q_F).

Figure 11.8*b* tells us that aggregate supply may be responsible for downturns as well. Our failure to achieve full employment may result from the unwillingness of producers to provide more goods at existing prices. That unwillingness may originate in simple greed, in rising costs, in resource shortages, or in government taxes and regulation. Whatever the cause, if the aggregate supply curve is AS_1 rather than AS_0 full employment will not be achieved with the demand AD_0. To get more output, the supply curve must shift back to AS_0. The mechanisms for shifting the aggregate supply curve in the desired direction are the focus of supply-side theories.

Eclectic Explanations

Not everyone blames either the demand side or the supply side exclusively. The various macro theories tell us that both supply and demand can help us achieve our policy goals or cause us to miss them. These theories also demonstrate how various shifts of the aggregate supply and demand curves can achieve any specific output or price level. Figure 11.8*c* illustrates how undesirable macro outcomes can be caused by shifts of both aggregate curves. Eclectic explanations of the business cycle draw from both sides of the market.

Policy Options

Aggregate supply and demand curves not only help illustrate the causes of the business cycle; they also imply a fairly straightforward set of policy options. Essentially, ***the government has three policy options:***

- ***Shift the aggregate demand curve.*** Find and use policy tools that stimulate or restrain total spending.
- ***Shift the aggregate supply curve.*** Find and implement policy levers that reduce the costs of production or otherwise stimulate more output at every price level.
- ***Do nothing.*** If we can't identify or control the determinants of aggregate supply or demand, then we shouldn't interfere with the market.

Historically, all three approaches have been adopted.

The classical approach to economic policy embraced the "do nothing" perspective. Prior to the Great Depression, most economists were convinced that the economy would self-adjust to full employment. If the initial equilibrium rate of output was too low, the resulting imbalances would alter prices and wages, inducing changes in market behavior. The aggregate supply and demand curves would naturally shift, until they reached the intersection at point E_0 where full employment (Q_F) prevails in Figure 11.8.

Recent versions of the classical theory—dubbed the new classical economics—stress not only the market's natural ability to self-adjust to *long-run* equilibrium, but also the inability of the government to improve *short-run* market outcomes. New classical economists point to the increasing ability of market participants to anticipate government policies—and to take defensive actions that thwart them.

Fiscal Policy

The Great Depression cast serious doubt on the classical self-adjustment concept. According to Keynes's view, the economy would *not* self-adjust. Rather, it might stagnate at point E_1 in Figure 11.8 until aggregate demand was forcibly shifted. An increase in government spending on goods and services might provide the necessary shift. Or a cut in taxes might be used to stimulate greater consumer and investor spending. These budgetary tools are the hallmark of fiscal policy. Specifically, **fiscal policy** is the use of government tax and spending powers to alter economic outcomes.

fiscal policy The use of government taxes and spending to alter macroeconomic outcomes.

Fiscal policy is an integral feature of modern economic policy. Every year the president and the Congress debate the budget. They argue about whether the economy needs to be stimulated or restrained. They then argue about the level of spending or taxes required to ensure the desired outcome. This is the heart of fiscal policy.

Monetary Policy

The government budget doesn't get all the action. As suggested earlier, the amount of money in circulation may also affect macro equilibrium. If so, then the policy arsenal must include some levers to control the money supply. These are the province of monetary policy. **Monetary policy** refers to the use of money and interest rates to alter economic outcomes.

monetary policy The use of money and credit controls to influence macroeconomic activity.

The Federal Reserve (the Fed) has direct control over monetary policy. The Fed is an independent regulatory body, charged with maintaining an "appropriate" supply of money. In practice, the Fed adjusts interest rates and the money supply in accordance with its views of macro equilibrium.

Supply-Side Policy

Fiscal and monetary policies focus on the demand side of the market. Both policies are motivated by the conviction that appropriate shifts of the aggregate demand curve can bring about desired changes in output or price levels. **Supply-side policies** offer an alternative; they seek to shift the aggregate supply curve.

supply-side policy The use of tax rates, (de)regulation, and other mechanisms to increase the ability and willingness to produce goods and services.

There are scores of supply-side levers. The most famous are the tax cuts implemented by the Reagan administration in 1981. Those tax cuts were designed to increase *supply*, not just demand (as traditional fiscal policy does). By reducing tax rates on wages and profits, the Reagan tax cuts sought to increase the willingness to supply goods at any given price level. The promise of greater after-tax income was the key incentive for the supply shift.

Republicans used a similar argument in 2003 to reduce the tax on capital gains (profits from the sale of acquired property) from 20 percent to 15 percent. Lower capital-gains tax rates encouraged people to invest more in factories, equipment, and office buildings. As investment increased, so did the capacity to supply goods and services. When the economy faltered, the Bush administration also sought a cut in taxes on corporate dividends, hoping to both reduce supply-side costs and increase consumer demand.

Other supply-side levers are less well recognized but nevertheless important. Your economics class is an example. The concepts and skills you learn here should increase your productive capabilities. This expands the economy's capacity. With a more educated workforce, a greater supply of goods and services can be produced at any given price level. Hence government subsidies to higher education might be viewed as part of supply-side policy. Government support for employment and training programs also shifts the aggregate supply curve to the right. Immigration policies that increase the inflow of workers get even quicker supply-side effects.

Government regulation is another staple of supply-side policy. Regulations that slow innovation or raise the cost of doing business reduce aggregate supply. Removing unnecessary red tape can facilitate more output and reduce inflationary pressures.

POLICY PERSPECTIVES

The Changing Choice of Policy Levers

The various policy levers in our basic macro model have all been used at one time or another. The "do nothing" approach prevailed until the Great Depression. Since that devastating experience, more active policy roles have predominated.

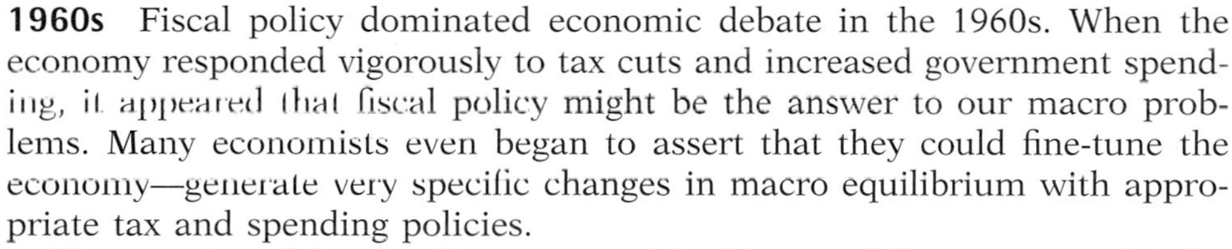

1960s Fiscal policy dominated economic debate in the 1960s. When the economy responded vigorously to tax cuts and increased government spending, it appeared that fiscal policy might be the answer to our macro problems. Many economists even began to assert that they could fine-tune the economy—generate very specific changes in macro equilibrium with appropriate tax and spending policies.

The promise of fiscal policy was tarnished by our failure to control inflation in the late 1960s. It was further compromised by the simultaneous outbreak of both inflation and unemployment in the 1970s. This new macro failure appeared to be chronic, immune to the cures proposed by fiscal policy. Solutions to our macro problems were sought elsewhere.

1970s Monetary policy was next in the limelight. The flaw in fiscal policy, it was argued, originated in its neglect of monetary constraints. More government spending, for example, might require so much of the available money supply that private spending would be crowded out. To ensure a net boost in aggregate demand, more money would be needed, a response only the Fed could make.

In the late 1970s the Fed dominated macro policy. It was hoped that appropriate changes in the money supply would foster greater macro stability. Reduced inflation and lower interest rates were the immediate objectives. Both were to be accomplished by placing greater restraints on the supply of money. Full employment was also anticipated, as investment and consumption spending responded positively to lower, and more predictable, interest and inflation rates.

The heavy reliance on monetary policy lasted only a short time. When the economy skidded into yet another recession, the search for effective policy tools resumed.

1980s Supply-side policies became important in 1980. In his 1980 presidential campaign, Ronald Reagan asserted that supply-side tax cuts, deregulation of markets, and other supply-focused policies would reduce both inflation and unemployment. According to Figure 11.8*c*, such an outcome appeared at least plausible. A rightward shift of the aggregate supply curve does reduce both prices and unemployment. Although the Reagan administration later embraced an eclectic mix of fiscal, monetary, and supply-side policies, its initial supply-side emphasis was very distinctive.

1990s The George H. Bush administration pursued a less activist approach. Bush Senior initially resisted tax increases but later accepted them as part of a budget compromise that also reduced government spending. When the economy slid into recession in 1990, President Bush maintained a hands-off policy. Like classical economists, Bush kept assuring the public that the economy would come around on its own. Not until the 1992 elections approached did he propose more active intervention. By then it was too late for him, however. Voters were swayed by Bill Clinton's promises to use tax cuts and increased government spending (fiscal policy) to create "jobs, jobs, jobs."

After he was elected, President Clinton reversed policy direction. Rather than delivering the promised tax cuts, Clinton pushed a tax *increase* through Congress. He also pared the size of his planned spending increases. This fiscal-policy retreat cleared the field for the reemergence of monetary policy as the decisive policy lever.

After he was re-elected in 1996, President Clinton shifted direction a bit. The Balanced Budget and Taxpayer Relief Acts of 1997 provided some tax cuts for consumers. However, it also cut the growth of government spending for the years 1999–2002. The net effect of the legislation was to reduce aggregate demand slightly. This leftward shift of aggregate demand helped restrain inflationary pressures as the economy approached full employment.

Current Policy The fiscal restraint of the late 1990s helped the federal budget move from deficits to surpluses. These budget surpluses grew so large and so fast that they prompted another turn in fiscal policy. One of the most heated issues in the 2000 presidential campaign was whether to use the federal budget surplus to cut taxes, increase government spending, or pay down the debt. By the time George W. Bush took office in January 2001, the economy had slowed so much that people feared another recession was imminent. This helped convince the Congress to pull the fiscal policy lever in the direction of stimulus. When the first round of tax cuts failed to shift AD far enough to the right, Congress followed up with two more rounds of tax cuts in 2002 and 2003. Bush Junior wasn't about to risk the same re-election fate as Bush Senior; he pushed the stimulus lever hard.

SUMMARY

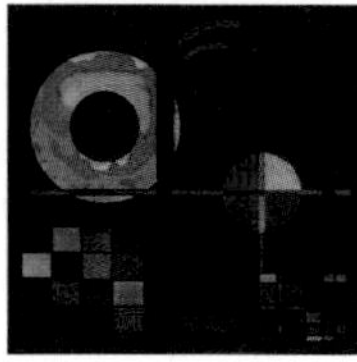

- The primary outcomes of the macro economy are output, prices, jobs, and international balances. These outcomes result from the interplay of internal market forces, external shocks, and policy levers.
- All of the influences on macro outcomes are transmitted through aggregate supply or aggregate demand. Aggregate supply and demand determine the equilibrium rate of output and prices. The economy will gravitate to that unique combination of output and price levels.
- The market's macro equilibrium may not be consistent with our nation's employment or price goals. Macro failure occurs when the economy's equilibrium is not optimal.
- Macro equilibrium may be disturbed by changes in aggregate supply (AS) or aggregate demand (AD). Such changes are illustrated by shifts of the AS and AD curves, and they lead to a new equilibrium. Recurring AS and AD shifts cause business cycles.

- Competing economic theories try to explain the shape and shifts of the aggregate supply and demand curves, thereby explaining the business cycle. Specific theories tend to emphasize demand or supply influences.
- Macro policy options range from doing nothing (the classical approach) to various strategies for shifting either the aggregate demand curve or the aggregate supply curve.
- Fiscal policy uses government tax and spending powers to alter aggregate demand. Monetary policy uses money and credit availability for the same purpose.
- Supply-side policies include all interventions that shift the aggregate supply curve. Examples include tax incentives, (de)regulation, and resource development.

Terms to Remember

Define the following terms:

macroeconomics	aggregate supply	business cycle
Say's Law	equilibrium (macro)	fiscal policy
aggregate demand	unemployment	monetary policy
real GDP	inflation	supply-side policy

Questions for Discussion

1. If the price level were below P_E in Figure 11.5, what macro problems would we observe? Why is P_E considered an equilibrium?
2. What factors might cause a rightward shift of the aggregate demand curve? What might induce a rightward shift of aggregate supply?
3. What kind of external shock would benefit an economy?
4. If all wages and prices fell by 20 percent, would you be better or worse off? Could you buy more goods?
5. What would a *horizontal* aggregate supply curve imply about producer behavior? How about a vertical AS curve?
6. If equilibrium is compatible with both buyers' and sellers' intentions, how can it be undesirable?
7. From 1996 to 2000, the U.S. stock market more than doubled in value. How might this have affected aggregate demand? What happens to aggregate demand when the stock market plunges?
8. President George H. Bush maintained a hands-off policy during the 1990–91 recession. How did he expect the economy to recover on its own?

Problems

1. Illustrate these events with AS or AD shifts:

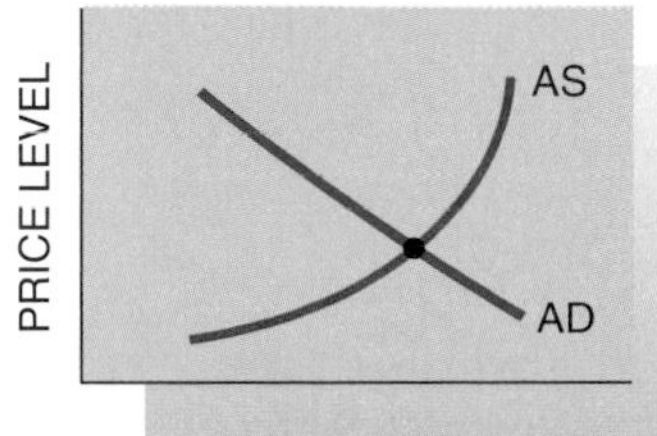

Government increases defense spending.

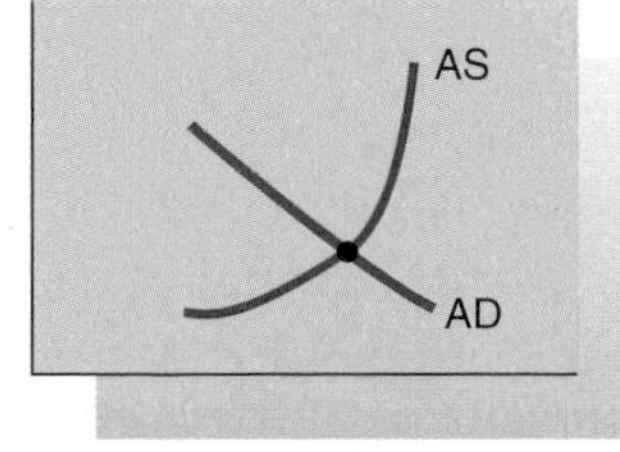

The Headline story on p. 263.

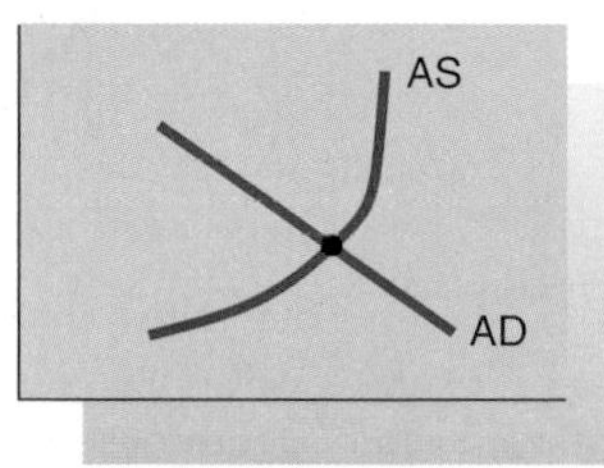

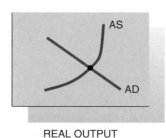

Imported raw materials get cheaper.

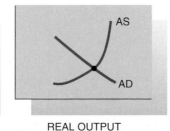

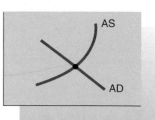

AS
AD
REAL OUTPUT

Congress cuts corporate income tax.

2. Based on the Headlines on p. 264,
   (*a*) Illustrate the AS and AD shifts that occur.
   (*b*) Identify the old (E_0) and new (E_1) macro equilibrium.
   (*c*) What macro ailments result?
   (*d*) How can the economy stay healthy in this case?
3. Graph the following aggregate supply and demand curves (be sure to draw to scale).

	Real GDP (in $ trillions)	
Price Level	Supplied	Demanded
100	7	17
110	10	11
140	13	8
200	15	7

   (*a*) What explains the shape of the AS curve?
   (*b*) What is the equilibrium price level?
   (*c*) What is the equilibrium output?
   (*d*) If the quantity of output demanded at every price level increases by $1 trillion, what happens to equilibrium output and prices? Graph your answer.
4. Draw a conventional aggregate demand curve on a graph. Then add three different aggregate supply curves, labeled

   S_1: Horizontal curve

   S_2: Upward-sloping curve

   S_3: Vertical curve

   all intersecting the AD curve at the same point.
   If AD were to increase (shift to the right), which AS curve would lead to
   (*a*) The biggest increase in output?
   (*b*) The largest jump in prices?
   (*c*) The least inflation?
5. The following schedule provides information with which to draw both an aggregate demand curve and an aggregate supply curve. Both curves are assumed to be straight lines.

Average Price (dollars per unit)	Quantity Demanded (units per year)	Quantity Supplied (units per year)
$1,000	0	1,000
100	900	100

   (*a*) At what price level does equilibrium occur?
   (*b*) What curve would have shifted if a new equilibrium were to occur at an output level of 700 and a price level of $700?
   (*c*) What curve would have shifted if a new equilibrium were to occur at an output level of 700 and a price level of $500?

(*d*) What curve would have shifted if a new equilibrium were to occur at an output level of 700 and a price level of $300?

(*e*) Compared to the initial equilibrium (*a*), how have the outcomes in (*b*), (*c*), and (*d*) changed price levels or output?

6. Graph the wealth effect described in the Headline on p. 263.

Web Activities

1. Log on to www.whitehouse.gov/fsbr/output.html. Find data on the current level of nonresidential fixed investment. What does the trend suggest is happening to aggregate demand?
2. Log on to www.bea.doc.gov/briefrm/tables/ebr6.htm. Find data on the personal savings rate percentage. At the bottom of the page, click on "Chart Saving Rate." All other things remaining constant, what does the trend suggest is happening to current consumption spending?
3. Log on to www.bea.doc.gov/briefrm/tables/ebr6.htm. Find data on current disposable income. All other things remaining constant, what does the trend suggest is happening to consumption and savings?
4. Log on to www.bea.doc.gov/briefrm/price.htm and observe the changes in the average price level. Using AS and AD analysis, discuss some possible explanations for the trends in these data.

Living Econ

What Do the Headlines Really Mean?

Whether on radio, on TV, or in the newspaper, most of us are exposed to the "news" every day. Until now you may have assumed you needed an advanced degree in economics to comprehend the economic impact of news stories concerning government policies, international affairs, or technological breakthroughs.

If you hear that the government is spending additional dollars, for example, to address a domestic concern, you know that this action will shift the aggregate demand curve to the right, potentially raising the price level and real GDP, ceteris paribus. On the other hand, a report about a technological advance that leads to productivity improvement across the economy will cause aggregate supply to shift to the right, lowering the price level and raising real GDP.

Of course, other factors are also affecting the economy at any given time, so the outcome may not be exactly as predicted. Nonetheless, you now have a set of tools to help you analyze the economic consequences of major events in the headlines.

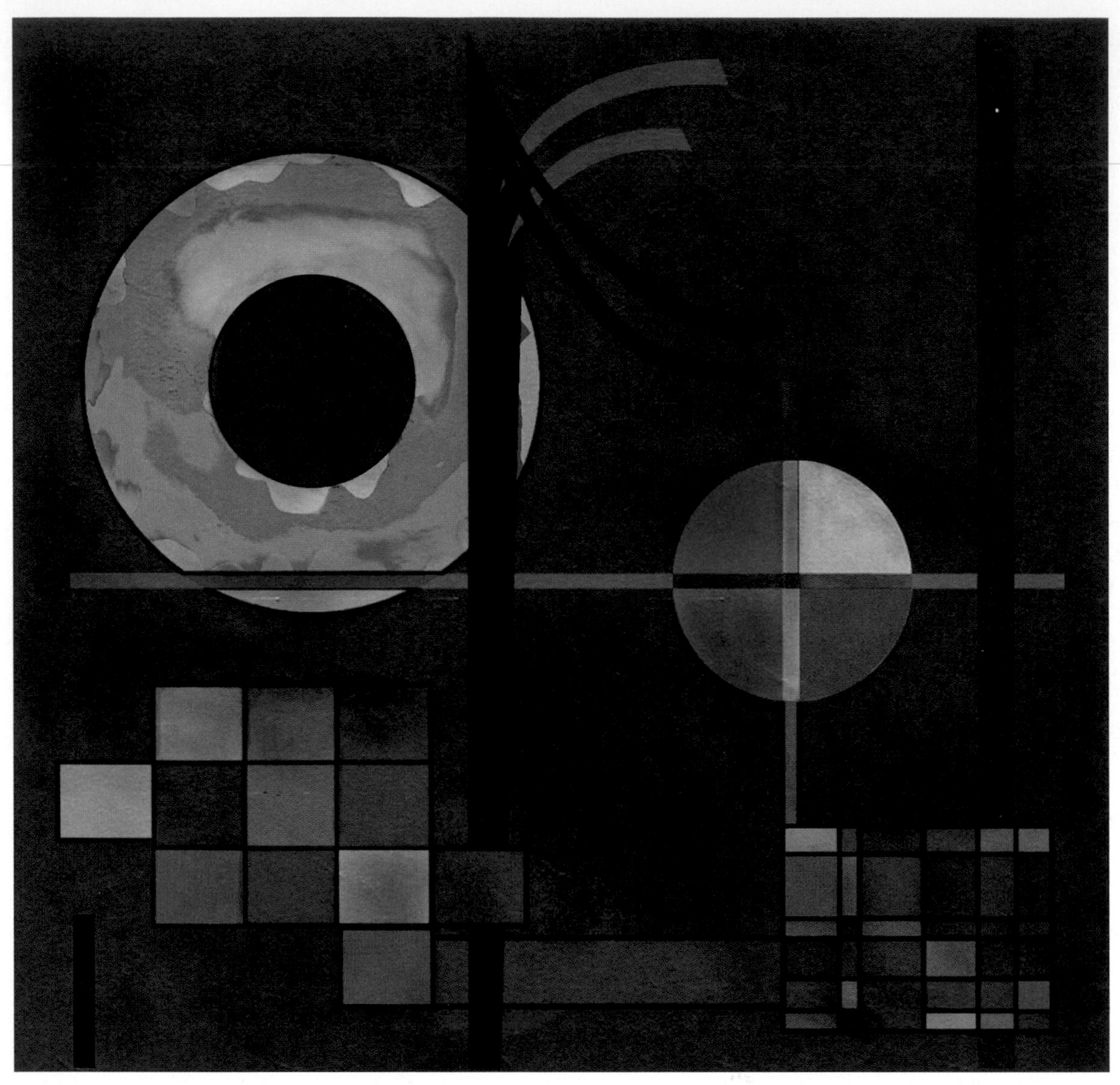

Fiscal Policy

CHAPTER 12

During the Great Depression of the 1930s, as many as 13 million Americans were out of work. They were capable people and eager to work. But no one would hire them. As sympathetic as employers might have been, they simply could not use any more workers. Consumers were not buying the goods and services already being produced. Employers were more likely to cut back production and lay off still more workers than to hire any new ones. As a consequence, an "army of the unemployed" was created in 1929 and continued to grow for nearly a decade. It was not until the outbreak of World War II that enough jobs could be found for the unemployed, and most of these "jobs" were in the armed forces.

The Great Depression was the springboard for the Keynesian approach to economic policy. John Maynard Keynes concluded that the ranks of unemployed persons were growing because of problems on the *demand* side of product markets. People simply were not able and willing to buy all the goods and services the economy was capable of producing. As a consequence, producers had no incentive to increase output or to hire more labor. So long as the demand for goods and services was inadequate, unemployment was inevitable.

Keynes sought to explain how a deficiency of demand could arise in a market economy, then to show how and why the government had to intervene. Keynes was convinced that government intervention was necessary to achieve our macroeconomic goals, particularly full employment. To that end, Keynes advocated aggressive use of fiscal policy, that is, deployment of the government's tax and spending powers to alter macro outcomes. He urged policymakers to use these powers to minimize the swings of the business cycle.

In this chapter we take a closer look at what Keynes intended. We focus on the following questions:

- Why did Keynes think the market was inherently unstable?
- How can fiscal policy help stabilize the economy?
- How will the use of fiscal policy affect the government's budget deficit?

Components of Aggregate Demand

fiscal policy The use of government taxes and spending to alter macroeconomic outcomes.

aggregate demand The total quantity of output demanded at alternative price levels in a given time period, ceteris paribus.

The premise of **fiscal policy** is that the **aggregate demand** for goods and services will not always be compatible with economic stability. As observed in Chapter 11 (e.g., Figure 11.7), recessions occur when aggregate demand declines; recessions persist when aggregate demand remains below the economy's capacity to produce. Inflation results from similar imbalances. If aggregate demand increases faster than output, prices tend to rise. The price level will keep rising until aggregate demand is compatible with the rate of production.

But why do such macro failures occur? Why shouldn't aggregate demand always reflect the economy's full employment potential?

To determine whether we are likely to have the right amount of aggregate demand, we need to take a closer look at spending behavior. Who buys the goods and services on which output decisions and jobs depend?

The *four major components of aggregate demand are*

C: ***consumption***
I: ***investment***
G: ***government spending***
X − M: ***net exports (exports minus imports)***

Consumption

consumption Expenditure by consumers on final goods and services.

Consumption refers to all household expenditures on goods and services—everything from groceries to college tuition. Just look around and you can see the trappings of our consumer-oriented economy. In the aggregate, consumption spending accounts for approximately two-thirds of total spending in the U.S. economy (Figure 12.1).

Because consumer spending looms so large in aggregate demand, any change in consumer behavior can have a profound impact on employment

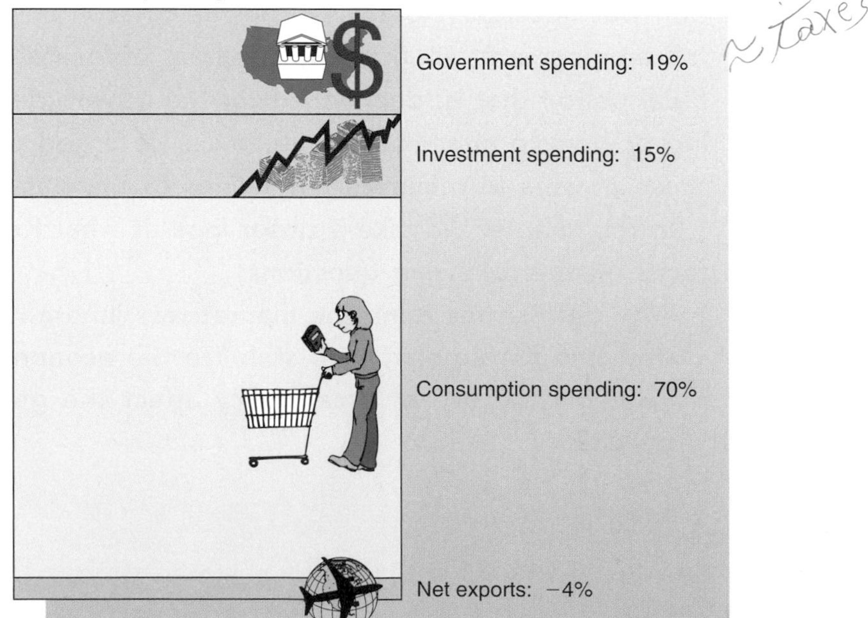

FIGURE 12.1
Components of Aggregate Demand
In 2002, the output of the U.S. economy was $10.5 trillion. Over two-thirds of that output consisted of consumer goods and services. The government sectors (federal, state, and local) demanded 19 percent of total output. Investment spending took another 15 percent. Finally, because imports exceeded exports, the impact of net exports on aggregate demand was negative.
Source: U.S. Department of Commerce.

EXPECTATIONS HEADLINE

Consumer Confidence Plunges to Two-Year Low

WASHINGTON—Consumer confidence plunged to its lowest level in two years as the holiday season failed to lift the spirit of Americans rattled by stock-market volatility and mounting fears of a significant economic slowdown.

The Conference Board said consumer confidence slid to 128.3 in December from a revised 132.6 a month earlier. December's decline marked the third consecutive decrease in the closely watched index, which has lost 14 points since September. The reading compares results with its base year of 1985 when the index was 100. A sharp decrease in household expectations about the future health of the economy accounted for much of the drop.

Although most sectors of the economy have begun to slow, the drop in consumer confidence is especially troubling because household fears about a recession can become a self-fulfilling prophecy. Consumer spending accounts for nearly two-thirds of the nation's total economic activity; shrinking consumer confidence would probably cause spending to slow.

That prospect was very much on the minds of Conference Board officials, who described the fall in confidence as "somewhat disconcerting."

"The latest decline in consumer confidence suggests that consumer spending will cool further as we enter 2001," said Lynn Franco, who oversees the monthly survey of 5,000 American households for the firm. "If expectations continue on this downward trend, a more severe economic slowdown may be on the horizon."

—Yochi J. Dreazen

Source: *The Wall Street Journal*, December 29, 2000, p. A2.

NOTE: Expectations for jobs and income affect current spending decisions. When expectations diminish, the rate of spending typically slows down.

and prices. Economists try to anticipate such changes by studying consumer behavior. Clues to consumer behavior are often found in surveys of consumer confidence. If consumer confidence is rising, consumer *spending* may increase. When consumer confidence plunged in late 2000 (see Headline), economists predicted the economy would stumble (they were right).

Investment

Investment refers to spending by business on new plant and equipment. When a corporation decides to build a new factory or modernize an old one, the resulting expenditure adds to aggregate demand. When farmers replace their old tractors, their purchases also increase total spending on goods and services.

Investment Expenditures on (production of) new plant and equipment (capital) in a given time period, plus changes in business inventories.

Changes in business inventory are also counted as investment. Retail stores stock their shelves with goods bought from other firms. E-commerce firms also rely on *someone* stocking goods for sale. Although they hope to resell these goods later, the inventory buildup reflects a demand for goods and services. If companies allow their inventories to shrink, then inventory investment would be negative. During the Great Depression not only was inventory investment negative but spending on plant and equipment also plummeted. As a result, total business investment plunged by 70 percent between 1929 and 1933. This plunge in investment spending wracked aggregate demand and eliminated millions of jobs.

Government Spending

Government spending is a third source of aggregate demand. The federal government currently spends roughly $2.5 trillion a year, and state and local governments collectively spend even more. Not all of that spending gets counted as part of aggregate demand, however. Aggregate demand refers to spending on goods and services. Much of what the government spends, however, are merely *income transfers*—payments to individuals for which no services are exchanged. Uncle Sam, for example, mails out close to $500 billion a year in Social Security checks. This doesn't represent a demand for goods and services. That money will become part of aggregate demand only when the Social Security recipients spend their transfer income on goods and services.

Only that portion of government budgets that gets spent on goods and services represents part of aggregate demand. Aggregate demand includes federal, state, and local spending on highways, schools, police, national defense, and all other goods and services the public sector provides. Such spending now accounts for nearly one-fifth of aggregate demand.

Net Exports

net exports Exports minus imports (X − M).

The fourth component of aggregate demand, **net exports,** is the difference between export and import spending. The demand of foreigners for American-made products shows up as U.S. exports. At the same time, Americans spend some of their income on goods imported from other countries. The difference between exports and imports represents the *net* demand for domestic output.

U.S. net exports are negative. This means that Americans are buying more goods from abroad than foreigners are buying from us. The net effect of trade is thus to reduce domestic aggregate demand. That is why net exports is a negative amount in Figure 12.1.

Equilibrium

The four components of aggregate demand combine to determine the shape and position of the aggregate demand curve. Notice that ***aggregate demand is not a single number but instead a schedule of planned purchases.*** The quantity of output market participants desire to purchase depends in part on the price level.

equilibrium (macro) The combination of price level and real output that is compatible with both aggregate demand and aggregate supply.

Suppose the existing price level is P_1, as seen in Figure 12.2, and that the curve AS represents aggregate supply. Full employment is represented by the output level Q_F. What we want to know is whether aggregate demand will be just enough to assure both price stability and full employment. This happy **equilibrium** occurs only if the aggregate demand curve intersects the aggregate supply curve at point *a*. The curve AD* achieves this goal.

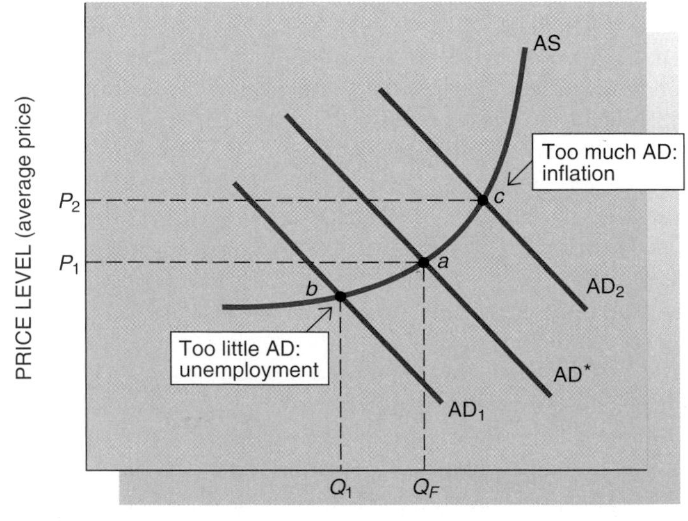

FIGURE 12.2
The Desired Equilibrium

The goal of fiscal policy is to achieve price stability and full employment, the desired equilibrium represented by point *a*. This equilibrium will occur only if aggregate demand is equal to AD*. Less demand (e.g., AD_1) will cause unemployment; more demand (e.g., AD_2) will cause inflation.

Inadequate Demand Aggregate demand may turn out to be less than perfect, however. Keep in mind that aggregate demand includes four different types of spending; that is,

$$AD = C + I + G + (X - M)$$

There is no evident reason why these four distinct components of aggregate demand would generate exactly the output Q_F at the price level P_1 in Figure 12.2. They could in fact generate *less* spending, as illustrated by the curve AD_1. In this case, aggregate demand falls short, leaving some potential output unsold at the equilibrium point *b*.

Excessive Demand The curve AD_2 illustrates a situation of excessive aggregate demand. The combined expenditure plans of market participants exceed the economy's full-employment output. The resulting scramble for available goods and services pushes prices up to the level P_2. This inflationary equilibrium is illustrated by the AS/AD_2 intersection at point *c*.

The Nature of Fiscal Policy

Clearly, we will fulfill our macroeconomic goals only if we get the right amount of aggregate demand (the curve AD* in Figure 12.2). But what are the chances of such a fortunate event? Keynes asserted that the odds were stacked against such an outcome. Indeed, Keynes concluded that ***it would be a minor miracle if C + I + G + (X − M) added up to exactly the right amount of aggregate demand.*** Consumers, investors, and foreigners all make independent decisions on how much to spend. Why should those separate decisions result in just enough demand to assure either full employment or price stability? It is far more likely that the level of aggregate demand will turn out to be wrong. In these circumstances, government spending must be the safety valve that expands or contracts aggregate demand as needed. ***The use of government spending and taxes to adjust aggregate demand is the essence of fiscal policy.*** Figure 12.3 puts fiscal

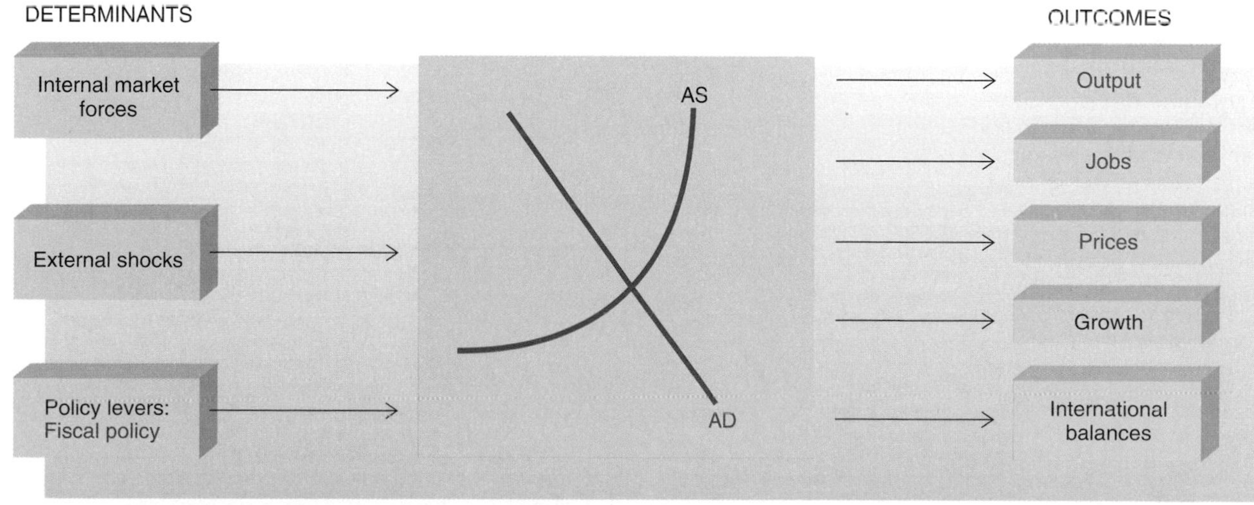

FIGURE 12.3 Fiscal Policy

Fiscal policy refers to the use of the government tax and spending powers to alter macro outcomes. Fiscal policy works principally through shifts of the aggregate demand curve.

policy into the framework of our basic macro model. In this figure, fiscal policy appears as a policy lever for adjusting macro outcomes.

Fiscal Stimulus

Suppose that aggregate demand has fallen short of our goals and unemployment rates are high. This scenario is illustrated again in Figure 12.4, this time with some numbers added. Full employment is reached when $6 trillion of output is demanded at current price levels, as indicated by Q_F. The quantity of output demanded at current price levels, however, is only $5.6 trillion ($Q_1$). Hence there is a gap between the economy's ability to produce (Q_F) and the amount of output people are willing to buy (Q_1) at the current price level (P_1). This **GDP gap** amounts to $400 billion in Figure 12.4. If nothing is done, $400 billion of productive facilities will be idled.

GDP gap The difference between full-employment output and the amount of output demanded at current price levels.

The goal here is to eliminate the GDP gap by *shifting* the aggregate demand curve to the right. In this case, spending has to increase by $400 billion per year to close the GDP gap. How can fiscal policy make this happen?

More Government Spending

The simplest solution to the demand shortfall would be to increase government spending. If the government were to step up its purchases of tanks, highways, schools, and other goods, the increased spending would add directly to aggregate demand. This would shift the aggregate demand curve rightward, moving us closer to full employment. Hence ***increased government spending is a form of fiscal stimulus.***

fiscal stimulus Tax cuts or spending hikes intended to increase (shift) aggregate demand.

Multiplier Effects It isn't necessary for the federal government to fill the entire gap between desired and current spending. In fact, if government spending did increase by $400 billion, aggregate demand would shift *beyond* point *a* in Figure 12.4. In that case we would quickly move from a situation of *inadequate* aggregate demand (AD_1) to a situation of *excessive* aggregate demand.

The solution to this riddle lies in the circular flow of income. According to the circular flow, ***an increase in spending results in increased incomes.***

FIGURE 12.4
Deficient Demand

The aggregate demand curve AD_1 results in only $5.6 trillion of final sales at current price levels (P_1). This is well short of full employment (Q_F), which occurs at $6.0 trillion of output. The fiscal-policy goal is to close the GDP gap by shifting the AD curve rightward until it passes through point *a*.

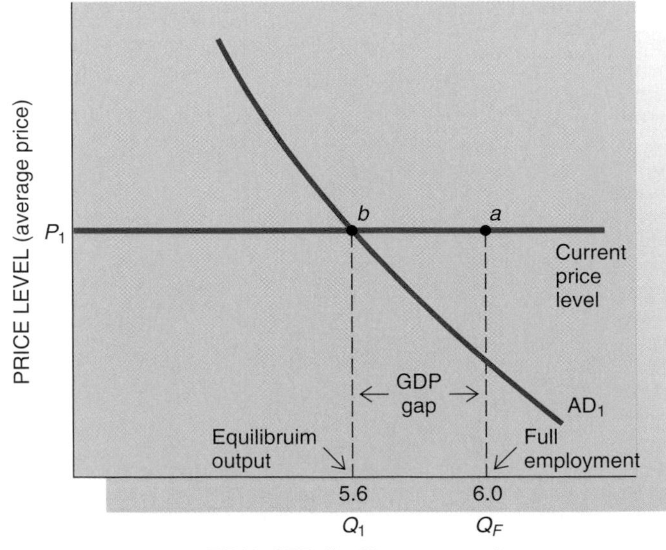

When the government increases its spending, it creates additional income for market participants. The recipients of this income will in turn spend it. Hence each dollar gets spent and respent several times. As a result, every dollar of government spending has a *multiplied* impact on aggregate demand.

Suppose that the government decided to spend an additional $100 billion per year on a fleet of cruise missiles. This $100 billion of new defense expenditure would add directly to aggregate demand. But that is only the beginning of a very long story. The people who build cruise missiles will be on the receiving end of a lot of income. Their fatter paychecks, dividends, and profits will enable them to increase their own spending.

What *will* the aerospace workers do with all that income? They have only two choices: ***all income is either spent or saved.*** Hence every dollar of income must go to consumer spending or to **saving.** From a macroeconomic perspective, the only important decision the aerospace workers have to make is what percentage of income to spend and what percentage to save (i.e., not spend). Any additional consumption spending contributes directly to aggregate demand. That portion of income that is saved (not spent) goes under the mattress or into banks or other financial institutions.

saving Income minus consumption: that part of disposable income not spent.

Suppose aerospace workers decide to spend 75 percent of any extra income they get and to save the rest (25 percent). We call these percentages the marginal propensity to consume and the marginal propensity to save, respectively. The **marginal propensity to consume (MPC)** is the fraction of additional income people spend. The **marginal propensity to save (MPS)** is the fraction of new income that is saved.

marginal propensity to consume (MPC) The fraction of each additional (marginal) dollar of disposable income spent on consumption.

marginal propensity to save (MPS) The fraction of each additional (marginal) dollar of disposable income not spent on consumption: 1 − MPC.

Figure 12.5 illustrates how the spending and saving decisions are connected. In this case we have assumed that the MPC equals 0.75. Hence, 75 cents out of any extra dollar gets spent. By definition, the remaining 25 cents gets saved. The MPC and MPS tell us how the aerospace workers will behave when their incomes rise.

According to these behavioral patterns, the aerospace workers will use their additional $100 billion of income as follows:

$$\begin{aligned}\text{Increased consumption} &= \text{MPC} \times \text{additional income}\\ &= 0.75 \times \$100 \text{ billion}\\ &= \$75 \text{ billion}\end{aligned}$$

$$\begin{aligned}\text{Increased saving} &= \text{MPS} \times \text{additional income}\\ &= 0.25 \times \$100 \text{ billion}\\ &= \$25 \text{ billion}\end{aligned}$$

Thus all of the new income is either spent ($75 billion) or saved ($25 billion).

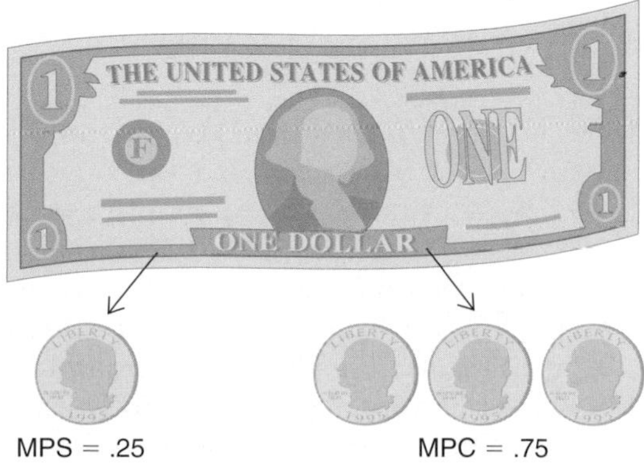

FIGURE 12.5
MPC and MPS

The marginal propensity to consume (MPC) tells us what portion of an extra dollar of income will be spent. The remaining portion will be saved. The MPC and MPS help us predict consumer behavior.

FIGURE 12.6
The Circular Flow

In the circular flow of income, money gets spent and respent multiple times. As a result of this multiplier process, aggregate demand increases by much more than the initial increase in government spending.

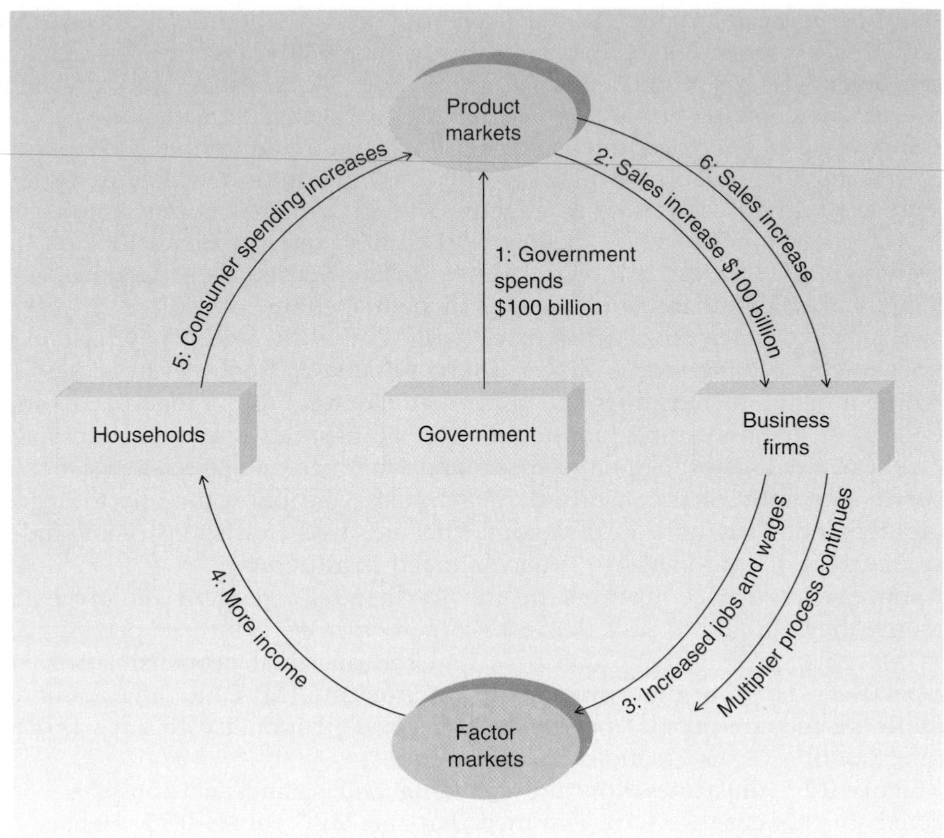

According to our calculations, the aerospace workers increase their consumer spending by $75 billion. This $75 billion of new consumption adds directly to aggregate demand. Hence aggregate demand has now been increased *twice:* first by the government expenditure on missiles ($100 billion) and then by the additional consumption of aerospace workers ($75 billion). Thus aggregate demand has increased by $175 billion as a consequence of the stepped-up defense expenditure. ***The fiscal stimulus to aggregate demand includes both the initial increase in government spending and all subsequent increases in consumer spending triggered by the government outlays.*** That combined stimulus is already up to $175 billion.

The stimulus of new government spending doesn't stop with the aerospace workers. The circular flow of income is a *continuing* process. The money spent by the aerospace workers becomes income to *other* workers. As their incomes rise, we expect their spending to increase as well. In other words, ***income gets spent and respent in the circular flow.*** This multiplier process is illustrated in Figure 12.6.

Spending Cycles Table 12.1 fills in the details of the multiplier process. Suppose the aerospace workers spend their $75 billion on new boats. This increases the income of boat builders. They, too, are then in a position to increase *their* spending.

Suppose the boat builders also have a marginal propensity to consume of 0.75. They will then spend 75 percent of their new income ($75 billion). This will add another $56.25 billion to consumption demand.

Notice in Table 12.1 what is happening to cumulative spending as the multiplier process continues. When the boat builders go on a spending spree,

Spending Cycles	Change in Spending during Cycle (billions per year)	Cumulative Increase in Spending (billions per year)
First cycle: government buys $100 billion worth of missiles	$100.00	$100.00
Second cycle: missile workers have more income, buy new boats (MPC = 0.75)	75.00	175.00
Third cycle: boat builders have more income, spend it on beer (0.75 × $75)	56.25	231.25
Fourth cycle: bartenders and brewery workers have more income ($56.25 billion), spend it on new cars (0.75 × $56.25)	42.19	273.44
Fifth cycle: autoworkers have more income, spend it on clothes (0.75 × $42.19)	31.64	305.08
Sixth cycle: apparel workers have more income, spend it on movies and entertainment (0.75 × $31.64)	23.73	328.81
Nth cycle and beyond		400.00

TABLE 12.1
The Multiplier Process at Work

Purchasing power is passed from hand to hand in the circular flow. The *cumulative* change in total expenditure that results from a new injection of spending into the circular flow depends on the MPC and the number of spending cycles that occur. The limit to multiplier effects is established by the ratio 1/(1 − MPC). In this case, MPC = 0.75, so the multiplier equals 4. That is to say, total spending will ultimately rise by $400 billion per year as a result of an increase in *G* of $100 billion per year.

there is a cumulative increase in spending:

Cycle 1: Government expenditure on cruise missiles	$100.00 billion
Cycle 2: Aerospace workers, purchase of boats	75.00 billion
Cycle 3: Boat builders' expenditure on beer	56.25 billion
Cumulative increase in spending after three cycles	$231.25 billion

As a result of the circular flow of spending and income, the impact of the initial government expenditure has already more than doubled.

Table 12.1 follows the multiplier process to its logical end. Each successive cycle entails less new income and smaller increments to spending. Ultimately, the changes get so small that they are not even noticeable. By that time, however, the *cumulative* change in spending is huge. The cumulative change in spending is $400 billion: $100 billion of initial government expenditure and an additional $300 billion of consumption induced by multiplier effects. Thus ***the demand stimulus initiated by increased government spending is a multiple of the initial expenditure.***

Multiplier Formula To compute the cumulative change in spending, we need not examine each cycle of the multiplier process. There is a shortcut. The entire sequence of multiplier cycles is summarized in a single number, aptly named the *multiplier*. The **multiplier** tells us how much *total* spending will change in response to an initial spending stimulus. The multiplier is computed as

multiplier The multiple by which an initial change in aggregate spending will alter total expenditure after an infinite number of spending cycles: 1/(1 − MPC).

- $$\text{Multiplier} = \frac{1}{1 - \text{MPC}}$$

In our case, where MPC = 0.75, the multiplier is

$$\text{Multiplier} = \frac{1}{1 - \text{MPC}}$$
$$= \frac{1}{1 - 0.75} = \frac{1}{0.25} = 4$$

Using this multiplier we can confirm the conclusion of Table 12.1 by observing that

$$\bullet\ \begin{array}{c}\text{Total change}\\ \text{in spending}\end{array} = \text{multiplier} \times \begin{array}{c}\text{initial change in}\\ \text{government spending}\end{array}$$
$$= \frac{1}{1 - \text{MPC}} \times \$100 \text{ billion per year}$$
$$= \frac{1}{1 - 0.75} \times \$100 \text{ billion per year}$$
$$= 4 \times \$100 \text{ billion per year}$$
$$= \$400 \text{ billion per year}$$

The impact of the multiplier on aggregate demand is illustrated in Figure 12.7. The AD_1 curve represents the inadequate aggregate demand that caused the initial unemployment problem (Figure 12.4). When the government increases its defense spending, the aggregate demand curve shifts rightward by \$100 billion to AD_2. This increase in defense expenditure sparks a consumption spree, shifting aggregate demand further, to AD_3. This combination of increased government spending (\$100 billion) and induced consumption (\$300 billion) is sufficient to restore full employment.

The multiplier packs a lot of punch. ***Every dollar of fiscal stimulus has a multiplied impact on aggregate demand.*** This makes fiscal policy easier. The multiplier also makes fiscal policy riskier, however, by exaggerating any intervention mistakes.

Tax Cuts

Although government spending is capable of moving the economy to its full-employment potential, increased *G* is not the only way to get there. The

FIGURE 12.7
Multiplier Effects

A \$100 billion increase in government spending shifts the aggregate demand curve to the right by a like amount (i.e., AD_1 to AD_2). Aggregate demand gets another boost from the additional consumption induced by multiplier effects. In this case, an MPC of 0.75 results in \$300 billion of additional consumption.

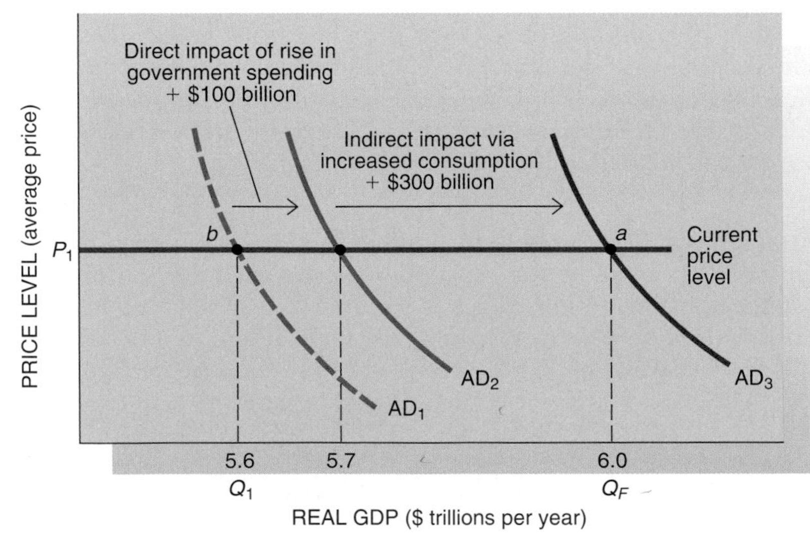

FISCAL STIMULUS HEADLINE

Retailers See Results from Child Tax Credit Checks

Retailers suddenly are ringing up strong sales, thanks in part to parents cashing in child tax credit checks.

The IRS mails out a third and final wave of rebate checks today. And the $180 billion retail industry, in the throes of back-to-school sales, is hankering for an even bigger share of the estimated $14 billion in checks.

About 24 million families will get an average $583, the IRS says. It's the result of a $350 billion tax package signed into law last May. Those dollars, along with an overall uptick in retail spending, is helping recharge the industry and could portend a robust holiday shopping season, retail's most critical period.

"Put a little money in people's pockets, and we'll spend. We're Americans," says Tad Shepperd, president of ShopperTrak, a company that measures general merchandise, apparel and furniture sales. The company said retail sales jumped 14% last week from the week before.

—Theresa Howard

Source: *USA Today*, August 8, 2003, p. 1B.

NOTE: Tax cuts increase disposable income and boost consumer spending. This shifts the AD curve rightward.

stimulus required to raise output and employment levels from Q_1 to Q_F could originate in C or I as well as from G. It could also come from abroad, in the form of increased demand for our exports. In other words, any big spender would help. Of course, the reason we are initially at Q_1 instead of Q_F in Figure 12.7 is that consumers and investors have chosen not to spend as much as is required for full employment.

The government might be able to stimulate more consumer and business spending with a tax cut. A tax cut directly increases the **disposable income** of the private sector. As soon as people get more income in their hands, they're likely to spend it. When they do, aggregate demand gets a lift. This is what happened in 2003. An increase in the child tax credit put an additional $14 billion into the hands of consumers. What did consumers do with this extra disposable income? As the accompanying Headline reports, they quickly spent most of it. The added consumer spending shifted the AD curve rightward.

disposable income After-tax income of consumers.

Taxes and Consumption How much of an AD shift we get from a personal tax cut depends on the marginal propensity to consume. If consumers squirreled away their entire tax cut, AD wouldn't budge. But an MPC of zero is an alien concept. People *do* increase their spending when their disposable income increases. So long as the MPC is greater than zero, a tax cut *will* stimulate more consumer spending.

Suppose again the MPC is 0.75. If taxes are cut by $100 billion, the resulting consumption spree amounts to:

- Intial increase in consumption = MPC × tax cut
  = 0.75 × $100 billion
  = $75 billion

Hence ***a tax cut that increases disposable incomes stimulates consumer spending.***

The initial consumption spree induced by a tax cut starts the multiplier process in motion. Once in motion, the multiplier picks up steam. The new consumer spending creates additional income for producers and workers, who will then use the additional income to increase their own consumption.

This will propel us along the multiplier path already depicted in Table 12.1. The cumulative change in total spending will be

- Cumulative change in spending = multiplier × initial change in consumption

In this case, the cumulative change is

$$\begin{aligned}\text{Cumulative change in spending} &= \frac{1}{1 - \text{MPC}} \times \$75 \text{ billion} \\ &= 4 \times \$75 \text{ billion} \\ &= \$300 \text{ billion}\end{aligned}$$

Here again we see that the multiplier increases the impact of a tax cut on aggregate demand. ***The cumulative increase in aggregate demand is a multiple of the initial tax cut.*** Thus the multiplier makes both increased government spending and tax cuts very powerful policy levers.

Taxes and Investment A tax cut may also be an effective mechanism for increasing investment spending. Investment decisions are guided by expectations of future profit, particularly after-tax profits. If a cut in corporate taxes raises potential after-tax profits, it should encourage additional investment. Once increased investment spending enters the circular flow, it has a multiplier effect on total spending like that which follows an initial change in consumer spending. Thus tax cuts for consumers or investors provide an alternative to increased government spending as a mechanism for stimulating aggregate spending.

Tax cuts designed to stimulate C and I have been used frequently. In 1963 President John F. Kennedy announced his intention to reduce taxes in order to stimulate the economy, citing the fact that the marginal propensity to consume for the average American family at that time appeared to be exceptionally high. His successor, Lyndon Johnson, concurred with Kennedy's reasoning. Johnson agreed to "shift emphasis sharply from expanding federal expenditure to boosting private consumer demand and business investment." He proceeded to cut personal and corporate taxes $11 billion.

One of the largest tax cuts in history was initiated by President Ronald Reagan in 1981. The Reagan administration persuaded Congress to cut personal taxes $250 billion over a three-year period and to cut business taxes another $70 billion. The resulting increase in disposable income stimulated consumer spending and helped push the economy out of the 1981–82 recession.

President George W. Bush proposed even larger tax cuts in 2001. He urged a $1.6 *trillion* tax cut, spread out over ten years. One of the principal arguments for the tax cut was the weak condition of the U.S. economy in early 2001. A tax cut, Bush argued, would not only increase disposable income, but also raise expectations for future income. Congress concurred, ultimately passing a $1.35 trillion tax cut, spread out over ten years. Continued weakness in the U.S. economy prompted further tax cuts in 2002 and again in 2003. As the following Headline reports, the 2003 tax cuts were designed to boost both consumer and business spending.

Inflation Worries

President Clinton had used the same Keynesian argument when he ran for president in 1992. With the economy still far short of its productive capacity (Q_F), he called for more fiscal stimulus. After he was elected, however, President Clinton changed his mind about the need for fiscal stimulus.

BOOSTING C, I HEADLINE

Tax Cuts Could Improve Growth

Consumer spending could get faster lift

WASHINGTON—The $350 billion tax package endorsed by President Bush Thursday could boost economic growth slightly this year . . .

Faucher's firm predicts the tax bill will improve economic growth by 0.25 percent this year and 0.5 percent in 2004.

In the short term, consumer spending could be helped by provisions in the bill that speed tax cuts for some married couples and cut income tax rates this year, rather than in 2004 and later . . .

Steven Stanley of RBS Greenwich Capital says the tax plan could address a big problem facing the economy: lack of business investment. The bill lets small businesses expense up to $100,000 in new equipment and lets some bigger firms depreciate assets faster. "It doesn't necessarily mean they'll invest in the next month or two, but over the next year or so, it should help," Stanley says.

—Sue Kirchhoff

Source: *USA Today*, May 23, 2003, p. 1B.

NOTE: Tax cuts may be used to increase both consumer and business spending. The added C and I shift AD rightward.

Rather than delivering the middle-class tax cut he had promised, Clinton instead decided to *raise* taxes. This abrupt policy U-turn was motivated in part by the recognition of how powerful the multiplier is. The economy was already expanding when Clinton was elected and the multiplier was at work. As each successive spending cycle developed, the economy would move closer to full employment. Any *new* fiscal stimulus would accelerate that movement. As a result, the economy might end up expanding so fast that it would overshoot the full-employment goal.

If too much fiscal stimulus were enacted, the resultant pressure might force prices higher. In other words, a tax cut in 1993 carried the risk of causing inflation. This risk is illustrated in Figure 12.2. ***Whenever the aggregate supply curve is upward-sloping, an increase in aggregate demand increases prices as well as output.*** Notice in Figure 12.2 how the price level starts creeping up as aggregate demand increases from AD_1 to AD^*. If aggregate demand expands further to AD_2, the price level really jumps. This suggests that the degree of inflation caused by increased aggregate demand depends on the slope of the aggregate supply curve. Only if the AS curve were horizontal would there be no risk of inflation. Keynes thought this might have been the case during the Great Depression. With so much excess capacity available, businesses were willing and able—indeed, eager—to supply more output at the existing price level. In 1993, the risk of inflation was greater. In 2003, the risk of inflation was much less.

Fiscal Restraint

The threat of inflation suggests that **fiscal restraint** may be an appropriate policy strategy at times. If excessive aggregate demand is causing prices to rise, the goal of fiscal policy will be to reduce aggregate demand, not stimulate it (see Figure 12.8).

fiscal restraint Tax hikes or spending cuts intended to reduce (shift) aggregate demand.

The means available to the federal government for restraining aggregate demand emerge again from both sides of the budget. The difference here is that we use the budget tools in reverse. We now want to *reduce* government spending or *increase* taxes.

FIGURE 12.8
Fiscal Restraint
Fiscal restraint is used to reduce inflationary pressures. The strategy is to shift the aggregate demand curve to the left with budget cuts or tax hikes.

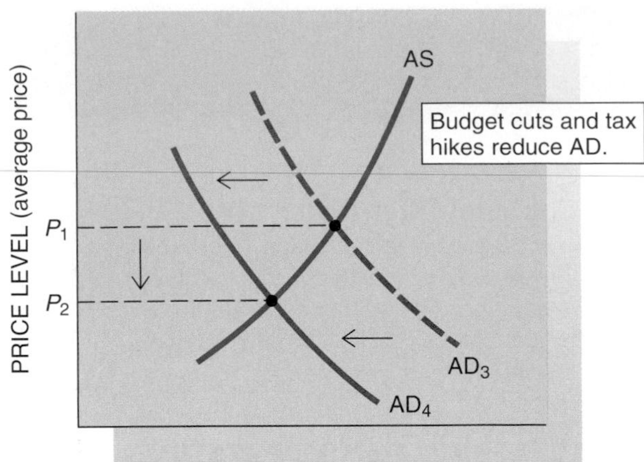

Budget Cuts

Cutbacks in government spending directly reduce aggregate demand. As with spending increases, the impact of spending cuts is magnified by the multiplier.

Multiplier Cycles Suppose the government cut military spending by $100 billion. This would throw a lot of aerospace employees out of work. Thousands of workers would get smaller paychecks, or perhaps none at all. These workers would be forced to cut back on their own spending. Hence aggregate demand would take two hits: first a cut in government spending, then induced cutbacks in consumer spending. The multiplier process works in both directions.

The marginal propensity to consume again reveals the power of the multiplier process. If the MPC is 0.75, the consumption of aerospace workers will drop by $75 billion when the government cutbacks reduce their income by $100 billion. (The rest of the income loss will be covered by a reduction in savings balances.)

From this point on the story should sound familiar. As detailed in Table 12.1, the $100 billion government cutback will ultimately reduce consumer spending by $300 billion. The *total* drop in spending is thus $400 billion. Like their mirror image, ***government cutbacks have a multiplied effect on aggregate demand.*** The total impact is equal to

- Cumulative reduction in spending = multiplier × initial budget cut

Tax Hikes

Tax increases can also be used to shift the aggregate demand curve to the left. The direct effect of a tax increase is a reduction in disposable income. People will pay the higher taxes by reducing their consumption and depleting their savings. The reduced consumption results in less aggregate demand. As consumers tighten their belts they set off the multiplier process, leading to a much larger cumulative shift of aggregate demand.

In 1982 there was great concern that the 1981 tax cuts had been excessive and that inflationary pressures were building up. To reduce that inflationary pressure, Congress withdrew some of its earlier tax cuts, especially those designed to increase investment spending. The net effect of the Tax Equity and Fiscal Responsibility Act of 1982 was to increase taxes roughly $90 billion for the years 1983–85. This shifted the aggregate demand curve leftward, reducing inflationary pressures (see Figure 12.8).

Problem	Solution	Policy Tools
Unemployment (recession)	Increase aggregate demand	Increase government spending Cut taxes
Inflation	Reduce aggregate demand	Cut government spending Raise taxes

TABLE 12.2
Fiscal Policy Guidelines
The Keynesian emphasis on aggregate demand results in simple guidelines for fiscal policy: reduce aggregate demand to fight inflation; increase aggregate demand to fight unemployment. Changes in government spending and taxes are the tools used to shift AD.

The Clinton tax increase of 1993 also restrained aggregate demand. The initial fiscal restraint from the tax increase and spending slowdown amounted to roughly $40 billion. This helped to slow the rate of economic growth and to keep inflation in check. The tax increases did nothing for President Clinton's popularity, however. After the Republican election victories in November 1994, President Clinton again decided that tax cuts were needed. In 1997 Clinton and the Congress agreed to a five-year package of tax cuts worth $80 billion.

Fiscal Guidelines

The basic rules for fiscal policy are so simple that they can be summarized in a small table. **The policy goal is to match aggregate demand with the full-employment potential of the economy. The fiscal strategy for attaining that goal is to shift the aggregate demand curve.** The tools for doing so are (1) changes in government spending and (2) changes in tax rates. Table 12.2 summarizes the guidelines developed by John Maynard Keynes for using those tools.

POLICY PERSPECTIVES

Unbalanced Budgets

The primary lever of fiscal policy is the federal government's budget. As we have observed, changes in either federal taxes or outlays are the mechanism for shifting the aggregate demand curve. The use of this mechanism has a troubling implication: ***The use of the budget to manage aggregate demand implies that the budget will often be unbalanced.*** In the face of a recession, for example, the government has sound reasons both to cut taxes and to increase its own spending. By reducing tax revenues and increasing expenditures simultaneously, however, the federal government will throw its budget out of balance.

Budget Deficit Whenever government expenditures exceed tax revenues, a **budget deficit** exists. The deficit is measured by the difference between expenditures and receipts:

budget deficit The amount by which government expenditures exceed government revenues in a given time period.

- Budget deficit = government spending > tax revenues

where spending exceeds revenues. In 2003 the federal budget deficit was nearly $400 billion. To pay for such deficit spending, the government had to borrow money, either directly from the private sector or from the banking sector. From 1970 to 1997 the federal budget was in the red (deficit) every year. As Figure 12.9 reveals, the deficits of the 1980s and early 1990s peaked at close to $300 billion in 1992. This string of deficits caused recurrent political crises. Several times the federal government had to shut down for days at a time, while Republicans and Democrats in Congress battled over how to cut the deficit. A majority of citizens even supported adding an

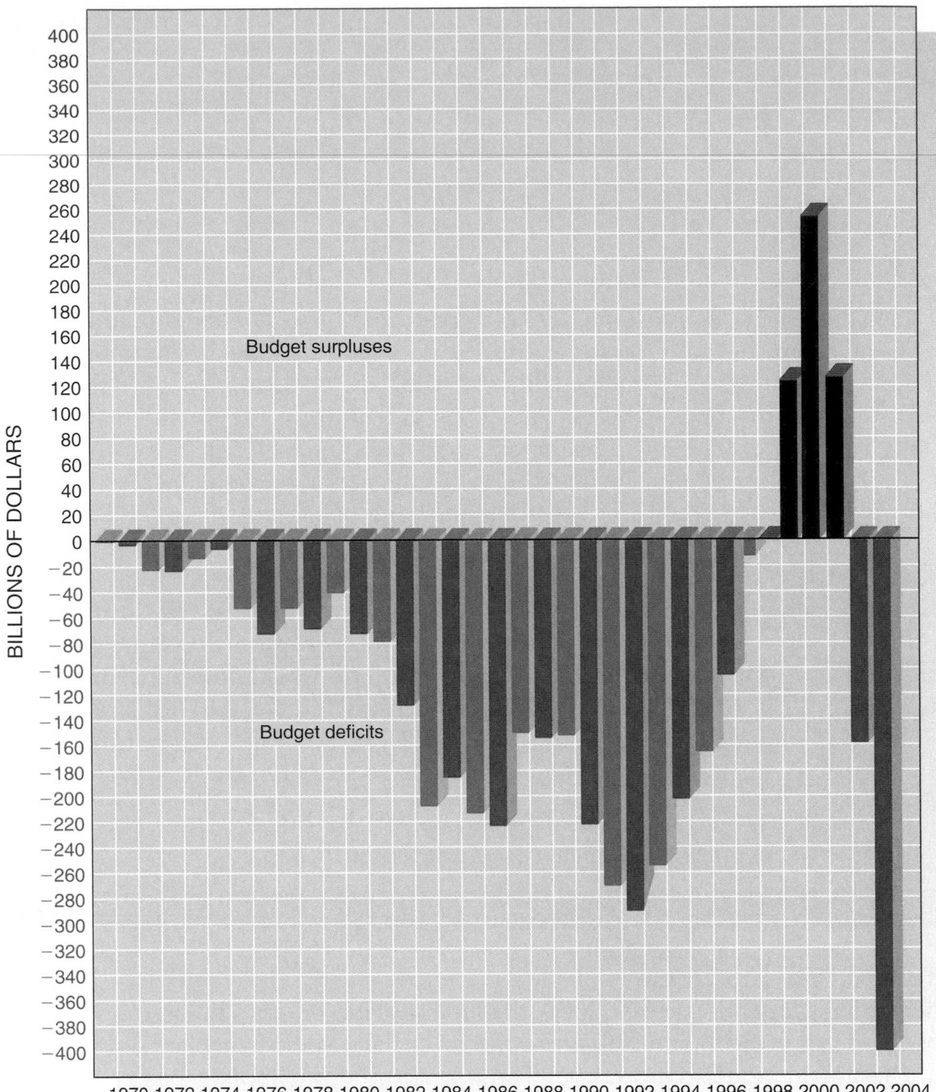

FIGURE 12.9
Unbalanced Budgets
From 1970 until 1997 the federal budget was in deficit every year. In the early 1980s, federal deficits increased dramatically. They soared further in the early 1990s as a result of a recession and the continued expansion of government programs. From 1998 to 2002 the budget was in surplus due to strong GDP growth and slowed federal spending. An economic slowdown, tax cuts, and a surge in defense spending returned the budget to deficit.
Source: Congressional Budget Office.

amendment to the U.S. Constitution that would *force* Congress to balance the budget every year.

Budget Surplus As the U.S. Congress was debating such an amendment, the deficit started shrinking. The record-breaking expansion of the U.S. economy and the stock market boom of the late 1990s swelled tax collections. The Balanced Budget Act of 1997 also slowed the growth of government spending. This combination of growing tax revenues and slower government spending shrunk the deficit dramatically.

By 1998 the deficit had completely vanished and a **budget surplus** appeared. For the first time in 30 years, tax revenues exceeded government spending.

budget surplus An excess of government revenues over government expenditures in a given time period.

- Budget surplus = government spending < tax revenues

The surpluses started out small but grew rapidly as the economy kept expanding. In 2000 the Congressional Budget Office projected a 10-year string of budget surpluses that would add up to over $4.5 trillion.

The transformation of the federal budget from deficit to surplus transformed political debates as well. In the 1980s and 1990s the central debate was how to reduce the deficit. In 1998–2000 the debate focused on how to use the surplus. Indeed, that was the central issue in the 2000 presidential campaign. George W. Bush wanted to use a big chunk of the surplus for tax cuts. Al Gore, by contrast, wanted to increase federal spending on domestic programs.

Countercyclical Policy For John Maynard Keynes, the choice would have been easy. From a Keynesian perspective, the desirability of a budget deficit or surplus depends on the health of the economy. If the economy is ailing, an injection of government spending or a tax cut would be appropriate. On the other hand, if the economy were booming, some fiscal restraint (spending cuts, tax hikes) would be called for. Hence Keynes would first examine the economy, then prescribe fiscal restraint or stimulus. He might even prescribe neither, sensing the economy was in optimal health. ***In Keynes's view, an unbalanced budget was perfectly appropriate if macro conditions called for a deficit or surplus.*** A balanced budget would be appropriate only if the resulting aggregate demand were consistent with full-employment equilibrium.

Keynes wouldn't have been enthusiastic about the budget proposals of either Gore or Bush. In 2000 the U.S. economy was pushing against its production possibilities. The national unemployment rate had even dipped below the low end of its full-employment range (4–6 percent). Inflation was low but rising. Whatever political appeal tax cuts or increased domestic spending might have had, Keynes would have preferred fiscal restraint, or at least neutrality. He would have used most of the budget surplus to pay off national debt incurred from prior budget deficits.

The debate on the proper use of budget surpluses ended abruptly in any case. The U.S. economy suddenly ran out of steam. The stock market, which had peaked in March 2000, kept falling well into 2001. With it, consumer and business confidence declined significantly and the U.S. economy fell into recession (March 2001). In September 2001 the terrorist attacks dealt the economy another blow.

The slowing economy reduced government tax revenues. Rising unemployment caused government spending to go up for unemployment benefits and other programs. On top of that, defense and homeland-security spending increased dramatically. Swiftly, budget surpluses disappeared and budget deficits re-emerged. Nevertheless, President Bush heeded Keynes's advice and pushed Congress to pass the largest-ever tax cut in 2001 and additional tax cuts in 2002 and 2003. Bush asserted that creating jobs in the short run was the most urgent task, even if it required deficit-financed fiscal stimulus. So the budget deficit skyrocketed (Figure 12.9). Bush hoped that subsequent economic growth and future fiscal restraint would shrink the huge budget deficit in later years.

SUMMARY

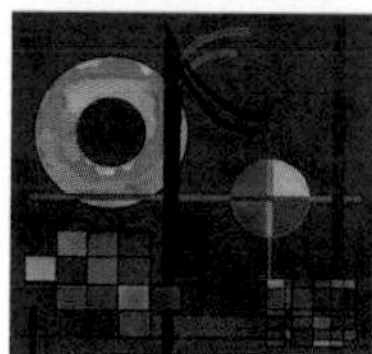

- The Keynesian explanation of macro instability requires government intervention to shift the aggregate demand curve to the desired rate of output. The government can do this by balancing aggregate spending with the economy's full-employment potential.
- To boost aggregate demand, the government may either increase its own spending or cut taxes. To restrain aggregate demand, the government may reduce its own spending or raise taxes.

- Any change in government spending or taxes will have a multiplied impact on aggregate demand. The additional impact comes from changes in consumption caused by changes in disposable income.
- The marginal propensity to consume tells how changes in disposable income affect consumer spending. The MPC is the fraction of each additional dollar spent (i.e., not saved).
- The size of the multiplier depends on the marginal propensity to consume. The higher the MPC, the larger the multiplier, where the multiplier = 1/(1 − MPC).
- Fiscal stimulus carries the risk of inflation. The steeper the upward slope of the AS curve, the greater is the risk of inflation.
- A balanced budget is appropriate only if the resulting aggregate demand is compatible with full employment and price stability. Otherwise, *unbalanced* budgets (deficits or surpluses) are appropriate.

Terms to Remember

Define the following terms:

fiscal policy
aggregate demand
consumption
investment
net exports
equilibrium (macro)
GDP gap
fiscal stimulus
saving
marginal propensity to consume (MPC)
marginal propensity to save (MPS)
multiplier
disposable income
fiscal restraint
budget deficit
budget surplus

Questions for Discussion

1. How long does it take you to spend any income you receive? What happens to the dollars you spend?
2. What is your MPC? Would a welfare recipient and a millionaire have the same MPC? What determines a person's MPC?
3. What do people do with that fraction of their income they save?
4. How long does the multiplier process take? How many cycles are likely to occur in a year's time? How will this alter the impact of fiscal policy?
5. Do fiscal policymakers really need to know the magnitudes of the MPC and multipliers? Could they get along as well without such information?
6. If the guidelines for fiscal policy (Table 12.2) are so simple, why does the economy ever suffer from unemployment or inflation?
7. Would a constitutional amendment that would require the federal government to balance its budget (incur no deficits) be desirable? Explain.
8. In the second quarter of 2003, defense spending surged by 44 percent, or nearly $30 billion. How did this surge affect GDP? Which nondefense industries were most likely affected?

Problems

1. If the marginal propensity to save is 0.05, how large is the multiplier? If the marginal propensity to save doubles to 0.10, what happens to the multiplier?
2. If the MPC were 0.8, how much spending would occur at step 5 in Figure 12.6? How many spending rounds would occur before consumer spending increased by $200 billion?

3. (*a*) The multiplier process depicted in Table 12.1 is based on an MPC of 0.75. Recompute the first five cycles using an MPC of 0.50.
   (*b*) What is the value of the multiplier in this case?
   (*c*) What is the multiplier when the MPC is (1) 0.80 and (2) 0.90?
4. Suppose the government increases education spending by $20 billion. How much additional *consumption* will this increase cause?
5. By how much would the 2003 child tax credit increase have shifted AD if the MPC was 0.80? (see Headline, p. 285).
6. If taxes were cut by $1 trillion and the MPC were 0.95, by how much would total spending
   (*a*) Increase in the first year with two spending cycles?
   (*b*) Increase over five years, with two spending cycles per year?
   (*c*) Increase over an infinite time period?
7. By how much more would the $11 trillion economy grow in the first two years of the Bush 2003 tax cuts, according to the Headline on p. 287?

Web Activities

1. Log on to www.whitehouse.gov/fsbr/output.html. Find data on the current level of nonresidential fixed investment.
   (*a*) What does the trend suggest is happening to aggregate demand?
   (*b*) Draw an AD/AS graph that represents the trend in these data.
2. Log on to www.house.gov/jec and click on the JEC index. Click on "Federal Spending." In general, how does the JEC suggest the federal government change fiscal spending? Why? What will be the likely macroeconomic impact, *ceteris paribus,* of this change in spending?
3. Log on to www.house.gov/jec/bud.htm, then click on the report on budget surpluses (halfway down the page). Read the report by the joint economic committee to determine whether the U.S. government is currently running a surplus or a deficit. What impact will this surplus (deficit) have on the macroeconomic equilibrium in the United States?

Living Econ

How Confident Are You?

You hear frequent media reports about the national debt, corporate earnings, and unemployment levels, but do you ever stop to consider how these reports affect your confidence? Not how good your hair looks or if your clothes are the hottest fashion, but how confident you are as a consumer.

Consumer confidence in the nation's economy plays a significant role in determining consumer spending. If stock market prices are falling and everyone around you is being laid off, your confidence as a consumer is likely to be negatively affected. In fact you might even fear a recession is near. How would you behave if you thought a recession was coming and you might lose your job? You would probably reduce your spending. And if that fear is deep enough, widespread enough, and enough people reduce their spending, what might happen to the economy? The decrease in spending might cause a recession.

What a self-fulfilling prophesy! If consumers behave as if they are confident about the economy and continue to spend as usual, the economy may temporarily survive a negative report card. However, if consumers think the "end" is near, they may hasten what they feared most in the first place, an economic downturn.

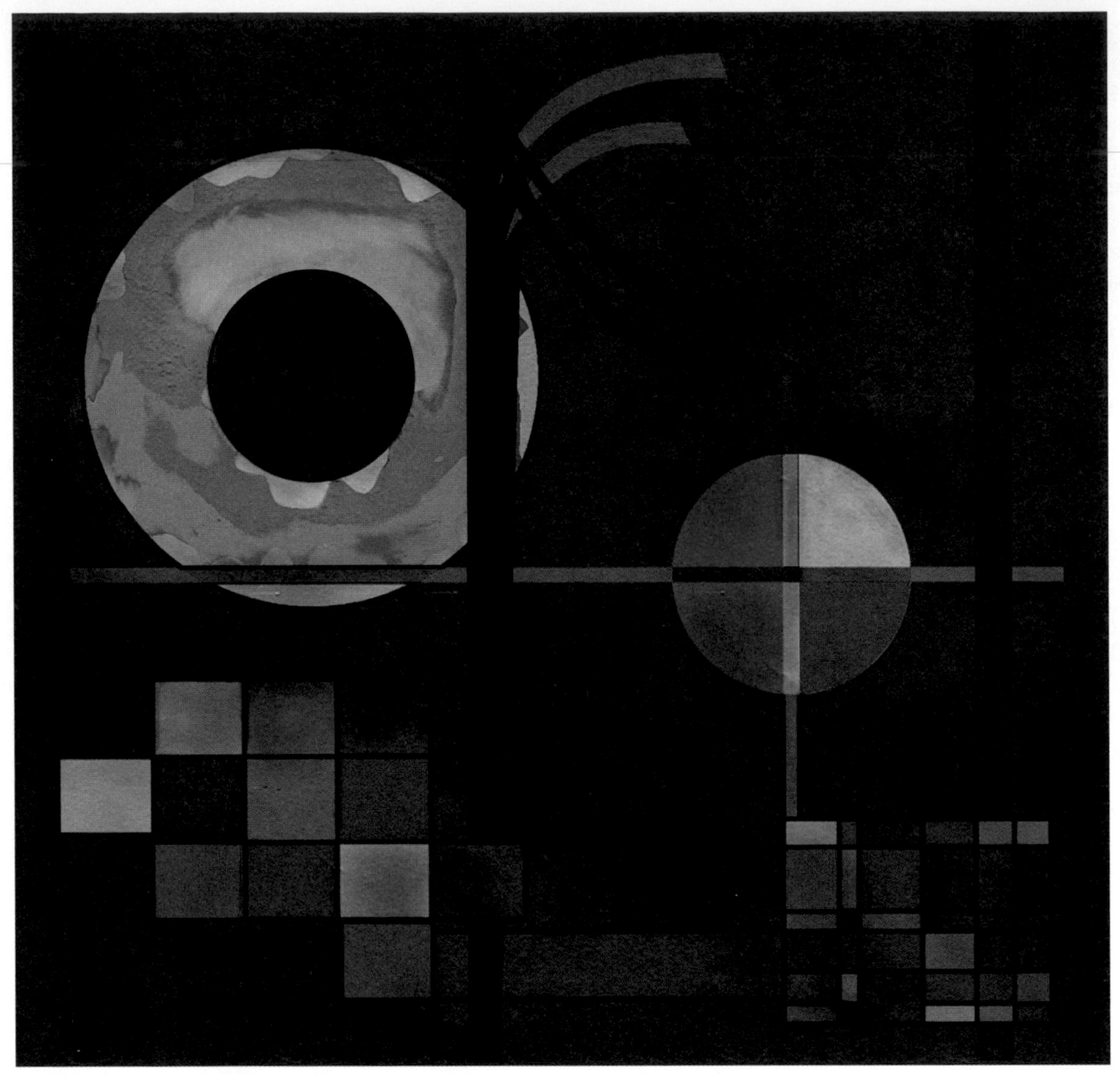

Money and Banks

CHAPTER 13

Sophocles, the ancient Greek playwright, had very strong opinions about the role of money. As he saw it, "Of evils upon earth, the worst is money. It is money that sacks cities, and drives men forth from hearth and home; warps and seduces native intelligence, and breeds a habit of dishonesty."

In modern times, people may still be seduced by the lure of money and fashion their lives around its pursuit. Nevertheless, it is hard to imagine an economy functioning without money. Money affects not only morals and ideals but also the way an economy works.

The purpose of this and the following chapter is to examine the role of money in the economy today. We begin with a very simple question:

- What is money?

As we shall discover, money isn't exactly what you think it is. Once we have established the characteristics of money, we go on to ask:

- Where does money come from?
- What role do banks play in the macro economy?

In the next chapter we look at how the Federal Reserve System controls the supply of money and thereby affects macroeconomic outcomes. We will then have a second policy lever in our basic macro model.

The Uses of Money

To appreciate the significance of money for a modern economy, imagine for a moment that there were no such thing as money. How would you get something for breakfast? If you wanted eggs for breakfast, you would have to tend your own chickens or go see Farmer Brown. But how would you pay Farmer Brown for his eggs? Without money, you would have to offer him goods or services that he could use. In other words, you would have to engage in primitive **barter—**the direct exchange of one good for another. You would get those eggs only if Farmer Brown happened to want the particular goods or services you had to offer and if the two of you could agree on the terms of the exchange.

barter The direct exchange of one good for another, without the use of money.

The use of money greatly simplifies market transactions. It's a lot easier to exchange money for eggs at the supermarket than to go into the country and barter with farmers. Our ability to use money in market transactions, however, depends on the grocer's willingness to accept money as a *medium of exchange.* The grocer sells eggs for money only because he can use the same money to pay his help and buy the goods he himself desires. He, too, can exchange money for goods and services. Accordingly, money plays an essential role in facilitating the continuous series of exchanges that characterize a market economy.

Money has other desirable features. The grocer who accepts your money in exchange for a carton of eggs doesn't have to spend his income immediately. He can hold onto the money for a few days or months, without worrying about its spoiling. Hence money is also a useful *store of value,* that is, a mechanism for transforming current income into future purchases. Finally, common use of money serves as a *standard of value* for comparing the market worth of different goods. A dozen eggs is more valuable than a dozen onions if it costs more at the supermarket.

We may identify, then, several essential characteristics of what we call money. Specifically, ***anything that serves all of the following purposes can be thought of as money:***

- ***Medium of exchange:*** is accepted as payment for goods and services (and debts).
- ***Store of value:*** can be held for future purchases.
- ***Standard of value:*** serves as a yardstick for measuring the prices of goods and services.

The great virtue of money is that it facilitates the market exchanges that permit specialization in production. In fact, efficient division of labor requires a system whereby people can exchange the things they produce for the things they desire. Money makes this system of exchange possible.

Many Types of Money

Although markets cannot function without money, they can get along without *dollars.* U.S. dollars are just one example of money. In the early days of Colonial America, there were no U.S. dollars. A lot of business was conducted with Spanish and Portuguese gold coins. Later, people used Indian wampum, then tobacco, grain, fish, and furs as mediums of exchange. Throughout the colonies, gunpowder and bullets were frequently used for small change. These forms of money weren't as convenient as U.S. dollars, but they did the job. So long as they served as a medium of exchange, a store of value, and a standard of value, they were properly regarded as money.

The first paper money issued by the U.S. federal government consisted of \$10 million worth of "greenbacks," printed in 1861 to finance the Civil War. The Confederate states also issued paper money to finance their side of the

BARTER **HEADLINE**

Goods Replace Rubles in Russia's Vast Web of Trade

Workers, paid in products, must make deals to survive; glasses, shoes, bras become new forms of currency

GUS-KHRUSTALNY, RUSSIA—Wrapped tightly against chilling winds, Valentina Novikova, a pensioner, stood expectantly at a lonely crossroads outside this old glass-and crystal-making town, her champagne flutes tucked neatly into cardboard boxes, stacked on makeshift birch tables. . . .

The glass and crystal sold on the roadside here are the lifeblood of the local economy. Workers are paid in glass, receive their social benefits in glass and must sell the glass to stay alive. The glass has become a kind of substitute money.

The workers and their glass factory are part of a vast transactional web of barter, trading and debt—all using surrogates for the Russian ruble—that by some estimates now accounts for more than half of the Russian economy.

Virtually every sector, every factory and every worker in Russia has been touched by the flood of surrogate money. What began a few years ago at a time of runaway inflation has persisted and become even more widespread as inflation has cooled yet industry remained moribund. From sheet metal to finished cars, from champagne glasses to shoes, goods are traded around Russia in lieu of money.

In Volgograd, workers at the Armina factory decided to go on strike this month, according to the newspaper *Izvestia*. The reason: Their monthly wage of about $50 is paid in brassieres. . . .

Movie theaters in the Siberian city of Altai started charging two eggs for admission because people had no cash to spare. But the theaters hit a problem in the winter, when hens lay fewer eggs and audiences began to dwindle. So now the movie houses are taking empty bottles as payment, turning them back in to the bottlers for cash.

—David Hoffman

NOTE: When people lose faith in a nation's currency, they must use something else as a medium of exchange. This greatly limits market activity.

Civil War. Confederate dollars became worthless, however, when the South lost and people no longer accepted Confederate currency in exchange for goods and services.

When communism collapsed in Eastern Europe, similar problems arose. In Poland, the zloty was shunned as a form of money in the early 1980s. Poles preferred to use cigarettes and vodka as mediums of exchange and stores of value. So much Polish currency (zlotys) was available that its value was suspect. The same problem undermined the value of the Russian ruble in the 1990s. Russian consumers preferred to hold and use American dollars rather than the rubles that few people would accept in payment for goods and services. Cigarettes, vodka, and even potatoes were a better form of money than Russian rubles. Notice in the accompanying Headline how movie tickets were sold in 1997 for eggs, not cash, and workers were paid in goods, not rubles.

The Money Supply

Cash vs. Money

In the U.S. economy today, such unusual forms of money are rarely used. Nevertheless, the concept of money includes more than the dollar bills and coins in your pocket or purse. Most people realize this when they offer to pay for goods with a check or debit card rather than cash. The money you have in a checking account can be used to buy goods and services or to pay debts, or it can be retained for future use. In these respects, your checking account balance is as much a part of your money as are the coins and dollars in your pocket or purse. In fact, if everyone accepted your checks (and if the checks could also operate vending machines and pay telephones), there would be no need to carry cash.

There is nothing unique about cash, then, insofar as the market is concerned. ***Checking accounts can and do perform the same market functions as cash.*** Accordingly, we must include checking account balances in our concept of **money.** The essence of money is not its taste, color, or feel but, rather, its ability to purchase goods and services.

money Anything generally accepted as a medium of exchange.

Transactions Accounts

In their competition for customers, banks have created all kinds of different checking accounts. Credit unions and other financial institutions have also created checking-account services. Although they have a variety of distinctive names, all checking accounts have a common feature: they permit depositors to spend their deposit balances easily, without making a special trip to the bank to withdraw funds. All you need is a checkbook, a debit card, an ATM card, or an Internet hookup.

Because all such checking-account balances can be used directly in market transactions (without a trip to the bank), they are collectively referred to as *transactions accounts*. The distinguishing feature of all **transactions accounts** is that they permit direct payment to a third party, without requiring a trip to the bank to make a withdrawal. The payment itself may be in the form of a check, a debit-card transfer, or an automatic payment transfer. In all such cases, ***the balance in your transactions account substitutes for cash, and is, therefore, a form of money.***

transactions account A bank account that permits direct payment to a third party (e.g., with a check).

Basic Money Supply

Because all transactions accounts can be spent as readily as cash, they are counted as part of our money supply. Adding transactions-account balances to the quantity of coins and currency held by the public gives us one measure of the amount of money available—that is, the basic **money supply.** The basic money supply is typically referred to by the abbreviation **M1.**

money supply (M1) Currency held by the public, plus balances in transactions accounts.

Figure 13.1 illustrates the actual composition of our money supply. The first component of MI is the cash people hold (currency in circulation

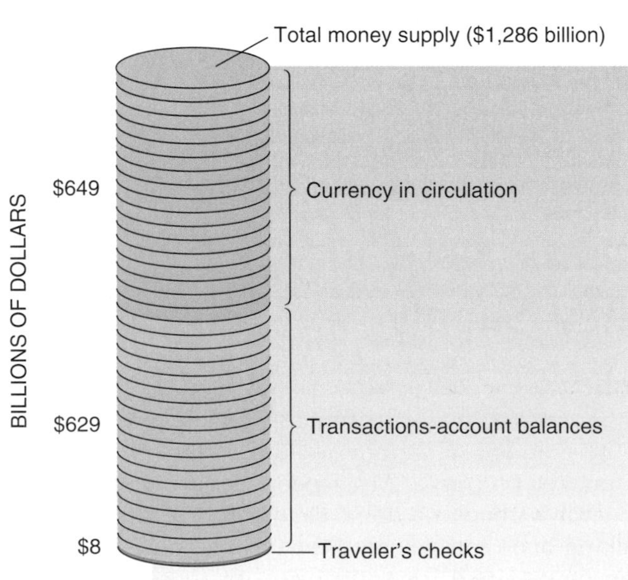

FIGURE 13.1
Composition of the Basic Money Supply (M1)

The money supply (M1) includes all cash held by the public plus balances people hold in transactions accounts (e.g., checking, NOW, ATS, and credit union share-draft accounts). Cash is only part of our money supply.

Source: Federal Reserve Board of Governors, September 2003.

MEDIUMS OF EXCHANGE HEADLINE

Writing Checks Going Out of Style

U.S. consumers and businesses make 80 billion retail payments annually, nearly 50 billion by check and 30 billion by electronic instruments, such as credit cards, debit cards and the Automated Clearing House (ACH). Check writing in 2000 compared with 21 years ago:

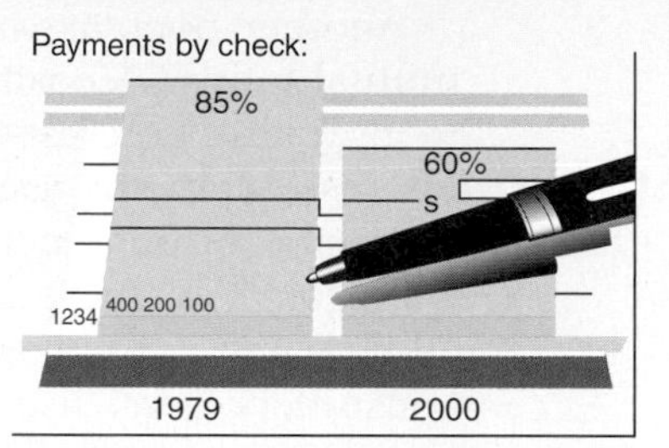

Source: *USA Today*, December 10, 2001, p. B1.

NOTE: Although people are writing fewer checks, checks are still the most common form of noncash payment. Checks are also used to pay most credit-card balances.

outside of commercial banks). Clearly, ***cash is only part of the money supply; most money consists of balances in transactions accounts.*** This really should not come as too much of a surprise. Most market transactions are still conducted in cash. But those cash transactions are typically small (e.g., for coffee, lunch, small items). They are vastly outspent by the 80 billion *non*-cash retail payments made each year. People prefer to use checks rather than cash for most large market transactions (see Headline). Checks are more convenient than cash, because they eliminate trips to the bank. Checks are also safer: lost or stolen cash is gone forever; checkbooks are easily replaced, at little or no cost.

Credit cards are another popular medium of exchange. People use credit cards for about one-third of all purchases. This use is not sufficient, however, to qualify credit cards as a form of money. Credit card balances must be paid by check or cash. Hence credit cards are simply a payment *service*, not a final form of payment (credit card companies charge fees and interest for this service). The cards themselves are not a store of value, in contrast to cash or bank account balances.

The last component of our basic money supply consists of traveler's checks issued by nonbank firms (e.g., American Express). These, too, can be used directly in market transactions, just like good old-fashioned cash.

Near Money

Transactions accounts are not the only substitute for cash. Even a conventional savings account can be used to finance market purchases. This use of a savings account may require a trip to the bank for a special withdrawal. But that is not too great a barrier to consumer spending. Many savings banks make that trip unnecessary by offering computerized withdrawals and transfers from their savings accounts, some even at supermarket service desks or cash machines. Others offer to pay your bills if you phone in instructions.

Not all savings accounts are so easily spendable. Certificates of deposit, for example, require a minimum balance to be kept in the bank for a specified number of months or years; early withdrawal results in a loss of interest. Funds held in certificates of deposit cannot be transferred automatically to a checking account (like passbook savings balances) or to a third party (like NOW-account balances). As a result, certificates of deposit are seldom used for everyday market purchases. Nevertheless, such accounts still function like "near money" in the sense that savers can go to the bank and withdraw cash if they really want to buy something.

Another popular way of holding money is to buy shares of money-market mutual funds. Deposits into money-market mutual funds are pooled and used to purchase interest-bearing securities (e.g., Treasury bills). The resultant interest payments are typically higher than those paid on regular checking accounts. Moreover, money-market funds can often be withdrawn *immediately,* just like those in transactions accounts. However, such accounts only allow a few checks to be written each month without paying a fee. Hence consumers don't use money-market funds as readily as other transactions accounts to finance everyday spending.

Additional measures of the money supply (M2, M3, etc.) have been constructed to account for the possibility of using money-market mutual funds and various other deposits to finance everyday spending. At the core of all such measures, however, are cash and transactions-account balances, the key elements of the basic money supply (M1). Accordingly, we will limit our discussion to just M1.

Aggregate Demand

Why do we care so much about the specifics of money? Does it really matter how people pay for their purchases?

Our concern about the specific nature of money stems from our broader interest in macro outcomes. As we have observed, total output, employment, and prices are all affected by changes in **aggregate demand.** How much money people have may be one of the determinants of their spending behavior. That's why it's important to know what "money" is and where it comes from.

aggregate demand The total quantity of output demanded at alternative price levels in a given time period, ceteris paribus.

Creation of Money

When people ponder where money comes from, they often have a simple answer: the government prints it. They may even have toured the Bureau of Engraving and Printing in Washington, D.C., and seen dollar bills running off the printing presses. Or maybe they visited the U.S. Mint in Denver or Philadelphia and saw coins being stamped.

There is something wrong with this explanation of the origin of money, however. As Figure 13.1 illustrates, ***most of what we call money is not cash but bank balances.*** Hence, the Bureau of Engraving and the two surviving U.S. mints may play only a minor role in creating money. The real power over the money supply must lie elsewhere.

Deposit Creation

To understand the origins of money, think about your own bank balance. How did you acquire a balance in your checking account? Did you deposit cash? Did you deposit a check? Or did you receive an automatic payroll transfer? If you typically make *non*cash deposits, your behavior is quite typical. Most deposits into transactions accounts are checks or computer transfers; hard cash is seldom used. When people get paid, for example, they typically deposit their paychecks at the bank. Some employers even arrange automatic payroll deposits, thereby eliminating the need to go to the bank at all. The employee never sees or deposits cash in these cases (see cartoon).

Less than half of our money supply consists of coins and currency. Most banking transactions entail check or computer deposits and payments.

Frank & Ernest reprinted by permission of Newspaper Enterprise Association. Inc.

If checks are used to make deposits, then the supply of checks provides an initial clue about where money comes from. Anyone can buy blank checks and sign them, of course. But banks won't cash checks without some assurance that there are funds in a bank to make the check good. Banks, in fact, hold checks for a few days to confirm the existence of sufficient account balances to cover the checks. Likewise, retailers won't accept checks unless they get some deposit confirmation or personal identification. The constraint on check writing, then, is not the supply of paper but the availability of transactions-account balances.

Like a good detective novel, the search for the origins of money seems to be going in a circle. It appears that transactions-account deposits come from transactions-account balances. This seeming riddle suggests that money creates money. But it offers no clue to us to how the money got there in the first place. Who created the first transactions-account balance? What was used as a deposit?

The solution to this mystery is totally unexpected: banks themselves create money. They don't print dollar bills. But they do make loans. The loans, in turn, become transactions-account balances and therefore part of the money supply. This is the answer to the riddle. Quite simply, ***in making a loan, a bank effectively creates money, because transactions-account balances are counted as part of the money supply.*** And you are free to spend that money, just as if you had earned it yourself.

To understand where money comes from, then, we must recognize two basic principles:

- Transactions-account balances are the largest part of the money supply.
- Banks create transactions-account balances by making loans.

In the following two sections we shall examine this process of creating money—**deposit creation**—more closely.

deposit creation The creation of transactions deposits by bank lending.

A Monopoly Bank

Suppose, to keep things simple, that there is only one bank in town, University Bank, and no one regulates bank behavior. Imagine also that you have been saving some of your income by putting loose change into a piggy bank. Now, after months of saving, you break the bank and discover that your thrift has yielded $100. You immediately deposit this money in a new checking account at University Bank.

Your initial deposit will have no immediate effect on the money supply (M1). The coins in your piggy bank were already counted as part of the money supply, because they represented cash held by the public. ***When you deposit cash or coins in a bank, you are changing the composition of the money supply, not its size.*** The public (you) now holds $100 less of coins but $100 more of transactions deposits. Accordingly, no money is lost or created by the demise of your piggy bank (the initial deposit).

What will University Bank do with your deposit? Will it just store the coins in its safe until you withdraw them (in person or by check)? That doesn't seem very likely. After all, banks are in business to earn a profit. And University Bank won't make much profit just storing your coins. To earn a profit on your deposit, University Bank will have to put your money to work. This means using your deposit as the basis for making a loan to someone else—someone who is willing to pay the bank interest for the use of money.

Typically, a bank does not have much difficulty finding someone who wants to borrow money. Many firms and individuals have expenditure desires that exceed their current money balances. These market participants are eager to borrow whatever funds banks are willing to lend. The question is, how much money can a bank lend? Can it lend your entire deposit? Or must University Bank keep some of your coins in reserve, in case you want to withdraw them? The answer may surprise you.

An Initial Loan Suppose that University Bank decided to lend the entire $100 to Campus Radio. Campus Radio wants to buy a new antenna but doesn't have any money in its own checking account. To acquire the antenna, Campus Radio must take out a loan from University Bank.

When University Bank agrees to lend Campus Radio $100, it does so by crediting the account of Campus Radio. Instead of giving Campus Radio $100 cash, University Bank simply adds $100 to Campus Radio's checking-account balance. That is to say, the loan is made with a simple bookkeeping entry.

This simple bookkeeping entry is the key to creating money. At the very moment University Bank lends $100 to the Campus Radio account, it creates money. Keep in mind that transactions deposits are counted as part of the money supply. Once the $100 loan is credited to its account, Campus Radio can use this new money to purchase its desired antenna, without worrying that its check will bounce.

Or can it? Once University Bank grants a loan to Campus Radio, both you and Campus Radio have $100 in your checking accounts to spend. But the bank is holding only $100 of **reserves** (your coins). In other words, the increased checking-account balance obtained by Campus Radio does not limit your ability to write checks. There has been a net *increase* in the value of transactions deposits, but no increase in bank reserves.

bank reserves Assets held by a bank to fulfill its deposit obligations.

Using the Loan What happens if Campus Radio actually spends the $100 on a new antenna? Won't this use up all the reserves held by the bank, and endanger your check-writing privileges? The answer is no.

Consider what happens when Atlas Antenna receives the check from Campus Radio. What will Atlas do with the check? Atlas could go to University Bank and exchange the check for $100 of cash (your coins). But Atlas probably doesn't have any immediate need for cash. Atlas may prefer to deposit the check in its own checking account at University Bank (still the only bank in town). In this way, Atlas not only avoids the necessity of going to the bank (it can deposit the check by mail), but also keeps its money in a safe place. Should Atlas later want to spend the money, it can simply write a check. In the meantime, the bank continues to hold its entire reserves (your coins) and both you and Atlas have $100 to spend.

Fractional Reserves Notice what has happened here. The money supply has increased by $100 as a result of deposit creation (the loan to Campus Radio). Moreover, the bank has been able to support $200 of transaction deposits (your account and either the Campus Radio or Atlas account) with only $100 of reserves (your coins). In other words, ***bank reserves are only a fraction of total transactions deposits.*** In this case, University Bank's reserves (your $100 in coins) are only 50 percent of total deposits. Thus the bank's **reserve ratio** is 50 percent—that is,

reserve ratio The ratio of a bank's reserves to its total transactions deposits.

- $\text{Reserve ratio} = \dfrac{\text{bank reserves}}{\text{total deposits}}$

The ability of University Bank to hold reserves that are only a fraction of total deposits results from two facts: (1) people use checks for most transactions, and (2) there is no other bank. Accordingly, reserves are rarely withdrawn from this monopoly bank. In fact, if people *never* withdrew their deposits in cash and *all* transactions accounts were held at University Bank, University Bank would not really need any reserves. Indeed, it could melt your coins and make a nice metal sculpture. So long as no one ever came to see or withdraw the coins, everybody would be blissfully ignorant. Merchants and consumers would just continue using checks, presuming that the bank could cover them when necessary. In this most unusual case, University Bank could continue to make as many loans as it wanted. Every loan made would increase the supply of money.

Reserve Requirements

If a bank could create money at will, if would have a lot of control over aggregate demand. In reality, no private bank has that much power. First of all, there are many banks available, not just a single monopoly bank. Hence ***the power to create money resides in the banking system, not in any single bank.*** Each of the thousands of banks in the system plays a relatively small role.

The second constraint on bank power is government regulation. The Federal Reserve System (the Fed) regulates bank lending. The Fed decides how many loans banks can make with their available reserves. Hence even an assumed monopoly bank could not make unlimited loans with your piggy bank's coins. ***The Federal Reserve System requires banks to maintain some minimum reserve ratio.*** The reserve requirement directly limits the ability of banks to grant new loans.

To see how Fed regulations limit bank lending (money creation), we have to do a little accounting. Suppose that the Federal Reserve had imposed a minimum reserve requirement of 75 percent on University Bank. That means the bank must hold reserves equal to at least 75 percent of total deposits.

A 75 percent reserve requirement would have prohibited University Bank from lending $100 to Campus Radio. That loan would have brought *total* deposits up to $200 (your $100 plus the $100 Campus Radio balance). But reserves (your coins) would still be only $100. Hence the ratio of reserves to deposits would have been 50 percent ($100 of reserves ÷ $200 of deposits). That would have violated the Fed's assumed 75 percent reserve requirement. A 75 percent reserve requirement means that University Bank must hold at all times **required reserves** equal to 75 percent of *total* deposits, including those created through loans.

required reserves The minimum amount of reserves a bank is required to hold by government regulation: equal to required reserve ratio times transactions deposits.

The bank's dilemma is evident in the following equation:

- $\text{Required reserves} = \text{required reserve ratio} \times \text{total deposits}$

To support $200 of total deposits, University Bank would need to satisfy this equation:

$$\text{Required reserves} = 0.75 \times \$200 = \$150$$

But the bank has only $100 of reserves (your coins) and so would violate the reserve requirement if it increased total deposits to $200 by lending $100 to Campus Radio.

University Bank can still issue a loan to Campus Radio. But the loan must be less than $100 in order to keep the bank within the limits of the required reserve formula. Thus ***a minimum reserve requirement directly limits deposit-creation possibilities.***

Excess Reserves

excess reserves Bank reserves in excess of required reserves.

Banks will sometimes hold reserves in excess of the minimum required by the Fed. Such reserves are called **excess reserves** and calculated as

- Excess reserves = total reserves − required reserves

Suppose again that University Bank's only deposit is the $100 in coins you deposited. Assume also a Fed reserve requirement of 75 percent. In this case, the initial ledger of the bank would look like this:

Assets		Liabilities	
Required reserves	$75	Your account balance	$100
Excess reserves	$25		
Total assets (your coins)	$100		

Notice two things in this T-account ledger. First, total assets equal total liabilities. This must always be the case, because someone must own every asset. Second, the bank has $25 of excess reserves. It is *required* to hold only $75; the remainder of its reserves ($25) are thus excess.

This bank is not fully using its lending capacity. ***So long as a bank has excess reserves, it can make additional loans.*** If it does, the nation's money supply will increase.

A Multibank World

In reality, there is more than one bank in town. Hence any loan University Bank makes may end up as a deposit in another bank rather than at its own. This complicates the arithmetic of deposit creation but doesn't change its basic character. Indeed, the existence of a multibank system makes the money-creation process even more powerful.

In a multibank world, ***the key issue is not how much excess reserves any specific bank holds but how much excess reserves exist in the entire banking system.*** If excess reserves exist anywhere in the system, then some banks still have unused lending authority.

The Money Multiplier

Excess reserves are the source of bank lending authority. If there are no excess reserves in the banking system, banks can't make any more loans.

Although an *absence* of excess reserves precludes further lending activity, the *amount* of excess reserves doesn't define the limit to further loans.

This surprising conclusion emerges from the way a multibank system works. Consider again what happens when someone borrows all of a bank's excess reserves. Suppose University Bank uses its $25 excess reserves to support a loan. If someone borrows that much money from University Bank, those excess reserves will be depleted. The money won't disappear, however. Once the borrower *spends* the money, someone else will *receive* $25. If that person deposits the $25 elsewhere, then another bank will acquire a new deposit.

If another bank gets a new deposit, the process of deposit creation will continue. The new deposit of $25 increases the second bank's *required* reserves as well as its *excess* reserves. We're talking about a $25 deposit. If the Federal Reserve minimum is 75 percent, then *required* reserves increase by $18.75. The remaining $6.25, therefore, represents *excess* reserves. This second bank can now make additional loans in the amount of $6.25.

Perhaps you are beginning to get a sense that the process of deposit creation will not come to an end quickly. On the contrary, it can continue indefinitely as loans get made and the loans are spent—over and over again. **Each loan made creates new excess reserves, which help fund the next loan.** This recurring sequence of loans and spending is very much like the income multiplier, which creates additional income every time income is spent. People often refer to deposit creation as the money-multiplier process, with the **money multiplier** expressed as the reciprocal of the required reserve ratio. That is

money multiplier The number of deposit (loan) dollars that the banking system can create from $1 of excess reserves; equal to 1 ÷ required reserve ratio.

- $$\text{Money multiplier} = \frac{1}{\text{required reserve ratio}}$$

The money-multiplier process is illustrated in Figure 13.2. When a new deposit enters the banking system, it creates both excess and required reserves. The required reserves represent leakage from the flow of money, since they cannot be used to create new loans. Excess reserves, on the other hand, can be used for new loans. Once those loans are made, they typically become transactions deposits elsewhere in the banking system. Then some additional leakage into required reserves occurs, and further loans are made. The process continues until all excess reserves have leaked into required reserves. Once excess reserves have all disappeared, the total value of new loans will equal initial excess reserves multiplied by the money multiplier.

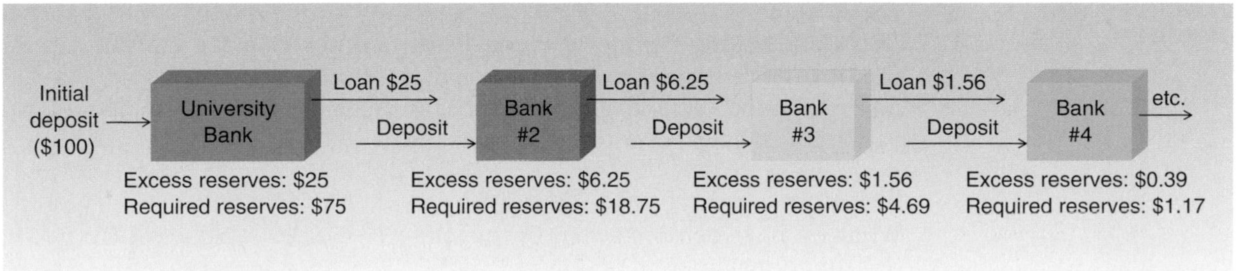

FIGURE 13.2 The Money-Multiplier Process

Each bank can use its excess reserves to make a loan. The loans will end up as deposits at other banks. These banks will then have some excess reserves and lending capacity. Bank #2 can lend 25 percent of the $25 deposit it receives.

Limits to Deposit Creation

The potential of the money multiplier to create loans is summarized by the equation

$$\bullet\ \frac{\text{Excess reserves of}}{\text{banking system}} \times \frac{\text{money}}{\text{multiplier}} = \frac{\text{potential}}{\text{deposit creation}}$$

Notice how the money multiplier worked in our previous example. The value of the money multiplier was equal to 1.33, which is 1.0 divided by the required reserve ratio of 0.75. The banking system started out with the $25 of excess reserves created by your initial $100 deposit. According to the money multiplier, then, the deposit-creation potential of the banking system was

$$\begin{matrix}\text{Excess reserves} \\ (\$25)\end{matrix} \times \begin{matrix}\text{money multiplier} \\ (1.33)\end{matrix} = \begin{matrix}\text{potential deposit} \\ \text{creation } (\$33.25)\end{matrix}$$

If all the banks fully utilize their excess reserves at each step of the money-multiplier process, the banking system could make loans in the amount of $33.25.

Excess Reserves as Lending Power

While you are reviewing the arithmetic of deposit creation, notice the critical role that excess reserves play in the process. A bank can make loans only if it has excess reserves. Without excess reserves, all of a bank's reserves are required, and no further liabilities (transactions deposits) can be created with new loans. On the other hand, a bank with excess reserves can make additional loans. In fact,

- ***Each bank may lend an amount equal to its excess reserves and no more.***

As such loans enter the circular flow and become deposits elsewhere, they create new excess reserves and further lending capacity. As a consequence,

- ***The entire banking system can increase the volume of loans by the amount of excess reserves multiplied by the money multiplier.***

By keeping track of excess reserves, then, we can gauge the lending capacity of any bank or, with the aid of the money multiplier, the entire banking system.

The Macro Role of Banks

The bookkeeping details of bank deposits and loans are complex and often frustrating. But they do demonstrate convincingly that ***banks can create money.*** Since virtually all market transactions involve the use of money, banks must have some influence on macro outcomes.

Financing Aggregate Demand

What we have demonstrated in this chapter is that banks perform two essential functions:

- Banks transfer money from savers to spenders by lending funds (reserves) held on deposit.
- The banking system creates additional money by making loans in excess of total reserves.

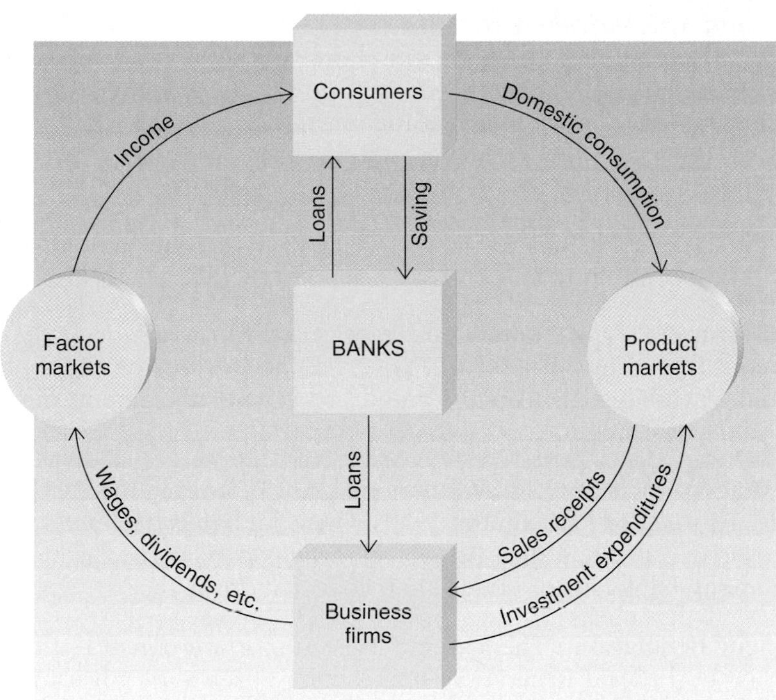

FIGURE 13.3
Banks in the Circular Flow

Banks help to transfer income from savers to spenders. They do this by using their deposits to make loans to business firms and consumers who desire to spend more money than they have. By lending money, banks help to maintain any desired rate of aggregate spending.

In performing these two functions, banks change not only the size of the money supply but aggregate demand as well. The loans banks offer to their customers will be used to purchase new cars, homes, business equipment, and other output. All of these purchases will add to aggregate demand. Hence ***increases in the money supply tend to increase aggregate demand.***

When banks curtail their lending activity, the opposite occurs. People can't get the loans or credit they need to finance desired consumption or investment. As a result, ***aggregate demand declines when the money supply shrinks.***

The central role of the banking system in the economy is emphasized in Figure 13.3. In this depiction of the circular flow, income flows from product markets through business firms to factor markets and returns to consumers in the form of disposable income. Consumers spend most of their income but also save (don't spend) some of it. This consumer saving could pose a problem for the economy if no one else were to step up and buy the goods and services consumers leave unsold.

The banking system is the key link between consumer savings and the demand originating in other sectors of the economy. To see how important that link is, imagine that *all* consumer saving was deposited in piggy banks rather than depository institutions (banks) and that no one used checks. Under these circumstances, banks could not transfer money from savers to spenders by holding deposits and making loans. The banks could not create the money needed to boost aggregate demand.

In reality, a substantial portion of consumer saving *is* deposited in banks. These and other bank deposits can be used as the bases of loans, thereby returning purchasing power to the circular flow. Moreover, because the banking system can make *multiple* loans from available reserves, banks don't have to receive all consumer saving in order to carry out their function. On the contrary, ***the banking system can create any desired level of money supply if allowed to expand or reduce loan activity at will.***

Constraints on Money Creation

If banks had unlimited power to create money (make loans), they could control aggregate demand. Their power isn't quite so vast, however. There are four major constraints on their lending activity.

Bank Deposits The first constraint on the lending activity of banks is the willingness of people to keep deposits in the bank. If people preferred to hold cash rather than checkbooks, banks would not be able to acquire or maintain the reserves that are the foundation of bank lending activity.

Willing Borrowers The second constraint on deposit creation is the willingness of consumers, businesses, and governments to borrow the money that banks make available. If no one wanted to borrow any money, deposit creation would never begin.

Willing Lenders The banks themselves may not be willing to satisfy all credit demands. This was the case in the 1930s when the banks declined to use their excess reserves for loans they perceived to be too risky. In the recession of 1990–91 many banks again closed their loan windows.

Government Regulation The last and most important constraint on deposit creation is the Federal Reserve System. In the absence of government regulation, individual banks would have tremendous power over the money supply and therewith all macroeconomic outcomes. The government limits this power by regulating bank lending practices. The levers of Federal Reserve policy are examined in the next chapter.

POLICY PERSPECTIVES

Digital Money

The Internet has created a virtual mall that millions of people visit every day. In 2003 roughly $60 *billion* of goods and services were sold at that mall. Yet, experts say the sales potential of the Internet has barely been tapped. Only a tiny fraction of the consumers who browse through the Internet mall actually buy something. As a result, Internet sales remain a very small fraction of gross domestic product.

E-retailers say *money* is the problem. You can't pay cash at the Internet mall. And you can't hand over a check in cyberspace. So the most common forms of money used in bricks-and-mortar malls can't serve as a medium of exchange in electronic malls.

Credit Cards Because cash and checks don't work in cyberspace, almost all Internet purchases are completed with credit cards. But dependence on credit cards limits the potential of e-commerce. To begin with, there is the question of security. Once you transmit your credit card number into cyberspace, you can't be 100 percent confident about its use. There are thousands of credit card thefts on the Internet. Hackers have even broken into databases that were supposed to provide security for credit card transactions.

Consumers also worry about privacy. Retail merchants compile databases on credit card purchasers. They even sell these data files to other merchants, unleashing a barrage of targeted advertising. Consumers don't want those marketing intrusions. And they don't want the world to know how often they visited a pornographic site or purchased sex toys in cyberspace.

E-Payments Dozens of Internet companies have tried to create alternative means of payment for cybershoppers. Some companies offer a quasi-banking service by storing purchasing power that consumers and e-retailers can access. To use this kind of e-cash, retailers have to install new software. Consumers must deposit e-cash with credit card advances. Digital "wallets" are a slight variation of digital cash. With wallets, however, the merchant actually receives a direct credit card charge rather than a form of Internet currency. Other companies simply act as umpires for specific purchases, holding final payment (via credit card) until the buyer is satisfied with the purchase.

Speed of Spending All of these digital means of payment are designed to make cyberspending faster and easier. When the credit card bills come due, however, consumers will still need real money (cash and checking-account balances) to pay for their purchases. Hence the amount of money available still counts; even in cyberspace. With easier and more secure payment mechanisms, however, virtual malls will allow consumers to spend money balances *faster,* thereby boosting aggregate demand.

SUMMARY

- In a market economy, money serves a critical function in facilitating exchanges and specialization, thus permitting increased output. "Money" in this context may refer to anything that serves as a medium of exchange, store of value, and standard of value.
- The most common measure of the money supply (M1) includes both cash and balances people hold in transactions accounts (e.g., checking, NOW, and ATS accounts).
- Banks have the power to create money simply by making loans. In making loans, banks create new transactions deposits, which become part of the money supply.
- The ability of banks to make loans—create money—depends on their reserves. Only if a bank has excess reserves—reserves greater than those required by federal regulation—can it make new loans.
- As loans are spent, they create deposits elsewhere, making it possible for other banks to make additional loans. The money multiplier (1 ÷ required reserve ratio) indicates the total value of deposits that can be created by the banking system from excess reserves.
- The role of banks in creating money includes the transfer of money from savers to spenders as well as deposit creation in excess of deposit balances. Taken together, these two functions give banks direct control over the amount of purchasing power available in the marketplace.
- The deposit-creation potential of the banking system is limited by government regulation. It is also limited by the willingness of market participants to hold deposits or borrow money. At times, banks themselves may be unwilling to use all their lending ability.

Terms to Remember

Define the following terms:

barter	aggregate demand	required reserves
money	deposit creation	excess reserves
transactions account	bank reserves	money multiplier
money supply (M1)	reserve ratio	

Questions for Discussion

1. Do eggs satisfy the three conditions for money? Did barter make it easier or more difficult to go to the movies in Russia? (See Headline on page 297.)
2. If a friend asked you how much money you had to spend, what items would you include in your response?
3. Why aren't credit cards counted as money?
4. Does money have any intrinsic value? If not, why are people willing to accept money in exchange for goods and services?
5. Have you ever borrowed money to buy a car, pay tuition, or for any other purpose? In what form did you receive the money? How did your loan affect the money supply? Aggregate demand?
6. Does the fact that your bank keeps only a fraction of your account balance in reserve make you uncomfortable? Why don't people rush to the bank and retrieve their money? What would happen if they did?
7. If people never withdrew cash from banks, how much money could the banking system potentially create? Could this really happen? What might limit deposit creation in this case?
8. If all banks heeded Shakespeare's admonition "Neither a borrower nor a lender be," what would happen to the supply of money?

Problems

1. What percentage of your monthly spending do you pay with (*a*) cash, (*b*) check, (*c*) credit card, or (*d*) automatic transfers? How do you pay off the credit-card balance? How does your use of cash compare with the composition of the money supply (Figure 13.1)?
2. How large is the money multiplier when the required reserve ratio is 0.05? If the required reserve ratio increases to 0.0667, what happens to the money multiplier?
3. How large a loan can Bank #4 in Figure 13.2 make?
4. What volume of loans can the banking system in Figure 13.2 support? If the reserve requirement were 50 percent, what would the system's lending capacity be?
5. Suppose that an Irish Sweepstakes winner deposits $10 million in cash into her transactions account at the Bank of America. Assume a reserve requirement of 25 percent and no excess reserves in the banking system prior to this deposit. Show the changes on the Bank of America balance sheet when the $10 million is initially deposited.
6. In December 1994, a man in Ohio decided to deposit all of the *8 million* pennies he had been saving for nearly 65 years. (His deposit weighed over 48,000 pounds!) With a reserve requirement of 20 percent, how did his deposit change the lending capacity of
   (*a*) His bank?
   (*b*) The banking system?

Web Activities

1. Log on to www.federalreserve.gov/releases/h3/about.htm and access the latest release.
   (*a*) What is the latest level of required reserves?
   (*b*) Are banks keeping excess reserves?
2. Log on to http://research.stlouisfed.org/fred2 and click on "Monetary Aggregates." What is the average money multiplier for the last two weeks?

3. Log on to www.federalreserve.gov/releases/h3/about.htm and access the latest release.
   (*a*) Calculate excess reserves for the latest month reported.
   (*b*) Assuming a reserve requirement of 0.05, how much additional lending capacity exists in the banking system?
4. Log on to www.federalreserve.gov/releases/h6/about.htm.
   (*a*) How does the Fed define the terms M1, M2, and M3?
   (*b*) Click on the most recent statistical release. What are the most recent estimates for M1, M2, and M3?

Living Econ

How Do I Create Money?

When you hear the words "money creation," your first thought might be of counterfeiting. Certainly it occurs, but in this chapter you learned that the banking system creates money by lending—and it's perfectly legal. Banks take in the deposits of those who save and then lend the dollars to those who spend. The "magic" of money creation occurs because banks can lend out the portion of the deposits they do not hold as required reserves.

What role do you play in this process? Well, each time you deposit dollars into the banking system you allow a bank to lend more dollars. And each time you borrow dollars, to buy a car or pay your college tuition, you contribute to the demand for loans. If you and many others decide to take your money out of the banking system and keep it under a mattress, money creation will shrink. Or, if you and many others decide to stop borrowing money, the money creation process will also be reduced. So, without even thinking about the impact, you and I are likely to influence the amount of money creation and, ultimately, the size of the money supply.

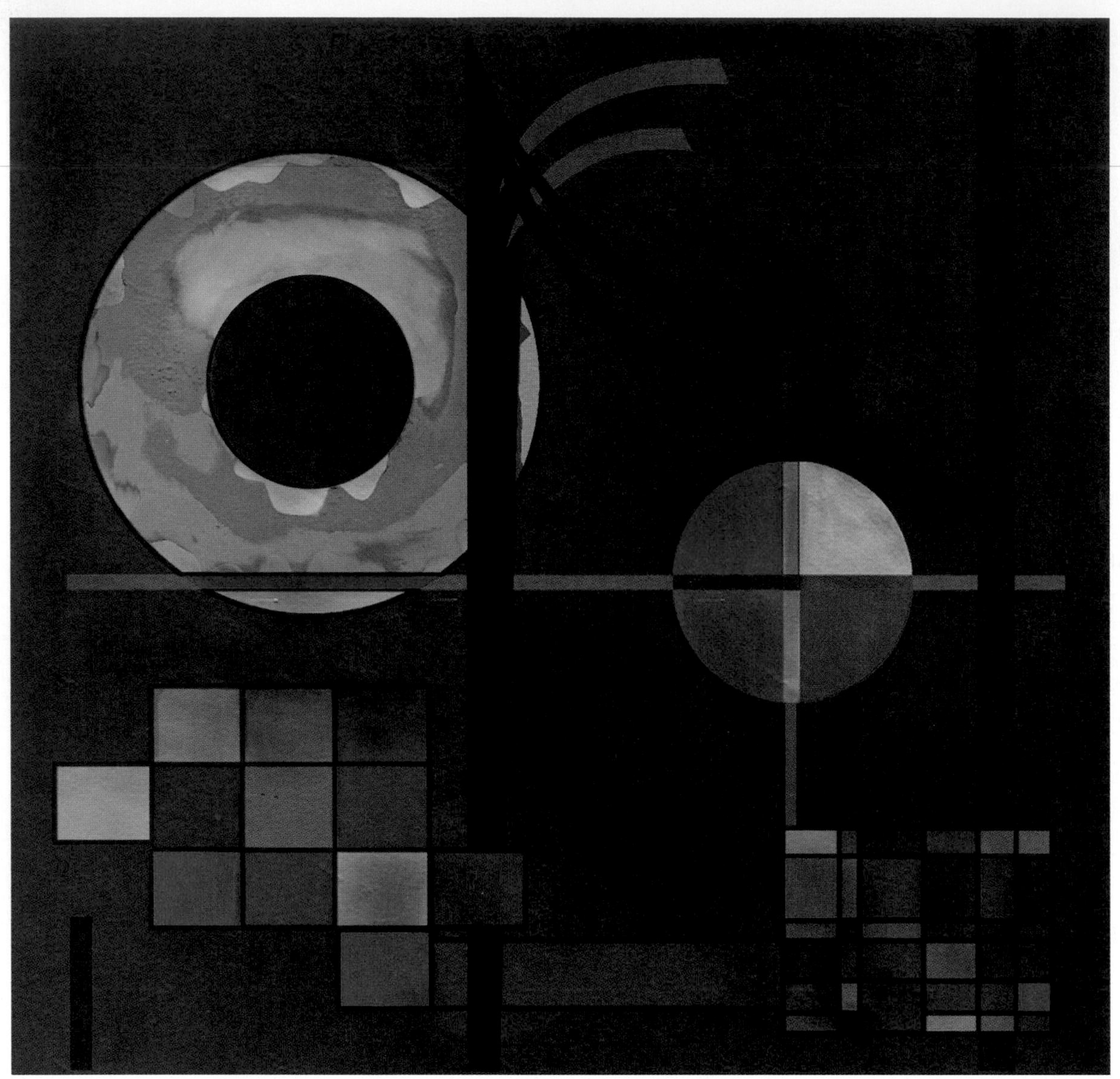

Monetary Policy

CHAPTER 14

Rarely do all the members of a congressional committee attend a committee hearing. But when Alan Greenspan is the witness, all 21 members of the U.S. Senate Committee on Banking, Housing, and Urban Affairs typically show up. So do staffers, lobbyists, and a throng of reporters and camera crews from around the world. They don't want to miss a word that Chairman Greenspan utters.

Tourists visiting the U.S. Capitol are often caught up in the excitement. Seeing all the press and the crowds, they assume some movie star is testifying. Maybe Kim Basinger is protesting animal abuses. Or Lars Ulrich, the drummer for Metallica, is pleading more copyright protection for music. Maybe Michael J. Fox is urging Congress to increase funding for research on Parkinson's disease. Or Clint Eastwood is asking Congress to ease the requirements of the Americans with Disabilities Act. Curious to see who's getting all the attention, the tourists often stand in line to get a brief look into the hearing room. Imagine their bewilderment when they finally get in: the star witness is a balding old man droning on about economic statistics. Who is *this* guy? they wonder, as they head for the exit.

"This guy" is often described as the most powerful person in the U.S. economy. Even the president seeks his advice and approval. Why? Because he is the chairman of the Federal Reserve, the government agency that controls the nation's money supply. As we saw in the previous chapter, changes in the money supply can alter aggregate demand. So whoever has a hand on the money-supply lever has a lot of power over macro economic outcomes. Which explains why so many people want to know what the Fed chairman thinks about the health of the economy.

monetary policy The use of money and credit controls to influence macroeconomic activity.

Why do so many people listen intently to the Fed chairman, Alan Greenspan?
AP/Wide World Photos

Figure 14.1 offers a bird's-eye view of how **monetary policy** fits into our macro model. Clearly, a lot of people think the monetary-policy lever is important. Otherwise, no one would be attending those boring congressional hearings at which the Fed chairman testifies. To understand why monetary policy is so important, we must answer two basic questions:

- How does the government control the amount of money in the economy?
- How does the money supply affect macroeconomic outcomes?

The Federal Reserve System

Control of the money supply in the United States starts with the Fed. The Federal Reserve System is actually a system of regional banks and central controls, headed by a chairman of the board.

Federal Reserve Banks

The core of the Federal Reserve System consists of 12 Federal Reserve banks, located in the various regions of the country. Each of these banks acts as a central banker for the private banks in its region. In this role,

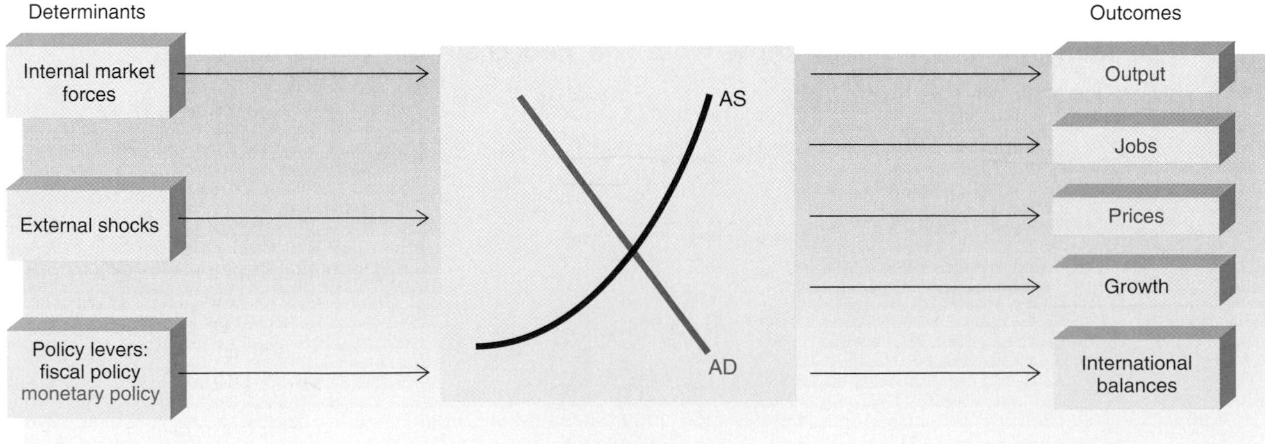

FIGURE 14.1 Monetary Policy

Monetary policy tries to alter macro outcomes by managing the amount of money available in the economy. By changing the money supply and/or interest rates, monetary policy seeks to shift aggregate demand.

the regional Fed banks perform many critical services, including the following:

- ***Clearing checks between private banks.*** Suppose the Bank of America in San Francisco receives a deposit from one of its customers in the form of a check written on a Chase Manhattan bank branch in New York. The Bank of America doesn't have to go to New York to collect the cash or other reserves that support that check. Instead, the Bank of America can deposit the check at its account with the Federal Reserve Bank of San Francisco. The Fed then collects from Chase Manhattan. This vital clearinghouse service saves the Bank of America and other private banks a great deal of time and expense. In view of the fact that over 40 *billion* checks are written every year, this clearinghouse service is an important feature of the Federal Reserve System.
- ***Holding bank reserves.*** What makes the Fed's clearinghouse service work is the fact that the Bank of America and Chase Manhattan both have their own accounts at the Fed. Banks are *required* to hold some minimum fraction of their transactions deposits in reserve. Nearly all of these reserves are held in accounts at the regional Federal Reserve banks. Only a small amount of reserves is held as cash in a bank's vaults. The accounts at the regional Fed banks provide greater security and convenience for bank reserves. They also enable the Fed to monitor the actual level of bank reserves.
- ***Providing currency.*** Because banks hold very little cash in their vaults, they turn to the Fed to meet sporadic cash demands. A private bank can simply call the regional Federal Reserve bank and order a supply of cash, to be delivered (by armored truck) before a weekend or holiday. The cash will be deducted from the bank's own account at the Fed. When all the cash comes back in after the holiday, the bank can reverse the process, sending the unneeded cash back to the Fed.
- ***Providing loans.*** The Federal Reserve banks may also loan reserves to private banks. This practice, called *discounting*, will be examined more closely in a moment.

The Board of Governors

At the top of the Federal Reserve System's organization chart (Figure 14.2) is the Board of Governors. The Board of Governors is the key decision

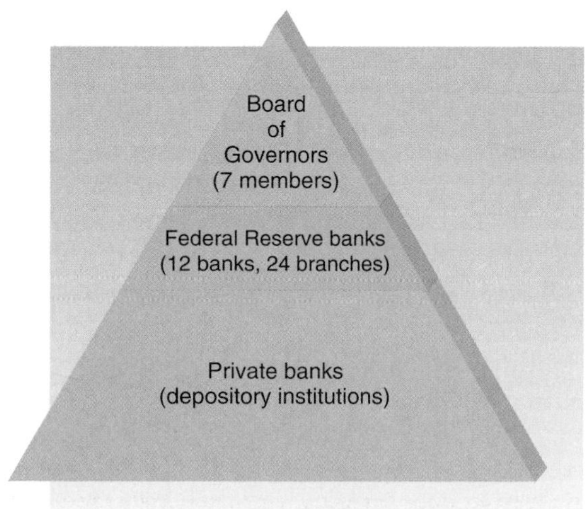

FIGURE 14.2
Structure of the Federal Reserve System

The broad policies of the Fed are determined by the seven-member Board of Governors. Alan Greenspan is the chairman of the Fed Board.

The 12 Federal Reserve banks provide central-banking services to individual banks in their respective regions. The private banks must follow Fed rules on reserves and loan activity.

maker for monetary policy. The Fed Board, located in Washington, D.C., consists of seven members appointed by the president of the United States and confirmed by the U.S. Senate. Board members are appointed for 14-year terms and cannot be reappointed. Their exceptionally long tenure is intended to give the Fed governors a measure of political independence. They are not beholden to any elected official and will hold office longer than any president.

The intent of the Fed's independence is to keep control of the nation's money supply beyond the immediate reach of politicians (especially members of Congress, elected for two-year terms). The designers of the Fed system feared that political control of monetary policy would cause wild swings in the money supply and macro instability. Critics argue, however, that the Fed's independence makes it unresponsive to the majority will.

The Fed Chairman

The most visible member of the Fed system is the Board's chairman. The chairman is selected by the president of the United States for a four-year term. The chairman may be reappointed for additional terms during his or her 14-year term as a governor. President Ronald Reagan first made Alan Greenspan the Fed chairman in 1987 and President George H. Bush reappointed him for another four-year term in 1991. President Clinton appointed him for two more four-year terms (in 1996 and 2000), and President George W. Bush reappointed him for one last term beginning in 2004. As a result, Greenspan has headed the Fed through five separate presidencies.

Monetary Tools

money supply (M1) Currency held by the public, plus balances in transactions accounts.

Our immediate interest is not in the structure of the Federal Reserve System but in the way the Fed can use its powers to alter the **money supply (M1).** ***The basic tools of monetary policy are:***

- ***Reserve requirements***
- ***Discount rates***
- ***Open-market operations***

Reserve Requirements

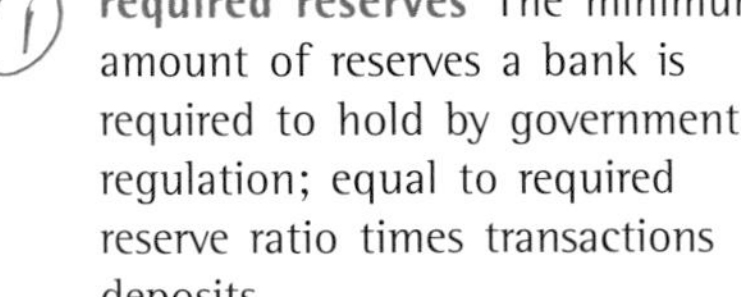

required reserves The minimum amount of reserves a bank is required to hold by government regulation; equal to required reserve ratio times transactions deposits.

In Chapter 13 we emphasized the need for banks to maintain some minimal level of reserves. The Fed requires private banks to keep a certain fraction of their deposits in reserve. These **required reserves** are held either in the form of actual vault cash or, more commonly, as credits (deposits) in the bank's reserve account at a regional Federal Reserve bank.

The Fed's authority to set reserve requirements gives it great power over the lending behavior of individual banks. ***By changing the reserve requirement, the Fed can directly alter the lending capacity of the banking system.***

Recall that the ability of the banking system to make additional loans—create deposits—is determined by two factors: (1) the amount of excess reserves banks hold and (2) the money multiplier—that is

$$\bullet \quad \begin{array}{c}\text{Available lending capacity}\\ \text{of banking system}\end{array} = \text{excess reserves} \times \text{money multiplier}$$

Changes in reserve requirements affect both variables on the right side of this equation, giving this policy tool a one-two punch.

	Required Reserve Ratio	
	25 Percent	20 Percent
1. Total deposits	$100 billion	$100 billion
2. Total reserves	30 billion	30 billion
3. Required reserves	25 billion	20 billion
4. Excess reserves	5 billion	10 billion
5. Money multiplier	4	5
6. Unused lending capacity	$20 billion	$50 billion

TABLE 14.1
The Impact of a Decreased Reserve Requirement

A decrease in the required reserve ratio raises both excess reserves (row 4) and the money multiplier (row 5). As a consequence, changes in the reserve requirement have a huge impact on the lending capacity of the banking system.

The impact of reserve requirements on the first of these variables is straightforward. **Excess reserves** are simply the difference between total reserves and the amount required by Fed rules—that is

excess reserves Bank reserves in excess of required reserves.

- Excess reserves = total reserves − required reserves

Accordingly, with a given amount of total reserves, ***a decrease in required reserves directly increases excess reserves.*** The opposite is equally apparent: an increase in the reserve requirement reduces excess reserves.

A change in the reserve requirement also increases the **money multiplier.** Recall that the **money multiplier** is the reciprocal of the reserve requirement (i.e., 1 ÷ reserve requirement). Hence ***a lower reserve requirement increases the value of the money multiplier.*** Both determinants of bank lending capacity thus are affected by reserve requirements.

money multiplier The number of deposit (loan) dollars that the banking system can create from $1 of excess reserves; equal to 1 ÷ required reserve ratio.

A Decrease in Required Reserves The impact of a decrease in the required reserve ratio is summarized in Table 14.1. In this case, the required reserve ratio is decreased from 25 to 20 percent. Notice that this change in the reserve requirement has no effect on the amount of initial deposits in the banking system (row 1 of Table 14.1) or the amount of total reserves (row 2). They remain at $100 billion and $30 billion, respectively.

What the decreased reserve requirement *does* affect is the way those reserves can be used. Before the increase, $25 billion in reserves was *required* (row 3) leaving $5 billion of *excess* reserves (row 4). Now, however, banks are required to hold only $20 billion (0.20 × $100 billion) in reserves, leaving them with $10 billion in excess reserves. Thus a decrease in the reserve requirement immediately increases excess reserves, as illustrated in row 4 of Table 14.1.

There is a second effect also. Notice in row 5 of Table 14.1 what happens to the money multiplier (1 ÷ reserve ratio). Previously it was 4 (= 1 ÷ 0.25); now it is 5 (= 1 ÷ 0.20). Consequently, a lower reserve requirement not only increases excess reserves but boosts their lending power as well.

A change in the reserve requirement, therefore, hits banks with a double whammy. ***A change in the reserve requirement causes***

- ***A change in excess reserves.***
- ***A change in the money multiplier.***

These changes lead to a sharp rise in bank lending power. Whereas the banking system initially had the power to increase the volume of loans by only $20 billion (= $5 billion of excess reserves × 4), it now has $50 billion (= $10 billion × 5) of unused lending capacity, as noted in the last row of Table 14.1.

HEADLINE RESERVE REQUIREMENTS

Central Bank in China Raises Reserve Requirement

Move to curb lending

SHANGHAI—China's central bank has raised the reserve requirement for financial institutions to stem rapid lending growth.

The People's Bank of China (PBOC) said at the weekend that from September 21, the deposit **reserve** ratio would be raised from 6 percent to 7 percent.

The PBOC statement said: "The Chinese economy has had a good start this year . . . but all regulatory departments agree there is an excessive increase in the current monetary lending."

The PBOC said the move was modest and would not cause overall lending to decrease this year. It is viewed as a response to the overheating of some parts of the economy.

Cheng Dinghua, of China Everbright Securities in Shanghai, said the central bank had few options because recent verbal admonishments against excessive lending had proved ineffective, and raising interest rates would have been too blunt an instrument.

He said: "Central bank officials are like reservoir supervisors—if the water flow is excessive for several consecutive months, they get worried about flooding in some areas."

—Richard McGregor

Source: *Financial Times*, August 25, 2003, p. 5.

NOTE: A change in reserve requirements is such a powerful monetary lever that it is rarely used. A change in the reserve requirements immediately changes both the amount of excess reserves and the money multiplier.

Changes in reserve requirements are a powerful weapon for altering the lending capacity of the banking system. The Fed uses this power sparingly, so as not to cause abrupt changes in the money supply and severe disruptions of banking activity. From 1970 to 1980, for example, reserve requirements were changed only twice, and then only by half a percentage point each time (e.g., from 12.0 to 12.5 percent). In December 1990, the Fed lowered reserve requirements, hoping to create enough extra lending power to push the stalled U.S. economy out of recession.

The central bank of China pushed this policy lever in the opposite direction in 2003. Fearful that excessive bank lending was overheating the economy, China *raised* the reserve requirement (see Headline).

The Discount Rate

discount rate The rate of interest charged by the Federal Reserve banks for lending reserves to private banks.

The second tool in the Fed's monetary-policy toolbox is the **discount rate.** This is the interest rate the Fed charges for *lending* reserves to private banks.

To understand how this policy tool is used, you have to recognize that banks are profit seekers. They don't want to keep idle reserves; they want to use all available reserves to make interest-bearing loans. In their pursuit of profits, banks try to keep reserves at or close to the bare minimum established by the Fed. In fact, banks have demonstrated an uncanny ability to keep their reserves close to the minimum federal requirement. As Figure 14.3 illustrates, the only time banks held huge excess reserves was in the Great Depression of the 1930s. Banks didn't want to make any more loans during the Depression and were fearful of panicky customers withdrawing their deposits.

Because banks continually seek to keep excess reserves at a minimum, they run the risk of occasionally falling below reserve requirements. A large borrower may be a little slow in repaying a loan, or deposit withdrawals may exceed expectations. At such times a bank may find that it doesn't have enough reserves to satisfy Fed requirements.

Banks could ensure continual compliance with reserve requirements by maintaining large amounts of excess reserves. But that is an unprofitable

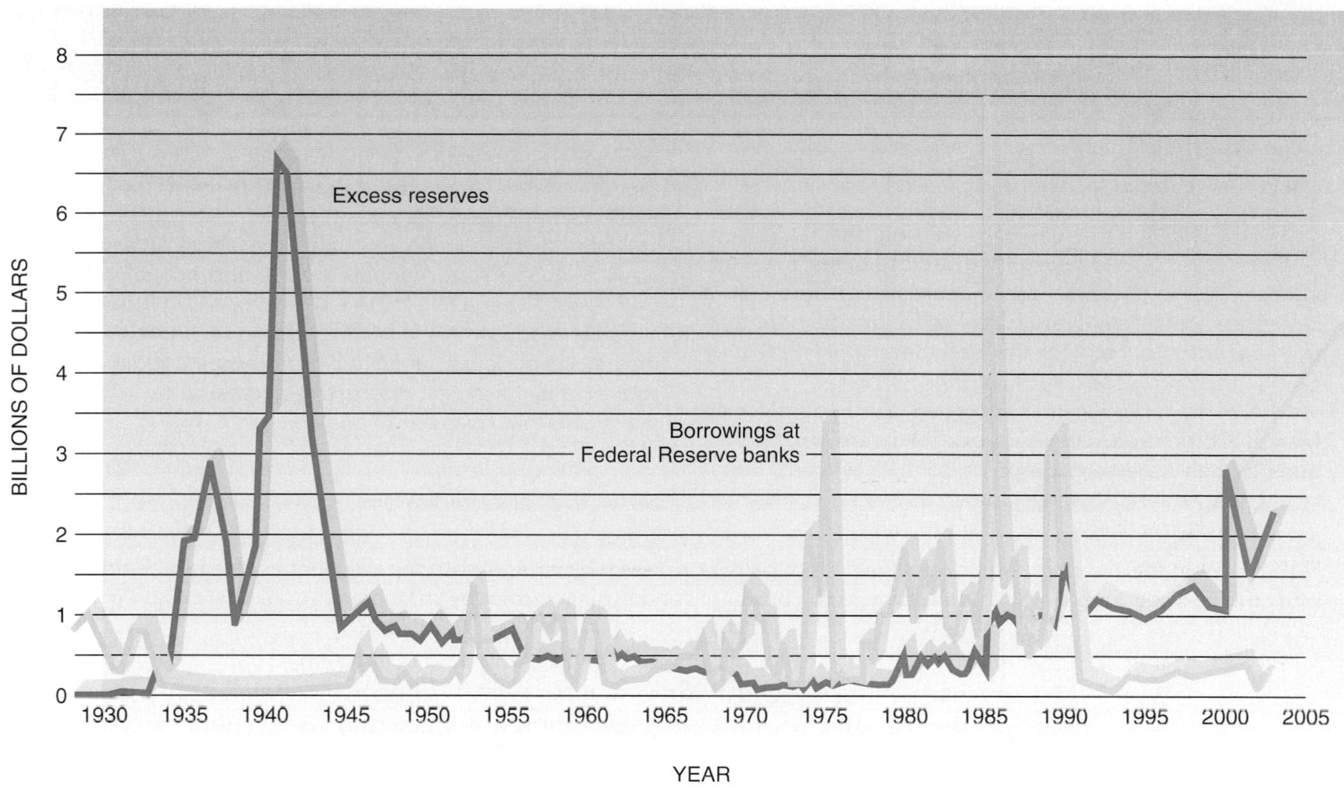

FIGURE 14.3 Excess Reserves and Borrowings

Excess reserves represent unused lending capacity. Hence banks strive to keep excess reserves at a minimum. The one exception to this practice occurred in the Great Depression, when banks were hesitant to make any loans.

In trying to minimize excess reserves, banks occasionally fall short of required reserves. At such times they may borrow from other banks (the federal funds market) or they may borrow reserves from the Fed. Borrowing from the Fed is called *discounting*.

Source: Federal Reserve System.

procedure. On the other hand, a strategy of maintaining minimum reserves runs the risk of violating Fed rules. Banks can pursue this strategy only if they have some last-minute source of extra reserves.

Federal Funds Market There are three possible sources of last-minute reserves. A bank that finds itself short of reserves can turn to other banks for help. If a reserve-poor bank can borrow some reserves from a reserve-rich bank, it may be able to bridge its temporary deficit and satisfy the Fed. Interbank borrowing is referred to as the *federal funds market*.

Securities Sales Another option available to reserve-poor banks is the sale of securities. Banks use some of their excess reserves to buy government bonds, which pay interest. If a bank needs more reserves to satisfy federal regulations, it may sell these securities and deposit the proceeds at the regional Federal Reserve bank. Its reserve position is thereby increased.

Discounting A third option for avoiding a reserve shortage is to *borrow* reserves from the Federal Reserve System itself. The Fed not only establishes rules of behavior for banks but also functions as a central bank, or banker's bank. Banks maintain accounts with the regional Federal Reserve banks, much the way you and I maintain accounts with a local bank. Individual

HEADLINE DISCOUNT RATES

Fed Cuts Key Rate by Half a Point

Increasingly worried that U.S. economic growth is close to stalling, Federal Reserve officials yesterday cut a key short-term interest rate to its lowest level in more than four decades to help lift the economy over what they called "this current soft spot."

The Fed's top policymaking group, the Federal Open Market Committee, cut its target for overnight interest rates by half a percentage point, to 1.25 percent. Separately, the Federal Reserve Board reduced a companion rate governing what banks pay when they borrow from regional Federal Reserve banks to 0.75 percent, the lowest in the Fed's 89-year history.

Those extraordinarily low rates are a sign of how seriously Fed Chairman Alan Greenspan and other Fed officials regard the failure of the U.S. economy to sustain a stronger recovery this year. They do not expect the economy to slip back into recession, but they are using the only tool at their disposal, interest rate cuts, in an effort to make sure that does not happen.

—John M. Berry

Source: *Washington Post*, November 7, 2002, p. 1.

NOTE: A cut in the discount rate lowers the cost of bank borrowing. By cutting both the discount and federal-funds rates the Fed sought to reduce interest rates to consumers and business, thereby stimulating more spending.

banks deposit and withdraw *reserve credits* from these accounts, just as we deposit and withdraw dollars. Should a bank find itself short of reserves, it can go the Fed's *discount window* and borrow some reserves. This process is called **discounting.** Discounting means the Fed is lending reserves directly to private banks.

discounting Federal Reserve lending of reserves to private banks.

The discounting operation of the Fed provides private banks with an important source of reserves, but not without cost The Fed, too, charges interest on the reserves it lends to banks, a rate of interest referred to as the *discount rate.*

The discount window provides a mechanism for directly influencing the size of bank reserves. ***By raising or lowering the discount rate, the Fed changes the cost of money for banks and therewith the incentive to borrow reserves.*** At high discount rates, borrowing from the Fed is expensive. High discount rates also signal the Fed's desire to restrain money-supply growth. Low discount rates, on the other hand, make it profitable for banks to borrow additional reserves and to exploit one's lending capacity to the fullest. This was the objective of the Fed's November 2002 discount rate reduction (see Headline).

Open-Market Operations

Reserve requirements and discount-window operations are important tools of monetary policy. But they do not come close to open-market operations in day-to-day impact on the money supply. ***Open-market operations are the principal mechanism for directly altering the reserves of the banking system.*** Since reserves are the lifeblood of the banking system, open-market operations have an immediate and direct impact on lending capacity. They are more flexible than changes in reserve requirements, thus permitting minor adjustments to lending capacity (and, ultimately, aggregate demand).

Portfolio Decisions To appreciate the impact of open-market operations, you have to think about the alternative uses for idle funds. Just about everybody has some idle funds, even if they amount to a few measly dollars in your pocket or a minimal balance in your checking account. Other consumers and corporations have great amounts of idle funds, even millions of dollars at any time. What we're concerned with here is what people decide to do with such funds.

People, and corporations, do not hold all of their idle funds in transactions accounts or cash. Idle funds are also used to purchase stocks, build up savings-account balances, and purchase bonds. These alternative uses of idle funds are attractive because they promise some additional income in the form of interest, dividends, or capital appreciation (e.g., higher stock prices).

Hold Money or Bonds? The open-market operations of the Federal Reserve focus on one of the portfolio choices people make—whether to deposit idle funds in transactions accounts or to purchase government bonds. In essence, the Fed attempts to influence this choice by making bonds more or less attractive, as circumstances warrant. It thereby induces people to move funds from banks to bond markets, or vice versa. In the process, reserves either enter or leave the banking system, thereby altering the lending capacity of banks.

Figure 14.4 depicts the general nature of Federal Reserve open-market operations. The process of deposit creation begins when people deposit money in the banking system. They can deposit either cash or checks. They cannot deposit bonds. Hence the size of potential deposits depends on how much of their wealth people hold in the form of money and how much in the form of bonds.

Open-Market Activity The Fed's interest in these portfolio choices originates in its concern over bank reserves. The more money people hold in the form of bank deposits, the greater the reserves and lending capacity of the banking system. If people hold more bonds and smaller bank balances, banks will have fewer reserves and less lending power. Recognizing this, ***the Fed buys or sells bonds in order to alter the level of bank reserves.*** This is the purpose of the Fed's bond market activity. In other words, **open-market operations** entail the purchase and sale of government securities (bonds) for the purpose of altering the flow of reserves into and out of the banking system.

open-market operations Federal Reserve purchases and sales of government bonds for the purpose of altering bank reserves

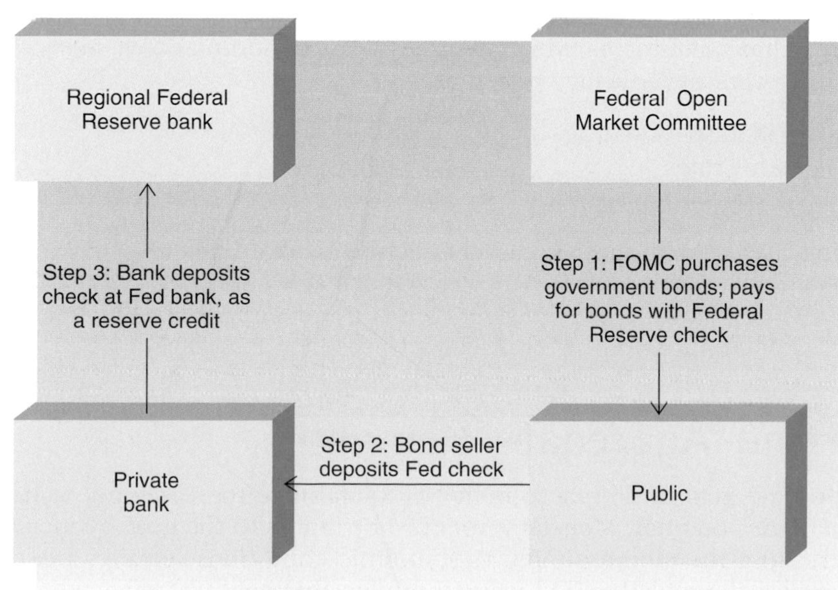

FIGURE 14.4
An Open-Market Purchase

The Fed can increase bank reserves by buying government securities from the public. The Fed check used to buy securities (step 1) gets deposited in a private bank (step 2). The bank returns the check to the Fed (step 3), thereby obtaining additional reserves (and lending capacity).

To decrease bank reserves, the Fed would sell securities, thus reversing the flow of reserves.

Buying Bonds Suppose the Fed wants to increase the money supply. To do so, it must persuade people to deposit a larger share of their financial assets in banks and hold less in other forms, particularly government bonds. How can the Fed do this? The solution lies in bond prices. If the Fed offers to pay a high price for bonds, people will sell some of their bonds to the Fed. They will then deposit the proceeds of the sale in their bank accounts. This influx of money into bank accounts will directly increase bank reserves.

Notice in Figure 14.4 that when the Fed buys a bond from the public, it pays with a check written on itself. The bond seller must deposit the Fed's check in a bank account if she or he wants to use the proceeds or simply desires to hold the money for safekeeping. The bank, in turn, deposits the check at a regional Federal Reserve bank, in exchange for a reserve credit. The bank's reserves are directly increased by the amount of the check. Thus ***by buying bonds, the Fed increases bank reserves.*** These reserves can be used to expand the money supply as banks put their newly acquired reserves to work making loans.

Selling Bonds Should the Fed desire to slow the growth in the money supply, it can reverse the whole process. Instead of offering to *buy* bonds, the Fed in this case will try to *sell* bonds. If it sets the price sufficiently low, individuals, corporations, and government agencies will want to buy them. When they do so, they write a check, paying the Fed for the bonds. The Fed then returns the check to the depositor's bank, taking payment through a reduction in the bank's reserve account. The reserves of the banking system are thereby diminished. So is the capacity to make loans. Thus ***by selling bonds, the Fed reduces bank reserves.***

To appreciate the significance of open-market operations, one must have a sense of the magnitudes involved. The volume of trading in U.S. government securities exceeds \$400 *billion* per day. The Fed alone owned over \$650 billion worth of government securities at the beginning of 2004 and bought or sold enormous sums daily. Thus open-market operations involve tremendous amounts of money and, by implication, potential bank reserves.

Powerful Levers

What we have seen in these last few pages is how the Fed can regulate the lending behavior of the banking system. By way of summary, we observe that the three levers of monetary policy are

- Reserve requirements
- Discount rates
- Open-market operations

By using these levers, the Fed can change the level of bank reserves and their lending capacity. Since bank loans are the primary source of new money, ***the Fed has effective control of the nation's money supply.*** The question then becomes, what should the Fed do with this policy lever?

Shifting Aggregate Demand

The ultimate goal of all macro policy is to stabilize the economy at its full-employment potential. Monetary policy contributes to the goal by increasing or decreasing the money supply as economic conditions require. Table 14.2 summarizes the tools the Fed uses to pursue this goal.

Problem	Solution	Policy Tools
Unemployment (slow GDP growth)	Increase aggregate demand	Buy bonds Lower discount rate Reduce reserve requirement
Inflation (excessive GDP growth)	Decrease aggregate demand	Sell bonds Raise discount rate Increase reserve requirement

TABLE 14.2
Monetary Policy Guidelines

Monetary policy works by increasing or decreasing aggregate demand, as macro conditions warrant. The tools for shifting AD include open-market bond activity, the discount rate, and bank reserve requirements.

Expansionary Policy

Suppose the economy is in recession, producing less than its full-employment potential. Such a situation is illustrated by the equilibrium point E_1 in Figure 14.5. The objective in this situation is to stimulate the economy, increasing the rate of output from Q_1 to Q_F.

We earlier saw how fiscal policy can help bring about the desired expansion. Were the government to increase its own spending, **aggregate demand** would shift to the right. A tax cut would also stimulate aggregate demand by giving consumers and business more disposable income to spend.

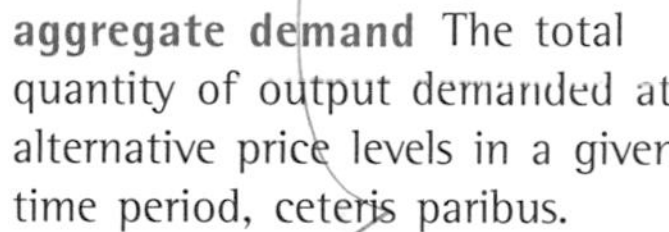

aggregate demand The total quantity of output demanded at alternative price levels in a given time period, ceteris paribus.

Monetary policy may be used to shift aggregate demand as well. If the Fed lowers reserve requirements, drops the discount rate, or buys more bonds, it will increase bank lending capacity. The banks in turn will try to use that expanded capacity and make more loans. By offering lower interest rates or easier approvals, the banks can encourage people to borrow and spend more money. In this way, an increase in the money supply will result in a rightward shift of the aggregate demand curve. In Figure 14.5 the resulting shift propels the economy out of recession (Q_1) to its full-employment potential (Q_F).

Restrictive Policy

Monetary policy may also be used to cool an overheating economy. Excessive aggregate demand may put too much pressure on our production capacity. As market participants bid against each other for increasingly scarce goods, prices will start rising.

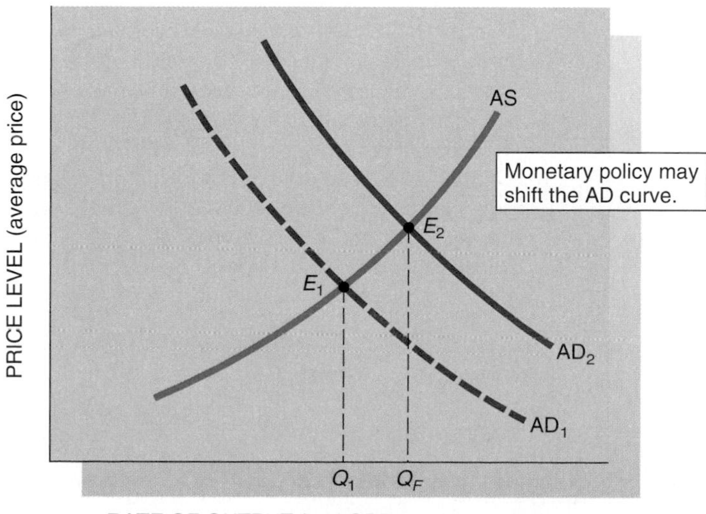

FIGURE 14.5
Demand-Side Focus

Monetary-policy tools change the size of the money supply. Changes in the money supply, in turn, shift the aggregate demand curve. In this case, an increase in M1 shifts demand from AD_1 to AD_2 restoring full employment (Q_F).

Tight monetary policy reduces aggregate demand and inflationary pressures.

The Dropouts—reprinted by permission of Howard Post.

The goal of monetary policy in this situation is to reduce aggregate demand, that is, to shift the AD curve leftward. To do this, the Fed can reduce the money supply by (1) raising reserve requirements, (2) increasing the discount rate, or (3) selling bonds in the open market. All of these actions will reduce bank lending capacity. The competition for this reduced pool of funds will drive up interest rates. The combination of higher interest rates and lessened loan availability will curtail investment, consumption, and even government spending. This was the intent of the Fed's monetary restraint in the spring of 2000 (see Headline). Worried that the U.S. economy was pressing against its production possibilities, the Fed moved to slow money-supply growth and nudge interest rates up a bit. The essence of this restrictive policy is captured in the accompanying cartoon.

HEADLINE MONETARY RESTRAINT

Increases in demand have remained in excess of even the rapid pace of productivity-driven gains in potential supply.

—Federal Open Market Committee

Fed Increases Dosage of Anti-Inflation Medicine

Half-point rate hike signals more aggressive stance as economy refuses to slow

The Federal Reserve's most aggressive interest rate increase in more than five years is a signal that frustrated policymakers have effectively ended their long-running argument about whether they should baby the "new economy." . . .

The Fed frets that the tightest job market in a generation and relentless consumer demand will eventually overwhelm supply, causing wages and inflation to take off. As long as pay and prices were subdued . . . the Fed was content to go slowly.

But recent signs that wages are surging and inflation is beginning to creep up "have added some genuine urgency to the situation," Robertson says. Hence the half-point increase and ominous language from the Fed about what's next.

In the statement accompanying the announcement of the rate increase Tuesday, the Fed said demand has "remained in excess" of the economy's ability to satisfy it, and that policymakers are "concerned" that the problem "will continue."

Analysts now say the Fed won't stop raising rates until it gets hard evidence of a slowdown. Signs would include sharply lower economic growth, stock markets with none of last year's fizz, and a major pullback in the consumer-spending binge that has fueled the economic boom.

—George Hager and Dina Temple-Raston

Source: *USA Today*, May 17, 2000, p. B1.

NOTE: When the Fed fears that aggregate demand is growing too fast, it tries to cool the economy down with higher interest rates.

Price vs. Output Effects

The successful execution of monetary policy depends on two conditions. The first condition is that aggregate demand will respond (shift) to changes in the money supply. The second prerequisite for success is that the aggregate supply curve have the right shape.

Aggregate Demand

The first prerequisite—responsive aggregate demand—usually isn't a problem. An increase in the money supply is typically gobbled up by consumers and investors eager to increase their spending. Only in rare times of economic despair (e.g., the Great Depression of the 1930s) do banks or their customers display a reluctance to use available lending capacity. In such situations, anxieties about the economy may overwhelm low interest rates and the ready availability of loans. If this happens, monetary policy will be no more effective than pushing on a string. In more normal times, however, increases in the money supply can shift aggregate demand rightward.

Aggregate Supply

The second condition for successful monetary policy is not so assured. As we first observed in Chapter 12, an increase in aggregate demand affects not only output but prices as well. How fast prices rise depends on **aggregate supply.** ***Specifically, the effects of an aggregate demand shift on prices and output depend on the shape of the aggregate supply curve.***

aggregate supply The total quantity of output producers are willing and able to supply at alternative price levels in a given time period, ceteris paribus.

Notice in Figure 14.5 what happened to output and prices when aggregate demand shifted rightward. This expansionary monetary policy *did* succeed in increasing output to its full-employment level. In the process, however, prices also rose. The price level of the new macro equilibrium (E_2) is higher than before the monetary stimulus (E_1). Hence the economy suffers from inflation as it moves toward full employment. The monetary-policy intervention is not an unqualified success.

Figure 14.6 illustrates how different slopes of the aggregate supply curve could change the impact of monetary policy. Figure 14.6*a* depicts the shape often associated with Keynesian theory. In Keynes's view, producers would not need the incentive of rising prices during a recession. They would willingly supply more output at prevailing prices, just to get back to full production. Only when capacity was reached would producers start raising prices. In this view, the aggregate supply curve is horizontal until full employment is reached, at which time it shoots up.

The horizontal aggregate supply curve in Figure 14.6*a* creates an ideal setting for monetary policy. If the economy is in recession (e.g., Q_1), expansionary policy (e.g., AD_1 to AD_2) increases output but not prices. If the economy is overheated, restrictive policy (e.g., AD_3 to AD_2) lowers prices but not output. In each case, the objectives of monetary policy are painlessly achieved.

Although a horizontal AS curve is ideal, there is no guarantee that producers and workers will behave in that way. The relevant AS curve is the one that mirrors producer behavior. Economists are in disagreement, however, about the true shape of the AS curve.

Figure 14.6*b* illustrates a different theory about the shape of the AS curve, a theory that gives the Fed nightmares. The AS curve is completely vertical in this case. The argument here is that the quantity of goods produced is primarily dependent on production capacity, labor-market efficiency, and other structural forces. These structural forces establish a natural rate of

FIGURE 14.6
Contrasting Views of Aggregate Supply

The impact of increased demand on output and prices depends on the shape of the aggregate supply curve.

(*a*) **Horizontal AS** In the simple Keynesian model, the rate of output responds fully and automatically to increases in demand until full employment (Q_F) is reached. If demand increases from AD_1 to AD_2, output will expand from Q_1 to Q_F without any inflation. Inflation becomes a problem only if aggregate demand increases beyond capacity—to AD_3, for example.

(*b*) **Vertical AS** Some critics assert that changes in the money supply affect prices but not output. They regard aggregate supply as a fixed rate of output, positioned at the long-run, "natural" rate of unemployment (here noted as Q_N). Accordingly, a shift of demand (from AD_4 to AD_5) can affect only the price level (from P_4 to P_5).

(*c*) **Sloped AS** The eclectic view concedes that the AS curve may be horizontal at low levels of output and vertical at capacity. In the middle, however, the AS curve is upward-sloping. In this case, both prices and output are affected by monetary policy.

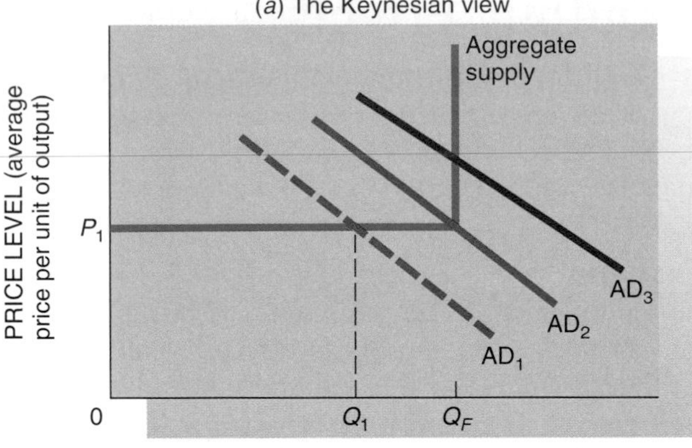

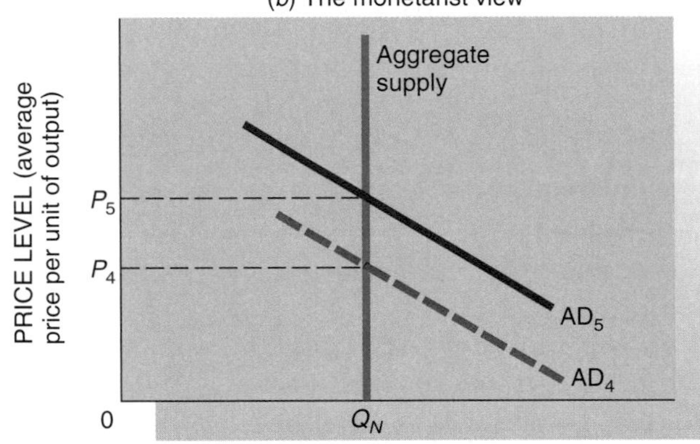

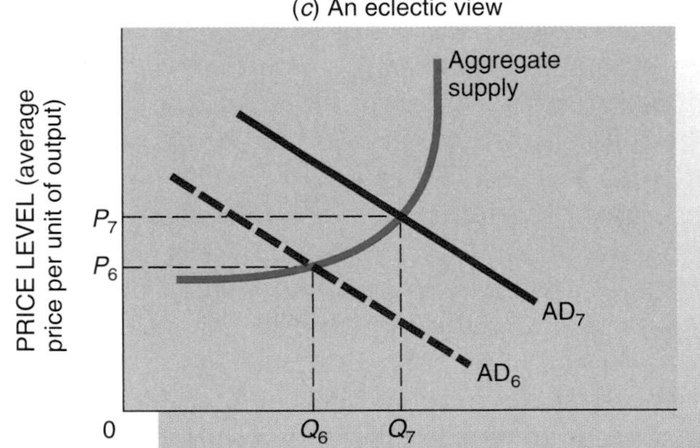

unemployment that is fairly immune to short-run policy intervention. From this perspective, there is no reason for producers to depart from this natural rate of output when the money supply increases. Producers are smart enough to know that both prices and costs will rise when spending increases. Hence rising prices will not create any new profit incentives for increasing output. Firms will just continue producing at the natural rate, with higher (nominal) prices and costs. As a result, increases in aggregate demand (e.g., AD_4 to AD_5) are not likely to increase output levels. Expansionary monetary policy only causes inflation in this case; the rate of output is unaffected.

The third picture in Figure 14.6 is much brighter. The AS curve in Figure 14.6*c* illustrates a middle ground between the other two extremes. This upward-sloping AS curve renders monetary policy effective but not perfectly so. ***With an upward-sloping AS curve, expansionary policy causes some inflation and restrictive policy causes some unemployment.*** There are no clear-cut winners or losers here. Rather, monetary (and fiscal) policy confronts a tradeoff between the goals of full employment and price stability.

Many economists believe Figure 14.6*c* best represents market behavior. The Keynesian view (horizontal AS) assumes more restraint in raising prices and wages than seems plausible. The monetarist vision (vertical AS) assumes instantaneous wage and price responses. The eclectic view (upward-sloping AS), on the other hand, recognizes that market behavior responds gradually and imperfectly to policy interventions.

POLICY PERSPECTIVES

Fixed Rules or Discretion?

The debate over the shape of the aggregate supply curve spotlights a central policy debate. Should the Fed try to fine-tune the economy with constant adjustments of the money supply? Or should the Fed instead simply keep the money supply growing at a steady pace?

Discretionary Policy The argument for active monetary intervention rests on the observation that the economy itself is constantly beset by expansionary and recessionary forces. In the absence of active discretionary policy, it is feared, the economy would tip first one way, then the other. To reduce such instability, the Fed can lean against the wind, restraining the economy when the wind accelerates, stimulating the economy when it stalls. This view of market instability and the attendant need for active government intervention reflects the Keynesian perspective. Applied to monetary policy, it implies the need for continual adjustments to the money supply.

Fixed Rules Critics of discretionary monetary policy raise two objections. Their first argument relies on the vertical AS curve (Figure 14.6*b*). They contend that expansionary monetary policy inevitably leads to inflation. Producers and workers can't be fooled into believing that more money will create more goods. With a little experience, they'll soon realize that when more money chases available goods, prices rise. To protect themselves against inflation, they will demand higher prices and wages whenever they see the money supply expanding. Such defensive behavior will push the AS curve into a vertical position.

Even if one concedes that the AS curve isn't necessarily *vertical,* one still has to determine how much slope it has. This inevitably entails some guesswork and the potential for policy mistakes. If the Fed thinks the AS curve is less vertical than it really is, its expansionary policy might cause too much inflation. Hence discretionary policy is as likely to cause macro problems as to cure them. Critics conclude that fixed rules for money-supply management are less prone to error. These critics, led by Milton Friedman, urge the Fed to increase M1 by a constant (fixed) rate each year.

The Fed's Eclecticism For a brief period (1979–82) the Fed adopted the policy of fixed money-supply targets. On October 6, 1979, the chairman of the Fed (Paul Volcker) announced that the Fed would begin focusing on the money supply, seeking to keep its growth within tight limits. The Fed's primary goal was to reduce inflation, which was then running at close to 14 percent a year. To slow the inflationary spiral, the Fed decided to limit sharply growth of the money supply.

The Fed succeeded in reducing money-supply growth and the inflationary spiral. But its tight-money policies sent interest rates soaring and pushed the economy into a deep recession (1981–82). Exactly three years after adopting fixed rules, the Fed abandoned them.

Instead of fixed rules for money-supply growth, the Fed then adopted an eclectic combination of (flexible) rules and (limited) discretion. Each year the Fed used to announce targets for money-supply growth. But the targets were very broad and not very stable. At the beginning of 1986, for example, the Fed set a target of 3 to 8 percent growth for M1. That wide target gave it plenty of room to adjust to changing interest rates and cyclical changes. But the Fed actually missed the target by a mile—M1 increased by 15 percent in 1986. In explaining this mile-wide miss to Congress, Chairman Volcker emphasized pragmatism. "Success in my mind." he asserted, "will not be measured by whether or not we meet some preordained, arbitrary target" but by our macroeconomic performance. Since the economy was growing steadily in 1987, and inflation was not increasing, he concluded that monetary policy had been a success. He ended his testimony by telling Congress that the Fed would no longer set targets for M1 but would instead keep an eye on broader money-supply measures and interest rates. In other words, the Fed would do whatever it thought necessary to promote price stability and economic growth.

Alan Greenspan is committed to the same brand of eclecticism. In early 1992, he refused to set a target for growth of the narrowly defined money supply (M1) and set very wide targets (2.5–6.5 percent) for broader measures of the money supply (M2). He wanted to stimulate the economy but also to keep a rein on inflation. To achieve this balancing act, Greenspan proclaimed that the Fed could not be bound to any one theory but must instead use a mix of money-supply and interest-rate adjustments to attain desired macro outcomes. So long as the economy continued growing, no one demanded a more specific policy plan. When the Fed's monetary restraint appeared to derail economic growth in 2000, however, critics again questioned how much discretion the Fed should have. They said the Fed was as responsible as anyone for the subsequent recession (March–November 2001). Less guesswork, they concluded, might be safer.

SUMMARY

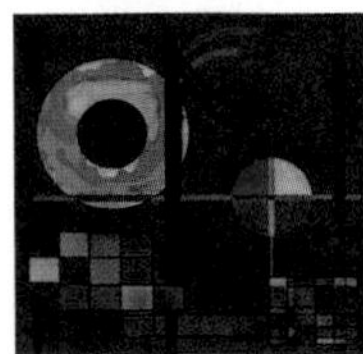

- The Federal Reserve System controls the nation's money supply by regulating the loan activity (deposit creation) of private banks (depository institutions).
- The core of the Federal Reserve System is the 12 regional Federal Reserve banks, which provide check-clearance, reserve deposit, and loan (discounting) services to individual banks. Private banks are required to maintain minimum reserves on deposit at one of the regional Federal Reserve banks.

- The general policies of the Fed are set by its Board of Governors. The Board's chairman is selected by the U.S. president and confirmed by Congress. The chairman serves as the chief spokesperson for monetary policy.
- The Fed has three basic tools for changing the money supply: reserve requirements, discount rates, and open-market operations (buying and selling of Treasury bonds). With these tools, the Fed can change bank reserves and their lending capacity.
- Changes in the money supply directly affect aggregate demand. Increases in M1 shift the aggregate demand curve rightward; decreases shift it to the left.
- The impact of monetary policy on macro outcomes depends on the slope of the aggregate supply curve. If the AS curve has an upward slope, a tradeoff exists between the goals of full employment and price stability.
- Advocates of discretionary monetary policy say the Fed must counter market instabilities. Advocates of fixed policy rules warn that discretionary policy may do more harm than good.

Terms to Remember

Define the following terms:

monetary policy	excess reserves	open-market operations
money supply (M1)	money multiplier	aggregate demand
	discount rate	aggregate supply
required reserves	discounting	

Questions for Discussion

1. Why do banks want to maintain as little excess reserves as possible? Under what circumstances might banks desire to hold excess reserves? (*Hint:* see Figure 14.3.)
2. Why do people hold bonds rather than larger savings-account or checking-account balances? Under what circumstances might they change their portfolios, moving their funds out of bonds into bank accounts?
3. If the Federal Reserve banks mailed everyone a brand-new $100 bill, what would happen to prices, output, and income? Illustrate with aggregate demand and supply curves.
4. How does an increase in the money supply get into the hands of consumers? What do they do with it?
5. Is a reduction in interest rates likely to affect spending on pizza? What kinds of spending are sensitive to interest-rate fluctuations?
6. If banks and credit card companies charged *zero* interest, would people spend and invest more? What would inhibit business or consumer borrowing?
7. Which aggregate supply curve in Figure 14.6 does the Fed chairman fear the most? Why?
8. Like all human institutions, the Fed makes occasional errors in altering the money supply. Would a constant (fixed) rate of money-supply growth eliminate errors?

9. Congress sometimes demands more control of monetary policy. Is this a good idea? Why is fiscal policy, but not monetary policy, entrusted to elected politicians?
10. Would you advocate monetary restraint or stimulus for today's economy? Who would disagree with you?

Problems

1. Suppose the following data apply:

Total bank reserves:	$5 billion
Total bank deposits:	$100 billion
Cash held by public:	$10 billion
Bonds held by public:	$220 billion
Stocks held by public:	$140 billion
Gross domestic product:	$5 trillion
Interest rate:	6 percent
Required reserve ratio:	0.04

   (*a*) How large is the money supply?
   (*b*) How much excess reserves are there?
   (*c*) What is the money multiplier?
   (*d*) What is the available lending capacity?

2. Assume that the following data describe the condition of the commercial banking system:

Total reserves:	$200 billion
Transactions deposits:	$800 billion
Cash held by public:	$100 billion
Reserve requirement:	0.20

   (*a*) How large is the money supply (M1)?
   (*b*) Are the banks fully utilizing their lending capacity? Explain.
   (*c*) What would happen to the money supply *initially* if the public deposited another $50 billion in cash in transactions accounts? Explain.
   (*d*) What would the lending capacity of the banking system be after such a portfolio switch?
   (*e*) How large would the money supply be if the banks fully utilized their lending capacity?
   (*f*) What three steps could the Fed take to offset that potential growth in M1?

3. Suppose the Federal Reserve decided to purchase $10 billion worth of government securities in the open market.
   (*a*) How will M1 be affected initially?
   (*b*) How will the lending capacity of the banking system be affected if the reserve requirement is 25 percent?
   (*c*) How will banks induce investors to utilize this expanded lending capacity?

4. Suppose the economy is initially in equilibrium at an output level of 100 and price level of 100. The Fed then manages to shift aggregate demand rightward by 20.
   (*a*) Illustrate the initial equilibrium (E_1) and the shift of AD.

(*b*) Show what happens to output and prices if the aggregate supply curve is (i) horizontal, (ii) vertical, and (iii) upward-sloping.

5. Illustrate the effects on bank reserves of an open-market sale (see Figure 14.4).
6. How did the money multiplier change when China increased its reserve requirement (Headline, p. 318)?

Web Activities

1. Log on to www.federalreserve.gov and read the description of the role of the Federal Reserve System. Summarize the role of the Federal Reserve System from this information.
2. Log on to www.federalreserve.gov/pubs/frseries/frseri.htm and find a description of the current structure of the Federal Reserve System. Summarize the structure of the Federal Reserve System from this information.
3. Log on to www.federalreserve.gov/policy.htm, then click on the Monetary Policy Report to Congress. Click on the most recent report, and access the section on Monetary Policy and Economic Outlook. Read the report and summarize the Fed's perception of the economy and its monetary policy response.
4. Log on to www.federalreserve.gov/releases/h15 and click on the most recent release data. Find the general trend for the federal funds interest rate. What have been the likely actions of the Fed that have caused the interest rates to move in the direction shown?

Living Econ

Why Should I Care about Interest Rates?

Most of us are affected by interest rates. There are your credit card interest rate, your car or student loan interest rate, and the interest rate paid by the bank on your savings account. But there is an even greater reason why you should care about interest rates. When interest rates rise or fall, overall economic growth slows down or speeds up, creating or destroying jobs and raising or lowering inflation.

In this chapter you learned that the Federal Reserve influences interest rates through monetary policy. If interest rates are increased, aggregate demand will decrease, potentially causing lower real GDP and a lower price level. Conversely, with lower interest rates the level of aggregate demand will increase, causing higher real GDP and a rise in the price level.

In the long run, the impact of interest rates on the overall economy, and ultimately your job prospects and purchasing power, will be more important than the immediate impact of interest rates on your loans or savings account. That's why you should pay attention to the Federal Reserve and its decisions.

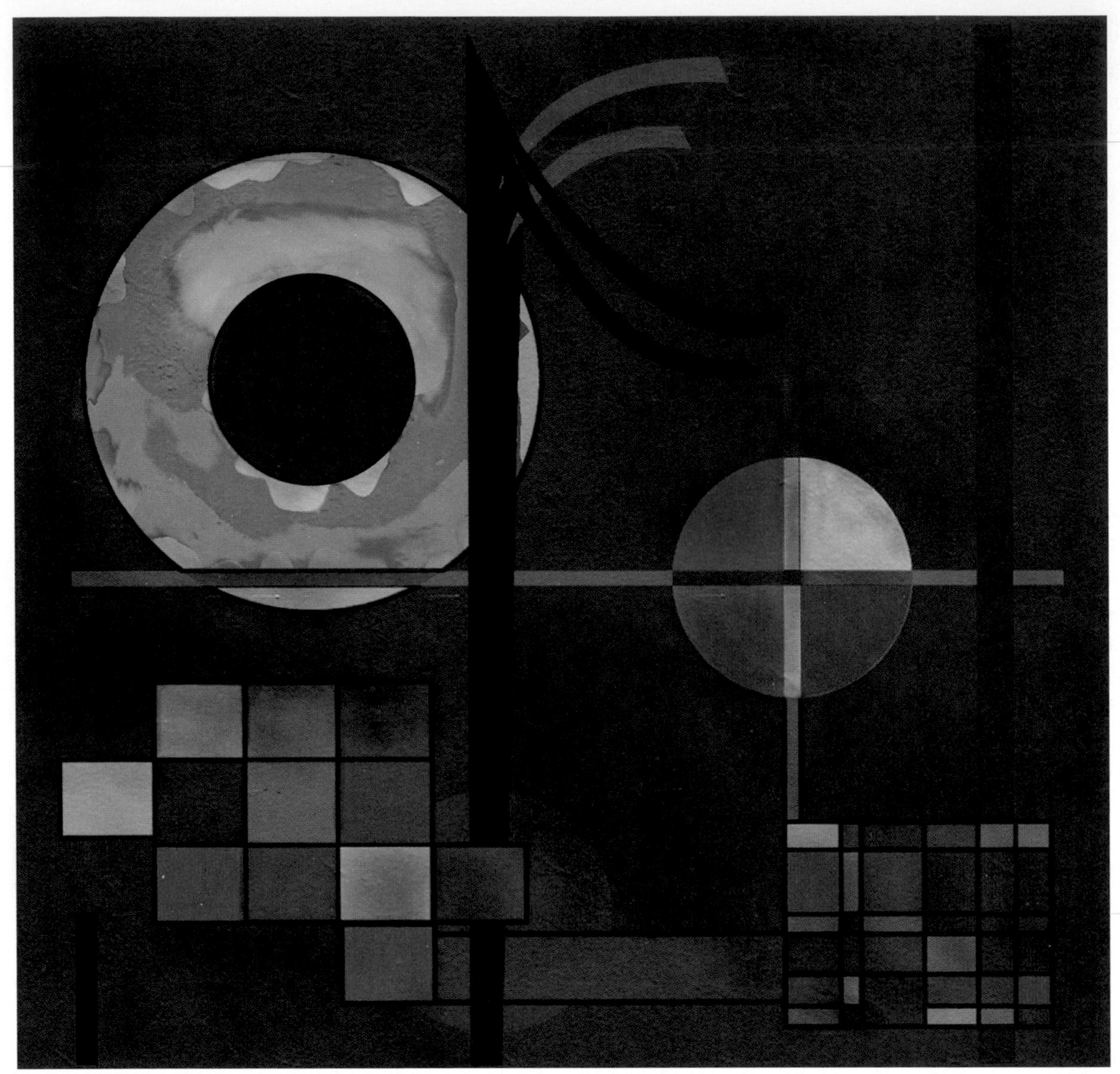

Economic Growth

CHAPTER 15

Economic growth is the fundamental determinant of the long-run success of any nation, the basic source of rising living standards, and the key to meeting the needs and desires of the American people.

—Economic Report of the President, 1992

Twenty-five years ago there were no fax machines, no cellular phones, no satellite TVs, and no DATs. Personal computers were still on the drawing board, and laptops weren't even envisioned. Home video didn't exist, and no one had yet produced microwave popcorn. Biotechnology hadn't yet produced any blockbuster drugs, and people used the same pair of athletic shoes for most sports.

New products are symptoms of our economic progress. Over time, we produce not only *more* goods and services but also *new* and *better* goods and services. In the process, we get richer: our material living standards rise.

Rising living standards are not inevitable, however. According to World Bank estimates, nearly 3 *billion* people—close to half the world's population—continue to live in abject poverty (incomes of less than $3 per day). Worse still, living standards in many of the poorest countries have *fallen* in the last decade. Living standards also fell in Eastern Europe when communism collapsed and a painful transition to market economies began. The former communist-bloc countries are counting on the power of free markets to jump-start their economies and raise living standards.

The purpose of this chapter is to take a longer-term view of economic performance. Most macro policy focuses on the *short-run* variations in output and prices we refer to as business cycles. There are *long-run* concerns as well. As we ponder the future of the economy beyond the next business cycle, we have to confront the prospects for economic growth. In that longer-run context three questions stand out:

- How important is economic growth?
- How does an economy grow?
- What policies promote economic growth?

We develop answers to these questions by first examining the nature of economic growth and then examining its sources and potential.

The Nature of Growth

Economic growth refers to increases in the output of goods and services. But there are two distinct ways in which output increases, and they have very different implications for our economic welfare.

Short-Run Changes in Capacity Use

The easiest kind of growth comes from increased use of our productive capabilities. In any given year there is a limit to an economy's potential output. This limit is determined by the quantity of resources available and our technological know-how. We have illustrated these short-run limits to output with a **production-possibilities** curve, as in Figure 15.1*a*. By using all of our available resources and our best expertise, we can produce any combination of goods on the production-possibilities curve.

production possibilities The alternative combinations of goods and services that could be produced in a given time period with all available resources and technology.

We do not always take full advantage of our productive capacity, however. The economy often produces a mix of output that lies *inside* our production possibilities, like point *A* in Figure 15.1*a*. When this happens, the short-run goal of macro policy is to achieve full employment—to move us from point *A* to some point on the production-possibilities curve (e.g., point *B*). The fiscal- and monetary-policy levers for attaining full employment were the focus of Chapters 12 to 14.

Long-Run Changes in Capacity

As desirable as full employment is, there is an obvious limit to how much additional output we can obtain in this way. Once we are fully utilizing our productive capacity, further increases in output are attainable only if we *expand* that capacity. To do so, we have to *shift* the production-possibilities curve outward, as in Figure 15.1*b*. Such shifts imply an increase in *potential* GDP—that is, our productive capacity.

Over time, increases in capacity are critical. Short-run increases in the utilization of existing capacity can generate only modest increases in output. Even high unemployment rates (e.g., 7 percent) leave little room

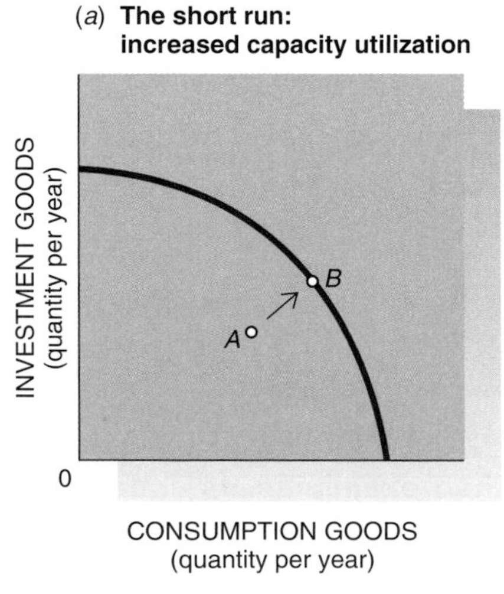

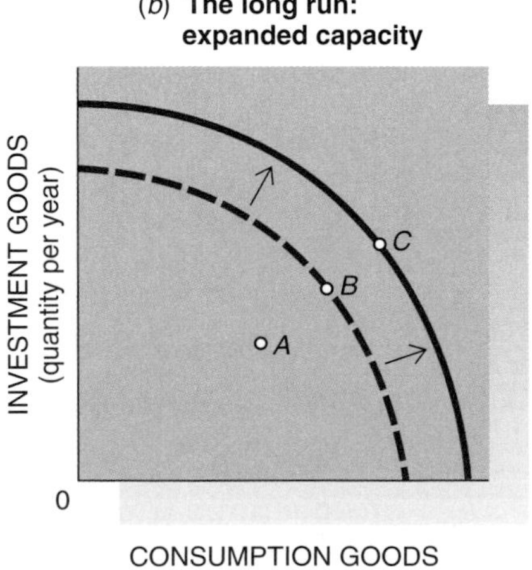

FIGURE 15.1
Two Types of Growth

Increases in output may result from increased use of existing capacity or from increases in that capacity itself. In part *a* the mix of output at point *A* does not make full use of production possibilities. Hence we can grow—get more output—by employing more of our available resources or using them more efficiently. This is illustrated by point *B* (or any other point on the curve).

Once we are on the production-possibilities curve, we can increase output further only by *increasing* our productive capacity. This is illustrated by the outward *shift* of the production-possibilities curve in part *b*.

for increased output. ***To achieve large and lasting increases in output we must push our production possibilities outward.*** For this reason, economists tend to define **economic growth** in terms of changes in *potential* GDP.

economic growth An increase in output (real GDP); an expansion of production possibilities.

Aggregate Supply Focus The unique character of economic growth can also be illustrated with aggregate supply and demand curves. Short-run macro policies focus on aggregate demand. Fiscal- and monetary-policy levers are used to shift the AD curve, trying to achieve the best possible combination of full employment and price stability. As we have observed, however, the aggregate supply (AS) curve sets a limit to demand-side policy. In the short run, the slope of the aggregate supply curve determines how much inflation we have to pay to get more output. In the long run, the position of the AS curve limits total output. To get a long-run increase in output, we must move the AS curve.

Figure 15.2 illustrates the supply-side focus of economic growth. Notice that ***economic growth—sustained increases in total output—is possible only if the AS curve shifts rightward.***

Nominal vs. Real GDP

We refer to *real* GDP, not *nominal* GDP, in our concept of economic growth. **Nominal GDP** is the current dollar value of output—that is, the average price level (*P*) multiplied by the quantity of goods and services produced (*Q*). Accordingly, increases in nominal GDP can result from either increases in the price level or increases in the quantity of output. In fact, nominal GDP can rise even when the quantity of goods and services falls. This was the case in 1991, for example. The total quantity of goods and services produced in 1991 was less than the quantity produced in 1990. Nevertheless, prices rose enough during 1991 to keep nominal GDP growing.

nominal GDP The total value of goods and services produced within a nation's borders, measured in current prices.

Real GDP refers to the actual quantity of goods and services produced. Real GDP avoids the distortions of inflation by valuing output in *constant* prices.

real GDP The inflation-adjusted value of GDP; the value of output measured in constant prices.

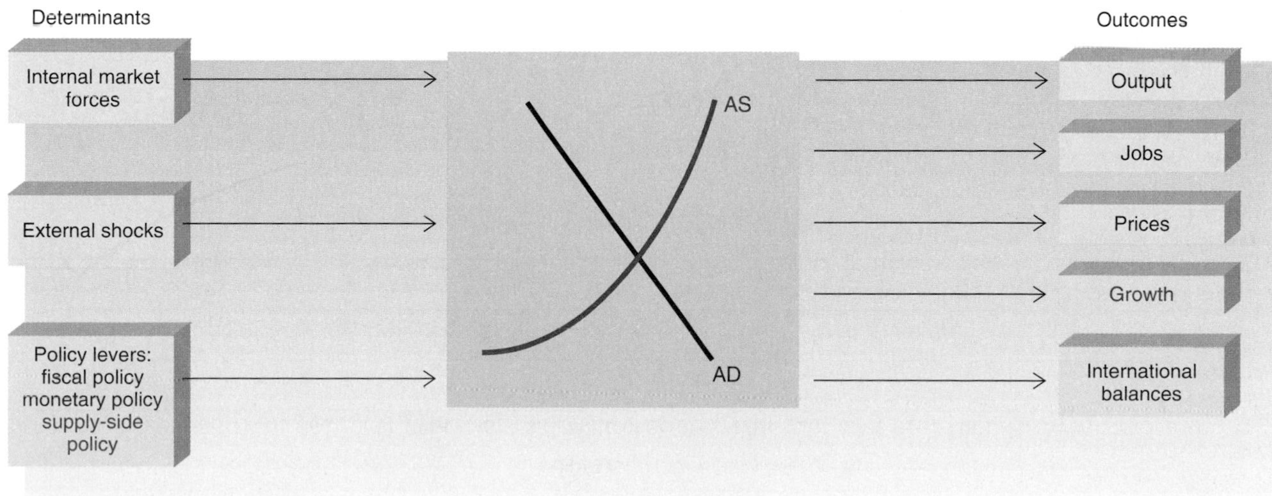

FIGURE 15.2 Supply-Side Focus

Short-run macro policy uses shifts of the aggregate demand curve to achieve economic stability. To achieve long-run *growth,* however, the aggregate supply curve must be shifted as well.

Growth Indexes

The GDP Growth Rate

growth rate Percentage change in real GDP from one period to another.

Typically, changes in real GDP are expressed in percentage terms, as a growth *rate*. The **growth rate** is simply the change in real output between two periods divided by total output in the base period. In 1990, for example, real GDP was \$6.708 trillion when valued in constant prices. Real GDP fell to \$6.676 trillion in 1991, again measured in constant prices. Hence the growth rate between 1990 and 1991 was

$$\text{Growth rate} = \frac{\text{change in real GDP}}{\text{base period GDP}} = \frac{-.032 \text{ trillion}}{6.708 \text{ trillion}} = -0.5\%$$

The negative growth rate in 1991 was far below the long-term average for the United States (just over 3 percent). As Figure 15.3 illustrates, growth rates are usually positive, although they vary greatly from year to year. Years of actual decline in real GDP (e.g., 1974, 1975, 1980, 1982, 1991) are relatively rare. They are a serious setback to economic growth, however, and always lower living standards.

The challenge for the future is to maintain higher rates of economic growth. After the recession of 1990–91, the U.S. economy got back on its long-term growth track. The growth rate even moved a bit above the long-term average for several years (1997–99). As the economy slowed in 2000, however, policymakers were challenged to maintain growth above 3 percent.

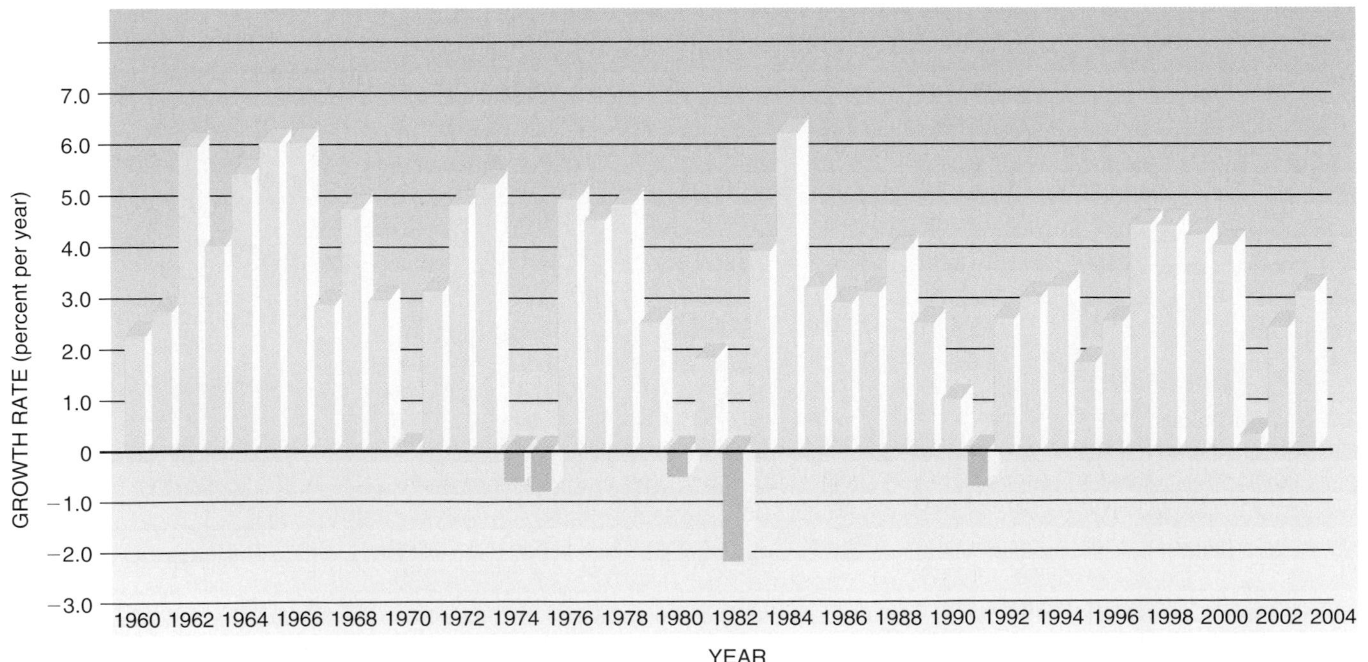

FIGURE 15.3 Recent U.S. Growth Rates

Total output typically increases from one year to another. The focus of policy is on the growth *rate*—that is, how fast real GDP increases from one year to the next. Historically, growth rates have varied significantly from year to year and even turned negative on occasion. The policy challenge is to foster faster, steadier GDP growth. Is this possible?

The Exponential Process At first blush, the challenge of raising the growth rate from 1 or 2 percent to 3 percent may appear neither difficult nor important. Indeed, the whole subject of economic growth looks rather dull when you discover that big gains in economic growth are measured in fractions of a percent. However, this initial impression is not fair. First of all, even one year's low growth implies lost output. Consider the recession of 1991 (see Figure 15.3). If we had just *maintained* the rate of total ouput in 1991—that is, achieved a *zero* growth rate rather than a 0.7 percent decline—we would have had $37 billion more worth of goods and services. That works out to $148 worth of goods and services per person. Lots of people would have liked that extra output.

Second, economic growth is a *continuing* process. Gains made in one year accumulate in future years. It's like interest you earn at the bank. If you leave your money in the bank for several years, you begin to earn interest on your interest. Eventually you accumulate a nice little bankroll.

The process of economic growth works the same way. Each little shift of the production-possibilities curve broadens the base for future GDP. As shifts accumulate over many years, the economy's productive capacity is greatly expanded. Ultimately, we discover that those little differences in annual growth rates generate tremendous gains in GDP.

This cumulative process, whereby interest or growth is compounded from one year to the next, is called an *exponential process*. To get a feel for its impact, consider the longer-run difference between annual growth rates of 3 and 5 percent. In 30 years, a 3 percent growth rate will raise our GDP to $27 trillion (in 2004 dollars). But a 5 percent growth rate would give us $48 trillion of goods and services in the same amount of time. Thus, in a single generation, 5 percent growth translates into a standard of living that is 80 percent higher than 3 percent growth. From this longer-term perspective, little differences in growth rates look very big.

GDP per Capita: A Measure of Living Standards

The exponential process looks even more meaningful when translated into *per capita* terms. **GDP per capita** is simply total output divided by total population. In 2003 the total output of the U.S. economy was roughly $11 trillion. Since there were 286 million of us to share that output, GDP per capita was

GDP per capita Total GDP divided by total population; average GDP.

$$\text{2003 GDP per capita} = \frac{\$11 \text{ trillion of output}}{286 \text{ million people}} = \$38{,}462$$

This does not mean that every man, woman, and child in the United States received $38,462 worth of goods and services in 2003. Rather, it simply indicates how much output was potentially available to the average person.

Growth in GDP per capita is attained only when the growth of output exceeds population growth. In the United States, this condition is usually achieved. In the 1990s our population grew by an average of only 1 percent a year. Hence our average economic growth rate of 3 percent was more than sufficient to ensure steadily rising living standards.

The accompanying Headline illustrates some of the ways rising per capita GDP has changed our lives. In the 20-year period between 1970 and 1990, the size of the average U.S. house increased by a third. Air conditioning went from the exception to the rule. And the percentage of college graduates nearly doubled. Had the economy grown more slowly, we wouldn't have gotten all these additional goods and services.

HEADLINE IMPROVED LIVING STANDARDS

What Economic Growth Has Done for U.S. Families

As the economy grows, living standards rise. The changes are so gradual, however, that few people notice. After 20 years of growth, though, some changes are remarkable. We now live longer, work less, and consume a lot more. Some examples:

	1970	1990
Average size of a new home (square feet)	1,500	2,080
New homes with central air conditioning	34%	76%
People using computers	<100,000	75.9 million
Households with color TV	33.9%	96.1%
Households with cable TV	4 million	55 million
Households with VCRs	0	67 million
Households with two or more vehicles	29.3%	54%
Median household net worth (real)	$24,217	$48,887
Households owning a microwave oven	<1%	78.8%
Heart transplant procedures	<10	2,125
Average workweek	37.1 hours	34.5 hours
Average daily time working in the home	3.9 hours	3.5 hours
Annual paid vacation and holidays	15.5 days	22.5 days
Women in the workforce	31.5%	56.6%
Recreational boats owned	8.8 million	16 million
Manufacturers' shipments of RVs	30,300	226,500
Adult softball teams	29,000	188,000
Recreational golfers	11.2 million	27.8 million
Attendance at symphonies and orchestras	12.7 million	43.6 million
Americans finishing high school	51.9%	77.7%
Americans finishing four years of college	13.5%	24.4%
Employee benefits as a share of payroll	29.3%	40.2%
Life expectancy at birth (years)	70.8	75.4
Death rate by natural causes (per 100,000)	714.3	520.2

Source: Federal Reserve Bank of Dallas, *1993 Annual Report.*

NOTE: Economic growth not only generated more and better output but also improved health and provided more leisure.

It's tempting to take the benefits of growth for granted. But that would be a serious mistake. As Figure 15.4 shows, rising GDP per capita is a relatively new phenomenon in the long course of history. World GDP per capita hardly grew at all for 1,500 years or so. It is only since 1820 that world output has grown significantly faster than the population.

Figure 15.4 also reveals that most of the non-Western world has not enjoyed the robust GDP growth we have experienced. Even today, many poor countries continue to suffer from a combination of slow GDP growth and fast population

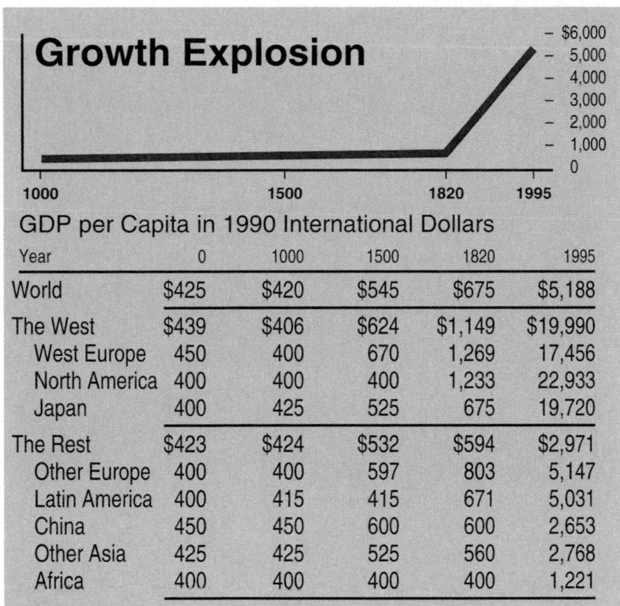

GDP per Capita in 1990 International Dollars

Year	0	1000	1500	1820	1995
World	$425	$420	$545	$675	$5,188
The West	$439	$406	$624	$1,149	$19,990
West Europe	450	400	670	1,269	17,456
North America	400	400	400	1,233	22,933
Japan	400	425	525	675	19,720
The Rest	$423	$424	$532	$594	$2,971
Other Europe	400	400	597	803	5,147
Latin America	400	415	415	671	5,031
China	450	450	600	600	2,653
Other Asia	425	425	525	560	2,768
Africa	400	400	400	400	1,221

FIGURE 15.4
The History of World Growth

GDP per capita was stagnant for centuries. Living standards started rising significantly around 1820. Even then, most growth in per capita GDP occurred in the West.

Source: Angus Maddison, "Poor until 1820," *Wall Street Journal*, January 11, 1999.

growth. Angola, for example, is one of the poorest countries in the world, with GDP per capita of less than $1,700. Yet its population continues to grow more rapidly (3.1 percent per year) than GDP (2.0 percent growth), further depressing living standards. The population of Nigeria grew by 2.9 percent per year in the 1990s, while GDP grew at a slower rate of only 2.5 percent. As a consequence, GDP per capita *declined* by more than 0.4 percent per year. Even that dismal record outstripped Haiti, where GDP itself *declined* by 0.4 percent a year in the 1990s while the population continued to grow at 2 percent a year.

By comparison with these countries, the United States has been most fortunate. Our GDP per capita has more than doubled since Ronald Reagan was president. This means that the average person today has twice as many goods and services as the average person had only a generation ago.

What about the future? Will we continue to enjoy substantial gains in living standards? It all depends on how fast output continues to grow in relation to population. Table 15.1 indicates some of the possibilities. If GDP per capita continues to grow at 2.0 percent per year—as it did in the 1990s—our average income will double again in 36 years.

Growth Rate (percent)	Doubling Time (years)
0.0	Never
0.5	144
1.0	72
1.5	48
2.0	36
2.5	29
3.0	24
3.5	21
4.0	18
4.5	16
5.0	14

TABLE 15.1
The Rule of 72

Small differences in annual growth rates cumulate into large differences in GDP. Shown here are the number of years it would take to double GDP at various growth rates.

Doubling times can be approximated by the rule of 72. Seventy-two divided by the growth rate equals the number of years it takes to double.

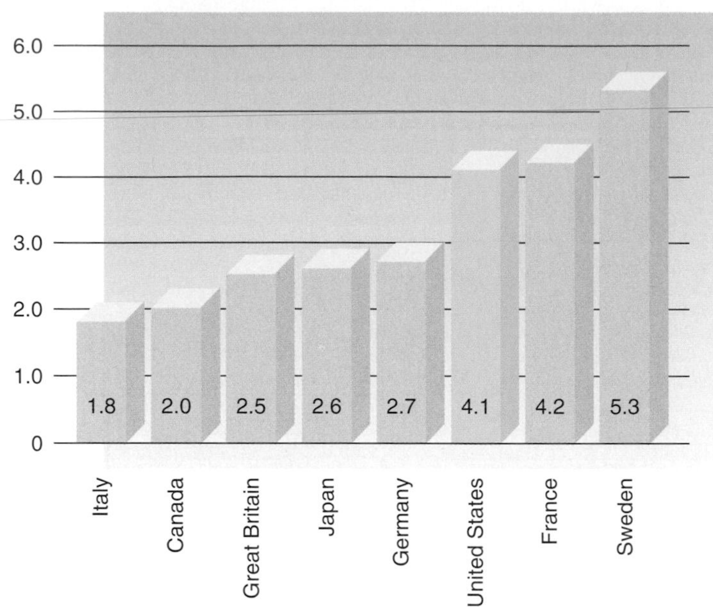

FIGURE 15.5
Comparative Productivity Gains
Manufacturing output per U.S. worker increased by 4.1 percent a year from 1991 to 2001. This track record was better than most industrialized nations.
Source: U.S. Bureau of Labor Statistics.

GDP per Worker: A Measure of Productivity

labor force All persons over age 16 who are either working for pay or actively seeking paid employment.

employment rate The proportion of the adult population that is employed.

productivity Output per unit of input, e.g., output per labor hour.

As the people in Angola, Haiti, and Nigeria know, these projected increases in total output may never occur. Someone has to *produce* more output if we want GDP per capita to rise. One reason our living standard rose in the 1990s is that the **labor force** grew faster than the population. The baby boomers born after World War II had completed college, raised families, and were fully committed to the workforce. The labor force also continued to expand with a steady stream of immigrants and women taking jobs outside the home. The **employment rate**—the percentage of the adult population actually working—rose from under 60 percent in 1980 to over 65 percent in 2003.

The employment rate cannot increase forever. At the limit, everyone would be in the labor market, and no further workers could be found. Sustained increases in GDP per capita are more likely to come from increases in output *per worker.* The total quantity of output produced depends not only on how many workers are employed but also on how productive each worker is. If **productivity** is increasing, then GDP per capita is likely to rise as well.

Historically, productivity gains have been the major source of economic growth. The average worker today produces *twice* as much output as his or her parents did. As Figure 15.5 confirms, substantial productivity gains are common among the world's richest nations. As a result, people in these countries can consume *more* each year even if they choose to work a bit less (e.g., longer vacations, earlier retirements).

Sources of Productivity Growth

If we want GDP per capita to keep going up, productivity will have to continue rising. Will it?

To answer this question, we need to examine the sources of productivity gains. ***The sources of productivity gains include***

- ***Higher skills***—an increase in labor skills.
- ***More capital***—an increase in the ratio of capital to labor.

Period	Average Annual Percentage Change in Labor Stock	Capital Stock	Output per Labor Hour
1959–65	0.9	3.8	3.3
1965–69	1.2	4.1	2.2
1969–73	0.4	3.5	2.6
1973–79	1.6	2.5	0.8
1979–85	1.6	2.2	0.9

Source: *Economic Report of the President,* 1988.

TABLE 15.2
Average Annual Growth Rate of Labor, Capital, and Productivity, 1959–1985

In the 1970s, the rate of capital growth slowed while the rate of labor growth increased. As a consequence, productivity gains declined. These trends were reversed in the late 1980s.

- ***Improved management***—better use of available resources in the production process.
- ***Technological advance***—the development and use of better capital equipment.

Labor Quality

As recently as 1950, less than 8 percent of all U.S. workers had completed college. Today over 30 percent of the workforce has completed four years of college. As a result, today's workers enter the labor market with much more knowledge. Moreover, they keep acquiring new skills by company-paid training programs, adult education classes, and distant-learning options on the Internet. As education and training levels rise, so does productivity.

Capital Investment

No matter how educated workers are, they still need tools, computers, and other equipment to produce most goods and services. Thus ***capital* investment *is a prime determinant of both productivity and growth.*** More investment gives the average worker more and better tools to work with.

investment Expenditures on (production of) new plant and equipment (capital) in a given time period, plus changes in business inventories.

While labor-force growth accelerated in the 1970s, the growth of capital slowed. As Table 15.2 indicates, the capital stock increased by 4.1 percent per year in the late 1960s. In the 1970s, however, the growth of capital slowed to only 2.5 percent per year; and in the early 1980s, it slowed even further. The stock of capital was still growing faster than the labor force (compare columns 1 and 2), but the difference was getting smaller. This means that although the average worker was continuing to get more and better machines, the rate at which he or she was getting them was slower. As a consequence, productivity growth declined (see column 3).

These trends reversed in the 1990s. Capital investment accelerated, with investments in computer networks and telecommunications surging by 10–12 percent a year. As a result, productivity gains accelerated into the 2.5–2.7 percent range. Those productivity gains shifted the production-possibilities curve outward, permitting output to expand with less inflationary pressure. In fact, real GDP grew by more than 4 percent per year in 1997–2000 without any added inflation.

Management

The quantity and quality of factor inputs do not completely determine the rate of economic growth. Resources, however good and abundant, must be organized into a production process and managed. Hence entrepreneurship and the quality of continuing management are major determinants of economic growth.

It is difficult to characterize differences in management techniques or to measure their effectiveness. However, much attention has been focused in recent years on the potential conflict between short-term profits and long-term productivity gains. By cutting investment spending, a firm can increase short-run profits. In doing so, however, a firm may also reduce its growth potential and ultimately its long-term profitability. When corporate managers become fixated on short-run fluctuations in the price of corporate stock, the risk of such a tradeoff increases.

Managers must also learn to motivate employees to their maximum potential. Workers who are disgruntled or alienated aren't likely to put out much effort. To maximize productivity, managers must develop personnel structures and incentives that make employees want to contribute to production.

Research and Development

A fourth and vital source of productivity advance is research and development (R&D). R&D is a broad concept that includes scientific research, product development, innovations in production technique, and the development of management improvements. R&D activity may be a specific, identifiable activity (e.g., in a research lab), or it may be part of the process of learning by doing. In either case, the insights developed from R&D generally lead to new products and cheaper ways of producing them. Over time, R&D is credited with the greatest contributions to economic growth. In his study of U.S. growth during the period 1929–82, Edward Denison concluded that 26 percent of *total* growth was due to "advances in knowledge." The relative contribution of R&D to productivity (output per worker) was probably twice that much.

There is an important link between R&D and capital investment. Part of each year's gross investment compensates for the depreciation of existing plant and equipment. However, new machines are rarely identical to the ones they replace. When you get a new computer, you're not just *replacing* an old one; you're *upgrading* your computing capabilities with more memory, faster speed, and a lot of new features. Indeed, the availability of *better* technology is often the motive for such capital investment. The same kind of motivation spurs businesses to upgrade machines and structures. Hence advances in technology and capital investment typically go hand in hand.

The fruits of research and development don't all reside in new machinery. New ideas may nurture products and processes that expand production possibilities, even without additional capital equipment. Biotechnology has developed strains of wheat and rice that have multiplied the size of harvests, with no additional farm machinery. The development of nonhierarchical databases revolutionized information technology, making it far less time-consuming to access and transmit data, with *less* hardware.

Policy Levers

To a large extent, the pace of economic growth is set by market forces—by the education, training, and investment decisions of market participants. Government policy plays an important role as well. Indeed, ***government policies can have a major impact on whether and how far the aggregate supply curve shifts.***

Education and Training

As noted earlier, the quality of labor largely depends on education and training. Accordingly, government policies that support education and training contribute directly to growth and productivity. From a fiscal-policy perspective, money spent on schools and training has a dual payoff: it stimulates the economy in the *short* run (like all other spending) and increases the *long*-run capacity to produce. Tax incentives for training have the same effect.

LABOR SUPPLY HEADLINE

O Canada, You're One Tough Cookie

Even wonder whether you have what it takes to be a Canadian? Would-be immigrants to that country are rated using a point system that gauges suitability in 10 areas, including age, education, occupation, and work experience.

Compared with the American system, which greatly favors family members of the newly settled, Canada is pragmatic: Having a close relative there earns you just 5 points toward the 70 needed to qualify for an immigration interview. Far more important are your skills—and your potential to contribute to Canada's future.

Ideally, you should be young but not too young. If you're between 21 and 44, you earn 10 points. Turn 49, and that number drops to zero. Zero is also the number of points awarded for not completing secondary school, while a master's degree earns you 16. But all that schooling is for naught unless Canada needs your skills. You say you're a historian? Congratulations! 18 points. A marriage counselor? Same. (Add another 10 if you have already arranged employment.) Not so fortunate are the hairstylist and machine operator, whose talents garner only 2 points. For skilled occupations, four or more years of work experience is a bonus. So, too, fluency in English or French—and, better still, both. *Voila!* Finally, 10 points may be awarded for "personal suitability" as determined by a visa officer, based on such characteristics as motivation, initiative and resourcefulness—qualities little considered in the American immigration process.

—Outlook

Source: *Washington Post*, December 23, 2001, p. B2.

NOTE: Immigrants are an important source of human capital. Should immigrants be selected on the basis of skills or wealth?

Immigration Policy

Both the quality and the quantity of labor are affected by immigration policy. Close to a million people immigrate to the United States each year. This influx of immigrants has been a major source of growth in the U.S. labor force—and thus a direct contributor to an outward shift of our production possibilities.

The impact of immigration on our productive capacity is not just a question of numbers but also the quality of these new workers. Recent immigrants have much lower educational attainments than native-born Americans and are less able to fill job vacancies in growing industries. This is largely due to immigration policy, which sets only country-specific quotas and gives preference to relatives of U.S. residents. Some observers have suggested that the United States should pay more attention to the educational and skill levels of immigrants and set preferences on the basis of potential productivity, as Canada and many other nations do (see Headline). In any case, we have to recognize that the sheer number of people entering the country makes immigration policy an important growth-policy lever.

Investment Incentives

Government policy also affects the supply of capital. As a rule, lower tax rates encourage people to invest more—to build factories, purchase new equipment, and construct new offices. Hence ***tax policy is not only a staple of short-term stabilization policy but a determinant of long-run growth as well.***

The tax treatment of capital gains is one of the most debated supply-side policy levers. Capital gains are increases in the value of assets. When stocks, land, or other assets are sold, any resulting gain is counted as taxable income. Many countries—including Japan, Italy, South Korea, Taiwan, and the Netherlands—do not levy any taxes on capital gains. The rest of the

European Union and Canada impose lower capital gains taxes than does the United States. Lowering the tax rate on capital gains might stimulate more investment and encourage people to reallocate their assets to more productive uses. When the capital-gains tax rate was cut from 28 to 20 percent in 1997, U.S. investment accelerated. That experience prompted President George W. Bush to push for further tax cuts in 2003. The capital-gains tax rate was cut to 15 percent for most people—and *eliminated* for low-income people.

Critics argue that a capital-gains tax cut overwhelmingly favors the rich, who own most stocks, property, and other wealth. This inequity, they assert, outweighs any efficiency gains. Advocates of capital-gains tax cuts say a little more inequality in the short run is justified if the resulting economic growth makes everyone better off in the long run.

Savings Incentives

saving Income minus consumption: that part of disposable income not spent.

Another prerequisite for faster growth is more **savings.** At full employment, a greater volume of investment is possible only if the rate of consumption is cut back. In other words, additional investment requires additional saving. Hence ***supply-side economists favor tax incentives that encourage saving as well as greater tax incentives for investment.*** This kind of perspective contrasts sharply with the Keynesian emphasis on stimulating consumption.

In the early 1980s Congress greatly increased the incentives for saving. First, banks were permitted to increase the rate of interest paid on various types of savings accounts. Second, the tax on earned interest was reduced. And finally, new forms of tax-free saving were created (e.g., Individual Retirement Accounts [IRAs]).

Despite these incentives, the U.S. saving rates declined during the 1980s. Household saving dropped from 6.2 percent of disposable income in 1981 to a low of 2.5 percent in 1987. Neither the tax incentives nor the high interest rates that prevailed in the early 1980s convinced Americans to save more. As a result, the U.S. saving rate fell considerably below that of other nations. American households continue to save relatively little, as the accompanying Headline confirms.

HEADLINE SAVING RATES

Americans Save Little

American households save very little. In 2002, the average American actually spent *more* income than he or she earned—the saving rate was *negative*. As shown here, the United States ranked at the bottom of the savers' list in 2002.

Supply-siders are especially concerned about low saving rates. They argue that Americans must save more, to finance increased investment and economic growth. Otherwise, they fear, the United States will fall behind other countries in the progression toward higher productivity levels and living standards.

Country	Saving Rate (2002)
Korea	19.2%
France	16.2
Japan	13.2
Germany	9.8
Canada	7.0
Great Britain	4.6
United States	**−0.2**

Note: Saving rate equals household saving divided by disposable income.

Source: Organization for Economic Cooperation and Development (OECD).

NOTE: Savings are a primary source of investment financing. Higher saving rates imply proportionately less consumption and more investment and growth.

Government Finances

The dependence of economic growth on investment and savings adds an important dimension to the debate over budget deficits. When the government borrows money to finance its spending, it dips into the nation's savings pool. Hence the government ends up borrowing funds that could have been used to finance investment. If this happens, the government deficit effectively crowds out private investment. This process of **crowding out**—of diverting available savings from investment to government spending—directly limits private investment. From this perspective, government budget deficits act as a constraint on economic growth.

crowding out A reduction in private-sector borrowing (and spending) caused by increased government borrowing.

From 1998 until 2001 the federal government generated a budget *surplus* every year. These surpluses turned the situation around. The surpluses not only eliminated government borrowing, but also *added* funds to money markets. This tended to drive down interest rates, stimulating private investment. In other words, crowding out was transformed to **crowding in.**

crowding in An increase in private-sector borrowing (and spending) caused by decreased government borrowing.

As we saw in earlier chapters, budget deficits aren't always bad. Nor are budget surpluses always good. Short-run cyclical instability may require fiscal policies that unbalance the federal budget. The concern for long-run growth simply adds another dimension to fiscal policy decisions: ***fiscal and monetary policies must be evaluated in terms of their impact not only on short-run aggregate demand but also on long-run aggregate supply.***

Deregulation

There are still other mechanisms for stimulating economic growth. The government intervenes directly in supply decisions by *regulating* employment and output behavior. In general, such regulations limit the flexibility of producers to respond to changes in demand. Government regulation also tends to raise production costs. The higher costs result not only from required changes in the production process but also from the expense of monitoring government regulations and filling out endless government forms. The budget costs and the burden of red tape discourage production and so limit aggregate supply. From this perspective, deregulation would shift the AS curve rightward.

Factor Markets Minimum-wage laws are one of the most familiar forms of factor-market regulation. The Fair Labor Standards Act of 1938 required employers to pay workers a minimum of 25 cents per hour. Over time, Congress has increased the minimum wage repeatedly (see Headline, p. 191), and further increases are in the works.

The goal of the minimum-wage law is to ensure workers a decent standard of living. But the law has other effects as well. By prohibiting employers from using lower-paid workers, it limits the ability of employers to hire additional workers. This hiring constraint limits job opportunities for immigrants, teenagers, and low-skill workers. Without that constraint, more of these workers would find jobs and gain valuable experience, shifting the AS curve rightward.

The government also sets standards for workplace safety and health. The Occupational Safety and Health Administration (OSHA), for example, sets limits on the noise levels at work sites. If noise levels exceed these limits, the employer is required to adopt administrative or engineering controls to reduce the noise level. Personal protection of workers (e.g., earplugs or earmuffs), though much less costly, will suffice only if source controls are not feasible. All such regulations are intended to improve the welfare of workers. In the process, however, these regulations raise the costs of production and inhibit supply responses.

Product Markets The government's regulation of factor markets tends to raise production costs and inhibit supply. The same is true of regulations imposed directly on product markets. A few examples illustrate the impact.

Transportation Costs At the federal level, various agencies regulate the output and prices of transportation services. Until 1984 the Civil Aeronautics Board (CAB) determined which routes airlines could fly and how much they could charge. The Interstate Commerce Commission (ICC) has had the same kind of power over trucking, interstate bus lines, and railroads. The routes, services, and prices for ships (in U.S. coastal waters and foreign commerce) have been established by the Federal Maritime Commission. In all these cases the regulations constrained the ability of producers to respond to increases in demand. Existing producers could not increase output at will, and new producers were excluded from the market. The easing of these restrictive regulations spurred more output, lower prices, and innovation in air travel, telecommunications, and land transportation. In the process, the AS curve shifted to the right.

Food and Drug Standards The Food and Drug Administration (FDA) has a broad mandate to protect consumers from dangerous products. In fulfilling this responsibility, the FDA sets health standards for the content of specific foods. A hot dog, for example, can be labeled as such only if it contains specific mixtures of skeletal meat, pig lips, snouts, and ears. By the same token, the FDA requires that chocolate bars must contain no more than 60 microscopic insect fragments per 100 grams of chocolate. The FDA also sets standards for the testing of new drugs and evaluates the test results. In all three cases, the goal of regulation is to minimize health risks to consumers.

Like all regulation, the FDA standards entail real costs. The tests required for new drugs are very expensive and time-consuming. Getting a new drug approved for sale can take years of effort and require a huge investment. The net results are that (1) fewer new drugs are brought to market and (2) those that do reach the market are more expensive than they would be in the absence of regulation. In other words, the aggregate supply of goods is shifted to the left.

Many—perhaps most—of these regulatory activities are beneficial. In fact, all were originally designed to serve specific public purposes. As a result of such regulation, we do get safer drugs, cleaner air, and less deceptive advertising. We must also consider the costs involved, however. All regulatory activities impose direct and indirect costs. These costs must be compared to the benefits received. ***The basic contention of supply-side economists is that regulatory costs are too high.*** To improve our economic performance, they assert, we must *deregulate* the production process, thereby shifting the aggregate supply curve to the right again.

Economic Freedom

Regulation and taxes are just two forms of government intervention that affect production possibilities. Governments also establish and enforce property rights, legal rights, and political rights. One of the greatest obstacles to postcommunist growth in Russia was the absence of legal protection. Few people wanted to invest in businesses that could be stolen or confiscated, with little hope of judicial redress. Nor did producers want to ship goods without ironclad payment guarantees. By contrast, producers in the United States are willing to produce and ship goods without prepayment, knowing that the courts, collection agencies, and insurance companies can help assure payment, if necessary.

INSTITUTIONAL FRAMEWORK — HEADLINE

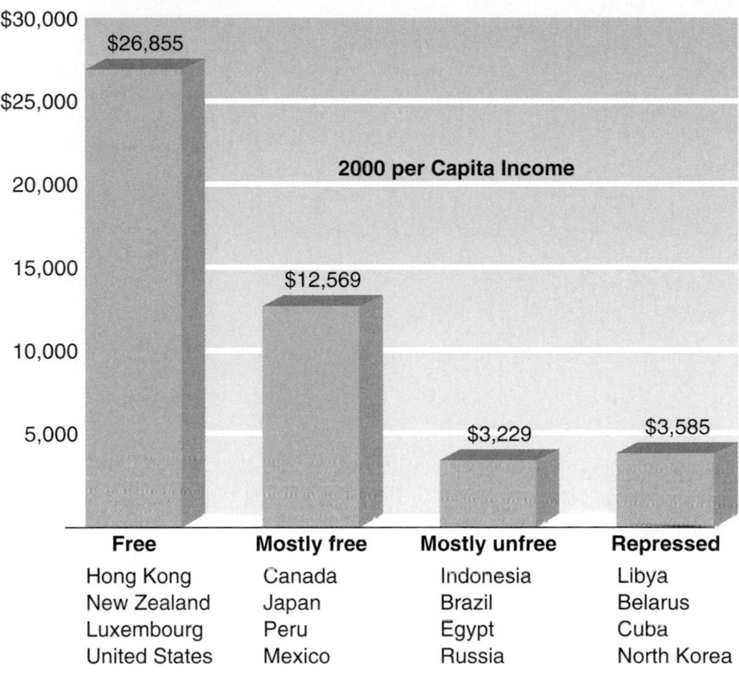

Source: Heritage Foundation, *2003 Index of Economic Freedom*, Washington, DC, 2003.

NOTE: A nation's institutional framework affects its economic growth. Nations with more open and less regulated economies grow faster.

It is difficult to identify all of the institutional features that make an economy business friendly. The Heritage Foundation, a conservative think tank, has constructed an index of economic freedom, using 50 different measures of government policy. Each year they rank the world's countries on this index, thereby identifying the most "free" economies (least government control) and the most "repressed" (most government control). According to Heritage, the nations with the most economic freedom not only have the highest GDP per capita (see Headline) but continue to grow the fastest.

POLICY PERSPECTIVES

Is More Growth Desirable?

The government clearly has a powerful set of levers for promoting faster economic growth. Many people wonder, though, whether more economic growth is really *desirable*. Those of us who commute on congested highways, worry about global warming, breathe foul air, and can't find a secluded camping site may raise a loud chorus of no's. But before reaching a conclusion let us at least determine what it is people don't like about the prospect of continued

HEADLINE POPULATION GROWTH

Keeping Up with the Patels and the Wangs

For years to come, the United States will be the only developed country on the list of fastest-growing nations. Why the U.S. boom? A steady influx of immigrants and a fertility rate of 2.04, higher than that of most developed nations.

Country	2000 Population	Projected Growth from 2000–05	Percentage Change
1. India	1.0 billion	80 million	8.0
2. China	1.3 bil.	46 mil.	3.5
3. Pakistan	141 mil.	19 mil.	13.4
4. Nigeria	114 mil.	16 mil.	14.0
5. Bangladesh	137 mil.	15 mil.	10.9
6. Indonesia	212 mil.	13 mil.	6.1
7. United States	283 mil.	13 mil.	4.5
8. Brazil	170 mil.	11 mil.	6.5
9. Dem. Republic of the Congo	51 mil.	9 mil.	17.6
10. Ethiopia	63 mil.	8 mil.	12.6

- World population in 2000: **6.1 Billion**
- Projected population in 2050: **8.3 Billion**
- Highest life expectancy: **Japan, 81.5 years**
- Lowest life expectancy: **Botswana, 38.1 years**
- Highest median age: **Japan, 41.2 years**
- Lowest median age: **Yemen, 15 years**

Source: *U.S. News & World Report*, March 12, 2001, p. 12.

NOTE: Continuing population growth implies that total output must also grow to maintain existing living standards. Still faster output growth is needed to raise living standards.

growth. Is it really economic growth per se that people object to or, instead, the specific ways GDP has grown in the past?

First of all, let us distinguish very clearly between economic growth and population growth. Congested neighborhoods, dining halls, and highways are the consequence of too many people, not of too many goods and services. And there's no indication that population growth will cease any time soon. As the accompanying Headline notes, the world's population is likely to increase by another 2 billion people by the year 2050.

Who's going to feed, clothe, and house all these people? Are we going to redistribute the current level of output, leaving everyone with less? Or should we try to produce *more* output so living standards don't fall? If we had *more* goods and services—if we had more houses and transit systems—much of the population congestion we now experience might be relieved. Maybe if we had enough resources to meet our existing demands *and* to build a solar-generated "new town" in the middle of Montana, people might move out of the crowded neighborhoods of Chicago and St. Louis. Well, probably not, but at least one thing is certain: with fewer goods and services, more people will have to share any given quantity of output.

Which brings us back to the really essential measure of growth, GDP per capita. Are there any serious grounds for desiring *less* GDP per capita, a reduced standard of living? And don't say yes just because you think we already have too many cars on our roads or calories in our bellies. That argument refers to the *mix* of output again and does not answer the question of whether or not we want *any* more goods or services per person. Increasing GDP per capita can take a million forms, including the educational services you are now consuming. The rejection of economic growth per se implies that none of those forms is desirable.

We could, of course, acquire more of the goods and services we consider beneficial simply by cutting back on the production of the things we consider unnecessary. But who is to say which mix of output is best, and how are we going to bring about the desired shift? The present mix of output may be considered bad because it is based on a maldistribution of income, deceptive advertising, or failure of the market mechanism to account for external costs. If so, it would seem more efficient (and politically more feasible) to address those problems directly rather than to attempt to lower our standard of living.

SUMMARY

- Economic growth refers to increases in real GDP. Short-run growth may result from increases in capacity utilization (e.g., less unemployment). In the long run, however, growth requires increases in capacity itself—rightward shifts of the long-run aggregate supply curve.
- GDP per capita is a basic measure of living standards. By contrast, GDP per worker gauges our productivity. Over time, increases in productivity have been the primary cause of rising living standards.
- Productivity gains can originate in a variety of ways. These sources include better labor quality, increased capital investment, research and development, and improved management.
- The policy levers for increasing growth rates include education and training, immigration, investment and saving incentives, and the broader institutional framework. All of these levers may increase the quantity or quality of resources.
- Budget deficits may inhibit economic growth by crowding out investment, that is, absorbing savings that would otherwise finance investment. Budget surpluses can have the opposite (crowding in) effect.
- The goal of economic growth implies that macroeconomic policies must be assessed in terms of their long-run supply impact as well as their short-term demand effects.
- Continued economic growth is desirable as long as it brings a higher standard of living for people and an increased ability to produce and consume socially desirable goods and services.

Terms to Remember

Define the following terms:

production possibilities	GDP per capita	saving
economic growth	labor force	crowding out
nominal GDP	employment rate	crowding in
real GDP	productivity	
growth rate	investment	

Questions for Discussion

1. In what specific ways (if any) does a college education increase a worker's productivity?
2. Why don't we consume all of our current output instead of sacrificing some present consumption for investment?
3. In 1866 Stanley Jevons predicted that economic growth would come to a halt when England ran out of coal, a doomsday that he reckoned would occur in the mid-1970s. How did we manage to avert that projection? Will an oil shortage cripple future growth?
4. Fertility rates in many developed nations (e.g., France) have dropped so low that they are approaching zero population growth. How will this affect economic growth? The standard of living?
5. Suppose that economic growth could only be achieved by increasing inequality (e.g., via tax incentives for investment). Would economic growth still be desirable?
6. Is limitless growth really possible? What forces do you think will be most important in slowing or halting economic growth?
7. Notice in the Headline on p. 338 how the time spent working on the job and at home has declined. How are these changes indicative of economic growth?
8. How would the following factors affect a nation's growth potential?
   (*a*) Legal protection of private property
   (*b*) High tax rates
   (*c*) Judicial corruption
   (*d*) Government price controls
   (*e*) Free trade
9. Should the United States adopt an immigration policy like Canada's (Headline, p. 343) or continue to give preference to family members?

Problems

1. China's output grew at an amazing rate at 10 percent per year in the 1990s. At that rate how long will it take for China's GDP to double? (see Table 15.1). With its population increasing at 0.6 percent per year, how long will it take for *per capita* GDP to double?
2. If real GDP is growing at 3 percent a year, how long will it take for
   (*a*) Real GDP to double?
   (*b*) Real GDP *per capita* to double if the population is increasing each year by
      i. 0 percent?
      ii. 1 percent?
      iii. 2 percent?
3. In 2000, approximately 64 percent of the adult population (220 million) was employed. If the employment rate increased to 65 percent,
   (*a*) How many more people would be working?
   (*b*) By how much would output increase if per worker GDP is $70,000?
4. According to the data in Figure 15.4, how fast did world GDP per capita grow from
   (*a*) 1000 to 1500?
   (*b*) 1500 to 1820?
   (*c*) 1820 to 1995?
5. Suppose that every additional 5 percentage points in the investment rate (I ÷ GDP) boost economic growth by 1 percentage point. Assume

also that all investment must be financed with consumer saving. The economy is now characterized by

GDP:	$6 trillion
Consumption:	5 trillion
Saving:	1 trillion
Investment:	1 trillion

If the goal is to raise the growth rate by 1 percent,
(*a*) By how much must investment increase?
(*b*) By how much must consumption decline for this to occur?
(*c*) Are consumers better or worse off as a result?

Web Activities

1. Log on to www.whitehouse.gov/fsbr/output.html. What is the U.S. economy's most recent growth rate?
2. Log on to www.whitehouse.gov/fsbr/output.html. What has been the trend in growth in the United States during the last three years?
3. Log on to www.heritage.org/index. Click on "Simple Search."
   (*a*) How does economic freedom in the United States compare to Hong Kong? Japan? China?
   (*b*) How would you expect future economic growth in the United States to compare to these nations? Explain.

Living Econ

How Does Exponential Growth Affect Me?

Which of these three options would you prefer: (1) $7,000 thirty years from today, (2) $3,000 today that you save at 3% interest for 30 years, or (3) $1,000 today that you save at 7% for 30 years? Well, because interest compounds year after year, the last option is superior by several hundred dollars. Over thirty years, a retirement account more than doubles at 3% interest and gains more than seven fold at a 7% return. This exponential growth explains why it is important to start saving early.

Exponential change also is evident in GDP growth. If the United States averages 3% real GDP growth and China is able to sustain real GDP growth of 7% per year, then the Chinese economy would catch up with the U.S. economy in thirty years. Of course, China's GDP *per capita* would still be less than the U.S. per capita GDP, and high growth rates such as 7% are rarely sustained over long time periods.

Whether we are talking about the growth of money or the growth of GDP, gains made in one year accumulate into additional gains for the future years. As a result, a smaller savings account—or a smaller economy—can grow to be significantly larger in the long run even with relatively small differences in interest—or growth—rates.

Theory and Reality

CHAPTER 16

There is no one solution. It isn't just a question of the budget. It isn't just the question of inflationary labor rates. It isn't just the question of sticky prices. It isn't just the question of what the Government does to keep prices up or to make regulations that tend to be inflationary. It isn't just the weather or just the drought. It is all these things. The interaction of these various factors is what is so terribly difficult for us to understand and, of course, what is so terribly difficult for us to deal with.

—Former Secretary of the Treasury W. Michael Blumenthal

Macroeconomic theory is supposed to explain the business cycle and show policymakers how to control it. But something is obviously wrong. Despite our relative prosperity, we have not consistently achieved the goals of full employment, price stability, and vigorous economic growth. All too often, either unemployment or inflation jumps unexpectedly or economic growth slows down. No matter how hard we try, the business cycle seems to persist.

What accounts for this gap between the promises of economic theory and the reality of economic performance? Are the theories inadequate? Or is sound economic advice being ignored? Many people blame the economists. They point to the conflicting theories and advice that economists offer and wonder what theory is supposed to be followed. If economists themselves can't agree, it is asked, why should anyone else listen to them?

Not surprisingly, economists see things a bit differently. First of all, they point out, the **business cycle** isn't as bad as it used to be. Since World War II, the economy has had many ups and downs, but none as severe as the Great Depression or earlier catastrophes. In the 1980s and again in the 1990s, the U.S. economy enjoyed uninterrupted economic expansions that were particularly long. The U.S. economy also exhibited resilience in the wake of the 2001 recession and terrorist attacks. So the economic record contains more wins than losses.

Second, economists place most of the blame for occasional losses on the real world, not on their theories. They complain that politics takes precedence over good economic advice. Politicians are reluctant, for example, to raise taxes or cut spending in order to control inflation. Their concern is winning the next election, not solving the country's economic problems.

business cycle Alternating periods of economic growth and contraction.

President Jimmy Carter anguished over another problem—the complexity of economic decision making. In the real world, neither theory nor politics can keep up with all our economic goals. As President Carter observed:

> We cannot concentrate just on inflation or just on unemployment or just on deficits in the federal budget or our international payments. Nor can we act in isolation from other countries. We must deal with all of these problems simultaneously and on a worldwide basis.

The purpose of this chapter is to confront these and other frustrations of the real world. In so doing, we will try to provide answers to the following questions:

- What is the ideal package of macro policies?
- How well does our macro performance live up to the promises of that package?
- What kinds of obstacles prevent us from doing better?

Policy Levers

The macroeconomic tools available to policymakers are summarized in Table 16.1. Although this list is brief, we hardly need a reminder at this point of how powerful each instrument can be. Every one of these major policy instruments can significantly change our answers to the basic economic questions of WHAT, HOW, and FOR WHOM to produce.

Fiscal Policy

fiscal policy The use of government taxes and spending to alter macroeconomic outcomes.

The basic tools of **fiscal policy** are contained in the federal budget. Tax cuts are supposed to stimulate spending by putting more income in the hands of consumers and businesses. Tax increases are intended to curtail spending and thus reduce inflationary pressures. Some of the major tax changes implemented in recent years are summarized in Table 16.2.

The expenditure side of the federal budget provides another fiscal-policy tool. Increases in government spending raise aggregate demand and so encourage more production. A slowdown in government spending restrains aggregate demand, lessening inflationary pressures. With government spending exceeding $2 trillion a year, changes in the federal budget can influence aggregate demand significantly. In the second quarter of 2003, for example,

TABLE 16.1
The Policy Levers

Economic policymakers have access to a variety of policy instruments. The challenge is to choose the right tools at the right time. The mix of tools required may vary from problem to problem.

Type of Policy	Policy Instruments
Fiscal	Tax cuts and increases
	Changes in government spending
Monetary	Open-market operations
	Reserve requirements
	Discount rates
Supply-side	Tax incentives for investment and saving
	Deregulation
	Education and training
	Immigration
	Trade policy

TABLE 16.2
Fiscal-Policy Milestones

1981	Economic Recovery Tax Act	Three-year consumer tax cut of $213 billion plus $59 billion of business tax cuts
1982	Tax Equity and Fiscal Responsibility Act	Raised business, excise, and income taxes by $100 billion over three years
1983	Social Security Act Amendments	Increased payroll taxes and cut future retirement benefits
1984	Deficit Reduction Act	Increased Income, business, and excise taxes by $50 billion over three years
1985	Gramm-Rudman-Hollings Act	Required a balanced budget by 1991 and authorized automatic spending cuts
1986	Tax Reform Act	Major reduction in tax rates coupled with broadening of tax base
1987	Gramm-Rudman-Hollings Reaffirmation	Postponed balanced-budget target until 1993
1990	Budget Enforcement Act	Eliminated deficit ceilings; imposed limit on discretionary spending
1993	Clinton's "New Direction"	Tax increases and spending cuts to reduce deficit, 1994–97
1994	Contract with America	Republicans propose tax cuts for personal income and capital gains
1997	Balanced Budget Act Taxpayer Relief Act	Package of tax cuts and spending cuts to balance budget by 2002
2001	Economic Growth and Tax Relief Reconciliation Act	$1.35 trillion in personal tax cuts spread over 10 years
2002	Job Creation and Worker Assistance Act	Tax cuts for businesses
2003	Jobs and Growth Tax Relief Act	$350 billion tax cut, including reduced dividend and capital gains taxes

federal spending increased by $34 billion, largely for national defense. With multiplier effects, that spending surge significantly increased aggregate demand. That fiscal stimulus was augmented with continuing tax cuts legislated in 2001, 2002, and May 2003.

Automatic Stabilizers Changes in the budget don't necessarily originate in presidential decisions or congressional legislation. Tax revenues and government outlays also respond to economic events. ***When the economy slows, tax revenues decline, and government spending increases automatically.*** The 2001 recession, for example, displaced 2 million workers and reduced the incomes of millions more. As their incomes fell, so did their tax liabilities. As a consequence, government tax revenues fell.

The recession also caused government spending to *rise.* The swollen ranks of unemployed workers increased outlays for unemployment insurance benefits, welfare, food stamps, and other transfer payments. None of this budget activity required new legislation. Instead, the benefits were increased *automatically* under laws already written. No *new* policy was required.

These recession-induced changes in tax receipts and budget outlays are referred to as **automatic stabilizers.** Such budget changes help stabilize the economy by increasing after-tax incomes and spending when the economy slows. Specifically, ***recessions automatically***

automatic stabilizer Federal expenditure or revenue item that automatically responds countercyclically to changes in national income—e.g., unemployment benefits, income taxes.

- ***Reduce tax revenues.***
- ***Increase government outlays.***
- ***Widen budget deficits.***

Economic expansions have the opposite effect on government budgets. When the economy booms, people have to pay more taxes on their rising incomes. They also have less need for government assistance. Hence tax receipts rise and government spending drops automatically when the economy heats up. These changes tend to shrink the budget deficit. This is exactly the kind of automatic deficit reduction that occurred in the late 1990s. While President Clinton and congressional Republicans were squabbling about how to reduce the federal deficit, the economy kept growing. Indeed, it grew so fast that the budget *deficit* turned into a budget *surplus* in 1998. Soon thereafter both the Democrats and Republicans claimed credit for that turn of events.

Discretionary Policy To assess political claims for deficit reduction, we need to distinguish *automatic* changes in the budget from *policy-induced* changes. Automatic changes in taxes and spending do not reflect current fiscal-policy decisions: they reflect laws already on the books. Discretionary fiscal policy entails only *new* tax and spending decisions. Specifically, ***fiscal policy refers to deliberate changes in tax or spending legislation.*** These changes can be made only by the U.S. Congress. Every year the president proposes specific budget and tax changes, negotiates with Congress, then accepts or vetoes specific acts that Congress has passed. The resulting policy decisions represent discretionary fiscal policy. Policymakers deserve credit (or blame) only for the effects of the discretionary policy decisions they make (or fail to make).

The distinction between automatic stabilizers and discretionary spending helps explain why the federal budget deficit jumped from $221 billion in **fiscal year** 1991 to nearly $270 billion in fiscal 1992. Ironically, Congress had *increased* tax rates in fiscal 1992, hoping to trim the deficit. Congress had also planned to slow the growth of government spending. Hence discretionary fiscal policy was slightly restrictive. These discretionary policies were overwhelmed, however, by the force of the 1990–91 recession. Automatic stabilizers caused tax revenues to fall and government transfer payments to rise. The net result was a much *larger* budget deficit in fiscal 1992, the opposite of what Congress had intended. The swollen deficit was a symptom of the economy's weakness, not a measure of fiscal-policy stimulus.

fiscal year (FY) The 12-month period used for accounting purposes: begins October 1 for federal government.

A similar chain of events plunged the federal budget into deficit in 2002–2004 (see Headline). Tax cuts and a surge in military spending threw the budget into a deficit situation. That much of the deficit increase was due to deliberate fiscal policy. The deficit widened even further, however, due to sluggish economic growth. The Bush administration hoped that faster GDP growth would keep a lid on projected deficits.

The opposite sequence occurred in 1996–2000. The economy grew faster in those years than anticipated. As a result, tax revenues increased, transfer payments declined, and the budget deficit shrank more rapidly than expected. Although President Clinton claimed credit for the deficit reduction, the Congessional Budget Office said that over two-thirds of the

ORIGINS OF DEFICITS HEADLINE

Budget Deficit May Surpass $450 Billion

War costs, tax cut, slow economy are key factors

War, tax cuts and a third year of a flailing economy may push this year's budget deficit past $450 billion, according to congressional sources familiar with new White House budget forecasts. That would be 50 percent higher than the Bush administration forecast five months ago.

The deficit projection due out today is nearly $50 billion more than economists anticipated just last week, and it underscores the continuing deterioration of the government's fortunes since 2000, when the Treasury posted a $236 billion surplus. That represents a fiscal reversal exceeding $680 billion.

"It's shock and awe," said a senior Republican Senate aide. . . .

The 2003 budget deficit—for the fiscal year ending Sept. 30 was exacerbated by the $79.2 billion emergency spending bill enacted at the outset of the Iraq war, which foresees $42 billion in spending in fiscal 2003. It also includes the initial costs of the 10-year, $350 billion tax cut enacted in May. . . .

But Republicans and many independent economists say the sluggish economy and rising jobless rate remain the largest factors in the worsening fiscal picture. Tax revenue has fallen for three straight years, a streak not seen since the Depression. Through June, tax collection is below the amount of taxes collected in the same period in 1999, according to the Congressional Budget Office.

"I consider this an amazing phenomenon," said CBO Director Douglas Holtz-Eakin.

—Jonathan Weisman

Source: *Washington Post*, July 15, 2003, p. 1.

Into the Red *U.S. government's surplus/deficit in billions of dollars*

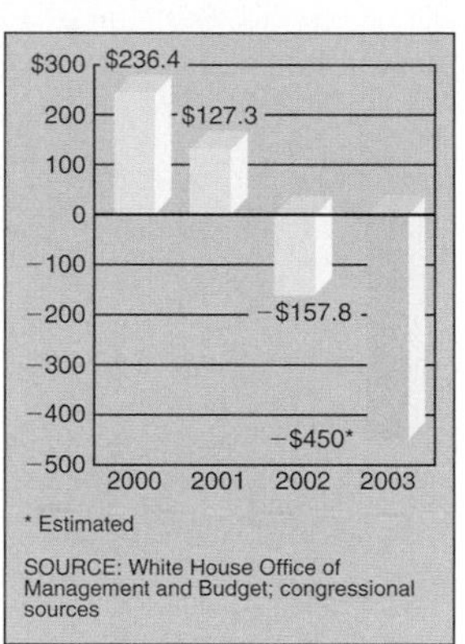

* Estimated

SOURCE: White House Office of Management and Budget; congressional sources

THE WASHINGTON POST

NOTE: The budget deficit is affected by both deliberate fiscal policy and cyclical changes in the economy. Tax cuts, a spending surge, and a sluggish economy all contributed to the budget deficits of 2002–04.

1996–2000 deficit reduction was due to the strong economy and automatic stabilizers.

Monetary Policy

The policy arsenal described in Table 16.1 also contains monetary tools. The tools of **monetary policy** include open-market operations, discount-rate change, and reserve requirements. The Federal Reserve uses these tools to change the **money supply.** In so doing, the Fed strives to shift the aggregate demand curve in the desired direction.

monetary policy The use of money and credit controls to influence macroeconomic activity.

money supply (M1) Currency held by the public, plus balances in transactions accounts.

The effectiveness of both fiscal and monetary policy depends on the shape of the aggregate supply (AS) curve. If the AS curve is horizontal, changes in the money supply (and related aggregate demand shifts) affect output only. If the AS curve is vertical, money-supply changes will affect prices only. In the typical case of an upward-sloping AS curve, changes in the money supply affect both prices and output.

Rules vs. Discretion Disagreements about the actual shape of the AS curve raise questions about how to conduct monetary policy. As discussed in Chapter 14, some economists urge the Fed to play an active role in adjusting

TABLE 16.3
Monetary-Policy Milestones

October 1979	Fed adopts monetarist approach, tightening money supply; interest rates soar
July 1982	Deep into recession, Fed votes to ease monetary restraint
October 1982	Fed abandons pure monetarist approach and expands money supply rapidly
1984	Reagan administration and Fed criticize each other's policies: Fed criticized for being too tight; Reagan criticized for being too stimulative
1986	Money supply increases by 15 percent
May 1987	Fed abandons money-supply targets as policy guides
June 1987	Alan Greenspan appointed chairman; money-supply growth decreases; discount rate increased
1989	Greenspan announces goal of zero inflation, slows money-supply growth
1991	In midst of recession Fed reverses monetary policy; interest rates fall to their lowest level in decades
1994	As growth accelerates and unemployment dips, Fed raises interest rates substantially
Feb. 1995	Fed reduces interest rates slightly when economy stalls in first quarter
1997	When unemployment rate drops below 5 percent, Fed nudges interest rates higher
1998	Fed cuts interest rates to offset shock of Asian crisis
1999–2000	Fed increases interest rates six times in one year
2001–2003	Fed reverses policy, cuts interest rates; continues cutting interest rates repeatedly until mid-2003

the money supply to changing economic conditions. Others suggest that we would be better served by fixed rules for money-supply growth. Fixed rules would make the Fed more of a passive mechanic rather than an active policymaker.

There are clear risks of error in discretionary policy. In 1979 and again in 1989 the Fed pursued restrictive policies that pushed the economy into recessions. In both cases, the Fed had to reverse its policies. (In Table 16.3 compare October 1982 to October 1979 and the years 1991 to 1989.) In 1999–2000 the Fed again raised interest rates substantially, in six separate steps. When the economy slowed abruptly at the end of 2000, critics said the Fed had again stepped too hard on the monetary brake. The Fed was forced to reverse course again in 2001.

Critics charge that the repeated U-turns in monetary policy prove that strict rules for money management would be better than Fed discretion. But fixed rules might not work better. The efficacy of fixed rules depends on consistent market responses to monetary-policy levers. This is not assured. In 1991 the Fed moved aggressively to stimulate aggregate demand with lower interest rates. But consumers and investors were unpersuaded. They used the lower interest rates to reduce their debts rather than buy more goods and services. A preprogrammed set of policy rules wouldn't have anticipated such a response. The 2000–01 economic slowdown was also aggravated by the unexpected but significant decline in consumer confidence (see Headline on next page). In principle at least, discretionary policy can adapt faster than fixed policy rules to such unanticipated events.

POLICY ADJUSTMENTS HEADLINE

Falling Consumer Confidence Could Alter Fed Outlook

The economy gave ominous signals Tuesday as orders for big-ticket goods fell sharply and consumer confidence dropped to the lowest in more than a year.

Even though consumers are still secure enough about short-term conditions to promise a healthy holiday shopping season, the long-term outlook is less certain.

That's why some analysts predict that the Federal Reserve will shift its closely watched "risk statement" to neutral when it meets Dec. 19.

Coming after the Fed has warned all year that inflation poses the greatest risk to the economy, a shift to neutral would be a sign that policymakers are now just as worried about growth slowing too much. Analysts would view that as evidence that interest rate cuts might not be far behind, which could boost the stock market and the economy.

—George Hager

Source: *USA Today*, November 9, 2000, p. 1.

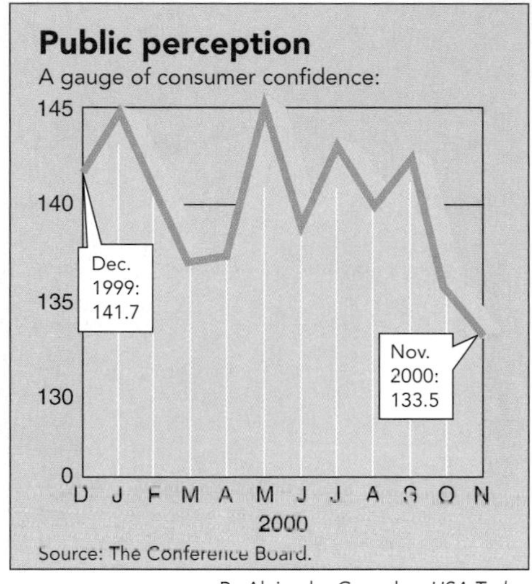

By Alejandro Gonzalez, *USA Today*.

NOTE: The Fed's decisions on monetary policy reflect its outlook for the economy. When the outlook changes, so must Fed policy.

Supply-Side Policy

Supply-side theory offers the third major set of policy tools. We have seen how ***the shape of the aggregate supply curve limits the effectiveness of fiscal and monetary policies.*** Shifts of the aggregate supply curve are also a prerequisite for economic growth. Supply-side policy focuses directly on these constraints. The goal of **supply-side policy** is to shift the aggregate supply curve to the right. Such rightward shifts not only promote long-term growth but also make short-run demand-side intervention more successful.

supply-side policy The use of tax rates, (de)regulation, and other mechanisms to increase the ability and willingness to produce goods and services.

The supply-side toolbox is filled with tools. Tax cuts designed to stimulate work effort, saving, and investment are among the most popular and powerful supply-side tools. Deregulation may also reduce production costs and stimulate investment. Expenditure on education, training, and research expands our capacity to produce. Immigration policy alters the size and skills of the labor force and thus affects aggregate supply as well.

In the 1980s, tax rates were reduced dramatically. The maximum marginal tax rate on individuals was cut from 70 percent to 50 percent in 1981, and then still further, to 28 percent, in 1987. The 1980s also witnessed major milestones in the deregulation of airlines, trucking, telephone service, and other industries (see Table 16.4). All of these policies helped shift the AS curve rightward.

TABLE 16.4
Supply-Side Milestones

1978	Airline Deregulation Act	Phased out federal regulations of airline routes, fares, and entry
1980	Motor Carrier Act	Eliminated federal restrictions on entry, routes, and fares in the trucking industry
1981	Economic Recovery Tax Act	Decreased marginal tax rates by 30 percent
1982	AT&T breakup	AT&T monopoly on phone service ended via antitrust action
1986	Tax Reform Act	Eliminated most tax preferences for investment and saving, but sharply reduced marginal tax rates
1990	Social Security Act amendments implemented	Payroll tax increased to 7.65 percent
1990	Americans with Disabilities Act	Employers must provide more handicap access
1990	Immigration Act	Increased immigration quotas, new preference for skilled workers
1990	Clean Air Act	Toughened pollution standards
1991	Surface Transportation Act	Accelerated highway and rail improvements
1993	Rebuild America Program	Increased infrastructure investment
1993	Family Leave Act	Employers required to offer unpaid leave
1994	NAFTA	North American trade barriers lowered
1996–97	Minimum wage	Minimum wage jumps from $4.25 to $5.15 per hour
1997	Taxpayer Relief Act	Capital gains tax reduced; tuition tax credits enacted
1998	Workforce Investment Act	Funds for skill-training programs
2001	Economic Growth and Tax Relief Reconciliation Act	Reduced marginal tax rates over 10 years
2002	Job Creation and Worker Assistance Act	Business tax cuts and incentives
2003	Jobs and Growth Tax Relief Act	Reduced taxes on dividends and capital gains

Government policies can also shift the AS curve leftward. When the minimum wage jumped to $5.15 an hour in 1997, the cost of supplying goods and services went up. A 1990 increase in the payroll tax boosted production costs as well. In the early 1990s, private employers were also burdened with higher labor costs associated with government-mandated fringe benefits (Family Leave Act of 1993) and accommodations for handicapped workers (Americans with Disabilities Act). All of these policies restrained aggregate supply.

President Clinton argued that the productive capacity of the economy could be expanded with greater investment in both *physical* capital and *human* capital. His Rebuild America program stepped up spending on highways and other public infrastructure. He also increased spending on education and urged private employers to provide more worker training. The 1998 tuition tax credit for college students was also intended to encourage more human capital investment.

Even welfare reform has supply-side implications. The 1996 Personal Responsibility and Work Opportunity Act established time limits for welfare dependence. When those limits were reached in 1998–99, more welfare recipients had to enter the labor market. When they did, aggregate supply shifted rightward.

Because tax rates are a basic tool of supply-side policy, fiscal and supply-side policies are often interwined. When Congress changes the tax laws, it almost always alters marginal tax rates and thus changes production incentives. Notice, for example, that tax legislation appears in Table 16.4 as well as in Table 16.2. The Taxpayer Relief Act of 1997 not only changed total tax revenues (fiscal policy) but also restructured production and investment incentives (supply-side policy). The Bush tax cuts of 2001 and 2003 also encouraged more production by reducing marginal tax rates for individuals and increasing tax incentives for business investment.

Idealized Uses

These fiscal, monetary, and supply-side tools are potentially powerful levers for controlling the economy. In principle, they can cure the excesses of the business cycle. To see how, let us review their use in three distinct macroeconomic settings.

Case 1: Recession

When output and employment levels fall far short of the economy's full-employment potential, the mandate for public policy is clear. The **GDP gap** must be closed. Total spending must be increased so that producers can sell more goods, hire more workers, and move the economy toward its productive capacity. At such times the most urgent need is to get people back to work.

GDP gap The difference between full-employment output and the amount of output demanded at current price levels.

How can a recession be ended? Keynesians emphasize the need to stimulate aggregate demand. They seek to shift the aggregate demand curve rightward by cutting taxes or boosting government spending. The resulting stimulus will set off a **multiplier** reaction, propelling the economy to full employment.

multiplier The multiple by which an initial change in aggregate spending will alter total expenditure after an infinite number of spending cycles; $1/(1 - MPC)$.

Modern Keynesians acknowledge that monetary policy might also help. Specifically, increases in the money supply may lower interest rates and thus give investment spending a further boost. To give the economy a really powerful stimulus, we might want to do everything at the same time, that is, cut taxes, increase government spending, and expand the money supply simultaneously. By taking such convincing action, we might also increase consumer confidence, raise investor expectations, and induce still greater spending and output.

Other economists offer different advice. So-called monetarists and other critics of government intervention see no point in discretionary policies. As they see it, the aggregate supply curve is vertical at the natural rate of unemployment (see Figure 14.6). Quick fixes of monetary or fiscal policy may shift the aggregate demand curve but won't change the aggregate supply curve. Monetary or fiscal stimulus will only push the price level up (more inflation), without reducing unemployment. In this view, the appropriate policy response to a recession is patience. As sales and output slow, interest rates will decline, and new investment will be stimulated.

Supply-siders confront these objections head-on. In their view, policy initiatives should focus on changing the shape and position of the aggregate supply curve. Supply-siders would emphasize the need to improve production incentives. They would urge cuts in marginal tax rates on investment and labor. They would also look for ways to reduce government regulation.

Different macro theories offer alternative explanations and policy options for macro failures.

By MAL. © Associated Features, Inc.

Case 2: Inflation

An overheated economy elicits a similar assortment of policy prescriptions. In this case the immediate goal is to restrain aggregate demand—that is, shift the aggregate demand curve to the left. Keynesians would do this by raising taxes and cutting government spending, relying on the multiplier to cool down the economy.

Monetarists would simply cut the money supply. If the AS curve is really vertical, changes in the money supply alter prices, not output. Therefore, inflation must reflect excessive money-supply growth or the anticipation of such growth. Monetarists would not only reduce money-supply growth but try to convince market participants that a more cautious monetary policy will be continued. That might rein in inflationary expectations.

Supply-siders would point out that inflation implies both too much money and not enough goods. They would look at the supply side of the market for ways to expand productive capacity. In a highly inflationary setting, they would propose more incentives to save. The additional savings would automatically reduce consumption while creating a larger pool of investable funds. Supply-siders would also cut taxes and regulations and lower import barriers that keep out cheaper foreign goods.

Case 3: Stagflation

stagflation The simultaneous occurrence of substantial unemployment and inflation.

Although serious inflations and recessions provide reasonably clear options for economic policy, there is a vast gray area between these extremes. Occasionally, the economy suffers from both inflation and unemployment at the same time—a condition called **stagflation.** In 1975, for example, the unemployment rate (8.5 percent) and the inflation rate (9.1 percent) were both far too high. With an upward-sloping aggregate supply curve, there is no easy way to bring both rates down at the same time. Any demand-side stimulus to attain full employment worsens inflation. Likewise, restrictive demand policies increase unemployment. Although any upward-sloping AS curve poses such a tradeoff, the position of the curve also determines how difficult the choices are. Figure 16.1 illustrates this stagflation problem.

There are no simple solutions for stagflation. Any demand-side initiatives must be designed with care, seeking to balance the competing threats of

FIGURE 16.1
Stagflation

Both unemployment and inflation may occur at the same time. This is always a potential problem with an upward-sloping AS curve. The further the AS curve is to the left, the worse the stagflation problem is likely to be. The curve AS_1, implies higher prices and more unemployment than AS_2 for any given level of aggregate demand.

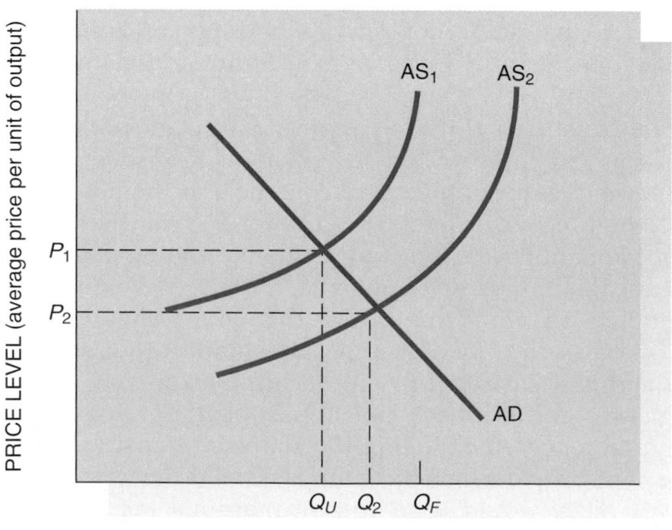

inflation and unemployment. This requires more attention to the specific nature of the supply constraints. Perhaps the early rise in the AS curve is due to **structural unemployment.** Prices may be rising in the telecommunications industry, for example, while unemployed workers are abundant in the housing industry. The higher prices and wages in telecommunications function as a signal to transfer resources from the housing industry into telecommunications. Such resource shifts, however, may not occur smoothly or quickly. In the interim, public policy can be developed to facilitate interindustry mobility or to alter the structure of supply or demand.

structural unemployment Unemployment caused by a mismatch between the skills (or location) of job seekers and the requirements (or location) of available jobs.

On the demand side, the government could decrease the demand for telecommunications by increasing excise taxes on phone services or by buying fewer computers for government use. It could increase the demand for houses by providing housing subsidies to poor people, greater home-related tax deductions for everyone, or lower interest rates in the mortgage market. On the supply side, the government could offer tax credits for housing construction, teach construction workers how to install and operate telecommunications equipment, or speed up the job-search process.

High tax rates or costly regulations might also contribute to stagflation. If either of these constraints exists, high prices (inflation) may not be a sufficient incentive for increased output. In this case, reductions in tax rates and regulation could shift the AS curve rightward, easing stagflation pressures.

Stagflation may have arisen from a temporary contraction (leftward shift) of aggregate supply that both reduces output and drives up prices. In this case, neither structural unemployment nor excessive demand is the culprit. Rather, an external shock (such as a natural disaster) or an abrupt change in world trade (such as higher oil prices) is the cause of stagflation. The high oil prices and supply disruptions that occurred during the Gulf War (1990–91) illustrate this problem. The Asian currency crisis of 1997–98 was another external shock. The 1999–2000 jump in world oil prices was yet another one. In all these circumstances, conventional policy tools are unlikely to provide a complete cure. In most cases the economy simply has to adjust to a temporary setback.

Fine-Tuning

Everything looks easy on the blackboard. Indeed economic theory seems to have all the answers for our macro problems. Some people even imagine that economic theory has the potential to fine-tune the economy, that is, to correct any and all macro problems that arise. Such **fine-tuning** would entail continual adjustments to policy levers. When unemployment is the problem, simply give the economy a jolt of fiscal or monetary stimulus; when inflation is worrisome, simply tap on the fiscal or monetary brakes. To fulfill our goals for content and distribution, we simply pick the right target for stimulus or restraint. With a little attention and experience, the right speed could be found and the economy guided successfully down the road to prosperity.

fine-tuning Adjustments in economic policy designed to counteract small changes in economic outcomes; continuous responses to changing economic conditions.

The Economic Record

The economy's track record does not live up to these high expectations. To be sure, the economy has continued to grow and we have attained an impressive standard of living. We have also had some great years when both unemployment and inflation rates were low, as in 1994–2000. Nor can we lose sight of the fact that even in a bad year our per capita income greatly exceeds the realities and even the expectations in most other countries of the world. Nevertheless, we must also recognize that our economic history is punctuated

FIGURE 16.2
The Economic Record

The Full Employment and Balanced Growth Act of 1978 established specific goals for unemployment (4 percent), inflation (3 percent), and economic growth (4 percent). We have rarely attained all those goals, however, as these graphs illustrate. Measurement, design, and policy implementation problems help explain these shortcomings.

Source: *Economic Report of the President*, 2003.

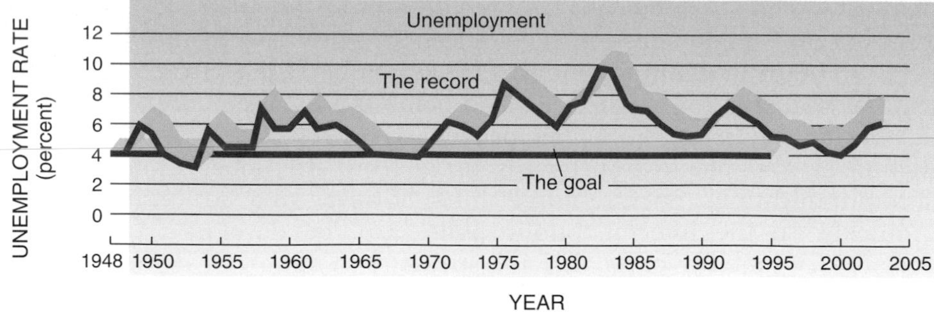

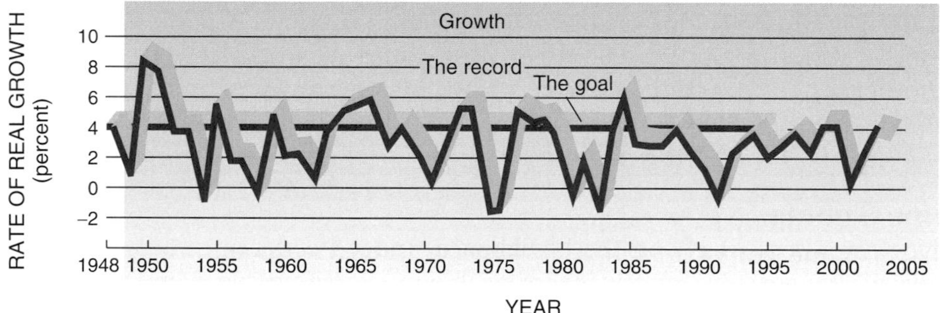

by periods of recession, high unemployment, inflation, and recurring concern for the distribution of income and mix of output.

The graphs in Figure 16.2 provide a quick summary of our experiences since 1946, the year the Employment Act committed the federal government to macro stability. It is evident that our economic track record is far from perfect. In the 1970s the record was particularly bleak: two recessions, high inflation, and persistent unemployment. The 1980s were better but still marred by two recessions, one of which sent the unemployment rate to a post–World War II record. Then inflation accelerated at the end of the 1980s, despite the fact that we were still a long way from the avowed goal of 4 percent unemployment. When more restrictive monetary and fiscal policies were implemented, the economy stumbled into another recession (1990–91).

In terms of real economic growth, the record is equally spotty. Output actually declined (i.e., recessions) in eight years and grew less than 3 percent in another nineteen. The 1990s got under way with virtually zero growth as the seven-year expansion of the 1980s petered out. After that,

COMPARATIVE PERFORMANCE HEADLINE

Macro Performance in the 1990s

The performance of the U.S. economy in the 1990s was better than that of most developed economies. Japan had the greatest success in restraining inflation (15 percent) but suffered from sluggish growth (1.5 percent per year). The United States grew faster and had less unemployment than Europe.

Performance (annual average percentage)	U.S.	Japan	Germany	United Kingdom	France	Italy	Canada
Real growth	2.4	1.5	2.4	1.6	1.8	1.4	1.8
Inflation	3.0	1.2	2.5	3.9	2.0	4.1	2.2
Unemployment	5.8	3.0	9.0	7.3	11.2	11.4	9.7

Source: *International Monetary Fund.*

NOTE: No nation gets a gold medal in all macro dimensions. Inflation, unemployment, and growth records reveal uneven performance.

however, the track record improved a lot. For eight years in a row the U.S. economy grew well. The unemployment rate fell to generational lows, with relatively little inflation. Even with the strong economy of the 1990s, however, 30 million Americans remained poor. Moreover, the distribution of income in 2000 was little changed from that of 1946. So not all our economic goals were met. Then all performance measures worsened when the economy slipped into another recession (March–November 2001) and terrorist attacks (September 2001) sidetracked the economy.

The economic performance of the United States is similar to that of other Western nations. The economies of most countries did not grow as fast as the U.S. economy in the 1980s or 1990s. But, as the accompanying Headline shows, some countries did a better job of restraining prices or reducing unemployment.

Why Things Don't Always Work

We have already noted the readiness of economists and politicians to blame each other for the continuing gap between our economic goals and performance. Rather than taking sides, however, we may note some general constraints on successful policymaking. In this regard, we can distinguish ***four obstacles to policy success:***

- ***Goal conflicts***
- ***Measurement problems***
- ***Design problems***
- ***Implementation problems***

Goal Conflicts

The first factor to note is potential conflicts in policy priorities. Suppose that the economy was suffering from stagflation and, further, that all macro policies involved some tradeoff between unemployment and inflation. Should fighting inflation or fighting unemployment get priority? Unemployed people will put the highest priority on attaining full employment. Labor unions and advocates for the poor will press for faster economic growth. Bankers, creditors, and people on fixed incomes will worry more about inflation. They will lobby for more restrictive fiscal and monetary policies. There is no way to satisfy everyone in such a situation.

In practice, these goal conflicts are often institutionalized in the decision-making process. The Fed is traditionally viewed as the guardian of price stability and tends to favor policy restraint. The president and Congress worry more about people's jobs and government programs, so lean toward policy stimulus. The end result may entail a mix of contradictory policies.

Distributional goals may also conflict with macro objectives. Anti-inflationary policies may require cutbacks in programs for the poor, the elderly, or needy students. These cutbacks may be politically impossible. Likewise, tight-money policies may be viewed as too great a burden for small businesses.

Although the policy levers listed in Table 16.1 are powerful, they cannot grant all our wishes. Since we still live in a world of scarce resources, ***all policy decisions entail opportunity costs.*** This means that we will always be confronted with tradeoffs: the best we can hope for is a set of compromises that yields optimal outcomes, not ideal ones.

Even if we all agreed on policy priorities, success would not be assured. We would still have to confront the more mundane problems of measurement, design, and implementation.

Measurement Problems

One reason firefighters are pretty successful in putting out fires before whole cities burn down is that fires are highly visible phenomena. Such visibility is not characteristic of economic problems, at least not in their more moderate manifestations. An increase in the unemployment rate from 5 to 6 percent, for example, is not the kind of thing you notice while crossing the street. Unless you lose your own job, the increase in unemployment is not likely to attract your attention. The same is true of prices; small increases in product prices are unlikely to ring many alarms. Hence both inflation and unemployment may worsen considerably before anyone takes serious notice. Were we as slow and ill-equipped to notice fires, whole neighborhoods would burn before someone rang the alarm.

Measurement problems are a very basic policy constraint. To formulate good economic policy, we must first determine the nature of our problems. To do so, we must measure employment changes, output changes, price changes, and other macro outcomes. Although the government spends vast sums of money to collect and process such data, the available information is always dated and incomplete. ***At best, we know what was happening in the economy last month or last week.*** The processes of data collection, assembly, and presentation take time, even in this age of high-speed computers. The average recession lasts about 11 months, but official data generally do not even confirm the existence of a recession until eight months after a downturn starts! The recession of 2001 was no exception, as the accompanying Headline shows.

Forecasts In an ideal world, policymakers would not only respond to economic problems that occur but also *anticipate* their occurrence and act to avoid them. If we foresee an inflation emerging, for example, we want to take immediate action to keep aggregate demand from increasing. That is to say, the successful firefighter not only responds to fires but also looks for hazards that might start one.

MEASUREMENT PROBLEMS HEADLINE

Despite Job Losses, the Recession Is Finally Declared Officially Over

The National Bureau of Economic Research said the U.S. economic recession that began in March 2001 ended eight months later, not long after the Sept. 11 terrorist attacks.

Most economists concluded more than a year ago that the recession ended in late 2001. But yesterday's declaration by the NBER—a private, nonprofit economic research group that is considered the official arbiter of recession timing—came after a lengthy internal debate over whether there can be an economic recovery if the labor market continues to contract. The bureau's answer: a decisive yes. . . .

The NBER committee is notoriously slow in making its declarations on the timing of the business cycle. Still, the 20 months it waited to declare the recession's end was slightly shorter than the 21 months it took to declare the end of the 1990–91 recession. That, too, was a so-called jobless recovery, though the job losses weren't as severe as they have been lately.

—Jon E. Hilsenrath

Source: *Wall Street Journal,* July 18, 2003, p. 1.

NOTE: Successful macro policy requires timely and accurate data on the economy. The measurement process is slow and imperfect, however.

Unfortunately, economic policymakers are again at a disadvantage. Their knowledge of future problems is even worse than their knowledge of current problems. ***In designing policy, policymakers must depend on economic forecasts,*** that is, informed guesses about what the economy will look like in future periods.

Macro Models Those guesses are often based on complex computer models of how the economy works. These models—referred to as *econometric macro models*—are mathematical summaries of the economy's performance. The models try to identify the key determinants of macro performance, then show what happens to macro outcomes when they change. As the accompanying Headline suggests, the apparent precision of such computer models may disguise "a black art."

An economist feeds the computer two essential inputs. One is a model of how the economy allegedly works. Such models are quantitative summaries of one or more macro theories. A Keynesian model, for example, will include equations that show multiplier spending responses to tax cuts. A monetarist model will show that tax cuts raise interest rates (crowding out), not total spending. And a supply-side model stipulates labor-supply and production responses. The computer can't tell which theory is right; it just predicts what it is programmed to see. In other words, the computer sees the world through the eyes of its economic master.

The second essential input in a computer forecast is the assumed values for critical economic variables. A Keynesian model, for example, must specify how large a multiplier to expect. All the computer does is carry out the required mathematical routines once it is told that the multiplier is relevant and what its value is. It cannot discern the true multiplier any better than it can pick the right theory.

Given the dependence of computers on the theories and perceptions of their economic masters, it is not surprising that computer forecasts often differ greatly. It's also not surprising that they are often wrong.

Even policymakers who are familiar with both economic theory and computer models can make some pretty bad calls. In January 1990, Fed

HEADLINE MACRO MODELS

Tough Calls in Economic Forecasting

Seers often peer into cracked crystal balls

In presenting his annual economic outlook last Thursday, the chairman of President Clinton's Council of Economic Advisers was having nothing to do with all the recession talk going around.

"Let me be clear," Martin Baily said,"we don't think that we're going into recession."

The same message was delivered the next day by Clinton in a Rose Garden economic valedictory. Citing the predictions of 50 private forecasters known as the Blue Chip Consensus—"the experts who make a living doing this," as he put it—Clinton assured Americans that the economy would continue to grow this year at an annual rate of 2 percent to 3 percent.

What the president and his adviser failed to mention was that "the experts" have not predicted any of the nine recessions since the end of World War II. . . .

"A recession, by its nature, is a speculative call."

On first blush, such humility may seem at odds with the aura surrounding the modern day forecaster. Using high-speed computers and sophisticated models of the U.S. economy, they constantly revise their two-year predictions for everything from unemployment to business investment to long-term interest rates, expressed numerically to the first decimal point.

But according to the forecasters themselves, what may appear to be a precise science is a black art, one that is constantly confounded by the changing structure of the economy and the refusal of investors, consumers and business executives to behave as rationally and predictably in real life as they do in the economic models.

"The reason we have trouble calling recessions is that all recessions are anomalies," said Joel Prakken, president of Macroeconomic Advisers of St. Louis, one of the nation's leading forecasting firms.

—Steven Pearlstein

Source: *Washington Post:*, January 15, 2001, p. 1.

NOTE: Even the most sophisticated computer models rely on basic assumptions about consumer and investor behavior. If the assumptions are wrong, the forecast will likely be wrong as well.

chairman Alan Greenspan assured Congress that the risk of a recession was as low as 20 percent. Although he said he "wouldn't bet the ranch" on such a low probability, he was confident that the odds of a recession were below 50 percent. Five months after his testimony, the 1990–91 recession began.

Martin Baily, chairman of President Clinton's Council of Economic Advisers, made the same mistake in January 2001. "Let me be clear," he told the press, "we don't think that we're going into recession." President Clinton echoed this optimism, projecting growth of 2–3 percent in 2001 (see Headline). Two months later the U.S. economy fell into another recession.

Design Problems

Forget all these bad forecasts for a moment and just pretend that we can, somehow, get a reliable forecast of where the economy is headed. The outlook, let us suppose, is bad. Now we are in the driver's seat, trying to steer the economy past looming dangers. We need to chart our course—to design an economic plan. What action should we take? How will the marketplace respond to any specific action we take? Will the aggregate demand curve respond as expected? What shape will the aggregate supply curve have? Which macro theory should we use to guide policy decisions?

Suppose, for example, that we adopt a Keynesian approach to ending a recession. Specifically, we cut income taxes to stimulate consumer spending.

DESIGN PROBLEMS HEADLINE

Japanese Tighten Belts

Many plan to save, not spend, tax cut

CHIBA, Japan—The proof is not in the pudding. It's in the soy sauce.

Every day just about every Japanese person uses soy sauce, on rice and fish and chicken and in cooking. Yuzaburo Mogi, family patriarch of the famous Kikkoman brand, can tell by people's soy sauce–buying habits that his nation's economy is in deep trouble.

"Food companies are usually not hit by recession, but this time we are having trouble," said Mogi, whose family has been making soy sauce for more than 300 years. "People who usually buy expensive soy sauce are buying cheaper sauce. And people who bought our cheaper soy sauce are now buying other brands."

The declining soy sauce index is a useful indicator to explain why one of the world's richest countries is in so much trouble. The heart of why the economy is expected to shrink for the first time in a quarter-century is simple: People are spending less. . . .

Prime Minister Ryutaro Hashimoto aimed a $30 billion rescue effort directly at consumers last week. He proposed a tax cut that would give a typical household as much as $500 this year and again next year.

But housewives, retirees and salarymen in this Tokyo suburb are not impressed with Hashimoto's rescue. They said it will not move them to spend more.

In hours of discussions, they talked about why they started saving more: fear that more jobs will be lost and wages cut, distrust of the government's ability to correct structural problems in the economy and a growing feeling that if they do not look out for themselves, no one will.

—Mary Jordan and Kevin Sullivan

Source: *Washington Post*, April 14, 1998, p. 1.

NOTE: The success of macro policy depends on how market participants respond to policy initiatives. Japanese consumers didn't follow the Keynesian script.

How do we know that consumers will respond as anticipated? Perhaps the marginal propensity to consume has changed. Maybe the level of consumer confidence has dropped. Any of these changes could frustrate even the best-intentioned policy, as Japanese policymakers learned in 1998–99 (see Headline above). The successful policymaker needs a very good crystal ball—one that will also foretell how market participants are going to respond to any specific actions taken.

Implementation Problems

Measurement and design problems can break the spirit of even the best policymaker (or his economic advisers). Yet measurement and design problems are only part of the story. A good idea is of little value unless someone puts it to use. Accordingly, to understand fully why things go wrong, we must also consider the difficulties of implementing a well-designed (and credible) policy initiative.

Congressional Deliberations Suppose that the president and his Council of Economic Advisers (perhaps in conjunction with the secretary of the Treasury and the director of the Office of Management and Budget) decide that the rate of aggregate spending is slowing down. A tax cut, they believe, is necessary to stimulate demand for goods and services. Can they simply go ahead and cut tax rates? No, because all tax changes must be legislated by Congress. Once the president decides on the appropriate policy initiative, he must ask Congress for authority to take the required action. This means a delay in implementing policy, and possibly no policy at all.

At the very least, the president must convince Congress of the desirability of his suggested action. The tax proposal must work its way through separate committees of both the House of Representatives and the Senate, get on the congressional calendar, and be approved in each chamber. If there are important differences in Senate and House versions of the tax-cut legislation, they must be compromised in a joint conference. The modified proposal must then be returned to each chamber for approval.

The same kind of process applies to the outlay size of the budget. Once the president has submitted his budget proposals (in January), Congress reviews them, then sets its own spending goals. After that, the budget is broken down into 13 different categories, and a separate appropriations bill is written for each one. These bills spell out in detail how much can be spent and for what purposes. Once Congress passes them, they go to the president for acceptance or veto.

In theory, all of these budget deliberations are to be completed in nine months. Budget legislation requires Congress to finish the process by October 1 (the beginning of the federal fiscal year). Congress rarely meets this deadline, however. In most years the budget debate continues well into the fiscal year. In some years, the budget debate is not resolved until the fiscal year is nearly over! The final budget legislation is typically over 1,000 pages long and so complex that few people understand all its dimensions.

This description of congressional activity is not an outline for a civics course; rather, it is an important explanation of why economic policy is not fully effective. ***Even if the right policy is formulated to solve an emerging economic problem, there is no assurance that it will be implemented. And if it is implemented, there is no assurance that it will take effect at the right time.*** One of the most frightening prospects for economic policy is that a policy design intended to serve a specific problem will be implemented much later, when economic conditions have changed. The policy's effect on the economy may then be the opposite of what was intended.

Figure 16.3 is a schematic view of why things don't always work out as well as economic theory suggests they might. There are always delays between the time a problem emerges and the time it is recognized. There are additional delays between recognition and response design, between design and implementation, and finally between implementation and impact. Not only may mistakes be made at each juncture, but even correct decisions may be overcome by changing economic conditions.

Politics vs. Economics Last but not least, we must confront the politics of economic policy. Tax hikes and budget cuts rarely win votes (see cartoon).

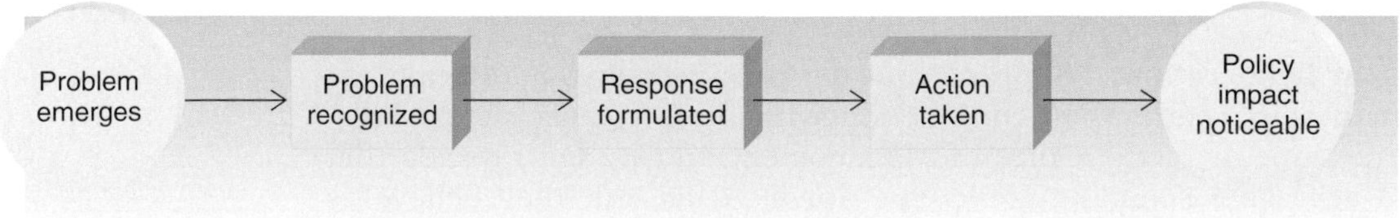

FIGURE 16.3 Policy Response: A Series of Time Lags

Even the best-intentioned economic policy can be frustrated by time lags. It takes time for a problem to be recognized, time to formulate a policy response, and still more time to implement that policy. By the time the policy begins to affect the economy, the underlying problem may have changed.

Budget cuts are not popular with voters—even when economic conditions warrant fiscal restraint.

On the other hand, tax cuts and pork-barrel spending tend to make voters happy. Accordingly, savvy politicians tend to stimulate the economy before elections, then tighten the fiscal restraints afterward. This creates a kind of *political* business cycle—a two-year pattern of short-run stops and starts. The conflict between the urgent need to get reelected and the necessity to manage the economy results in a seesaw kind of instability.

The politics of fiscal policy were clearly visible in 1999. With a presidential election approaching, both the Republicans and the Democrats wanted to use the budget to win votes. The Republicans pushed huge tax cuts; the Democrats promised more social spending (see Headline). Unfortunately, neither form of fiscal stimulus was appropriate for an economy already fully employed and showing signs of inflationary pressure. Two

POLITICS VS. ECONOMICS HEADLINE

Budget Economics, Politics Collide

The good news for critics of the big GOP tax packages now moving through Congress is that many economists say tax cuts are a terrible idea right now, since they would probably accelerate consumer spending, pouring gasoline on the fire of an already hot economy.

But the bad news for the critics, many of whom want to use the federal budget surplus to boost spending instead of cutting taxes, is that a lot of those same economists think more government spending is an equally terrible idea—for the same reason.

They fear that further stimulating a booming economy could trigger a destructive outburst of inflation. . . .

"You really wonder, does Congress not understand this?" said Nicholas S. Perna, chief economist with the Fleet Financial Group in Boston. "If financial markets get spooked by the consequences of big tax cuts and big spending increases, [they] might raise interest rates.". . .

The question of what consumers would do with a tax cut is at the core of the economic debate over whether the cuts are a good idea. If people react to lower taxes by buying more cars, clothes and CDs, that "demand-side" stimulus might push the economy to the point at which inflation takes off. But some economists argue that if consumers react by saving more of their money and working longer hours because they could keep more of what they earned, that "supply-side" stimulus would not overheat the economy.

Trouble is, economists say tax cuts often have both demand-side and supply-side effects, and they can disagree wildly over which is bigger, when it kicks in, and so on.

—George Hager

Source: *Washington Post*, July 28, 1999, p. El.

NOTE: Tax cuts and increased spending are always politically appealing even if not economically desirable. Politics can derail sound economic advice.

years later, when some fiscal stimulus was more appropriate, lobbyists and politicians spent months arguing over who would get the tax cuts the economy needed.

In theory, the political independence of the Fed's Board of Governors provides some protection from ill-advised but politically advantageous policy initiatives. In practice, however, the Fed's relative obscurity and independence may backfire. The president and the Congress know that if they don't take action against inflation—by raising taxes or cutting government spending—the Fed can and will take stronger action to restrain aggregate demand. This is a classic case of having one's cake and eating it too. Elected officials win votes for not raising taxes or not cutting some constituent's favorite spending program. They also take credit for any reduction in the rate of inflation brought about by Federal Reserve policies. To top it off, Congress and the president can also blame the Fed for driving up interest rates or starting a recession if monetary policy becomes too restrictive.

Finally, we must recognize that policy design is obstructed by a certain lack of will. Neither the man in the street nor the elected public official is constantly attuned to economic goals and activities. Even students enrolled in economics courses have a hard time keeping their minds on the economy and its problems. The executive and legislative branches of government, for their part, are likely to focus on economic concerns only when economic problems become serious or voters demand action. Otherwise, policymakers are apt to be complacent about economic policy as long as economic performance is within a tolerable range of desired outcomes.

POLICY PERSPECTIVES

Hands Off or Hands On?

In view of the goal conflicts and the measurement, design, and implementation problems that policymakers confront, it is less surprising that things sometimes go wrong than that things often work out right. The maze of obstacles through which theory must pass before it becomes policy explains many economic disappointments. On this basis alone, we may conclude that ***consistent fine-tuning of the economy is not compatible with either our design capabilities or our decision-making procedures.***

Hands-Off Policy Some critics of economic policy take this argument a few steps further. If fine-tuning isn't really possible, they say, we should abandon discretionary policies altogether. Typically, policymakers seek minor adjustments in interest rates, unemployment, inflation, and growth. The pressure to do something is particularly irresistible in election years. In so doing, however, policymakers are as likely to worsen the economic situation as to improve it. Moreover, the potential for such short-term discretion undermines people's confidence in the economy's future.

Critics of discretionary policies say we would be better off with fixed policy rules. They would require the Fed to increase the money supply at a constant rate. Congress would be required to maintain balanced budgets or at least to offset deficits in sluggish years with surpluses in years of high growth. Such rules would prevent policymakers from over- or understimulating the economy. They would also add a dose of certainty to the economic outlook.

Milton Friedman has been one of the most persistent advocates of fixed-policy rules instead of discretionary policies. With discretionary authority, Friedman argues,

> the wrong decision is likely to be made in a large fraction of cases because the decision makers are examining only a limited area and not taking into account the cumulative consequences of the policy as a whole. On the other hand, if a general rule is adopted for a group of cases as a bundle, the existence of that rule has favorable effects on people's attitudes and beliefs and expectations that would not follow even from the discretionary adoption of precisely the same policy on a series of separate occasions.[1]

The case for a hands-off policy stance is based on practical, not theoretical, arguments. Everyone agrees that flexible, discretionary policies *could* result in better economic performance. But Friedman and others argue that the practical requirements of monetary and fiscal management are too demanding and thus prone to failure. Moreover, required policies may be compromised by political pressures.

Hands-On Policy Critics of fixed rules acknowledge occasional policy blunders but emphasize that the historical record of prices, employment, and growth has improved since active fiscal and monetary policies were adopted. Without flexibility in the money supply and the budget, they argue, the economy would be less stable and our economic goals would remain unfulfilled. They say the government must maintain a hands-on policy of active intervention.

The historical evidence does not provide overwhelming support for either policy stance. Victor Zarnowitz showed that the U.S. economy has been much more stable since 1946 than it was in earlier periods (1875–1918 and 1919–45). Recessions have gotten shorter and economic expansions longer. But a variety of factors—including a shift from manufacturing to services, a larger government sector, and automatic stabilizers—have contributed to this improved macro performance. The contribution of discretionary macro policy is less clear. It is easy to observe what actually happened but almost impossible to determine what would have occurred in other circumstances. It is also evident that there have been noteworthy occasions—the September 11 terrorist attacks, for example—when something more than fixed rules for monetary and fiscal policy was called for, a contingency even Professor Friedman acknowledges. Thus occasional flexibility is required, even if a nondiscretionary policy is appropriate in most situations.

Finally, one must contend with the difficulties inherent in adhering to any fixed rules. How is the Fed, for example, supposed to maintain a steady rate of growth in M1? The supply of money (M1) is not determined exclusively by the Fed. It also depends on the willingness of market participants to buy and sell bonds, to maintain bank balances, and to borrow money. Since all of this behavior is subject to change at any time, maintaining a steady rate of M1 growth is an impossible task.

The same is true of fiscal policy. Government spending and taxes are directly influenced by changes in unemployment, inflation, interest rates, and growth. These automatic stabilizers make it virtually impossible to maintain any fixed rule for budget balancing. Moreover, if we eliminated the automatic stabilizers, we would risk greater instability.

[1]Milton Friedman. *Capitalism and Freedom* (Chicago: University of Chicago Press, 1962), p. 53.

Modest Expectations The clamor for fixed policy rules is more a rebuke of past policy than a viable policy alternative. We really have no choice but to pursue discretionary policies. Recognition of measurement, design, and implementation problems is important for an understanding of the way the economy functions. But even though it is impossible to reach all our goals, we cannot abandon conscientious attempts to get as close as possible to goal fulfillment. If public policy can create a few more jobs, a better mix of output, a little more growth and price stability, or an improved distribution of income, those initiatives are worthwhile.

SUMMARY

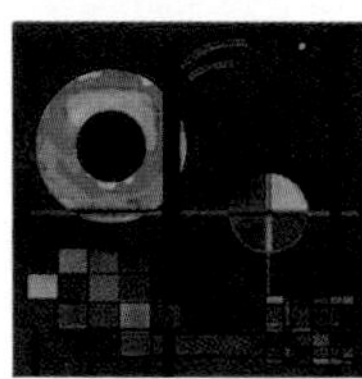

- The government possesses an array of policy levers, each of which can significantly alter macroeconomic outcomes. To end a recession, we can cut taxes, expand the money supply, or increase government spending. To curb inflation, we can reverse each of these policy levers. To overcome stagflation, we can combine fiscal and monetary levers with improved supply-side incentives.
- Although the potential of economic theory seems impressive, the economic record does not look as good. Persistent unemployment, recurring economic slowdowns, and nagging inflation suggest that the realities of policymaking are more difficult than theory implies.
- To a large extent, the failures of economic policy are a reflection of scarce resources and competing goals. Even when consensus exists, however, serious obstacles to effective economic policy remain. These obstacles include:
  (*a*) *Measurement problems.* Our knowledge of economic performance is always dated and incomplete. We must rely on forecasts of future problems.
  (*b*) *Design problems.* We don't know exactly how the economy will respond to specific policies.
  (*c*) *Implementation problems.* It takes time for Congress and the president to agree on an appropriate plan of action. Moreover, the agreements reached may respond more to political needs than to economic needs.

  For all these reasons, the fine-tuning of economic performance rarely lives up to its theoretical potential.
- Many people favor rules rather than discretionary macro policies. They argue that discretionary policies are unlikely to work and risk being wrong. Critics respond that discretionary policies are needed to cope with ever-changing economic circumstances.

Terms to Remember

Define the following terms:

business cycle
fiscal policy
automatic stabilizer
fiscal year (FY)
monetary policy
money supply (M1)
supply-side policy
GDP gap
multiplier
stagflation
structural unemployment
fine-tuning

Questions for Discussion

1. What policies would Keynesian, monetarists, and supply-siders advocate for
   (*a*) Restraining inflation?
   (*b*) Reducing unemployment?
2. Should economic policies respond immediately to any changes in reported unemployment or inflation rates? When should a response be undertaken?
3. Suppose that it is an election year and that aggregate demand is growing so fast that it threatens to set off an inflationary movement. Why might Congress and the president hesitate to cut back on government spending or raise taxes, as economic theory suggests is appropriate?
4. In his fiscal 1997 budget, President Clinton proposed decreases in defense spending to help reduce the budget deficit. Should military spending be subject to macroeconomic constraints? What programs should be expanded or contracted to bring about needed changes in the budget?
5. What is the "amazing phenomenon" referred to in the Headline on p. 357?
6. Are we better off or worse off as a result of the discretionary macro policies of the last two years? How can you tell?
7. Suppose that the economy is slumping into recession and needs a fiscal-policy boost. Voters, however, are opposed to larger federal deficits. What should policymakers do?
8. Outline a macro policy package for attaining full employment and price stability in the next 12 months. What obstacles, if any, will impede attainment of these goals?
9. What should the Fed have done in late 2000 when consumer confidence started falling (see Headline, p. 359)? Would that entail fine-tuning?
10. Democrats labeled President Bush's 2001 tax-cut plan as a "giveaway to the rich" because it gave the richest taxpayers the largest tax cuts. Corporate America also complained that there were no *business* tax cuts in the Bush plan. How would such criticism affect the lag time for fiscal policy?

Problems

1. The 1997 fiscal policy package included roughly \$200 billion in government spending cuts and \$70 billion in tax cuts. If all the tax cuts were given to households, by how much would aggregate demand shift (*a*) initially and (*b*) ultimately as a result of the policy package?
2. Suppose the federal budget is balanced but that automatic stabilizers increase tax revenues by \$20 billion per year and decrease transfer payments (e.g., welfare, unemployment benefits) by \$8 billion per year for every 1 percentage point change in the real GDP growth. Using this information, complete the following table:

Change in GDP Growth Rate	Change in Tax Revenue	Change in Transfer Payments	Change in Budget Balance
−2%			
+1%			
+3%			

3. On the basis of the information in the preceding question, what will happen to the federal budget balance if the economy falls into a recession of −2.0 percent from a growth path of +2.5 percent?
4. The following table presents hypothetical data on government expenditure, taxes, exports, imports, inflation, unemployment, and pollution for three levels of equilibrium income (GDP). A government decision maker is trying to determine the optimal level of government expenditures, with each of the three columns being a possible choice. At the time of the choice the inflation index is 1.0. Dollar amounts are in billions per year.

	Nominal GDP		
	$7,000	$8,000	$9,000
Government expenditure	$700	$800	$900
Taxes	$600	$800	$1,000
Exports	$300	$300	$300
Imports	$100	$300	$500
Inflation (index)	1.00	1.04	1.15
Unemployment rate	10%	4%	3.5%
Pollution index	1.00	1.80	2.00

(*a*) Compute the federal budget balance, balance of trade, and real GDP for each level of nominal GDP.

(*b*) What government expenditure level would best accomplish each of the following goals?

Lowest taxes
Largest trade surplus
Lowest pollution
Lowest inflation rate
Lowest unemployment rate
Highest amount of public goods and services
Highest real income
Balancing the federal budget
Achieving a balance of trade
Maintaining price stability
Achieving full employment

(*c*) What government expenditure levels would most flagrantly violate each of the preceding goals?

(*d*) Which policy would be in the best interests of the country?

(*e*) What policies, in addition to changes in government expenditures, might the government use to attain more of its desired goals?

Web Activities

1. Log on to www.cbo.gov. Click on current economic and budget projections. Access the most recent update.
   (*a*) What is the CBO's projection for economic growth in the coming year?
   (*b*) Can monetary policy be used to help improve this forecast? If so, how?
   (*c*) Can fiscal policy be used to help improve this forecast? If so, how?

2. Log on to www.dismal.com and click on the link for economic indicators.
   (*a*) What does this chart suggest about economic growth in the United States?
   (*b*) Why might these data be unreliable in predicting growth in the next 12 months?
3. Log on to w3.access.gpo.gov/eop and click on the Economic Report of the President. Look on the last page of the report. How does U.S. economic growth compare to other major industrial nations' economic growth during the last 20 years?

Should I Vote My Pocketbook?

Living Econ

Research shows that economic circumstances greatly influence voter behavior. At election time, if there is high unemployment, rising prices, or falling incomes, voters typically will punish those who currently hold office and elect the "other guy." Conversely, a strong economy is likely to help the incumbents to be re-elected.

However, this chapter explains that economic policies often are delayed in terms of their impact on the economy. Also, there is a lag in measuring economic data so that today's economic news may describe yesterday's economy. That being the case, an incumbent political leader may have initiated the correct policy action, but the necessary time may not have elapsed for the economy to fully respond to the policy and for the results to be measured.

In practice, voters tend to be very impatient, rewarding or punishing those in office for recent economic successes or problems while neglecting the longer-term picture. Informed voters should not expect a quick impact from policy actions. In order to make wise decisions today, voters may need to consider the decisions made years ago.

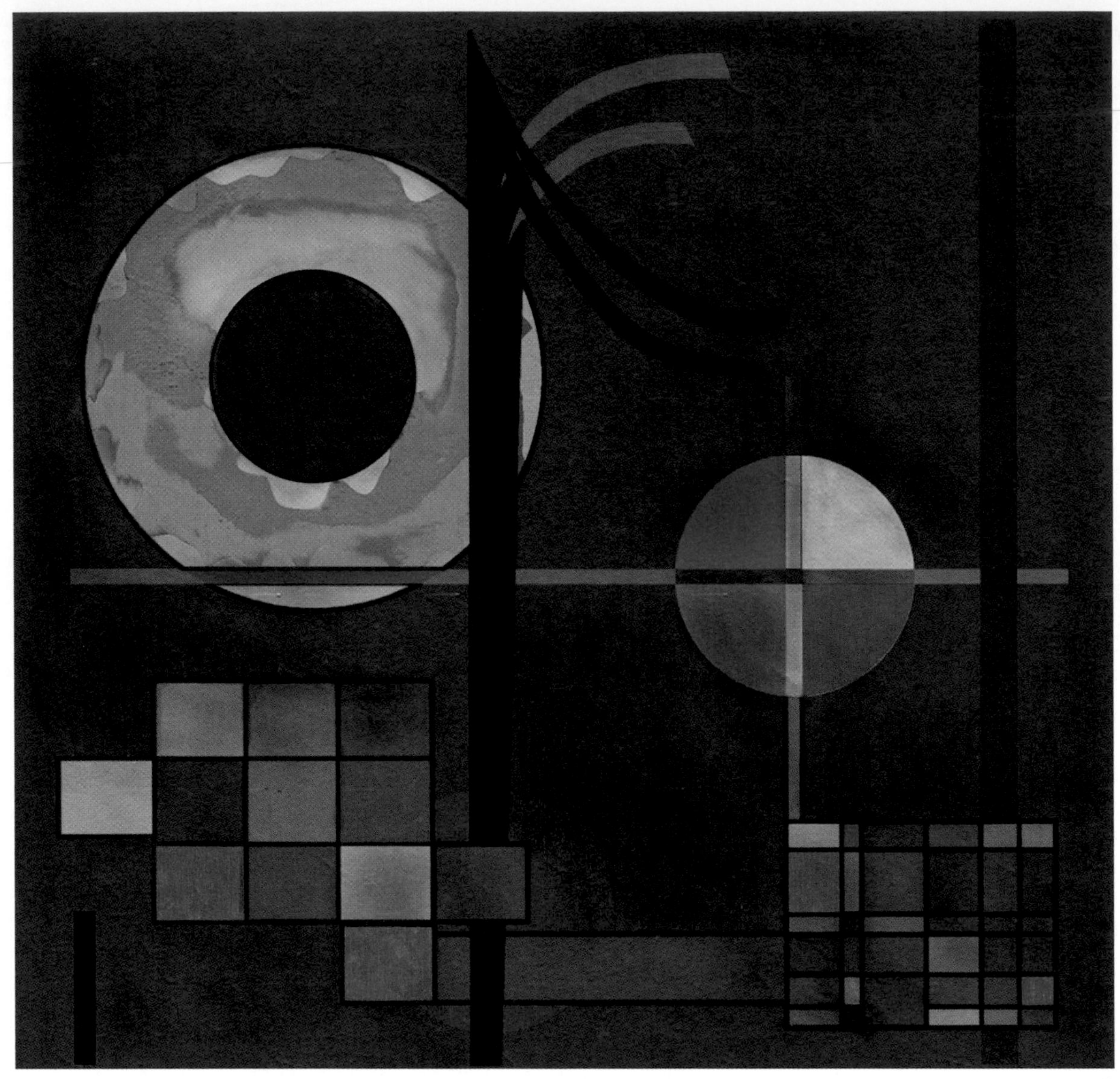

International Trade

CHAPTER 17

World travelers have discovered that Big Macs taste pretty much the same everywhere, but a Big Mac's price can vary tremendously. In 2003 a Big Mac was priced at 16,155 rupiah at the McDonald's in Jakarta, Indonesia. The same Big Mac cost 2.75 euros in Rome, 55 baht in Bangkok, and 6.35 francs in Geneva. So even those American travelers who don't want to sample foreign cuisine at least have to figure out foreign prices.

Similar problems affect even those consumers who stay at home. In 2003 American kids were clamoring for GameBoy SP machines produced in Japan. But how much would they have to pay? In Japan the machines were selling for 10,000 yen. What did that translate into in American dollars? In that same year American steel companies and wheat farmers were complaining that foreign producers were selling their products too cheaply. They wanted the government to protect them from unfair foreign competition.

Why does life have to be so complicated? Why doesn't everyone just use American dollars? Or why can't each nation simply produce for its own consumption so we don't have to worry about unfair foreign competition?

This chapter takes a bird's-eye view of how America interacts with the rest of the world. Of particular interest are the following questions:

- How is the international value of the dollar established?
- Why do we trade so much?
- Who benefits and who loses from imports, exports, and changes in the value of the dollar?

As we'll see, international trade *does* diminish the job and income opportunities for specific industries and workers. But those individual losses are overwhelmed by the gains the average consumer gets from international trade.

U.S. Trade Patterns

To understand how international trade affects our standard of living, it's useful to have a sense of *how much* we actually trade.

Imports

Baseball is often called the all-American sport. But the balls used in professional baseball are made in other countries. The same is true of coffee. Only a tiny fraction of the beans used to brew American coffee are grown in the United States (in Hawaii). All those PlayStation 2 machines and new Apple iPods are also produced abroad. The fact is that many of the products we consume are produced primarily or exclusively in other nations. All of these products are part of America's **imports.**

imports Goods and services purchased from foreign sources.

All told, America imports over $1.4 trillion worth of products from the rest of the world. Most of these products are *goods* like coffee, baseballs, and steel. The rest of the imports are *services,* like travel (on Air France or Aero Mexico); insurance (Lloyds of London), or entertainment (foreign movies). Together, imports account for about 14 percent of U.S. GDP.

Exports

While we are buying baseballs, coffee, video-game machines, and oil from the rest of the world, foreigners are buying our **exports.** In 2002 we exported $682 billion of goods, including farm products (wheat, corn, soybeans, tobacco), machinery (computers, aircraft, automobiles and auto parts), raw materials (lumber, iron ore, and chemicals). We also exported $292 billion of such services as tourism, insurance, and software.

exports Goods and services sold to foreign buyers.

As with our imports, our exports represent a relatively modest fraction of total GDP. Whereas we export 10–11 percent of total output, other developed countries export as much as 25–45 of their output (see Headline). Kuwait, for example, is considered a relatively prosperous nation, with a GDP per capita twice that of the world average. But how prosperous would it be if no one bought the oil exports that now account for nearly half of its output?

Even though the United States has a low export ratio, many American industries are very dependent on export sales. We export 25 to 50 percent of our rice, corn, and wheat production each year, and still more of our soybeans. Clearly, a decision by foreigners to stop eating American agricultural products would devastate a lot of American farmers. Such companies as Boeing (planes), Caterpillar Tractor (construction and farm machinery), Weyerhaeuser (logs, lumber), Eastman Kodak (film), Dow (chemicals), and Sun Microsystems (computer workstations) sell over one-fourth of their output in foreign markets. Pepsi and Coke are battling it out in the soft-drink markets of such unlikely places as Egypt, Abu Dhabi, Burundi, and Kazakhstan.

Trade Balances

As the figures indicate, our imports and exports were not equal in 2002. Quite the contrary: we had a large imbalance in our trade flows, with many more imports than exports. The trade balance is computed simply as the difference between exports and imports; that is

- Trade balance = exports − imports

trade deficit The amount by which the value of imports exceeds the value of exports in a given time period.

During 2002 we imported more than we exported and so had a negative trade balance. A negative trade balance is called a **trade deficit.** In 2002 the

EXPORT RATIOS HEADLINE

Exports in Relation to GDP

Exports of goods and services account for 11 percent of total U.S. output. Although substantial, this trade dependence is relatively low by international standards. Germany, for example, exports one-third of its total output, while Belgium exports more than 80 percent of its annual production (especially diamonds and chocolates). Myanmar, by contrast, is virtually a closed economy.

Source: The World Bank, *World Development Indicators, 2003*.

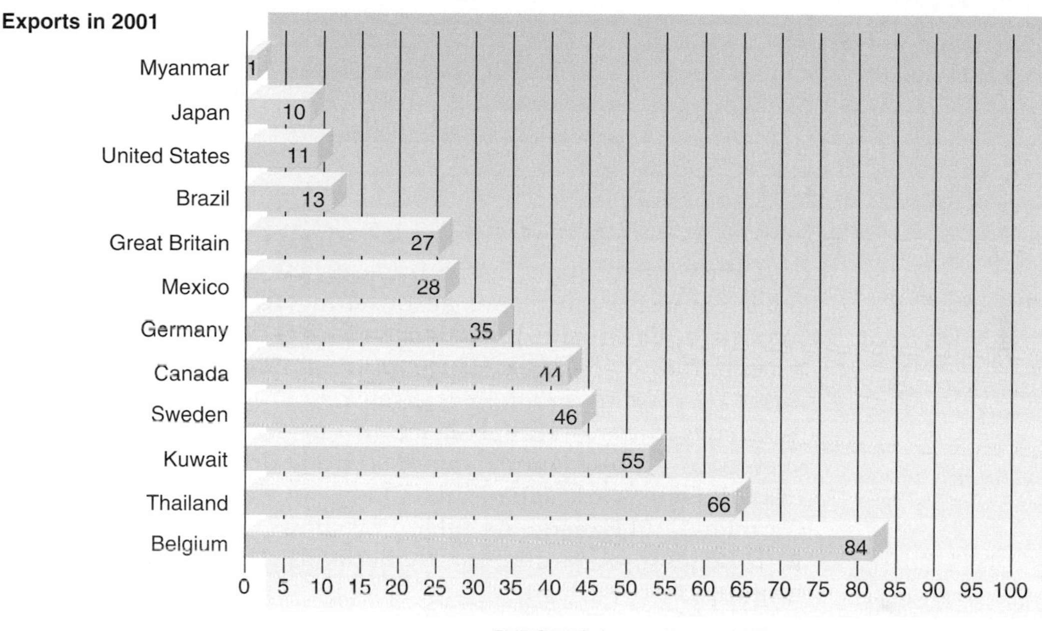

NOTE: The ratio of exports to total output is a measure of trade dependence. Most countries are much more dependent on trade than the United States.

United States had a negative trade balance of $418 billion. As Table 17.1 shows, this overall trade deficit reflected divergent patterns in goods and services. The United States had a very large deficit in *merchandise* trade, mostly due to auto and oil imports. In *services* (e.g., travel, finance, consulting), however, the United States enjoyed a modest surplus. When the merchandise and services accounts are combined, the United States ends up with a trade deficit.

	(In billions of dollars)		
Product Category	Exports	Imports	Surplus (Deficit)
Merchandise	$682	$1,165	$(483)
Services	292	227	65
Total trade	974	1,392	(418)

Source: U.S. Department of Commerce.

TABLE 17.1
Trade Balances

Both merchandise (goods) and services are traded between countries. The United States typically has a merchandise deficit and a services surplus. When combined, an overall trade deficit remained in 2002.

TABLE 17.2
Bilateral Trade Balances
The U.S. merchandise trade deficit of $483 billion in 2002 was the net result of bilateral deficits and surpluses. We had very large trade deficits with Japan and China, but small trade surpluses with the Netherlands, Belgium, Australia, and Hong Kong. International trade is *multi*national, with surpluses in some countries being offset by trade deficits elsewhere.

Country	Trade Balance (in billions of dollars)
Top deficit countries	
China	−103
Japan	−70
Canada	−50
Mexico	−37
Germany	−36
Top surplus countries	
Netherlands	+8.5
Australia	+6.6
Belgium	+3.5
Hong Kong	+3.3
United Arab Emirates	+2.7

Source: U.S. Department of Commerce.

trade surplus The amount by which the value of exports exceeds the value of imports in a given time period.

If the United States has a trade deficit with the rest of the world, then other countries must have an offsetting **trade surplus.** On a global scale, imports must equal exports, since every good exported by one country must be imported by another. Hence ***any imbalance in America's trade must be offset by reverse imbalances elsewhere.***

Whatever the overall balance in our trade accounts, bilateral balances vary greatly. For example, our 2002 trade deficit incorporated huge bilateral trade deficits with Japan and China, and also large deficits with Mexico, Germany, and Canada. As Table 17.2 shows, however, we had trade surpluses with Belgium, Australia, the Netherlands, Hong Kong, and the United Arab Emirates.

Motivation to Trade

Many people wonder why we trade so much, particularly since (1) we import many of the things we also export (e.g., computers, airplanes, clothes); (2) we *could* produce many of the other things we import; and (3) we seem to worry so much about imports and trade deficits. Why not just import those few things that we cannot produce ourselves, and export just enough to balance that trade?

Although it might seem strange to be importing goods we could produce ourselves, such trade is entirely rational. Indeed, our decision to trade with other countries arises from the same considerations that motivate individuals to specialize in production. Why don't you grow your own food, build your own shelter, and record your own songs? Presumably because you have found that you can enjoy a much higher standard of living (and better music) by working at just one job, then buying other goods in the marketplace. When you do so, you're no longer self-sufficient. Instead, you are *specializing* in production, relying on others to produce the array of goods and services you want. When countries trade goods and services, they are doing the same thing—*specializing* in production, then *trading* for other desired goods. Why do they do this? Because ***specialization increases total output.***

To demonstrate the economic gains from international trade, we'll examine the production possibilities of two countries. We want to demonstrate that two countries that trade can together produce more total output than they could in the absence of trade. If they can produce more, ***the gain from trade will be increased world output and thus a higher standard of living in both countries.***

Production and Consumption without Trade

Consider the production possibilities of just two countries—say, the United States and France. For the sake of illustration, we shall assume that both countries produce only two goods, bread and wine. To keep things simple, we will also transform the familiar **production-possibilities** curve into a straight line, as in Figure 17.1.

production possibilities The alternative combinations of goods and services that could be produced in a given time period with all available resources and technology.

The curves in Figure 17.1 suggest that the United States is capable of producing much more bread than France is. After all, we have a greater abundance of land, labor, and other factors of production. With these resources, we assume the United States is capable of producing up to 100 zillion loaves of bread per year, if we devote all of our resources to that purpose. This

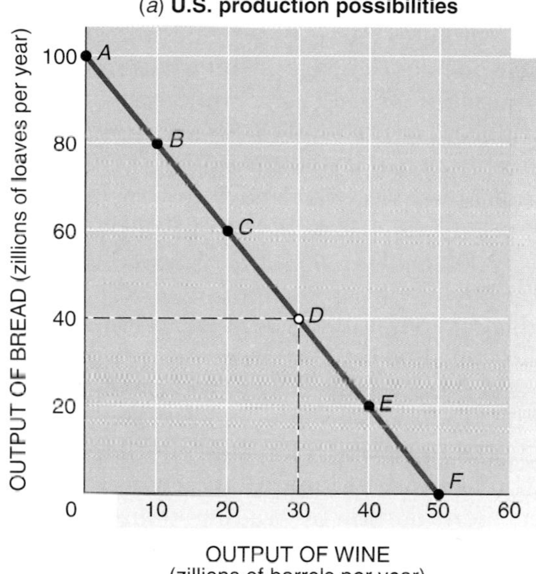

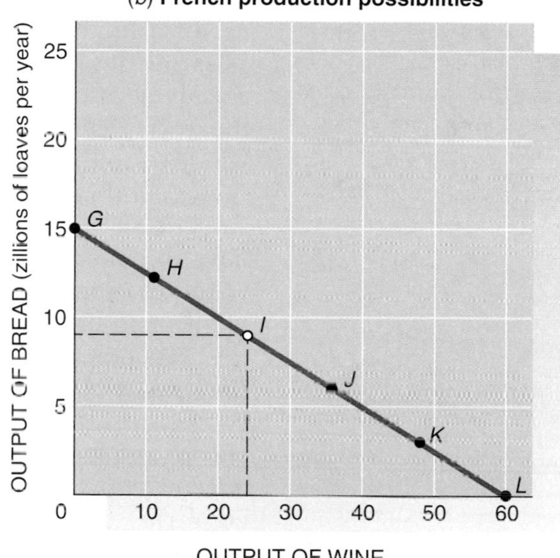

U.S. Production Possibilities		
	Bread (zillions of loaves)	Wine (zillions of barrels)
A	100	0
B	80	10
C	60	20
D	40	30
E	20	40
F	0	50

French Production Possibilities		
	Bread (zillions of loaves)	Wine (zillions of barrels)
G	15	0
H	12	12
I	9	24
J	6	36
K	3	48
L	0	60

FIGURE 17.1 Consumption Possibilities without Trade

In the absence of trade, a country's consumption possibilities are identical to its production possibilities. The assumed production possibilities of the United States and France are illustrated in the graphs and the corresponding schedules. Before entering into trade, the United States chose to produce and consume at point *D*, with 40 zillion loaves of bread and 30 zillion barrels of wine. France chose point *I* on its own production-possibilities curve. By trading, each country hopes to increase its consumption beyond these levels.

capability is indicated by point A in Figure 17.1a, and row A in the accompanying production-possibilities schedule. France (Figure 17.1b), on the other hand, confronts a *maximum* bread production of only 15 zillion loaves per year (point G) because it has little available land, less fuel, and fewer potential workers.

The assumed capacities of the two countries for wine production are 50 zillion barrels for us (point F) and 60 zillion for France (point L), reflecting France's greater experience in tending vines. Both countries are also capable of producing alternative *combinations* of bread and wine, as evidenced by their respective production-possibilities curves (points B–E for the United States and H–K for France).

We have seen production-possibilities curves before. We are looking at them again to emphasize that

- The production-possibilities curve defines the limits to what a country can produce.
- In the absence of trade, a country cannot consume more than it produces.

consumption possibilities The alternative combinations of goods and services that a country could consume in a given time period.

Accordingly, a production-possibilities curve also defines the **consumption possibilities** for a country that does not engage in international trade. Like a truly self-sufficient person, a nation that doesn't trade can only consume the goods and services it produces. If the United States closed its trading windows and produced the mix of output at point D in Figure 17.1, then that is the combination of wine and bread we would have to consume. If a self-sufficient France produced at point I, then that is the mix of output it would have to consume.

International trade opens a whole new set of options. International trade breaks the link between *production* possibilities and *consumption* possibilities. Nations no longer have to consume exactly what they produce. Instead, they can *export* some goods and *import* others. This will change the mix of goods *consumed* even if the mix *produced* stays the same. Now here's the real surprise. When nations specialize in production, not only does the *mix* of consumption change, but the quantity of consumption *increases* as well. Both countries end up consuming *more* output by trading than by being self-sufficient. In other words,

- ***With trade, a country's consumption possibilities exceed its production possibilities.***

To see how this startling outcome emerges, we'll examine how countries operate without trade and then with trade.

Initial Conditions Assume we start without any trade. The United States is producing at point D and France is at point I (Figure 17.1). These output mixes have no special significance; they are just one of many possible production choices each nation could make. Our focus here is on the *combined* output of the two countries. Given their assumed production choices, their combined output is:

	Bread Output (zillions of loaves)	Wine Output (zillions of barrels)
U.S. (at point *D*)	40	30
France (at point *I*)	9	24
World total	49	54

Trade Increases Specialization and World Output

Now comes the tricky part. We increase total (combined) output of these two countries by trading.

At first blush, increasing total output might seem like an impossible task. Both countries, after all, are already fully using their limited production possibilities. Such pessimism is unwarranted, however. Take another look at the production possibilities confronting the United States. Suppose that the United States were to produce at point *C* rather than point *D* in Figure 17.1*a*. At point *C* we could produce 60 zillion loaves of bread and 20 zillion barrels of wine. That combination is clearly possible since it lies on the U.S. production-possibilities curve. We didn't start at point *C* because the output mix at point *D* was assumed to be better for consumers. *Now,* however, we can use trade to break the link between production and consumption.

Suppose the French were also to change their mix of output. The French earlier produced at point *I*. Now we will move them to point *K*, where they can produce 48 zillion barrels of wine and 3 zillion loaves of bread. France might not want to consume this mix of output, but it clearly can produce it.

Now consider the consequences of these changes in each nation's *production* for their combined (total) output. Like magic, total output of both goods has increased. This is illustrated in Table 17.3. Both the old (pretrade) and new output mixes in each country are shown, along with their combined totals. The combined output of bread has increased from 49 to 63 zillion loaves. And combined output of wine has increased from 54 to 68 zillion barrels. Just by changing the mix of output produced in each country, we have increased *total* world output. This additional output creates the potential for making both countries better off than they were in the absence of trade.

The reason the United States and France weren't producing at points *C* and *K* before is that they simply didn't want to consume those particular combinations of output. The United States wanted a slightly more liquid combination than that represented by point *C* and the French could not survive long at point *K*. Hence they chose points *D* and *I*. Nevertheless, our discovery that points *C* and *K* result in greater *total* output suggests that everybody can be happier if we all cooperate. The obvious thing to do is to *specialize* in production, then start exchanging wine for bread in international trade. In this case the United States specialized in bread production when it moved from point *D* to point *C*. France specialized in wine production when it moved form point *I* to point *K*.

The increase in the combined output of both countries is the gain from trading. In this case the net gain is 14 zillion loaves of bread and 14 zillion barrels of wine (Table 17.3). By trading, the United States and France can divide up this increase in output and end up consuming more goods than they did before.

There is no sleight of hand going on here. Rather, ***the gains from trade are due to specialization in production.*** When each country goes it alone,

	Old Mix of Output		New Mix of Output	
	Bread	Wine	Bread	Wine
United States	40	30	60	20
	(point *D*)		(point *C*)	
France	9	24	3	48
	(point *I*)		(point *K*)	
World total	49	54	63	68

TABLE 17.3
Gains from Specialization

The combined total output of two countries can increase by simply altering the mix of output in each country. Here world output increases by 14 zillion loaves of bread and 14 zillion barrels of wine.

it is a prisoner of its own production-possibilities curve; it must make its production decisions on the basis of its own consumption desires. When international trade is permitted, however, each country can concentrate on those goods it makes best. Then the countries trade with each other to acquire the goods they desire to consume.

Comparative Advantage

By now it should be apparent that international trade *can* generate increased output. But how do we get from here to there? Which products should countries specialize in? How much should they trade?

Opportunity Costs

In the previous example, the United States specialized in bread production, and France specialized in wine production. This wasn't an arbitrary decision. Rather, those decisions were based on the relative costs of producing both products in each nation. Bread production was relatively cheap in the United States but expensive in France. Wine production was more costly in the United States but relatively cheap in France.

How did we reach such conclusions? There is nothing in Figure 17.1 that reveals actual production costs, as measured in dollars or French francs. That doesn't matter, however, because economists measure costs not in *dollars* but in terms of *goods* given up.

Reexamine America's production possibilities (Figure 17.1) from this basic economic perspective. Notice again that the United States can produce a maximum of 100 zillion loaves of bread. To do so, however, the United States must sacrifice the opportunity of producing 50 zillion barrels of wine. Hence the true cost—the **opportunity cost—**of 100 zillion bread loaves is 50 zillion barrels of wine. In other words, we're paying half a barrel of wine for every loaf of bread.

opportunity cost The most desired goods or services that are forgone in order to obtain something else.

Although the opportunity costs of bread production in the United States might appear outrageous, note the even higher opportunity costs that prevail in France. According to Figure 17.1*b*, the opportunity cost of producing a loaf of bread in France is a staggering 4 barrels of wine. To produce a loaf of bread, the French must use factors of production that could have been used to produce 4 barrels of wine.

A comparison of the opportunity costs prevailing in each country exposes the nature of what we call **comparative advantage.** The United States has a *comparative* advantage in bread production because less wine has to be given up to produce bread in the United States than in France. In other words, the opportunity costs of bread production are lower in the United States than in France. ***Comparative advantage refers to the relative (opportunity) costs of producing particular goods.***

comparative advantage The ability of a country to produce a specific good at a lower opportunity cost than its trading partners.

A country should specialize in what it is *relatively* efficient at producing, that is, goods for which it has the lowest opportunity costs. In this case, the United States should produce bread because its opportunity cost (½ barrel of wine) is less than France's (4 barrels of wine). Were you the production manager for the whole world, you would certainly want each country to exploit its relative abilities, thus maximizing world output. Each country can arrive at that same decision itself by comparing its own opportunity costs to those prevailing elsewhere. ***World output, and thus the potential gains from trade, will be maximized when each country pursues its comparative advantage.*** It does so by exporting goods that entail low domestic opportunity costs and importing goods that involve higher domestic opportunity costs.

Absolute Costs Don't Count

In assessing the nature of comparative advantage, notice that we needn't know anything about the actual costs involved in production. Have you seen any data suggesting how much labor, land, or capital is required to produce a loaf of bread in either France or the United States? For all you and I know, the French may be able to produce both a loaf of bread and a barrel of wine with fewer resources than we are using. Such an **absolute advantage** in production might exist because of their much longer experience in cultivating both grapes and wheat, or simply because they have more talent.

absolute advantage The ability of a country to produce a specific good with fewer resources (per unit of output) than other countries.

We can envy such productivity, but it should not alter our production and international trade decisions. All we really care about are *opportunity costs*—what we have to give up in order to get more of a desired good. If we can get a barrel of imported wine for less bread than we have to give up to produce that wine ourselves, we have a comparative advantage in producing bread. In other words, as long as we have a *comparative* advantage in bread production, we should exploit it. It doesn't matter to us whether France could produce either good with fewer resources. For that matter, even if France had an absolute advantage in *both* goods, we would still have a *comparative* advantage in bread production, as we have already confirmed. The absolute costs of production were omitted from the previous illustration because they were irrelevant.

To clarify the distinction between absolute advantage and comparative advantage, consider this example. When Charlie Osgood joined the Willamette Warriors' football team, he was the fastest runner ever to play football in Willamette. He could also throw the ball farther than most people could see. In other words, he had an *absolute advantage* in both throwing and running. Charlie would have made the greatest quarterback *or* the greatest end ever to play football. *Would have*. The problem was that he could play only one position at a time. Thus the Willamette coach had to play Charlie either as a quarterback or as an end. He reasoned that Charlie could throw only a bit farther than some of the other top quarterbacks but could far outdistance all the other ends. In other words, Charlie had a *comparative advantage* in running and was assigned to play as an end.

Terms of Trade

The principle of comparative advantage tells nations how to specialize in production. As we saw, the United States specialized in bread production and France specialized in wine. We haven't yet determined, however, how much output each country should *trade*. How much bread should the United States export? How much wine should it expect to get in return? We are clever Yankee traders, to be sure. But beyond that, is there any way to determine the **terms of trade,** the quantity of good *A* that must be given up in exchange for good *B*?

terms of trade The rate at which goods are exchanged; the amount of good A given up for good B in trade.

Limits to the Terms of Trade

Our first clue to the terms of trade lies in each country's domestic opportunity costs. ***A country will not trade unless the terms of trade are superior to domestic opportunity costs.*** In our example, the opportunity cost of a barrel of wine in the United States is 2 loaves of bread. Accordingly, we will not export bread unless we get at least 1 barrel of wine in exchange for every 2 loaves of bread we ship overseas. In other words, we will not play the game unless the terms of trade are superior to our own opportunity costs, thus providing us with some benefit.

No country will trade unless the terms of exchange are better than its domestic opportunity costs. Hence we can predict that ***the terms of trade between any two countries will lie somewhere between their respective opportunity costs in production.*** That is to say, a loaf of bread in international trade will be worth at least ½ barrel of wine (the U.S. opportunity cost) but no more than 4 barrels (the French opportunity cost).

The Market Mechanism

Exactly where the terms of trade end up in the range of 0.5–4.0 barrels of wine per loaf of bread will depend on how market participants behave. Suppose that Henri, an enterprising Frenchman, visited the United States before the advent of international trade. He noticed that bread was relatively cheap, while wine was relatively expensive, the opposite of the price relationship prevailing in France. These price comparisons brought to his mind the opportunity for making a fast franc. All he had to do was bring over some French wine and trade it in the United States for a large quantity of bread. Then he could return to France and exchange the bread for a greater quantity of wine. *Alors!* Were he to do this a few times, he would amass substantial profits.

Our French entrepreneur's exploits will not only enrich him but will also move each country toward its comparative advantage. The United States ends up exporting bread to France and France ends up exporting wine to the United States, exactly as the theory of comparative advantage suggests. The activating agent is not the Ministry of Trade and its 620 trained economists, however, but simply one enterprising French trader. He is aided and encouraged by the consumers and producers in each country. American consumers are happy to trade their bread for his wines. They thereby end up paying less for wine (in terms of bread) than they would otherwise have to. In other words, the terms of trade Henri offers are more attractive than the prevailing (domestic) relative prices. On the other side of the Atlantic, Henri's welcome is equally warm. French consumers are able to get a better deal by trading their wine for his imported bread than by trading with the local bakers.

Even some producers are happy. The wheat farmers and bakers in America are eager to deal with Henri. He is willing to buy a lot of bread and even to pay a premium price for it. Indeed, bread production has become so profitable in the United States that a lot of people who used to grow and mash grapes are now starting to grow wheat and knead dough. This alters the mix of U.S. output in the direction of more bread, exactly as suggested earlier in Figure 17.1.

In France the opposite kind of production shift is taking place. French wheat farmers start to plant grapes so they can take advantage of Henri's generous purchases. Thus Henri is able to lead each country in the direction of its comparative advantage, while raking in a substantial profit for himself along the way.

Where the terms of trade and the volume of exports and imports end up depends in part on how good a trader Henri is. It will also depend on the behavior of the thousands of individual consumers and producers who participate in the market exchanges. In other words, trade flows depend on both the supply and the demand for bread and wine in each country. ***The terms of trade, like the price of any good, will depend on the willingness of market participants to buy or sell at various prices.*** All we know for sure is that the terms of trade will end up somewhere between the limits set by each country's opportunity costs.

Protectionist Pressures

Although the potential gains from world trade are impressive, we should not conclude that everyone will be smiling at the Franco-American trade celebration. On the contrary, some people will be very upset about the trade routes that Henri has established. They will not only boycott the celebration but actively seek to discourage us from continuing to trade with France.

Microeconomic Losers

Consider, for example, the winegrowers in western New York. Do you think they are going to be very happy about Henri's entrepreneurship? Americans can now buy wine more cheaply from France than they can from New York. Before long we may hear talk about unfair foreign competition or about the greater nutritional value of American grapes (see Headline). The New York winegrowers may also emphasize the importance of maintaining an adequate grape supply and a strong wine industry at home, just in case of nuclear war.

Joining with the growers will be the farm workers and all of the other workers, producers, and merchants whose livelihood depends on the New York wine industry. If they are aggressive and clever enough, the growers will also get the governor of the state to join their demonstration. After all, the governor must recognize the needs of his people, and his people definitely don't include the wheat farmers in Kansas who are making a bundle from international trade. New York consumers are, of course, benefiting from lower wine prices, but they are unlikely to demonstrate over a few cents a bottle. On the other hand, those few extra pennies translate into millions of dollars for domestic wine producers.

The wheat farmers in France are no happier about international trade. They would dearly love to sink all those boats bringing wheat from America, thereby protecting their own market position.

IMPORT COMPETITION HEADLINE

Whining over Wine

A new type of wine bar has sprung up on Capitol Hill, and it's not likely to tickle the palate of a dedicated oenophile. California wine makers are hawking a bill that could slap higher tariffs on imported wine, and Congress shows some sign of becoming intoxicated with what the wine makers have to offer. First introduced last summer, the Wine Equity Act, as the measure is called, is already sponsored by 345 Congressmen and 60 Senators.

The wine makers aren't putting all their grapes into one bottle. Behind the scenes they have been making common cause with the American Grape Growers Alliance for Fair Trade, a group that represents many of the farmer cooperatives that supply domestic wineries. In a suit they filed with the Commerce Department and International Trade Commission in January, the growers complained that the Europeans, and particularly the Italians, are unfairly subsidizing their wine producers. If their suit is upheld, the ITC could impose stiff duties on the imports. The importers say there is no good evidence of substantial government subsidies.

Source: *Fortune*, February 20, 1984, p. 41.

NOTE: Imports reduce sales, jobs, profits, and wages in import-competing industries. This is the source of micro resistance to international trade.

If we are to make sense of international trade policies, then, we must recognize one central fact of life: some producers have a vested interest in restricting international trade. In particular, ***workers and producers who compete with imported products—who work in import-competing industries—have an economic interest in restricting trade.*** This helps to explain why GM, Ford, and Chrysler are unhappy about auto imports, and why workers in Massachusetts want to end the importation of Italian shoes. It also explains why the textile producers in South Carolina think Taiwan and Korea are behaving irresponsibly when they sell cotton shirts and dresses in the United States. Complaints of other losers from trade appear in the next Headline.

Although imports typically mean fewer jobs and less income for some domestic industries, exports represent increased jobs and incomes for other industries. Producers and workers in export industries gain from trade. Thus on a microeconomic level, there are identifiable gainers and losers from international trade. ***Trade not only alters the mix of output but also redistributes income from import-competing industries to export industries.*** This potential redistribution is the source of political and economic friction.

The Net Gain

We must be careful to note, however, that the microeconomic gains from trade are greater than the microeconomic losses. It's not simply a question of robbing Peter to enrich Paul. On the contrary, we must remind ourselves that consumers in general enjoy a higher standard of living as a result of international trade. As we saw earlier, trade increases world efficiency and

HEADLINE TRADE RESISTANCE

A Litany of Losers

Some excerpts from congressional hearings on trade:

In the past few years, sales of imported table wines . . . have soared at an alarming rate. . . . Unless this trend is halted immediately, the domestic wine industry will face economic ruin. . . . Foreign wine imports must be limited.

—Wine Institute

The apparel industry's workers have few other alternative job opportunities. They do want to work and earn a living at their work. Little wonder therefore that they want their jobs safeguarded against the erosion caused by the increasing penetration of apparel imports.

—International Ladies' Garment Workers' Union

We are never going to strengthen the dollar, cure our balance of payments problem, lick our high unemployment, eliminate an ever-worsening inflation, as long as the U.S. sits idly by as a dumping ground for shoes, TV sets, apparel, steel and automobiles, etc. It is about time that we told the Japanese, the Spanish, the Italians, the Brazilians, and the Argentinians, and others who insist on flooding our country with imported shoes that enough is enough.

—United Shoe Workers of America

We want to be friends with Mexico and Canada. . . . We would like to be put in the same ball game with them. . . . We are not trying to hinder foreign trade . . . (but) plants in Texas go out of business (17 in the last 7 years) because of the continued threat of fly-by-night creek bed, river bank Mexican brick operations implemented overnight.

—Brick Institute of America

Trade policy should not be an absolute statement of how the world ought to behave to achieve a textbook vision of "free trade" or "maximum efficiency." It should . . . attempt to achieve the best results for Americans.

—United Auto Workers

NOTE: Workers and owners in import-competing industries always depict imports as a threat to the American way of life. In reality, trade raises American living standards.

total output. Accordingly, we end up slicing up a larger pie rather than just reslicing the same old smaller pie.

Barriers to Trade

The microeconomic losses associated with imports give rise to a constant clamor for trade restrictions. People whose jobs and incomes are threatened by international trade tend to organize quickly and air their grievances. Moreover, they are assured of a reasonably receptive hearing, both because of the political implications of well-financed organizations and because the gains from trade are widely diffused. If successful, such efforts can lead to a variety of trade restrictions.

Tariffs

One of the most popular and visible restrictions on trade is the **tariff,** a special tax imposed on imported goods. Tariffs, also called *customs duties,* were once the principal source of revenue for governments. In the eighteenth century, tariffs on tea, glass, wine, lead, and paper were imposed on the American colonies to provide extra revenue for the British government. The tariff on tea led to the Boston Tea Party in 1773 and gave added momentum to the American independence movement. In modern times, tariffs have been used primarily as a means of import protection to satisfy specific microeconomic or macroeconomic interests. The current U.S. tariff code specifies tariffs on over 9,000 different products—nearly 50 percent of all U.S. imports. Although the average tariff is only 5 percent, individual tariffs vary widely. The tariff on cars, for example, is only 2.5 percent, while cotton sweaters confront a 17.8 percent tariff.

tariff A tax (duty) imposed on imported goods.

The attraction of tariffs to import-competing industries should be obvious. ***A tariff on imported goods makes them more expensive to domestic consumers, and thus less competitive with domestically produced goods.*** Among familiar tariffs in effect in 2004 were \$0.20 per gallon on Scotch whiskey and \$0.76 per gallon on imported champagne. These tariffs made American-produced spirits look like relatively good buys and thus contributed to higher sales and profits for domestic distillers and grape growers. In the same manner, imported baby food is taxed at 34.6 percent, footwear at 20 percent, and imported stereos at rates ranging from 4 to 6 percent. In each of these cases, domestic producers in import-competing industries gain (see photo). The losers are domestic consumers, who end up paying higher prices; foreign producers, who lose business; and world efficiency, as trade is reduced.

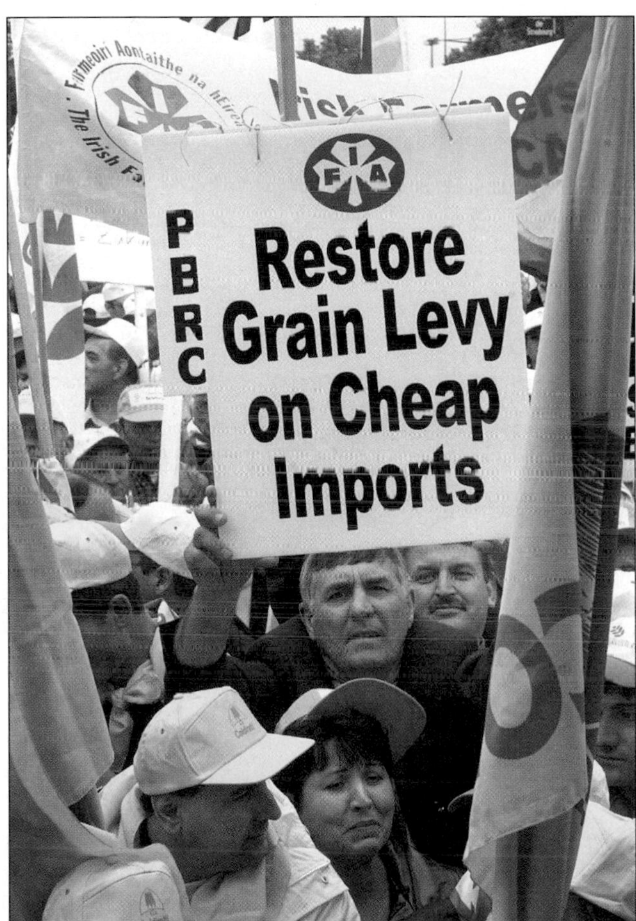

Producers who compete with cheaper imports welcome tariff (levy) protection. Here, Irish farmers are protesting cheap grain imports.

AP/Wide World Photos

Quotas

Tariffs reduce the flow of imports by raising import prices. As an alternative barrier to trade, a country can impose import **quotas,** numerical restrictions on the quantity of a particular good that may be imported. The United States maintained a quota on imported petroleum from 1959 to 1973. Other goods that have been (and most of which still are) subject to import quotas

quota A limit on the quantity of a good that may be imported in a given time period.

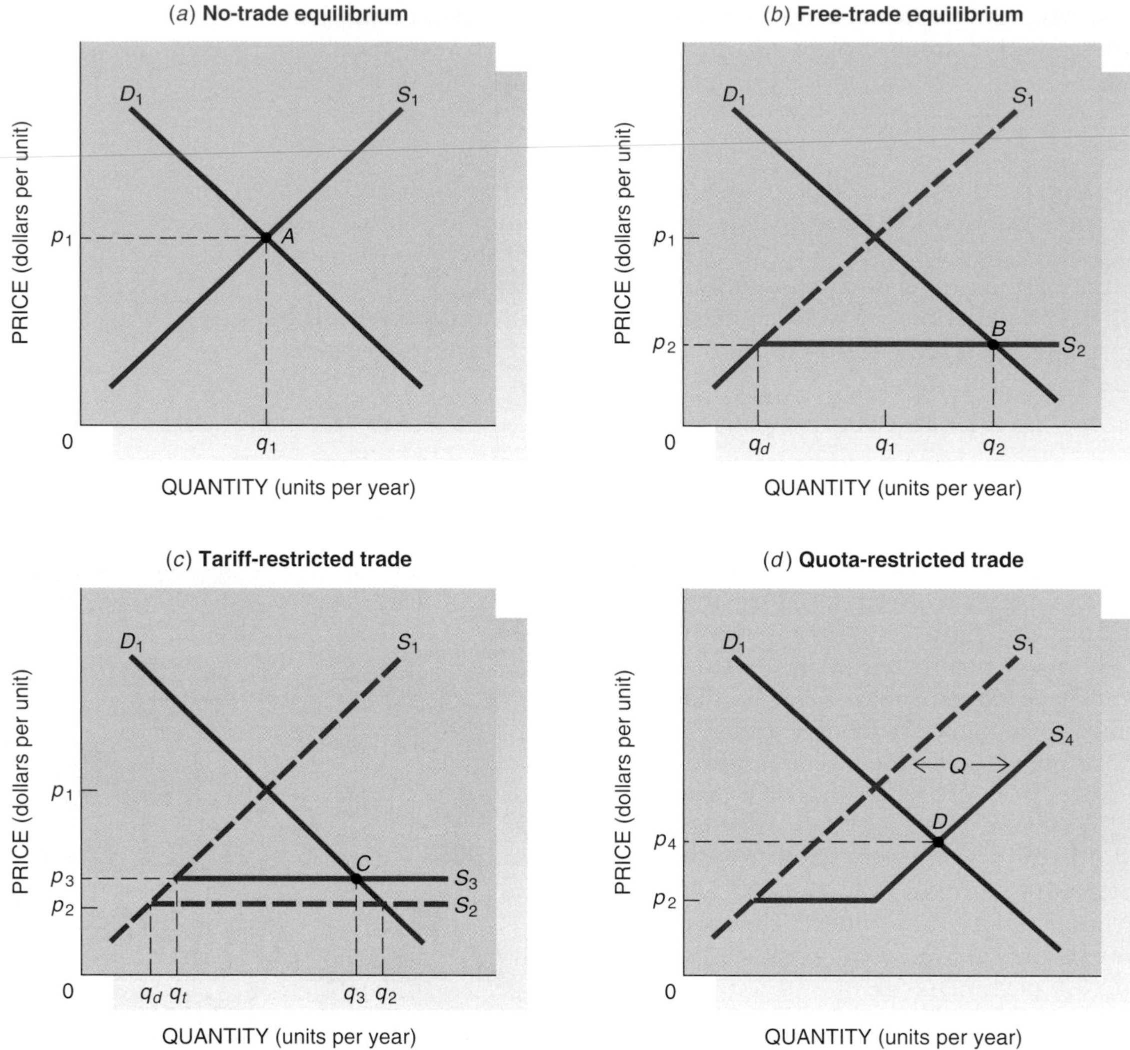

FIGURE 17.2 The Impact of Trade Restrictions

In the *absence of trade,* the domestic price and sales of a good will be determined by domestic supply and demand curves (point *A* in part *a*). Once trade is permitted, the market supply curve will be altered by the availability of imports. With *free trade* and unlimited availability of imports at price p_2, a new market equilibrium will be established at world prices (point *B* in part *b*).

Tariffs raise domestic prices and reduce the quantity sold (point *C* in part *c*). *Quotas* put an absolute limit on imported sales and thus give domestic producers a great opportunity to raise the market price (point *D* in part *d*).

in the United States are sugar, meat, dairy products, textiles, cotton, peanuts, steel, cloth diapers, and even ice cream. According to the U.S. Department of State, approximately 12 percent of our imports are subject to import quotas.

Quotas, like all barriers to trade, reduce world efficiency and invite retaliatory action. Moreover, quotas are especially harmful because of their impact on competition and the distribution of income. To see this impact, we may compare market outcomes in four different contexts: no trade, free trade, tariff-restricted trade, and quota-restricted trade.

equilibrium price The price at which the quantity of a good demanded in a given time period equals the quantity supplied.

Figure 17.2*a* depicts the supply-and-demand relationships that would prevail in a closed (no-trade) economy. In this situation, the **equilibrium price** of textiles is completely determined by domestic demand and supply curves. The equilibrium price is p_1, and the quantity of textiles consumed is q_1.

Suppose now that trade begins and foreign producers are allowed to sell textiles in the American market. The immediate effect of this decision will be a rightward shift of the market supply curve, as foreign supplies are added to domestic supplies (Figure 17.2*b*). If an unlimited quantity of textiles can be bought in world markets at a price of p_2, the new supply curve will look like S_2 (infinitely elastic at p_2). The new supply curve (S_2) intersects the old demand curve (D_1) at a new equilibrium price of p_2 and an expanded consumption of q_2. At this new equilibrium, domestic producers are supplying the quantity q_d while foreign producers are supplying the rest ($q_2 - q_d$). Comparing the new equilibrium to the old one, we see that **trade results in reduced prices and increased consumption.**

Domestic textile producers are unhappy, of course, with their foreign competition. In the absence of trade, the domestic producers would sell more output (q_1) and get higher prices (p_1). Once trade is opened up, the willingness of foreign producers to sell unlimited quantities of textiles at the price p_2 puts a limit on the price behavior of domestic producers. Accordingly, we can anticipate some lobbying for trade restrictions.

Figure 17.2*c* illustrates what would happen to prices and sales if the United Textile Producers was successful in persuading the government to impose a tariff. Let us assume that the tariff raises imported textile prices from p_2 to p_3. The higher price p_3 makes it more difficult for foreign producers to undersell domestic producers. Domestic production expands from q_d to q_t, imports are reduced from $q_2 - q_d$ to $q_3 - q_t$ and the market price of textiles rises. Domestic textile producers are clearly better off, whereas consumers and foreign producers are worse off. In addition, the U.S. Treasury will collect increased tariff revenues.

Now consider the impact of a textile *quota*. Suppose that we eliminate tariffs but decree that imports cannot exceed the quantity Q. Because the quantity of imports can never exceed Q, the supply curve is effectively shifted to the right by that amount. The new curve S_4 (Figure 17.2*d*) indicates that no imports will occur below the world price p_2, and that above that price the quantity Q will be imported. Thus the *domestic* supply curve determines subsequent prices. Foreign producers are precluded from selling greater quantities as prices rise further. This outcome is in marked contrast to that of tariff-restricted trade (Figure 12.3*c*), which at least permits foreign producers to respond to rising prices. Accordingly, ***quotas are a much greater threat to competition than tariffs, because quotas preclude additional imports at any price.*** The Headline on the next page suggests how costly such protection can be.

Import quotas tend to push both domestic and import prices higher, making consumers worse off.

From *Herblock at Large* (Pantheon Books, 1987). Used by permission of Herblock Cartoons.

Nontariff Barriers

Tariffs and quotas are the most visible barriers to trade, but they are only the tip of the iceberg. Indeed, the variety of protectionist measures that have been devised is testimony to the ingenuity of the human mind. At the turn of the century, the Germans were officially committed to a policy of

HEADLINE IMPORT QUOTAS

Sugar Quota a Sour Deal

Very little sugarcane is grown in the United States. Most domestically produced sugar comes from the sugar beet. The rest of our sugar is imported from tropical countries.

The 12,000 domestic sugar beet growers have convinced Congress to protect their industry to ensure a secure supply of sugar in a war. The U.S. Department of Agriculture guarantees the sugar beet growers a minimum of 18 cents per pound for their output. To keep prices at that level, the U.S. Congress limits sugar imports to 1.6 million tons a year. As a result, domestic sugar prices are typically twice as high as world sugar prices. In 2001, the price of sugar in U.S. markets was 22 cents per pound, versus only 10 cents in world markets. This price difference cost American consumers nearly $1.5 billion in 2001 alone. Foreign producers and workers who were excluded from the U.S. market also lost out. Between 1983 and 1990, over 400,000 workers in Caribbean nations lost their jobs as a result of shrinking U.S. sugar quotas.

Who benefits from these sugar quotas? The list includes

- The 12,000 American sugar beet farmers who produce over 7 million tons of sugar per year.
- Producers of sugar substitutes (e.g., corn syrups).
- Those nations and producers that get a share of the U.S. quota.
- Former and current members of Congress who receive fees and campaign contributions for perpetuating the sugar quota system.

NOTE: Import restrictions make both domestic consumers and foreign producers worse off. They enrich domestic producers, however.

extending equal treatment to all trading partners. The Germans, however, wanted to lower the tariff on cattle imports from Denmark without extending the same break to Switzerland. Accordingly, the Germans created a new and higher tariff on "brown and dappled cows reared at a level of at least 300 meters above sea level and passing at least one month in every summer at an altitude of at least 800 meters." The new tariff was, of course, applied equally to all countries. But Danish cows never climb that high, so they were not burdened with the new tariff.

With the decline in tariffs over the last 20 years, nontariff barriers have increased. The United States uses product standards, licensing restrictions, restrictive procurement practices, and other nontariff barriers to restrict roughly 15 percent of imports. Japan makes even greater use of nontariff barriers, restricting nearly 30 percent of imports in such ways.

In 1999–2000, the European Union banned imports of U.S. beef, arguing that the use of hormones on U.S. ranches created a health hazard for European consumers. Although both the U.S. government and the World Trade Organization disputed that claim, the ban was a highly effective nontariff trade barrier. The United States responded by slapping 100 percent tariffs on dozens of European products.

Exchange Rates

Up until now, we've made no mention of how people *pay* for goods and services produced in other countries. In fact, the principle of comparative advantage is based only on opportunity costs; it makes no reference to monetary prices. Yet when France and the United States started specializing in production, market participants had to *purchase* wine and bread to get trade flows started. Remember Henri, the mythical French entrepreneur? He got trade started by buying bread in the United States for export to France. That meant he had to make purchases in *dollars* and sales in *euros*. ***So long as each nation has its own currency, every trade will require use of two different currencies at some point.***

If you've ever traveled to a foreign country, you know the currency problem. Stores, hotels, vending machines, and restaurants price their products in local currency. So you've got to exchange your dollars for local currency when you travel (a service import). That's when you learn how important the **exchange rate** is. The exchange rate refers to the value of one currency in terms of another currency. If $1 exchanges for 5 euros, then a euro is worth 50 cents.

exchange rate The price of one country's currency expressed in terms of another country's currency.

Global Pricing

Exchange rates are a critical link in the global pricing of goods and services. Whether a bottle of French wine is expensive or not depends on two factors: (1) the French price of the wine, expressed in euros, and (2) the dollar-euro exchange rate. Specifically,

$$\bullet \quad \frac{\text{Dollar price of}}{\text{imported good}} = \frac{\text{foreign price}}{\text{of good}} \times \frac{\text{dollar price of}}{\text{foreign currency}}$$

Hence if French wine sells for 60 euros per bottle in France and a euro is worth 50 cents, the American price of imported French wine is

$$\begin{aligned} &= 60 \text{ euros} \times \$.50 \text{ per euro} \\ &= \$30.00 \end{aligned}$$

Appreciation/Depreciation

The formula for global pricing highlights how important exchange rates are for trade flows. ***Whenever exchange rates change, so does the global price of all imports and exports.***

Suppose the dollar were to get stronger against the euro. That means the exchange rate would change in favor of the dollar. Say the dollar would buy 4 euros instead of 2. That **currency appreciation** of the dollar would cut the dollar price of French wine in half. Americans would respond by buying more imported wine.

currency appreciation An increase in the value of one currency relative to another.

The appreciation of the dollar implies a **currency depreciation** for the euro. Previously, a euro was worth 50 cents; now it's worth only 35 cents. Hence French consumers will have to pay more euros for an American loaf of bread. Stuck with a depreciated currency, they may decide to buy fewer imported loaves of bread. As the above equation implies, ***if the value of a nation's currency declines,***

currency depreciation A decrease in the value of one currency relative to another.

- ***Its exports become cheaper.***
- ***Its imports become more expensive.***

Imagine how Brazilians felt in January 1999, when their currency (the real) depreciated by more than 70 percent. That abrupt depreciation made all foreign-made products too expensive for Brazilians. But it made Brazil a bargain destination for U.S. travelers.

Foreign Exchange Markets

The changes in exchange rates that alter global prices are really no different in principle from other price changes. An exchange rate is, after all, simply the *price* of a currency. Like other market prices, an exchange rate is determined by supply and demand.

Figure 17.3 depicts a foreign exchange market, in this case, the supply and demand for euros is the focus. On the demand side of the market is everyone who has some use of euros, including U.S. travelers to Europe, U.S. importers of European products, and foreign investors who want to buy European stocks, bonds, and factories. The cheaper the euro, the greater the quantity of euros demanded.

The supply of euros comes from similar sources. German tourists visiting Disney World *supply* euros when they *demand* U.S. dollars. When Daimler Benz bought Chrysler in 2000, it needed billions of U.S. dollars, many of which it purchased with euros. European consumers who buy American-made products set off a chain of transactions that *supplies* euros in exchange for dollars. The higher the price of the euro, the more they are willing to supply.

The intersection of the supply and demand curves in Figure 17.3 establishes the equilibrium price of the euro, that is, the prevailing exchange rate. As we have seen, however, exchange rates change. As with other prices, ***exchange rates change when either the supply or the demand for a currency shifts.*** If American students suddenly decided to enroll in European colleges, the demand for euros would increase. This rightward shift of the euro-demand curve would cause the euro to *appreciate,* as shown in Figure 17.4. Such a euro appreciation would increase the cost of studying in Europe. But the euro appreciation would make it cheaper for European students to attend U.S. colleges.

China's government has used a cheap currency to increase its exports. By keeping the dollar price of the yuan low, China effectively lowers the price of its exports and raises the price of its imports (see Headline). This helps China achieve huge export surpluses (see Table 17.2) but angers U.S. and European producers who must compete against cheap Chinese products.

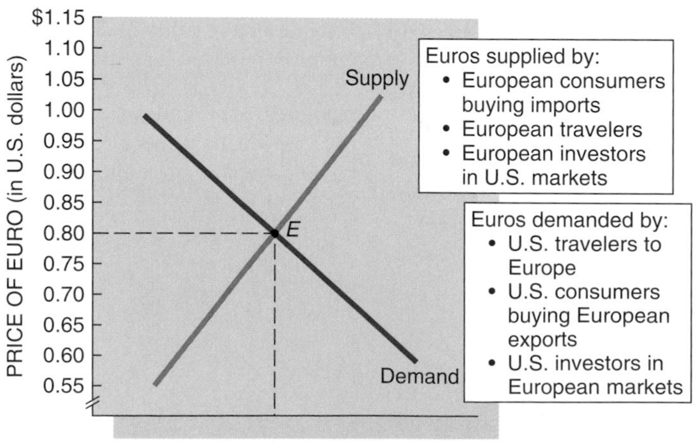

FIGURE 17.3 The Euro Market

Exchange rates are set in foreign-exchange markets by the international supply and demand for a currency. In this case the equilibrium price is 80 U.S. cents for the euro.

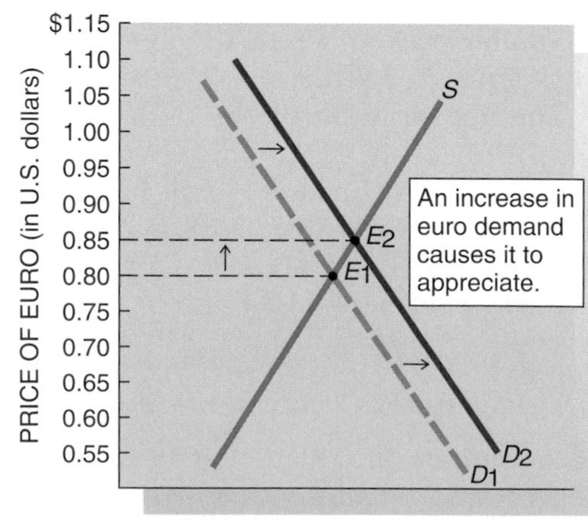

FIGURE 17.4 Currency Appreciation

If the demand for a currency increases, its value will rise (appreciate). Shifts of a currency's demand or supply curves will alter exchange rates.

CURRENCY DEPRECIATION

HEADLINE

China Quickly Rebuffs Pressure from U.S. to Strengthen Its Currency

China said it won't let its currency rise against the dollar, rebuffing U.S. Treasury Secretary John Snow before he even finished asking and setting the stage for political wrangling in the U.S. over trade relations with the world's fastest-growing major economy. . . .

Some American manufacturers contend that an artificially weak yuan is making it too hard to compete against Chinese companies, already a threat because of China's cheap labor and overbuilt factory capacity. The National Association of Manufacturers estimates that Chinese goods are 40 percent cheaper than they should be and blames China for a large portion of 71,000 jobs lost in America in July. Europeans are voicing similar complaints. . . .

The normally reticent European Central Bank has also expressed concern. Wim Duisenberg, the bank's president, indirectly called on China earlier this summer to rethink its peg. Italian government officials have spoken of trade sanctions. With the yuan as weak against the euro as it is against the dollar, Europeans are beginning to believe the exchange rate is fueling the double-digit increases in Chinese imports and chipping away at the European Union's already-shrinking manufacturing sector.

—Peter Wonacott
Michael M. Phillips

Source: *Wall Street Journal,* September 3, 2003, p. 1.

NOTE: When a nation's currency depreciates (devalues), its exports become cheaper and its imports become more expensive.

POLICY PERSPECTIVES

Policing World Trade

Trade policy is a continuing conflict between the benefits of comparative advantage and pleadings of protectionists. Free trade promises more output, greater efficiency, and lower prices. At the same time, free trade threatens profits, jobs, and wealth in specific industries.

Politically, the battle over trade policy favors protectionist interests over consumer interests. Few consumers understand how free trade affects them. Moreover, consumers are unlikely to organize political protests just because the price of orange juice is 35 cents per gallon higher. By contrast, import-competing industries have a large economic stake in trade restrictions and can mobilize political support easily. After convincing Congress to pass new quotas on textiles in 1990, the Fiber Fabric Apparel Coalition for Trade (FFACT) mustered 250,000 signatures and 4,000 union members to march on the White House demanding that President Bush sign the legislation.

President Clinton faced similar political resistance when he sought congressional approval of NAFTA in 1993 and GATT in 1994. Indeed, the political resistance to free trade was so intense that Congress delayed a vote on GATT until after the November 1994 elections. This forced President Clinton to convene a special postelection session of Congress for the sole purpose of ratifying the GATT trade agreement.

President George W. Bush confronted the same kind of political power in 2002. He wanted to increase Republican votes in the steel-producing states of Pennsylvania, Ohio, and Illinois. To secure those votes, he raised tariffs on steel products to a prohibitive 30 percent (see following Headline). That saved a few steel jobs in the short run but hurt steel-using industries (e.g., appliances, autos, housing) and foreign steel producers.

TARIFFS HEADLINE

Bush Sets Tariffs on Steel Imports

President Bush imposed temporary quotas yesterday of up to 30 percent on most imported steel in an effort to give the ailing U.S. industry a chance to modernize and restructure. . . .

Industry executives, union leaders and politicians from steel-producing states generally hailed the president's decision . . .

The president's decision was a blow to steel-consuming industries—such as makers of auto parts and home appliances—which conducted a furious lobbying campaign to dissuade him from adopting the tariff recommendations of the U.S. International Trade Commission. They argued that any tariffs would not only amount to a tax on consumers but would cost more jobs in their industries than would be saved at U.S. steel mills . . .

Private economists predict the tariff regime will increase domestic prices by 6 percent to 8 percent in the first year. If fully passed on to consumers—not a sure thing by any means—that would raise the price of a $30,000 car by about $50 or a washing machine by fewer than $5. . . .

Ben Goodrich and Gary Hufbauer, economists at the Institute of International Economics, estimate that overall, the 30 percent tariffs will cost U.S. consumers more than $8 billion, which would only partially be offset by the added profits and employment in the steel industry. . . .

As expected, the tariff order was immediately criticized by leading steel-producing countries. European officials warned that the action could force them to impose similar tariffs, while Russia said it would have a "serious impact on the atmosphere of relations" between the two countries. An appeal to the World Trade Organization appeared inevitable.

—Steven Pearlstein

Source: *Washington Post,* March 6, 2002, p. E1.

NOTE: Tariffs protect some domestic producers from import competition but raise costs for producers and consumers who buy the protected product.

GATT The political resistance to free trade is not unique to the United States. International trade creates winners and losers in every trading nation. Recognizing this, the countries of the world decided long ago that multinational agreements were the most effective way to overcome domestic protectionism. Broad trade agreements can address the entire spectrum of trade restrictions, rather than focusing on one industry at a time. Multinational agreements can also muster political support by offering greater *export* opportunities as *import* restrictions are lifted.

In 1947 the General Agreement on Tariffs and Trade (GATT) was signed by 23 of the world's largest trading nations. The GATT pact committed these nations to pursue free-trade policies and to extend equal access ("most favored nation" status) to domestic markets for all GATT members. This goal was pursued with periodic rounds of multilateral trade agreements. Because each round of negotiations entailed hundreds of industries and products, the negotiations typically dragged on for six to ten years. At the end of each round, however, trade barriers were always lower. When GATT was first signed, in 1947, tariff rates in developed countries averaged 40 percent. The first seven GATT rounds pushed tariffs down to an average of 6.3 percent, and the 1986–94 Uruguay Round lowered them further, to 3.9 percent.

WTO The 117 nations that signed the 1994 Uruguay agreement also decided that a stronger mechanism was needed to enforce free-trade agreements. To that end, the World Trade Organization (WTO) was created to replace GATT. If a nation feels its exports are being unfairly excluded from another country's market, it can file a complaint with the WTO. This is exactly what the United States did when the European Union (EU) banned U.S. beef imports. The WTO ruled in favor of the United States. When the EU failed to lift its import ban, the WTO authorized the United States to impose retaliatory tariffs on European exports.

The European Union turned the tables on the United States in 2003. They complained to the WTO that U.S. tariffs on steel violated trade rules. The WTO agreed and gave the EU permission to impose retaliatory tariffs on $2.2 billion of U.S. exports. That prompted the Bush administration to scale back the tariffs in December 2003.

In effect, the WTO is now the world's trade police force. It is empowered to cite nations that violate trade agreements and even to impose remedial action when violations persist. Why do sovereign nations give the WTO such power? Because they are all convinced that free trade is the surest route to GDP growth.

WTO Protests Although freer trade clearly boosts economic growth, some people say that's not an unmixed blessing. Environmentalists question the very desirability of continued economic growth. They worry about the depletion of resources, congestion and pollution, and the social friction that growth often promotes. Labor organizations worry that global competition will depress wages and working conditions. And many Third World nations are concerned about playing by trade rules that always seem to benefit rich nations (e.g., copyright protection, import protection).

These varied concerns hit the streets when the WTO initiated the "Millenium Round" of trade negotiations in November 1999. Thousands of protestors showed up in Seattle to demand that the WTO pay more attention to social goals other than GDP growth. Yet another round of negotiations began in Doha, Qatar, in 2001. In the "Doha Round" the key issue is agricultural trade. In September 2003 a bloc of poor nations walked out of the negotiations to protest the trade barriers that rich nations erect to limit farm imports from poor nations. The 148 nations in attendance pledged to fashion new trade rules by January 2005.

SUMMARY

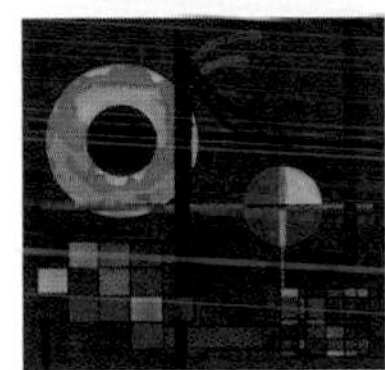

- International trade permits each country to concentrate its resources on those goods it can produce relatively efficiently. This kind of productive specialization increases world output.
- In determining what to produce and offer in trade, each country will exploit its comparative advantage—its *relative* efficiency in producing various goods. One way to determine where comparative advantage lies is to compare the quantity of good *A* that must be given up in order to get a given quantity of good *B* from domestic production. If the same quantity of *B* can be obtained for less *A* by engaging in world trade, we have a comparative advantage in the production of good *A*. Comparative advantage rests on a comparison of relative opportunity costs.
- The terms of trade—the rate at which goods are exchanged—are subject to the forces of international supply and demand. The terms of trade will lie somewhere between the opportunity costs of the trading partners.
- Resistance to trade emanates from workers and firms that must compete with imports. Even though the country as a whole stands to benefit from trade, these individuals and companies may lose jobs and incomes in the process.
- The means of restricting trade are many and diverse. Tariffs discourage imports by making them more expensive. Quotas limit the quantity of a good that may be imported. Nontariff barriers are less visible but also effective in curbing imports.

- International trade requires converting one nation's currency into that of another. The exchange rate is the price of one currency in terms of another.
- Changes in exchange rates (currency appreciation and depreciation) occur when supply or demand for a currency shifts. When a nation's currency appreciates, its exports become more expensive and its imports cheaper.
- The World Trade Organization (WTO) polices multilateral trade agreements to keep trade barriers low.

Terms to Remember

Define the following terms:

imports	consumption possibilities	tariff
exports	opportunity cost	quota
trade deficit	comparative advantage	equilibrium price
trade surplus	absolute advantage	exchange rate
production possibilities	terms of trade	currency appreciation
		currency depreciation

Questions for Discussion

1. Suppose a lawyer can type faster than any secretary. Should the lawyer do her own typing? Can you demonstrate the validity of your answer?
2. Can you identify three services Americans import? How about three exported services?
3. If a nation exported much of its output but imported little, would it be better or worse off? How about the reverse; that is, exporting little but importing a lot?
4. Suppose we refused to sell goods to any country that reduced or halted its exports to us. Who would benefit and who would lose from such retaliation? Can you suggest alternative ways to ensure import supplies?
5. Domestic producers often base their claim for import protection on the fact that workers in country X are paid substandard wages. Is this a valid argument for protection?
6. How would each of these events affect the supply or demand for Japanese yen?
   (*a*) Stronger U.S. economic growth.
   (*b*) A decline in Japanese interest rates.
   (*c*) Higher inflation in the United States.
7. Is a stronger dollar good or bad for America? Explain.
8. Who won and who lost from the steel tariffs (see Headline, p. 398)?
9. Could government-induced currency depreciations act as barriers to trade? Should nations pursue such a policy (see Headline, p. 397)?

Problems

1. Suppose the following table reflects the domestic supply and demand for compact discs (CDs):

Price ($)	16	14	12	10	8	6	4	2
Quantity supplied	8	7	6	5	4	3	2	1
Quantity demanded	2	4	6	8	10	12	14	16

(*a*) Graph these market conditions and identify the equilibrium price and sales.
(*b*) Now suppose that foreigners enter the market, offering to sell an unlimited supply of CDs for $6 apiece. Illustrate and identify (1) the market price, (2) domestric consumption, and (3) domestic production.
(*c*) If a tariff of $2 per CD is imposed, what will happen to (1) the market price, (2) domestic consumption, and (3) domestic production?

2. Alpha and Beta, two tiny islands off the east coast of Tricoli, produce pearls and pineapples. The production-possibilities schedules in the table below describe their potential output in tons per year:
(*a*) Graph the production possibilities confronting each island.
(*b*) What is the opportunity cost of pineapples on each island (before trade)?
(*c*) Which island has a comparative advantage in pearl production?

Alpha		Beta	
Pearls	Pineapples	Pearls	Pineapples
0	30	0	20
2	25	10	16
4	20	20	12
6	15	30	8
8	10	40	4
10	5	45	2
12	0	50	0

3. Suppose the two islands in problem 2 agree that the terms of trade will be 1 pineapple for 1 pearl and that trade soon results in an exchange of 10 pearls for 10 pineapples.
(*a*) If Alpha produced 6 pearls and 15 pineapples and Beta produced 30 pearls and 8 pineapples before they decided to trade, how much would each be producing after trade became possible? Assume that the two countries specialize just enough to maintain their consumption of the item they export, and make sure each island trades the item for which it has a comparative advantage.
(*b*) How much would the combined production of pineapples increase for the two islands due to trade? How much would the combined production of pearls increase?
(*c*) How could both countries produce and consume even more?

4. What is the equilibrium euro price of the U.S. dollar
(*a*) In Figure 17.3?
(*b*) In Figure 17.4?
(*c*) Did the dollar appreciate or depreciate in Figure 17.4?

5. In what country is the U.S. dollar price of a Big Mac (p. 379) the highest with the following exchange rates?
(*a*) 7.945 rupiah = $1
(*b*) .8 euros = $1
(*c*) 38 baht = $1
(*d*) 1.70 swiss francs = $1

6. If a Gameboy SP costs 10,000 yen in Japan, how much will it cost in U.S. dollars if the exchange rate is as follows?
   (*a*) 120 yen = $1
   (*b*) 1 yen = $0.00833
   (*c*) 100 yen = $1
7. How much added income did U.S. sugar beet farmers earn as a result of higher sugar prices (Headline, p. 394)?

Web Activities

1. What is the current price of a McDonald's Big Mac? What is the price of a Big Mac expressed in euros? To make the conversion, log on to www.oanda.com/converter/classic and convert the U.S. dollar price into euros.
2. Log on to www.cia.gov/cia/publications/factbook. Click on two nations of interest to you and find the resource strengths of these nations. To find this information, you need to click on the "Economy" button.
   (*a*) Are these resources used in the production of the nations' exports?
   (*b*) Does this trade pattern follow the principle of comparative advantage?
   (*c*) Who are the nations' primary trading partners?
   (*d*) Do the nations' geographical locations affect with whom they trade? Explain.
3. Log on to www.wto.org/english/res_e/statis_e/chp_1_e.pdf and find the table that lists the leading exporters and importers of world trade. List the top 10 exporters and importers in world merchandise trade, including the value and share of world trade, for the most recent year reported.
4. Log on to www.census.gov/indicator/www/ustrade.html. What is the current balance of trade for the United States? Has this balance been increasing or decreasing?

Living Econ

Should I Travel Abroad during a Recession?

One factor to consider when planning to travel abroad is the value of your home currency in terms of the other nation's currency. Foreign exchange markets provide an opportunity to apply the demand and supply tools from Chapter 3. In fact, without thinking through the demand and supply analysis, it is easy to make an incorrect prediction about the rise or fall of currency values.

Consider this scenario. During a U.S. recession, U.S. consumers reduce their spending on goods and services including imports. When the demand for imports decreases, the supply of dollars falls in the currency market. The supply curve shifts to the left causing a rise in the value of the dollar. If the dollar has more value, it buys more of the foreign currency, and your food, lodging, and entertainment just got cheaper while abroad.

Other aspects of a recession may complicate your decision to travel overseas, such as lower income, higher interest rates, or declining stock values. And certainly there are additional factors that influence the supply of and demand for U.S. dollars. But in every case, understanding currency markets requires a careful application of supply and demand, a tool kit you can carry with you beyond this course.

Glossary

Numbers in parentheses indicate the chapters in which the definitions appear.

A

absolute advantage The ability of a country to produce a specific good with fewer resources (per unit of output) than other countries. (*17*)

aggregate demand The total quantity of output demanded at alternative price levels in a given time period, *ceteris paribus.* (*11*) (*12*) (*13*) (*14*)

aggregate supply The total quantity of output producers are willing and able to supply at alternative price levels in a given time period, *ceteris paribus.* (*11*) (*14*)

antitrust Government intervention to alter market structure or prevent abuse of market power. (*9*)

automatic stabilizer Federal expenditure or revenue item that automatically responds countercyclically to changes in national income—e.g., unemployment benefits, income taxes. (*16*)

average total cost (ATC) Total cost divided by the quantity produced in a given time period. (*5*)

B

bank reserves Assets held by a bank to fulfill its deposit obligations. (*13*)

barriers to entry Obstacles that make it difficult or impossible for would-be producers to enter a particular market, e.g., patents. (*6*) (*7*)

barter The direct exchange of one good for another, without the use of money. (*3*) (*13*)

budget deficit The amount by which government expenditures exceed government revenues in a given time period. (*12*)

budget surplus An excess of government revenues over government expenditures in a given time period. (*12*)

business cycle Alternating periods of economic growth and contraction. (*10*) (*11*) (*16*)

C

capital intensive Production processes that use a high ratio of capital to labor inputs. (*2*)

ceteris paribus The assumption of nothing else changing. (*1*) (*3*) (*4*)

comparative advantage The ability of a country to produce a specific good at a lower opportunity cost than its trading partners. (*17*)

competitive firm A firm without market power, with no ability to alter the market price of the goods it produces. (*6*)

competitive market A market in which no buyer or seller has market power. (*6*)

competitive profit-maximization rule Produce at that rate of output where price equals marginal cost. (*6*)

Consumer Price Index (CPI) A measure (index) of changes in the average price of consumer goods and services. (*10*)

consumption Expenditure by consumers on final goods and services. (*12*)

consumption possibilities The alternative combinations of goods and services that a country could consume in a given time period. (*17*)

contestable market An imperfectly competitive industry subject to potential entry if prices or profits increase. (*7*)

crowding in An increase in private-sector borrowing (and spending) caused by decreased government borrowing. (*15*)

crowding out A reduction in private-sector borrowing (and spending) caused by increased government borrowing. (*15*)

currency appreciation An increase in the value of a currency relative to another. (*17*)

currency depreciation A decrease in the value of a currency relative to another. (*17*)

D

deflation A decrease in the average level of prices of goods and services. (*10*)

demand The ability and willingness to buy specific quantities of a good at alternative prices in a given time period, *ceteris paribus.* (*3*) (*4*)

demand curve A curve describing the quantities of a good a consumer is willing and able to buy at alternative prices in a given time period, *ceteris paribus*. (*3*) (*4*)

demand for labor The quantities of labor employers are willing and able to hire at alternative wage rates in a given time period. *ceteris paribus.* (*8*)

demand schedule A table showing the quantities of a good a consumer is willing and able to buy at alternative prices in a given time period, *ceteris paribus.* (*3*)

deposit creation The creation of transactions deposits by bank lending. (*13*)

derived demand The demand for labor and other factors of production results from (depends on) the demand for final goods and services produced by these factors. (*8*)

discounting Federal Reserve lending of reserves to private banks. (*14*)

discount rate The rate of interest charged by the Federal Reserve banks for lending reserves to private banks. (*14*)

disposable income After-tax income of consumers. (*12*)

E

economic cost The value of all resources used to produce a good or service; opportunity cost. (*5*)

economic growth An increase in output (real GDP); an expansion of production possibilities. (*1*) (*2*) (*15*)
economics The study of how best to allocate scarce resources among competing uses. (*1*)
economies of scale Reductions in minimum average costs that come about through increases in the size (scale) of plant and equipment. (*7*)
efficiency (technical) Maximum output of a good from the resources used in production. (*6*)
emission charge A fee imposed on polluters, based on the quantity of pollution. (*9*)
employment rate The proportion of the adult population that is employed. (*15*)
equilibrium (macro) The combination of price level and real output that is compatible with both aggregate demand and aggregate supply. (*11*) (*12*)
equilibrium price The price at which the quantity of a good demanded in a given time period equals the quantity supplied. (*3*) (*6*) (*17*)
equilibrium wage The wage at which the quantity of labor supplied in a given time period equals the quantity of labor demanded. (*8*)
excess reserves Bank reserves in excess of required reserves. (*13*) (*14*)
exchange rate The price of one country's currency expressed in terms of another country's currency. (*17*)
exports Goods and services sold to foreign buyers. (*2*) (*17*)
externalities Costs (or benefits) of a market activity borne by a third party; the difference between the social and private costs (or benefits) of a market activity. (*1*) (*2*) (*9*)

F

factor market Any place where factors of production (e.g., land, labor, capital, entrepreneurship) are bought and sold. (*3*)
factors of production Resource inputs used to produce goods and services, e.g., land, labor, capital, entrepreneurship. (*1*) (*2*) (*5*)
fine-tuning Adjustments in economic policy designed to counteract small changes in economic outcomes; continuous responses to changing economic conditions. (*16*)
fiscal policy The use of government taxes and spending to alter macroeconomic outcomes. (*11*) (*12*) (*16*)
fiscal restraint Tax hikes or spending cuts intended to reduce (shift) aggregate demand. (*12*)
fiscal stimulus Tax cuts or spending hikes intended to increase (shift) aggregate demand. (*12*)
fiscal year (FY) The 12-month period used for accounting purposes; begins October 1 for federal government. (*16*)
fixed costs Costs of production that do not change when the rate of output is altered, e.g., the cost of basic plant and equipment. (*5*)
free rider An individual who reaps direct benefits from someone else's purchase (consumption) of a public good. (*9*)
full employment The lowest rate of unemployment compatible with price stability; variously estimated at between 4 and 6 percent unemployment. (*10*)

G

GDP gap The difference between full-employment output and the amount of output demanded at current price levels. (*12*) (*16*)
GDP per capita Total GDP divided by total population; average GDP. (*15*)
government failure Government intervention that fails to improve economic outcomes. (*1*) (*3*) (*9*)
gross domestic product (GDP) The total value of goods and services produced within a nation's borders in a given time period. (*2*)
growth rate Percentage change in real GDP from one period to another. (*15*)

H

human capital The knowledge and skills possessed by the workforce. (*2*)

I

imports Goods and services purchased from foreign sources. (*2*) (*17*)
income transfers Payments to individuals for which no current goods or services are exchanged, e.g., Social Security, welfare, unemployment benefits. (*2*)
inflation An increase in the average level of prices of goods and services. (*10*) (*11*)
inflation rate The annual rate of increase in the average price level. (*10*)
in-kind income Goods and services received directly, without payment in a market transaction. (*2*)
investment Expenditures on (production of) new plant and equipment (capital) in a given time period, plus changes in business inventories. (*1*) (*2*) (*12*) (*15*)
investment decision The decision to build, buy, or lease plant and equipment; to enter or exit an industry. (*5*)

L

labor force All persons over age 16 who are either working for pay or actively seeking paid employment. (*10*) (*15*)
labor supply The willingness and ability to work specific amounts of time at alternative wage rates in a given time period, *ceteris paribus*. (*8*)
laissez faire The doctrine of "leave it alone," of nonintervention by government in the market mechanism. (*1*) (*3*)
law of demand The quantity of a good demanded in a given time period increases as its price falls, *ceteris paribus*. (*3*) (*4*)
law of diminishing marginal utility The marginal utility of a good declines as more of it is consumed in a given time period. (*4*)
law of diminishing returns The marginal physical product of a variable input declines as more of it is employed with a given quantity of other (fixed) inputs. (*5*) (*8*)
law of supply The quantity of a good supplied in a given time period increases as its price increases, *ceteris paribus*. (*3*)
long run A period of time long enough for all inputs to be varied (no fixed costs). (*5*)

M

macroeconomics The study of aggregate economic behavior, of the economy as a whole. (*1*) (*10*) (*11*)

marginal cost (MC) The increase in total cost associated with a one-unit increase in production. (*5*) (*6*)

marginal cost pricing The offer (supply) of goods at prices equal to their marginal cost. (*6*) (*7*)

marginal physical product (MPP) The change in total output associated with one additional unit of input. (*5*) (*8*)

marginal propensity to consume (MPC) The fraction of each additional (marginal) dollar of disposable income spent on consumption. (*12*)

marginal propensity to save (MPS) The fraction of each additional (marginal) dollar of disposable income not spent on consumption; 1 − MPC. (*12*)

marginal revenue (MR) The change in total revenue that results from a one-unit increase in quantity sold. (*7*)

marginal revenue product (MRP) The change in total revenue associated with one additional unit of input. (*8*)

marginal utility The change in total utility obtained by consuming one additional (marginal) unit of a good or service consumed. (*4*)

market Any place where goods are bought and sold. (*3*)

market demand The total quantities of a good or service people are willing and able to buy at alternative prices in a given time period; the sum of individual demands. (*3*) (*4*) (*7*)

market failure An imperfection in the market mechanism that prevents optimal outcomes. (*1*) (*9*)

market mechanism The use of market prices and sales to signal desired outputs (or resource allocations). (*1*) (*3*) (*6*) (*9*)

market power The ability to alter the market price of a good or service. (*6*) (*7*) (*9*)

market shortage The amount by which the quantity demanded exceeds the quantity supplied at a given price; excess demand. (*3*)

market structure The number and relative size of firms in an industry. (*6*)

market supply The total quantities of a good that sellers are willing and able to sell at alternative prices in a given time period, *ceteris paribus.* (*3*) (*6*)

market supply of labor The total quantity of labor that workers are willing and able to supply at alternative wage rates in a given time period, *ceteris paribus.* (*8*)

market surplus The amount by which the quantity supplied exceeds the quantity demanded at a given price; excess supply. (*3*)

microeconomics The study of individual behavior in the economy, of the components of the larger economy. (*1*)

mixed economy An economy that uses both market and nonmarket signals to allocate goods and resources. (*1*)

monetary policy The use of money and credit controls to influence macroeconomic activity. (*11*) (*14*) (*16*)

money Anything generally accepted as a medium of exchange. (*13*)

money multiplier The number of deposit (loan) dollars that the banking system can create from $1 of excess reserves; equal to 1 ÷ required reserve ratio. (*13*) (*14*)

money supply (M1) Currency held by the public, plus balances in transactions accounts. (*13*) (*14*) (*16*)

monopoly A firm that produces the entire market supply of a particular good or service. (*2*) (*6*) (*7*)

multiplier The multiple by which an initial change in aggregate spending will alter total expenditure after an infinite number of spending cycles; 1/(1 − MPC). (*12*) (*16*)

N

natural monopoly An industry in which one firm can achieve economies of scale over the entire range of market supply. (*7*)

net exports Exports minus imports (*X* − *M*). (*12*)

nominal GDP The total value of goods and services produced within a nation's borders, measured in current prices. (*10*) (*15*)

nominal income The amount of money income received in a given time period, measured in current dollars. (*10*)

O

open-market operations Federal Reserve purchases and sales of government bonds for the purpose of altering bank reserves. (*14*)

opportunity cost The most desired goods and services that are forgone in order to obtain something else. (*1*) (*3*) (*6*) (*8*) (*17*)

opportunity wage The highest wage an individual would earn in his or her best alternative job. (*8*)

optimal mix of output The most desirable combination of output attainable with existing resources, technology, and social values. (*9*)

P

patent Government grant of exclusive ownership of an innovation. (*7*)

per capita GDP Total GDP divided by total population; average GDP. (*2*)

personal distribution of income The way total personal income is divided up among households or income classes. (*2*)

predatory pricing Temporary price reductions designed to drive out competition. (*7*)

price ceiling Upper limit imposed on the price of a good. (*3*)

price elasticity of demand The percentage change in quantity demanded divided by the percentage change in price. (*4*)

price floor Lower limit imposed on the price of a good. (*3*)

price stability The absence of significant changes in the average price level; officially defined as a rate of inflation of less than 3 percent. (*10*)

private costs The costs of an economic activity directly borne by the immediate producer or consumer (excluding externalities). (*9*)

private good A good or service whose consumption by one person excludes consumption by others. (*9*)

production decision The selection of the short-run rate of output (with existing plant and equipment). (*5*) (*6*) (*7*)

production function A technological relationship expressing the maximum quantity of a good attainable from different combinations of factor inputs. (*5*)
production possibilities The alternative combinations of goods and services that could be produced in a given time period with all available resources and technology. (*1*) (*10*) (*15*) (*17*)
productivity Output per unit of input, e.g., output per labor hour. (*2*) (*15*)
product market Any place where finished goods and services (products) are bought and sold. (*3*)
profit The difference between total revenue and total cost. (*5*) (*6*)
profit-maximization rule Produce at that rate of output where marginal revenue equals marginal cost. (*7*)
progressive tax A tax system in which tax rates rise as incomes rise. (*2*)
public good A good or service whose consumption by one person does not exclude consumption by others. (*9*)

Q

quota A limit on the quantity of a good that may be imported in a given time period. (*17*)

R

real GDP The inflation-adjusted value of GDP; the value of output measured in constant prices. (*2*) (*10*) (*11*) (*15*)
real income Income in constant dollars; nominal income adjusted for inflation. (*10*)
recession A decline in total output (real GDP) for two or more consecutive quarters. (*10*)
regressive tax A tax system in which tax rates fall as incomes rise. (*2*)
relative price The price of one good in comparison with the price of other goods. (*10*)
required reserves The minimum amount of reserves a bank is required to hold by government regulation; equal to required reserve ratio times transactions deposits. (*13*) (*14*)
reserve ratio The ratio of a bank's reserves to its total transactions deposits. (*13*)

S

saving Income minus consumption; that part of disposable income not spent. (*12*) (*15*)
Say's Law Supply creates its own demand. (*11*)
scarcity Lack of enough resources to satisfy all desired uses of those resources. (*1*)
shift in demand A change in the quantity demanded at any (every) given price. (*3*)
short run The period in which the quantity (and quality) of some inputs cannot be changed. (*5*)
social costs The full resource costs of an economic activity, including externalities. (*9*)
stagflation The simultaneous occurrence of substantial unemployment and inflation. (*16*)
structural unemployment Unemployment caused by a mismatch between the skills (or location) of job seekers and the requirements (or location) of available jobs. (*16*)
supply The ability and willingness to sell (produce) specific quantities of a good at alternative prices in a given time period, *ceteris paribus*. (*3*) (*5*) (*6*)
supply-side policy The use of tax rates, (de)regulation, and other mechanisms to increase the ability and willingness to produce goods and services. (*11*) (*16*)

T

tariff A tax (duty) imposed on imported goods. (*17*)
terms of trade The rate at which goods are exchanged; the amount of good *A* given up for good *B* in trade. (*17*)
total cost The market value of all resources used to produce a good or service. (*5*)
total revenue The price of a product multiplied by the quantity sold in a given time period, $p \times q$. (*4*) (*6*)
total utility The amount of satisfaction obtained from entire consumption of a product. (*4*)
trade deficit The amount by which the value of imports exceeds the value of exports in a given time period. (*17*)
trade surplus The amount by which the value of exports exceeds the value of imports in a given time period. (*17*)
transactions account A bank account that permits direct payment to a third party (e.g., with a check). (*13*)
transfer payments Payments to individuals for which no current goods or services are exchanged, e.g., Social Security, welfare, unemployment benefits. (*9*)

U

unemployment The inability of labor-force participants to find jobs. (*10*) (*11*)
unemployment rate The proportion of the labor force that is unemployed. (*10*)
utility The pleasure or satisfaction obtained from a good or service. (*4*)

V

variable costs Costs of production that change when the rate of output is altered, e.g., labor and material costs. (*5*)
voluntary restraint agreement (VRA) An agreement to reduce the volume of trade in a specific good; a "voluntary" quota. (*17*)

Note: **Boldface** indicates glossary terms defined in the text.

N

O